AN ENTIRE YEAR'S RECIPES FROM
AMERICA'S FAVORITE FOOD MAGAZINE

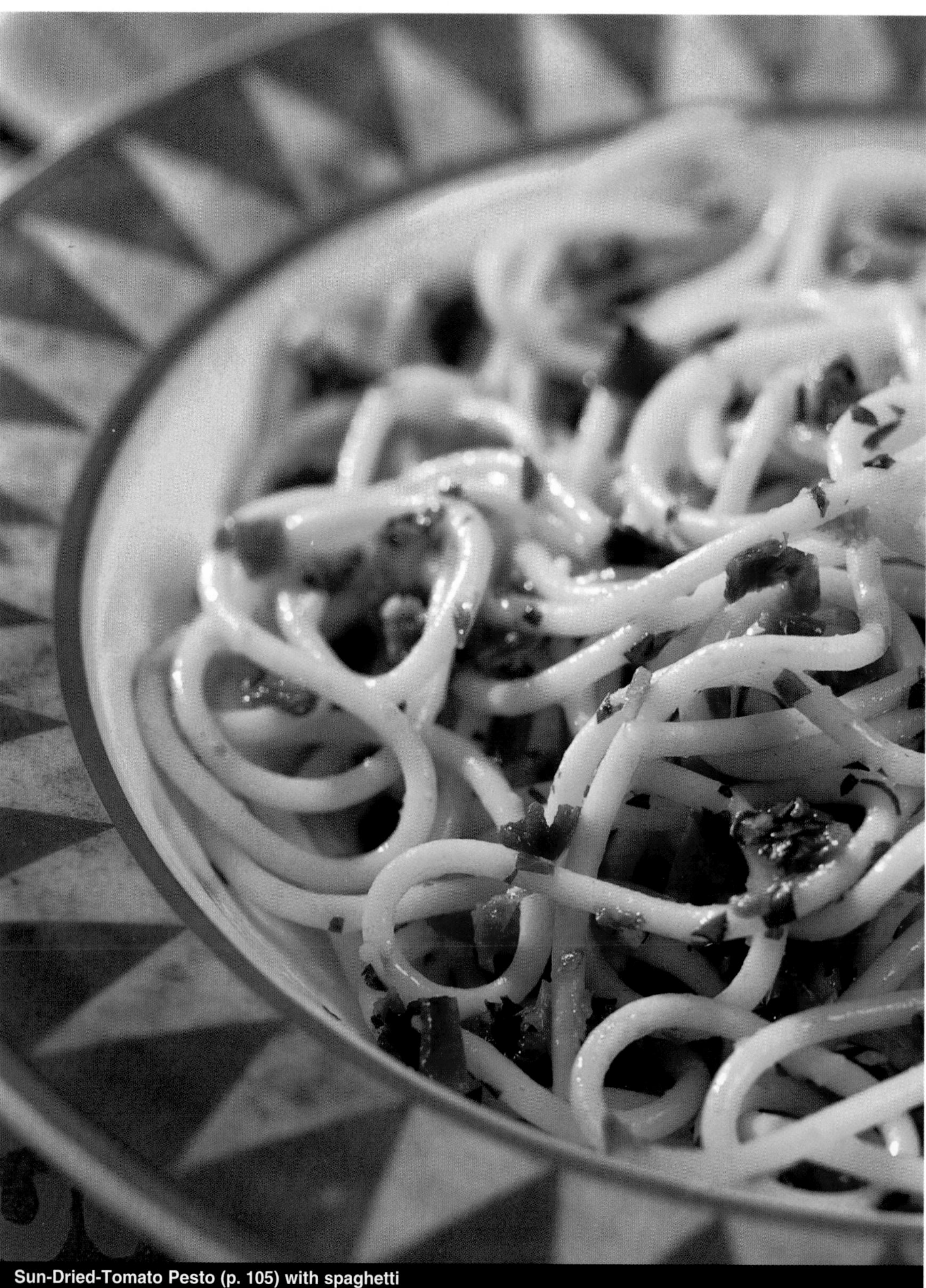

Sun-Dried-Tomato Pesto (p. 105) with spaghetti

1996 Food & Wine

AN ENTIRE YEAR'S RECIPES FROM AMERICA'S FAVORITE FOOD MAGAZINE

American Express Publishing Corporation
New York

Cover Photo: **Ann Stratton** (Shrimp Escabeche with Ginger-Grilled Pineapple, p. 38)
Back Photo: **Geoff Lung** (Ice-Cream Sandwiches, p. 441)

American Express Publishing Corporation

Library of Congress Cataloging-in-Publication Data
1996 Food & wine : an entire year's recipes from
America's favorite food magazine.
p. cm.
Includes index.
ISBN 0-916103-34-X
1. Cookery. I. Food & wine (New York, N.Y.)
TX714.A199 1997
641.5--dc21 96-37982
CIP

Published by American Express Publishing Corporation
1120 Avenue of the Americas, New York, New York 10036

Manufactured in the United States of America

CONTENTS

Frisée Salad with Beans and Warm Bacon Dressing (p. 274)

FOREWORD

In 1996, I experienced The Cooking Paradox: I had less time to prepare delicious meals and a greater urge to make them. What to do? Well, when you're the editor in chief of a fabulous food magazine, the answer is easy—ask the talented editors and test-kitchen staff to come up with recipes and menus that will make your life, and the lives of the readers, easier. So in this collection of recipes from the past year you'll find some outstanding, innovative dishes that can be made simply and quickly. Some of my favorites for summer were the rubs and marinades for grilling (pages 347 to 350), and for winter, the Minestrone with Tomatoes and Rice (page 85) and the Roast Beef Tenderloin with Madeira and Prunes (page 239) served with Horseradish Scalloped Potatoes (page 308). Thanks to the efforts of Food Editor Tina Ujlaki and her crew, my year was filled with more fun, more friends and more great food. What could be better?

DANA COWIN
Editor in Chief
FOOD & WINE Magazine

Lemon Lover's Tart (p. 397)

For your convenience, recipes that have appeared in our "Low-Fat Cooking" and "Good Food Fast" columns (or in articles specifically dealing with low-fat or quick cooking) have been marked:

LF for low-fat **Q** for quick

CHAPTER 1

~

HORS D'OEUVRES

Clockwise from top: Tempura Crab Bites (p. 20), Baked Tortilla Crisps (with Pepper and Corn Salsa, p. 357), Scallop Dumplings with Garlic Chives (p. 21), Curried Coconut Yogurt Dip (p. 17)

CRISP BREAD SQUARES WITH HOT RED PEPPER

Leave the ruler in the desk drawer and consider the measurements for these bread squares just a suggestion; a little variation in their size only accentuates their rustic charm.

4 SERVINGS

3 tablespoons cold-pressed olive oil
4 garlic cloves, lightly crushed
3 or 4 slivers fresh hot red chile, or a pinch of crushed red pepper
4 big thick slices of sturdy country bread, cut into ¾-inch cubes
Fine sea salt
Dried Mediterranean oregano

In a large skillet, combine the oil, garlic and chile. Cook over low heat until the garlic is light golden. Add the bread cubes and toss over moderate heat until golden and crisp on the outside but still somewhat soft within, about 5 minutes. Remove from the heat. Season with salt and oregano and toss. Serve warm or at room temperature.—VIANA LA PLACE

BAKED TORTILLA CRISPS

These healthy chips are great with Two-Tomato Salsa with Poblanos (p. 355), Roasted-Tomato Salsa (p. 355) and Pepper and Corn Salsa (p. 357).

10 SERVINGS

10 low-fat flour or corn tortillas
Coarse salt

Preheat the oven to 350°. Cut each tortilla into six wedges. Arrange the wedges in one layer on two nonstick baking sheets; sprinkle with salt. Bake until crisp and golden, about 12 minutes for the flour and 18 minutes for the corn. Halfway through, shift the pans.—BOB CHAMBERS

SUPER BOWL SNACK

Here's our version of that football favorite, the Chex party mix.

MAKES ABOUT 9 CUPS

4 tablespoons melted butter
1½ tablespoons lime juice
1 tablespoon soy sauce
1 tablespoon Worcestershire sauce
1 tablespoon chili powder
1 teaspoon ground cumin
1 teaspoon salt
7 cups Chex cereal
2 cups small pretzels
2 cups Pepperidge Farm Cheddar Goldfish Crackers
1 cup cocktail peanuts
½ cup pecan pieces

1. Heat the oven to 250°. In a small bowl, combine the butter, lime juice, soy sauce and Worcestershire sauce. In another small bowl, combine the chili powder, cumin and salt.
2. In a large bowl, combine the cereal, pretzels, crackers, peanuts and pecans. Add the butter mixture and toss to coat; add the spices and toss again.
3. Spread the cereal mixture in two large roasting pans. Bake for about 45 minutes, stirring occasionally, until dry; let cool. (**MAKE AHEAD:** The mix can be stored in an airtight container for up to 4 days. To recrisp, briefly heat in the oven.)—GRACE PARISI

HERB POTATO MAXIMES

Charlie Palmer serves these sophisticated yet playful potato bites at Aureole, his Manhattan restaurant. They're also featured in his book Great American Food *(Random House).*

MAKES 20

½ cup clarified butter
2 large Idaho potatoes
Twenty 1½-inch fresh chives
20 fresh tarragon leaves
20 tiny fresh chervil sprigs
Coarse salt

1. Heat the oven to 275°. Brush a heavy, flat baking sheet with clarified butter. Peel and rinse the potatoes; pat dry. Using a mandoline, cut the potatoes into paper-thin lengthwise slices.
2. Lay half the potato slices next to one another but not touching on the baking sheet; place one piece of each herb in the center of each slice, leaving a border around the herbs. Pat the remaining slices dry; lay them evenly on top of the herbs and press firmly. Brush with clarified butter; season with salt. Bake for 25 to 30 minutes, turning the sheet, until golden.—CHARLIE PALMER

GRITZ CHEESE CRACKERS LF

MAKES ABOUT 100 CRACKERS

1 cup instant grits
1 cup bread flour or all-purpose flour
¾ teaspoon salt
½ teaspoon baking soda
¼ teaspoon cayenne pepper
2½ tablespoons cold unsalted butter, cut into ¼-inch pieces
½ cup freshly grated Parmesan cheese (about 2 ounces)
⅔ cup low-fat (1.5%) buttermilk

1. Preheat the oven to 350°. In a bowl, mix the grits, flour, salt, baking soda and cayenne. Rub in the butter until the mixture resembles coarse meal. Stir in the Parmesan and make a well in the center. Add the buttermilk and stir to form a stiff dough. Knead on a lightly floured surface until smooth. Wrap in plastic and let stand for 15 minutes.

2. Cut the dough into quarters. Set one quarter on a lightly floured surface; cover the remaining pieces with plastic. Roll out the dough to 1⁄16 inch thick. Using a 2-inch round biscuit cutter or a glass, cut out rounds of dough and arrange them on a nonstick baking sheet. Bake for 12 to 14 minutes, or until golden and crisp. Transfer to a rack and let cool. Repeat with the remaining dough. (**MAKE AHEAD:** The crackers can be stored in an airtight container for up to 2 weeks.) —GRACE PARISI

Q & A: HORS D'OEUVRES

Q: How many hors d'oeuvres should I make, and how many different types?

A: A good rule of thumb for hors d'oeuvres is six to eight pieces per person per hour. For fewer than eight people, one or two types of hors d'oeuvres will be fine. For eight or more people, you'll want to serve four kinds, with one from each of the following categories: fish or shellfish, cheese, vegetables and meat.

Q: How big should the hors d'oeuvres be?

A: Bite-size is ideal, especially for hors d'oeuvres that are delicate or crumbly. The exceptions are things that can be dipped, like endive spears.

Q: What are your favorite instant hors d'oeuvres?

A: White, rye or pumpernickel bread, cut into rounds, toasted and topped with caviar, pâté, mousse, cured meats or fish, cheese or a mixture of finely diced tomato, crème fraîche, Tabasco, minced fresh chives and salt.

Q: Do you have any tips for serving hors d'oeuvres?

A: Be creative: Instead of using doilies, use a bed of mixed dried spices with different colors and shapes. Arrange cheese canapés on a bed of shelled almonds, walnuts or pecans, or on grated Parmesan; put seafood canapés on a bed of very coarse sea salt or seaweed.—DANIEL BOULUD

CRISP PHYLLO BITES PROVENÇAL

MAKES ABOUT 5 DOZEN PIECES

- 2 tablespoons olive oil
- 1½ pounds fresh spinach, stemmed and washed
- 3 garlic cloves, minced
- 6 tablespoons chopped sun-dried tomatoes
- 3 tablespoons pitted and chopped Niçoise olives
- Pinch of cayenne pepper
- 6 sheets of phyllo dough
- 3 tablespoons unsalted butter, melted
- ¾ cup freshly grated Parmesan cheese
- Freshly grated nutmeg
- 12 anchovies, halved lengthwise

1. Preheat the oven to 400°. Heat the oil in a large skillet. Add the spinach and garlic in batches and cook over moderate heat until the spinach wilts. Transfer to a colander and squeeze out all the water; if the spinach isn't dry, the rolls won't be crisp. Chop the spinach and mix it with the tomatoes, olives and cayenne.

2. Lay a sheet of phyllo on a work surface with the short side directly in front of you. Brush with butter and sprinkle with 1 tablespoon of the Parmesan and a pinch of nutmeg. Spread about ¼ cup of the spinach filling in a narrow strip across the short edge of the phyllo. Lay four anchovy halves over the filling and roll up tightly. Brush the roll with butter and sprinkle with 1 tablespoon of the Parmesan. Place on a baking sheet. Repeat with the remaining ingredients, leaving ample space between the rolls. Bake on the top shelf of the oven for 10 to 12 minutes, or until golden brown and crisp. Let the rolls cool slightly before slicing at an angle into bite-size pieces.—DANIEL BOULUD

VEGETABLE-CHIP MEDLEY LF

These crisp, delectable chips have more vegetable flavor and a lot less fat than commercial versions—less than half a gram per cup. They cook quickly in the microwave, but can also be baked in a 250° oven for about forty-five minutes. A mandoline, available at kitchenware stores, makes slicing easy.

MAKES ABOUT 6 CUPS

- 1 small sweet potato, peeled and sliced crosswise 1/16 inch thick
- 2 medium unpeeled red potatoes, sliced crosswise 1/16 inch thick
- 3 large radishes, sliced 1/16 inch thick
- 1 small butternut squash, narrow end only, peeled and sliced crosswise 1/16 inch thick
- 1 large thick carrot, sliced crosswise 1/16 inch thick
- 1 small boniato (batata), peeled and sliced crosswise 1/16 inch thick (optional)
- 1 small yuca (cassava), peeled and sliced crosswise 1/16 inch thick (optional)
- Vegetable cooking spray
- Salt
- 1 ripe plantain, peeled and sliced crosswise 1/16 inch thick

1. Blanch the sweet-potato slices in a large saucepan of boiling water for 1 minute. Transfer to paper towels and pat dry. Blanch all the remaining vegetables except the plantain, one vegetable at a time; pat dry. Keep the vegetables separate after blanching.

2. Lightly coat a large microwave-safe plate with cooking spray. Arrange the sweet-potato slices, without overlapping, on the plate and season with salt. Microwave on high for 5 minutes. Toss the slices and cook for about 2 minutes more, or until crisp. Spread the chips on a platter to cool; transfer to a bowl. Repeat with the remaining blanched vegetables, cooking each vegetable separately until the slices stiffen, about 7 minutes per batch. Spray the plate before cooking each batch.

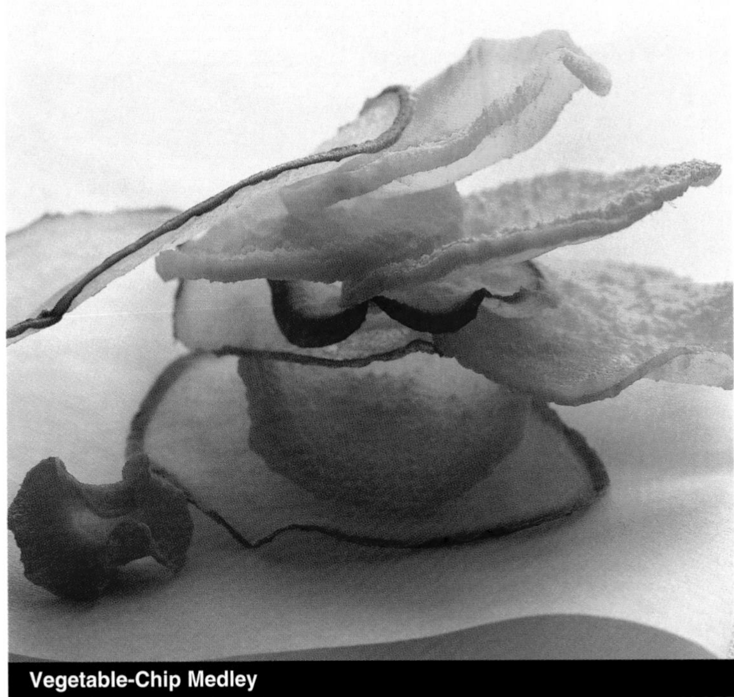

Vegetable-Chip Medley

3. Arrange the plantain slices on the sprayed plate. Microwave for about 6 minutes, or until starting to brown. Let cool. If necessary, microwave 1 to 2 minutes longer, until crisp. (MAKE AHEAD: The chips can be stored in an airtight container up to 1 week. Recrisp in a 250° oven.) —GRACE PARISI

EGGPLANT CAVIAR LF

4 SERVINGS

- 1 large eggplant, halved lengthwise
- 1 tablespoon olive oil
- 1 small French baguette (about 6 ounces), sliced 1/4 inch thick
- Vegetable cooking spray
- 1 medium red bell pepper, cut into 1/8-inch dice
- 1 small onion, minced
- 2 garlic cloves, minced
- 1 large tomato, peeled, seeded and cut into 1/8-inch dice
- 3 tablespoons fresh lemon juice
- Salt and freshly ground pepper
- 2 tablespoons minced chives
- 1 tablespoon minced fresh basil

1. Preheat the oven to 350°. Brush the cut-sides of the eggplant with 1 teaspoon of the olive oil. Set the eggplant, cut-side down, on a baking sheet and roast for about 1 hour, or until tender and collapsed. Let cool.

2. Arrange the bread slices on another baking sheet and spray lightly with cooking spray. Bake for about 8 minutes, or until golden and crisp.

3. Heat 1 teaspoon of the olive oil in a nonstick skillet. Add the red pepper, onion and garlic and cook over moderate heat, stirring occasionally, until the vegetables are softened but not browned, about 6 minutes. Transfer to a bowl and let cool. ➤

4. Using a spoon, scrape the eggplant flesh from the skin; discard the skin. Finely chop the flesh and add the eggplant to the sautéed vegetables. Stir in the tomato, lemon juice and the remaining 1 teaspoon oil. Season with salt and pepper and refrigerate until slightly chilled. (**MAKE AHEAD:** The eggplant caviar can be refrigerated for up to 1 day; store the croutons at room temperature. Let the eggplant stand at room temperature for 20 minutes before serving.) Stir the chives and basil into the eggplant caviar and serve with the croutons.—HUBERT KELLER

CHILES WITH BEER AND CHEESE

Serve these chiles with oven-dried or fried tortillas. We've called for Cheddar or Muenster cheese, but Mexican Chihuahua or Asadero is best; if you can find a market that sells either one, by all means try it.

6 SERVINGS

- 3 tablespoons vegetable oil
- 1 cup thinly sliced white onion
- Salt
- 1 pound poblano or Anaheim chiles (about 6 medium chiles), charred and peeled, with stems, seeds and veins removed and flesh cut into narrow strips
- 1 cup strong beer
- 6 ounces medium-sharp Cheddar or domestic Muenster cheese, cut into thin slices

1. Heat the oil in a deep, nonreactive, medium skillet or shallow flameproof casserole. Add the onion; season with salt. Cook over moderate heat until translucent.

2. Add the chile strips, cover the pan and cook until just tender but not soft, about 4 minutes. Add the beer, increase the heat to high and boil, uncovered, until it is absorbed, about 7 minutes.

3. Spread the cheese slices over the chiles. Heat until melted. Serve at once.—DIANA KENNEDY

Chiles with Beer and Cheese

CHILACA-CHILE SNACK

You can use poblano chiles in this recipe, but they do not have the sweet, deep flavor of chilacas. Serve this combination with corn tortillas.

8 SERVINGS

- 8 chilaca chiles or 7 small poblano chiles, charred and peeled, with stems, seeds and veins removed
- 2 tablespoons fresh lime juice
- 2 tablespoons finely chopped white onion
- 3 tablespoons finely crumbled *queso fresco* or cream cheese
- ¼ cup crème fraîche or sour cream

Tear or cut the chiles lengthwise into thin strips. Place in a medium bowl and stir in the rest of the ingredients. Set aside for the flavors to meld, about 30 minutes. Just before serving, stir thoroughly. Serve at room temperature.—DIANA KENNEDY

PEELING CHILES

Charring and steaming chiles not only loosens the skins effectively but also enhances the flavor of the flesh. Follow these three steps:

1. Place the chile directly over an open flame or under a broiler and turn until blistered and charred. Do this quickly so that the flesh does not cook. If your chiles are wrinkled and not too fresh or if you are using a broiler, rub the skins lightly with vegetable oil before charring.

2. Immediately put the chiles into a plastic or paper bag or under a damp cloth and set aside to steam for about ten minutes. Do not rinse the chiles in cold water as some cookbooks suggest; they will lose flavor.

3. If you have sensitive skin, put on thin rubber or surgical gloves before you start this step. Slide your hands over the chiles and slip off the blackened skin. Don't worry about picking off each bit of skin; that would take forever.

CURRIED COCONUT YOGURT DIP

Serve this cooling dip with vegetables, shrimp, chicken wings or, my favorite, fried pappadums, *the thin Indian crackers made from lentil flour.*

MAKES ABOUT 2 CUPS

2 cups plain low-fat yogurt
2 tablespoons shredded unsweetened coconut*
1 cup unsweetened coconut milk
1 tablespoon fresh lime juice
¼ to ½ teaspoon minced fresh habanero or Scotch bonnet chile
1 tablespoon Madras curry powder
1 medium scallion, finely chopped
2 tablespoons minced fresh cilantro

*Available at specialty-food shops

1. Line a strainer with a coffee filter and set it over a bowl; spoon in the yogurt and let it drain in the refrigerator until thickened, about 3 hours. Discard the liquid.
2. In a small skillet, toast the shredded coconut over high heat, stirring, until golden, about 3 minutes; let cool.
3. In a medium bowl, combine the thickened yogurt, coconut milk, lime juice, the minced chile and the curry powder. (MAKE AHEAD: The dip can be refrigerated for up to 3 days; leave the toasted coconut out at room temperature. Allow the dip to return to room temperature before serving.) Stir in the scallion and cilantro and garnish with the toasted coconut.—GRACE PARISI

ROASTED-RED-PEPPER AND GOAT-CHEESE DIP

Sweet red peppers complement tangy goat cheese in this smooth, creamy dip. Serve it with vegetables or breadsticks.

MAKES ABOUT 2½ CUPS

3 large red bell peppers
11 ounces mild goat cheese, softened
3 ounces cream cheese, softened
2 tablespoons heavy cream
Salt and freshly ground pepper
1 tablespoon finely chopped fresh flat-leaf parsley

1. Roast the bell peppers over a gas flame or under the broiler, turning, until charred all over. Transfer to a bowl, cover with plastic and let steam for 20 minutes. Peel the peppers, discarding the peels, cores, ribs and seeds.
2. Transfer the peppers to a food processor or blender and process until finely chopped; set aside ½ cup. Add the goat cheese and cream cheese to the processor and puree until smooth. With the machine on, add the cream and process just until combined. Transfer to a bowl and stir in the reserved chopped peppers. Season with salt and pepper. (MAKE AHEAD: The dip can be refrigerated for up to 3 days. Allow to return to room temperature.) Stir in the parsley and serve.—GRACE PARISI

BLACK-BEAN AND CHILE DIP

The smoky anchos and beans go well with vegetables and tortilla chips.

MAKES ABOUT 2½ CUPS

2 ancho chiles, broken into 2-inch pieces
Two 15-ounce cans black beans, drained and rinsed
2 garlic cloves
1 large jalapeño chile, finely chopped
3 tablespoons fresh lime juice
¾ teaspoon ground cumin
1 teaspoon Worcestershire sauce
3 tablespoons minced fresh cilantro
2 scallions, white parts minced, green parts thinly sliced

In a small bowl, cover the anchos with 1 cup of hot water. Let soak until softened, about 15 minutes. Drain, reserving the soaking liquid; transfer the chiles to a food processor. Add 2 cups of the beans, the garlic, jalapeño, lime juice, cumin, Worcestershire and 2 tablespoons of the soaking liquid; process until pureed. Transfer to a bowl; stir in the remaining beans. (MAKE AHEAD: The dip can be refrigerated for up to 2 days. Let return to room temperature before serving.) Stir in the cilantro and the scallion whites. Garnish with the scallion greens and serve.—GRACE PARISI ➤

INSTANT DIP

Here's a sun-dried-tomato dip that can be put together in minutes. The recipe makes about 1 cup of dip. Heat 2 teaspoons of olive oil in a small skillet. Add 1 minced large garlic clove and cook over moderate heat until golden. Add ¼ cup minced sun-dried tomatoes; cook until heated through. Off the heat, stir in 6 ounces of soft goat cheese, 3 ounces softened cream cheese and freshly ground pepper.

SWEET-AND-SOUR ONIONS

If you can find the small, flat, yellow- or red-skinned onions sold as cipolline, by all means use them in this recipe, following the peeling method in Step 1 below.

4–8 SERVINGS

- 1 pound small white or red onions (about 20)
- 3 tablespoons extra-virgin olive oil
- 2 bay leaves
- 2 tablespoons red-wine vinegar
- 1 tablespoon sugar
- Salt and freshly ground pepper

1. Using a paring knife, trim the root and stem ends of the onions. In a medium saucepan of boiling water, cook the onions over moderate heat until they are just beginning to soften, about 5 minutes. Drain the onions immediately and remove their peels.
2. Meanwhile, heat the olive oil in a nonreactive medium saucepan. Add the bay leaves and cook over moderately low heat until fragrant, about 1 minute. Add the peeled onions and cook, stirring occasionally, until the onions are just beginning to brown around the edges, about 7 minutes. Add the red-wine vinegar and sugar and season with salt and pepper. Increase the heat to moderate and cook the onions, stirring frequently, until the mixture starts to caramelize, about 2 minutes. Remove the bay leaves. Transfer the onions to a bowl and stir them gently to coat them with the syrup. Serve the onions at room temperature.—NANCY HARMON JENKINS

ROASTED AND STUFFED PEPPERS

For a neater presentation that avoids the use of toothpicks, lay each piece of roasted pepper on a small sheet of plastic wrap, spread the bread-crumb mixture on the pepper and then use the plastic wrap to roll it up into a firm, tight package, twisting the ends to secure them. Steam the packages briefly, then unwrap the rolled stuffed peppers and finish cooking them on a baking sheet in the oven.

4–8 SERVINGS

- 1½ tablespoons golden raisins
- 4 large red or yellow bell peppers
- 1½ tablespoons chopped capers
- 1½ tablespoons pine nuts, lightly toasted
- 2 rinsed and boned salted anchovies or 4 small oil-packed anchovy fillets, finely chopped
- ⅓ cup dry bread crumbs
- 1½ tablespoons minced fresh flat-leaf parsley
- Salt and freshly ground black pepper
- 1 tablespoon extra-virgin olive oil, plus more for brushing

1. Soak the raisins in a small bowl of hot water until softened, about 15 minutes. Meanwhile, roast the peppers directly over a gas flame or under a broiler, turning frequently, until the skins are charred all over and the peppers just begin to collapse. Transfer the peppers to a bowl, cover them tightly with plastic wrap and let steam for 20 minutes. Peel, core and seed the peppers. Cut them lengthwise into quarters, removing any membranes as you go.
2. Preheat the oven to 425°. In a small bowl, combine the capers, pine nuts, anchovies, dry bread crumbs, parsley and drained raisins. Season with salt and black pepper. Add the oil to make a thick paste.
3. Lightly brush a baking sheet with oil. On a large work surface, lay out all the pepper pieces, skinned-side down; place a heaping teaspoon of the bread-crumb mixture at the widest end of each piece. Beginning at that end, firmly roll up the peppers and secure with toothpicks.
4. Bake the peppers for about 15 minutes, or until warmed through with lightly browned tops. Serve immediately or at room temperature.—NANCY HARMON JENKINS

CRISP PARMESAN BASKETS FILLED WITH GOAT CHEESE

To dress up the finished hors d'oeuvres, top the goat cheese with thin shavings from a fresh truffle.

MAKES ABOUT 32 BASKETS

- 2 cups very finely grated Parmesan cheese (about 8 ounces)
- 8 ounces goat cheese, softened
- ½ tablespoon olive oil
- ½ teaspoon sherry vinegar
- 1 tablespoon chopped fresh herbs, such as chives, cilantro or parsley, or a combination
- 3 to 4 tablespoons milk
- Salt and freshly ground pepper
- 2 tablespoons each of halved and pitted Niçoise olives, walnut pieces and tiny fresh herb sprigs, for garnish

1. Preheat the oven to 400°. Spoon six evenly spaced tablespoon-size mounds of the grated

Crisp Parmesan Baskets Filled with Goat Cheese

Parmesan onto a heavy nonstick baking sheet. Pat each mound into a fairly even 3-inch round. Bake the rounds for about 3 minutes, or until the cheese is bubbling and golden brown. Working quickly, remove the lacy rounds from the baking sheet and drape them over an upturned paper egg carton to mold them slightly. The baskets will crisp up as they cool. Repeat with the remaining Parmesan. (MAKE AHEAD: The Parmesan baskets will keep in an airtight container for up to 1 day.)

2. In a small bowl, combine the goat cheese, olive oil, sherry vinegar and chopped herbs and stir until smooth. Add the milk, 1 tablespoon at a time, until the cheese is easily spreadable. Season with salt and pepper. Using 2 teaspoons, fill each basket with a little dollop of goat cheese; you can also use a pastry bag fitted with a small tip. Decorate the baskets with the garnishes and serve.—DANIEL BOULUD

SHRIMP REMOULADE

Remoulade sauce is a kind of herb-packed mayonnaise. Instead of making it from scratch, you can leave out the eggs and oil and blend in two cups of prepared mayonnaise.

12 SERVINGS

REMOULADE SAUCE:

- ½ cup cider vinegar
- ¼ cup yellow mustard
- ¼ cup Creole mustard*
- ¼ cup ketchup
- 2 tablespoons sweet paprika
- 1 teaspoon cayenne pepper
- 2 garlic cloves, minced
- Dash of hot sauce
- 1 teaspoon salt
- 1 cup chopped scallions
- ½ cup finely chopped celery
- ½ cup finely chopped fresh flat-leaf parsley
- 3 large eggs
- 1⅓ cups vegetable oil

SPICED SHRIMP:

- 1½ cups coarse salt
- 1 cup loosely packed dried whole cayenne peppers
- ¼ cup whole black peppercorns
- 6 lemons, halved
- 3 large garlic cloves, peeled
- 8 bay leaves
- 2 medium onions, chopped
- 2 pounds medium shrimp, shelled and deveined, tails left on
- 3 pounds ice (about 12 cups)

- 1 small head red or green cabbage, finely shredded
- 1 medium carrot, cut into 2-by-⅛-inch matchsticks
- 1 medium red bell pepper, cut into 2-by-⅛-inch matchsticks

*Available at specialty-food shops

1. Make the remoulade sauce: In a blender, combine the vinegar, mustards, ketchup, paprika, cayenne, garlic, hot sauce, salt, scallions, celery, parsley and eggs on high speed until smooth. With the machine on, add the oil in a thin steady stream until the mixture is thick. Transfer to a bowl and refrigerate until slightly chilled.

2. Make the spiced shrimp: In a large pot, combine the salt, peppers, peppercorns, lemons, garlic, bay leaves, onions and 2 gallons of water and bring to a boil over moderately high heat; cook for 15 minutes. Add the shrimp; cook until just pink, about 2 minutes. Using a slotted spoon, transfer the shrimp to a large bowl. Add the ice to the bowl and strain 4 cups of the hot cooking liquid over the shrimp. Let the shrimp soak for 5 minutes, then drain. (MAKE AHEAD: The remoulade and shrimp can be covered and refrigerated separately for up to 1 day.)

3. In a large bowl, toss the cabbage, carrot and red bell pepper with some of the sauce. Mound on a platter, arrange the shrimp on top and serve the remaining sauce on the side. —COMMANDER'S PALACE, NEW ORLEANS

FRIED SHRIMP DUMPLINGS

Spring-roll wrappers are thinner but sturdier than wonton wrappers and make especially crisp fried dumplings.

MAKES 20 DUMPLINGS

- 1 large dried tree-ear mushroom, or 2 dried shiitake-mushroom caps
- 1 pound medium shrimp
- 1 medium carrot, coarsely chopped
- 1 small onion, coarsely chopped

1½ tablespoons fish sauce (nuoc mam)
¼ teaspoon Asian sesame oil
¼ teaspoon salt
½ teaspoon freshly ground pepper
10 spring-roll wrappers, or 40 wonton wrappers
1 large egg, lightly beaten
2 cups vegetable oil, for frying
Nuoc Cham (p. 353)

1. In a small bowl, cover the dried mushroom with hot water. Let stand until softened, about 5 minutes. Drain and coarsely chop. Peel and devein the shrimp, reserving twenty with their tails. Coarsely chop the rest.

2. In a food processor, finely chop the carrot. Add the onion and mushroom and finely chop. Add the chopped shrimp, the fish sauce, sesame oil, salt and pepper; process just until blended.

3. If using spring-roll wrappers: Cut the wrappers in half diagonally to form two triangles. Lay two of the triangles on a work surface with the long side facing down; keep the remaining wrappers covered with a damp towel. Place a whole shrimp in the center of each wrapper with the tail sticking up beyond the tip of the triangle. Spread one scant tablespoon of the chopped filling over each shrimp; brush the edges of the wrappers with a little beaten egg. Fold the longest side of each wrapper up and over the shrimp, wrapping the ends tightly around it. **If using wonton wrappers:** Lay one on a work surface and brush the edges with egg. Set a shrimp in the center, with the tail sticking out of the wrapper. Spread with 1 tablespoon of the filling and cover with another wrapper. Repeat with the remaining wrappers, shrimp and filling. (**MAKE AHEAD:** The spring-roll dumplings can be refrigerated for 1 day. Don't make the wonton ones ahead.)

4. In a heavy saucepan, heat the vegetable oil to 350° over moderately high heat. Fry three or four of the dumplings at a time, turning once, until they are golden brown and crisp, 4 to 5 minutes. If necessary, lower the heat so that the oil won't smoke. Drain the dumplings briefly on paper towels, then transfer them to a platter and keep warm. Serve the dumplings with a bowl of Nuoc Cham.—MARCIA KIESEL

BUYING AND STORING WONTON SKINS

• Look for wonton skins (also called wonton wrappers) in the refrigerated produce section and the freezer section of supermarkets and Asian markets. They usually come in twelve-ounce transparent plastic packages containing fifty or more sheets. Thinner wonton skins are sometimes available in Chinatown stores and some supermarkets; a package of the thinner skins contains almost twice as many sheets per comparable weight—about a hundred in a twelve-ounce package. The thin skins are rarely labeled as such, but they may have a black dot on the package or be called *siu mei* skins. These more delicate wrappers suit light fillings, such as the seafood mousse in the Scallop Dumplings with Garlic Chives. The thicker, chewier skins are sturdy enough for any meat or vegetable stuffing.

• Try these brands: Frieda's (national), Nasoya (Northeast), Azumaya (South, Southwest and West), Twin Dragon (Midwest) and New Hong Kong (West).

• Store wonton skins in the refrigerator for up to ten days, or freeze them in airtight bags for up to two months; defrost them overnight in the refrigerator before using.

TEMPURA CRAB BITES WITH SOY GINGER DIPPING SAUCE

6–8 SERVINGS

2 large egg whites
1 cup plus 2 tablespoons cornstarch
2 tablespoons dry white wine
1 tablespoon hot sauce
2 teaspoons coarse salt
6 jumbo soft-shell crabs, cleaned
¼ cup low-sodium soy sauce
1 scallion, thinly sliced
1 tablespoon rice vinegar
1¼ teaspoons Asian sesame oil
1 teaspoon finely grated ginger
½ teaspoon sugar
3 cups vegetable oil, for frying

1. In a large shallow dish, blend the egg whites with the 2 tablespoons cornstarch and the white wine, hot sauce and salt. Add the soft-shell crabs to the cornstarch mixture and coat thoroughly. Arrange the soft-shell crabs snugly in the dish, cover and refrigerate for up to 2 hours.

CLEANING SOFT-SHELL CRABS

1. Turn each crab upside down. With scissors, cut off the face. Remove the brain sac from behind the eyes.
2. Lift the "apron" from the abdomen of the crab and cut it off where it joins the body.
3. Turn the crab right-side up and lift the flap where the shell comes to a point; then pull or scrape off the crab's spongy gills.

Cutting off the face of the crab

Scraping off the gills

2. In a small serving bowl, combine the soy sauce, sliced scallion, vinegar, sesame oil, ginger, sugar and 2½ tablespoons of water.
3. In a large deep saucepan, heat the vegetable oil to 375°. Spread the remaining 1 cup cornstarch on a large plate. Working with two at a time, remove the crabs from the marinade and dredge them in the cornstarch, shaking off any excess. Using tongs, add the crabs to the hot oil and fry, turning once, until they are cooked through and very crisp, about 4 minutes. Transfer the crabs to a rack to drain.
4. Cut the crabs at their natural separations into pieces that can be picked up easily. Serve the tempura crab bites hot, with the soy ginger dipping sauce on the side.—MARCIA KIESEL

SCALLOP DUMPLINGS WITH GARLIC CHIVES

Garlic chives have a subtle but distinctive garlicky flavor. Look for them at Asian or farmers' markets or specialty produce shops. For the tiny pleated dumplings, use thin round wonton skins (see "Buying and Storing Wonton Skins," opposite page). If you can't find them, follow the directions below for cutting the square ones.

MAKES 36 DUMPLINGS

- 2 tablespoons vegetable oil
- ½ pound garlic chives or 6 ounces ordinary chives, trimmed and cut into 1-inch pieces
- 1 scallion, cut into several pieces
- 1 teaspoon minced fresh ginger
- ½ pound sea scallops
- 1 tablespoon plum wine* or sherry
- 2 teaspoons soy sauce
- 2 teaspoons cornstarch
- 1 teaspoon Asian sesame oil
- ½ teaspoon salt
- ½ teaspoon freshly ground pepper
- 36 thin wonton skins
- Orange Sweet-and-Sour Sauce, Spicy Fish Sauce, Soy Vinegar Sauce or Spiced Salt (see "Wonton Dipping Sauces," p. 27)

*Available at Asian markets

1. Heat 1 tablespoon of the vegetable oil in a skillet. Add the garlic chives. Sauté over moderately high heat, stirring often, until wilted. Transfer to a bowl to cool.
2. In a food processor, combine the scallion and ginger; pulse until the scallion is finely chopped. Add the scallops, plum wine, soy sauce, cornstarch, sesame oil, salt and pepper. Pulse until the scallops are finely chopped. Add the garlic chives. Pulse just until evenly incorporated but not smooth.
3. If using square wonton skins, spread them out on a work surface and cut them with a 3½-inch round biscuit cutter. Keep all but twelve skins covered with a towel while you proceed. Spoon a heaping teaspoon of the filling into the center of each wonton skin. Draw the edges up and pleat evenly (see photo, below). Pinch the pleated edge to form a little bun. Repeat

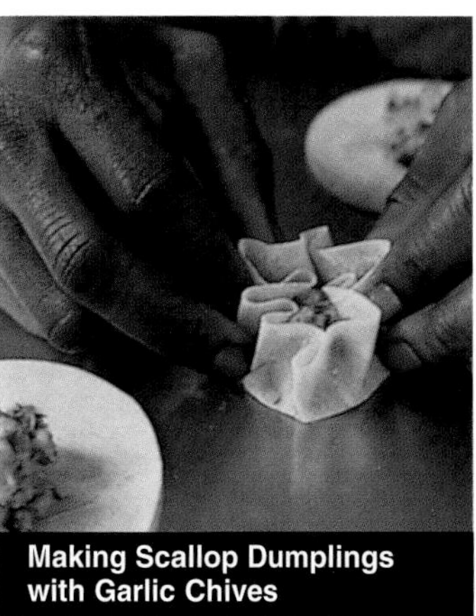
Making Scallop Dumplings with Garlic Chives

with the remaining wonton skins and filling.

4. Pour the remaining tablespoon vegetable oil onto a small plate. Dip the bottom of each dumpling in the oil. In a bamboo steamer basket, arrange the dumplings so that they do not touch. Cover and steam over boiling water for 10 minutes. (**MAKE AHEAD:** The dumplings can be refrigerated for up to 1 day or frozen for up to 2 weeks. Reheat in a steamer or a microwave oven.) Serve warm with the sauces.—ROSA ROSS

GOLDEN ROASTED OYSTERS

To eat one of these delicious oysters on the half-shell, drizzle lemon juice on top, then add a drop of hot sauce and slide the oyster into your mouth. And there's a surprise: a slice of artichoke hiding under the garlicky topping.

12 SERVINGS

- 6 large artichokes, stems trimmed
- 2 tablespoons olive oil, plus more for drizzling
- 1 tablespoon minced garlic
- Salt and freshly ground pepper
- 2 tablespoons fresh lemon juice
- 2 teaspoons minced fresh oregano
- 4 cups fresh bread crumbs (from about 2 baguettes)
- ¼ cup freshly grated Parmesan cheese
- ¼ cup minced fresh flat-leaf parsley
- 2 tablespoons unsalted butter, melted
- 4 dozen freshly shucked large oysters on the half-shell
- Coarse salt, for the platters
- Sweet paprika, for dusting
- Lemon wedges and Louisiana hot sauce

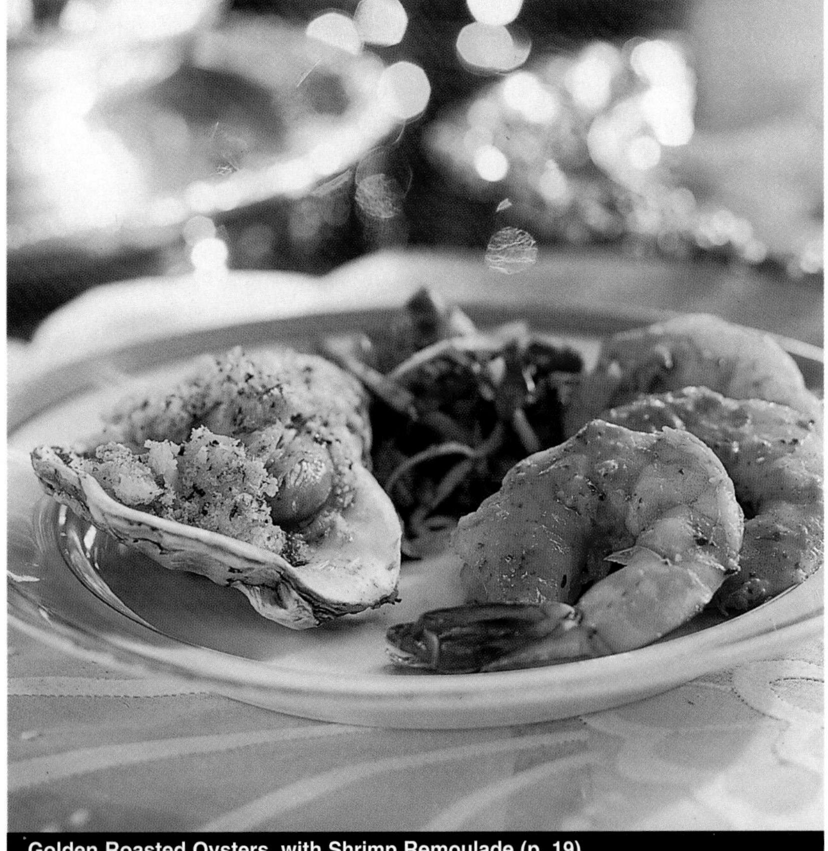

Golden Roasted Oysters, with Shrimp Remoulade (p. 19)

1. Arrange the artichokes in a large steaming basket, stem-end down. Set the basket in a large pot with 2 inches of water, cover and bring to a boil over high heat. Reduce the heat to moderate and steam the artichokes until tender when pierced with a knife, about 25 minutes. Transfer to a platter. When the artichokes are cool enough to handle, remove the artichoke leaves. Using a teaspoon, scrape out the hairy chokes. Cut each artichoke bottom into seven slices, then cut the large center slices in half.

2. In a large nonreactive skillet, warm 1 tablespoon of the olive oil over moderate heat. Add the garlic and cook until fragrant, about 1 minute. Add the artichoke slices, season with salt and pepper and cook, stirring, until lightly browned, about 4 minutes. Add the lemon juice and oregano and stir gently. Remove from the heat and add the remaining 1 tablespoon olive oil.

3. In a large bowl, mix the bread crumbs with the Parmesan, parsley, ¾ teaspoon salt, ¼ teaspoon pepper and the butter. (**MAKE AHEAD:** The artichokes and seasoned bread crumbs can be refrigerated separately for up to 1 day.)

4. Preheat the oven to 450°. Set the oysters in their shells on large baking sheets, fitting them snugly to prevent tilting. Put one artichoke slice and a pinch of the cooked garlic on each oyster, drizzle with olive oil and mound a scant 2 tablespoons of the bread crumbs on top.

5. Roast the oysters in the upper third of the oven for about 10 minutes, or until golden brown and bubbling. Meanwhile, cover serving platters with a layer of coarse salt. Sprinkle the roasted oysters with paprika and set them on the salt. Serve immediately with lemon wedges and hot sauce.—JAMIE SHANNON

OYSTER PATTIES

These rich patties in a crisp crust are like a taste of old New Orleans.

MAKES 12 PATTIES

DOUGH:

- 2 sticks (½ pound) cold unsalted butter, cut into tablespoons
- 2¼ cups all-purpose flour
- ½ cup ice water

FILLING:

- 1 stick (4 ounces) unsalted butter
- 4 celery ribs, finely chopped
- 2 medium leeks, white and light green parts, thinly sliced
- 1 large onion, finely chopped
- 1 tablespoon minced garlic
- 1 quart shucked oysters, in their liquor
- 1 tablespoon plus 1 teaspoon finely chopped fresh thyme
- 2 cups fresh bread crumbs
- 2 cups thinly sliced scallions (about 8 large scallions)
- Coarse salt and cracked black pepper
- ¼ cup freshly grated Pecorino Romano cheese
- Louisiana hot sauce

1. Make the dough: In a large bowl, using a pastry cutter or two knives, cut the butter into the flour until it resembles small peas. Add 6 tablespoons of the ice water and stir just until the dough can be gathered into a ball. Add more water, 1 tablespoon at a time, if the dough is too dry. Divide the dough into twelve equal portions and pat into ½-inch-thick disks. Wrap individually in plastic and refrigerate at least 1 hour or overnight.

2. Working with one disk at a time (keep the rest refrigerated), roll out the dough on a floured surface to a 6-inch round and fit it into a ½-cup ramekin or a 4-by-1-inch tart pan with a removable bottom. Trim the overhang. Refrigerate the pastry shells until well chilled.

3. Preheat the oven to 400°. **Make the filling:** In a large saucepan, melt the butter over moderate heat. Add the celery, leeks, onion and garlic and cook, stirring, until tender, about 10 minutes. Drain the oysters and reserve 1 cup of their liquor. Add the thyme and reserved oyster liquor to the pan and cook for 10 minutes. Add the oysters, bread crumbs and scallions and cook until the oysters are just cooked through, 3 to 5 minutes. Season with salt and pepper.

4. Spoon the oyster filling evenly into the pastry shells and sprinkle each with 1 teaspoon of the cheese. Place the ramekins directly on a rack in the lower third of the oven and bake for about 25 minutes, or until the tops of the patties are golden and bubbling and the crusts are golden. During baking, to make sure the patties brown evenly, move the front ramekins to the back of the oven and vice versa. Cool the patties slightly before serving or serve at room temperature. (**MAKE AHEAD:** The patties can be kept at room temperature for up to 3 hours.) Pass the hot sauce separately.—JAMIE SHANNON

CLAMS WITH LEMON CREAM AND SEVRUGA CAVIAR

Medium mussels can be substituted for the clams, and the dish can also be made without the caviar.

MAKES 2 DOZEN CLAMS

- 2 dozen mahogany or littleneck clams, scrubbed and rinsed
- 1 cup dry white wine
- 2 tablespoons minced shallots
- 1 fresh thyme sprig
- Freshly ground pepper
- 3 tablespoons heavy cream
- 1½ teaspoons fresh lemon juice
- 1 teaspoon minced fresh chives
- 1½ to 2 ounces sevruga or osetra caviar
- Salt
- 2 dozen fresh chervil leaves and tiny lemon triangles (see "Lemons," next page), for garnish

1. In a large nonreactive saucepan, combine the clams with the wine, shallots, thyme sprig and a pinch of pepper. Cover and cook over high heat until the clams just open, about 8 minutes. With a slotted spoon, transfer the clams to a bowl; strain and reserve 1½ teaspoons of the liquid. Remove the empty half-shell from each clam and reserve.

2. In a small bowl, combine the cream, lemon juice, chives and the reserved cooking liquid. Fold in the caviar. Season with salt and pepper. (**MAKE AHEAD:** The clams and cream can be made early in the day and refrigerated.)

3. Just before serving, spoon the caviar cream over each clam and garnish with the chervil and lemon wedges.—DANIEL BOULUD

LEMONS

One lemon can make both the juice and the garnish for Clams with Lemon Cream and Sevruga Caviar. Peel the lemon with a sharp knife, removing all the bitter white pith. Cut in between the membranes to release the sections into a bowl. Squeeze the membranes to extract the juice and use it in the recipe. Cut a few of the sections into tiny triangles to top the clams and cream.

Clams with Lemon Cream and Sevruga Caviar

BAKED MUSSELS

The Mediterranean mussel has a more delicate flavor and a creamier texture than our common Atlantic blue mussels, but both work beautifully in this dish. Mediterranean mussels cultivated in Puget Sound are available by mail from Taylor United in Shelton, Washington (360-426-6178). If you order mussels for this dish, ask for medium grade.

8 SERVINGS

- 2 pounds small-to-medium mussels, scrubbed, with beards removed
- Dry white wine, if needed
- ¼ cup fresh bread crumbs
- 3 tablespoons finely chopped fresh flat-leaf parsley
- 2 tablespoons minced garlic
- 2 tablespoons freshly grated Pecorino or Parmigiano-Reggiano cheese
- ½ teaspoon crumbled dried oregano
- ¼ cup extra-virgin olive oil

1. Preheat the oven to 425°. Discard any mussels that are gaping, keeping only those that are firmly closed. Place the mussels in a deep skillet with 3 tablespoons of water and cook over moderately high heat, stirring frequently. As the mussels open, transfer them to a large platter with a slotted spoon.

2. When all of the mussels are cooked, strain the liquid in the pan through a sieve lined with several layers of cheesecloth. (You should have ¼ cup of liquid; if not, make up the balance with a little dry white wine.) Remove the mussels from their shells, reserving one half-shell for each mussel; set the shells on a baking sheet and fill each one with a mussel.

3. In a small bowl, combine the bread crumbs, parsley, garlic, grated cheese and oregano. Evenly sprinkle the bread crumbs over the mussels, then drizzle the oil and the strained mussel liquid over them.

4. Bake the mussels in the oven for about 10 minutes, or until the tops are brown and crisp. Serve hot or at room temperature. (Do not reheat or the mussels will toughen.)—NANCY HARMON JENKINS

SMOKED-TROUT AND ROASTED-GARLIC DIP

This luxurious smoky dip goes nicely with pita crisps, vegetables, breadsticks and (best of all) toasted brioche. It's also fantastic as a spread for bagels at breakfast or brunch.

MAKES ABOUT 2½ CUPS

- 1 large unpeeled head of garlic, top quarter trimmed off
- ½ teaspoon minced fresh thyme, plus 5 whole sprigs
- 1 fresh rosemary sprig
- 1 teaspoon olive oil
- ½ pound smoked trout fillets, skin removed, meat flaked
- ¾ pound cream cheese, softened
- ½ cup half-and-half
- 2 teaspoons minced lemon zest
- Freshly ground pepper

1. Preheat the oven to 400°. Set the garlic cut-side up on a large square of foil and top with 3 thyme sprigs, the rosemary and the olive oil. Wrap tightly in foil and roast for about 1 hour, or until softened and caramelized. Let cool in the foil. Squeeze the softened garlic cloves from the

CRÈME FRAÎCHE

Crème fraîche is made by fermenting heavy cream. Thick, rich and tangy, it is delicious with both savory foods, like Smoked Salmon Tartare, and sweet ones. To make it, whisk three tablespoons buttermilk with one cup heavy cream. Cover and let stand at room temperature for up to twelve hours; then refrigerate.

skins into a bowl and mash the garlic with a fork.

2. In a food processor, pulse the trout until finely chopped. Add the cream cheese, half-and-half and lemon zest and process until combined. Add to the roasted garlic, along with the minced thyme and pepper. (MAKE AHEAD: The dip can be refrigerated for up to 4 days; let return to room temperature before serving.) Garnish with the remaining 2 thyme sprigs.—GRACE PARISI

SMOKED SALMON TARTARE

Smoked salmon is chopped by hand and blended with crème fraîche and dill. Don't try to make this in a food processor—the mixture will turn mushy.

Champagne or a dry white wine goes nicely with this unusual smoked tartare. Try a fresh and fragrant French Sancerre, an oak-aged California or New Zealand Fumé Blanc or a California or French Riesling.

8 SERVINGS

- ½ pound thinly sliced smoked salmon
- ¼ cup crème fraîche (see box, above)
- ¼ cup chopped fresh dill, plus additional for garnish
- Toasted baguette slices

Lay each slice of salmon flat on a cutting board and cut into matchstick-size strips, then cut crosswise into ¼-inch dice. In a medium bowl, toss the salmon gently with the crème fraîche and the ¼ cup dill. (MAKE AHEAD: The tartare can be refrigerated for up to 2 hours.) Transfer the tartare to a serving bowl and garnish with the additional dill. Serve with the toasted baguette slices.—PATRICIA WELLS

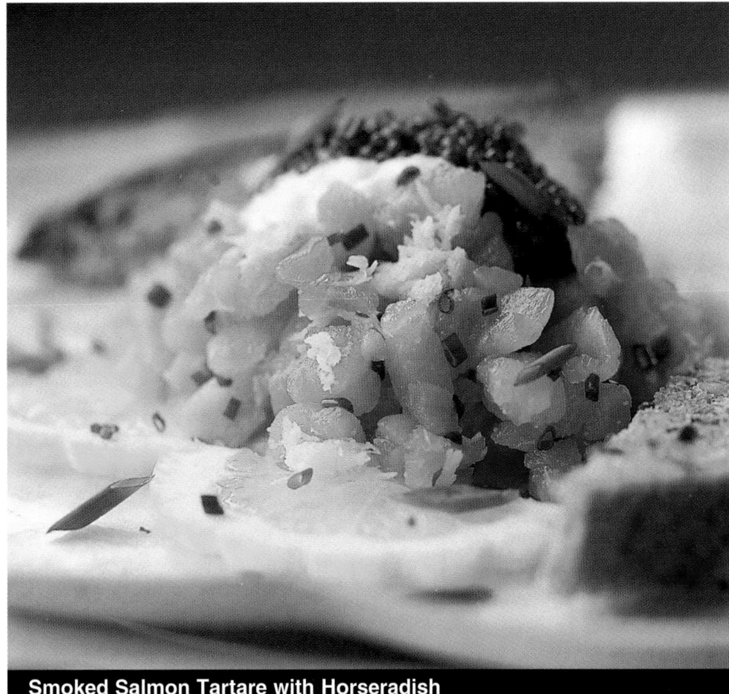

Smoked Salmon Tartare with Horseradish

SMOKED SALMON TARTARE WITH HORSERADISH

Serve chilled aquavit with this smoked salmon, or pick a highly aromatic wine, such as a California Viognier—especially the 1994 McDowell or the 1994 Arrowood.

4 SERVINGS

- 6 ounces smoked salmon
- 2 tablespoons chopped chives
- 2 tablespoons finely grated fresh or drained bottled horseradish
- 2 tablespoons sour cream
- 1 tablespoon fresh lemon juice
- 1 ounce sevruga caviar (optional)
- 6 slices whole grain toast, halved diagonally

Cut the salmon into ¼-inch dice; transfer to a bowl and stir in 1 tablespoon of the chives and the horseradish. In a bowl, combine the sour cream and lemon juice. Mound the salmon tartare on plates and drizzle with the lemon cream. Garnish the salmon with a dollop of caviar and the remaining chives. Serve with the toasts.—MARCUS SAMUELSSON ➤

CHICKEN-LIVER PÂTÉ

This recipe makes more than enough for eight; any extra will come in handy as a ready-made snack. The pâté can be refrigerated for up to four days. Spread one tablespoon of melted butter over the surfaces to seal the pâté and prevent discoloration.

MAKES 4 CUPS

- 2 pounds chicken livers, lobes separated and well trimmed
- ½ cup milk
- ½ pound sliced bacon
- 1 stick unsalted butter (4 ounces)
- Salt and freshly ground pepper
- 1 shallot, minced
- 1 garlic clove, minced
- 6 tablespoons Cognac
- 2 tablespoons minced fresh flat-leaf parsley
- 1 teaspoon minced fresh thyme
- 1 cup heavy cream
- 1 baguette, thinly sliced and toasted, for serving

1. In a medium bowl, soak the chicken livers in the milk for 30 minutes to remove any bitterness; drain and pat dry.

2. In a large heavy skillet, cook the bacon over moderate heat until crisp, about 8 minutes. Remove and drain on paper towels. Reserve 1 tablespoon of the fat.

3. Melt 1 tablespoon of the butter in the bacon fat over moderately high heat. When the butter stops foaming, add one-third of the chicken livers to the pan and season with salt and pepper. Cook without stirring until browned, about 2 minutes per side. The livers should be pink inside but not bloody. Transfer them to a plate. Repeat with the two remaining batches of livers, using ½ tablespoon butter for each batch.

4. Melt 1 tablespoon of the butter in the skillet. Add the shallot and garlic and cook, stirring, until slightly softened, about 2 minutes. Add the Cognac, parsley and thyme and boil for 1 minute.

5. Scrape the contents of the skillet into a food processor and add the chicken livers, the bacon and the remaining 5 tablespoons butter. Puree until smooth. Add the cream and process to blend. Season with salt and pepper. Spoon the pâté into four 1-cup crocks, smooth the tops and refrigerate until cold, at least 1 hour. Serve the pâté with the toasts.—DIANA STURGIS

VARIATIONS

• For a vegetarian version of Traditional Wontons, steam 1½ pounds stemmed fresh spinach until it is just wilted; squeeze dry and coarsely chop. In a small saucepan, mix 1 tablespoon cornstarch and 3 tablespoons water and simmer over low heat until thickened, about 1 minute. Stir in the spinach. Substitute for the pork in Step 2.

• To turn plain wonton skins into a tasty snack, brush one side lightly with oil, cut into thin strips and toss in a flavored salt (such as Spiced Salt, opposite page) or a mix of salt and pepper. Spread the strips on a baking sheet and toast in a preheated 350° oven for 5 to 8 minutes, or until lightly browned and crisp.

TRADITIONAL WONTONS

These wontons can be deep-fried, boiled or steamed. Serve them with one of the dipping sauces on the opposite page for an irresistible hors d'oeuvre.

MAKES 60 WONTONS

- 2 cups shredded napa cabbage
- ½ pound ground pork or chicken
- ½ cup lightly packed fresh cilantro leaves, finely chopped
- 2 scallions, minced
- 1 garlic clove, minced
- 1 teaspoon minced fresh ginger
- 1 teaspoon soy sauce
- 1 teaspoon Asian sesame oil
- ½ teaspoon salt
- ½ teaspoon freshly ground pepper
- 60 wonton skins
- 2 to 3 cups vegetable oil, for deep-frying (optional)
- Orange Sweet-and-Sour Sauce, Spicy Fish Sauce, Soy Vinegar Sauce or Spiced Salt (see "Wonton Dipping Sauces," opposite page)

1. In a medium saucepan of boiling water, blanch the cabbage for 2 minutes. Drain the cabbage and let cool slightly. Then squeeze out the excess water from the cabbage.

2. In a bowl, combine the cabbage with the ground pork, chopped cilantro leaves, scallions, garlic, ginger, soy sauce, Asian sesame oil, salt and pepper. Toss well.

3. Lay out 10 wonton skins on a work surface; keep the remainder of the skins covered with a damp towel. Place a rounded ½ teaspoon of filling in the center of each skin; dampen the edges and fold over to form a triangle. Press out the air and seal the edges. Dampen the two points farthest from each other and pinch them together to form a hat, or tortellini, shape. Put the filled wontons on a flour-dusted baking sheet and cover them with a clean towel. Repeat the procedure with the remaining skins and filling.

4. To deep-fry the wontons: Heat the vegetable oil to almost 400° in a wok. Add the filled wontons in batches of ten and cook, turning once, until they are lightly browned, 2 to 3 minutes. Using a slotted spoon, transfer to paper towels to drain. **To boil the wontons:** Bring a large saucepan of water to a boil. Add the wontons in batches and cook until they float to the top. Transfer the wontons to a colander to drain. **To steam the wontons:** In a bamboo steamer basket, arrange the wontons so that they do not touch. Cover and steam over boiling water for 10 minutes.

5. To serve, transfer the wontons to a platter and pass one or more of the dipping sauces separately.—ROSA ROSS

WONTON DIPPING SAUCES

Orange Sweet-and-Sour Sauce

MAKES 1 CUP

- 1 whole small dried red chile
- ⅔ cup fresh orange juice
- ¼ cup cider vinegar
- 2 tablespoons orange marmalade
- ½ teaspoon grated fresh ginger
- ¼ teaspoon salt

In a small nonreactive saucepan, simmer all the ingredients over low heat for 5 minutes. Let cool.

Spicy Fish Sauce

MAKES ABOUT ¼ CUP

- 2 tablespoons fresh lime juice
- 1 tablespoon fish sauce*
- 1 teaspoon chili paste
- ½ teaspoon sugar
- ½ teaspoon coarsely chopped fresh cilantro

*Available at Asian markets

Combine all the ingredients and stir to dissolve the sugar thoroughly. Let stand for 5 minutes.

Soy Vinegar Sauce

MAKES ¼ CUP

- 3 tablespoons soy sauce
- 1 tablespoon rice vinegar

In a small bowl, stir together the soy sauce and vinegar.

Spiced Salt

MAKES ABOUT ¼ CUP

- 1 teaspoon cumin seeds
- 1 teaspoon fennel seeds
- 1 teaspoon Szechuan peppercorns
- ½ teaspoon freshly ground black pepper
- 2 tablespoons coarse salt

In a small dry skillet, toast the cumin seeds, the fennel seeds and the Szechuan peppercorns over moderately low heat, stirring often, until they are aromatic, about 3 minutes. Let them cool. Grind in a spice grinder or a mortar and transfer the spices to a bowl. Add the black pepper and salt and mix well. Use as a dip for any fried food or as a dry rub in cooking.—ROSA ROSS

DEEP-FRIED SAVORY TARTS

As an alternative to frying, the tarts can be brushed with egg wash and baked in a preheated 375° oven for fifteen minutes, or until the tarts are golden and puffed.

MAKES 60–70 TARTS

DOUGH:

- 1 teaspoon active dry yeast
- 1 cup milk
- 3 tablespoons extra-virgin olive oil
- 3 tablespoons dry white wine
- 7 cups unbleached flour, plus more for kneading
- 1 teaspoon salt

ONION-AND-OLIVE STUFFING:

- 3 tablespoons extra-virgin olive oil
- 1 pound onions, halved lengthwise and thinly sliced crosswise
- 2 canned plum tomatoes, drained and coarsely chopped (½ cup)
- ⅓ cup minced fresh flat-leaf parsley
- 20 Kalamata olives, pitted and coarsely chopped
- 1 tablespoon capers
- 4 oil-packed anchovy fillets, coarsely chopped

3 tablespoons freshly grated Parmigiano-Reggiano cheese
Salt and freshly ground pepper

SPICY PORK STUFFING:

One 1-inch-thick slice of stale country bread, crust removed
½ pound lean ground pork
1 large egg
½ cup freshly grated Parmigiano-Reggiano cheese
½ cup finely chopped fresh flat-leaf parsley
1 teaspoon crushed red pepper
1 teaspoon freshly ground black pepper
½ teaspoon crumbled dried oregano
1 teaspoon salt

Extra-virgin olive oil, for deep-frying

1. Make the dough: In a small bowl, mix the yeast with 1 cup of warm water and let stand until frothy, about 10 minutes. Meanwhile, warm the milk in a small saucepan. Stir in the oil and wine.
2. In a large bowl, combine 2 cups of the flour with the dissolved yeast. Add the milk mixture to the dough and gradually stir in the remaining 5 cups flour and the salt. The dough should be very soft, but if it is too wet to knead by hand, add more flour. Turn the dough out onto a lightly floured work surface and knead until satiny and smooth, about 5 minutes. Place the dough in a lightly oiled bowl, cover with a damp kitchen towel and set aside in a warm place to rise until doubled in bulk, about 1 hour.
3. Make the onion-and-olive stuffing: Heat the oil in a large nonreactive skillet. Add the onions and cook over moderately low heat until softened but not browned, about 12 minutes. Stir in the tomatoes and cook until they begin to dissolve, about 5 minutes. Remove from the heat and stir in the parsley, olives, capers, anchovies and cheese. Season with salt and pepper.
4. Make the spicy pork stuffing: Soak the bread in warm water until softened, and then squeeze out as much water as possible. Tear the bread into small pieces. In a medium bowl, combine the bread, ground pork, egg, cheese, parsley, crushed red pepper, black pepper, oregano and salt. Knead the mixture thoroughly with your hands.
5. Punch down the dough and pull off sixty to seventy walnut-size pieces. Roll them into little balls and set the balls on a lightly floured baking sheet. Cover with a dampened cloth and let rise until billowy and nearly doubled in bulk, about 1 hour.
6. Working with a few pieces of dough at a time, roll out each ball on a lightly floured surface to a thin 4-inch round. Place 1 tablespoon of a filling on each circle, just to one side of the center. Lightly brush the edges with water, fold in half to enclose the filling and seal the edges with a fork. Set each tart on a rack as it is finished; repeat with the remaining dough and filling. Let the tarts dry for at least 15 minutes after the last one is completed.
7. In a deep skillet, heat 1½ inches of oil to 380°. Working in batches of four or five, carefully slide the tarts into the hot oil and fry until golden on both sides, about 5 minutes. Using a slotted spoon, transfer the tarts to a rack to drain. Serve immediately.—NANCY HARMON JENKINS

BACARO-STYLE FRIED MEATBALLS WITH POTATO

These meatballs are delightfully soft because they contain a large proportion of mashed potatoes. Although they are best the moment they are made, they're quite good cold. The traditional version calls for an equal mixture of three ground meats—beef, veal and pork—but I find the all-beef the most succulent.

ABOUT 40 MEATBALLS

½ pound boiling potatoes
3 tablespoons vegetable oil, plus more for frying
1 teaspoon minced garlic
½ teaspoon chopped fresh rosemary
1 pound ground beef chuck
Salt and freshly ground pepper
3 thin slices firm-textured white bread, crusts trimmed
½ cup milk
2 tablespoons chopped flat-leaf parsley
2 large eggs
½ cup freshly grated Parmesan cheese
1 cup fine, dry bread crumbs

1. In a medium saucepan, cover the potatoes with cold water and boil gently over moderately high heat until tender.
2. Meanwhile, in a large skillet, combine the 3 tablespoons vegetable oil with ½ teaspoon of the garlic and the rosemary. Cook over moderately high heat, stirring frequently, until the garlic is fragrant but not colored. Add the ground beef and break it up with a wooden spoon. Season the meat

with salt and pepper and cook, stirring from time to time, until it is evenly browned. Empty the meat into a colander set over a bowl to drain off the fat. Transfer the meat to a large bowl.

3. In a small bowl, soak the bread in the milk for a few minutes; it should absorb as much as possible.

4. Drain the potatoes as soon as they are tender. Peel while still hot and mash through a food mill or ricer into the bowl with the meat. Add the milk-soaked bread and the remaining ½ teaspoon garlic, the parsley, 1 egg and the Parmesan. Mix thoroughly.

5. Break the remaining egg into a small bowl and beat it lightly with 2 tablespoons water. Spread the bread crumbs on a plate. Lightly roll the meat mixture into 1-inch balls. Dip the meatballs first in the beaten egg, lifting them out one at a time and letting any excess egg drip back into the bowl, and then roll them in the bread crumbs. Set the meatballs on a platter. (**MAKE AHEAD:** The meatballs can stand for up to 1 hour before frying.)

6. Pour ½ inch of vegetable oil into a large skillet and turn the heat to high; the oil is ready when a piece of bread added to the skillet sizzles immediately. Add as many meatballs as will fit loosely in the pan. Fry, turning as necessary, until evenly browned all over, about 4 minutes. Adjust the heat as needed if the oil becomes too hot. Transfer the browned meatballs to a wire rack set over a tray or paper towels. Fry the remaining meatballs in batches. Transfer to a warmed platter and serve piping hot, or serve at room temperature.—MARCELLA HAZAN

CRISP PHYLLO BITES WITH ASPARAGUS AND PROSCIUTTO

MAKES ABOUT 3½ DOZEN PIECES

- 6 long, fairly thick asparagus spears, stems peeled
- Freshly ground pepper
- 9 thin slices of lean prosciutto (2 to 3 ounces)
- 6 sheets of phyllo dough
- 3 tablespoons unsalted butter, melted
- ½ cup freshly grated Parmesan cheese
- Freshly grated nutmeg

1. In a saucepan of boiling salted water, blanch the asparagus until crisp-tender, about 2 minutes. Refresh under cold water and pat very dry with paper towels.

2. Season the asparagus spears with pepper and roll them in the prosciutto; you will need about 1½ slices to cover each spear.

3. Preheat the oven to 400°. Lay one sheet of the phyllo on a work surface with the short end directly in front of you. Brush it with butter and sprinkle with 1 tablespoon of the Parmesan and a pinch of nutmeg. Set a wrapped asparagus spear on the short end of the phyllo and roll it up snugly. Brush the roll with butter, dust it lightly with more Parmesan and set it on a baking sheet. Repeat with the remaining ingredients, arranging the rolls at least 2 inches apart on the sheet.

4. Bake the rolls on the top shelf of the oven for 10 to 12 minutes, or until golden brown and crisp. Let the rolls cool slightly before slicing them at an angle into bite-size pieces.—DANIEL BOULUD

Crisp Phyllo Bites with Asparagus and Prosciutto

VENETIAN WAFERS

This traditional Italian snack is frequently served with sparkling wine. The super-simple version here is from Recipes 1-2-3 *(Viking).*

MAKES 24 WAFERS

- 24 slices *soppressata* salami
- ½ cup freshly grated Parmesan cheese
- 2 tablespoons fennel seeds

1. Preheat the oven to 500°. Place the *soppressata* slices side by side on a large baking sheet. Sprinkle 1 teaspoon of the cheese on each slice to cover evenly, then sprinkle each with ¼ teaspoon fennel seeds.

2. Bake the wafers for 5 to 7 minutes, or until sizzling. Remove from the oven and serve while still warm. The wafers will be crisp.—ROZANNE GOLD

CHAPTER 2

~

FIRST COURSES

Ratatouille Taco Towers

RATATOUILLE TACO TOWERS LF

These unusual tacos are made by filling tortillas with earthy Provençal vegetables and garnishing them with a little spoonful of fragrant pesto sauce.

4 SERVINGS

RATATOUILLE:

1 tablespoon olive oil
1 medium red onion, finely chopped
1 medium red bell pepper, finely chopped
1 medium yellow bell pepper, finely chopped
1 small zucchini, finely chopped
½ small eggplant, finely chopped
2 medium tomatoes, finely chopped
4 garlic cloves, minced
2 tablespoons minced fresh basil
2 teaspoons minced fresh thyme
Salt and freshly ground black pepper

BASIL PESTO:

1 tablespoon olive oil
1 teaspoon pine nuts
1 tablespoon finely chopped fresh basil
½ teaspoon minced garlic
Salt and freshly ground black pepper

Four 6-inch flour tortillas

1. Make the ratatouille: Preheat the oven to 400°. Heat the oil in a large nonstick skillet. Add the onion and cook over moderate heat, stirring, until translucent, about 3 minutes. Add the red and yellow bell peppers and cook until just tender, about 3 minutes. Add the zucchini and eggplant and cook until just tender, about 4 minutes. Add the tomatoes, garlic, basil and thyme, season with salt and black pepper and toss to combine. Spread the mixture in a medium baking dish and roast for about 10 minutes, or until softened and beginning to brown. Transfer to a plate to cool. Lower the oven temperature to 375°. (**MAKE AHEAD:** The ratatouille can be refrigerated for up to 1 day. Let return to room temperature before proceeding.)

2. Make the basil pesto: In a mortar, work all the ingredients together to form a puree.

3. Lay the tortillas out on a work surface. Spread half of the ratatouille on the tortillas, leaving a ½-inch border around the edges. Roll up the tortillas and secure each one with a toothpick. Set the rolls, seam-side down, on a baking sheet and bake for about 10 minutes, or until crisp, lightly golden and heated through.

4. Slice the ends off each roll and remove the toothpicks. Cut each roll in half diagonally and set two halves upright on each of four plates. Spoon the remaining ratatouille around the taco towers, garnish with a spoonful of pesto and serve.—VINCENT GUERITHAULT

TOMATO RAVIOLI WITH ROASTED-TOMATO SAUCE

The smoky tomato flavors call for a gutsy, fruity, uncomplicated red with plenty of intense, ripe flavors. Among the possible choices: the 1992 Louis M. Martini Barbera, the 1994 Quivira Zinfandel from California or the 1994 Paul Jaboulet Aîné Saint-Joseph Le Grand Pompée from France.

8 SERVINGS

PASTA:

1 cup all-purpose flour
1 teaspoon coarse salt
1 large egg
1 tablespoon extra-virgin olive oil

8 small fresh basil leaves, plus 1 cup of leaves
8 roasted-tomato halves from Roasted Tomatoes (p. 362)
Salt and freshly ground pepper
Extra-virgin olive oil
1 tablespoon fresh tarragon leaves
¼ cup small fresh dill sprigs
¼ cup fresh flat-leaf parsley leaves
1 cup fresh chervil leaves
Roasted-Tomato Sauce (recipe follows)

1. Make the pasta: In a standing mixer fitted with the paddle, blend the flour and salt. In a small bowl, beat the egg with the oil and 1 tablespoon water. With the mixer on the lowest speed, slowly add the beaten egg and mix until the dough comes together in a loose ball.

2. Turn the dough out onto a work surface and knead it into a smooth, firm ball. Cover the dough with plastic wrap and let rest at room temperature for 20 minutes to 1 hour. (**MAKE AHEAD:** The dough can also be wrapped in plastic and refrigerated for up to 1 day.)

3. Pat the ball of pasta dough into a disk. Using a pasta machine, gradually roll the pasta dough through successively narrower settings, ending with the thinnest. Cut the dough into eight 5-inch squares and cover. ➤

4. Bring a medium saucepan of salted water to a boil. Fill a bowl with cold water. Boil the pasta squares one at a time for 30 seconds each; drop the pasta into the cold water as soon as it's done, then drain on paper towels.
5. Place a basil leaf in the center of each pasta square, top it with a tomato half and season with salt and pepper. Fold the pasta over the tomato half as you would fold a letter, then fold in the ends. Transfer the ravioli, folded-side down, to a rimmed baking sheet lined with parchment paper and brush them with a little olive oil. (**MAKE AHEAD:** The ravioli can be refrigerated for up to 1 day.)
6. Preheat the oven to 450°. Pour enough very hot water around the ravioli to just cover the bottom of the pan. Bake the ravioli for about 3 minutes, or until heated through.
7. In a large bowl, toss the remaining 1 cup basil leaves with the tarragon, dill, parsley and chervil. Add 1 teaspoon oil; season with salt and pepper. Toss well.
8. Set one ravioli on each plate and spoon the tomato sauce around them. Garnish with the herb salad and serve immediately.

Tomato Ravioli with Roasted-Tomato Sauce

Roasted-Tomato Sauce

MAKES ABOUT 1½ CUPS

- 2 roasted-tomato halves from Roasted Tomatoes (p. 362)
- 6 roasted garlic cloves from Roasted Tomatoes (p. 362), peeled
- 1 cup tomato juices from Roasted Tomatoes (p. 362), warmed
- 2 tablespoons extra-virgin olive oil
- Salt and freshly ground pepper

In a blender, combine the roasted-tomato halves, the roasted garlic cloves and the tomato juices and puree. With the machine running, slowly add the olive oil to make a smooth, thick sauce. Transfer the sauce to a small nonreactive saucepan and season with salt and pepper. Just before serving, rewarm the sauce gently until almost hot.—TOM COLICCHIO

VEGETABLE TORTA WITH TOMATO COULIS

Even out of season, farms in Mexico and greenhouses in the United States and abroad supply all the vegetables you'll need for this dish.

8 SERVINGS

- 6 large unpeeled garlic cloves
- ¼ cup olive oil
- 2 medium zucchini, sliced lengthwise ¼ inch thick
- 1 pound plum tomatoes, sliced crosswise ¼ inch thick
- Salt and freshly ground pepper
- 1 medium eggplant, peeled and sliced crosswise ¼ inch thick
- 1 large red bell pepper
- 11 ounces soft, mild goat cheese, at room temperature
- Tomato Coulis (recipe follows)

1. Preheat the oven to 400°. Wrap the garlic cloves in foil and roast for 40 minutes, or until soft and golden.
2. Meanwhile, brush two heavy baking sheets with some of the

oil. Arrange the zucchini on one sheet and the tomatoes on the other, in a single layer. Brush the zucchini with oil. Season the vegetables with salt and pepper and roast for about 20 minutes, or until just beginning to brown; switch the baking sheets halfway through. Transfer the vegetables to a platter.

3. Brush the baking sheets with more oil and arrange the eggplant in a single layer. Brush the eggplant with oil and season with salt and pepper. Roast for about 20 minutes, until soft and just beginning to brown. Let cool.

4. Roast the bell pepper directly over a gas flame or under the broiler until blackened all over. Transfer to a paper bag, seal and let steam for 20 minutes. Peel and core the pepper, discarding the seeds and ribs. Slice the pepper into ¼-inch-wide strips.

5. Lower the oven temperature to 325°. Squeeze the garlic pulp from the skins into a medium bowl. Add the goat cheese, season with salt and pepper and mash to a paste.

6. Line the bottom of a 9-inch springform pan with parchment paper and brush the paper with the remaining oil. Line the bottom with the zucchini strips in a decorative pattern. Arrange half of the tomatoes and bell-pepper strips over the zucchini. Spoon half of the goat-cheese mixture in small dollops all over the tomatoes and peppers. Cover with half of the eggplant slices, overlapping them slightly. Top the eggplant with the remaining tomatoes and bell-pepper strips. Dot with the remaining goat cheese and top with the remaining eggplant. Cover with a piece of oiled parchment paper and press down to compress the torta. (**MAKE AHEAD:** The torta can be refrigerated at this point for up to 3 days.)

7. Bake the torta for about 20 minutes, or until it is warmed through. Let cool for 10 minutes, then remove the sides of the springform pan. Remove the parchment paper, place a large plate over the torta and invert. Carefully remove the pan bottom and the parchment paper. Serve the torta in wedges with the coulis spooned alongside.

Tomato Coulis

MAKES ABOUT 1½ CUPS

1 tablespoon unsalted butter
1 tablespoon olive oil
1 small onion, finely chopped
1 garlic clove, minced
1½ pounds plum tomatoes
½ cup dry white wine
Pinch of crushed red pepper
Pinch of salt

In a nonreactive medium saucepan, melt the butter in the oil over moderate heat. Add the onion and garlic and cook until translucent. Add the tomatoes, wine, crushed red pepper and salt and cook until the tomatoes are soft, about 25 minutes. Pass the sauce through a food mill or strainer into a small bowl, pressing on the solids to extract the juices. Serve warm.—GRACE PARISI

ZUCCHINI WITH MOZZARELLA AND OLIVES

Warm sautéed zucchini slices melt slivers of fresh mozzarella, while a sprinkling of chopped olives adds salty flavor to this simple, summery dish. Serve with crusty bread.

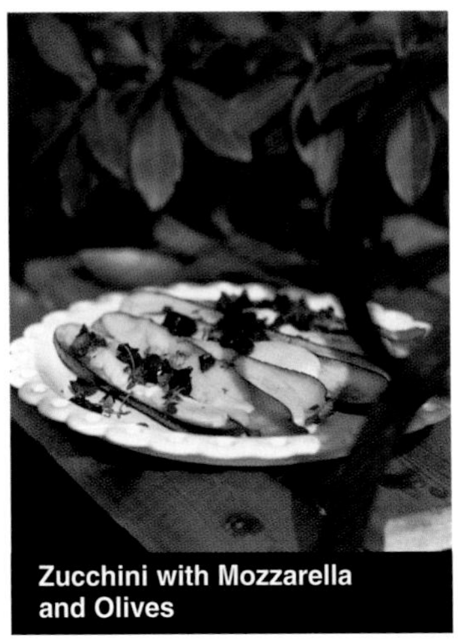
Zucchini with Mozzarella and Olives

An assertive dry white wine, such as the 1995 Vietti Roero Arneis from Italy or the 1994 Eyrie Vineyards Pinot Gris from Oregon, would add its own accent to the mozzarella and zucchini and stand up to the olives.

6 SERVINGS

About ¼ cup extra-virgin olive oil
Five 6-inch-long zucchini, sliced lengthwise ¼ inch thick
Salt and freshly ground pepper
½ pound fresh mozzarella, halved and cut into ¼-inch-thick slices
1½ teaspoons minced fresh thyme
2 tablespoons finely chopped black olives, such as Niçoise

1. In a skillet, heat 1 tablespoon of the oil until almost smoking. Season the zucchini with salt and pepper and add about a quarter of the slices to the skillet in a single layer. Cook over moderately high heat, turning once, until lightly browned, about 1 minute per side. Transfer the zucchini slices to a platter, loosely fanning them out to resemble their original shape. Insert pieces of mozzarella between the warm slices; cover the slices with foil and keep warm.

2. Cook the remaining zucchini, using 1 tablespoon of oil per batch; layer the just-cooked zucchini slices with slices of mozzarella. Sprinkle the thyme and the olives over the zucchini and serve warm or at room temperature.—MARCIA KIESEL

TOMATO AND FETA BRUSCHETTA

The sharp, herbal character of Sauvignon Blanc is tailor-made to cope with the acidity of tomatoes, the bite of onion and the tang of feta in this dish. Look for forthright bottlings, such as the 1995 Chimney Rock Fumé Blanc from California or the 1995 Casa Lapostolle Sauvignon Blanc from Chile.

8 SERVINGS

2½ tablespoons extra-virgin olive oil
1 tablespoon fresh thyme leaves
1½ teaspoons red-wine vinegar
1 teaspoon minced fresh hot chile, such as jalapeño or serrano
1 medium red onion, thinly sliced
4 ounces feta cheese, preferably Bulgarian, crumbled
Salt and freshly ground pepper
Eight ½-inch-thick slices from a large loaf of peasant bread
2 large ripe tomatoes, sliced ½ inch thick

1. In a medium bowl, combine the oil, thyme, vinegar and chile. Fold in the onion and feta and season with salt and pepper.

2. Toast the bread. Spread the feta mixture on the pieces of toast and arrange the tomato slices on top, cutting them in half if necessary. Season with salt and pepper and serve.—MARCIA KIESEL

BUYING TOMATOES

The redder, the better. For cooking, the best value is an ordinary plum tomato. For eating raw, you may want to splurge on a greenhouse variety. Keep any tomato out on the counter until it's fully ripe.—JULIA CALIFANO

Fallen Goat-Cheese Soufflé

FALLEN GOAT-CHEESE SOUFFLÉS LF

8 SERVINGS

5 medium red bell peppers, roasted, peeled, cored and seeded
⅓ cup chicken stock or canned low-sodium broth, skimmed of fat
¼ cup minced fresh herbs, such as parsley, dill and chives
Salt and freshly ground pepper
Vegetable cooking spray
¼ cup plain dry bread crumbs
¾ cup low-fat ricotta cheese
5½ ounces soft fresh goat cheese
3 tablespoons grated aged goat cheese
1 cup plus 2 tablespoons skim milk
3 tablespoons cornstarch

5 large egg whites, at room temperature

1. Put the roasted peppers in a blender and puree with the stock. Strain into a nonreactive saucepan, stir in 2 tablespoons of the mixed herbs and season with salt and pepper.
2. Preheat the oven to 350°. Coat eight ½-cup ramekins with vegetable cooking spray. Season the bread crumbs with salt and pepper and use them to coat the ramekins. In a food processor, puree the ricotta, the fresh and aged goat cheeses, the remaining 2 tablespoons herbs, 1 teaspoon of salt and ¼ teaspoon pepper until smooth.
3. In a small bowl, stir 2 tablespoons of the milk into the cornstarch until smooth. In a medium saucepan, bring the remaining 1 cup milk to a boil. Remove the pan from the heat and whisk in the dissolved cornstarch until smooth. Stir in the cheese mixture and let cool.
4. Beat the egg whites with a pinch of salt until stiff peaks form. Stir one-third of the whites into the cheese mixture, then fold in the remaining whites. Spoon the soufflé mixture into the ramekins and set them in a baking dish. Add water to reach halfway up the sides of the ramekins and bake for about 35 minutes, or until the tops are browned. Transfer to a wire rack to cool for 15 minutes.
5. Make a pool of the red-pepper sauce on eight plates. Unmold the soufflés and place them, browned-side up, on top of the red-pepper sauce and serve.—BOB CHAMBERS

MINT FRITTATA

4–8 SERVINGS

3 tablespoons extra-virgin olive oil
1 small onion, finely chopped
1 cup loosely packed fresh mint leaves
8 large eggs, lightly beaten
3 tablespoons freshly grated Parmigiano-Reggiano cheese
Salt and freshly ground pepper

1. Preheat the broiler and adjust a rack so that the top of the skillet will be about 6 inches from the heat. In a 10- to 12-inch ovenproof skillet, heat 2 tablespoons of the oil. Add the onion and cook over moderately low heat until softened but not browned, 6 to 8 minutes. Scrape the onion into a small bowl, add the mint and let cool completely.
2. In a medium bowl, combine the eggs, cheese and mint mixture. Season with salt and pepper.
3. Return the skillet to moderately high heat and add the remaining 1 tablespoon oil. Swirl the pan to coat the bottom and sides with the oil. Add the beaten eggs and cook, occasionally lifting the set sides to allow the uncooked eggs to seep underneath, until the bottom is golden and set, 5 to 7 minutes.
4. Place the frittata under the broiler for about 30 seconds to cook and brown the top. Cut it into wedges or small squares and serve hot, warm or at room temperature.—NANCY HARMON JENKINS

JUICY TIDBITS

• It's no pulp fiction: the pulp in fruit and vegetable juice is full of nutrients that contain antioxidant, anticarcinogenic and anti-inflammatory agents. Squeeze the juice yourself or buy a commercial juice with pulp in it.
• Fresh-squeezed juice contains folic acid, which may prevent birth defects and heart disease.
• If you must buy juice, tomato is a good choice. Partly as a result of their acidity, tomatoes lose fewer nutrients in processing than fruits like apples do. Veggie-packed V8 juice is a healthy alternative to the juice of freshly squeezed greens.

SHRIMP COCKTAIL WITH BLOODY-MARY SORBET LF

For this creative first course, you can buy any juice made with greens (like parsley, spinach, celery or chard) from a juice bar or health-food store. On the West Coast, look for the widely available bottled Hansen's mixed-greens juice. You can use V8 juice instead of the greens juice, but you'll lose the color contrast with the tomato sorbet.

6 SERVINGS

3 tablespoons sugar
4 ripe plum tomatoes, peeled, seeded and coarsely chopped
½ cup tomato juice
1½ tablespoons tomato paste
1 tablespoon fresh lemon juice
Salt and ground white pepper
Tabasco sauce
2 tablespoons minced fresh chives
18 medium shrimp, shelled and deveined with the tails left on
¼ cup plus 2 tablespoons savory greens juice

2 tablespoons dry vermouth
2 tablespoons sour cream
6 cilantro sprigs and 6 celery ribs with leafy tops, for garnish

1. In a small saucepan, stir the sugar with ¼ cup of water over moderate heat until dissolved; let the syrup cool.

2. In a blender, process the tomatoes, tomato juice, tomato paste, lemon juice, sugar syrup, salt and pepper until smooth. Add the Tabasco and chives. Transfer to an ice-cream maker and freeze according to the manufacturer's instructions. Alternatively, freeze the sorbet in a nonreactive baking dish until firm. Scrape into crystals with a fork.

3. In a medium saucepan of boiling water, cook the shrimp until pink throughout, about 2 minutes. Drain, rinse with cold water and pat dry.

4. Scoop the sorbet into six martini glasses. Spoon 1 tablespoon greens juice and 1 teaspoon vermouth into each glass and garnish with 1 teaspoon of sour cream, a cilantro sprig and a celery rib. Arrange three shrimp around the rim of each glass and serve.—HANS RÖCKENWAGNER

Shrimp Escabeche with Ginger-Grilled Pineapple

SHRIMP ESCABECHE WITH GINGER-GRILLED PINEAPPLE LF

Traditionally, escabeche is made by pickling fried fish. This low-fat version features sautéed shrimp in a cilantro marinade with tangy grilled pineapple.

6 SERVINGS

1 teaspoon olive oil
12 large shrimp, shelled and deveined
Fine sea salt and ground pepper
1 medium onion, finely chopped
½ teaspoon minced garlic
½ cup fresh orange juice
¼ cup fresh lime juice
2 tablespoons minced scallion
2 tablespoons minced fresh cilantro
1 tablespoon plus 1 teaspoon minced fresh ginger
1 tablespoon Asian sesame oil
1 large ripe pineapple, peeled, quartered lengthwise and cored
1 teaspoon sesame seeds

1. Heat the oil in a large nonstick skillet. Season the shrimp with salt and pepper and cook over high heat for 1 minute. Add the onion and garlic and cook, stirring occasionally, until the shrimp are cooked through, about 2 minutes more. Stir in the orange juice, 2 tablespoons of the lime juice, the scallion and the cilantro, transfer to a bowl and let cool.
2. Meanwhile, in another bowl, combine the remaining 2 tablespoons lime juice with the ginger, sesame oil, ½ teaspoon salt and ¼ teaspoon pepper. Brush the pineapple with this mixture and let stand at room temperature for 30 minutes.
3. In a dry skillet, toast the sesame seeds over high heat, shaking the pan, until fragrant, about 2 minutes.
4. Light a grill or preheat the broiler. Grill or broil the pineapple for about 2 minutes per side, turning once, until it is lightly browned. Cut each quarter crosswise into six pieces and arrange the pieces on six plates. Set two shrimp on each plate, spoon on a little of the orange-juice marinade and sprinkle with the sesame seeds.—ALLEN SUSSER

SHRIMP IN GARLIC SAUCE

You can't go to the Basque country without trying gambas al ajillo, *a classic seafood tapas dish and one of the simplest and most delicious of all shrimp preparations.*

🍷 *1993 or 1994 Torres Fransola*

6 SERVINGS

- ¾ cup olive oil
- 4 medium garlic cloves, thinly sliced
- 1½ pounds medium shrimp, shelled and deveined
- 5 small dried red chiles*
- Salt
- 1 thin loaf of French or Italian bread, for serving

*Available at specialty-food stores and most supermarkets

1. In a large, heavy nonreactive skillet, combine the oil and the garlic and cook over moderate heat, stirring occasionally with a wooden spoon, until the garlic is lightly golden, about 1 minute. Add the shrimp and dried red chiles and cook, stirring frequently, just until the shrimp are opaque throughout, 3 to 4 minutes. Immediately remove the skillet from the heat and season the shrimp lightly with salt.
2. Serve the shrimp at once in their oil with the bread for sopping it up.—JOSU ZUBIKARAI

STEAMED HERBED SHRIMP IN COCONUT MILK

6 SERVINGS

- 18 medium shrimp, shelled
- 4 teaspoons fresh lime juice
- ½ cup minced shallots
- ¼ teaspoon turmeric, plus a pinch
- 1 cup thick unsweetened coconut milk*
- 1 large egg, lightly beaten
- 2 fresh red Thai chiles,* 1 minced, 1 thinly sliced
- 2 tablespoons minced fresh lemongrass,* white bulb only
- ½ tablespoon tamarind concentrate* dissolved in ½ tablespoon boiling water
- 1 tablespoon Thai fish sauce*
- ½ teaspoon granulated sugar

Steamed Herbed Shrimp in Coconut Milk

- ½ teaspoon salt
- 2 tablespoons fresh coriander (cilantro) leaves

*Available at Asian markets

1. In a bowl, toss the shrimp with 1 teaspoon of the lime juice, 1 teaspoon of the shallots and the pinch turmeric. Let marinate at room temperature for 20 minutes.
2. In a bowl, beat the coconut milk with the egg. Stir in the remaining lime juice, shallots and turmeric, plus the minced chile, lemongrass, tamarind liquid, fish sauce, sugar and salt. Pour the mixture into six ½-cup ramekins or heatproof bowls and set three shrimp in the center of each. Arrange the ramekins on a wide rack set in a wok or large saucepan over 2 inches of simmering water. Wrap foil around the rack to secure, if necessary. Cover the wok and steam over low heat until the custards are just set and the shrimp are cooked, about 8 minutes. Garnish with the chile slices and the coriander and serve.—THAI COOKING SCHOOL, THE ORIENTAL HOTEL, BANGKOK ➤

PANFRIED SOFT-SHELL CRABS WITH WILTED ESCAROLE

4 SERVINGS

- 1½ teaspoons extra-virgin olive oil
- 1 large head of escarole, cored and cut into ½-inch-wide strips
- 2 large garlic cloves, minced
- 2 anchovy fillets, finely chopped, plus 1 teaspoon oil from the jar
- 2 tablespoons fresh lemon juice
- 5 tablespoons unsalted butter
- ½ cup all-purpose flour
- Salt and freshly ground pepper
- 4 medium soft-shell crabs, cleaned
- 3 tablespoons vegetable oil

1. Warm the olive oil in a nonreactive medium saucepan. Add the escarole and cook over high heat, stirring, until the escarole is wilted. Reduce the heat to moderate, 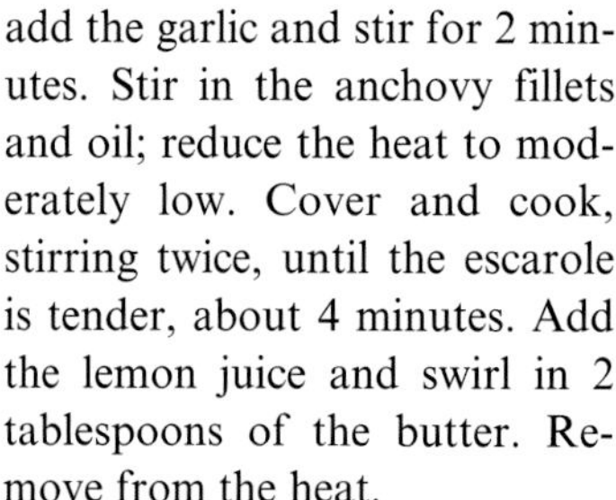add the garlic and stir for 2 minutes. Stir in the anchovy fillets and oil; reduce the heat to moderately low. Cover and cook, stirring twice, until the escarole is tender, about 4 minutes. Add the lemon juice and swirl in 2 tablespoons of the butter. Remove from the heat.

2. On a large flat plate, mix the flour with 1 teaspoon salt and ½ teaspoon pepper. Pat the crabs dry with paper towels. Dredge the crabs in the flour, shaking off the excess.

3. In a large skillet, heat the vegetable oil until shimmering. Add the remaining 3 tablespoons butter; when it stops sizzling, put in the crabs, under-side up. Fry the crabs over high heat, turning once, until they are crisp and cooked through, about 7 minutes. Reduce the heat if the oil gets too smoky.

4. Gently reheat the escarole and taste for seasoning. Spoon the escarole and lemon sauce onto plates, set the crabs on top and serve hot.—MARCIA KIESEL

Panfried Soft-Shell Crabs with Wilted Escarole

WHITE BEANS WITH CLAMS

Beans are commonly used in Basque cuisine. Here they are paired with shellfish in a light Basque stew.

🍷 *1993 Guelbenzu Navarra*

6 SERVINGS

- 1¾ cups dried navy beans
- 1 small onion, finely chopped
- 1 medium green bell pepper, finely chopped
- 1 bottle clam juice (8 to 10 ounces)
- 3 dozen small clams (4 pounds), such as littlenecks, well rinsed
- Coarsely chopped flat-leaf parsley

1. Soak the beans overnight in a bowl of cold water. (Alternatively, in a large saucepan, cover the beans generously with cold water and bring to a boil; simmer for 2 minutes, remove from the heat, cover and let sit for 1 hour.) Drain and rinse the beans; transfer them to a medium flameproof casserole. Add 1 quart of water, the onion and green pepper and bring to a boil. Reduce the heat to low and simmer for 45 minutes. Add the clam juice, cover partially and simmer, stirring occasionally, until the beans are tender, about 40 minutes.

2. Add the clams. Cover the pan tightly and cook over moderate heat; remove any opened clams after 5 minutes and check every 2 minutes thereafter. There should be enough liquid to keep the beans moist; add a few tablespoons of water if needed.

3. Spoon the beans and the clams into warm bowls, garnish with the parsley and serve.—JOSU ZUBIKARAI

CLAM RAGOUT WITH BACON AND ROASTED TOMATOES

4 SERVINGS

- 6 ounces slab bacon or pancetta, sliced ½ inch thick and cut into 2-inch pieces
- 1 tablespoon extra-virgin olive oil, plus more for serving
- 2 garlic cloves, thinly sliced
- 1 shallot, thinly sliced
- 4 roasted-tomato halves from Roasted Tomatoes (p. 362)
- ½ cup dry white wine
- 3 dozen littleneck clams, scrubbed and rinsed
- 4 cups packed baby mustard greens or watercress

Clam Ragout with Bacon and Roasted Tomatoes

1. In a large nonreactive saucepan, cook the bacon over moderately low heat until lightly browned and crisp, about 15 minutes. Transfer the bacon to a plate and pour off the fat. Add the olive oil to the pan along with the garlic and shallot and cook over moderate heat, stirring, until fragrant, about 2 minutes. Add the tomato halves and cook until warmed through.
2. Add the wine and simmer for 3 minutes, then add the clams. Cover and cook, stirring occasionally, until the clams open, about 12 minutes. Uncover, stir in the mustard greens and cook just until wilted. Gently stir in the bacon.
3. Ladle the ragout into four soup plates or shallow bowls and drizzle 1 teaspoon of olive oil over each serving.—TOM COLICCHIO

BAKED MUSSELS, POTATOES AND ZUCCHINI

This recipe may seem complex, but the mussels, tomato sauce and potatoes can be prepared well ahead of time. For best results, use waxy red-skinned potatoes or semi-waxy Yellow Finns but not starchy baking potatoes like Idahos.

4–8 SERVINGS

- 2 pounds medium mussels, scrubbed and debearded
- ½ cup extra-virgin olive oil
- 2 medium onions, halved lengthwise and thinly sliced crosswise
- 2 garlic cloves, finely chopped
- 5 large plum tomatoes, peeled, seeded and sliced
- 1 pound waxy potatoes, peeled and sliced ⅛ inch thick
- 2 small zucchini, thinly sliced
- 1 cup finely chopped fresh flat-leaf parsley
- ¼ cup torn fresh basil leaves
- ½ teaspoon crumbled dried oregano
- Salt and freshly ground pepper
- 1 cup dry bread crumbs
- 3 tablespoons freshly grated Parmigiano-Reggiano cheese

1. Preheat the oven to 375°. Place the mussels in a deep skillet and add 3 tablespoons of water. Cook over moderately high heat, stirring frequently. As the mussels just open, transfer them to a large platter with a slotted spoon. (They will continue cooking later.) Strain the liquid through a sieve lined with several layers of dampened cheesecloth and reserve. (You should have about ¼ cup of liquid.) Remove the mussels from their shells.
2. Heat 2 tablespoons of the oil in a large nonreactive skillet. Add half of the sliced onions and all of the garlic and cook over low heat until softened but not browned, about 7 minutes. Add the tomatoes, raise the heat to moderate and cook until they have cooked down to a thick sauce, about 10 minutes.
3. Meanwhile, bring a medium saucepan of water to a rolling boil. Add the potato slices and cook until just tender, 7 to 10 minutes. Drain well.
4. Brush the bottom of a deep 2-quart ceramic baking dish with 1 tablespoon of the oil. Spread a third of the tomato sauce over the bottom. Top with half of the remaining raw onions followed by half of the mussels, zucchini slices and potatoes. Sprinkle with half of the parsley, basil and oregano, 1 tablespoon of the oil, and salt and pepper. Cover with another third of the tomato sauce and repeat the layering with the remaining ingredients, ending with the tomato sauce. Sprinkle the bread crumbs, grated cheese and the remaining 3 tablespoons oil over the top.
5. In a small bowl, combine the reserved mussel liquid with ¼ cup of hot water. Pour the liquid gently down the side of the baking dish to keep the vegetables from sticking. Cover the dish with a double layer of aluminum foil and bake for about 1 hour, or until the potatoes are very tender; remove the foil during the last 15 minutes to brown the top. Let cool slightly, then serve hot or at room temperature.—NANCY HARMON JENKINS

STEAMED MUSSELS IN GUEUZE

Wheaty-flavored Gueuze beer makes a subtly sweet poaching liquid to complement the briny mussels. Or use a slightly tangy Blanche de Bruges or any pale ale. Serve with crusty bread.

4 SERVINGS

- 2 tablespoons unsalted butter
- 1 celery rib, minced
- 3 small shallots, minced
- 1 garlic clove, minced
- 2 fresh thyme sprigs
- 1¼ cups Gueuze beer
- 1 tablespoon minced fresh parsley
- 2 pounds small mussels, scrubbed and debearded
- Salt and freshly ground pepper

Melt the butter in a nonreactive saucepan. Add the celery, shallots, garlic and thyme and cook over moderate heat, stirring, until the vegetables soften. Add the beer and parsley and bring to a boil over high heat. Add the mussels, cover and steam, shaking the pan, until they open, about 5 minutes. Scoop the mussels into bowls, discarding any that don't open. Season the broth with salt and pepper and pour over the mussels.—CASSANDRA DOOLEY

STUFFED SQUID

These pretty little pockets of squid have their tops cut open to show off the stuffing inside. For best results, you should buy the smallest, freshest whole squid you can find.

6 SERVINGS

12 fresh uncleaned squid of even size (about 3 pounds)
2 cups dry bread crumbs
2 eggs, lightly beaten
3 garlic cloves, 2 finely chopped and 1 minced
1 small onion, finely chopped
⅓ cup plus 3 tablespoons finely chopped fresh flat-leaf parsley
3 tablespoons milk
6 tablespoons extra-virgin olive oil
½ cup freshly grated Pecorino or Parmigiano-Reggiano cheese (see box, above)
2 canned plum tomatoes, drained and chopped
8 large green olives, pitted and coarsely chopped
Salt and freshly ground pepper
½ cup dry white wine, plus more if needed
Lemon wedges, for serving

1. Clean the squid: Rub the thin purplish membranes off with your fingers, being careful to keep the bodies and hoods attached. (It isn't necessary to remove all the scraps but the squid will be more attractive without them.) Set the squid on a cutting board and cut a slit in the hoods from the base to the top, leaving the tentacles attached. Pull out and discard the innards, including the bony strip called the beak. Rinse the squid thoroughly inside and out; set aside to drain. Using scissors or a sharp knife, remove the very long tentacle and the fanlike fins (on either side of the hood) from each of the squid; chop them into small pieces.

2. In a medium bowl, mix the bread crumbs with the eggs, finely chopped garlic, onion and ⅓ cup parsley. Add the milk and 3 tablespoons of the oil to form a moist paste. Mix in the cheese, tomatoes, olives and the chopped squid tentacles and fins and season with salt and pepper. Stuff each squid hood loosely with the mixture.

3. In a nonreactive skillet large enough to hold all the squid in a single layer, heat the remaining 3 tablespoons oil. Add the minced garlic and the remaining 3 tablespoons parsley and cook over moderate heat just until the garlic is opaque, about 30 seconds. Add the stuffed squid to the pan in a single layer and cook until browned, about 3 minutes per side. Add the wine to the pan, cover and reduce the heat to low. Cook until the squid is tender, about 30 minutes; if the pan begins to look dry, add a little more wine.

4. Spoon the small amount of sauce remaining in the pan over the squid and serve immediately with the lemon wedges.—NANCY HARMON JENKINS

PECORINO

The cheese used in Italy's Apulia region, though called Pecorino, is a mixture of ewe's and cow's milk. It is not the sharp cheese known as Pecorino Romano. If you can't find Pecorino from Apulia, Sardinia or Tuscany to use in the Stuffed Squid recipe, use Parmigiano-Reggiano instead.

PIQUILLO PEPPERS STUFFED WITH CODFISH

Dried salt cod is a staple of Basque cooking. Before it is cooked, it must be soaked to eliminate excess salt and to rehydrate. In this recipe, allow thirty-six hours for soaking.

🍷 *1989 Chivite Navarra Reserva*

4 SERVINGS

½ pound skinless, boneless salt cod, preferably a thick center-cut piece
4½ tablespoons olive oil
1½ tablespoons all-purpose flour
2 cups milk
16 roasted piquillo peppers (from two 6-ounce jars), drained (see box, next page)
1 Spanish onion (about 8 ounces), coarsely chopped
1 medium carrot, thinly sliced crosswise
1 fresh parsley sprig, plus 1 tablespoon finely chopped parsley
1 garlic clove, finely chopped

1½ tablespoons dry sherry
Kosher salt

1. In a large bowl, soak the salt cod in plenty of fresh water in the refrigerator for 36 hours; change the water at least five times. Drain. Cut the cod crosswise into ¼-inch strips.
2. In a medium saucepan, warm 3 tablespoons of the oil over moderate heat. Add the salt cod; cook, stirring gently, to heat through, about 3 minutes. Stir in 1 tablespoon of the flour until incorporated. Gradually mix in the milk. Reduce the heat to low and simmer, stirring often, until the mixture has thickened, about 25 minutes. Cool to room temperature.
3. Keeping the peppers intact, remove any seeds and carefully stuff each pepper with a heaping tablespoon of the cod mixture.
4. In a large nonreactive skillet, warm the remaining 1½ tablespoons of the oil over moderately low heat. Add the onion, carrot, parsley sprig and garlic. Cook, stirring occasionally, until the onion is soft, about 12 minutes. Blend in the remaining ½ tablespoon flour and then stir in 1 cup of water. Bring to a boil, cover and cook for 10 minutes to blend the flavors. Uncover, stir in the sherry and simmer for 3 minutes. Transfer to a food processor and puree until completely smooth. Pour the sauce back into the skillet. Season with coarse salt.
5. Carefully place the stuffed peppers in the sauce. Cover and simmer gently over low heat until heated through, about 3 minutes. Transfer the peppers to serving plates and then spoon the sauce around them. Sprinkle the chopped parsley on top and serve at once.—TERESA BARRENECHEA

PIQUILLO PEPPERS

Piquillo peppers are a delicacy grown predominantly in the Basque province of Alava and in Navarre. They're hand-picked and roasted in brick ovens, and then peeled and preserved in brine. In the U.S., bottled peppers are available at specialty-food stores or by mail order from Zingerman's Delicatessen (422 Detroit Street, Ann Arbor, MI 48104; 313-769-1625). You can substitute fresh pimientos or small red bell peppers.

SMOKED SALMON WITH LEMON-DRESSED MESCLUN Q

8 SERVINGS

¾ pound thinly sliced smoked salmon
3 tablespoons fresh lemon juice
¼ cup olive oil
Salt and freshly ground pepper
6 ounces mesclun
1 large European seedless cucumber, peeled and thinly sliced
1 small bunch of chives, coarsely chopped

Arrange the salmon on eight salad plates. In a large bowl, whisk together the lemon juice and oil and season with salt and pepper. Add the mesclun, cucumber and chives and toss well. Arrange the dressed salad alongside the salmon and serve.—NICO MARTIN

SWEET-POTATO PANCAKES WITH CAVIAR Q

8 SERVINGS

2 large sweet potatoes, peeled and cut into 2-inch pieces
2 tablespoons honey
About 1 stick unsalted butter (4 ounces), softened
1 cup milk
2 large eggs, lightly beaten
1½ cups all-purpose flour
1 tablespoon baking powder
1 teaspoon salt
½ teaspoon cayenne pepper
¾ cup sour cream
2 ounces caviar, preferably osetra

1. Bring a medium saucepan of lightly salted water to a boil. Add the sweet potatoes and cook over moderately high heat until tender, about 15 minutes. Drain well and return to the saucepan. Add the honey and 4 tablespoons of the butter. Mash until smooth.
2. In a small bowl, combine the milk and eggs and stir into the sweet-potato puree. In another bowl, stir together the flour, baking powder, salt and cayenne. Add the dry ingredients to the puree, stirring just until blended.
3. Melt 1 tablespoon of the butter in each of two large nonstick skillets. Spoon rounded tablespoons of the sweet-potato batter into the skillets, flattening each pancake slightly to form a 2-inch round. Fry over moderately high heat, turning once, until golden and crisp, about 1 minute per side. Transfer to a large baking sheet. Repeat the process with the remaining butter and batter; you should have 32 pancakes. (**MAKE AHEAD:** The pancakes can

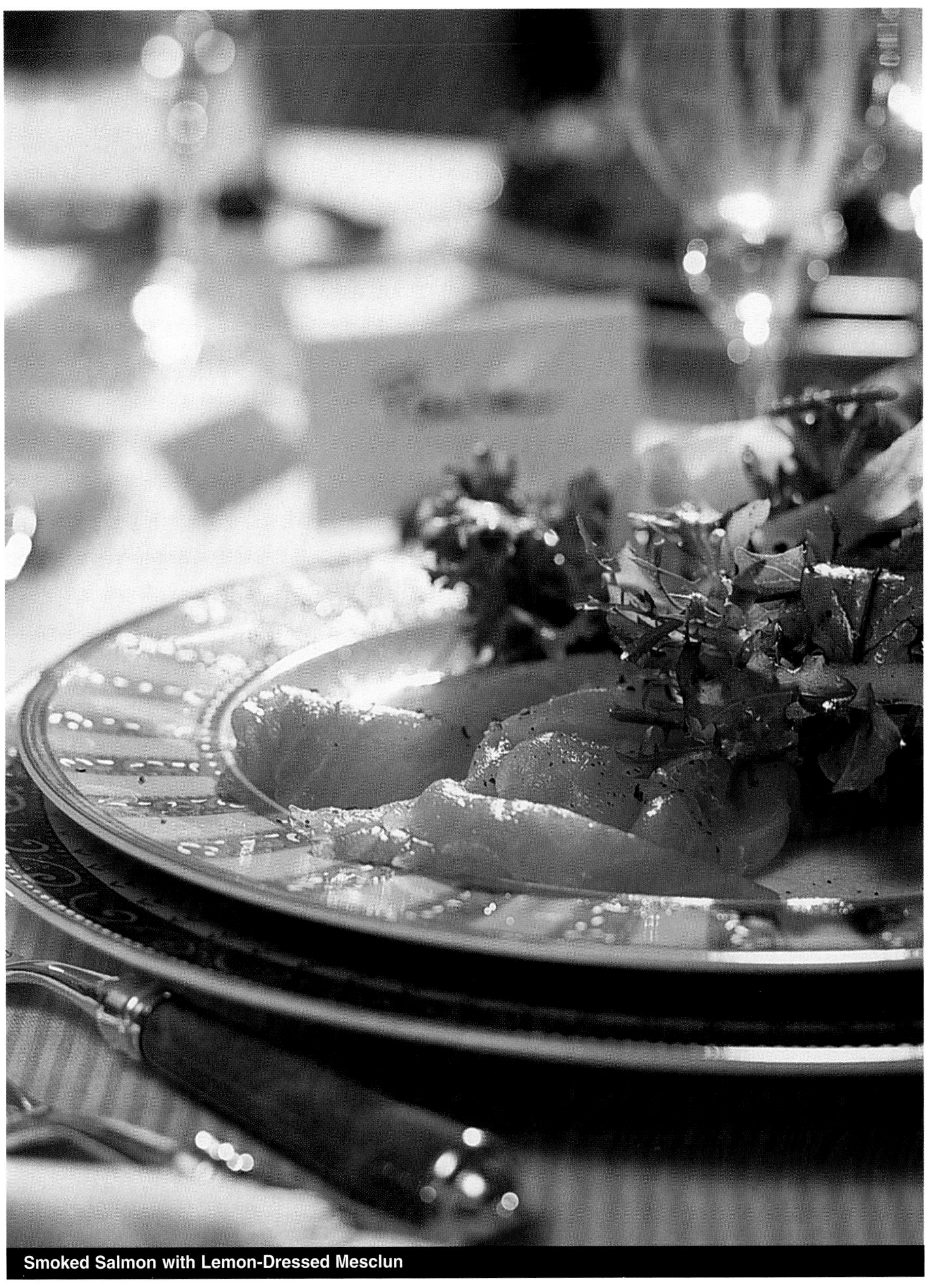

Smoked Salmon with Lemon-Dressed Mesclun

stand at room temperature for 2 hours. Reheat in a 325° oven for 5 minutes before serving.)

4. To serve, arrange four sweet-potato pancakes on each of eight small plates. Garnish each of the pancakes with a dollop of sour cream and a small spoonful of caviar.—TANYA HOLLAND

ALSATIAN ONION TART

8 SERVINGS

- 3 slices of lean bacon, cut crosswise into ¼-inch strips
- 2 large onions, quartered lengthwise and very thinly sliced crosswise (about 4 cups)
- ¼ teaspoon ground cumin
- Pinch of cayenne pepper
- Pinch of cloves
- Pinch of nutmeg
- Salt
- Flaky Pie Dough (recipe follows)
- 2 large eggs
- 2 tablespoons all-purpose flour
- 1 cup heavy cream
- Freshly ground black pepper
- ¼ cup shredded imported Swiss cheese

Alsatian Onion Tart

1. Preheat the oven to 350°. In a large heavy saucepan, cook the bacon over moderately high heat, stirring often, until translucent, 2 to 3 minutes. Add the onions, cumin, cayenne, cloves, nutmeg and ¼ teaspoon salt and cook until the onions soften slightly. Reduce the heat to moderately low and cook, stirring often, until the onions are very soft but not browned, about 30 minutes. Remove from the heat and let cool to room temperature.

2. Meanwhile, roll out the pie dough to a ⅛-inch-thick round. Transfer it to a 9½-inch fluted tart pan with a removable bottom. Trim the edges. Prick the bottom of the dough with a fork and line with foil and pie weights or dried beans. Bake the shell for about 15 minutes, or until lightly browned around the edges. Remove the foil and the weights and bake the shell for 10 to 15 minutes longer, or until the bottom is golden brown and completely dry.

3. In a medium bowl, whisk the eggs with the flour until smooth. Whisk in the cream, then stir in the onion mixture. Season with 1 teaspoon salt and ½ teaspoon pepper. Pour the filling into the baked shell and sprinkle the shredded Swiss on top. Bake for 30 to 35 minutes, or until the top is golden brown and the custard is set. Let cool slightly before serving. (**MAKE AHEAD:** The tart can be refrigerated for up to 2 days. Reheat it slowly in a 325° oven until warmed through.)

Flaky Pie Dough

MAKES ENOUGH FOR ONE 9½-INCH PIE SHELL

- 1 cup plus 2 tablespoons all-purpose flour
- ½ teaspoon salt
- 4 tablespoons cold unsalted butter, cut into ½-inch dice
- 2 tablespoons cold vegetable shortening, cut into small pieces
- 3 tablespoons ice water

In a food processor, pulse the flour with the salt. Add the butter and the shortening and pulse until the mixture resembles coarse meal with some pieces the size of peas. Drizzle in the ice water. Pulse just until small clumps form. Transfer the dough to a lightly floured work surface and knead it gently a few times. Flatten the pie dough into a disk and wrap well in plastic. Chill until firm, at least four hours. (**MAKE AHEAD:** The dough can be refrigerated for up to 2 days, or frozen.)—MICHEL KELLER

LEEK AND BACON QUICHE

MAKES TWO 9-INCH QUICHES

- 2 cups all-purpose flour
- Salt
- 1 stick plus 2 tablespoons cold unsalted butter (5 ounces), cut into ½-inch pieces
- 1 large egg yolk
- ¼ cup ice water
- ¾ pound thickly sliced bacon, cut into ⅓-inch dice
- 2 medium leeks, white and tender green, sliced crosswise ⅛ inch thick

Freshly ground pepper
4 large whole eggs
2 cups heavy cream
½ pound Gruyère cheese, grated (about 2 cups)

1. In a large bowl, combine the flour and ½ teaspoon salt. Using your fingers or a pastry blender, rub or cut the butter into the flour until it resembles coarse meal. In a measuring cup, combine the egg yolk with the ice water. Stir the yolk mixture into the flour mixture until the dough comes together. Gather the dough into a ball, then divide it in half and pat each half into a 6-inch disk. Wrap each disk in plastic and chill until firm, about 2 hours or overnight.
2. Preheat the oven to 375°. On a lightly floured surface, roll out one piece of the dough into a 14-inch round. Transfer to a 9-inch fluted tart pan with a removable bottom, fitting it evenly into the pan without stretching. Repeat with the remaining dough. Trim the overhanging dough to ½ inch and fold it into the tart pan to strengthen the sides.
3. Line the tart shells with foil and fill with pie weights, rice or beans. Bake in the center of the oven for 20 minutes. Remove the foil and weights and bake for about 10 minutes longer, or until the shells are light golden and fully cooked; if the bottoms bubble, lightly press down with a fork. Transfer the pans to a rack and let the tart shells cool.
4. In a large skillet, cook the bacon over moderately high heat until brown and crisp, about 8 minutes. Transfer to paper towels to drain, then transfer to a small bowl. Pour off all but 1 tablespoon of the rendered fat from the skillet. Add the leeks to the skillet and cook over moderately high heat, stirring occasionally, until softened but not browned, about 2 minutes. Add to the bacon in the bowl; season with salt and pepper. In a medium bowl, combine the eggs and cream and season with salt and pepper.
5. Sprinkle ½ cup of the Gruyère into each tart shell and top with the bacon mixture. Stir the custard, pour it over the bacon filling in each tart shell and sprinkle with the remaining cheese. Bake for about 30 minutes, or until the custard is set and a knife inserted in the center comes out clean.
6. Preheat the broiler. Broil each quiche for about 30 seconds to brown the top. Transfer to a wire rack and let rest for 10 minutes before serving. (MAKE AHEAD: The quiches can be refrigerated overnight or frozen for up to 1 month. If frozen, thaw overnight in the refrigerator. Allow the quiches to return to room temperature before reheating them in a 325° oven.) —GRACE PARISI

RIOJA-STYLE POTATO AND CHORIZO-SAUSAGE STEW

A famous peasant dish, this stew is typical of the Rioja region of Spain.

🍷 *1987 López de Heredia Bosconia Rioja Reserva*

4 SERVINGS

¼ cup plus 2 tablespoons olive oil
1 medium Spanish onion, finely chopped
2 Spanish chorizo sausages (about 3 ounces each), cut into ¼-inch dice
5 baking potatoes, peeled and cut into coarse 1-inch chunks (see "Potato Tip," above)
1 tablespoon hot paprika
Kosher salt

1. In a large nonreactive saucepan, warm the oil over moderate heat. Add the onion and cook, stirring, until translucent, about 5 minutes. Add the chorizo and cook, stirring, until it is heated through, about 1 minute. Add the potatoes, paprika and 1 tablespoon of coarse salt; stir well. Add 4 cups of water and bring to a boil over high heat. Reduce the heat to low, partially cover and simmer, stirring occasionally, until the potatoes are tender when pierced and the stew has thickened slightly, about 30 minutes.
2. Uncover the stew, increase the heat to high and bring to a boil, stirring occasionally to incorporate the oil on the surface into the stew. If desired, crush some of the potatoes against the side of the pan to thicken the stew. Season with coarse salt if necessary. Ladle the stew into shallow soup bowls and serve at once.—TERESA BARRENECHEA

POTATO TIP

Here's an old peasant trick for cutting potatoes so the maximum amount of starch is released into the stew: Instead of cutting all the way through with a knife, insert the knife tip at one end of the potato and work it like a wedge to break off chestnut-size pieces.

CHAPTER 3

~

SALADS

Poached-Salmon Salad

POACHED-SALMON SALAD

If you find spring onions, fresh fava beans, sugar snap peas or young string beans, by all means use them in this salad. If pink beets are unavailable, use red beets but dress them separately so that they won't discolor the other vegetables.

8 SERVINGS

- 1¾ pounds skinless center-cut salmon fillet
- 1½ tablespoons plus 2 teaspoons coarse salt
- 3 bay leaves
- 1 cup finely diced cooked pink Chioggia beets
- ⅔ cup finely diced young carrots
- ½ cup finely diced celery hearts
- 1 large shallot, minced
- 2 tablespoons drained capers
- Freshly ground pepper
- Juice of 1 lemon
- ¼ cup extra-virgin olive oil
- 2 tablespoons minced chives
- 2 tablespoons fresh chervil leaves

1. Using small pliers or tweezers, remove any bones from the salmon. Cut the fillet in half lengthwise, then slice each piece crosswise and on an angle about ¼ inch thick. Transfer the salmon to a platter.

2. In a deep 10-inch skillet, bring 2 quarts of water to a boil with 1½ tablespoons of the salt and the bay leaves. Reduce the heat so that the water barely simmers. Working quickly, poach eight to ten slices of the salmon at a time for no more than 30 seconds; using a slotted spatula, transfer the salmon to paper towels to drain. Arrange the slices on a platter in a single layer and let cool while you poach the rest. (**MAKE AHEAD:** The salmon can be refrigerated, covered, for up to 1 day. Bring to room temperature before proceeding.)

3. In a medium bowl, combine the beets, carrots, celery, shallot and capers. Add the remaining 2 teaspoons salt, some pepper, the lemon juice and the olive oil. Mix well.

4. Casually arrange the salmon slices on eight plates. Scatter the diced vegetables all over the salmon and the plates. Drizzle any remaining dressing over the salads. Garnish the salads with the chives and the chervil leaves and serve.—PAUL BERTOLLI

Beet and Smoked-Trout Salad with Chive Oil

BEET AND SMOKED-TROUT SALAD WITH CHIVE OIL

Leftover chive oil makes a delicious addition to tomato sandwiches, grilled fish or chicken and almost any pizza.

🍷 *A light, fruity white wine with lively acidity harmonizes with the sweet beets and contrasts with the smoky trout. Consider a classic German wine, such as the 1994 Kerpen Wehlener Sonnenuhr Riesling Spätlese or the 1994 Haag Brauneberger Juffer Riesling Spätlese.*

4 SERVINGS

CHIVE OIL:

- ½ cup chopped fresh chives
- ½ cup canola or vegetable oil
- Salt

BEET SALAD:

3 cups rice vinegar
¼ cup sugar
2 tablespoons mustard seeds
1 tablespoon anise seeds
1 tablespoon cumin seeds
2 large beets, peeled and sliced crosswise ⅓ inch thick
1 tablespoon fresh lemon juice
Olive oil, for brushing
Salt and freshly ground pepper
¾ pound smoked trout fillets, skinned and coarsely flaked
4 cups mâche or mesclun mix
2 teaspoons finely grated lemon zest

1. Make the chive oil: In a blender, puree the chives with the canola oil. Scrape into a small bowl; season with salt. (**MAKE AHEAD:** The chive oil can be refrigerated for up to 5 days. Let it return to room temperature before using.)

2. Make the beet salad: In a large nonreactive saucepan, combine the vinegar, sugar, mustard, anise, cumin and 4 cups water. Boil over high heat until reduced by half, about 15 minutes. Add the beets; reduce the heat to moderately high. Cook until tender, about 30 minutes. Let cool in the liquid. Transfer 2 tablespoons of the cooking liquid to a small bowl. Add the lemon juice.

3. Light a grill or heat a lightly oiled grill pan or cast-iron skillet. Pat the beet slices dry with paper towels. Brush on both sides with the olive oil and grill for about 2 minutes per side, or until lightly charred. Transfer to a large plate and season with salt and pepper.

4. Arrange the beet slices in a circle on four plates, overlapping the slices slightly. Scatter the trout over the beets and drizzle about 1 tablespoon chive oil and 2 teaspoons lemon beet juice around each plate. Mound the mâche in the center, sprinkle with a little chive oil and the lemon zest and serve.—MATTHEW LAKE

CHEF'S TIP

The mustard anise liquid used to pickle the beets for the Beet and Smoked-Trout Salad can be used for almost any sturdy, sweet vegetable like carrots and red bell peppers; it even works for spicy chiles. Experiment with different amounts of spices.

GRILLED-SCALLOP SALAD

This salad is simple and elegant with complex flavors.

6 SERVINGS

2 plum tomatoes, peeled, seeded and cut into ¼-inch dice
1 tablespoon minced shallot
2 teaspoons balsamic vinegar
2 tablespoons fresh lemon juice
½ teaspoon coarsely cracked black pepper
Salt
⅓ cup plus 1 tablespoon extra-virgin olive oil
2 teaspoons vegetable oil
Six ¼-inch-thick crosswise slices of red onion

Grilled-Scallop Salad

6 loosely packed cups frisée, tough stems removed
18 jumbo sea scallops
Freshly ground pepper

1. In a small bowl, combine the tomatoes, shallot and vinegar. In another small bowl, whisk together the lemon juice, the cracked black pepper and the salt. Gradually whisk in ⅓ cup of the olive oil. (**MAKE AHEAD:** The tomatoes and dressing can stand separately at room temperature for up to 4 hours.)
2. In a large nonstick skillet, heat the vegetable oil. Add the onion slices in a single layer and cook over moderately high heat until golden, about 3 minutes per side. Transfer the onions to a plate and separate into rings.
3. In a large bowl, thoroughly toss the frisée with two-thirds of the dressing. Mound the salad onto six plates and top with the onion rings.
4. Light a grill or heat a grill pan over moderately high heat. In a bowl, toss the scallops with the remaining 1 tablespoon olive oil and season them with salt and ground pepper. Grill the scallops until golden and just cooked through, about 1½ minutes per side. Arrange three of the scallops around the edge of each salad and spoon the tomatoes on top. Drizzle the remaining dressing over the scallops and serve at once.—BRIGIT LEGERE BINNS

GRILLED-SQUID SALAD WITH MANGO

This simple salad contrasts the smoky grilled squid and chipotle chile with the refreshing arugula and diced mango.

8 SERVINGS

¼ cup rice vinegar
2 tablespoons fresh lime juice
1 tablespoon honey
1 teaspoon minced seeded chipotle chile in adobo*
2 tablespoons finely shredded fresh mint
2 tablespoons finely chopped fresh cilantro
¼ cup olive oil
Salt and freshly ground pepper
1¼ pounds cleaned small squid
Vegetable oil, for brushing
½ cup cooked black beans, drained and rinsed
½ cup finely diced mango
3 cups arugula leaves, torn into bite-size pieces

*Available at Latin American markets and specialty-food stores

1. In a small bowl, combine the vinegar, lime juice, honey, chipotle chile, shredded mint and chopped cilantro. Whisk in the olive oil and season the mixture with salt and pepper.
2. Light a charcoal grill or heat a grill pan over moderate heat. Brush the squid with vegetable oil and sprinkle with salt and pepper. Grill for about 3 minutes per side, turning once, or until lightly charred. Transfer to a cutting board and cut the squid into 1-inch pieces.
3. In a large bowl, combine the squid, black beans, mango and two-thirds of the dressing. Arrange the arugula on a platter and drizzle with the remaining dressing. Top the dressed arugula with the squid salad and serve.—BOBBY FLAY

Grilled-Squid Salad with Mango

LOBSTER AND CELERY-ROOT SALAD WITH PESTO

🍷 *Most lobster dishes call for crisp whites, but the roasted peppers make a light red possible. Try an Italian Merlot, such as the 1992 Conti Brandolini d'Adda Vistorta, or a California alternative like the 1992 St. Supéry Dollarhide Ranch.*

4 SERVINGS

PESTO:
1 cup (packed) fresh basil leaves
2 garlic cloves, halved
¼ cup extra-virgin olive oil
½ teaspoon coarse salt
2 tablespoons freshly grated Parmesan cheese

SALAD:
2 medium red bell peppers
2 garlic cloves, minced
3 tablespoons extra-virgin olive oil

1 large celery root, quartered lengthwise and peeled
1 tablespoon fresh lemon juice
½ cup mayonnaise
Coarse salt and freshly ground pepper
Two 1½-pound live lobsters
1½ tablespoons good-quality balsamic vinegar
Fresh basil sprigs, for garnish

1. Make the pesto: In a mortar or mini-processor, work the basil and garlic together to form a paste. With the machine on, add 3 tablespoons of the oil in a steady stream until the mixture is smooth. Add the salt and Parmesan and process to blend. Scrape the pesto into a small bowl and pour the remaining 1 tablespoon oil on top; cover and refrigerate.

2. Make the salad: Roast the red bell peppers over a gas flame or under the broiler until charred all over. Transfer the peppers to a paper bag and let steam for 10 minutes. Discard the skin, cores, ribs and seeds and halve each pepper. Put the peppers in a shallow bowl and add the garlic and 2 tablespoons of the oil. Let marinate in the refrigerator for 2 hours. (**MAKE AHEAD:** The pesto and peppers can be refrigerated separately overnight. Let the peppers return to room temperature before serving.)

3. Using a mandoline, cut the celery root into very thin strips, about ½ inch wide; alternatively, use a knife to cut it into fine julienne strips. Transfer to a large bowl and toss with the lemon juice. In a medium bowl, combine the pesto and mayonnaise. Add the celery root, season with salt and pepper and toss well.

4. Bring a large saucepan of water to a boil. Plunge the lobsters in head first, then cover and cook until they're red all over, about 10 minutes; transfer to a bowl and let cool.

5. Detach the lobster tails from the bodies. Using shears, cut through the underside of the tail shells and remove the meat. Halve the tail meat lengthwise and discard the intestinal veins. Twist off the claws, crack them and remove the meat. Transfer the lobster meat to a bowl.

6. Mound the celery-root salad on four plates. Toss the lobster meat with the remaining 1 tablespoon oil, season with salt and pepper and arrange on top of the salad. Drain the oil from the roasted peppers into a small bowl. Scrape off the garlic from the peppers and set a pepper half on each plate. Stir the vinegar into the pepper oil, season with salt and pepper and spoon around each salad. Garnish with basil and serve.—GILLES EPIE

CHEF'S TIP

Cutting celery root like long strands of pasta, as in Lobster and Celery-Root Salad with Pesto, is a great trick—it's unexpected and attractive. If you don't have a mandoline, you can julienne the celery root with a knife.

Lobster and Celery-Root Salad

MUSSEL AND POTATO SALAD

Cooking the mussels for this tasty, mustard-dressed salad produces a cooking liquid that can be refrigerated for up to two days and used to enhance other seafood dishes. This recipe is from Jacques Pépin's Kitchen: Cooking with Claudine *(KQED).*

4 SERVINGS

3 to 3½ pounds medium mussels, debearded
½ cup dry white wine
1 pound medium red potatoes
4 small scallions, white and tender green, minced
2 garlic cloves, finely chopped
1 tablespoon red-wine vinegar
1 tablespoon Dijon mustard
⅓ cup extra-virgin olive oil
½ teaspoon salt
1 teaspoon freshly ground pepper
3 cups mesclun (about 2 ounces)

1. In a large bowl, cover the mussels with cold water. If they are sandy, rub them against one another. Transfer to another bowl of cold water. Repeat the process, rinsing out the bowl each time, until there is no sand left.

2. Transfer the mussels to a large nonreactive pot and add the wine and ½ cup of water. Cover and bring to a boil. Cook,

Mussel and Potato Salad

tossing occasionally, for about 7 minutes. As they open, transfer them to a bowl; discard any that do not open. Slowly pour the mussel cooking liquid into a bowl, leaving any grit behind. Reserve the liquid in the refrigerator for another use. Let the mussels cool, then remove them from their shells, discarding any remaining beards, and transfer the mussels to another bowl.

3. Meanwhile, in a medium saucepan, cover the potatoes with cold water and bring to a boil over high heat. Reduce the heat to low and boil gently until tender, about 20 minutes. Drain the potatoes and let cool slightly. Slice the lukewarm potatoes crosswise ¼ inch thick. Add the potatoes and scallions to the mussels in the bowl.

4. In a small bowl, combine the garlic, vinegar, mustard, oil, salt and pepper. Add the dressing to the mussels and potatoes and toss the salad gently. Arrange the greens on four plates and spoon the salad on top. Serve the salad warm or at room temperature.—JACQUES PÉPIN

ANTIPASTO SALAD WITH GRILLED CHICKEN

This salad contains all my favorite foods: roasted peppers, olives and spinach. The salami Parmesan crisps were inspired by the cookbook author Rozanne Gold.

🍷 *The sharp, lively flavors in this salad call for a straightforward dry white to cleanse the palate between bites. Consider a Rioja, such as the 1994 Marqués de Cáceres Blanco or the 1994 Bodegas Montecillo Cumbrero Blanco.*

4 SERVINGS

- ½ cup plus 2 tablespoons extra-virgin olive oil
- 3 tablespoons fresh lemon juice
- 2 large garlic cloves, thinly sliced
- Salt and freshly ground pepper
- 4 boneless chicken-breast halves with skin, tenders separated, breasts lightly pounded
- 3 red bell peppers
- ¼ pound thinly sliced Genoa salami or pancetta
- 2 tablespoons freshly grated Parmesan cheese
- 6 ounces assorted brine-cured olives, such as Kalamata, Niçoise and green Sicilian, pitted and coarsely chopped (½ cup)
- 1 medium shallot, minced
- 1 tablespoon chopped capers
- 3 tablespoons red-wine vinegar
- 1 teaspoon Dijon mustard
- 3 tablespoons finely chopped flat-leaf parsley
- 1 pound fresh spinach, tough stems removed
- 6 small radishes, cut into 1-by-¼-inch matchsticks or thin wedges

1. In a large nonreactive baking dish, combine ¼ cup of the olive oil with the lemon juice and garlic. Season with salt and pepper. Add the chicken breasts and tenders, turn to coat and let marinate at room temperature for 1 hour, turning once.

2. Meanwhile, preheat the broiler. Broil the red peppers as close to the heat as possible, turning with tongs, until black all over. Transfer the charred peppers to a bowl, cover with plastic wrap and let cool for 10 minutes. Peel, seed and core the peppers, and then cut the peppers into 3-by-¼-inch strips.

3. Turn the oven down to 425°. Arrange the salami slices in one layer on a baking sheet and sprinkle with the Parmesan. Bake the salami slices for about 10 minutes, or until browned. Transfer the salami to paper towels to drain. When the slices are cool enough to handle, break them into 1-inch pieces.

4. In a medium bowl, combine the olives, shallot, capers, vinegar, mustard and salt and pepper to taste. Stir in the remaining 6 tablespoons olive oil; don't worry if the dressing separates.

5. Heat a grill pan or cast-iron skillet over moderate heat. When the pan is hot, season the chicken with salt and pepper and grill or pan-fry until browned and crusty, about 4 minutes per side for the breasts and 3 minutes per side for the tenders. Let the chicken rest for 15 minutes, then slice the pieces crosswise ½ inch thick. Reserve any juices. (**MAKE AHEAD:** All of the elements can be refrigerated, covered, for up to 2 days.) ➤

6. Just before serving, stir the parsley and any accumulated chicken juices into the dressing. In a large bowl, combine the spinach, radishes, roasted peppers and salami chips and toss with half of the dressing. Mound on four large plates or a large platter; arrange the chicken on top. Spoon the remaining dressing over the chicken.—GRACE PARISI

BLT SALAD Q

Back in the Fifties, short-order cooks dubbed the bacon, lettuce and tomato sandwich the BLT. It's a classic combination that deserves a new lease on life. So hold the white bread and mayo. Cook the bacon, marinate the tomatoes, add arugula and a basil dressing and you've created a BLT salad.

The best match is a crisp Sauvignon Blanc. Consider the 1995 Morgan or the 1995 Chateau Souverain, both from California.

4 SERVINGS

- ¼ cup plus ½ tablespoon olive oil
- 1½ tablespoons balsamic vinegar
- 2 tablespoons finely chopped fresh basil, plus small whole leaves for garnish
- ¼ teaspoon salt
- Pinch of freshly ground pepper
- 2 medium tomatoes, cored, seeded and coarsely chopped
- 8 thick slices bacon, cut crosswise into ¾-inch strips
- 2 large bunches of arugula, thick stems discarded
- Pan-Roasted Garlic Potatoes (recipe follows)
- ¼ cup finely chopped Vidalia or other sweet onion
- ½ cup crumbled blue cheese

1. Combine the olive oil, vinegar, chopped basil, salt and pepper. Toss 1 tablespoon of this dressing with the tomatoes. In a skillet, cook the bacon until crisp. Drain on paper towels.

2. Toss the arugula with the remaining dressing and arrange on four large plates. Scatter the bacon and potatoes over the arugula and sprinkle the chopped onion and the blue cheese on top. Scatter the marinated tomatoes and the basil leaves over the salad and serve.

Pan-Roasted Garlic Potatoes

4 SERVINGS

- 2 tablespoons olive oil
- 8 large unpeeled garlic cloves

QUICK DINNER

BLT SALAD (P. 56)

PAN-ROASTED GARLIC POTATOES (P. 56)

ICE CREAM WITH CARAMELIZED PEACHES (P. 419)

GAME PLAN:

- **Make the dressing for the salad.**
- **Marinate the tomatoes.**
- **Sauté the garlic and potatoes.**
- **Fry the bacon.**
- **Prepare the rest of the salad.**
- **Caramelize the peaches.**

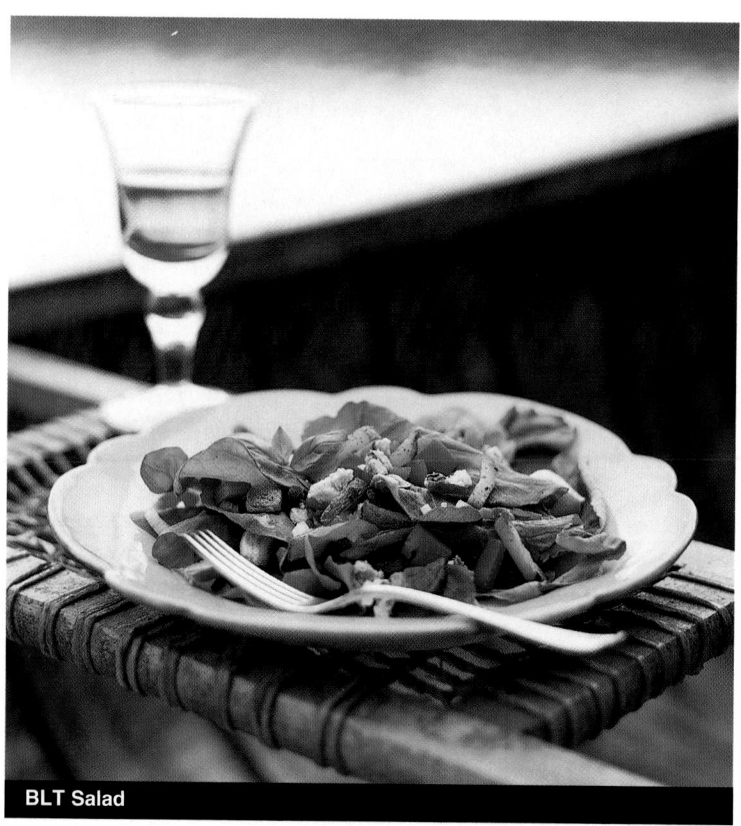

BLT Salad

1 pound new potatoes, quartered and sliced crosswise ⅜ inch thick
1 teaspoon coarse salt
¼ teaspoon freshly ground pepper

1. In a heavy 12-inch skillet, heat the oil. Add the garlic and cook over moderate heat, stirring occasionally, until golden, about 5 minutes.
2. Add the potatoes and sprinkle with the salt and pepper. Cook, stirring occasionally, until golden brown and tender, about 25 minutes. Serve warm or at room temperature; remove the garlic skins before serving if you prefer.—JUDITH SUTTON

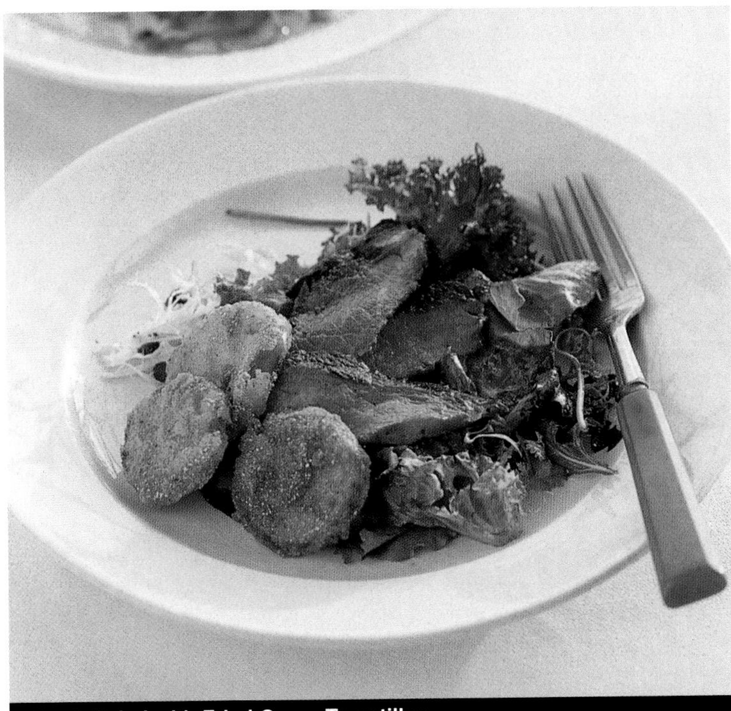

Steak Salad with Fried Green Tomatillos

STEAK SALAD WITH FRIED GREEN TOMATILLOS

Unripe tomatoes can be substituted for the tomatillos. Sprinkle leftover cumin oil on salads or roast lamb or chicken. It can be refrigerated for up to one month.

🍷 *The tomatillos and the dressing call for a young, light red that can stand up to their bite—a Spanish Rioja, such as the 1991 Bodegas Montecillo Viña Cumbrero, or a California Sangiovese, such as the 1994 Flora Springs.*

4 SERVINGS

VINAIGRETTE:
2 tablespoons ground cumin
1¼ cups mild olive oil
2 tablespoons Champagne vinegar
Salt and freshly ground pepper

STEAK AND FRIED TOMATILLOS:
1 pound boneless strip steak or sirloin, about ¾ inch thick
Salt and freshly ground pepper
½ cup buttermilk
½ cup yellow or white cornmeal
½ cup all-purpose flour
3 medium tomatillos, husked, rinsed, cored and cut into ¼-inch slices
2 tablespoons unsalted butter
2 tablespoons olive oil
4 ounces mesclun

1. Make the vinaigrette: In a blender or mini-processor, blend the cumin with 1 tablespoon of water. Add the olive oil and blend for 3 minutes. Transfer to a bowl; let the cumin oil stand for at least 30 minutes or up to 1 day. Strain through a tea strainer or a cheesecloth-lined sieve. Put the vinegar in a bowl and whisk in ⅓ cup of the cumin oil in a steady stream. Season with salt and pepper.
2. Make the steak and fried tomatillos: Heat a grill pan or large cast-iron skillet. Season the steak on both sides with salt and pepper and grill or panfry over high heat, turning once, until browned, about 3½ minutes per side for medium-rare. Transfer the steak to a carving board and let rest for 10 minutes.
3. Pour the buttermilk into a shallow bowl and season with salt and pepper. In another shallow bowl, combine the cornmeal and flour and season with salt and pepper. Dip the tomatillo slices in the buttermilk, then coat them on both sides with the cornmeal mixture. Melt the butter in the olive oil in a large skillet. Add the tomatillos and fry over moderate heat, turning once, until golden and crisp, about 2 minutes per side. Transfer the tomatillos to a paper-towel-lined plate; keep warm. ➤

4. In a bowl, toss the mesclun with half of the vinaigrette and divide among four plates. Thinly slice the steak against the grain. Fan the steak slices on the greens and arrange the fried tomatillos alongside. Drizzle the remaining vinaigrette over the salads and serve.—ANNE AND DAVID GINGRASS

TENDER ROSE SALAD

It may seem like overkill, but this delicate salad makes an ideal first course for Roasted Squab with Rose Petals (p. 219).

2 SERVINGS

- 1 tablespoon Rose-Petal Vinegar (recipe follows)
- 1 tablespoon canola oil
- 1/4 teaspoon coarse salt
- 1/4 teaspoon freshly ground pepper
- 6 cups (lightly packed) assorted tender salad greens, such as mâche, Boston lettuce, purslane
- 1/2 cup (lightly packed) fragrant edible rose petals (see "Roses by Mail," p. 219)

Tender Rose Salad

In a large bowl, combine the vinegar, oil, salt and pepper. Add the greens and toss. Sprinkle the rose petals on top and toss gently. Serve.

Rose-Petal Vinegar

MAKES ABOUT 1 1/2 CUPS

- 2 cups (tightly packed) fragrant edible red-rose petals (see "Roses by Mail," p. 219)
- 1 1/2 cups white-wine vinegar

1. Push the edible rose petals into a clean 12- to 16-ounce glass bottle, using a chopstick to pack the petals down if necessary. Then set a funnel into the top of the bottle.

2. In a small nonreactive saucepan, warm the white-wine vinegar over moderate heat until it is hot to the touch. Pour the hot vinegar through the funnel and into the bottle. Using a chopstick, push the rose petals down to disperse them in the vinegar. Allow the vinegar to cool to room temperature and then secure the lid or trim a cork to fit the top of the bottle.

3. Let the vinegar sit in a cool dark spot until bright red and fragrant, about 1 week. Strain the vinegar to remove the petals. (**MAKE AHEAD:** The vinegar will keep at room temperature for up to 6 months.)—MARCIA KIESEL

MESCLUN WITH SUN-DRIED-TOMATO VINAIGRETTE Q

I like to make twice as much dressing as I need for two reasons: a smaller amount would be impractical to do in my blender—and I like to have leftovers for another day.

6 SERVINGS

- 5 medium basil leaves
- 1 small shallot, halved
- 6 oil-packed sun-dried-tomato halves, drained (2 tablespoons)
- 1 tablespoon balsamic vinegar
- ½ teaspoon Dijon mustard
- 3 tablespoons olive oil
- 6 ounces mesclun

Salt and freshly ground pepper

In a blender, puree the basil, shallot, tomatoes, vinegar, mustard and 6 tablespoons of water until smooth. Blend in the olive oil. In a bowl, toss the mesclun with ⅓ cup of the dressing. Season with salt and pepper and serve.—GRACE PARISI

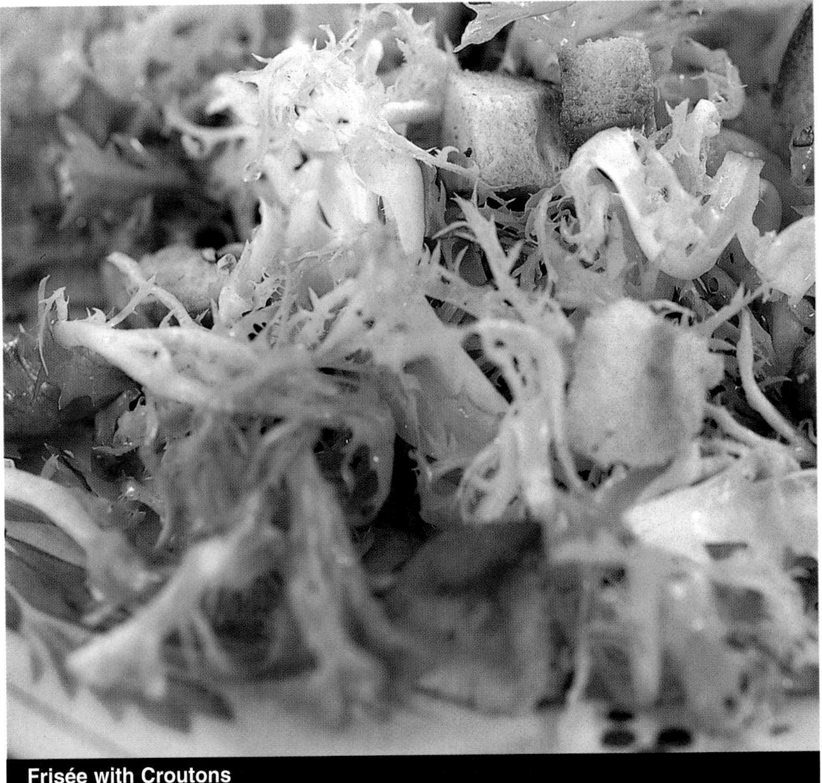

Frisée with Croutons

FRISÉE WITH CROUTONS

You can substitute any curly endive for the frisée; select heads with the whitest inner leaves. This recipe is from Jacques Pépin's Kitchen: Cooking with Claudine *(KQED).*

4 SERVINGS

- One 4-inch piece of leftover baguette (about 1½ ounces), cut into ½-inch cubes
- 3 tablespoons plus 2 teaspoons extra-virgin olive oil
- 1 large garlic clove, finely chopped
- 1 tablespoon Dijon mustard
- 2 teaspoons red-wine vinegar
- ¼ teaspoon salt
- ¼ teaspoon freshly ground pepper
- 1 large or 2 small heads frisée, torn into 2-inch pieces

1. Preheat the oven to 400°. In a medium bowl, toss the baguette cubes with the 2 teaspoons oil. Spread the bread on a baking sheet and bake for about 10 minutes, or until the cubes are nicely browned.

2. In a large bowl, mix the garlic, mustard, vinegar, salt and pepper together. Stir in the remaining 3 tablespoons oil.

3. Just before serving, add the frisée to the bowl and toss with the dressing. Divide among four salad plates and sprinkle the croutons on top.—JACQUES PÉPIN

SALAD OF MIXED GREENS WITH SESAME DRESSING

8 SERVINGS

- 1 tablespoon green-peppercorn mustard or plain Dijon mustard
- 1 tablespoon balsamic vinegar

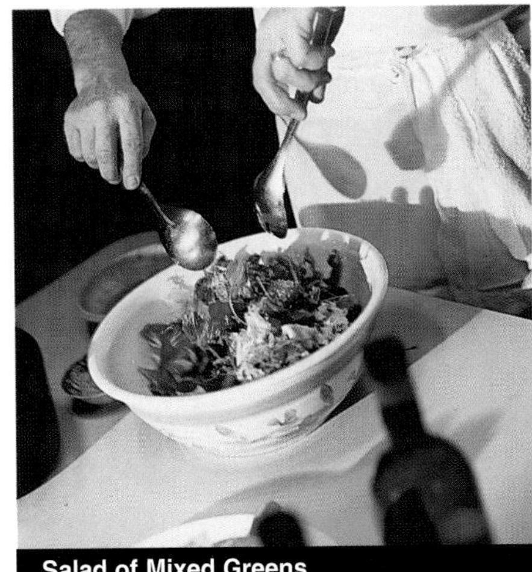

Salad of Mixed Greens

- 1 tablespoon raspberry vinegar
- 1 teaspoon honey

Salt and freshly ground pepper

- 3 tablespoons vegetable oil
- 1 tablespoon Asian sesame oil

12 cups mixed salad greens
2 tablespoons sesame seeds, toasted

In a large salad bowl, mix the green-peppercorn or Dijon mustard with the balsamic vinegar, raspberry vinegar, honey, salt and freshly ground pepper. Whisk in the vegetable oil and the Asian sesame oil. Add the salad greens to the dressing and toss well. Sprinkle the toasted sesame seeds on top of the salad and serve.—JACKY RUETTE

ESCAROLE SALAD WITH GARLIC DRESSING

When I buy escarole at the market, I search for large heads that are mostly white inside. I cut away the darkest green outer leaves, which are tougher and tend to be more bitter, and reserve them for soup. I use only the sweet and tender lighter green and white inner leaves.

4–6 SERVINGS

2 teaspoons Dijon mustard
2 teaspoons red-wine vinegar
1 teaspoon minced garlic
¼ teaspoon salt
¼ teaspoon freshly ground pepper
⅓ cup canola oil
1¼ pounds escarole, cored, cut into 2-inch pieces, washed and dried

In a small bowl, mix together the mustard, red-wine vinegar, garlic, salt and pepper. Gradually whisk in the canola oil in a steady stream until incorporated; the dressing may separate and that's all right. Put the escarole in a large bowl and toss with the dressing 5 minutes before serving the salad.—JACQUES PÉPIN

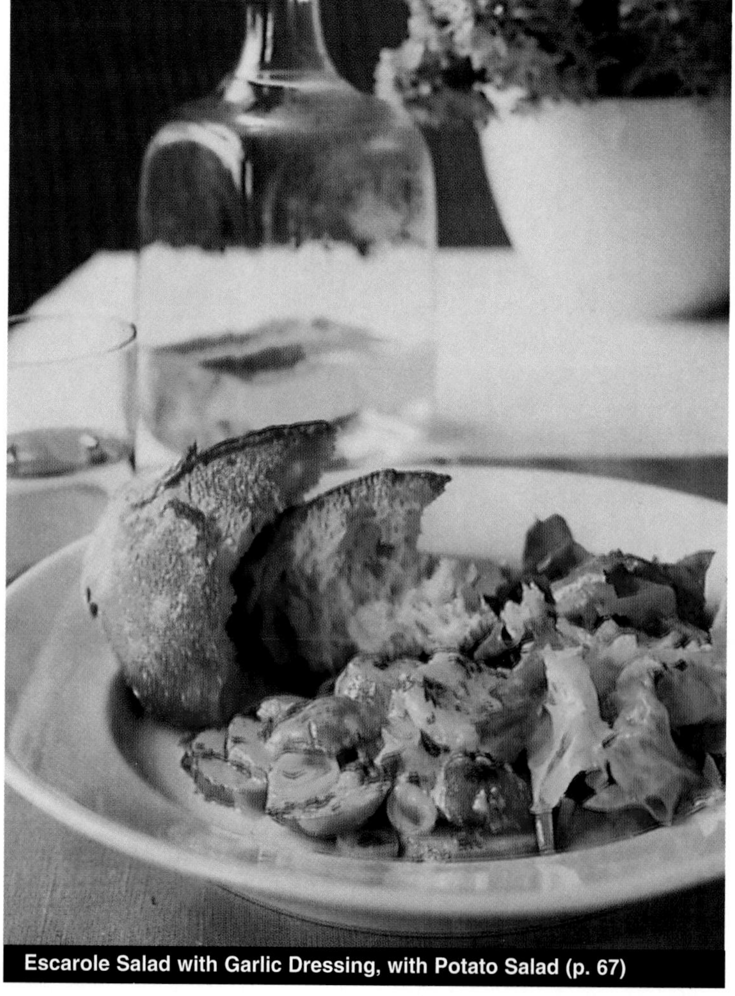

Escarole Salad with Garlic Dressing, with Potato Salad (p. 67)

MESCLUN SALAD WITH PARMESAN DRESSING Q

12 SERVINGS

1 garlic clove
2 tablespoons freshly grated Parmesan cheese
2 tablespoons red-wine vinegar
1 tablespoon balsamic vinegar
½ teaspoon oregano
¼ teaspoon salt
½ teaspoon freshly ground pepper
⅓ cup olive oil
¾ pound mesclun
⅓ cup pine nuts

In a blender or mini-processor, combine the garlic, Parmesan, red-wine vinegar, balsamic vinegar, oregano, salt and pepper and process until smooth. With the machine on, add the oil in a steady stream and process until smooth. Transfer the dressing to a large bowl, add the mesclun and pine nuts and toss.—SUSAN SHAPIRO JASLOVE

RADICCHIO SALAD WITH PARMESAN PEPPER CROSTINI Q

Crisp, cheesy, peppery toasts dress up a simple salad. For a garnish that is even easier, top the salad with delicate shavings of Parmesan.

8 SERVINGS

CROSTINI:

- 2 tablespoons unsalted butter, softened
- ¼ cup freshly grated Parmesan cheese
- 2 teaspoons freshly ground pepper

Twenty-four ¼-inch-thick baguette slices

SALAD:

- 2 tablespoons balsamic vinegar
- ¼ cup plus 2 tablespoons extra-virgin olive oil
- ½ teaspoon salt
- 1 large head of radicchio (about 10 ounces), torn into 2-inch pieces
- 4 Belgian endives, sliced crosswise 2 inches thick

1. Make the crostini: Preheat the oven to 400°. In a small bowl, combine the butter, Parmesan and pepper until smooth. Spread ½ teaspoon of Parmesan butter on each slice of bread and arrange on a baking sheet. (**MAKE AHEAD:** The crostini can stand for up to 2 hours in a cool place.)

2. Bake the crostini for about 8 minutes, or until golden.

3. Meanwhile, **make the salad:** In a large bowl, whisk together the vinegar, oil and salt. Add the radicchio and endives and toss. Arrange the salad on eight small plates, garnish with the crostini and serve.—PEGGY RYAN

GARLIC CAESAR SALAD LF

6 SERVINGS

Two ½-inch-thick slices of peasant bread, crusts trimmed, bread cut into ½-inch cubes

- 1 teaspoon olive oil
- 1 large head of romaine lettuce, torn into bite-size pieces
- ½ cup Caesar Salad Dressing (recipe follows)
- ¼ cup freshly grated Parmesan cheese

1. Preheat the oven to 350°. In a bowl, toss the bread cubes with the oil and spread in a single layer on a baking sheet. Toast for about 8 minutes, until golden and crisp. Let cool.

2. Combine the lettuce and the croutons in a large bowl. Toss with the dressing. Sprinkle with the Parmesan and toss again.

Caesar Salad Dressing

MAKES ABOUT 1½ CUPS

- ½ cup vegetable or chicken stock or canned low-sodium broth
- ¼ cup blanched garlic puree (see box, above)
- 1 medium shallot, minced
- 2 anchovy fillets, patted dry and minced, or 1 teaspoon anchovy paste
- 1 tablespoon Dijon mustard
- 2 tablespoons fresh lemon juice
- 2 tablespoons red-wine vinegar
- ¼ cup extra-virgin olive oil

Salt and freshly ground pepper

In a small bowl, combine the stock, garlic puree, shallot, anchovies, mustard, lemon juice and vinegar. In a slow steady stream, whisk in the olive oil until incorporated. Season with salt and pepper. (**MAKE AHEAD:** The dressing can be refrigerated for up to 2 days. Let return to room temperature before using.)—JIM ACKARD

BLANCHED GARLIC

Blanched garlic may be used in place of roasted in almost any dressing or condiment. Blanching is quicker than roasting, and adds no fat. To make half a cup of blanched garlic puree, peel the cloves from two large heads of garlic. Put the cloves in a pan, add water to cover and bring to a boil over high heat. Drain and return to the pan. Repeat the process three more times until softened. Transfer to a bowl and mash with a fork until smooth.

CRISPED CHEESE WITH MIXED GREENS LF

4 SERVINGS

- 1 pound plum tomatoes, cored and halved lengthwise
- 2 tablespoons minced shallots
- ¼ cup balsamic vinegar
- 2 teaspoons Dijon mustard

Salt and freshly ground pepper

- ½ cup grated Gruyère cheese
- 1 tablespoon freshly grated Parmesan cheese
- 2 tablespoons coarsely chopped fresh chives
- 6 cups assorted salad greens

1. Preheat the broiler. Set the tomatoes, cut-side down, on a nonstick baking sheet and broil for 5 minutes. Remove the tomato skins and broil for another 2 minutes, or until just browned. Turn cut-side up and broil for about 4 minutes, or until blackened. Transfer the tomatoes with any pan juices to a food processor and pulse until coarsely chopped. Add the shallots, vinegar and mustard. Season with salt and pepper; process until smooth. Transfer the dressing to a bowl.

2. In a small bowl, toss the Gruyère and Parmesan cheeses with ⅛ teaspoon each salt and pepper. Sprinkle in an even layer in a large nonstick skillet to form an 8-inch disk. Cook over moderate heat, spooning off the fat, until lightly browned, about 4

Mesclun and Fresh-Herb Salad with Goat Cheese

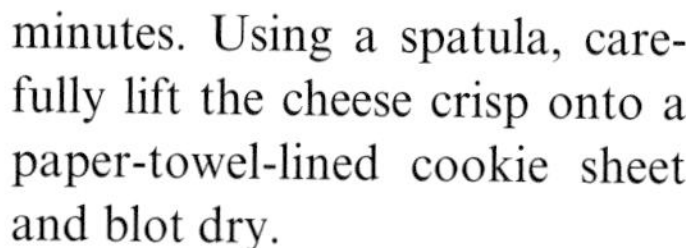

minutes. Using a spatula, carefully lift the cheese crisp onto a paper-towel-lined cookie sheet and blot dry.

3. Stir the chives into the dressing. Toss the greens with 6 tablespoons of the dressing; reserve the remaining dressing for another salad. Arrange the salad on four plates and crumble the crisped cheese on top.—BOB CHAMBERS

MIXED GREENS WITH GOAT CHEESE AND PECANS

The washed and dried greens, as well as the cleaned scallions, can be wrapped in paper towels and refrigerated in plastic bags for up to two days.

8 SERVINGS

- 1 cup pecan halves (4 ounces)
- 2 tablespoons fresh lemon juice
- 1½ tablespoons balsamic vinegar
- 1 tablespoon minced shallot
- 1 large garlic clove, minced
- 1 teaspoon salt
- ¼ teaspoon freshly ground pepper
- Scant ½ cup olive oil
- 1 bunch of scallions
- 4 ounces pepperoni (optional)
- 1 head of romaine lettuce, preferably red leaf
- 2 bunches of watercress, large stems discarded
- 6 ounces fresh, tangy goat cheese

1. Preheat the oven to 350°. Spread the pecans on a small baking sheet and toast in the oven for about 5 minutes, or until fragrant.

2. In a bowl, whisk together the lemon juice, vinegar, shallot, garlic, salt and pepper. Gradually whisk in the oil. (MAKE AHEAD: The pecans and dressing can be stored separately in covered jars for up to 2 days.)

3. Just before serving, thinly slice the scallions and the pepperoni. Tear the lettuce and the watercress into bite-size pieces and place them in a bowl. Add the scallions and pepperoni slices and the pecans. Shake the dressing, drizzle it over the salad and toss well. Crumble in the goat cheese, toss the salad again and serve.—DIANA STURGIS

MESCLUN AND FRESH-HERB SALAD WITH GOAT CHEESE

12 SERVINGS

- 1 tablespoon Dijon mustard
- 1 tablespoon minced shallot
- 1 teaspoon minced garlic
- 2 tablespoons white-wine vinegar mixed with 2 tablespoons water
- ½ cup canola oil
- ¼ cup extra-virgin olive oil
- Salt and freshly ground pepper
- One 11-ounce log of pepper-coated goat cheese, cut into 12 slices
- ¾ pound mesclun
- 1 cup fresh flat-leaf parsley
- ¼ cup snipped fresh chives
- ½ cup small fresh basil leaves
- 2 tablespoons fresh tarragon leaves
- 2 tablespoons fresh chervil leaves

1. In a bowl, whisk together the mustard, shallot, garlic and diluted vinegar. Gradually whisk in the canola oil and olive oil in a thin stream. Season generously with salt and pepper. (MAKE AHEAD: The vinaigrette can be refrigerated overnight.)

2. Preheat the broiler. Set the goat-cheese slices on a baking sheet and sprinkle lightly with the vinaigrette. Broil for 1 minute, or just until the cheese is warmed through.

3. Meanwhile, toss the mesclun and all the fresh herbs with the remaining vinaigrette. Mound the salad on individual plates and top each serving with a slice of warm goat cheese.—WALDY MALOUF

GRILLED-VEGETABLE SALAD WITH PISTACHIO VINAIGRETTE

The secret to this delicious salad is the way the nutty pistachio oil contrasts with the sweet balsamic vinegar. The oil is also wonderful sprinkled over broiled fish, shrimp or toasted bread.

4 SERVINGS

¼ cup olive oil
1 large garlic clove, minced
1 tablespoon minced fresh flat-leaf parsley
2 teaspoons minced fresh thyme
Coarse salt and freshly ground pepper
½ pound fresh chanterelle mushrooms, thickly sliced if large
½ pound thin asparagus, trimmed
3 tablespoons balsamic vinegar
5 tablespoons Toasted-Pistachio Oil (recipe follows)
6 cups mesclun (about 6 ounces)

1. Preheat the oven to 500°. In a small bowl, combine the olive oil, garlic, flat-leaf parsley, thyme, and salt and pepper to taste. Spread the chanterelle mushrooms on a baking sheet and toss with half of the herb-oil mixture. Roast 4 to 5 minutes, stirring, until the mushrooms are tender and browned. Transfer to a plate.

2. On the baking sheet, toss the asparagus with the remaining herb oil and roast for 6 to 7 minutes, stirring, until tender and browned. Cut the asparagus into 2-inch lengths and add to the mushrooms.

3. In a bowl, blend 1½ tablespoons of the vinegar with 2 tablespoons of the pistachio oil and toss with the mesclun. Season with ½ teaspoon salt and ¼ teaspoon pepper and mound the salad onto four plates.

4. Add the roasted mushrooms and the asparagus to the bowl, toss with the remaining balsamic vinegar and arrange on the salads. Drizzle the remaining pistachio oil over and around each of the salads.

Toasted-Pistachio Oil

MAKES ABOUT 1¾ CUPS

½ pound salted pistachios, shelled
1½ cups olive oil
2 teaspoons coarse salt

1. Preheat the oven to 350°. Toast the pistachios for about 4 minutes, or until fragrant. Let cool. Transfer to a food processor and finely grind.

2. In a small saucepan, warm the olive oil over moderate heat. Add it to the ground pistachios and process until blended. Pour the pistachio oil into a jar, stir in the salt and let stand overnight at room temperature. (**MAKE AHEAD:** The pistachio oil can be refrigerated for up to 2 weeks.)—GEORGE MAHAFFEY

Beet, Basil and Watercress Salad

BEET, BASIL AND WATERCRESS SALAD

8 SERVINGS

¾ cup packed light brown sugar
2 cups balsamic vinegar
¼ cup plus 5 teaspoons red-wine vinegar
2 bay leaves
5 whole black peppercorns
2 pounds small beets, trimmed
2 tablespoons grainy mustard
3 tablespoons minced onion
¼ cup extra-virgin olive oil
Salt and freshly ground pepper
8 radishes, thinly sliced
¾ pound watercress, large stems discarded
1 cup loosely packed small fresh basil leaves
3 ounces aged goat cheese

1. In a large nonreactive saucepan, combine the brown sugar, balsamic vinegar, the ¼ cup red-wine vinegar, the bay leaves and the peppercorns. Add the beets and 4 cups of water. Place a plate over the beets to keep them submerged and bring the water to a boil over high heat. Reduce the heat to low and simmer the beets until tender, about 1 hour and 15 minutes; allow the beets to cool in the cooking liquid. Peel the cooked beets and cut them into thin wedges.

2. In a small bowl, combine the remaining 5 teaspoons of red-wine vinegar with the mustard and the minced onion. Whisk in the olive oil in a thin stream until emulsified. Season the dressing with salt and pepper.

3. In a large bowl, toss the beet wedges and the radish slices with the dressing. Add the watercress and fresh basil leaves and toss. Mound the salad on eight plates and finely grate the goat cheese on top of each serving. Serve at once.—ALI SEEDSMAN

RASPBERRY-DRESSED COLESLAW

This colorful two-cabbage slaw gets a double dose of fruit flavor from fresh raspberries and raspberry vinegar. Leave plenty of time to refrigerate the coleslaw before serving—the longer it sits, the more intense the berry taste will be.

8 SERVINGS

- Scant ¼ cup fresh raspberries
- 3 tablespoons raspberry vinegar
- 3 tablespoons finely chopped fresh tarragon
- Salt and freshly ground pepper
- ¼ cup plus 2 tablespoons olive oil
- ¾ pound red cabbage, thinly sliced
- ¾ pound green cabbage, thinly sliced

1. In a blender or a food processor, combine the raspberries, raspberry vinegar and 1½ tablespoons of the tarragon; season with salt and pepper and blend until pureed. With the machine on, add the olive oil to the vinaigrette in a steady stream.

2. In a large bowl, toss the red and green cabbages together; add the vinaigrette and toss to coat. Season the slaw with salt and pepper and refrigerate for at least 1 hour or up to 4 hours. Just before serving, stir in the remaining 1½ tablespoons tarragon.—PAMELA MORGAN

JICAMA-AND-CARROT SALAD WITH LIME Q

This salad is great with meat or poultry that is prepared or served with an Asian-style marinade or sauce.

4 SERVINGS

- ½ large jicama (about 1½ pounds), peeled and cut into ⅛-by-1½-inch sticks
- 4 carrots, coarsely grated
- 6 tablespoons olive oil
- 3 tablespoons fresh lime juice
- ½ jalapeño chile, ribs and seeds removed, minced
- ¾ teaspoon salt

In a bowl, toss together all the ingredients.—STEPHANIE LYNESS

CELERY-ROOT AND CARROT SALAD

The celery root can be shredded in a food processor, but you'll get a thicker and smoother result if you cut the vegetables into julienne strips on a mandoline. This salad improves overnight in the refrigerator.

8 SERVINGS

- 2 large fresh kumquats, seeded and finely chopped
- ¼ cup fresh orange juice
- ¼ cup sour cream
- 2 tablespoons hot and sweet mustard
- 2 small garlic cloves, minced
- 1½ teaspoons salt
- ½ teaspoon freshly ground pepper
- 2 large celery roots (3 pounds), trimmed, quartered and peeled
- 3 tablespoons fresh lemon juice
- ½ pound carrots, peeled and cut into 2-by-¼-inch julienne strips
- 1 cup pecan halves (4 ounces), toasted and coarsely crumbled

1. In a bowl, combine the kumquats, orange juice, sour cream, mustard, garlic, salt and pepper. (**MAKE AHEAD:** The dressing can be refrigerated, covered, for up to 2 days.)

2. Using a mandoline or the large shredding disk of a food processor, cut the celery roots into 2-by-¼-inch julienne strips. Transfer the strips to a very large bowl and toss them with the lemon juice to prevent discoloration. Add the carrot strips and the kumquat dressing and toss. Cover the salad and refrigerate for 1 day.

3. Taste the salad for seasoning. Transfer it to a large platter and scatter the toasted pecans on top.—MARCIA KIESEL

VEGETABLE CARPACCIO

For this refreshing starter, the nearly transparent slices of vegetables are enhanced with a lightly tangy, caper-dotted dressing. Slicing the vegetables paper-thin serves several functions: It allows the juices locked in the fibers to come to the surface, encourages greater absorption of the dressing and tenderizes dense vegetables such as artichokes and carrots. Using a mandoline-type slicer ensures neat, thin shavings.

4 SERVINGS

A small handful of large, firm radishes
1 large carrot
1 celery rib from the heart
1 firm leek, white and tender green only
1 small fennel bulb, halved and cored
Half a lemon, plus 3 tablespoons fresh lemon juice
1 teaspoon Dijon mustard
3 tablespoons cold-pressed olive oil, plus more for drizzling
1 heaping tablespoon drained small capers
Fine sea salt
1 firm medium artichoke
A small chunk of Parmesan cheese, for shaving
Freshly ground pepper

Vegetable Carpaccio

1. Trim and very thinly slice the radishes, carrot, celery, leek and fennel bulb using a manual mandoline-type slicer.

2. In a large bowl, combine the 3 tablespoons lemon juice with the mustard and beat lightly with a fork; beat in the 3 tablespoons olive oil. Stir in the drained capers and season with sea salt.

3. Trim the artichoke, rubbing the cut portions with the lemon half as you go to prevent discoloration. Cut off the stem and pull off all the dark outer leaves around the base. Cut the artichoke crosswise about 1½ inches from the base to remove the remaining leaves. Scoop out the hairy choke and trim around the top and bottom of the heart.

4. Slice the artichoke heart very thin. Toss with the dressing. Add the sliced vegetables; toss gently.

5. Arrange the carpaccio on a platter or plates. Using a vegetable peeler, shave Parmesan on top. Season with pepper, drizzle with oil and serve.—VIANA LA PLACE

PEAR, ARUGULA AND PECORINO SALAD

🍷 *The sharp and sweet flavors go best with a simple and direct Pinot Grigio, such as the 1995 Livio Felluga or the 1995 Albola.*

4 SERVINGS

2 juicy medium-sized pears, such as Bartlett, quartered, cored and sliced lengthwise ⅛ inch thick
1 tablespoon plus 1 teaspoon fresh lemon juice
2 teaspoons olive oil
Coarse salt and freshly ground pepper
1 large bunch of arugula, trimmed
1 cup Pecorino Romano cheese shavings (about 1 ounce)

In a medium bowl, gently toss the pear slices with the lemon juice and the olive oil and season them with salt and pepper. Make a bed of the arugula on each of four salad plates. Arrange the pear mixture on top. Scatter the Pecorino shavings over each of the salads and serve.—MICHELE SCICOLONE

FOOD-PROCESSOR CELERY-ROOT REMOULADE

The julienne disk of the food processor makes easy work of cutting the tough vegetables for this salad. If you don't have one, slice the celery root with the slicing disk, stack the slices and cut them into fine julienne strips by hand.

6 SERVINGS

One 2-pound celery root, peeled and cut into 2-by-3-inch pieces
1 tablespoon salt
1 tablespoon fresh lemon juice
2 tablespoons Dijon mustard
½ tablespoon finely grated peeled fresh ginger
¼ cup canola oil
1 tablespoon white-wine vinegar
Salt and freshly ground white pepper

1. In a food processor fitted with the julienne blade, cut the celery root into julienne strips.
2. In a large bowl, stir the salt with the lemon juice. Add the celery root and toss to coat thoroughly. Set aside for 30 to 45 minutes.
3. Meanwhile, make the remoulade: In a blender or food processor, combine the mustard and ginger and process until smooth. Add 1½ tablespoons of hot water and pulse to combine. With the machine on, slowly add the oil and vinegar and blend until the sauce is smooth and emulsified. Season with salt and white pepper to taste.
4. Drain the celery-root julienne; rinse well and pat completely dry. Transfer the celery-root julienne to a medium bowl and toss it with the remoulade. Cover the salad and refrigerate for at least 1 hour. Serve chilled.—MARDEE HAIDIN REGAN

SPICY GRILLED-EGGPLANT SALAD

For the Thai chiles, you can substitute the same amount of fresh bird chiles or half the quantity of fresh red serrano or cayenne chiles.

4 SERVINGS

1 tablespoon coarsely chopped fresh coriander (cilantro) root,* plus ¼ cup leaves
1 tablespoon chopped pickled garlic,* plus 1 tablespoon garlic brine
8 garlic cloves, 6 coarsely chopped, 2 minced
Coarse salt
1 medium semi-hot fresh green chile, such as poblano, seeded and chopped
4 fresh red Thai chiles,* seeded and chopped
1 tablespoon palm sugar*
1½ tablespoons fresh lime juice
1½ tablespoons Thai fish sauce*
3 pounds eggplant, sliced lengthwise ½ inch thick
¼ cup vegetable oil
2 hard-cooked large eggs, quartered
2 shallots, thinly sliced
1 tablespoon dried shrimp*

*Available at Asian markets

1. In a mortar, crush the coriander root, the pickled garlic and brine and the chopped garlic to a paste. Work in ½ teaspoon salt and the chiles. Stir in the palm sugar, then add the lime juice and fish sauce.
2. Light a grill or preheat the broiler. Brush the eggplant slices on both sides with the vegetable oil and season them with salt. Grill the eggplant slices over low heat, turning once, for about 3 minutes per side, or until they are tender and browned. Alternatively, broil the eggplant slices on two large baking sheets for about 3 minutes per side. Arrange the eggplant slices on a platter and top with the hard-cooked eggs. Drizzle the sauce over and sprinkle the salad with the minced garlic, the shallots, the dried shrimp and the coriander leaves.—THAI COOKING SCHOOL, THE ORIENTAL HOTEL, BANGKOK

FARMERS' MARKET SALAD

You can also use the tasty, tangy parsley dressing from this salad as a vegetable dip and for a potato or a pasta salad.

6–8 SERVINGS

PARSLEY DRESSING:
3 cups (packed) fresh flat-leaf parsley
½ medium onion, coarsely chopped
1 medium garlic clove, quartered
3 tablespoons red-wine vinegar
¼ cup plus 1 tablespoon extra-virgin olive oil
1 teaspoon coarse salt
¼ teaspoon freshly ground pepper

SALAD:

1 pound fresh bush or runner beans, such as green Kentucky Wonder, Blue Lake or yellow wax
¾ pound young lettuces
Salt and freshly ground pepper
6 to 8 radishes, thinly sliced
6 to 8 large hard-boiled eggs, halved

1. Make the parsley dressing: Puree the parsley, onion, garlic, vinegar, olive oil, coarse salt and freshly ground pepper in a blender. Transfer the dressing to a small bowl. (**MAKE AHEAD:** The dressing can be refrigerated for up to 1 day. Let return to room temperature before serving.)
2. Make the salad: In a saucepan of boiling salted water, cook the beans until just tender, about 5 minutes. Drain and refresh with cold water. Cut the beans into 2-inch lengths.
3. In a very large bowl, toss the lettuces with about ⅔ cup of the parsley dressing. Season the salad with salt and pepper and transfer it to a shallow serving bowl. Add the beans to the first bowl, toss them with about 2 tablespoons of the parsley dressing and season with salt and pepper. Scatter the beans and the radishes over the salad, arrange the hard-boiled eggs around the edge and drizzle on the remaining dressing.—MARCIA KIESEL

FLAVORS' ROASTED POTATO SALAD

8 SERVINGS

3 pounds unpeeled new potatoes, quartered
1 tablespoon olive oil
Coarse salt and freshly ground pepper
⅔ cup mayonnaise
2 tablespoons Dijon mustard
¼ cup finely chopped fresh dill
1 garlic clove, minced

1. Preheat the oven to 400°. In a medium roasting pan, toss the potatoes with the oil and season with salt and pepper. Roast the potatoes for about 40 minutes, tossing occasionally, until they are tender and browned. Let the potatoes cool completely.
2. In a small bowl, combine the mayonnaise, mustard, dill and garlic. Toss with the roasted potatoes and season the salad with salt and pepper. (**MAKE AHEAD:** The salad can be refrigerated for up to 2 hours. Let return to room temperature before serving.)—PAMELA MORGAN

POTATO SALAD

4–6 SERVINGS

2½ pounds medium red-skinned potatoes
⅓ cup plus 2 tablespoons olive oil
1 medium leek, white and tender green, thinly sliced
½ cup chopped onion, rinsed and patted dry
½ cup coarsely chopped fresh flat-leaf parsley
¼ cup coarsely chopped fresh chervil
1½ teaspoons finely chopped garlic
3 tablespoons Dijon mustard
3 tablespoons dry white wine
2 tablespoons red-wine vinegar
¾ teaspoon salt
½ teaspoon freshly ground pepper

1. Put the potatoes in a medium saucepan, cover with cold water and bring to a boil over high heat. Cook the potatoes until they are just tender when pierced with a knife, about 25 minutes. Drain and set aside for about 30 minutes to dry out, then cut into ⅛-inch slices.
2. Heat 2 tablespoons of the olive oil in a medium skillet. Add the leek and cook over high heat until it is just wilted but not browned, about 1½ minutes. Transfer the leek to a large bowl and stir in the onion, parsley, chervil, garlic, mustard, white wine, vinegar, salt, pepper and the remaining ⅓ cup oil. Gently fold in the potatoes and serve the salad warm or at room temperature.—JACQUES PÉPIN ➤

COOKING POTATOES

When cooking potatoes for potato salad, drain them as soon as they are tender and set them aside for about half an hour before slicing them. During this resting period, any water the potatoes have absorbed during cooking will evaporate, and their flesh will be creamier than if they had been sliced immediately after draining. Make certain, too, that the potatoes are thoroughly cooked. I'd much rather have my potatoes overcooked and breaking apart than undercooked.—JACQUES PÉPIN

PRECIOUS POTATO SALAD

The flavorful tiny new potatoes in this salad are available at farmers' markets. Italian white-truffle oil adds a rich flavor, but you can substitute an extra tablespoon of extra-virgin olive oil.

2 SERVINGS

- ½ pound tiny new potatoes, such as fingerlings
- 2 tablespoons extra-virgin olive oil
- 1 tablespoon white-truffle oil
- 1½ tablespoons fresh lemon juice
- ¼ teaspoon finely grated lemon zest
- ½ teaspoon salt
- ¼ teaspoon freshly ground pepper
- ¼ pound mâche (see box, below)
- 1½ tablespoons finely chopped fresh spearmint

1. In a steamer basket set over 1 inch of boiling water, steam the potatoes until tender, about 15 minutes. Meanwhile, in a small bowl, combine the olive oil, truffle oil, lemon juice, lemon zest, salt and pepper.

2. In a bowl, toss the mâche with 1 tablespoon of the dressing; arrange on a platter. Add the potatoes and toss with the remaining dressing. Mound the potatoes on the mâche and sprinkle with the mint.—MARCIA KIESEL

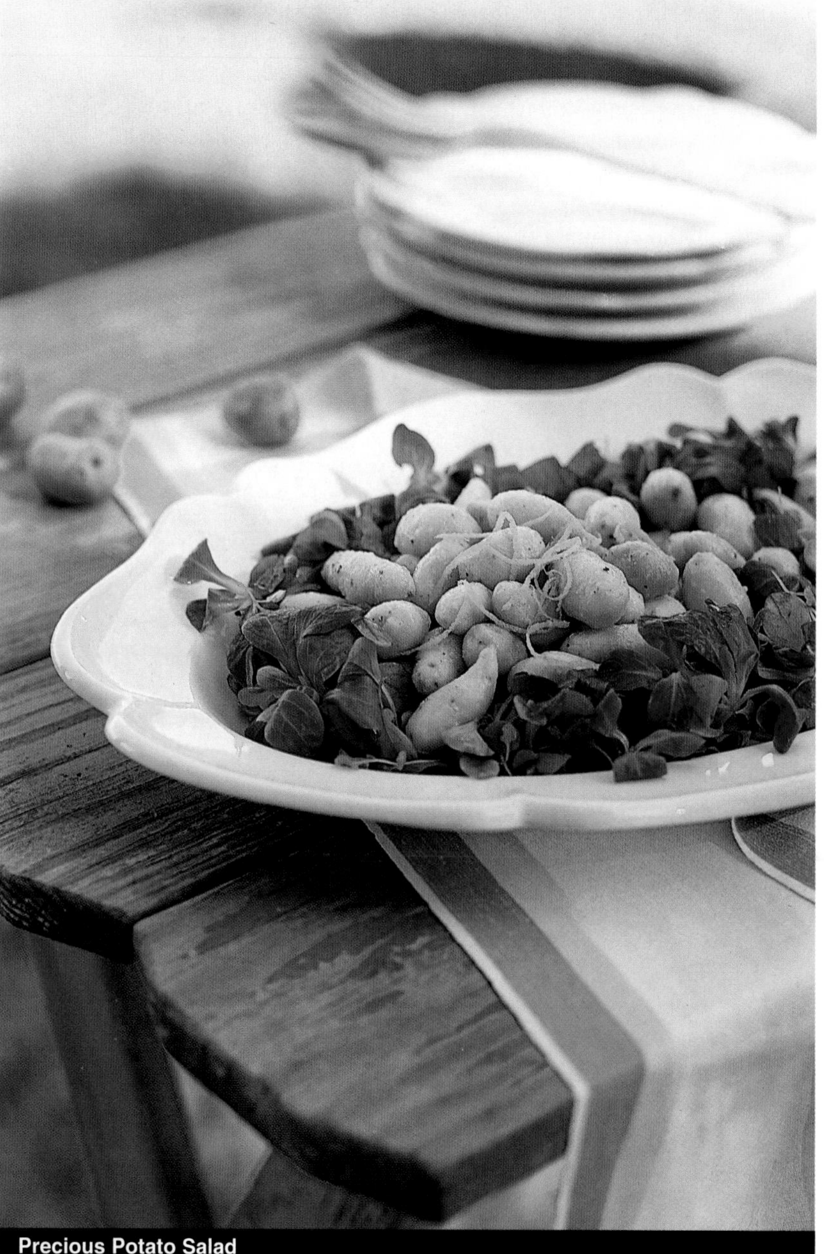

Precious Potato Salad

MÂCHE

Also known as lamb's lettuce or field salad, mâche has small, rounded, dark-green leaves. Wild mâche appears in the spring; however, the plant is cultivated commercially year-round. It doesn't keep well—buy it just before you plan to use it. The small heads, or clusters of leaves, are sold with the roots still attached. Trim off the roots, keeping the heads intact, and wash the leaves gently but thoroughly. Because the leaf clusters are so attractive, mâche is also a popular garnish.

FRICO SALAD

This salad was inspired by a wonderful meal I enjoyed at Frico Bar in New York City. The restaurant is named after an Italian snack—shredded Montasio cheese that is fried in a skillet into a crisp disk and often served with a full-flavored topping. Here I've substituted imported provolone cheese for the hard-to-find Montasio.

🍷 *A simple but characterful white is the best choice. Look for a Pinot Blanc from Alsace, such as the 1994 Lucien Albrecht Pinot Blanc d'Alsace, or an Oregon Pinot Gris, such as the 1994 King Estate.*

4 SERVINGS

DRESSING:

1 tablespoon red-wine vinegar
1 tablespoon dry white wine
2 teaspoons Dijon mustard
1 teaspoon anchovy paste
½ teaspoon salt
¼ teaspoon freshly ground pepper
1 garlic clove, minced
1 shallot, minced
¼ cup olive oil

SALAD:

1 pound medium red potatoes
2½ tablespoons olive oil
1 pound shiitake mushrooms, stemmed, caps thickly sliced
Salt and freshly ground pepper
1 tablespoon unsalted butter
1 garlic clove, minced
1 shallot, minced
¼ cup white wine
2 teaspoons fresh lemon juice
½ teaspoon chopped fresh thyme
½ teaspoon chopped fresh rosemary
½ pound Italian provolone cheese, coarsely grated (2⅔ cups)
10 cups tightly packed trimmed watercress (4 bunches)
2 cups tightly packed radicchio leaves, torn into bite-size pieces (from 1 large head)

1. Make the dressing: In a small bowl, blend all the ingredients and set aside.

2. Make the salad: In a medium saucepan, cover the potatoes with cold water and bring to a boil over high heat. Boil until tender, about 15 minutes. Drain and let the potatoes cool slightly. Peel the potatoes and slice them ¼ inch thick.

3. In a large nonreactive skillet, warm 1½ tablespoons of the olive oil over high heat. When the oil is hot, add the mushrooms in an even layer and cook undisturbed until browned on the bottom, about 3 minutes. Reduce the heat to moderately high, season with salt and pepper and sauté until tender, about 4 minutes. Add the butter, garlic and shallot, reduce the heat to moderately low and cook, stirring, until the shallot is tender, about 4 minutes. Scrape the mushrooms onto a plate.

4. Set the skillet over high heat. Add the remaining 1 tablespoon oil and when it is very hot, add the potatoes in an even layer. Season with salt and pepper and cook undisturbed until brown on the bottom, about 4 minutes. Turn the potatoes and stir in the mushrooms. Add the wine and cook, stirring, until absorbed. Add the lemon juice, thyme and rosemary and remove from the heat. Season with salt and pepper.

5. Warm a nonstick medium skillet over moderate heat for 1 minute. Measure out ⅓ cup of the grated cheese and sprinkle it into the skillet in a 6-inch round. Cook the cheese until it melts and becomes a lightly browned disk, about 4 minutes. Loosen the *frico* from the skillet and slide it onto a plate to cool; it will crisp up as it cools. Repeat to make seven more disks. (**MAKE AHEAD:** The potato and mushroom filling and the *frico* disks can stand at room temperature for up to 6 hours.)

6. Set four *frico* disks on a work surface. Reheat the potatoes and mushrooms in the skillet and spoon the mixture evenly onto the disks. Drizzle about ½ tablespoon of the dressing over each serving and top with a second *frico* disk. With a large sharp knife, quarter each filled *frico*.

7. In a large bowl, toss the watercress and the radicchio thoroughly with the remaining dressing. Mound the greens on four large plates and arrange a quartered *frico* on top of each of the salads. Serve the salads immediately with knives and forks.—MARCIA KIESEL

PAN-ROASTED GNOCCHI SALAD WITH PANCETTA

Store-bought gnocchi can be substituted for the homemade ones in this savory salad.

8 SERVINGS

GNOCCHI:

2 large Idaho potatoes
½ cup heavy cream
3 large egg yolks
¼ cup freshly grated Parmesan cheese
Pinch of ground nutmeg
1 teaspoon minced fresh thyme

1 teaspoon coarse salt
¼ teaspoon freshly ground pepper
1 cup all-purpose flour

SALAD:
¼ cup plus ½ tablespoon sherry vinegar
Coarse salt and freshly ground pepper
2 tablespoons truffle oil plus ¼ cup olive oil or ¼ cup plus 2 tablespoons olive oil
6 ounces thickly sliced pancetta, cut into ¼-inch-thick strips
2 tablespoons unsalted butter
1 shallot, thinly sliced
1 large garlic clove, minced
2 teaspoons minced fresh thyme
½ pound frisée, torn into bite-size pieces
1 cup shaved fresh Parmesan cheese (about 2 ounces)
1 tablespoon minced fresh chives

1. Make the gnocchi: Preheat the oven to 375°. Bake the potatoes for about 45 minutes, or until soft. Let cool slightly, then peel and pass them through a ricer or coarse sieve into a bowl. Stir in the cream, egg yolks, Parmesan, nutmeg, thyme, salt and pepper. Stir in the flour to make a soft, slightly sticky dough. Shape into a ball, wrap in plastic and refrigerate for at least 1 hour or overnight.

2. Divide the dough into three pieces. On a lightly floured surface, roll each piece of the dough into a 16-inch-long rope, about ½ inch wide. Cut crosswise into ¾-inch pieces. Lightly dust with flour and roll each piece down the back of a fork with your thumb to make long grooves on the gnocchi. Spread the gnocchi on a floured baking sheet. Refrigerate until chilled, about 2 hours.

3. Cook the gnocchi in two batches in a saucepan of boiling salted water until they float to the surface, about 2 minutes. Transfer them to a bowl of ice water, then to paper towels.

4. Make the salad: In a bowl, season the sherry vinegar with salt and pepper. Whisk in the truffle and olive oils.

5. Preheat the oven to 500°. In a nonreactive ovenproof skillet, cook the pancetta over moderately high heat, stirring, until crisp and browned. Transfer to a plate and discard the fat. Add the butter to the skillet, and when it is golden, add the gnocchi. Cook until they brown around the edges, about 3 minutes. Put the skillet in the oven and roast the gnocchi for about 5 minutes, stirring often, until browned all over. Add to the pancetta.

6. Add the shallot to the skillet and sauté until lightly browned. Add the garlic and thyme and cook for 1 minute. Stir in the gnocchi, pancetta and the sherry vinaigrette and season with salt and pepper.

7. In a large bowl, toss the frisée with the contents of the skillet. Mound the salad on eight plates. Garnish with the Parmesan shavings and chives and serve.—NICK MORFOGEN

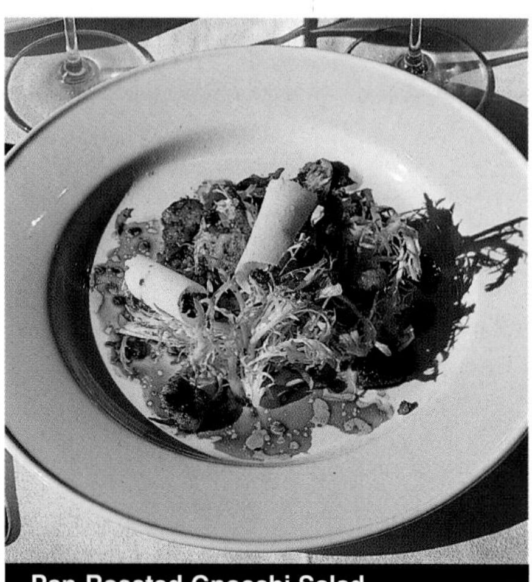
Pan-Roasted Gnocchi Salad

BARLEY-AND-CORN SALAD

Start this salad the day before you plan to serve it—it needs to be refrigerated overnight for the flavors to mingle.

8–10 SERVINGS

1 cup barley (about ½ pound)
½ pound green beans
1 cup fresh or frozen baby lima beans
1 cup fresh or frozen corn kernels
1 medium red onion, finely chopped
Coarse salt and freshly ground pepper
Scant 1 teaspoon ground cumin
⅓ cup fresh lemon juice
1 tablespoon honey mustard
⅓ cup light vegetable oil

1. Bring 9 cups of water to a boil in a large saucepan. Stir in the barley and simmer over low heat until tender, about 1 hour. Drain, rinse well with cold water, then drain again and transfer to a large bowl.

2. Bring a medium saucepan of salted water to a boil. Add the green beans and cook until tender, about 3 minutes. Using a slotted spoon, transfer the beans to a colander and rinse; add to the barley in the bowl. Add the lima beans and corn kernels to the boiling water and cook until tender, about 2 minutes. Drain, rinse with cold water and add to the barley along with the onion. Season the salad with salt and pepper to taste.

3. In a small dry skillet, toast the cumin over low heat, stirring, until fragrant, about 2 minutes. Transfer to a bowl and add the lemon juice and mustard. Slowly stir in the oil until emulsified and season with salt and pepper. Toss this dressing with the barley salad, cover and refrigerate overnight to allow the flavors to blend. Let return to room temperature, then season with salt and pepper and toss before serving.—PAMELA MORGAN

TUNISIAN COUSCOUS SALAD

8–10 SERVINGS

3 medium red bell peppers
10 ounces instant couscous (about 1½ cups)
Salt
¼ cup olive oil
¼ cup fresh lemon juice
1 teaspoon ground cumin
Pinch of cayenne pepper
Freshly ground black pepper
1 pound ripe beefsteak tomatoes, peeled, seeded and cut into ½-inch dice
1 large seedless cucumber, peeled and cut into ½-inch dice
½ cup Moroccan or other small, oil-cured black olives, pitted and coarsely chopped
2 scallions, white and tender green, minced
1 large garlic clove, minced
2 tablespoons finely chopped fresh flat-leaf parsley

1. Roast the bell peppers over a gas flame or under a broiler, turning, until charred all over. Transfer the peppers to a paper bag and let steam for 10 minutes. Remove the skin, cores, seeds and ribs and cut the peppers into ½-inch dice.

2. In a saucepan, bring 2¼ cups of water to a boil. Stir in the couscous and ½ teaspoon salt. Cover and let stand until tender, about 5 minutes. In a small bowl, combine the olive oil, lemon juice, cumin and cayenne and season with salt and pepper.

3. Fluff the couscous with a fork. Add the roasted peppers, tomatoes, cucumber, olives, scallions and garlic. Pour the dressing over the couscous and toss to combine. Let stand at room temperature for at least 1 hour or up to 4 hours. Just before serving, stir in the parsley.—MATTHEW KENNEY

GRILLED-TOFU SALAD

If you can't find firm tofu, you can use regular tofu as follows: Place the tofu blocks between two baking sheets and weigh down the top one with two or three heavy cans. Let stand at room temperature for thirty minutes, occasionally pouring off the excess liquid. Proceed with the recipe.

6 SERVINGS

Two 1-pound blocks of firm tofu
2 medium garlic cloves, minced
2 tablespoons honey
2 tablespoons peanut oil, plus more for grilling
2 tablespoons soy sauce
1 tablespoon black-bean chili paste
1 bunch of watercress, tough stems removed (about 3 loosely packed cups)
¾ cup Miso Carrot Dressing (recipe follows)

Tunisian Couscous Salad

1. Slice each of the tofu blocks into ½- to ¾-inch-thick slices. Pat the slices dry.

2. In a small bowl, stir together the garlic, honey, 2 tablespoons peanut oil, the soy sauce and the black-bean chili paste. Spread half of this marinade in the bottom of a large nonreactive baking dish and top with the tofu slices. Spread the remaining marinade over the tofu, covering it completely. (**MAKE AHEAD:** The tofu can stand at room temperature up to 1 hour before grilling.)

3. Preheat a stovetop grill or the broiler. If using a grill, lightly brush the surface with peanut oil. Grill or broil the tofu, turning once, until caramelized and

SOY GLOSSARY

TOFU White and silky, it's made from curdled fresh soy milk and sold in both firm and soft densities. Try it in stir-fries or dips.

MISO Often used in instant soups, miso is a combination of soybeans and a grain, such as rice, that is aged for one to three years. It can also bring rich flavor to glazes, dips and dressings.

SOY SAUCE This salty dark-brown sauce, available in many varieties, combines the liquid of fermented soybeans with wheat. *Tamari* is made with soybeans alone.

SOY MILK A creamy liquid from crushed whole soybeans, it is often sold in shelf-stable containers, either plain or sweetened and flavored.

SOY FLOUR Made from ground roasted soybeans, it can be used as a substitute for white flour in recipes for baked goods like breads and muffins.

EDAMAME (SWEET SOYBEANS) Pods are harvested when young and tender. The beans, when steamed and salted, are good for snacking.

TEMPEH Chewy yet tender, it's a fermented mixture of whole soybeans and a grain such as millet or rice. Plain or flavored varieties can be added to soups or stews.

ROASTED SOYBEAN POWDER Made from roasted, ground soybeans, it can be found at Asian markets and is used in Japanese confectionery.

brown, 2 to 3 minutes per side. Let cool. Cut each piece into wide strips if desired.

4. To serve, line plates or a platter with the watercress and set the tofu on top. Drizzle the dressing on the salad.

Miso Carrot Dressing

MAKES 1¼ CUPS

- 2 small carrots, coarsely chopped
- 2 small garlic cloves, peeled
- One ¾-inch piece of fresh ginger
- ⅔ cup fresh carrot juice
- 2 tablespoons yellow miso
- 1 tablespoon rice-wine vinegar
- 1 tablespoon olive oil
- ¼ teaspoon sugar
- 2 teaspoons minced fresh basil
- 2 teaspoons minced fresh cilantro

In a blender, combine the carrots, garlic, ginger, carrot juice, miso, vinegar, oil and sugar and blend until perfectly smooth. Transfer to a jar. (**MAKE AHEAD:** The dressing can be refrigerated for up to 4 days.) Just before serving, stir in the basil and cilantro.—GRACE PARISI

Grilled-Tofu Salad

FRESH CRANBERRY-BEAN SALAD

Freshly shelled beans are the key here; you can replace the cranberry beans with lima beans or black-eyed peas.

4–6 SERVINGS

- 4 ounces yellow wax beans
- 1½ pounds fresh cranberry beans, shelled (about 3 cups)
- 3½ tablespoons extra-virgin olive oil
- 2 tablespoons fresh lemon juice
- 1 small garlic clove, minced
- 1 large tomato, cut into ½-inch dice
- 2 tablespoons finely chopped onion

Salt and freshly ground pepper

1. In a large saucepan of boiling salted water, cook the yellow beans until tender, about 2 minutes. Using a slotted spoon, transfer the beans to a colander and refresh with cold water. Add the cranberry beans to the boiling water and cook over moderate heat until tender, about 15 minutes. Drain the beans, transfer to a large bowl and let cool slightly. Cut the yellow beans into 2-inch lengths and add them to the bowl.

2. In a small bowl, combine the oil, lemon juice and garlic. Add dressing to the beans along with the tomato and onion. Season with salt and pepper and toss well. (**MAKE AHEAD:** The salad can be refrigerated for up to 4 hours.) Serve slightly chilled or at room temperature.—MARCIA KIESEL

CHAPTER 4

~

SOUPS

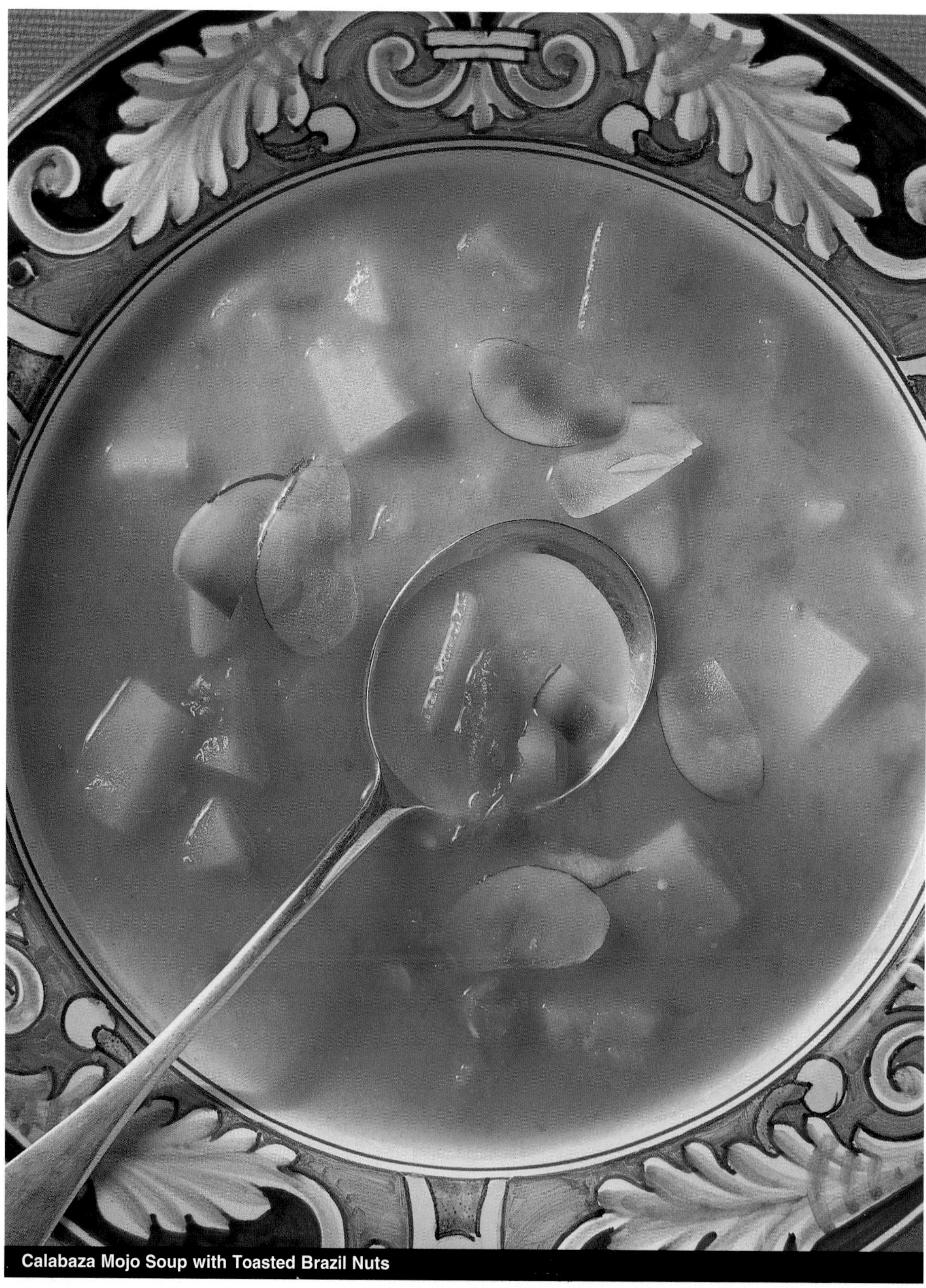

Calabaza Mojo Soup with Toasted Brazil Nuts

CALABAZA MOJO SOUP WITH TOASTED BRAZIL NUTS

This sweet and spicy soup is named for the brightly colored calabaza, the Latin American squash that's also known as West Indian pumpkin, and the Cuban seasoning blend called mojo. *Buttercup squash can be substituted for the calabaza. If you don't have the time to slice Brazil nuts, you can substitute a quarter cup sliced almonds.*

6 SERVINGS

- ¼ cup olive oil
- 1 medium onion, finely chopped
- 1 medium tomato, peeled, seeded and coarsely chopped
- 1 small garlic clove, minced
- 1 small fresh Thai or bird chile or 1 large serrano chile, seeded and minced
- 3 pounds calabaza squash, peeled and cut into ½-inch dice
- 4 cups vegetable stock or canned broth
- 2 cups fresh orange juice
- Salt
- 6 whole shelled Brazil nuts, thinly sliced

1. Heat 3 tablespoons of the oil in a large nonreactive saucepan. Add the onion and cook over moderately high heat, stirring, until softened, about 5 minutes. Add the tomato, garlic and chile and cook, stirring, for 5 minutes. Add the calabaza, stock and orange juice and bring to a boil. Reduce the heat to low, add 1 teaspoon salt and simmer until the calabaza is very soft, about 25 minutes.

2. Meanwhile, preheat the oven to 375°. On a baking sheet, drizzle the sliced Brazil nuts with the remaining 1 tablespoon oil. Bake for about 4 minutes, or until golden. Season with salt. (**MAKE AHEAD:** The soup can be prepared to this point and refrigerated for 1 day. Rewarm before proceeding. Let the nuts stand at room temperature.)

3. Using a slotted spoon, transfer 1½ cups of the vegetables to a food processor or blender and puree until smooth. Stir the puree back into the soup and season with salt. Ladle the soup into shallow bowls and garnish with the Brazil nuts.—ALLEN SUSSER

VEGETABLE TEA

Here's a vegetarian update of classic beef consommé.

4 SERVINGS

- 2 tomatoes, seeded and chopped
- 7 carrots, sliced
- 2 onions, sliced
- ½ leek, sliced
- 1 celery rib, sliced
- 2 garlic cloves, smashed
- 2 shallots, sliced
- 1 bay leaf
- 1 sprig fresh parsley
- 1 sprig fresh thyme
- 1 sprig fresh tarragon
- 8 black peppercorns
- Truffle oil, for garnish

1. In a 2-quart glass canning jar, combine the tomatoes, carrots, onions, leek, celery, garlic, shallots, bay leaf, parsley, thyme, tarragon and peppercorns. Add 3 cups of water to fill the jar almost to the top. Seal the jar, set it in a medium saucepan and add enough water to the pan to reach about halfway up the sides of the jar. Bring to a boil over moderately high heat and cook for 2½ hours; replenish the water in the pan as needed. Let the jar cool completely before opening.

2. Strain the tea through a fine sieve into a saucepan, pressing lightly on the vegetables, and boil

Vegetable Tea

over high heat until reduced to 2½ cups, about 25 minutes. Ladle the tea into bowls, garnish with blanched vegetable strips, if you like, and add a few drops of truffle oil.—CHRISTOPHER GROSS

BLENDER GAZPACHO

The blender makes instant work of this cold Spanish soup. Since gazpacho improves with age, make it ahead of time whenever possible. Although the olive oil is optional in this recipe, it adds real dimension to the flavor and texture of the soup. Even if you leave it out of the gazpacho, drizzle a tad on top at serving time.

6 SERVINGS

- 2 pounds ripe tomatoes, peeled, seeded and coarsely chopped, or one 28-ounce can best-quality plum tomatoes, chopped
- 1 medium onion, preferably a sweet variety such as Vidalia or Walla Walla, coarsely chopped
- 1 large cucumber, peeled
- ½ green bell pepper, coarsely chopped
- ½ red bell pepper, coarsely chopped
- 2 scallions, coarsely chopped
- 3 garlic cloves
- ⅓ cup extra-virgin olive oil
- 3 tablespoons sherry vinegar or balsamic vinegar
- 1 to 2 teaspoons hot-pepper sauce
- 1 teaspoon ground cumin
- ½ to 1 cup chilled tomato juice
- Salt and freshly ground black pepper
- Croutons, chopped fresh herbs, sliced scallions or diced avocado, for garnish

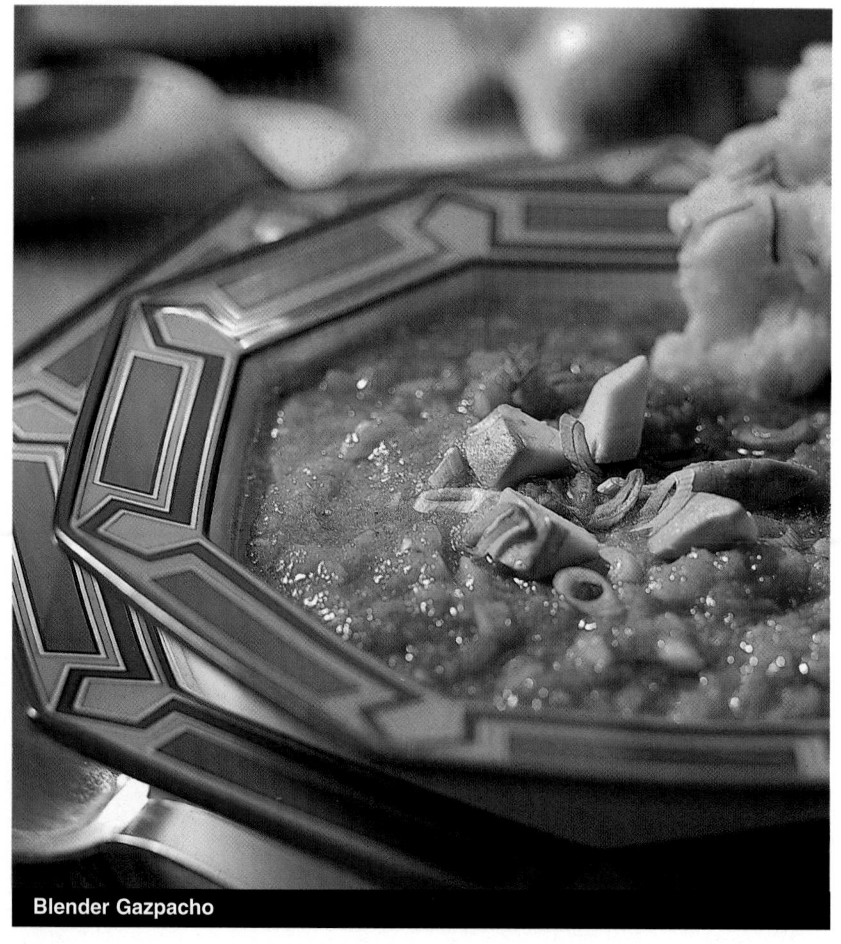
Blender Gazpacho

1. In a large bowl, stir together the tomatoes, onion, cucumber, bell peppers, scallions and garlic. Working in 2-cup batches, whirl the mixture in a blender until finely chopped but not pureed. Return the mixture to the bowl and stir in the oil, vinegar, hot-pepper sauce and cumin. Add enough of the cold tomato juice to make the gazpacho soupy but not too thin. Season generously with salt and black pepper.

2. Cover the bowl and refrigerate the soup until very cold, at least a couple of hours or for up to 2 days. Stir the gazpacho and ladle it into bowls, or pour it at table from a wide-mouth pitcher. Garnish with croutons, herbs, scallions or diced avocado.—MARDEE HAIDIN REGAN

ASIAN MUSHROOM AND LEEK SOUP

If you are unable to find lemongrass, substitute a quarter teaspoon finely grated lemon zest.

🍷 *The aromatic pungency of leeks and mushrooms finds a harmonious echo in Pinot Noir. Serve a light-bodied example from California, such as the 1993 Hess Select or the 1994 Monterey Vineyard, on the cool side to contrast with the warm soup.*

4–6 SERVINGS

- ½ ounce dried shiitake or porcini mushrooms
- 3 tablespoons vegetable oil
- 2 medium shallots, minced
- 1 large leek, white and tender green, halved lengthwise and thinly sliced crosswise
- 4 ounces white mushrooms, stems discarded, caps thinly sliced
- 1 tablespoon minced fresh ginger
- ½ teaspoon Madras curry powder
- 6 cups vegetable stock or canned broth
- ½ cup unsweetened coconut milk
- 1 teaspoon cornstarch
- Coarse salt and freshly ground pepper
- ½ pound wild mushrooms, preferably chanterelles, thinly sliced
- 1 tablespoon minced fresh lemongrass (tender white bulb only)
- 1 tablespoon fresh lemon juice
- 1 tablespoon coarsely chopped fresh chives

1. In a small bowl, cover the dried mushrooms with hot water and let soak until softened, about 30 minutes. Drain and rinse off any grit. Discard the stems and thinly slice the mushrooms.

2. Heat 1 tablespoon of the oil in a large saucepan. Add the shallots and cook over high heat, stirring, until lightly browned, about 2 minutes. Add the leek, white and dried mushrooms, ginger and curry powder and cook over moderate heat, stirring, for 3 minutes. Pour in the stock and coconut milk and bring to a boil.

3. In a bowl, blend the cornstarch with 1 tablespoon of water until smooth. Stir the paste into the soup and bring to a boil over moderately high heat. Reduce the heat to low and simmer the soup for 30 minutes. Season with salt and pepper. (**MAKE AHEAD:** The soup can be prepared to this point and refrigerated for 2 days. Rewarm before proceeding.)

4. Heat the remaining 2 tablespoons oil in a medium skillet. Add the wild mushrooms and sauté over high heat until softened, about 2 minutes. Season the mushrooms with salt and pepper.

5. Divide the sautéed wild mushrooms among four to six soup bowls. Stir the lemongrass and the lemon juice into the soup. Ladle the soup into the bowls and garnish with the chopped chives.—SUSANNA FOO

Asian Mushroom and Leek Soup

RED-PEPPER AND FENNEL SOUP

Spicy fennel adds an edge to this smooth roasted-pepper soup.

8–10 SERVINGS

- 6 large red bell peppers
- 3 tablespoons olive oil
- 8 medium carrots, coarsely chopped
- 2 medium fennel bulbs, halved, cored and coarsely chopped, leafy tops reserved
- 2 medium leeks, white and tender green, coarsely chopped
- 1 small Spanish onion, coarsely chopped
- 2 garlic cloves, coarsely chopped
- ½ cup dry white wine
- 2 tablespoons Pernod (optional)

Red-Pepper and Fennel Soup

Vegetarian Hot-and-Sour Soup

4 fresh thyme sprigs
1 teaspoon fennel seeds
Salt and freshly ground pepper
2 tablespoons coarsely chopped fresh basil
2 tablespoons coarsely chopped fresh flat-leaf parsley

1. Roast the peppers directly over a gas flame or under the broiler, turning, until charred. Transfer to a paper bag and let steam for 15 minutes. Peel the peppers, discarding the cores, ribs and seeds; coarsely chop the peppers.
2. Heat the oil in a large nonreactive saucepan. Add the carrots, fennel, leeks, onion and garlic and cook over moderate heat, stirring occasionally, until the vegetables are softened but not browned, about 8 minutes. Add the roasted peppers, white wine, Pernod, thyme, fennel seeds and 4 cups of water and season with salt and pepper. Reduce the heat to low, cover and simmer until the vegetables are soft, about 40 minutes.
3. Transfer the soup to a blender and blend until smooth. Season with salt and pepper. (**MAKE AHEAD:** The soup can be refrigerated overnight.) Stir in the basil and parsley and thin with a little water if the soup is thick. Serve warm, at room temperature or chilled, garnished with the leafy fennel tops.—PAMELA MORGAN

VEGETARIAN HOT-AND-SOUR SOUP LF

Although the chewy lily buds and tree-ear mushrooms add layers of texture to this soup, they can be omitted.

4 SERVINGS

40 dried lily buds (½ ounce)*
¼ cup small dried tree-ear mushrooms* or dried shiitake-mushroom caps
5 cups chicken stock or canned low-sodium broth
½ cup drained canned bamboo shoots, rinsed and julienned
2 teaspoons minced fresh ginger
¼ teaspoon salt
3 tablespoons red-wine vinegar
Crushed red pepper
3 tablespoons cornstarch mixed with 3 tablespoons water
1 large egg
1 large egg white
2½ tablespoons black soy sauce,* or 3 tablespoons light soy sauce plus a pinch of sugar
4 ounces firm tofu, cut into ⅓-inch dice
1 teaspoon Asian sesame oil
2 tablespoons finely sliced scallions

*Available at Asian markets and by mail order from the Oriental Pantry (1-800-828-0368)

1. In separate bowls, cover the lily buds and mushrooms with hot water. Let soak until softened, about 30 minutes. Drain and thoroughly rinse the lily buds and mushrooms. Trim the tough ends from the buds and halve them crosswise. If using shiitakes, coarsely chop them.
2. In a large nonreactive saucepan, combine the stock, lily buds, mushrooms, bamboo shoots, ginger and salt. Cover and bring to a boil over moderately high heat. Reduce the heat and simmer for 10 minutes. Stir in the vinegar

"Creamy" Mushroom Soup with Mushroom Chips (p. 83)

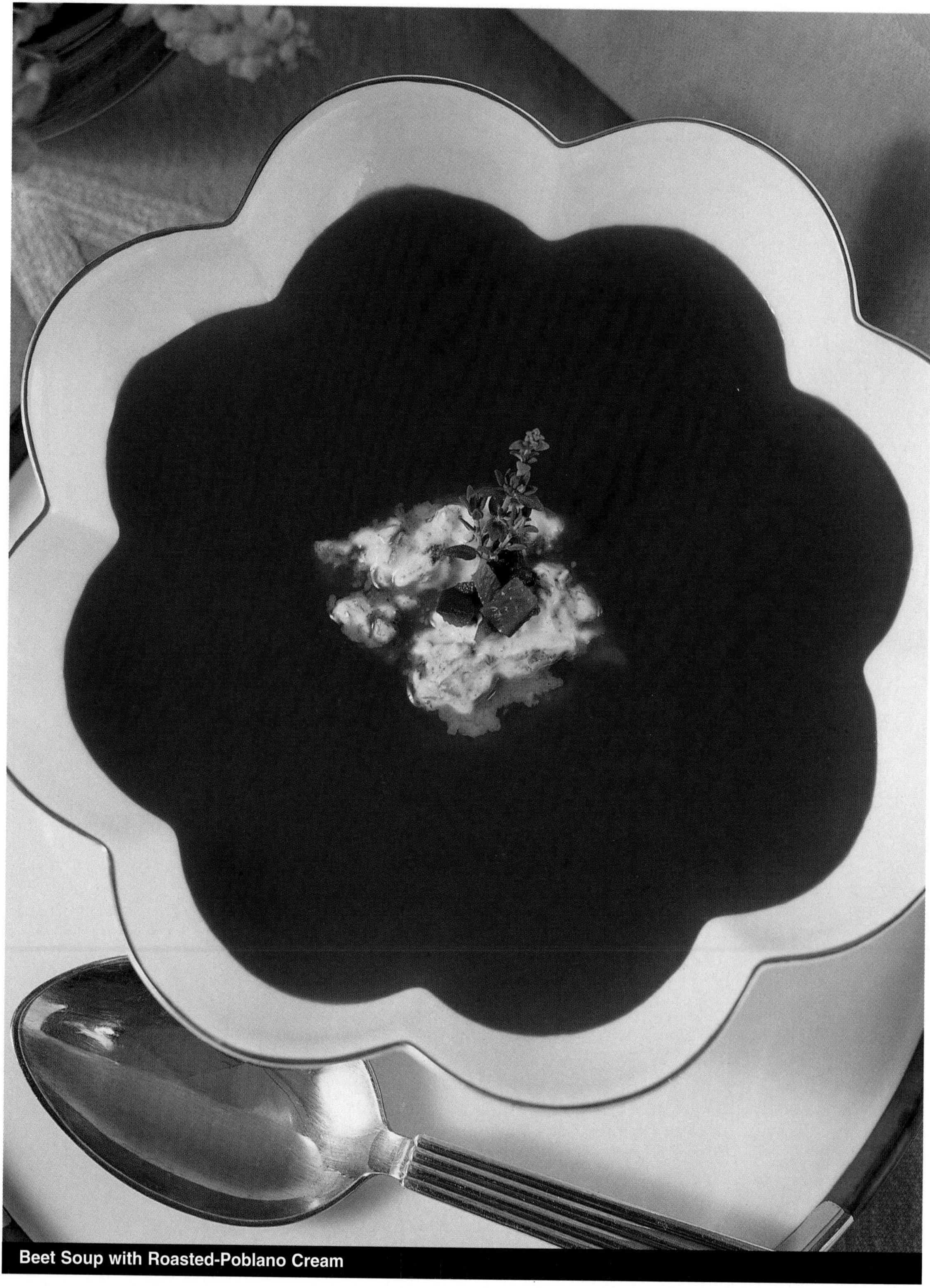

Beet Soup with Roasted-Poblano Cream

and 1½ teaspoons crushed red pepper and boil over moderately high heat for 2 minutes.

3. Beat the cornstarch mixture into the soup in a steady stream. In a bowl, combine the egg and the egg white and beat into the soup. Stir in the soy sauce, tofu and sesame oil and cook over moderate heat until warmed through. Season with crushed red pepper and garnish with the scallions.—EILEEN YIN-FEI LO

"CREAMY" MUSHROOM SOUP WITH MUSHROOM CHIPS

The illusion of cream in this silky soup comes from thoroughly pureeing it in a blender. Do use the Rich Chicken Stock; it makes all the difference.

8 SERVINGS

- 2 pounds oyster mushrooms, large stems removed (see Note)
- 3 tablespoons unsalted butter, plus 2 tablespoons melted
- Salt and freshly ground pepper
- 2 large shallots, minced
- ½ pound cremini mushrooms, sliced lengthwise
- ¼ cup dry white wine
- 3 tablespoons all-purpose flour
- 8 cups Rich Chicken Stock (recipe follows)
- 1 tablespoon fresh lemon juice
- 3 tablespoons minced fresh chives

1. Preheat the oven to 450°. In a large bowl, toss the oyster mushrooms with the 2 tablespoons of melted butter and season with salt and pepper. Arrange the mushrooms on a large rimmed baking sheet in a single layer and bake for about 20 minutes, or until the mushrooms have begun to brown and crisp. Remove any crisp mushrooms to a plate; continue baking the rest for 10 minutes, or until crisp.

2. Meanwhile, in a large nonreactive saucepan, melt the 3 tablespoons butter over moderate heat. When the foam subsides, add the shallots and reduce the heat to low. Cook, stirring a few times, until softened, about 5 minutes. Increase the heat to moderately high and add the cremini mushrooms. Season with salt and pepper and cook, stirring, until wilted, about 4 minutes. Add the wine and boil until reduced by half, about 3 minutes. Stir in the flour until well blended. Gradually whisk in the stock and bring to a simmer. Reduce the heat to low, cover and cook until the mushrooms are very tender, about 15 minutes.

3. Working in batches, puree the soup in a blender until completely smooth. (MAKE AHEAD: The soup and the mushroom chips can be refrigerated for up to 1 day. Recrisp the chips in a 400° oven.) Reheat the soup. Season with the lemon juice, salt and pepper. Ladle into rimmed soup plates and garnish with the chips and chives.

NOTE: If you can't find oyster mushrooms, use thinly sliced cremini or white mushrooms for the chips instead.

Rich Chicken Stock

MAKES ABOUT 8 CUPS

- 4 pounds chicken wings
- 2 whole chicken legs
- 1 medium onion, halved
- 1 bay leaf
- 2 teaspoons salt

In a small stockpot, cover the chicken parts with 12 cups water. Bring to a boil over high heat. Skim the surface and reduce the heat to low. Add the onion, bay leaf and salt, cover partially and simmer for 1 hour. Slowly strain the stock into a clean pan and boil over high heat, skimming occasionally, until reduced to 8 cups, about 20 minutes. If using immediately, skim off as much fat as possible. Or let cool to room temperature and refrigerate for up to 3 days. Skim off the fat before using.—MARCIA KIESEL

BEET SOUP WITH ROASTED-POBLANO CREAM

For a sweeter flavor, wrap the beets in foil and bake them in a 350° oven for about forty-five minutes instead of boiling them.

8 SERVINGS

- 2 pounds large beets
- 2 tablespoons unsalted butter
- 1 large red onion, thinly sliced
- 6 fresh thyme sprigs
- 4 garlic cloves, minced
- 5 cups chicken stock or canned low-sodium broth
- Salt and freshly ground pepper
- 4 large poblano or Anaheim chiles
- 1 teaspoon olive oil
- ½ cup sour cream
- 1 tablespoon fresh lime juice

1. In a large saucepan, cover the beets with cold water and bring to a boil over high heat. Reduce the heat to moderate and simmer the beets until tender, about 25 minutes. Drain the beets and let them cool slightly, then peel and cut into 2-inch chunks with a small sharp knife. ➤

2. In a large nonreactive saucepan, melt the butter over moderate heat. Add the onion and the thyme sprigs and cook, stirring, until the onion is translucent, about 4 minutes. Reduce the heat to moderately low and add the garlic. Cook until softened, about 5 minutes. Add the beets, stock and a large pinch each of salt and pepper. Increase the heat to moderate, cover and simmer for 10 minutes. Remove from the heat, uncover and let stand for 5 minutes. Discard the thyme sprigs.

3. Working in batches, puree the soup in a blender until it is very smooth. Season with salt and pepper and let cool completely.

4. Roast the chiles directly over a gas flame or under the broiler, turning, until charred all over. Transfer to a large bowl, cover with plastic wrap and let steam for 5 minutes. Peel the chiles and remove the seeds, then transfer to an airtight container and strain any accumulated juices on top. Coat the chiles with the olive oil and season lightly with salt and pepper. (**MAKE AHEAD:** Pour the soup into airtight containers and freeze for up to 1 month. The chiles can also be frozen for up to 1 month. Thaw both in the refrigerator overnight before proceeding.)

5. To serve, rewarm the soup over moderate heat, stirring often. Chop the chiles and put them in a small bowl. Fold in the sour cream. Season the soup with salt, pepper and the lime juice and ladle it into bowls. Dollop or swirl about 2 tablespoons of the chile cream in each serving.—MARCIA KIESEL

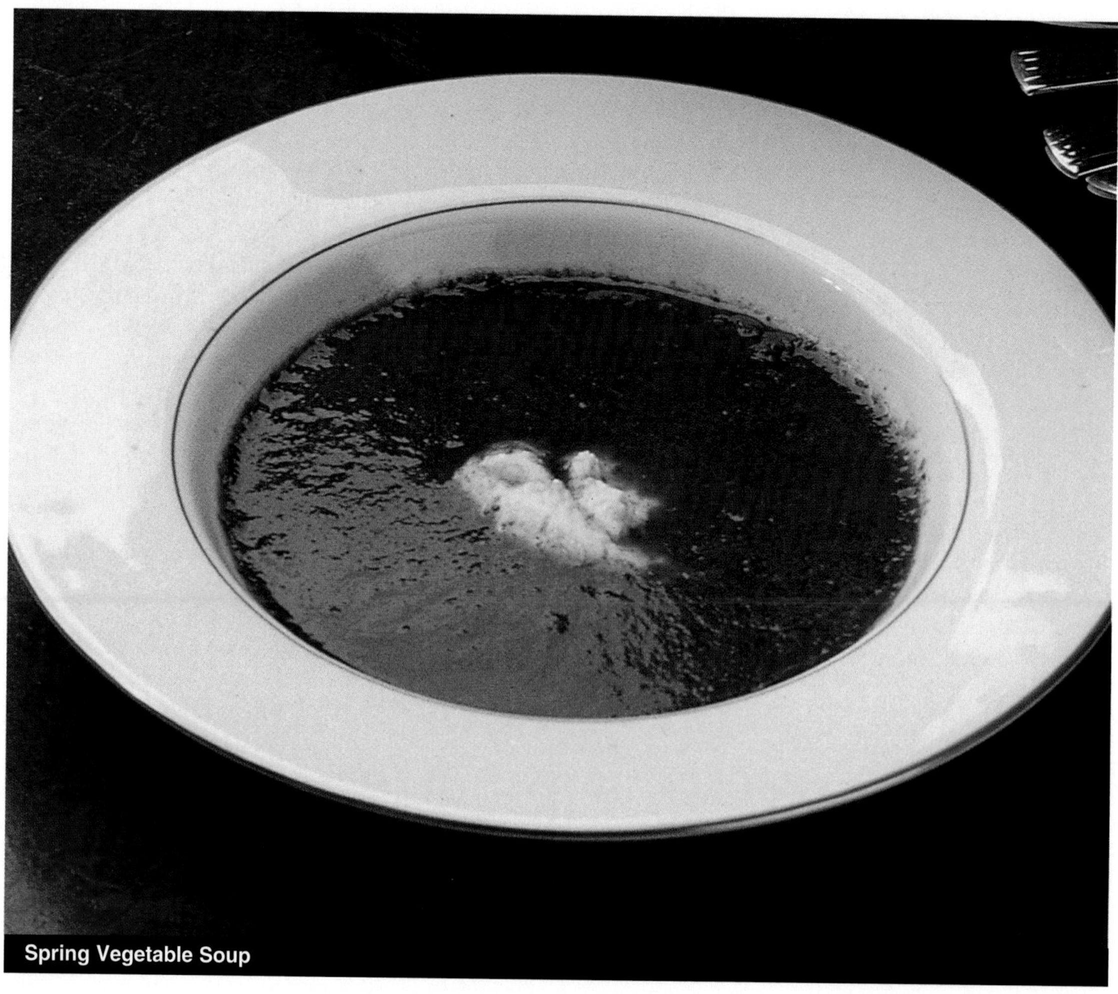

Spring Vegetable Soup

VICHYSSOISE

8 SERVINGS

½ cup vegetable oil
5 large shallots, thinly sliced
3 tablespoons unsalted butter
3 large leeks, white and tender green, thinly sliced crosswise
1 small onion, thinly sliced
½ cup dry white wine
8 cups chicken stock
1½ pounds red potatoes, peeled and cut into 2-inch chunks
2 bay leaves
Salt and freshly ground pepper
2½ cups milk
1 cup light cream
½ cup minced fresh chives

1. In a saucepan, heat the oil over moderately high heat until shimmering. Add the shallots and cook over moderately low heat, stirring often, until golden, about 5 minutes. Transfer the shallots to paper towels.

2. Melt the butter in a large nonreactive saucepan. Add the leeks and onion and cook over moderately low heat, stirring, until softened but not browned, about 12 minutes. Add the wine and cook over moderately high heat until reduced by half, about 3 minutes. Add the stock, potatoes, bay leaves and salt and pepper to taste. Bring to a boil, then simmer over low heat, partially covered, until the potatoes are tender, about 25 minutes.

3. Working in batches, puree the soup in a blender, then transfer to a bowl and let cool. Stir in the milk and cream. Refrigerate until chilled, at least 4 hours or overnight. Season with salt and pepper and garnish with the chives and shallots.—MARCIA KIESEL

SPRING VEGETABLE SOUP

In this vibrant, fresh-tasting soup, each vegetable makes a distinctive contribution: leeks, asparagus and peas give it body, sorrel provides acidity, watercress offers a peppery note and spinach enhances the color. A dollop of fresh ricotta cheese tops it all.

8 SERVINGS

2 tablespoons pure olive oil
2 small leeks, trimmed and diced
½ pound tender asparagus, cut into 1-inch pieces
1 cup freshly shelled young peas
1 ounce fresh sorrel or borage leaves
Coarse salt
1 pound fresh young spinach leaves
1 ounce watercress, stemmed
Ice
Freshly ground pepper
½ cup fresh ricotta cheese
Extra-virgin olive oil, for drizzling

1. Warm the pure olive oil in a heavy, nonreactive 6-quart saucepan. Add the leeks, asparagus, peas, sorrel and 2 teaspoons coarse salt and cook until warmed through. Add 1 cup of water, cover and sweat the vegetables over moderate heat until the water has evaporated, about 10 minutes.

2. Add another 7 cups of water and bring to a boil. Reduce the heat and simmer for 5 minutes. Increase the heat to high; add the spinach and watercress. Cook, stirring to submerge the leaves, until wilted, about 2 minutes.

3. Transfer the soup to a bowl set in a larger bowl of ice. Stir the soup frequently to chill it quickly and thoroughly. Once the soup is completely cold, pour it into a blender and puree until smooth. Season with salt and pepper.

4. To serve, gently reheat the soup. Spoon it into warmed soup plates or bowls. Garnish each serving with 1 tablespoon ricotta and a drizzle of extra-virgin olive oil and serve.—PAUL BERTOLLI

Minestrone with Tomatoes and Rice

MINESTRONE WITH TOMATOES AND RICE

This soup needs only a simple, straightforward dry red that will complement its mild vegetable flavors instead of competing with them. A young, fresh Rioja from Spain would work particularly well. Look for the 1990 Sierra Cantabria or the 1991 Conde de Valdemar.

4–6 SERVINGS

¼ cup olive oil
1 small onion, finely chopped
1 medium red bell pepper, cut into ½-inch dice
1 medium carrot, cut into ½-inch dice

1 medium Idaho potato, peeled and cut into 1-inch dice
1 small zucchini, cut into 1-inch dice
1 small yellow squash, cut into 1-inch dice
1 Japanese eggplant or ½ small eggplant, cut into ½-inch dice
½ cup arborio rice
One 28-ounce can Italian peeled tomatoes, drained and coarsely chopped
Salt and freshly ground black pepper
½ teaspoon crushed red pepper
1 small stalk of broccoli—cut into 1-inch florets, stem peeled and cut into ½-inch pieces
¼ small head of cauliflower, cut into 1-inch florets
1 medium celery rib, cut into ½-inch dice
½ cup frozen baby peas
Freshly grated Parmesan cheese, for serving

1. Heat the oil in a large nonreactive saucepan. Add the onion and bell pepper and cook over moderately high heat, stirring occasionally, until softened and lightly browned, about 6 minutes. Add the carrot, potato, zucchini, yellow squash and eggplant. Cook, stirring often, for 5 minutes.
2. Add the rice to the saucepan and toss well to coat the grains with oil. Add the tomatoes, 1 teaspoon salt, ¼ teaspoon black pepper, the crushed red pepper and 6 cups of water and bring to a boil over moderately high heat. Add the broccoli, cauliflower, celery and peas and cook, stirring, until all the vegetables and the rice are tender, about 35 minutes. Season the soup with salt and pepper. (**MAKE AHEAD:** The soup can be refrigerated for 1 day. Reheat before serving.) Ladle the soup into bowls and serve, passing the Parmesan cheese at the table.—LUCA MARCATO

ARTICHOKE PARMESAN SOUP

Although I prefer to prepare this with fresh artichokes, I'm aware that many cooks may not have the patience for trimming artichoke bottoms. I have tried this recipe with artichokes in a jar and find the flavor too dull. However, frozen artichokes—usually sold in nine-ounce packages labeled artichoke hearts—are a worthy substitute.

4 SERVINGS

1 lemon, halved
4 large artichokes (about 3 pounds)
¼ cup extra-virgin olive oil
2 medium shallots, minced
Sea salt
1 cup white wine, preferably Chardonnay
3 cups chicken stock or canned low-sodium broth
1 tablespoon unsalted butter
One 2-ounce chunk of Parmigiano-Reggiano cheese, shaved into strips with a vegetable peeler

1. Squeeze the lemon juice into a large bowl of cold water and add the lemon halves. Break off or cut the stem from the base of the artichokes. Using your hands, snap off the tough outer leaves near the base of the artichokes. Continue snapping off leaves until only the central cone of yellow leaves with pale green tips remain. Using a large sharp knife, trim the top cone of leaves to just below the green tips. Trim any tough dark-green areas from the base with a small knife. Cut the artichoke hearts in half. Using a small spoon or a melon baller, scrape out and discard the hairy chokes. Cut each half lengthwise into four even slices. Place the artichoke slices in the acidulated water.
2. In a large nonreactive saucepan, combine 2 tablespoons of the oil with the shallots and a pinch of sea salt and cook over moderate heat, stirring often, until softened but not brown. Stir in the remaining 2 tablespoons oil. Drain and add the artichoke slices and cook until slightly softened, about 2 minutes. Pour the wine all over the artichokes, increase the heat to moderately high and simmer until almost evaporated, about 7 minutes. Add the stock and reduce the heat. Cover and simmer gently until the flavors have mingled, about 20 minutes.
3. Transfer the soup to a food mill with a fine disk and puree. Discard any fibrous artichoke pieces that remain in the food mill. Return the soup to the pan; you should have about 3 cups. If the soup is too thin, return it to the saucepan and boil until it is reduced and thickened. (**MAKE AHEAD:** The soup can be refrigerated for several hours. Rewarm gently over moderately low heat.)
4. Just before serving, whisk the butter into the hot soup over moderate heat until it is melted and incorporated. Pour the soup into heated soup plates or bowls and scatter the strips of Parmigiano-Reggiano on top. Serve immediately.—PATRICIA WELLS

GRILLED-VEGETABLE SOUP WITH GOAT-CHEESE TOASTS Q

This easy, chunky vegetable soup is a meal in itself.

4 SERVINGS

1 small eggplant, sliced lengthwise ½ inch thick
1 medium zucchini, sliced lengthwise ½ inch thick
1 medium yellow squash, sliced lengthwise ½ inch thick
1 medium red onion, cut crosswise into 4 slices
2 teaspoons olive oil, plus more for brushing
½ each medium red and yellow bell pepper, halved lengthwise, or 1 whole red or yellow bell pepper, quartered lengthwise
2 garlic cloves, minced
1½ pounds ripe tomatoes, coarsely chopped
3 cups chicken stock or canned low-sodium broth
Salt and freshly ground pepper
1 tablespoon finely chopped fresh basil
1½ teaspoons finely chopped fresh oregano
4 thick slices of country bread
3 ounces mild goat cheese, at room temperature
1 tablespoon heavy cream (optional)

1. Light a grill or preheat the broiler. Brush the eggplant, zucchini, squash and onion with oil. Grill the pepper quarters, skin-side down, for about 12 minutes, or until charred. Grill the eggplant, zucchini, squash and onion, turning occasionally, until tender but still firm: 6 to 8 minutes for the zucchini, squash and onion and 8 to 10 minutes for the

Making Artichoke Parmesan Soup

Grilled-Vegetable Soup with Goat-Cheese Toasts

eggplant. Peel and seed the peppers and cut all the grilled vegetables into ½-inch dice.
2. Heat the 2 teaspoons oil in a large nonreactive saucepan. Add the garlic and stir over moderate heat until fragrant. Add the tomatoes, stock and salt and pepper to taste and simmer, stirring, for 10 minutes. Add the grilled vegetables, 1½ teaspoons of the basil and the oregano and simmer, stirring, for 3 minutes longer.
3. Grill the bread until toasted. Combine the cheese, the remaining 1½ teaspoons basil and a generous grinding of pepper and stir until smooth; stir in the cream. Spread the goat cheese on the warm toasts and serve with the soup.—JUDITH SUTTON

TOASTED-BREAD AND ONION SOUP

This soup is an ideal vehicle for leftover sourdough bread. The recipe is from Jacques Pépin's Kitchen: Cooking with Claudine *(KQED).*

4 SERVINGS

1½ tablespoons peanut oil
2 medium onions, thinly sliced
5 cups chicken stock or other homemade stock or canned low-sodium broth
Salt and freshly ground pepper
½ pound sourdough baguette, cut into ½-inch cubes
1 cup grated Gruyère cheese (about 4 ounces)

1. Preheat the oven to 400°. Heat the peanut oil in a large saucepan. Add the onions and cook over high heat, stirring, until nicely browned, 8 to 10 minutes. Add the stock, season with salt and pepper and bring to a strong boil.
2. Meanwhile, spread out the bread cubes on a baking sheet and toast for about 8 minutes, or until lightly golden. Transfer the cubes to a large soup tureen and sprinkle the cheese on top. Pour the boiling soup into the tureen and mix. Ladle into soup plates or bowls and serve.—JACQUES PÉPIN

WINTER MINESTRONE WITH TUSCAN KALE PESTO

If you can't find a prosciutto bone, substitute a pound of smoked ham hocks. Shred the meat from the ham hocks and add to the soup before serving.

🍷 *A light, tart red would stand up to the garlicky pesto that underscores the varied flavors in this soup. A Sangiovese, such as the 1993 Avignonesi from Italy or the 1994 Martin Brothers Il Palio from California, would be ideal.*

8–10 SERVINGS

½ pound dried cranberry or pinto beans (1⅓ cups), rinsed and picked over
1 prosciutto bone
¼ cup olive oil
1 large fennel bulb, trimmed, cored and cut into ⅓-inch dice
2 large onions, cut into ⅓-inch dice
4 medium celery ribs, cut into ⅓-inch dice
2 medium leeks, white and tender green, quartered lengthwise and sliced crosswise ¼ inch thick
2 medium carrots, cut into ⅓-inch dice
Coarse salt and freshly ground black pepper
1¼ pounds Savoy cabbage, finely shredded
1 bay leaf
Crushed red pepper
2 teaspoons minced fresh thyme
2 teaspoons minced fresh rosemary
½ cup freshly grated Parmesan cheese (about 1½ ounces)
Tuscan Kale Pesto (recipe follows)

1. In a bowl, cover the beans with water and let soak overnight. Alternatively, in a saucepan, cover the beans with water and bring to a boil over moderate heat. Remove from the heat and let soak, covered, for 1 hour.
2. Drain and rinse the beans. In a large enameled cast-iron casserole, combine the beans and the prosciutto bone with 10 cups of water. Bring to a boil over moderately high heat, then reduce the heat to moderately low and simmer until the beans are tender but still intact, 1½ to 2 hours.
3. Meanwhile, heat the oil in a large saucepan. Add the fennel, onions, celery, leeks and carrots and season with salt and black

Toasted-Bread and Onion Soup

pepper. Cook over moderate heat, stirring frequently, until the vegetables are softened, 15 to 20 minutes. Add the cabbage, bay leaf and 1 teaspoon crushed red pepper and cook, stirring, for 5 minutes.

4. Add the sautéed vegetables to the beans with the thyme and rosemary. If necessary, add more water to cover the vegetables. Bring to a boil over moderately high heat, then reduce the heat and simmer until the cabbage is tender, about 30 minutes. Season with salt, black pepper and crushed red pepper. (MAKE AHEAD: The soup can be refrigerated for 2 days. Rewarm before serving.) Discard the prosciutto bone. Ladle the soup into bowls and serve with the Parmesan and the pesto.

Tuscan Kale Pesto

MAKES ABOUT 1½ CUPS

1 pound kale, ribs removed, leaves coarsely chopped
¾ cup extra-virgin olive oil
1 large garlic clove, quartered
Coarse salt

Bring a large saucepan of salted water to a boil. Add the kale, cover and cook over moderately high heat for 10 minutes. Drain and rinse with cold water. Squeeze the excess water from the kale and transfer the kale to a food processor. Add the olive oil, garlic and 1 teaspoon coarse salt and process until smooth. Season with more salt. (MAKE AHEAD: The pesto can be refrigerated for 1 day. Let return to room temperature before using.) —JOHANNE KILLEEN AND GEORGE GERMON

PRESSURE-COOKER SPLIT-PEA SOUP

The dried chipotle chiles give this soup a distinctive smoky flavor without the traditional ham hock or ham bone.

6–8 SERVINGS

2 tablespoons oil
1 tablespoon thinly sliced garlic
2 cups coarsely chopped onion
1 teaspoon whole cumin seeds
2 dried chipotle chiles,* seeded and snipped into bits
5 cups boiling water
One 15-ounce can crushed tomatoes
2 cups green split peas (about 1 pound), picked over and rinsed
4 large carrots, cut into 1½-inch chunks
Salt and freshly ground black pepper
¼ cup chopped fresh cilantro

*Available at specialty-food shops and Latin markets

1. Heat the oil in a pressure cooker. Add the garlic and cook over moderately high heat until lightly browned. Stir in the onion,

USING A PRESSURE COOKER

Forget about the time Aunt Tillie's pea soup ended up on the kitchen ceiling. Forget, too, about her favorite pressure-cooker recipes for mushy, overcooked food. If you want to put a delicious, nourishing meal on the table in, say, fifteen minutes, you need a pressure cooker—one of the new models that have enough safety backup mechanisms to make them idiot-proof.

Here's how the pressure cooker works its magic: When the tightly sealed cooker is set over high heat, steam pressure builds and the internal temperature rises, increasing the boiling point from the standard 212° to 250°. Under high pressure (about fifteen pounds per square inch), the fiber in food is tenderized, and flavors mingle in record time. What's more, fewer nutrients are lost because cooking is so fast and because nutrient-rich steam condenses in the pot instead of being lost in the air.

Some points to consider before making Pressure-Cooker Split-Pea Soup, Pinto-Bean and Beef Chili (p. 248), Saffron Risotto (p. 317) or the chicken and vegetable stocks on p. 100:

- **All the recipes are designed to be prepared in a six-quart (or larger) cooker, although you can use a two-and-a-half-quart pan for the risotto.**
- **Do not fill the pressure cooker to more than half to three-quarters of the total capacity, depending on the ingredients and the manufacturer's specifications. There must be room inside for the pressure to build.**
- **Larger pots take longer to come up to pressure, but the pressure-cooking time remains the same.**
- **Calculate the cooking time from the moment that high pressure is reached. On newer pressure cookers, watch for the appropriate line on the pressure indicator. For best results, use a timer.**

cumin and chipotles and cook, stirring frequently, until the onion is translucent, about 2 minutes. Add the water, tomatoes, split peas and carrots.

2. Lock the lid of the pressure cooker in place and bring to high pressure over high heat. Lower the heat just enough to maintain high pressure and cook for 15 minutes. If time permits, allow the pressure to come down naturally. Otherwise, release the pressure by setting the cooker under cold running water. Remove the lid, tilting it away from you to allow any excess steam to escape.

3. Season the soup with salt and black pepper. If it seems thick, thin it with a little water. Stir in the chopped cilantro just before serving.—LORNA J. SASS

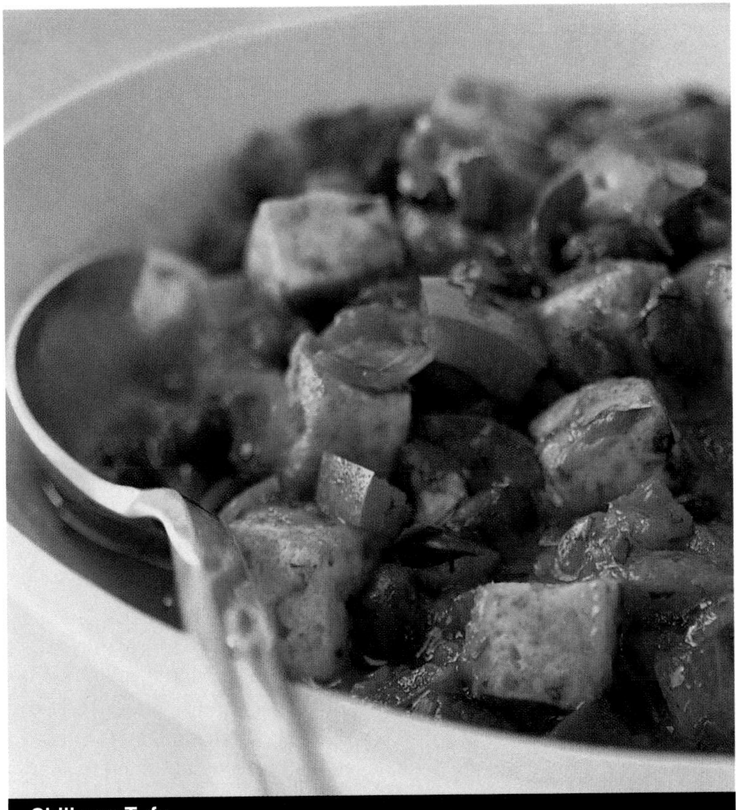

Chili con Tofu

CHILI CON TOFU

For a more substantial, spicy chili, use the same weight of tempeh in place of the tofu. Since tempeh is not packed in water, there is no need to pat it dry before sautéing, but stir in up to one extra cup of water in Step 4 when adding the beans.

6 SERVINGS

- ¼ cup plus 2 tablespoons olive oil
- 3 medium red onions, finely chopped
- 4 medium garlic cloves, minced
- 2 large poblano chiles, seeded and finely chopped
- 1 large red bell pepper, seeded and finely chopped
- 1 medium jalapeño chile, minced
- ⅓ cup pure chile powder
- 1 teaspoon ground cumin
- One 35-ounce can Italian peeled tomatoes in juice
- 1 cup canned tomato sauce
- ½ teaspoon dried oregano
- Salt
- One 1-pound block of extra-firm tofu, drained and patted dry
- One 19-ounce can black beans, drained
- ½ cup finely chopped fresh cilantro

1. In a large, heavy, nonreactive casserole, heat ¼ cup of the oil. Stir in the onions, garlic, poblanos, bell pepper, jalapeño, ¼ cup of the chile powder and the cumin. Cook over moderate heat, stirring occasionally, until slightly softened but not browned, about 10 minutes.

2. Coarsely chop the tomatoes and add them to the casserole with their juice and the tomato sauce. Stir in the oregano and 2 teaspoons salt and bring to a simmer over moderate heat. Reduce the heat to moderately low and simmer, stirring occasionally, until all the vegetables are soft, about 15 minutes.

3. Meanwhile, cut the tofu into ½-inch dice and pat dry. Place in a bowl and toss with the remaining 4 teaspoons chile powder. In a large nonstick skillet, heat the remaining 2 tablespoons oil. Add the tofu and cook over moderately high heat for 3 minutes to lightly toast the chile powder. Season with ¼ teaspoon salt. Transfer the tofu to the casserole. Add ⅓ cup of water to the skillet and scrape the bottom with a wooden spoon to loosen the browned bits. Add the liquid from the skillet to the casserole.

4. Stir the beans into the chili and simmer, stirring frequently, until the flavors are blended, about 10 minutes. (**MAKE AHEAD:** This chili is best if it stands for at least 1 hour or is refrigerated overnight.) Before serving, stir half of the chopped fresh cilantro into the chili; sprinkle the rest on top.—DIANA STURGIS

COOKING BEANS

To cook dried beans, first soak them overnight in water to cover by 3 inches. Drain, rinse and put the beans in a pot. Cover amply with water and simmer until tender, 45 minutes to 1 hour. Salt the beans once they're fully cooked and store them in their liquid.—MARCELLA HAZAN

WINTER WHITE-BEAN SOUP

12 SERVINGS

- 1 pound Great Northern beans, picked over, rinsed and soaked overnight in cold water
- 12 cups chicken stock or 6 cups canned low-sodium broth mixed with 6 cups water
- 1 onion, thinly sliced
- 1 carrot, thinly sliced
- 1 celery rib, thinly sliced
- 3 large garlic cloves, sliced
- Bouquet garni made with 2 teaspoons black peppercorns, 2 fresh thyme sprigs and 1 bay leaf, tied in cheesecloth
- 2 meaty smoked ham hocks
- Salt and freshly ground pepper

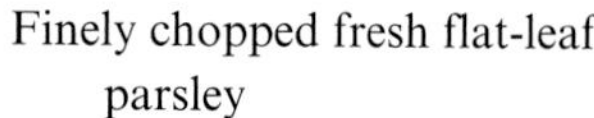

- Finely chopped fresh flat-leaf parsley

1. Drain the beans and rinse them thoroughly. Put the beans in a large pot, add the stock, onion, carrot, celery, garlic, bouquet garni and ham hocks and bring to a boil over high heat. Cover partially and simmer over moderate heat until the beans are tender, about 1¾ hours. Transfer the ham hocks to a plate; discard the bouquet garni.

2. Pass the beans through a food mill and return the puree to the soup pot. Season with salt and pepper. Pull all the meat from the ham hocks and shred it into bite-size pieces; add the meat to the soup. (**MAKE AHEAD:** The soup can be refrigerated for several days. Reheat the soup gently; add a little water if it seems too thick.)

3. Bring the soup to a boil and simmer for 10 minutes, stirring occasionally. Season well and stir in the parsley just before serving.—WALDY MALOUF

Cannellini Soup

CANNELLINI SOUP

If you really love beans, all you want in a bean soup is beans. There is very little liquid in this soup, but you can certainly add more broth or water if

Winter White-Bean Soup

you prefer it soupier. At the other extreme, you can add less and make it thick enough to serve as a side dish to accompany a nice roast.

4–6 SERVINGS

- ½ cup extra-virgin olive oil
- 1 teaspoon chopped garlic
- 2 cups cooked cannellini beans, drained and rinsed if canned
- Salt and freshly ground pepper
- 1 cup homemade beef broth or ⅓ cup canned beef stock diluted with ⅔ cup water
- 2 tablespoons chopped fresh flat-leaf parsley
- Toasted thick slices of crusty bread

1. Put the oil and the garlic in a saucepan. Cook over moderate heat, stirring, until the garlic is a pale gold. Add the beans and a pinch of salt and pepper. Cover and cook gently for 5 minutes.

2. Transfer ½ cup of the beans to a food mill, add the broth and puree back into the pan. Simmer the soup for 5 minutes, then season with salt and pepper. Swirl in the parsley. Ladle the soup over the bread and serve.—MARCELLA HAZAN

BLACK-BEAN SOUP WITH BANANAS

Pancetta adds a delicious complexity to this creamy, chunky soup, as does the mixture of olive oil, red-wine vinegar and Tabasco that's stirred in at the end. This recipe is from Jacques Pépin's Kitchen: Cooking with Claudine *(KQED).*

MAKES ABOUT 4 QUARTS

- 1 pound dried black beans, picked over, rinsed and soaked overnight in cold water to cover
- ½ cup (4 ounces) brown rice
- ¾ pound lean pancetta or bacon, cut into ¼-inch dice
- 2 medium onions, cut into 1-inch dice
- 8 garlic cloves, coarsely chopped
- 1 tablespoon *herbes de Provence*
- 1 tablespoon chili powder
- One 14-ounce can chopped tomatoes
- Salt
- 2 tablespoons virgin olive oil
- 2 tablespoons red-wine vinegar
- 1½ teaspoons Tabasco
- 4 ripe bananas
- 2 tablespoons fresh lemon juice
- ½ teaspoon freshly ground pepper

1. Drain and rinse the beans and put them in a large heavy saucepan or casserole. Add the rice, pancetta and 3 quarts of cool water and bring to a boil over high heat, stirring occasionally. Skim any foam that rises to the surface. Reduce the heat to very low, cover and simmer for 1 hour.

2. Stir in the onions, garlic, *herbes de Provence,* chili powder, tomatoes and salt to taste and bring to a boil. Reduce the heat to very low, cover and cook for 1½ hours longer.

3. Using a handheld electric mixer, beat the soup for 5 to 10 seconds to emulsify it a bit. Alternatively, puree 2 cups of the soup in a food processor or blender and then return it to the saucepan. The point is to thicken the soup somewhat while maintaining its overall chunkiness. (**MAKE AHEAD:** Let the soup cool, then refrigerate it for up to 5 days or freeze. Reheat the soup before proceeding.)

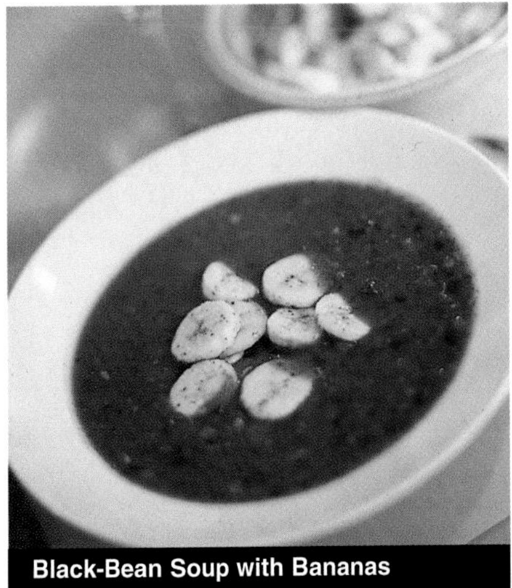

Black-Bean Soup with Bananas

4. In a small bowl, combine the oil, vinegar and Tabasco, then stir this mixture into the soup. Slice the bananas ¼ inch thick and place them in a bowl. Toss with the lemon juice and sprinkle with the pepper. Serve the soup in bowls and pass the bananas separately.—JACQUES PÉPIN

THREE-CHILE POTATO SOUP

This tangy Southwestern-style soup features three kinds of fresh chiles and a splash of beer.

🍷 *A beer such as Dos Equis or Guinness Extra Stout has just enough sweet richness and bite to balance the array of spicy flavors in the soup.*

6–8 SERVINGS

- 4 large plum tomatoes, halved lengthwise
- ¼ cup plus 1 tablespoon olive oil
- 8 cups vegetable stock or canned broth
- 6 medium poblano chiles
- 6 medium fresh Anaheim chiles
- 3 medium onions, cut into ½-inch dice

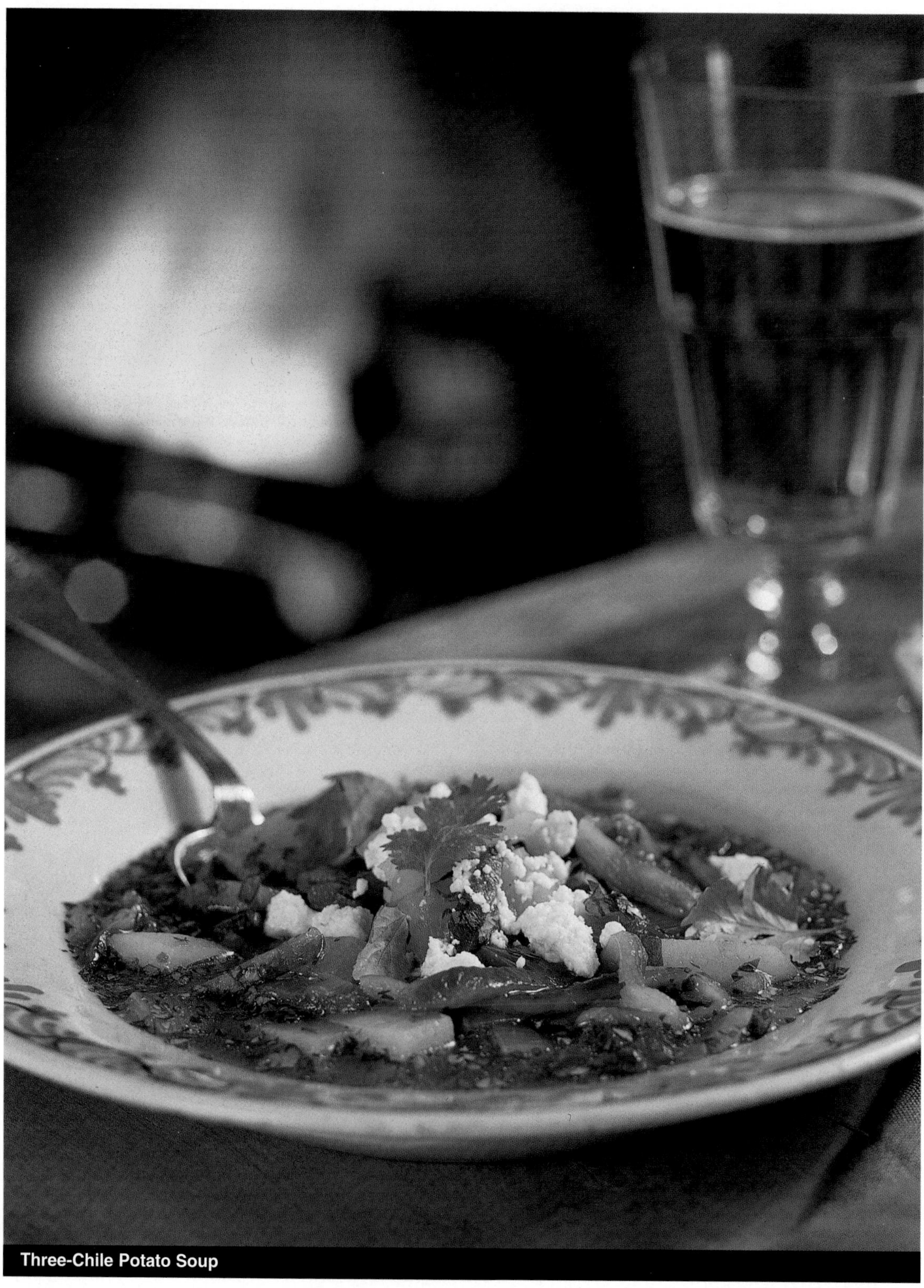

Three-Chile Potato Soup

2 jalapeño chiles, seeded and minced
1 tablespoon minced garlic
1 cup amber beer, such as Dos Equis
2 large Idaho potatoes, peeled and cut into ½-inch dice
1 tablespoon fresh lime juice
2 tablespoons achiote paste, optional (see Note)
1 tablespoon sugar
Salt and freshly ground pepper
1 cup finely chopped fresh cilantro, plus ¼ cup whole leaves for garnish
½ cup crumbled tangy white cheese, such as *queso fresco*, *ricotta salata* or a dry goat cheese

1. Preheat the broiler. Arrange the tomatoes, cut-side down, on a baking sheet and drizzle with the 1 tablespoon oil. Broil about 3 minutes, or until the skins are charred. Transfer to a large nonreactive saucepan, add the vegetable stock and bring to a boil over high heat. Reduce the heat to low and simmer for 20 minutes. Strain the stock.

2. Meanwhile, roast the poblano and Anaheim chiles directly over a gas flame or under the broiler until charred all over. Transfer the chiles to a paper bag and let steam for 5 minutes. Peel the chiles and discard the stems, ribs and seeds. Cut the chiles into 2-by-¼-inch strips.

3. Heat the remaining ¼ cup oil in the large nonreactive saucepan. Add the onions, jalapeños and garlic and cook over moderately high heat, stirring occasionally, until the onions are softened, about 5 minutes. Add the beer and boil for 3 minutes. Add the strained stock, roasted chiles, potatoes, lime juice, achiote paste and sugar. Lower the heat to moderate and simmer until the potatoes are tender, about 20 minutes. Season with salt and pepper. (**MAKE AHEAD:** The soup can be refrigerated for 1 day. Rewarm before serving.) Stir in the chopped cilantro. Ladle the soup into shallow bowls. Garnish with the cheese and the cilantro leaves.

NOTE: Achiote paste, made from annatto seeds, adds an ocher color to the soup; it's available at Latin American markets.—KEVIN RATHBUN

MISO CLAM SOUP

Clams and their broth create a wonderful brininess that lightens the richness of a traditional miso soup.

6 SERVINGS

3 dozen littleneck clams, scrubbed
3 tablespoons dark miso
6 ounces silken tofu, cut into ½-inch cubes
3 medium scallions, thinly sliced crosswise

1. In a large saucepan, bring 4 cups of water to a boil over high heat. Add the clams, cover and boil until they open, about 4 minutes. Using tongs, transfer the clams to a large plate. Remove the clams from the shells and reserve; discard the shells.

2. Slowly pour the broth from cooking the clams into a large bowl, stopping when you reach the grit on the bottom. Rinse the pan and put it back on the stove.

SECRETS OF GREAT SOUP

You'll get the best results from any vegetable-soup recipe when you follow these guidelines:

• Make the soup ahead of time; the flavors will blend after a day or two. Before serving the soup, warm it gently so fragile ingredients don't fall apart, then stir in just enough stock or water to replace the liquid that has been absorbed by items like beans or rice. Reheat again. If your recipe calls for pasta, cook it separately and add it to the soup right before serving so that the noodles don't get too soft.

• You can substitute one vegetable for another, but stay in the same family. If you can't find kale, for example, use another hearty green; if you don't have turnips, add rutabagas instead. And if you're tired of pasta, replace it with rice or one-inch cubes of toasted peasant bread.

• Don't be afraid to adjust the consistency of the soup. If it's too thick, add stock or water. If it's too thin, simmer until slightly reduced, or stir in some pureed cooked beans, potatoes or a few tablespoons of cornmeal. (Be sure to simmer the soup until the cornmeal softens.)

• Intensify flavor with last-minute additions. Among the options: a handful of fresh chopped herbs, such as cilantro or basil; a drizzle of extra-virgin olive oil, a spoonful of pesto or a squeeze of lemon juice; a sprinkling of slivered Brazil nuts or pecans.

Pour the clam broth back into the saucepan and whisk in the miso until smooth. Bring the soup to a simmer over moderate heat. Add the tofu and cook for 4 minutes.

3. Return the clams to the soup to heat through. Sprinkle the scallions on top and serve immediately.—MARCIA KIESEL

SEAFOOD GUMBO WITH OKRA

Gumbo is a defining dish of Louisiana cooking. This version is packed with seafood and delivers a real Creole punch. You can ask your fishmonger to crack the crabs for you. Any firm smoked pork sausage can replace the andouille.

12 SERVINGS

1½ to 2 pounds large hard-shell crabs
¾ cup vegetable oil
¾ cup sifted all-purpose flour
4 large onions, chopped
1 medium bunch of celery, cut into ½-inch dice (5 cups)
4 medium green or red bell peppers, cut into ½-inch dice
2 tablespoons minced garlic
1 teaspoon crushed red pepper
Pinch each of dried oregano, basil and thyme
4 bay leaves
Salt and freshly ground pepper
1 pound andouille sausage, sliced
1 pound okra, sliced ½ inch thick
1 pound medium shrimp, shelled and deveined
1 quart shucked oysters, in their liquor
8 cups cooked white rice, for serving
Louisiana hot sauce, for serving

1. Pull off the top shells of the crabs and discard. Remove and discard the gills. Cut the crabs in half. Crack the claws with a rolling pin or mallet.

2. Heat the oil in a large, heavy saucepan or small stockpot until smoking, about 5 minutes. Gradually add the flour and cook over high heat, stirring constantly, until the roux is the color of chocolate, 3 to 5 minutes; do not let it burn. Add the onions and cook for 1 minute. Add the celery and cook for 30 seconds, then stir in the bell peppers, scraping the bottom of the pot. Stir in the garlic, crushed red pepper, oregano, basil, thyme and bay leaves and season with salt and pepper.

3. Gradually add 2 quarts of cold water to the pot, stirring constantly. Add the crabs, sausage and okra, cover the pot and bring to a boil. Reduce the heat to moderately low, cover partially and cook for 1 hour; skim often. Add the shrimp and cook for 10 minutes. Add the oysters and their liquor and bring just to a boil over moderate heat. Serve immediately, passing the rice and hot sauce separately.—JAMIE SHANNON

TROUT IN GINGERED DASHI WITH SUSHI RICE

This Japanese-inspired dish features seasoned rice balls and sautéed trout in a light, fragrant broth called dashi. *It's made with flakes of dried bonito, kombu (seaweed) and water. All the Japanese ingredients called for are available at Japanese markets and well-stocked health-food stores.*

8 SERVINGS

BROTH:

One 4-by-10-inch piece of kombu (seaweed)
1 cup loosely packed bonito flakes
¾ cup sake
¼ cup Japanese soy sauce
¼ cup mirin (sweet Japanese cooking wine)
½ teaspoon ginger juice (see Note)

SUSHI RICE:

1 cup short-grain sushi rice
¼ cup rice vinegar
1½ tablespoons sugar
1 tablespoon black sesame seeds
1 medium carrot, cut into 2-by-⅛-inch matchsticks
½ cup loosely packed snow peas (about 2 ounces), cut into 2-by-⅛-inch matchsticks
One 2-inch piece of daikon radish, peeled and cut into 2-by-⅛-inch matchsticks
½ cup loosely packed canned bamboo shoots, drained, rinsed and cut into 2-by-⅛-inch matchsticks
4 trout fillets with skin (about 7 ounces each), each cut diagonally into 4 pieces
Salt
¼ cup all-purpose flour
1 tablespoon canola oil
½ teaspoon Asian sesame oil
Fresh ginger, cut into fine julienne strips (optional)

1. Make the broth: In a medium saucepan, cover the kombu with 4 cups of water. Simmer over low heat, partially covered, until the kombu is very tender and the broth is flavorful, about 1 hour and 15 minutes. Discard the kombu and add the bonito flakes and ½ cup cold water to the pan.

Bring the broth to a boil and boil for 30 seconds. Remove from the heat and let the bonito flakes sink to the bottom of the pan.

2. Strain the broth into a clean saucepan. Add the sake, soy sauce and mirin and bring just to a boil. Remove the pan from the heat. Stir in the ginger juice. (**MAKE AHEAD:** The broth can stand at room temperature for up to 2 hours.)

3. Meanwhile, **make the sushi rice**: Rinse the rice, stirring it with your fingers until the water runs clear. In a medium saucepan, combine the rice with 1 cup cold water, cover tightly and bring to a boil over high heat. Reduce the heat to low and cook until the rice is tender, about 20 minutes. Remove from the heat and let stand, covered, for 15 minutes.

4. In a small bowl, combine the rice vinegar and sugar and stir until the sugar dissolves. Turn the rice out onto a tray and toss with the sweetened vinegar. Let cool completely. Using moistened hands, roll the rice into sixteen 1-inch balls and sprinkle with the black sesame seeds.

5. In a saucepan of boiling salted water and working with one vegetable at a time, blanch the carrot, snow peas, daikon and bamboo shoots until just tender, about 1 minute each. Drain the vegetables and pat dry.

6. Reheat the broth. Season the trout with salt. Lightly dust with the flour, shaking off any excess.

7. In a large nonstick skillet, heat the canola and sesame oils over high heat. Add half of the trout, skin-side up. Cook the trout over high heat until golden, about 2 minutes. Turn and cook until just done, about 1 minute longer. Transfer the cooked trout to a plate and keep warm. Repeat with the remaining trout.

8. To serve, place two rice balls in each soup plate. Top each rice ball with a piece of trout and some of the julienned vegetables. Ladle the hot broth around the rice balls, garnish with the ginger julienne and serve.

NOTE: To make ½ teaspoon of ginger juice, put 1 teaspoon finely grated fresh ginger in a fine sieve and press firmly with the back of a wooden spoon to extract the juice.—ALI SEEDSMAN

CHICKEN SOUP WITH MEATBALLS

Masa harina, *a flour made from corn that has been treated with lime, is used in classic tortilla and tamale recipes. It is available at most supermarkets. This recipe first appeared in* Food From My Heart *(Macmillan).*

6–8 SERVINGS

- 2 Anaheim or California long green chiles
- 1 large ripe tomato or ¼ cup tomato puree
- ¼ cup *masa harina*
- 1 pound lean ground beef or ½ pound each lean ground beef and pork
- 4 medium garlic cloves, 3 minced and 1 whole

Salt and freshly ground pepper

- ¼ cup lard or vegetable oil
- 1 tablespoon all-purpose flour
- 2 quarts chicken stock or canned low-sodium broth
- ¼ cup finely chopped scallions
- 3 tablespoons finely chopped fresh cilantro
- 3 tablespoons finely chopped fresh mint

Seafood Gumbo with Okra

1. Preheat the broiler. Place the chiles and the tomato, if using, on a baking sheet and broil, turning occasionally, until blistered and charred all over. Transfer to a paper bag and set aside to steam for

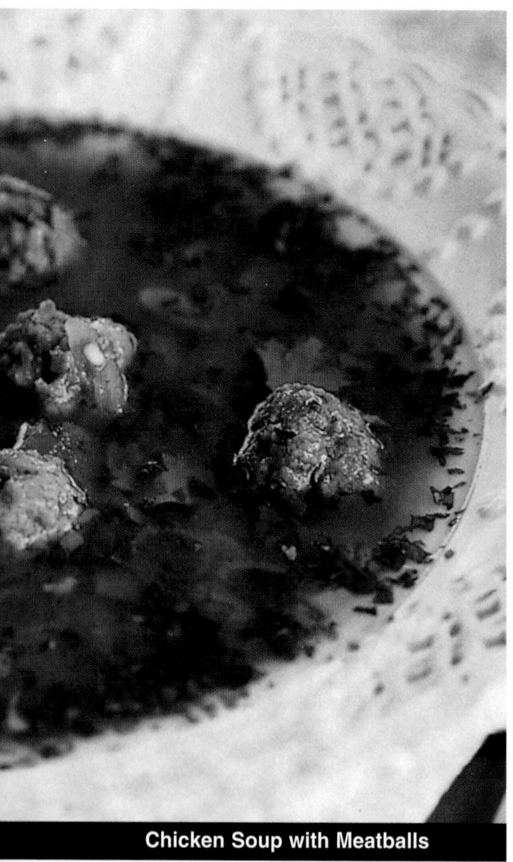
Chicken Soup with Meatballs

10 minutes. Using a small knife, scrape off the blackened skins. Discard the stems, seeds and ribs and finely chop the chiles. Seed and finely chop the tomato.

2. In a large bowl, combine the *masa harina* with ¼ cup of warm water. Add the ground meat, one-third of the minced garlic, ½ teaspoon salt and a generous grinding of black pepper. Mix well with your hands and shape into forty 1-inch balls.

3. In a medium nonreactive skillet, melt 2 tablespoons of the lard. Add the whole garlic clove and cook over moderately high heat for 20 to 30 seconds, pressing it with the back of a spoon. Discard the garlic and remove the pan from the heat. Whisk the flour into the lard and cook over moderate heat, stirring, until golden, about 1 minute.

4. Bring the chicken stock to a simmer in a large saucepan. Gradually whisk about ½ cup of the stock into the flour mixture, then whisk this into the simmering stock to smoothly combine. Simmer the soup over moderately low heat until very slightly thickened, about 5 minutes.

5. Heat the remaining 2 tablespoons lard in the skillet over moderately high heat. Add the scallions, roasted chiles and tomato (or tomato puree if using) and the remaining minced garlic. Reduce the heat to moderate and cook until the scallions and garlic are slightly softened, about 2 minutes. Stir into the soup along with the cilantro and mint and simmer for 5 minutes. Add the meatballs and simmer over low heat for 15 minutes. Season with salt and black pepper. Serve the soup warm.—ZARELA MARTINEZ

FENNEL AND TOMATO SOUP WITH ITALIAN SAUSAGES Q

For a less spicy dish, use all sweet sausages.

4 SERVINGS

- 1 tablespoon olive oil
- 1 large fennel bulb (about 1 pound), cut into ⅓-inch dice
- 1 large onion, diced
- 1 large garlic clove, minced
- 1 tablespoon tomato paste
- 4½ cups chicken stock or canned low-sodium broth
- One 14-ounce can Italian plum tomatoes with their juice, coarsely chopped
- Salt and freshly ground pepper
- ½ pound sweet Italian sausage
- ½ pound hot Italian sausage
- ¾ cup orzo
- 2 cups shredded fresh spinach leaves

1. In a large nonreactive saucepan, heat the oil. Add the fennel and onion; cook over moderate heat, stirring, until the onion is translucent and beginning to brown, about 5 minutes. Add the garlic; cook, stirring, until fragrant, about 1 minute. Blend in the tomato paste. Add the stock and the tomatoes with their juice. Season with salt and pepper; bring to a simmer. Reduce the heat, cover and simmer gently for 20 minutes.

2. Meanwhile, heat a large heavy skillet. Prick the sausages all over with a fork; add to the pan. Cook over moderately low heat, turning, until browned and cooked through, about 20 minutes. Drain on paper towels and let cool slightly. Halve lengthwise, then cut into ⅓-inch pieces.

3. Bring the soup to a boil, add the orzo and cook, stirring occasionally, until al dente, about 10 minutes. Add the spinach and the sausages and cook, stirring, until the spinach is wilted and the sausages are heated through, 2 to 3 minutes. (**MAKE AHEAD:** The soup can be made up to 1 day ahead.)—JUDITH SUTTON

VEGETABLE STOCK

MAKES 2 QUARTS

- 2 celery ribs, coarsely chopped
- 3 carrots, coarsely chopped
- 1 medium leek, coarsely chopped
- 1 large onion, quartered

1 large bunch of spinach (about 1 pound)
1 large fresh thyme sprig
1 bunch fresh flat-leaf parsley
6 unpeeled garlic cloves, halved lengthwise
12 whole black peppercorns

Combine all of the ingredients and 4 quarts of water in a large saucepan or small stockpot and bring to a boil over high heat. Cover partially, reduce the heat to moderately low and simmer until the broth is flavorful and reduced to 2 quarts, about 1½ hours. Slowly pour the stock through a fine strainer into a large heatproof bowl, leaving behind any particles at the bottom of the pan; press lightly on the solids to extract the liquid. Let cool completely before refrigerating.—GRACE PARISI

CHICKEN STOCK

The most versatile of all stocks, this can be used in meat, seafood and chicken dishes.

MAKES 2 QUARTS

6 pounds chicken bones, backs, legs or wings
3 celery ribs, cut into 2-inch pieces
2 medium carrots, cut into 2-inch pieces
2 medium unpeeled onions, quartered

1. Combine all of the ingredients with 3 quarts of cold water in a large saucepan or small stockpot and bring to a boil over high heat. Reduce the heat to moderate and simmer for 20 minutes, skimming frequently. Reduce the heat to low and partially cover the pan, leaving only a small opening between the lid and the pan. Simmer until the stock is flavorful, about 2½ hours.
2. Slowly pour the stock through a fine strainer into a large heatproof bowl, leaving behind any particles at the bottom of the pan; press on the solids to extract the liquid. Clean the pan, return the stock to it and boil until reduced to 2 quarts. Let cool completely before refrigerating.—GRACE PARISI

FISH STOCK

Use fish frames—the fish head and bones that remain once a fish has been filleted—from lean, white-fleshed fish such as red snapper, flounder, halibut, tilefish and porgy. Red snapper yields a particularly tasty stock.

MAKES ABOUT 2½ QUARTS

3½ pounds fish frames (see above)
1½ tablespoons olive oil
2 medium leeks, white and tender green, thinly sliced
1 shallot, thinly sliced
1 small celery rib, thinly sliced
3 fresh thyme sprigs
2 fresh parsley sprigs
½ cup dry white wine
1 bay leaf
1 medium tomato, chopped
Coarse salt

1. Rinse the fish frames thoroughly under cold water. In a large nonreactive saucepan or small stockpot, warm the oil over moderate heat. Add the leeks, shallot, celery, thyme, parsley and fish frames, bending them to fit into the pan if necessary. Cook, stirring occasionally, until the fish frames turn white and the vegetables are fragrant, about 4 minutes.
2. Add the wine and cook for 1 minute. Add 2½ quarts of water, the bay leaf, tomato and a large pinch of salt. Increase the heat to moderately high and bring to a gentle simmer. Skim and reduce the heat to low. Simmer for 20 minutes, skimming often. Slowly pour the stock through a fine strainer into a large heatproof bowl, leaving behind any particles at the bottom of the pan. Season lightly with salt. Let cool before refrigerating.—MARCIA KIESEL ➤

STORING STOCK

• Store homemade meat or chicken stock in the refrigerator for one week or freeze for up to three months. Fish stock is best used fresh but can be frozen for up to two weeks. Vegetable stock is also best fresh, but can be refrigerated for up to four days; it loses flavor when frozen.

• Save widemouthed jars for refrigerating stock. (This shape makes it easier to scoop off fat.) For freezing, try sturdy plastic storage bags. To prevent spills when filling a bag, stand it in a widemouthed jar and seal the bag tightly before removing.

• If storage space is a problem, boil strained, defatted meat or chicken stock until reduced by half. Pour this intensely flavored stock (demiglace) into a square baking pan and refrigerate or freeze until firm but not frozen. At this point, cut the demiglace into cubes, seal in a plastic bag and freeze. Add water for a lighter stock.

SHORT-ORDER STOCKS

Because a pressure cooker extracts gelatin from bones so quickly, it makes deeply flavored meat, poultry and fish stocks in no time. This Chicken Stock takes just thirty minutes to make; the Vegetable Stock, only ten.

CHICKEN STOCK

MAKES ABOUT 2½ QUARTS

- 2½ to 3 pounds chicken backs, necks and wings
- 2 celery stalks, cut into 3 to 4 chunks
- 2 large carrots, cut into 3 to 4 chunks
- 1 large onion, coarsely chopped
- 1 to 2 parsnips, cut into 3 to 4 chunks (optional)
- A few leek greens
- ¼ teaspoon whole black peppercorns
- 1 teaspoon salt, or to taste
- 10 sprigs parsley
- 2 bay leaves
- 3 quarts (12 cups) cold water

1. Put all the ingredients in a 6-quart cooker; be sure not to exceed the maximum capacity level advised by the manufacturer. Lock the lid in place and bring to high pressure over high heat. Cook for 30 minutes. Let the pressure drop naturally. Carefully remove the lid, tilting it away from you to allow steam to escape.

2. Let the stock cool slightly, then strain. Cover and refrigerate. Skim off the fat before using or freezing.

VEGETABLE STOCK

MAKES 7 CUPS

- 2 quarts water
- 2 large onions, quartered
- 2 large garlic cloves
- 3 large carrots, cut into chunks
- 3 large celery ribs, in large chunks
- ¼ cup dried sliced mushrooms, such as porcini (¼ ounce)
- 2 large bay leaves
- 20 fresh parsley sprigs or a small bunch of parsley stems
- 8 cups assorted vegetables, such as corncobs and husks, asparagus stalks, broccoli stems, leek greens, wilted salad greens and peeled winter squash

1. Bring the water to a boil in the pressure cooker while you trim and cut the vegetables. Add all the ingredients to the pot. (Do not go over the maximum fill line indicated by the manufacturer.) Lock the lid in place and bring to high pressure over high heat. Lower the heat just enough to maintain high pressure and cook for 10 minutes. Allow the pressure to come down naturally or use a quick-release method. Remove the lid, tilting it away from you to allow any excess steam to escape.

2. Let the vegetable stock cool slightly. Strain the stock, pressing the vegetables against the side of the strainer with a large spoon to extract all the liquid. Cover the stock and refrigerate or freeze.—LORNA J. SASS

RICH BEEF STOCK

It's best to remove the marrow from inside the beef shanks and freeze it for another use.

MAKES ABOUT 2 QUARTS

- 2 tablespoons vegetable oil
- 4 pounds beef shanks, cut crosswise about 1 inch thick, meat removed from the bones and cut into 2-inch chunks
- 1 medium onion, chopped
- 1 large carrot, thickly sliced
- 1 medium celery rib, thickly sliced
- 1 head of garlic, halved crosswise
- 2 teaspoons coarse salt
- 6 fresh parsley stems
- 3 fresh thyme sprigs
- 3 allspice berries
- 1 bay leaf
- 1 tablespoon dried porcini mushrooms

1. Preheat the oven to 450°. Warm the oil in a large flameproof roasting pan set over two burners on high heat. When the oil is hot, add the beef shank bones and the meat and cook, stirring, until the meat starts to brown, about 3 minutes. Set the pan on the bottom shelf of the oven and roast for about 25 minutes, or until the meat and bones are deeply browned. Add the onion, carrot, celery and garlic and stir well. Return the pan to the bottom shelf and roast for about 20 minutes, or until the vegetables are deeply browned around the edges.

2. Scrape the contents of the roasting pan into a large saucepan or small stockpot. Set the roasting pan over two burners on moderately high heat. When very hot, add 1 cup of water and scrape up the browned bits on the bottom of the pan. Boil the liquid for about 2 minutes and then pour it into the saucepan.

3. Add 3½ quarts of water, the salt, parsley, thyme, allspice, bay leaf and porcini. Bring to a boil over high heat and skim. Reduce the heat to low and simmer the stock, skimming often, until deep brown and flavorful, about 1½ hours. Season with a little salt if desired. Slowly pour the stock through a fine strainer into a large heatproof bowl, leaving behind any particles at the bottom of the pan; press lightly on the solids to extract the liquid. Let cool completely before refrigerating.—MARCIA KIESEL

MAKING STOCK

Canned broth and bouillon cubes are available in every supermarket. There's nothing wrong with using them, but they don't taste anything like homemade. Because soups, stews and other dishes get much of their character from stock, we prefer the kind we make ourselves.

Making stock is easy; it's largely a matter of chopping vegetables, adding them to a pot with meaty bones and letting the mixture cook on its own. The huge advantage of anything homemade over ready-made is that you can control the quality. Use the best ingredients and the stock will be natural (no additives) and full of flavor. You can add salt to taste or skip it entirely—a big plus in recipes that call for reducing the stock, which would make canned stock too salty. And because refrigeration solidifies the fat into a layer that lifts right off, homemade stock can be virtually fat free.

CHAPTER 5

~

PASTA

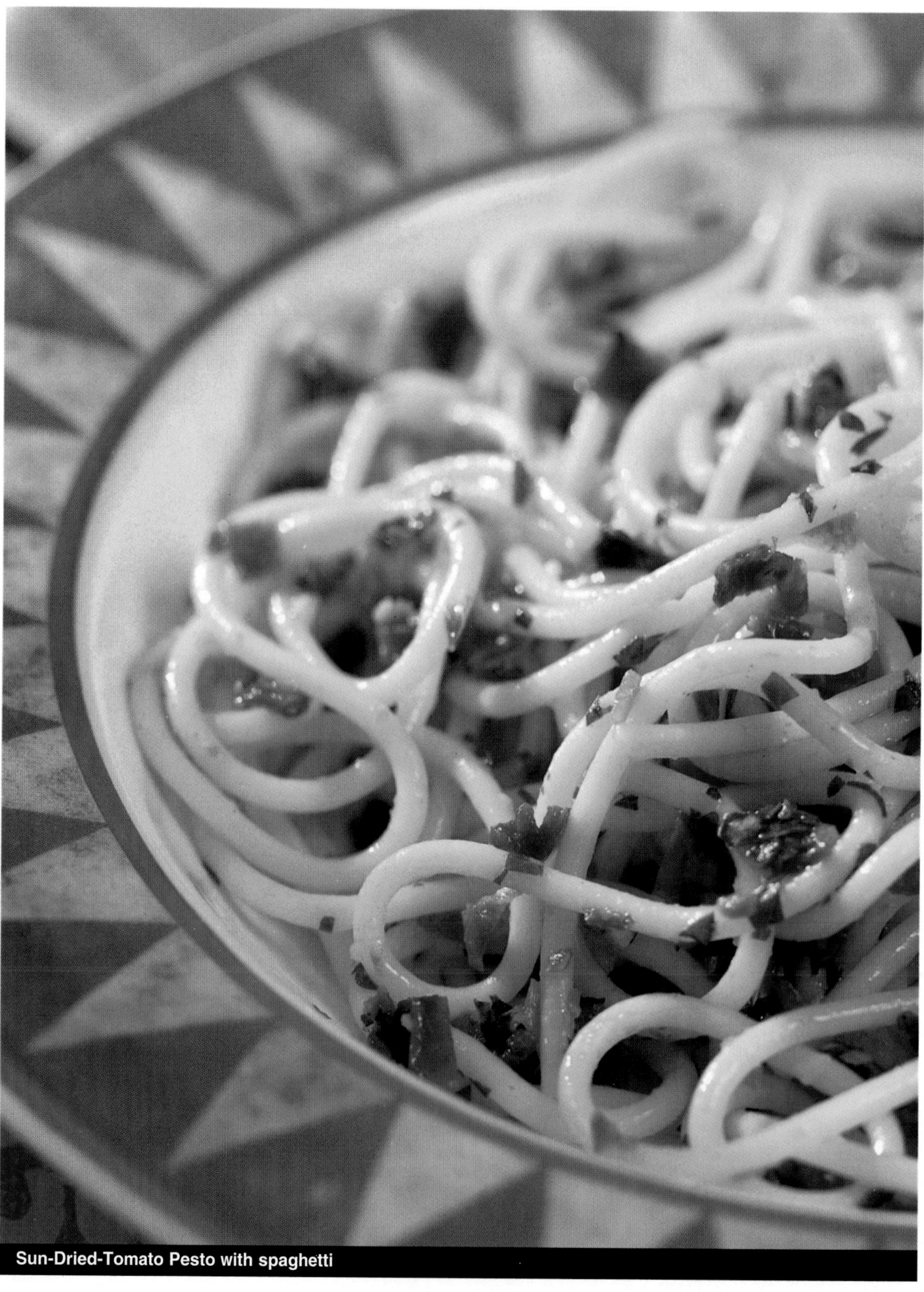

Sun-Dried-Tomato Pesto with spaghetti

SUN-DRIED-TOMATO PESTO Q

The leathery quality and concentrated flavor of sun-dried tomatoes make them ideal for a flavorful pesto, which is great with spaghetti or spaghettini. Cook and drain one pound of pasta, reserving approximately one cup of the pasta-cooking water and leaving the pasta dripping wet. Toss the pasta with the pesto, adding some of the reserved cooking water as needed.

4–6 SERVINGS

- 1 cup firmly packed drained sun-dried tomatoes in oil (from two 8-ounce jars), or ⅔ cup dry-packed sun-dried tomatoes (1½ ounces)
- 2 large garlic cloves, minced
- ½ teaspoon finely chopped fresh oregano or ¼ teaspoon dried
- ¼ teaspoon salt
- Pinch of crushed red pepper
- ½ cup extra-virgin olive oil
- ¼ cup finely chopped fresh flat-leaf parsley
- 2 tablespoons freshly grated Pecorino cheese

1. Finely chop the oil-packed tomatoes. Alternatively, if using dry-packed tomatoes, place them in a small bowl with just enough hot water to cover until they soften, about 20 minutes. Drain them in a strainer set over a small bowl and squeeze out excess water; reserve the soaking liquid. Finely chop the tomatoes.

2. In a medium bowl, combine the tomatoes, garlic, oregano, salt and crushed red pepper. Add the olive oil and mix thoroughly with a wooden spoon. Stir in ¼ cup of water or tomato-soaking liquid. (**MAKE AHEAD:** The pesto can be refrigerated for up to 1 month; coat lightly with olive oil and cover tightly. Let return to room temperature before proceeding.) Just before serving, stir in the parsley and cheese.—JULIA DELLA CROCE

QUICK SOUTHERN ITALIAN TOMATO SAUCE Q

This is one of the quickest yet most delicious tomato sauces you can make. You can sieve it and use it as a basic sauce for all manner of dried pasta. Unsieved, it is very chunky and thick and thus suitable for ribbon or strand pasta cuts or short macaroni cuts, such as pennette (short quills) or medium shells. Serve this sauce over one pound of pasta, with freshly grated Pecorino or Parmigiano-Reggiano cheese.

4 SERVINGS

- 4 cups canned peeled tomatoes in their liquid
- 4 large garlic cloves, lightly crushed
- ¼ cup plus 2 tablespoons extra-virgin olive oil
- ½ teaspoon salt
- Freshly ground pepper
- 1 tablespoon finely chopped fresh basil or fresh flat-leaf parsley

1. Drain the canned tomatoes in a strainer set over a medium bowl. Scoop out and discard any seeds from the tomatoes. Using your hands, a fork or a potato masher, crush the tomatoes well and place them in a separate bowl; reserve their liquid for another use.

2. In a medium nonreactive saucepan, cook the garlic in the olive oil over moderate heat until golden. Add the tomatoes and the salt; season with pepper. Stir in the basil and simmer gently for 15 minutes. Discard the garlic. To make a smooth sauce, leave the garlic cloves in and pass the sauce through a food mill. (**MAKE AHEAD:** Omit the basil, cover the sauce tightly and refrigerate for up to 5 days or freeze for up to 3 months. Before serving, stir in the basil and reheat the sauce gently.)—JULIA DELLA CROCE ➤

CANNED-TOMATO TIPS

WHOLE PEELED TOMATOES should not be too firm or tinged with green, and there should be lots of tomatoes and a relatively small amount of liquid. Those packed in puree or in juice can be used interchangeably if the recipe calls for drained tomatoes.

CRUSHED, OR CHOPPED, TOMATOES are an acceptable substitute if you don't want to do your own chopping, but beware of those that have been reduced so much that they are more like a thick puree. In addition, watch out for brands with oregano or basil, which can muddle the flavor.

TOMATO PASTE should be used judiciously as a thickener or for a touch of color or flavor. It is too concentrated to use in large quantities.

TOMATO SAUCE—avoid it. It is really strained tomatoes and is too thin to make an authentic Italian sauce.

QUICK TOMATO SAUCE WITH BUTTER Q

This variation on Quick Southern Italian Tomato Sauce (previous page) relies on butter instead of olive oil to smooth out the acidity of the tomatoes. The sauce is suitable for both fresh and dried pasta, and this recipe makes enough sauce to serve with one-and-a-half pounds of pasta.

6 SERVINGS

- 5 cups canned peeled tomatoes in their liquid
- 1 small onion, minced
- 1 stick unsalted butter (4 ounces)
- ½ teaspoon salt
- 3 tablespoons finely chopped fresh basil, flat-leaf parsley or mint
- Freshly ground pepper

1. Drain the tomatoes in a strainer set over a bowl. Scoop out and discard any seeds from the tomatoes. Crush the tomatoes well and place them in a separate bowl; reserve their liquid for another use.

2. In a large nonreactive saucepan, cook the onion in 6 tablespoons of the butter over moderately low heat until golden. Add the tomatoes and salt and simmer over moderate heat for 20 minutes. (**MAKE AHEAD:** The sauce can be tightly covered and refrigerated for up to 5 days or frozen for up to 3 months.)

3. Just before serving, stir in the remaining 2 tablespoons butter and the basil and season with pepper.—JULIA DELLA CROCE

Spaghetti with Garlic, Olive Oil and Tomato Paste

SPAGHETTI WITH GARLIC, OLIVE OIL AND TOMATO PASTE Q

A red wine with bright fruit flavors or a white wine with high acidity would work well. Choose either the Etna Bianco or the Etna Rosso from the Sicilian producer Murgo.

2 SERVINGS

- ¼ cup extra-virgin olive oil
- 2 tablespoons tomato paste
- 1½ teaspoons minced garlic
- Coarse salt
- ½ pound imported dried spaghetti or spaghettini
- 2 tablespoons chopped fresh flat-leaf parsley
- 1 tablespoon finely shredded fresh basil
- Finely julienned scallions, for garnish (optional)

1. Fill a stockpot with 6 quarts of water, cover and bring to a boil.

2. In a nonreactive skillet large enough to hold the pasta, combine the oil, tomato paste, garlic and 1 teaspoon salt. Cook over moderately low heat, stirring occasionally, until the garlic is golden, about 5 minutes. Remove from the heat.

3. Add 3½ tablespoons coarse salt to the water and add the spaghetti. Cover partially until the water just returns to a boil, then uncover, stir the pasta and cook until al dente.

4. Drain the spaghetti, add it to the skillet and toss well. Add the parsley and basil and toss again. Transfer to plates, garnish with the scallions and serve immediately.—JOHANNE KILLEEN AND GEORGE GERMON

SPAGHETTI WITH HANDMADE PESTO

In Liguria, the home of pesto, cooks use a few leaves of parsley, marjoram and spinach to preserve the vibrant green of the basil sauce, since pesto has a tendency to turn brown when it meets hot pasta. Try to use organically grown herbs whenever possible. You may be surprised to find no pine nuts in this pesto, but I think that their sweetness and creamy texture dull the herbal intensity of the sauce.

4–6 SERVINGS

- 2 cups (loosely packed) small fresh basil leaves
- Leaves from 1 small sprig of marjoram
- 4 flat-leaf parsley leaves
- 1 tender spinach leaf, stemmed
- ¼ teaspoon coarse sea salt
- 2 medium garlic cloves, lightly crushed
- ⅓ cup freshly grated Parmesan cheese, plus more for the table
- 3 tablespoons freshly grated Pecorino Romano cheese, plus more for the table
- About ½ cup extra-virgin olive oil
- 1 pound spaghetti or spaghettini

1. Wipe the herbs and the spinach clean with a dry towel; if they are not organic, wipe them with a lightly dampened towel.

2. Put the sea salt in a large mortar. Add a few basil leaves, torn into fragments, and 1 garlic clove. Start grinding with the pestle in a circular motion until everything is reduced to a fine texture. Add a few more basil leaves and the spinach and grind and gently pound to the same consistency. Continue pounding the basil and herbs, adding the second garlic clove halfway through, until all the leaves are ground to a fine texture; keep scraping the pesto down into the bottom of the mortar as you work.

3. With the pestle, gradually stir in the cheeses; you will have a very dense mixture. Scrape the pesto off the pestle and down from the sides of the mortar. Add the oil in a thin steady stream, stirring it in with the pestle in a circular motion until fully incorporated. One-half cup of oil makes a very loose pesto; use less for a thicker pesto.

4. Cook the spaghetti in a large pot of boiling salted water until al dente. Drain the spaghetti, reserving ¼ cup of the cooking water. Transfer the spaghetti to a large bowl and toss it with the pesto and 2 tablespoons of the

Spaghetti with Handmade Pesto

pasta-cooking water; add more of the water if necessary. Serve the spaghetti immediately, passing additional cheese at the table.—VIANA LA PLACE

UNPLUGGED MENU

Inspired by the tastes and traditions of Italy, this simple, unfussy menu relies on ingredients of the finest quality—and no appliances whatsoever. The recipes have been adapted from *Unplugged Kitchen* (Morrow).

🍷The simple, lively flavors of the Vegetable Carpaccio require nothing more than a straightforward, refreshing dry white to set them off. Among dry, crisp Italian whites that would work perfectly with the first course here are the 1994 Santi Pinot Grigio and the 1994 Pieropan Soave. Serve the same wine with the Prosciutto di Parma and the Spaghetti with Handmade Pesto, or try a deeper, more characterful Italian white with enough tart acidity to contrast with the oil of the main dish. The 1993 Livio Felluga Terre Alte or the 1993 La Scolca Gavi would be a good choice.

PROSCIUTTO DI PARMA

VEGETABLE CARPACCIO (P. 65)

CRISP BREAD SQUARES WITH HOT RED PEPPER (P. 13)

SPAGHETTI WITH HANDMADE PESTO (P. 107)

BRUSCHETTA WITH CANNOLI CREAM (P. 450)

FRESH STRAWBERRIES

ESPRESSO

LEMON THYME ORZO Q

4 SERVINGS

- 1 cup orzo
- ½ cup chicken stock or canned low-sodium broth
- 1½ teaspoons finely chopped lemon zest
- 1 teaspoon dried thyme
- Salt and freshly ground pepper
- 1 tablespoon unsalted butter
- ⅓ cup freshly grated Parmesan cheese

1. Bring a large saucepan of water to a boil. Salt the water and add the orzo. Cook until barely al dente, 8 to 10 minutes.
2. Drain the orzo and return it to the saucepan. Add the chicken stock, lemon zest, thyme, ½ teaspoon salt and ¼ teaspoon pepper. Cook over moderately high heat, stirring occasionally, until the orzo absorbs most of the liquid. Stir in the butter and Parmesan cheese just before serving.—PAUL GRIMES

PAPPARDELLE WITH OLIVES, THYME AND LEMON Q

🍷 *Try a bold red from southern Italy, such as a Primitivo di Manduria from Savese. Or for a white, choose a great Verdicchio from Umani Ronchi or La Monacesca.*

2 SERVINGS

- 16 Kalamata olives, pitted
- 2 tablespoons extra-virgin olive oil
- Zest of 1 lemon, minced

Pappardelle with Olives, Thyme and Lemon

One 3-inch strip of orange zest, minced
¼ teaspoon crushed red pepper
½ cup fresh flat-leaf parsley leaves
1 tablespoon fresh thyme leaves
Coarse salt
½ pound imported dried pappardelle

1. Fill a stockpot with 6 quarts of water, cover and bring to a boil.
2. Meanwhile, in a mini-processor, combine the olives, olive oil, lemon and orange zests, red pepper, parsley, thyme and ½ teaspoon salt. Pulse until very fine but not pureed. Transfer the paste to a warm serving bowl.
3. Add 3½ tablespoons salt to the boiling water and then the pappardelle. Cover partially until the water just returns to a boil, then uncover, stir the pasta and cook until al dente. Drain the pappardelle well, reserving ¼ cup of the pasta water.
4. Toss the pappardelle with the olive paste, adding some of the pasta-cooking water, 1 tablespoon at a time, if the pasta seems dry. Serve immediately.—JOHANNE KILLEEN AND GEORGE GERMON

Tonnarelli with Caper Pesto

TONNARELLI WITH CAPER PESTO Q

🍷 *Regaleali is a terrific producer of Sicilian wine. The best choice is either the Regaleali Bianco or the elegant Regaleali Nozze d'Oro, which emphasizes the Sauvignon Blanc grape.*

2 SERVINGS

¼ cup extra-virgin olive oil
2 large garlic cloves
¼ cup peeled and seeded tomatoes
1½ tablespoons capers in salt, rinsed and patted dry (see Note)
1 cup loosely packed fresh flat-leaf parsley leaves
¼ cup loosely packed fresh oregano leaves (see Note)
1 tablespoon good-quality red-wine vinegar
Coarse salt
½ pound imported dried tonnarelli, linguine or spaghettini
½ cup freshly grated Pecorino Romano cheese (optional)

1. Fill a stockpot with 6 quarts of water, cover and bring to a boil.
2. In a small saucepan, combine the oil with the garlic and bring to a boil, cooking briskly until the garlic is golden. Remove from the heat and let cool; swirl the pan to hasten the cooling.
3. Transfer the garlic and oil to a blender or mini-processor. Add the tomato pulp and the capers and pulse until chopped. Add the parsley and oregano and pulse until chunky, then add the vinegar.
4. Add 3½ tablespoons salt to the boiling water and then the tonnarelli. Cover partially until the water just returns to a boil, then uncover, stir the pasta and

cook until al dente. Drain the tonnarelli, reserving ½ cup of the pasta water. Toss the pasta with the caper paste. If the tonnarelli is dry, add some of the pasta water, 1 tablespoon at a time. Garnish with Pecorino Romano if desired and serve immediately.

NOTE: If you cannot find capers in salt, you can use brine-packed capers, with these modifications: double the amount called for in the recipe and add ⅛ teaspoon coarse salt to give them a boost. So as not to overwhelm the delicate taste of the capers, reduce the oregano to 2 tablespoons.—JOHANNE KILLEEN AND GEORGE GERMON

TOMATO, BACON AND HOT-PEPPER SAUCE Q

This Roman sauce is called all'arrabbiata, *or "angry," owing to the spicy heat of the crushed red pepper. It is traditionally served on penne (use one pound here) with freshly grated Pecorino, which has a salty tang suited to the piquant sauce.*

4 SERVINGS

2½ cups canned peeled tomatoes in juice
2 ounces thinly sliced pancetta or lean bacon
1 garlic clove, minced
2 tablespoons extra-virgin olive oil
About ½ teaspoon crushed red pepper
½ teaspoon salt

1. Drain the tomatoes in a strainer set over a bowl. Scoop out and discard any seeds from the tomatoes. Coarsely chop the tomatoes and add them to the liquid in the bowl.

2. If using pancetta, slice it into ¼-inch strips. If using lean bacon, drop it into a medium saucepan of boiling water and blanch for 30 seconds. Drain, rinse in cold water and drain again. Cut the bacon crosswise into ¼-inch strips.

3. In a medium nonreactive saucepan, cook the garlic in the olive oil over moderate heat until it begins to color. Reduce the heat to moderately low and add the pancetta or bacon, cooking them until browned. Stir in the peeled tomatoes and their liquid, ¼ teaspoon of the crushed red pepper and the salt. Simmer, stirring occasionally, until the sauce thickens, about 20 minutes. If desired, add up to ¼ teaspoon of additional crushed red pepper. (**MAKE AHEAD:** The sauce can be refrigerated for up to 5 days or frozen for up to 3 months.) —JULIA DELLA CROCE

TOMATO EQUIVALENTS

Your recipe calls for three cups of tomatoes. When you get to the market, you wonder how many fresh or canned tomatoes you should buy. Here are some figures to take the guesswork out of shopping.

FRESH PEELED PLUM TOMATOES

2½ pounds	=	3 cups seeded, chopped, drained		
	=	2½ cups seeded, chopped, cooked		
	=	2½ cups canned peeled in juice or puree		
CANNED PEELED TOMATOES IN THEIR JUICE OR PUREE				
35-ounce can	=	4 cups	=	2½ to 3 cups drained
28-ounce can	=	3 cups	=	2 to 2½ cups drained
16-ounce can	=	2 cups	=	1 cup drained
CANNED CRUSHED/CHOPPED TOMATOES				
28-ounce can	=	3 cups		
CANNED TOMATO PASTE				
6-ounce can	=	¾ cup		

ANGEL-HAIR PASTA WITH ANCHO-CHILE SAUCE

In Mexico, sopa seca, *or dry soup, is served as a pasta course would be in Italy. This version can be a separate course or a lunch dish. The avocado, cheese and limes that accompany it are a necessary counterbalance to the ancho chiles.*

4 SERVINGS

4 ancho chiles, stems, seeds and veins removed
About 2½ cups chicken stock or water
2 whole cloves
1 garlic clove, coarsely chopped
⅛ teaspoon cumin seeds
Salt
¼ cup vegetable oil
4 ounces angel-hair pasta or very fine vermicelli, preferably in nests or skeins
⅓ cup finely grated *queso añejo* or Romano cheese
Avocado slices, for serving
Quartered limes, for serving

1. In a nonreactive medium saucepan, cover the chiles with water and simmer for 5 minutes.

Remove the pan from the heat and let the chiles soak until soft, 5 minutes more. Drain.

2. Pour ¼ cup of the stock into a blender, add the cloves, garlic and cumin seeds and blend until smooth. Season with salt. Add 1 cup of the stock and the drained chiles, a few at a time, and blend until smooth, adding more stock if necessary.

3. Heat the vegetable oil in a large heavy saucepan. Add the angel-hair pasta and fry, turning, until it has turned a deep golden color, about 3 minutes (keep the nests intact). Strain off excess oil.

4. Add the blended sauce to the pasta in the skillet and fry over moderate heat for about 3 minutes, scraping the bottom of the pan to prevent sticking. Cover and cook over low heat, adding the remaining stock a little at a time to prevent sticking, until the pasta is just cooked through, 5 to 8 minutes.

5. Transfer to a serving dish, sprinkle with the cheese and serve with the avocado and limes.—DIANA KENNEDY

Angel-Hair Pasta with Ancho-Chile Sauce

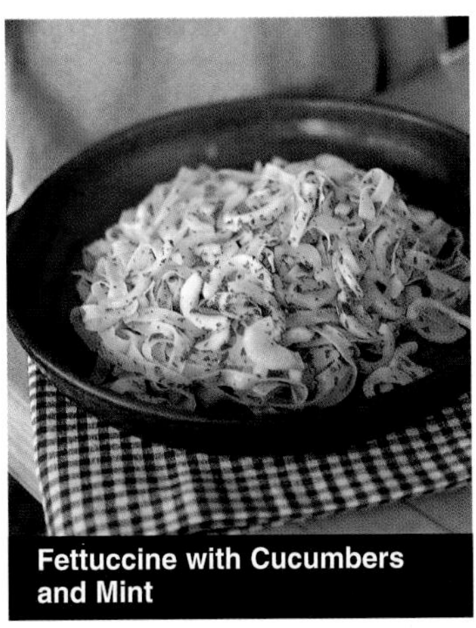

Fettuccine with Cucumbers and Mint

FETTUCCINE WITH CUCUMBERS AND MINT Q

A lovely Pinot Bianco from Puiatti or a Müller-Thurgau from Pojer e Sandri would complement this delicate dish.

2 SERVINGS

- 3 kirby cucumbers (about 1 pound)
- 3 tablespoons unsalted butter
- Coarse salt
- ½ pound imported dried fettuccine, tagliatelle or spaghettini
- ½ cup loosely packed shredded fresh mint

1. Fill a stockpot with 6 quarts of water. Cover the pot and bring the water to a boil.

2. Peel the cucumbers and halve them lengthwise. Scoop out the seeds. Slice the cucumbers crosswise ¼ inch thick.

3. In a large skillet, combine the butter, cucumbers and 1 teaspoon salt. Cook over moderately high heat, tossing or stirring frequently, until the cucumbers are tender but still slightly crisp, about 5 minutes.

4. Meanwhile, add 3½ tablespoons salt to the boiling water and then the fettuccine. Cover partially until the water just returns to a boil, then uncover, stir the pasta and cook until al dente. Drain, reserving ½ cup of the pasta water.

5. Add the fettuccine to the cucumbers and toss them together over moderate heat to coat the strands with butter. Add some of the pasta water, 1 tablespoon at a time, to moisten if necessary. Remove the skillet from the heat, add the mint and toss. Serve the pasta immediately.—JOHANNE KILLEEN AND GEORGE GERMON ➤

PAPPARDELLE WITH ROMANO BEANS

For this lightly creamy, vegetable-packed pasta, you can substitute any green beans for the flat Romano beans.

🍷 *A California Chardonnay, such as the 1994 Gloria Ferrer or the 1994 Jekel Gravelstone, would wrap this dish in its own fruity flavors and showcase the richness of the basil and sour cream.*

4–6 SERVINGS

- ¾ pound fresh Romano beans, trimmed
- 2 tablespoons unsalted butter
- 1 tablespoon olive oil
- 1 medium red bell pepper, thinly sliced
- 1 large scallion, white and green separated and thinly sliced lengthwise
- ¼ cup sour cream, at room temperature
- ¾ pound fresh pappardelle or fettuccine

Pappardelle with Romano Beans

Salt and freshly ground pepper
2 tablespoons minced fresh basil

1. In a medium saucepan of boiling salted water, cook the beans until tender, about 4 minutes. Drain; refresh with cold water. Cut the beans into 2-inch lengths.
2. In a large skillet, melt 1 tablespoon of the butter in the oil. Add the red pepper and the white of the scallion and toss over high heat for 1 minute. Add ½ cup of water, reduce the heat to moderately low, cover and cook until the pepper is tender, about 4 minutes. Add the beans and cook until warmed through. Stir in the sour cream and scallion greens and remove from the heat.
3. Meanwhile, in a large saucepan of boiling salted water, cook the pappardelle, stirring, until al dente, about 3 minutes. Drain the noodles and transfer to a platter. Toss with the remaining 1 tablespoon butter. Season the vegetable mixture with salt and pepper, spoon over the pasta and garnish with the basil.—MARCIA KIESEL

LINGUINE WITH BITTER GREENS AND PANCETTA Q

Bitter greens go well with Barbera—a Barbera d'Asti from Trinchero or Bricco Mondalino, or a Barbera d'Alba from Sandrone or Conterno Fantino.

2 SERVINGS

- 2 tablespoons extra-virgin olive oil
- 1½ teaspoons minced garlic
- 1 ounce pancetta, cut into ¼-inch dice
- ⅛ teaspoon crushed red pepper
- 1½ cups chicken stock or canned low-sodium broth
- Coarse salt

Q & A: CHEESE

Q: What's the role of fat in cheese?

A: Fat is what gives cheese its voluptuousness, what builds and carries its flavors. With a few exceptions (such as mascarpone, some chèvres and cream cheese), the blander the cheese, the lower its fat content. One ounce of low-fat cottage cheese averages less than a third of a gram of fat.

Q: Are high-fat cheeses taboo?

A: Of course not. I personally have sworn off triple crèmes, but other high-fat cheeses deliver such big flavor that a little goes a long way. Parmesan is a particular favorite of mine. Believe it or not, even part-skim versions contain seven grams of fat per ounce—as much as a buttery Camembert. But just a tablespoon of grated Parmesan (with less than two grams of fat) can add kick to a "skinny" Alfredo sauce made with milk instead of heavy cream. Then there's sharp, ripe Cheddar, which weighs in at nine grams of fat per ounce. That's a hefty amount. But shred just half an ounce of Cheddar onto a baked potato and you'll end up with about two-thirds less fat and fifty percent fewer calories than if you had added the same quantity of butter.

Q: What about low-fat cheeses?

A: When processing cheese to reduce the amount of fat in it, manufacturers often add vegetable gums for smoothness. As the percentage of fat decreases, the percentage of protein increases, which can sometimes account for a rubbery texture. There is one "light" cheese I do like, however: Jarlsberg Lite, a nutty, sweet-tart Gruyère-type with only three-and-a-half grams of fat per ounce.

Q: Does cheese have any redeeming nutritional virtues?

A: Plenty. It's a powerhouse of top-quality calcium, protein, phosphorous (which helps build strong bones and teeth) and vitamin A. One ounce of Monterey Jack, for example, supplies the following amounts of the government's recommended daily values: calcium, 21 percent; protein, 14 percent; phosphorous, 13 percent; and vitamin A, 14 percent. But, alas, many cheeses are also loaded with sodium. If you're sensitive to salt, scrutinize labels.

Q: Which is the easiest cheese to digest: goat, cow or sheep?

A: Because of their protein makeups, cheeses that are made from goat milk or sheep milk (Roquefort is the best-known sheep cheese) are more digestible than cheeses made from cow milk. But for people with lactose (milk sugar) intolerance, goat and sheep cheeses are no better than cow cheese. All three varieties contain similar amounts of lactose.—JEAN ANDERSON

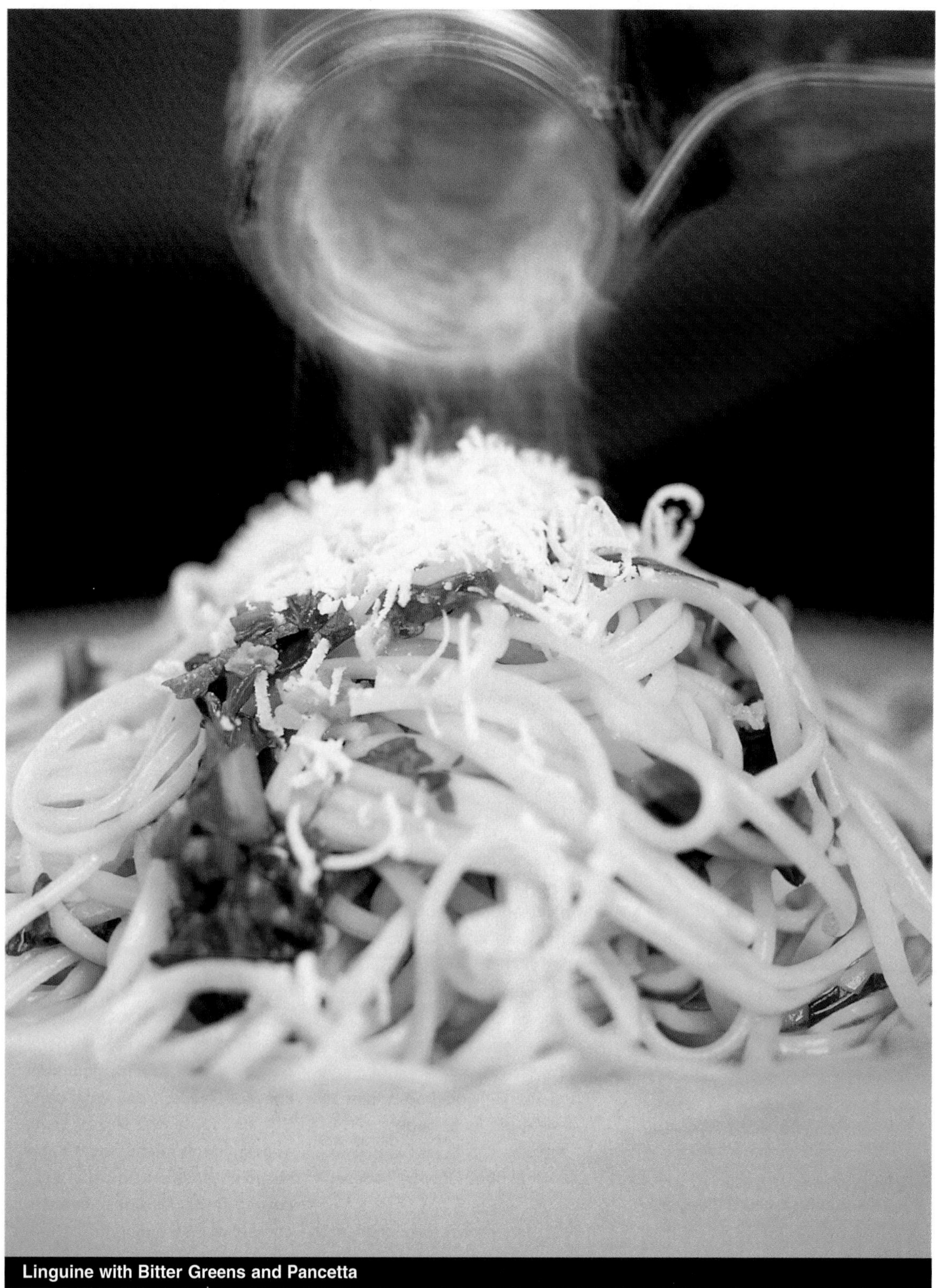

Linguine with Bitter Greens and Pancetta

½ pound imported dried thin linguine or spaghetti
1 small bunch arugula (about 5 ounces), finely shredded (about 2 cups)
3 tablespoons freshly grated Parmigiano-Reggiano cheese

1. Fill a stockpot with 6 quarts of water, cover and bring to a boil.
2. In a large skillet, combine the oil, garlic, pancetta and red pepper and cook over high heat until the garlic is golden. Add the stock and bring to a boil. Lower the heat to moderately high and boil gently until the liquid is reduced by half, about 6 minutes.
3. Meanwhile, put 3½ tablespoons salt in the boiling water and add the linguine. Cover partially until the water just returns to a boil, then uncover, stir the pasta and cook until barely al dente. Drain the linguine, reserving ¼ cup of the pasta water.
4. Add the linguine to the skillet. Cook over moderate heat, tossing occasionally, until al dente. Add the reserved pasta water, 1 tablespoon at a time, if the linguine seems dry. Fold in the arugula, transfer to a bowl, sprinkle with the Parmigiano-Reggiano and serve immediately.—JOHANNE KILLEEN AND GEORGE GERMON

NEW WORLD PAPPARDELLE Q

Lageder makes a Lagrein that's worth finding. A youthful Rosso di Montalcino would be terrific, too.

2 SERVINGS

2 large ears of corn, shucked
1½ pounds ripe tomatoes, cored and cut into ½- to 1-inch dice
¼ cup extra-virgin olive oil
¼ cup finely chopped fresh cilantro
¼ to ½ habanero chile, seeded and minced
Coarse salt
½ pound imported dried pappardelle

New World Pappardelle

1. In a medium saucepan of boiling salted water, cook the ears of corn until barely tender, about 2 minutes. Remove and let cool slightly, then cut the kernels from the cobs with a sharp knife. In a large stainless steel bowl, toss the corn with the diced tomatoes, olive oil, chopped cilantro, habanero chile and 1 teaspoon salt.

2. Meanwhile, fill a stockpot with 6 quarts of water; cover and bring to a boil. Add 3½ tablespoons salt to the water; then add the pappardelle. Partially cover the stockpot until the water just returns to a boil, then uncover the pot, stir the pappardelle and cook until al dente.

3. While the pappardelle cooks, carefully hold the metal bowl containing the corn-and-tomato mixture over the boiling pasta water, shaking it occasionally, until the tomatoes are just warmed through. Drain the pappardelle and add it to the bowl. Toss the pasta and sauce well and serve immediately.—JOHANNE KILLEEN AND GEORGE GERMON

Riccioli Pasta with Caramelized Corn

RICCIOLI PASTA WITH CARAMELIZED CORN

The unusual shape of this pasta is created by wrapping thin strips of fresh pasta around a large knitting needle. You can also use a thin-handled wooden spoon. Or you can skip the riccioli altogether and substitute about one pound fresh or three-quarters of a pound dried pappardelle.

🍷 *The heavy cream and smoky bacon in this dish require a red wine for contrast—but one with enough tartness to stand up to the tomatoes. That points to a Chianti, such as the 1990 Villa Sant'Anna or the 1991 Rocca di Castagnoli.*

4–6 SERVINGS

PASTA:

3 cups all-purpose flour
Salt and freshly ground pepper
4 to 5 large eggs
½ cup cornmeal

SAUCE:

1 tablespoon olive oil
3 ounces thickly sliced smoked bacon, cut into ½-inch dice

CHEF'S TIP

Riccioli, like most delicate homemade pastas, is best served with a light sauce that won't weigh it down. It's just right with the creamy corn in Riccioli Pasta with Caramelized Corn, but too fragile to be tossed with a chunky, heavy sauce.

1 medium onion, finely chopped
½ teaspoon minced garlic
3 cups fresh corn kernels
½ cup chicken stock or canned low-sodium broth
1½ cups heavy cream
1 teaspoon minced fresh thyme
Salt and freshly ground pepper
2 large plum tomatoes, seeded and finely diced
1 teaspoon balsamic vinegar
1 scallion green, cut lengthwise into very fine julienne

1. Make the pasta: In a food processor, pulse the flour with ½ teaspoon salt and ¼ teaspoon pepper. With the machine on, add four of the eggs, one at a time. If the mixture is too dry to gather into a ball, beat the last egg to mix and add as much of it as needed. Process until the pasta dough is smooth and elastic, about 3 minutes. Cover with a bowl and let the dough rest for 15 minutes.

2. Divide the pasta dough into four equal pieces. Working with one piece at a time and keeping the rest covered, roll the dough through successively narrower settings of a pasta machine, ending with the narrowest setting. Cut the pasta lengthwise into 1-inch-wide strips. Lay the long strips on a work surface; cover with kitchen towels. Repeat with the three remaining pieces of pasta dough.

3. Spread the cornmeal on two large baking sheets. Working with one strip of dough at a time, wind the pasta around a thick knitting needle in a tight spiral. Slide the pasta off the needle onto a prepared baking sheet so that it forms a loose coil. Allow the pasta to dry for about 1 hour. (**MAKE AHEAD:** The pasta can be refrigerated uncovered for up to 1 day.)

4. Make the sauce: Heat 1½ teaspoons of the olive oil in a large skillet. Add the smoked bacon and cook over moderate heat until most of the fat is rendered, about 5 minutes. Add the onion and the garlic and cook, stirring, until the vegetables are translucent, about 4 minutes.

5. Add all but ⅓ cup of the corn kernels to the skillet and cook over moderately high heat, stirring, until the corn is browned, about 4 minutes. Add the chicken stock and bring to a boil. Add the heavy cream and boil, stirring, until the mixture is reduced by about one-third, 3 to 5 minutes. Add the minced fresh thyme and season well with salt and pepper.

6. Heat the remaining 1½ teaspoons olive oil in a nonreactive skillet. Add the remaining ⅓ cup of corn kernels and sauté over moderate heat until the kernels are toasted, about 3 minutes. Add the tomatoes and the vinegar and season with salt and pepper. Cook, stirring, until the tomatoes are just soft, about 2 minutes.

7. Cook the riccioli in a large saucepan of boiling salted water, stirring occasionally, until the pasta is al dente, about 4 minutes. Drain, transfer the pasta to a bowl and toss with the creamed-corn sauce. Garnish the riccioli with the toasted corn and julienned scallion and serve.—BARBARA LYNCH

ZITI AND PORTOBELLOS

This dish needs a red with plenty of acidity, such as the 1994 Santa Cristina from Antinori.

8 SERVINGS

2 tablespoon unsalted butter
4 tablespoons olive oil
6 onions, chopped
Salt
1 teaspoon sugar
2 pounds of Portobello mushrooms, stems removed, caps halved and sliced crosswise ¼ inch thick
6 tablespoons chopped fresh flat-leaf parsley
Freshly ground black pepper
1½ pounds ziti
8 ounces soft goat cheese, crumbled
3 tablespoons freshly grated Parmesan, plus more for serving

1. In a large skillet, melt 1 tablespoon of the butter in 2 tablespoons of the oil. Add the onions, 1 teaspoon salt and the sugar and cook over moderate heat, stirring frequently, until the onions are well browned, 20 to 30 minutes. Transfer the onions to a bowl.

2. In the same skillet, melt the remaining 1 tablespoon butter in another 1 tablespoon oil. Add the mushrooms and ½ teaspoon salt and cook over moderate heat, stirring occasionally, until tender and browned, about 8 minutes. Add the onions and parsley. Season with salt and pepper.

3. In a large pot of boiling salted water, cook the ziti until al dente, about 13 minutes; reserve 1½ cups of the pasta water and drain the ziti. ➤

4. In a large bowl, toss the ziti with 1 cup of the reserved pasta water, the mushroom mixture, the goat cheese, the Parmesan and the remaining 1 tablespoon oil. If the pasta seems dry, add more of the pasta water. Serve immediately, passing additional Parmesan at the table.—SUSAN LANTZIUS

BAKED VEGETABLE PASTA LF

8 SERVINGS

- 2 medium red bell peppers
- 2 medium yellow bell peppers
- 1 small butternut squash, halved lengthwise, seeds discarded
- 1 tablespoon vegetable oil
- 1 large eggplant, cut into ½-inch cubes
- 4 ounces mushrooms, stems discarded and caps cut into ½-inch cubes
- Salt and freshly ground pepper
- 2 medium leeks (white and tender green), finely chopped
- 1 medium onion, finely chopped

Ziti and Portobellos

- 2 garlic cloves, minced
- 4 cups low-fat (2%) milk
- 2 tablespoons unsalted butter
- ⅓ cup all-purpose flour
- 2 medium bunches of arugula, large stems discarded
- ¾ pound penne pasta
- ½ pint cherry tomatoes, halved
- ¼ cup plus 2 tablespoons freshly grated Parmesan cheese

1. Roast the red and yellow bell peppers over a gas flame or under a broiler until charred all over. Transfer to a paper bag and let steam for 10 minutes. Peel the peppers and discard the stems, ribs and seeds. Cut the peppers into ½-inch squares and transfer to a large bowl.

2. Preheat the oven to 450°. Set the butternut squash, cut-side down, in a baking dish and add ½ inch of hot water. Bake for about 50 minutes, or until lightly browned; let cool. Remove the skin, cut the flesh into ½-inch cubes and add to the peppers.

3. Meanwhile, brush a nonstick baking sheet with 1 teaspoon of the vegetable oil. Spread the eggplant and the mushrooms on the baking sheet. Roast in the oven with the butternut squash for about 25 minutes, or until browned. Toss the eggplant and mushrooms with the peppers and squash and season with salt and pepper. Lower the oven temperature to 400°.

4. Heat the remaining 2 teaspoons oil in a saucepan. Add the leeks and the onion and cook over moderately high heat, stirring, until golden, about 5 minutes. Add the garlic and cook for 1 minute. Add the milk and bring to a simmer. Remove the pan from the heat, cover and let stand for 5 minutes. Strain, reserving the milk and the leek mixture separately.

5. Wipe out the saucepan and melt the butter in it. Add the flour and whisk over moderate heat until lightly golden, about 3 minutes. Whisk in the milk until smooth. Raise the heat to moderately high, add the leek mixture and cook, stirring, until thickened, about 4 minutes. Season with salt and pepper. (MAKE AHEAD: The vegetables and sauce can be refrigerated separately for 1 day. Rewarm the sauce before proceeding.)

6. Bring a saucepan of salted water to a boil. Add the arugula and blanch for 30 seconds. Using a slotted spoon, transfer the arugula to a colander, rinse and squeeze out the excess liquid. Add the penne to the boiling water and cook until al dente, about 9 minutes. Drain the pasta and moisten with 2 tablespoons of the cooking water.

7. Add the tomatoes and the arugula to the eggplant mixture. Spread one-third of the leek sauce in a large gratin or baking dish. Cover with one-third of the pasta, half of the vegetables and 2 tablespoons of the Parmesan. Repeat with another layer of leek sauce, pasta, vegetables and Parmesan. Top with the remaining pasta and leek sauce and sprinkle with the remaining Parmesan. Bake the pasta for about 35 minutes, or until it is heated through and golden.—BOB CHAMBERS

Baked Vegetable Pasta

BAKED FUSILLI WITH ROASTED VEGETABLES Q

To save cooking time, cut the vegetables into small pieces.

4–6 SERVINGS

- 2 medium red onions, halved and sliced ¼ inch thick
- 4 medium carrots, halved lengthwise and sliced crosswise ¼ inch thick
- 2 small zucchini, quartered lengthwise and sliced crosswise ¼ inch thick
- 1 small red bell pepper, cut into ¼-inch dice
- 2 tablespoons olive oil
- 1 garlic clove, minced
- Salt
- ¾ pound fusilli
- 1½ cups heavy cream
- ½ cup canned chopped tomatoes in puree
- 2 tablespoons finely chopped fresh flat-leaf parsley
- 6 ounces Fontina cheese, shredded (about 1½ cups)
- ½ cup freshly grated Parmesan cheese
- Freshly ground black pepper

1. Preheat the oven to 450°. Put a large pot of water on to boil. Toss the onions, carrots, zucchini and bell pepper with the oil; spread on two large baking sheets. Roast for 20 to 25 minutes, stirring several times, until caramelized and golden brown. Transfer to a bowl, add the garlic and toss well. Reduce the oven temperature to 425°.

2. Meanwhile, salt the boiling water, add the fusilli and cook, stirring occasionally, until al dente, about 11 minutes. Drain.

3. Add the pasta to the vegetables along with the cream, tomatoes, parsley, Fontina and ¼ cup of the Parmesan. Season with salt and pepper; stir. Transfer to a 13-by-9-inch baking pan; top with the remaining cheese. (**MAKE AHEAD:** The pasta can be assembled up to 8 hours in advance and refrigerated. Remove from the refrigerator when you turn the oven on and increase the baking time as necessary.) Bake for 15 to 20 minutes, or until bubbling and golden brown. Let rest for 5 minutes before serving.—JUDITH SUTTON

Baked Fusilli with Roasted Vegetables

VEGETABLE CANNELLONI

Wonton skins welcome all manner of fillings—savory or sweet, meaty or vegetarian, whether Asian or Italian or Eastern European in inspiration. This recipe wraps them around a vegetable filling for an easy variation on cannelloni.

8 SERVINGS

- 4 dried black or shiitake mushrooms
- 2 teaspoons vegetable oil
- 1¼ pounds bok choy, stems reserved for another use and leaves finely chopped
- 4 scallions, minced, plus 2 thinly sliced scallions for garnish
- 2 teaspoons minced fresh ginger
- 1 cup ricotta cheese
- 1 large egg yolk
- ¼ teaspoon freshly ground black pepper
- Salt
- 24 wonton skins
- 4 tablespoons unsalted butter, melted
- 2 cups plus 2 tablespoons hot Mushroom Broth (recipe follows)

1. Soak the mushrooms in 1 cup of warm water until soft, 10 to 15 minutes. Drain and discard the stems. Finely dice the mushroom caps.

2. Heat the vegetable oil in a medium skillet. Add the bok choy, minced scallions and ginger and sauté over moderately high heat until wilted. Stir in the mushrooms. Transfer the vegetables to a bowl and let cool. Stir in the ricotta cheese, the egg yolk, the freshly ground black pepper and ½ teaspoon salt.

3. Bring a medium pot of water to a boil and stir in 1 tablespoon of salt. Dip the wonton skins in the water one at a time and then spread the wonton skins out on a clean towel. ➤

Vegetable Cannelloni

WONTONS

"Swallowing clouds"—the literal meaning of the Chinese characters for *wontons*—suggests the sensuous delight the Chinese take in eating these little bundles of food neatly wrapped in noodles. And they aren't alone, judging from the worldwide popularity of dumplings, ravioli, kreplach and dozens of other similar "packaged" foods. Now ready-made wonton skins, or wrappers, make it easy to reproduce many of these variations at home—and to create your own. The skins, available at most supermarkets, are paper-thin sheets of dough made of flour, water, egg and salt, a mixture comparable to fresh Italian egg pasta. The stretching and rolling of the dough until it is very thin lends it elasticity, making wonton skins ideal for pinching, folding and twisting into different shapes. Each sheet measures about three-and-one-half inches square (round skins are also available). The thin sheets are dusted with cornstarch to keep them from sticking together.

4. Preheat the oven to 350°. Using a pastry brush, grease an 8-by-11-inch baking dish with some of the melted butter. Spoon 1 tablespoon of the vegetable filling into the center of each wonton skin and roll up to form a log. Place the cannelloni in a single layer, just touching, in the prepared baking dish. Drizzle the cannelloni with the remaining melted butter and the 2 tablespoons broth. Bake the cannelloni for 10 minutes, or until cooked through.
5. Place three cannelloni in each of eight soup plates and spoon ¼ cup of the broth around each serving. Garnish with the sliced scallions and serve.

Mushroom Broth

MAKES 4 CUPS

- 2 ounces dried black or shiitake mushrooms
- 1 tablespoon canola oil
- 3 tablespoons minced shallots
- 10 ounces white mushrooms, quartered
- 2 quarter-size slices of fresh ginger

1. In a small bowl, soak the dried mushrooms in 2 cups of warm water until soft, 10 to 15 minutes.
2. Heat the oil in a heavy medium saucepan. Add the shallots; cook over moderate heat until wilted, about 2 minutes. Add the white mushrooms and ginger. Stir in the dried mushrooms and their soaking liquid along with 6 cups of cold water. Bring to a boil, then simmer over moderate heat until the broth is reduced to 4 cups, about 40 minutes. Strain the broth. (**MAKE AHEAD:** The broth can be refrigerated for up to 2 days or frozen for up to 1 month.) —ROSA ROSS

FETTUCCINE WITH MASCARPONE AND EGG Q

A Roman wine would be suitable. Consider a good Frascati from Villa Simone or the white or red from Paola Di Mauro's label Colle Picchioni.

2 SERVINGS

- 2 large eggs
- 3 tablespoons mascarpone cheese
- ½ cup freshly grated Parmigiano-Reggiano cheese, plus more for serving
- Coarse salt
- Freshly ground pepper
- ½ pound imported dried fettuccine

1. Fill a stockpot with 6 quarts of water, cover and bring to a boil. In a medium stainless steel bowl, beat the eggs with the mascarpone, the ½ cup Parmigiano-Reggiano, ½ teaspoon salt and ¼ teaspoon pepper. Set aside.
2. Add 3½ tablespoons of salt to the boiling water and add the fettuccine. Cover partially just until the water returns to a boil, then uncover, stir the pasta and cook until al dente.
3. While the fettuccine is cooking, carefully hold the metal bowl just slightly over the boiling water to warm the egg and cheese mixture, stirring occasionally. When the fettuccine is cooked, drain and add it to the bowl; toss well. Serve the pasta immediately, passing the extra Parmigiano at the table.—JOHANNE KILLEEN AND GEORGE GERMON

FRESH-SAGE AND GOAT-CHEESE RAVIOLI

If gyoza *wrappers are hard to find, use readily available wonton wrappers for these simple-to-assemble ravioli.*

6 SERVINGS

- 6 ounces goat cheese
- ½ cup heavy cream
- 2 teaspoons finely chopped fresh sage, plus 6 small sage sprigs for garnish
- 1 medium shallot, finely chopped
- Salt and freshly ground pepper
- 24 *gyoza* wrappers
- Flour, for sprinkling
- Infused Vegetable Stock (recipe follows)
- Pinch of cayenne pepper
- 1 stick plus 2 tablespoons cold unsalted butter (5 ounces), cut into tablespoons

1. In a small bowl, mash the goat cheese with ⅓ cup of the heavy cream, the chopped sage, shallot and salt and pepper to taste.
2. On a lightly floured surface, make the ravioli: Brush the edges of 4 *gyoza* wrappers with a wet brush. Scoop 1 tablespoon of the goat cheese into the center of each of two wrappers; top each with a second wrapper. Press around the edges to seal, flattening the filling and pressing out as much air as possible. Transfer to a lightly floured plate. Repeat to make ten more ravioli; sprinkle lightly with flour as you layer them on the plate. Cover with a kitchen towel. (**MAKE AHEAD:** The ravioli can be refrigerated for up to 4 hours.)
3. In a small saucepan, combine the stock with the remaining heavy cream, ¼ teaspoon salt and the cayenne and simmer

until reduced to ½ cup, about 10 minutes. Turn the heat to very low and whisk in the cold butter, a few pieces at a time. Remove the sauce from the heat and partially cover.

4. In a large deep skillet of boiling salted water, simmer the ravioli until translucent, about 2 minutes. Using a slotted spoon, transfer the ravioli to paper towels to drain very briefly. Arrange two ravioli on each of six warmed small plates and spoon the sauce on top. Garnish with the sage sprigs and serve at once.

Infused Vegetable Stock

MAKES ABOUT 1¼ CUPS

1¾ cups vegetable stock or broth
¼ cup dry white wine
2 teaspoons white-wine vinegar
One ½-inch slice of onion
1 bay leaf
1 fresh parsley sprig
1 fresh thyme sprig
3 small slices of carrot
5 whole black peppercorns

Combine the ingredients in a nonreactive saucepan and simmer for 15 minutes. Remove from the heat and set aside for 10 minutes, then strain.—BRIGIT LEGERE BINNS

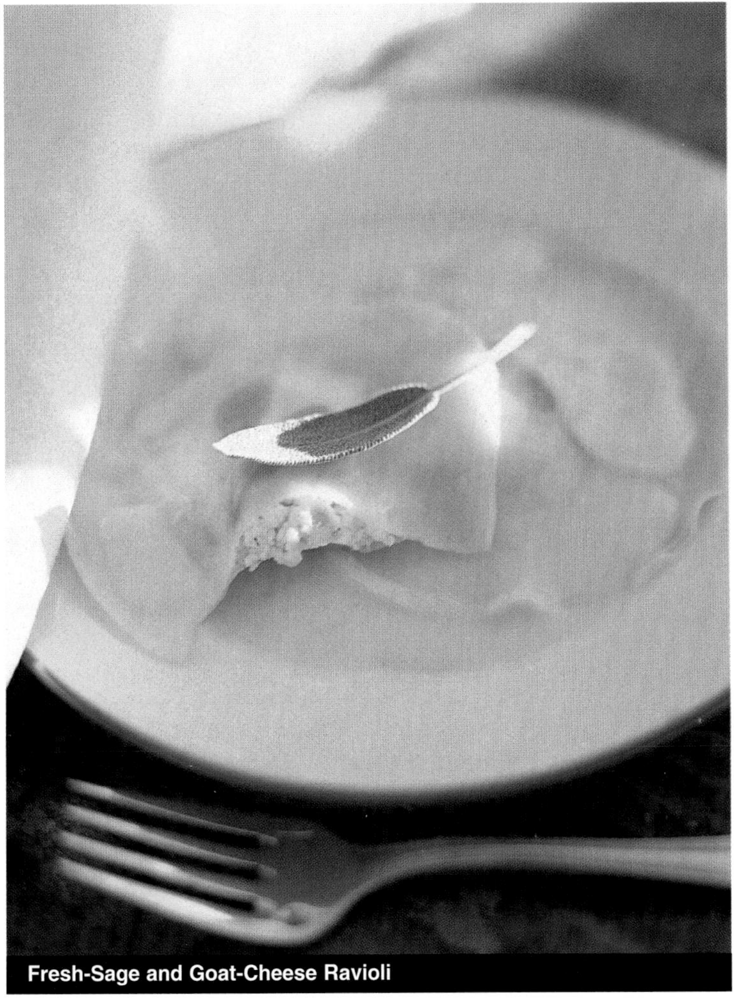

Fresh-Sage and Goat-Cheese Ravioli

SPAGHETTINI WITH POTATOES, SAGE AND GORGONZOLA Q

This dish would work with a Grumello, Inferno or Sassella from a Valtellina producer like Nino Negri or Rainoldi. Another especially good choice: Nebbiolo delle Langhe from Clerico or Roberto Voerzio.

2 SERVINGS

½ pound medium red potatoes, peeled and cut into ½-inch dice
Coarse salt
½ pound spaghettini
Scant ¼ cup crumbled Gorgonzola cheese (about 2 ounces)
3 tablespoons unsalted butter, cut into small pieces
Scant 1 tablespoon finely chopped fresh sage
Freshly ground pepper

1. In a small saucepan, cover the potatoes with cold water and bring to a boil. Cook until tender, about 5 minutes. Drain and set aside.

2. At the same time, fill a stockpot with 6 quarts of water, cover and bring to a boil. Add 3½ tablespoons salt to the water and add the spaghettini. Cover partially until the water just returns to a boil, then uncover, stir the pasta and cook until al dente. Drain, reserving ¼ cup of the pasta water.

3. Meanwhile, in a serving bowl large enough to hold the spaghettini, mash the Gorgonzola with the butter and sage using the back of a spoon. Add the spaghettini and potatoes, season with pepper and toss gently but thoroughly. Add 1 or 2 tablespoons of the pasta water if necessary. Serve at once.—JOHANNE KILLEEN AND GEORGE GERMON

PAD THAI

Here's a version of pad thai *made with rice vermicelli. It packs a spicy punch; for a milder dish, cut down on the chiles.*

4 SERVINGS

- ½ pound dried rice vermicelli*
- 8 small dried hot chiles, such as Chinese or cayenne, stems and seeds discarded
- 1 large dried semihot chile, such as guajillo, pasilla or New Mexico, stem and seeds discarded
- Boiling water
- 1 small shallot, coarsely chopped
- 1 tablespoon sugar
- 3 tablespoons Thai fish sauce (nam pla)*
- 1½ tablespoons tamarind concentrate* dissolved in 1½ tablespoons boiling water
- 1 teaspoon fresh lime juice
- 2 cups plus 3½ tablespoons vegetable oil
- ¼ cup diced soft tofu, patted dry (½ inch)
- 2 tablespoons unsalted peanuts
- 2 tablespoons coarsely chopped dried shrimp*
- 2 large eggs, lightly beaten
- Coarse salt
- ½ pound medium shrimp, shelled, deveined and halved lengthwise
- 2 cups mung bean sprouts
- Lime wedges, for serving

*Available at Asian markets

1. In a large bowl, cover the rice vermicelli with cold water and let soak until pliable, about 20 minutes. Drain the vermicelli.

2. In a medium bowl, cover all the chiles with boiling water. Let soak until softened, about 10 minutes. Drain and coarsely chop the chiles.

3. In a mortar or mini-processor, grind the softened chiles, shallot and sugar to a paste. Work in the fish sauce, tamarind liquid and lime juice. Set the chile paste aside.

4. In a wok or a medium saucepan, heat 2 cups of the oil until shimmering. Add the tofu and deep-fry over moderately high heat until golden brown, about 4 minutes. Using a slotted spoon, transfer to paper towels to drain. Add the peanuts to the oil and deep-fry until golden brown, about 2 minutes; drain on paper towels. Fry the dried shrimp until crisp, about 1 minute, then drain on paper towels. Reserve the oil for future frying or discard it.

5. Heat the wok over moderately high heat. When it is very hot, after about 2 minutes, add ½ tablespoon of the remaining oil and heat until it is shimmering. Season the eggs with salt and lightly stir-fry until they start to set. Shape the eggs into an 8-inch round, flatten it slightly, then turn the egg cake over and cook until firm, about 10 seconds more. Transfer the egg cake to a work surface and cut it into long 1-inch-wide strips.

6. Heat the remaining 3 tablespoons oil in the wok over moderately high heat until almost smoking. Add the chile paste and stir-fry until fragrant, about 4 minutes. Add the fresh shrimp and stir-fry until bright pink, about 3 minutes. Add ⅓ cup of water and the soaked rice vermicelli and stir-fry until tender, about 3 more minutes. Add more water if necessary to keep the noodles moist. Add the egg strips and toss again. Transfer the noodles to a platter and garnish with the fried tofu, peanuts, dried shrimp and bean sprouts. Serve with lime wedges.—THAI COOKING SCHOOL, THE ORIENTAL HOTEL, BANGKOK

CLAM SAUCE Q

The success of this simple sauce depends on fresh clams and excellent, fruity, extra-virgin olive oil. Linguine is the pasta of choice, with spaghetti a close runner-up. Add one pound of cooked pasta to the clam sauce in the skillet and toss for a few minutes to combine; some of the sauce will be absorbed by the pasta but plenty of liquid will remain. Serve the pasta in bowls with its brothy sauce and a sprinkling of parsley. Outside of Italy, it is commonplace to see waiters offering grated cheese at the table for this dish, but not in Italy. Grated cheese should simply never be added to seafood sauces for pasta.

4–6 SERVINGS

- 4 dozen littleneck clams, or 4 pounds West Coast steamer clams or cockles
- Flour or cornmeal, for purging the clams
- ½ cup extra-virgin olive oil
- 3 tablespoons finely chopped fresh flat-leaf parsley

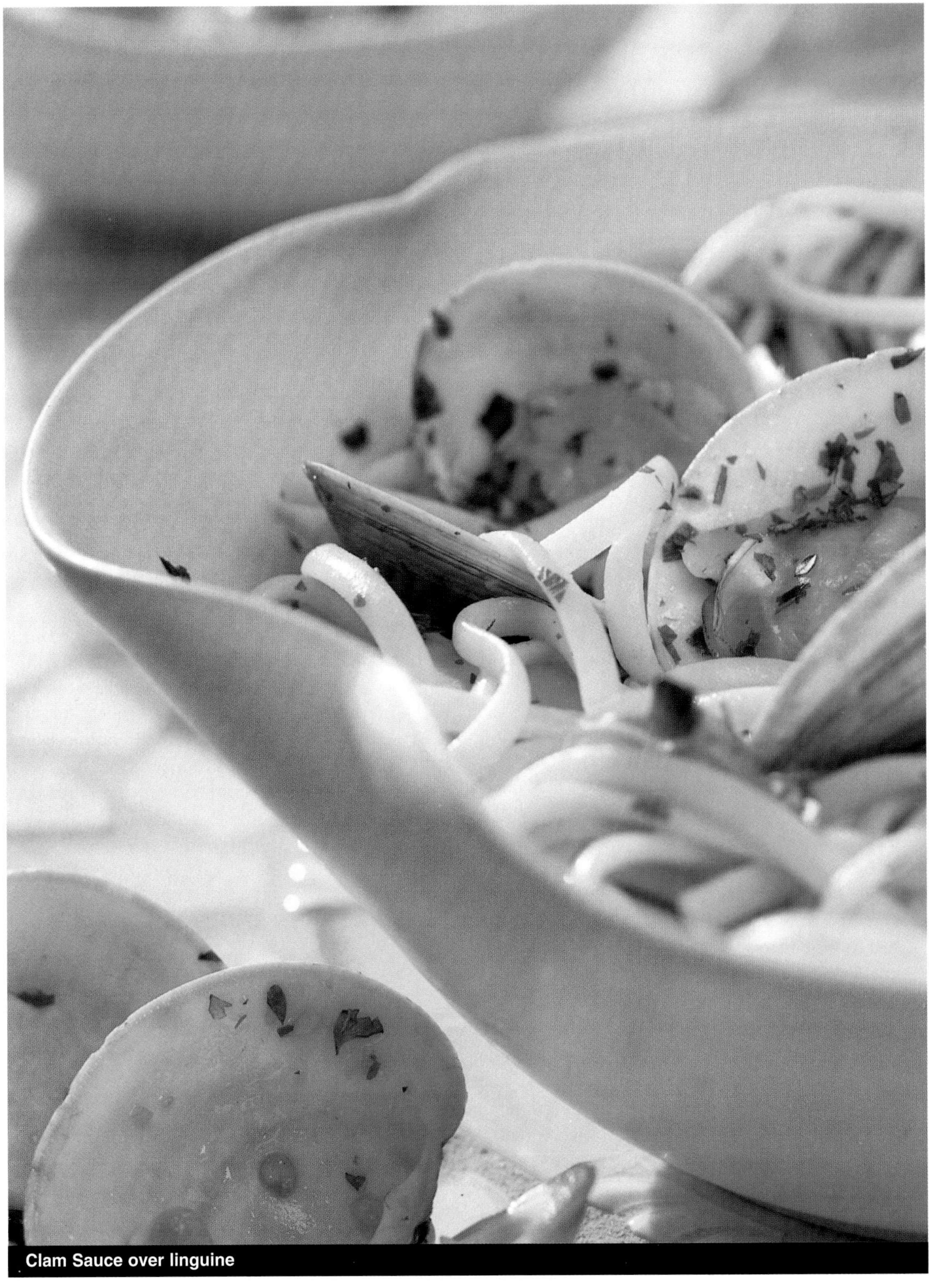

Clam Sauce over linguine

1 teaspoon finely chopped fresh oregano or ½ teaspoon dried
¼ teaspoon crushed red pepper
5 large garlic cloves, minced
½ cup dry white wine

1. Place the clams in a large bowl and cover with cool water. Stir a handful of flour or cornmeal into the water so that the clams will purge themselves of sand or other foreign matter. Refrigerate for at least 3 hours or overnight. When you are ready to use the clams, scrub them well with a clean, stiff brush.
2. In a deep nonreactive sauté pan or saucepan large enough to hold the clams, combine the oil, parsley, oregano and crushed pepper. Stir in the garlic and cook gently over moderate heat until softened but not colored, about 4 minutes. Pour in the wine and cook for about 3 minutes to burn off the alcohol. Add the clams and cover immediately. Increase the heat to high and cook until the clams open, 8 to 12 minutes, depending on the kind of clams. Discard any clams that do not open. Set aside a few clams with their shells for garnishing. Then remove the remaining clams from their shells; discard the shells and return the clams to the broth to heat through.—JULIA DELLA CROCE

QUICK SAUCES

For every slow-cooked Italian *ragù*, there's a sauce that can be whipped up in the length of time it takes to boil the water for pasta. The many speedy sauces—Clam Sauce, Sausage and Broccoli-Rabe Sauce (p. 135), Saffron, Tomato and Sausage Sauce (p. 133), Sun-Dried-Tomato Pesto (p. 105), Tomato, Bacon and Hot-Pepper Sauce (p. 110), Quick Southern Italian Tomato Sauce (p. 105) and Quick Tomato Sauce with Butter (p. 106)—all use uncomplicated techniques, and can be made in thirty minutes or less. Because the ingredients are few and therefore unmasked, their quality must be impeccable. Preparation begins with a well-stocked pantry full of fruity, extra-virgin olive oil and good factory-produced dried semolina pasta, *pasta secca*, which is made from hard durum wheat. Canned tomatoes are also a must for many of the quick, tomato-based sauces.

CRAB CURRY WITH RICE VERMICELLI

The very spicy chile paste here is great in coconut-milk-based dishes. Store leftover paste in a jar in the refrigerator.

4 SERVINGS

½ pound dried rice vermicelli*
1 tablespoon vegetable oil
3 tablespoons Naam Ya Chile Paste (recipe follows)
2 cups thin unsweetened coconut milk*
1 cup thick unsweetened coconut milk*
3 tablespoons Thai fish sauce (nam pla)*
1 teaspoon palm sugar*
1 pound cooked crabmeat, such as king crab, blue claw or Dungeness, picked over and torn into large pieces
1 cup mung bean sprouts
1 cup small fresh basil leaves

*Available at Asian markets

1. In a large bowl, cover the rice vermicelli with cold water and let soak until pliable, about 20 minutes. Drain the vermicelli.
2. Heat the vegetable oil in a wok or large saucepan. Add the chile paste and stir-fry over moderately high heat until fragrant, about 4 minutes. Add the thin coconut milk and bring to a simmer. Add the thick coconut milk, fish sauce, palm sugar and crabmeat and simmer until the curry is heated through, about 2 minutes.
3. Meanwhile, bring a large saucepan of water to a boil. Add the rice vermicelli and cook, stirring, until just tender, about 2 minutes. Drain the vermicelli and transfer to a large shallow serving bowl. Spoon the crab curry on top and garnish with the bean sprouts and basil leaves.

Naam Ya Chile Paste

MAKES ABOUT ¾ CUP

12 large dried semihot chiles, such as guajillo, pasilla or New Mexico, stems and seeds discarded
5 small dried hot chiles, such as Chinese or cayenne, stems and seeds discarded
¼ cup finely chopped fresh lemongrass,* white bulb only
5 quarter-size slices of peeled fresh galangal,* finely chopped

Linguine with Clams, Green Tomatoes and Saffron

1 teaspoon black peppercorns, crushed
5 small shallots, chopped
3 garlic cloves, chopped
½ teaspoon coarse salt
¼ teaspoon turmeric
1 tablespoon minced lime zest
1 tablespoon shrimp paste*

*Available at Asian markets

1. In a large bowl, cover the chiles with boiling water and let soak until softened, about 20 minutes. Drain and coarsely chop.
2. In a mortar or mini-processor, grind the lemongrass, galangal and peppercorns to a paste. Work in the shallots, garlic, salt, turmeric and lime zest. Add the soaked chiles and pound to a puree. Stir in the shrimp paste. (MAKE AHEAD: The curry paste can be refrigerated for up to 1 month.) —THAI COOKING SCHOOL, THE ORIENTAL HOTEL, BANGKOK

LINGUINE WITH CLAMS, GREEN TOMATOES AND SAFFRON Q

Abruzzo, home of some of the world's best saffron, inspired the wine choice. Valentini is an exceptional producer of Trebbiano d'Abruzzo (white) and Montepulciano d'Abruzzo (red); either works beautifully.

2 SERVINGS

Coarse salt
½ pound imported dried thin linguine or spaghetti
¼ cup extra-virgin olive oil
1 small onion, halved and thinly sliced lengthwise
2 teaspoons minced garlic
Small pinch of saffron threads
¼ teaspoon crushed red pepper
2 small green tomatoes (about ¾ pound total), cored, seeded and chopped, juices reserved
18 littleneck clams, scrubbed

1. Fill a stockpot with 6 quarts of water, cover and bring to a boil. Add 3½ tablespoons salt to the water and add the linguine. Cover partially just until the water returns to a boil, then uncover, stir the pasta and cook until almost al dente. Drain the linguine, reserving ¼ cup of the pasta water.
2. Meanwhile, heat the olive oil in a large nonreactive skillet. Add the onion and the garlic and cook over high heat until the garlic is barely golden, about 2 minutes. Add the saffron, the crushed red pepper, the green tomatoes and their juices and the clams. Cover tightly and cook over moderately low heat until the clams have opened fully, about 7 minutes. Discard any clams that don't open.
3. Add the linguine to the skillet with the clam mixture and cook for 1 minute, tossing well. If the linguine seems dry, add some of the pasta-cooking water, 1 tablespoon at a time. Serve immediately.—JOHANNE KILLEEN AND GEORGE GERMON ➤

TEN PASTA TIPS

1. **Start with good imported dried pasta. Our favorite brands are De Cecco, Delverde, Latini and Rustichella d'Abruzzo.**
2. **Use an ample amount of water—six quarts for a pound of pasta. Cover the pot so the water comes to a boil quickly.**
3. **Salt the water just before adding the pasta; use about three-and-a-half tablespoons of coarse salt for six quarts of water.**
4. **To prevent the pasta from sticking together, stir it frequently while it cooks. Never add oil to the water.**
5. **Use spring-loaded tongs for stirring pasta in boiling water and in sauces, as well as for serving.**
6. **Reserve some of the cooking water before you drain the pasta. If a sauce is too thick, a little pasta water will lighten it; if it's too thin, add pasta water and then reduce it.**
7. **Never rinse pasta. The starch that clings to the strands is important to the taste and texture.**
8. **If adding pasta to a sauce, undercook by a minute or two so it can simmer in the sauce and absorb its flavor.**
9. **Serve pasta the moment it's done—it never gets better. To keep it steaming, heat your serving bowls.**
10. **Use top-quality ingredients. For canned tomato products, we like organic Muir Glen brand best.**—JOHANNE KILLEEN AND GEORGE GERMON

LINGUINE WITH TOMATO, TUNA, GARLIC, FENNEL AND LEMON Q

We use tuna packed in olive oil; look for a good brand from Italy or Spain. If tomatoes are out of season, substitute one cup canned tomato pulp.

This dish needs a wine with some concentration and body. One option: Sella & Mosca's Vermentino di Sardegna.

2 SERVINGS

Coarse salt
½ pound imported dried thin linguine
¼ cup extra-virgin olive oil
2 teaspoons minced garlic
½ teaspoon crushed red pepper
½ teaspoon fennel seeds
One 5-ounce can imported tuna packed in olive oil, drained
1½ pounds ripe tomatoes, peeled, seeded and coarsely chopped, juices reserved
½ teaspoon minced lemon zest
2 tablespoons finely chopped fresh flat-leaf parsley

1. Fill a stockpot with 6 quarts of water, cover and bring to a boil. Put 3½ tablespoons salt in the water and add the linguine. Cover partially until the water just returns to a boil, then uncover, stir the pasta and cook until almost al dente. Drain, reserving some of the pasta water.

2. Meanwhile, in a large nonreactive skillet, heat the olive oil. Add the garlic, red pepper and fennel seeds and cook over moderate heat, stirring, until the garlic is just golden. Add the tuna and ½ teaspoon salt, raise the heat to high and cook until the tuna begins to sizzle; be careful not to break it up too much. Add the tomatoes and their juices and bring to a boil, then simmer over moderate heat until softened, about 4 minutes. Stir in the lemon zest.

3. Add the linguine to the sauce and cook over moderately low heat for 1 minute. Add a little of the pasta water, 1 tablespoon at a time, if the pasta seems dry. Serve the pasta immediately, garnished with the parsley.—JOHANNE KILLEEN AND GEORGE GERMON

PENNE WITH SMOKED CHICKEN AND MASCARPONE Q

A plate of sliced tomatoes with basil, sprinkled with olive oil, makes a nice accompaniment for this pasta. Buy extra mascarpone to serve with fresh figs and thin butter cookies for dessert.

4–6 SERVINGS

1 pound penne rigate
½ cup mascarpone cheese
2 tablespoons sherry vinegar
1 tablespoon extra-virgin olive oil
½ pound young green beans, cut into 1½-inch lengths and blanched until al dente
½ pound zucchini, cut into 1½-by-⅓-inch sticks
2 shallots, thinly sliced
1 pound boneless smoked chicken breast, skinned, trimmed of fat and shredded (see box, opposite page)
⅛ teaspoon crushed red pepper
Salt
2 tablespoons minced parsley

1. In a large pot of boiling salted water, cook the penne until al dente, about 12 minutes. Drain the pasta, reserving about ½ cup of the cooking liquid.

SMOKED CHICKEN

The secret of Penne with Smoked Chicken and Mascarpone is using flavorful smoked chicken breasts. We love the individually packed boneless ones from Nodine's Smokehouse in Goshen, Connecticut; 1-800-222-2059.

2. Meanwhile, in a small nonreactive saucepan, combine the mascarpone and sherry vinegar. Cook over low heat until melted; keep warm.

3. Heat the olive oil in a large nonreactive skillet. Add the green beans and zucchini. Sauté until tender and lightly browned. Stir in the shallots; cook until softened. Add the smoked chicken and crushed red pepper, season with salt and cook just until warmed through.

4. In a large bowl, toss the pasta with the vegetables and the mascarpone sauce; add some of the reserved cooking liquid if the pasta seems dry. Sprinkle with the parsley and serve.—GRACE PARISI

FARFALLE WITH PROSCIUTTO, PEAS AND TOMATOES

This dish is perfect when fresh peas are in season, especially if you can also get the tender shoots, or leaves.

4 SERVINGS

- 1½ pounds fresh peas, shelled, or 1½ cups frozen baby peas, thawed
- 4 ounces prosciutto di Parma, sliced ¼ inch thick and cut into ¼-inch dice

Penne with Smoked Chicken and Mascarpone

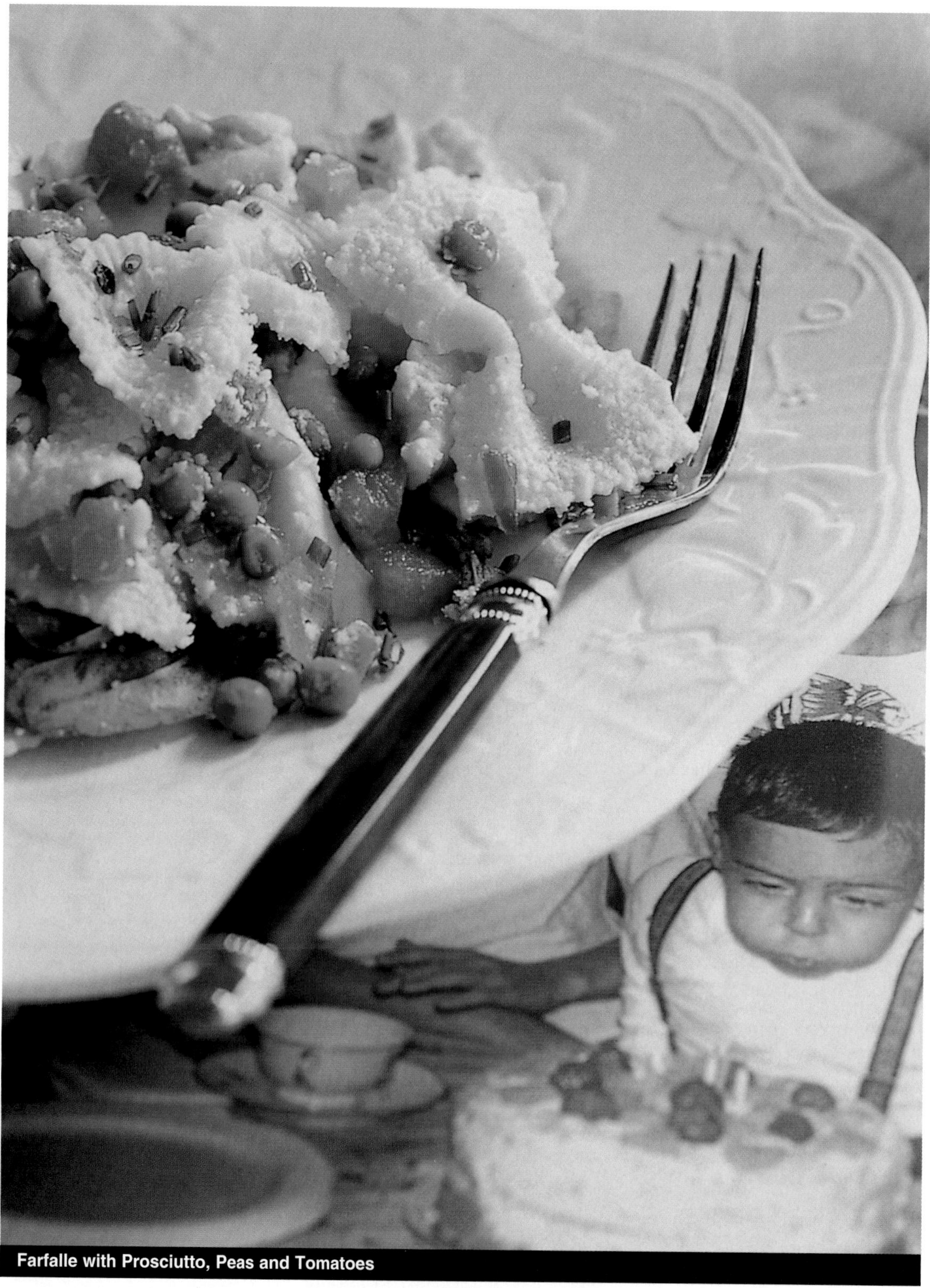

Farfalle with Prosciutto, Peas and Tomatoes

1½ cups loosely packed pea shoots or 1-inch pieces of arugula
4 large ripe plum tomatoes, peeled, seeded and cut into ¼-inch dice
6 tablespoons freshly grated Parmesan cheese, plus more for serving
1 stick unsalted butter (4 ounces), softened
1 small garlic clove, minced
1 teaspoon fresh lemon juice
½ teaspoon freshly ground pepper
½ teaspoon finely chopped fresh thyme
1 pound farfalle
1 tablespoon snipped fresh chives
Salt and freshly ground white pepper

1. In a small saucepan of boiling salted water, cook the fresh peas just until tender, about 7 minutes. Drain.

2. Bring a large pot of salted water to a boil. Meanwhile, in a serving bowl, combine the prosciutto, peas, pea shoots, tomatoes and the 6 tablespoons of Parmesan. Combine the butter, garlic, lemon juice, pepper and thyme and beat until blended.

3. Cook the farfalle in the boiling water until al dente, about 15 minutes. Drain well, reserving ¼ cup of the cooking water. Add the pasta to the prosciutto and peas and dot with the garlic butter. Toss well, adding enough of the reserved pasta-cooking water to melt the cheese. Sprinkle the chives on top and season with salt and white pepper. Serve at once. Pass additional cheese separately.—ALFRED PORTALE

POTATO GNOCCHI WITH TOMATO PROSCIUTTO SAUCE LF

Baking potatoes, usually called Idaho potatoes or russets, are the best for making gnocchi; since they're drier than other varieties, they'll produce lighter dumplings. Oven-roasting the potatoes also helps make the dough drier by evaporating moisture from the tubers.

🍷 *The bright flavors of a Chianti Classico Riserva would suit the tartness of this tomato sauce nicely. We recommend looking for the 1993 Antinori Peppoli or the 1990 Vignamaggio Mona Lisa.*

4 SERVINGS

GNOCCHI:

2 pounds medium baking potatoes
1 teaspoon salt
About 1 cup all-purpose flour

SAUCE:

1 tablespoon olive oil
1 medium onion, minced
One 28-ounce can crushed tomatoes
Salt and freshly ground pepper
2 ounces thinly sliced prosciutto, trimmed of fat and cut into thin strips
2 tablespoons minced fresh basil

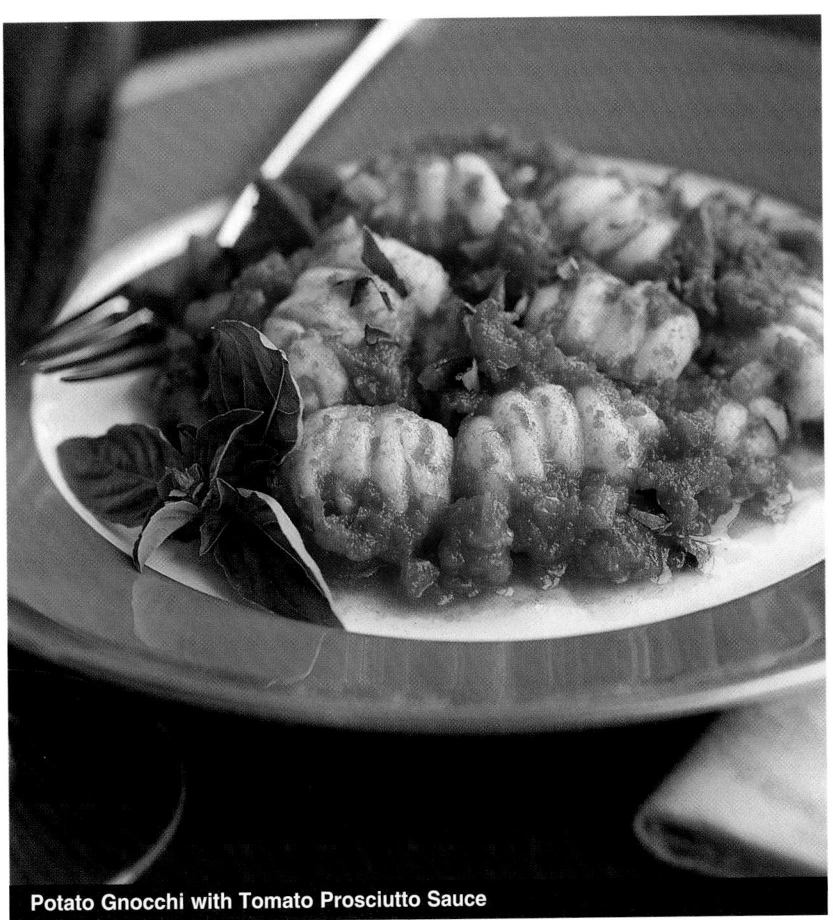

Potato Gnocchi with Tomato Prosciutto Sauce

Linguine with Prosciutto and Gorgonzola

1. Make the gnocchi: Preheat the oven to 400°. Prick the potatoes once or twice with a small knife and bake for about 45 minutes, or until tender in the center when pierced. Let cool slightly.

2. Peel the potatoes and pass them through a potato ricer or food mill into a large bowl. Let cool completely. Stir in the salt. Gradually stir in about half of the flour until the mixture becomes stiff. Transfer the mixture to a lightly floured surface and knead in as much of the remaining flour as necessary until the dough is no longer sticky.

3. Line two baking sheets with wax paper and dust them with flour. Divide the dough into eight equal pieces. Set one piece of dough on a floured surface; keep the remaining dough covered with an inverted bowl. Using your hands, roll out the piece of dough to a ½-inch-thick rope and then cut the rope into ¾-inch lengths.

4. Dip a fork in flour. Roll each piece of dough down the back of the tines; press gently with your thumb so the tines leave ridges. Alternatively, flatten the gnocchi by pressing each one gently with a fork. Set the gnocchi on the prepared baking sheets without letting them touch. Repeat with the remaining pieces of dough.

5. Make the sauce: Heat the olive oil in a large nonreactive skillet. Add the onion and cook over moderately high heat, stirring, until tender, about 5 minutes. Add the tomatoes and season with salt and pepper. Bring to a simmer, then reduce the heat to low and cook for 20 minutes, stirring occasionally. (**MAKE AHEAD:** The gnocchi and sauce can stand at room temperature for up to 2 hours. Rewarm the sauce before serving.)

6. Bring a large pot of water to a boil. Add 2 tablespoons of salt, then half the gnocchi, a few at a time; simmer until they float to the surface. With a slotted spoon, transfer the gnocchi to a rack to drain; don't pile or they'll stick together. Repeat the procedure with the remaining gnocchi.

7. Stir the prosciutto and basil into the tomato sauce. Spoon the gnocchi onto four large plates, top with the tomato sauce and serve.—MICHELE SCICOLONE

LINGUINE WITH PROSCIUTTO AND GORGONZOLA Q

To get great flavor and save time, use California Sun Dry brand julienne-cut sun-dried tomatoes with herbs, straight from the jar. Serve the pasta with a lightly dressed green salad and a crusty loaf of Italian bread.

4–6 SERVINGS

1 pound thin linguine
1 tablespoon extra-virgin olive oil
2 shallots, thinly sliced
One ¼-inch-thick slice of prosciutto, cut into 3-by-¼-inch matchsticks
½ cup drained, oil-packed sun-dried tomatoes, cut into thin strips
Crushed red pepper
Salt and freshly ground black pepper
¾ cup chicken stock or canned low-sodium broth
¼ pound Italian Gorgonzola cheese
2 tablespoons finely chopped flat-leaf parsley

1. In a large pot of boiling salted water, cook the pasta until al dente. Drain, reserving ½ cup cooking liquid. Return the pasta to the pot. Cover partially; keep warm.

2. Meanwhile, heat the oil in a large nonreactive skillet. Add the shallots and cook over moderately high heat for 1 minute. Stir in the prosciutto and sun-dried tomatoes. Season with crushed red pepper, salt and black pepper and cook for 5 minutes. Add ¼ cup of the stock and stir up any browned bits clinging to the bottom of the pan. Pour the sauce over the pasta and toss well.

3. Add the remaining ½ cup stock and the Gorgonzola to the skillet and stir over moderate heat until creamy. Strain the sauce over the pasta, add the parsley and toss, adding some of the reserved cooking liquid if the pasta seems dry. Serve the pasta at once.—GRACE PARISI

SAFFRON, TOMATO AND SAUSAGE SAUCE Q

The saffron in this sauce is characteristic of Sardinian cooking. Not only does it add a subtly rich flavor but it also imparts a deep golden cast to the red of the tomato. This sauce is traditionally served with malloreddus (see box, right), but you can substitute cavatelli (ridged elongated pasta shells), gnocchetti (little gnocchi) or conchiglie (shells). Use one pound of pasta and serve with freshly grated Parmesan.

🍷 *The sweet tomato sauce, with its hint of fennel and saffron, would flatten the taste of a subtle red. So choose one with tart, pointed flavors of its own, such as a Barbera d'Alba from Italy. Among possible choices: the 1991 Ceretto or the 1993 Bruno Giacosa.*

Saffron, Tomato and Sausage Sauce with cavatelli

MALLOREDDUS

Malloreddus—saffron-tinted semolina or cornmeal dumplings, similar to gnocchi, which are unique to Sardinia—are exported from Italy in small quantities. You can order them from Dean & DeLuca (1-800-221-7714) and Balducci's (1-800-225-3822; specify No. 4706).

4–6 SERVINGS

2½ cups canned peeled tomatoes in puree, or 1½ cups canned peeled tomatoes in juice plus 3 tablespoons tomato paste
1 tablespoon extra-virgin olive oil
1 large red or yellow onion, finely chopped

1	pound sweet fennel-flavored Italian sausages, casings off
⅛	teaspoon saffron threads (about 15 threads) or saffron powder

Salt

Fusilli with Fennel Sausage

Sausage and Broccoli-Rabe Sauce with orecchiette

1. Drain the tomatoes in a strainer set over a medium bowl and reserve the liquid. Working over the strainer, scoop out and discard any excess seeds from the tomatoes with your fingers. Coarsely chop the tomatoes and add to the liquid in the bowl.
2. In a large nonreactive saucepan, warm the oil over moderate heat. Add the onion and cook until softened, about 10 minutes. Add the sausage meat and cook, stirring occasionally, until it is browned, about 8 minutes. If using tomatoes in puree, stir them into the meat. If using tomatoes in juice and tomato paste, stir in the paste until dissolved, then add the chopped tomatoes and their juice.
3. In a small dry skillet, toast the saffron threads over low heat for 1 minute. Crush the threads between your fingers and stir them into the sauce. Alternatively, stir in the saffron powder. Season the sauce with salt and simmer over moderately low heat, stirring occasionally, until it is nicely thickened, about 25 minutes. (**MAKE AHEAD:** The sauce can be refrigerated for up to 5 days or frozen up to 3 months.) —JULIA DELLA CROCE

FUSILLI WITH FENNEL SAUSAGE

Here's a hearty pasta dish that will stick to your ribs. It's a mix of well-seasoned pork sausage with a hint of fennel and a dense, reduced red-wine sauce. The wine replaces water or stock, adding additional acidity, balance, character and flavor. Search out a well-seasoned pork sausage sold either in bulk or in casings (you'll need to remove the meat from the casings).

🍷 *This pasta can take a big wine. I love it with a fine Piedmont red, such as a Dolcetto d'Alba.*

4–6 SERVINGS.

1	pound sausage meat, broken into small pieces
½	teaspoon fennel seeds
3	tablespoons tomato paste
2	cups red wine, such as Chianti
2	large eggs, at room temperature
¼	cup freshly grated Parmigiano-Reggiano cheese (1 ounce)
½	teaspoon freshly ground pepper
1	pound fusilli or penne

1. In a nonreactive skillet large enough to hold the pasta, brown the sausage meat over moderately high heat, breaking it up into fine bits. Stir in the fennel seeds and tomato paste and cook for 3 minutes. Slowly pour the wine all over the sausage, reduce the heat to moderate and simmer until most of the wine has evaporated, about 15 minutes.
2. Meanwhile, whisk the eggs in a small bowl. Whisk in the Parmigiano-Reggiano cheese and the pepper.
3. In a large pot of boiling salted water, cook the fusilli, stirring it occasionally, until tender but firm to the bite. Lightly drain the fusilli, reserving 1 cup of the pasta-cooking water.
4. Add the pasta to the skillet and toss thoroughly until well coated. Remove from the heat and quickly stir in the egg mixture, tossing with forks until each piece of pasta is evenly coated. Add the reserved pasta

water a few tablespoons at a time until the pasta is nicely coated with sauce. Serve the pasta immediately in warmed bowls.—PATRICIA WELLS

SAUSAGE AND BROCCOLI-RABE SAUCE Q

Both the sharp, bitter flavor of broccoli rabe and its vitamins are best preserved by steaming, but if you prefer a milder flavor, boil it. The traditional pasta shapes used here are orecchiette (little ears), gnochetti (little gnocchi) and cavatelli (ridged elongated pasta shells). Cook and drain one pound of pasta, leaving it very moist. Toss the pasta with the sauce and a quarter cup extra-virgin olive oil.

🍷 *This zesty dish needs a refreshing but assertive red that can balance the attractive bitter-salty flavors. Not surprisingly, there are a number of flavorful Italian reds that will work well in this context, among them Chianti Classico. Look for such bottlings as the 1990 Monsanto or the 1990 Castello di Ama.*

4–6 SERVINGS

2 pounds broccoli rabe
Salt
2 tablespoons extra-virgin olive oil
¾ pound sweet Italian sausages, casings removed
4 medium garlic cloves, minced
¼ teaspoon crushed red pepper

1. Wash the broccoli rabe thoroughly and remove any yellow leaves. Trim the stems. Using a small sharp knife, peel any thick, tough stems. Rinse and drain. Coarsely chop into 1-inch pieces. Bring 4½ quarts of water to a rolling boil, salt the water and add the broccoli rabe. Cover partially, return to a boil and cook for 1 minute. Drain, reserving ½ cup of the cooking water.

2. In a large, deep, nonreactive skillet, warm the oil. Add the sausage meat. Cook over moderately low heat, stirring occasionally, until browned, about 10 minutes. Stir in the garlic and crushed red pepper and cook until the garlic is softened, about 3 minutes. Add the broccoli rabe and the reserved cooking water. Cover and cook, stirring occasionally, until the broccoli rabe is tender, 8 to 10 minutes.—JULIA DELLA CROCE

LASAGNA WITH SPINACH AND SAUSAGE Q

It's important to use nine-by-four-inch no-boil lasagna noodles, available at supermarkets, so that the layers will fit in the pan without overlapping; otherwise the noodles will be gummy.

🍷 *Ingredients like sausage, cheese and tomatoes call for an assertive red. A spicy California Zinfandel, such as the 1992 Beringer or the 1993 Niebaum-Coppola Edizione Pennino, would match the heartiness of the dish and have just enough tannins to contrast with the sausage and cheese.*

12 SERVINGS

¼ cup plus 1 tablespoon olive oil
1 pound ground turkey
1 pound hot Italian sausage, casings removed, meat crumbled
2 large onions, coarsely chopped
6 large garlic cloves, minced
Four 28-ounce cans peeled Italian tomatoes, drained and liquid reserved

QUICK DINNER

LASAGNA WITH SPINACH AND SAUSAGE
(P. 135)

MESCLUN SALAD WITH PARMESAN DRESSING
(P. 60)

CRUSTY ITALIAN BREAD

VANILLA ICE CREAM AND RASPBERRY SORBET

GAME PLAN:

- **Cook the turkey and sausage meat and make the tomato sauce.**
- **Make the spinach filling.**
- **Assemble and bake the lasagna.**
- **Make the Parmesan dressing and toss the salad.**

Lasagna with Spinach and Sausage

¼ cup tomato paste
1 tablespoon oregano
½ teaspoon crushed red pepper
Salt and freshly ground black pepper
1 pound frozen chopped spinach, thawed and squeezed dry
2 pounds ricotta cheese
1 pound shredded mozzarella cheese
Eighteen 9-by-4-inch no-boil lasagna noodles (about ¾ pound)
1 cup freshly grated Parmesan cheese (about 3 ounces)

1. Preheat the oven to 450°. Heat two large nonreactive saucepans. Add 1 tablespoon of the oil and the ground turkey to one saucepan and add the sausage to the other. Cook the meats over high heat, stirring to break them up, until cooked through, about 6 minutes. Transfer the meats to a colander. Add 2 tablespoons oil to each saucepan, then divide the onions between the pans and cook, stirring, until slightly softened, about 5 minutes. Add half of the garlic to each pan and cook for 1 minute.
2. Using your hands, crush half of the drained tomatoes into each saucepan, then divide the tomato paste, oregano and crushed red pepper between the pans. Cook the sauce over high heat, stirring, until the tomatoes are softened and the sauce is thickened, about 10 minutes. Combine the two pans of sauce; you should have 8 cups. If necessary, stir in enough of the reserved tomato liquid to make 8 cups. Add the cooked meat to the sauce and season with salt and black pepper.
3. Meanwhile, in a medium bowl, combine the spinach with the ricotta and mozzarella and season well with salt and black pepper.
4. Spread ½ cup of tomato sauce in each of two nonreactive 9-by-13-inch baking dishes. Arrange 3 lasagna noodles in each. Cover each pan of noodles with 1 cup of sauce. Dollop one-quarter of the spinach filling over the sauce in each pan. Top with another layer of noodles, sauce and the remaining spinach filling and cover with the remaining noodles. Divide the remaining sauce between the pans, spreading it to cover the noodles. Sprinkle each lasagna with ½ cup of Parmesan cheese.
5. Cover the pans with foil and bake the lasagnas for 15 minutes. Remove the foil and bake for about 5 minutes more, or until the lasagnas are bubbling. Let stand for at least 5 minutes before serving. (**MAKE AHEAD:** The cooked lasagnas can be refrigerated for 2 days or frozen for 1 month. Let the frozen lasagnas thaw overnight in the refrigerator. Cover with foil and rewarm in a 375° oven.) —SUSAN SHAPIRO JASLOVE

Veal, Lemon and Pine-Nut Sauce with farfalle

VEAL, LEMON AND PINE-NUT SAUCE

Pine nuts provide an interesting texture and a nutty flavor in this meat sauce. The sauce is designed for an inexpensive cut of veal, such as the shoulder, which will stand up to lengthy cooking. This recipe makes enough sauce for three-quarters of a pound of short-cut dried pasta, such as farfalle (butterflies), conchiglie (shells), gemelli (twins) or pennette (short quills).

4–6 SERVINGS

Four 1-inch-thick boneless veal shoulder steaks (10 to 12 ounces each)
¼ cup all-purpose flour, for dredging
2 tablespoons unsalted butter
2 tablespoons sunflower or corn oil
½ cup dry white wine
1 tablespoon finely chopped fresh rosemary or ½ teaspoon crushed dried rosemary
2 cups chicken stock or canned low-sodium broth, plus extra for reheating
Two 2-inch strips of lemon zest
½ teaspoon salt
1 tablespoon pine nuts, coarsely chopped
¼ teaspoon freshly ground white or black pepper

1. Trim any excess fat from the veal steaks and cut each in half. Spread the flour on a piece of wax paper or a large plate.

2. In a large, heavy, deep, nonreactive skillet with a lid, heat half of the butter and oil until sizzling hot. Dredge the veal in the flour and add half to the skillet. Cook over moderately high heat, turning once, until brown on both sides, about 15 minutes. Transfer to a platter and add the remaining 1 tablespoon each butter and oil to the skillet. Add the remaining meat and cook until brown, as above. Transfer the meat to the platter.

3. Add the wine and rosemary to the skillet and cook, stirring with a wooden spoon, until the wine evaporates, about 1 minute. Stir in about ⅓ cup of the stock. Return the veal to the skillet in a single layer, cover and simmer over moderately low heat until the stock is absorbed, about 10 minutes. Stir in about ¼ cup more stock at 10-minute intervals or as needed to keep the meat moist.

4. After 1 hour, add the lemon zest. Continue to cook the veal over low heat, covered, until tender, 45 to 60 minutes longer; continue to add the remaining stock at 10-minute intervals as necessary. Stir in the salt and pine nuts about 15 minutes before the meat is done. Transfer the veal to a work surface, slice it about ¼ inch thick or cut it into ½-inch dice and return it to the sauce. Stir in the pepper. (**MAKE AHEAD:** The sauce can be refrigerated for up to 3 days. Rewarm the sauce over low heat, stirring in about ¼ cup extra chicken stock.) —JULIA DELLA CROCE

CHAPTER 6

~

FISH & SHELLFISH

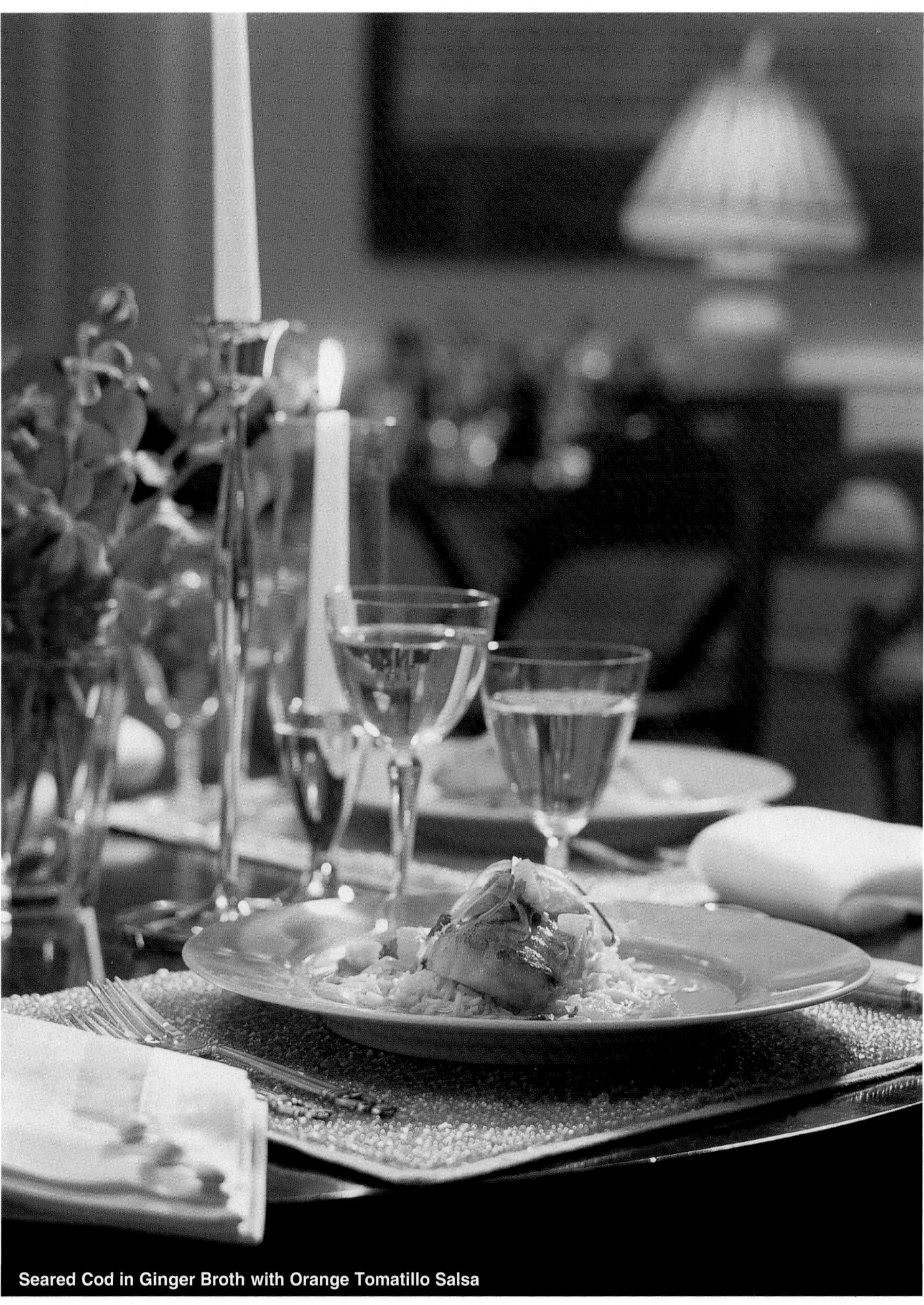

Seared Cod in Ginger Broth with Orange Tomatillo Salsa

SEARED COD IN GINGER BROTH WITH ORANGE TOMATILLO SALSA Q

Thick white fish fillets are the perfect foil for tangy sweet salsa and buttery broth; tilefish or striped-bass fillets can be substituted for the cod. After removing the zest from the orange for the broth, use the fruit in the colorful salsa.

8 SERVINGS

1 large onion, thinly sliced
1 medium carrot, coarsely chopped
1 medium celery rib, coarsely chopped
4 garlic cloves, halved
One 4-inch piece of unpeeled fresh ginger, rinsed and thinly sliced
Six ½-inch-thick strips of orange zest
1 tablespoon coriander seeds or 1 teaspoon ground coriander
1 teaspoon whole white peppercorns
1 large star-anise pod
Salt
2 cups dry white wine
1½ cups basmati or jasmine rice
2 tablespoons olive oil
Eight 7-ounce skinless, boneless cod fillets, about 2 inches thick
Freshly ground black pepper
3 tablespoons unsalted butter, softened
Orange Tomatillo Salsa (recipe follows)
Fresh cilantro sprigs, for garnish

1. In a large nonreactive saucepan, combine the onion, carrot, celery, garlic, ginger, orange zest, coriander, peppercorns, star anise and 2 teaspoons salt. Add the wine and 3 cups water; bring to a boil over high heat. Cook until reduced to 2½ cups, about 25 minutes. Strain the broth.

2. In a medium saucepan, cover the rice with 3 cups of water; add ½ teaspoon salt. Bring to a boil over moderately high heat. Reduce the heat, cover and cook until the rice is tender, about 17 minutes. Let stand, covered.

3. Divide the oil between two large nonstick skillets. Season the cod with salt and pepper; put four fillets in each skillet. Cook over high heat without turning until the bottoms are nicely browned, about 5 minutes. (MAKE AHEAD: The cod can stand at room temperature for 30 minutes. Transfer to a plate. Reheat the skillets before returning the fish to them.) Carefully turn the fillets. Pour the broth into the skillets. Simmer over moderately high heat until the cod is just opaque throughout, about 6 minutes.

4. Mound the rice in eight shallow bowls or soup plates and then set the fillets on top, browned-side up. Pour all the broth in one skillet. Whisk in the butter over moderately high heat until incorporated. Divide the broth among the bowls, garnish the fish with the salsa and cilantro and serve. ➤

PEELING GINGER

Whether or not to peel ginger is actually a matter of choice. Chinese cooks always peel it; unpeeled ginger is considered "dirty" ginger. But the skin of washed fresh ginger is paper-thin and harmless, and when you're using slices to season a sauce and plan to discard them, as in Seared Cod in Ginger Broth, it hardly seems worth the trouble. If you do choose the refinement of removing the skin, a stainless-steel vegetable peeler or paring knife will do the trick.—LAUREN MUKAMAL CAMP

ELEGANT DINNER

🍷 Set off the spicy pancakes with a tart, fruity California Brut sparkling wine, such as Domaine Carneros or Mumm Cuvée Napa. With the fish, serve a savory California Sauvignon Blanc, such as the 1994 Bernardus or the 1994 Murphy-Goode Reserve Fumé.

SWEET-POTATO PANCAKES WITH CAVIAR (P. 44)

SEARED COD IN GINGER BROTH WITH ORANGE TOMATILLO SALSA (P. 141)

CHOCOLATE MOLE BREAD PUDDING (P. 447)

GAME PLAN:

- **Assemble the bread pudding—make the chocolate cream; cut up the bread and soak it.**
- **Cut up the sweet potatoes and put them on to cook.**
- **Bake the bread pudding.**
- **Make the sweet-potato batter and fry the pancakes.**
- **Start the main course—make the ginger broth and orange salsa; cook the rice; sear the fish.**
- **Ten minutes before serving the first course, reheat the sweet-potato pancakes, then garnish them.**
- **Ten minutes before serving the main course, finish cooking the fish in the ginger broth.**

Orange Tomatillo Salsa

MAKES ABOUT 1½ CUPS

- 3 medium tomatillos, husked, rinsed, cored and coarsely chopped
- 1 large navel orange, peeled and coarsely chopped
- 1 small red onion, halved and thinly sliced
- 1 small jalapeño chile, seeded and minced
- 3 tablespoons fresh lime juice
- ¼ cup coarsely chopped fresh cilantro
- 1 teaspoon honey
- 2 tablespoons olive oil
- Salt and freshly ground pepper

In a medium bowl, combine all the ingredients except the salt and pepper. Let stand at room temperature for up to 1 hour. Season with salt and pepper before serving.—TANYA HOLLAND

ROASTED COD WITH POTATOES AND LEEKS Q

Use a food processor or mandoline to slice the potatoes very thin.

4 SERVINGS

- 3½ tablespoons unsalted butter
- 3 large leeks, white and tender green, split, thinly sliced crosswise and thoroughly rinsed (about 3 cups)
- 2 cups thinly sliced mushrooms (about 5 ounces)
- Salt and freshly ground pepper
- 2 tablespoons finely chopped fresh flat-leaf parsley
- 1½ pounds red potatoes, peeled and very thinly sliced
- 1½ cups chicken stock or canned low-sodium broth
- 1½ pounds cod fillet in one piece
- 2 teaspoons olive oil
- 1 large plum tomato, diced

1. Preheat the oven to 450°. In a large skillet, melt 1 tablespoon of the butter. Add the leeks and cook over moderately high heat, stirring, until softened, 2 to 3 minutes. Add the mushrooms, season with salt and pepper and cook, stirring, until the vegetables are tender and the juices have evaporated, about 5 minutes. Stir in 1 tablespoon of the parsley and remove from the heat.

2. Coat a 13-by-9-inch baking pan with 1 tablespoon of the butter. Layer one-third of the potato slices in the pan, overlapping slightly; sprinkle with salt and pepper. Spoon half of the leek mixture over the potatoes, top with another layer of potatoes and season with salt and pepper. Repeat with the remaining leeks and potatoes. Sprinkle with salt and pepper, dot with the remaining 1½ tablespoons butter and pour the stock around the edges. Bake in the upper third of the oven for 25 minutes, or until the potatoes are tender. If the potatoes start to overbrown, cover loosely with foil.

3. Rub the cod with the oil, season with salt and pepper and set it on the potatoes. Scatter the tomato and the remaining 1 tablespoon parsley over the fish. Bake uncovered for 8 to 10 minutes, or until just cooked through. Serve immediately, spooning any pan juices over the potatoes.—JUDITH SUTTON

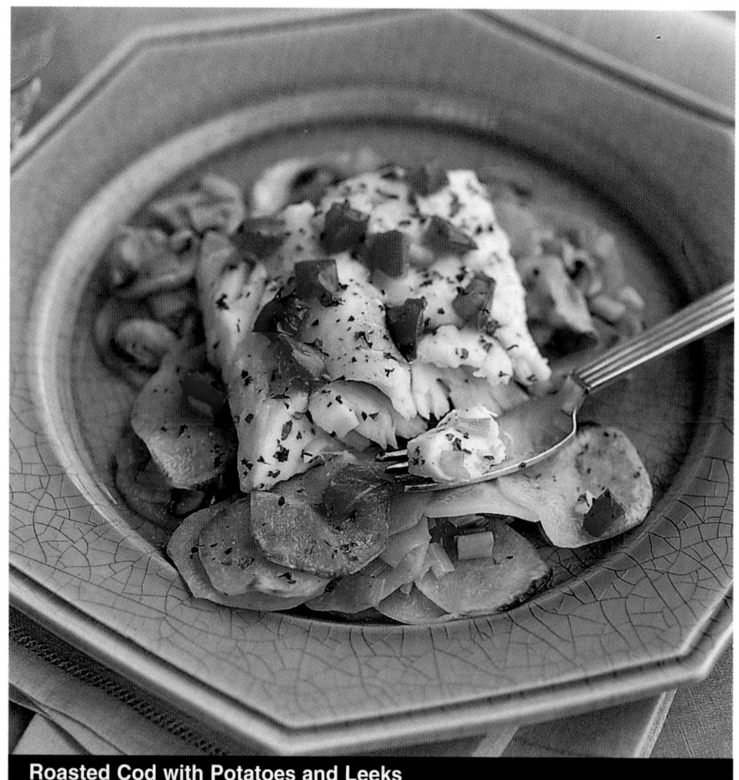
Roasted Cod with Potatoes and Leeks

CHEF'S TIP

Generally I cook fish in a hot skillet, but I've recently discovered that when I'm cooking Potato-Crusted Cod, starting the fish in an unheated pan prevents the crust from falling off or burning.—MICHAEL SCHLOW

Potato-Crusted Cod with Parsley Vinaigrette

POTATO-CRUSTED COD WITH PARSLEY VINAIGRETTE

The secret for this crisp fish is using dried potato flakes, also known as instant mashed potatoes. Do not use potato granules.

🍷 *Since cod is a mild fish, all that's needed is a simple, refreshing white wine, such as a Pinot Grigio from Italy. Among the possible choices: the 1995 Castello d'Albola or the 1995 Mezzacorona.*

4 SERVINGS

½ cup fresh flat-leaf parsley leaves
3 ice cubes
½ cup plus 3 tablespoons olive oil
2 tablespoons sherry vinegar
2½ teaspoons fresh lemon juice
Large pinch of sugar
Salt and freshly ground pepper
2 medium carrots, cut into 2-by-½-inch sticks
1½ cups fresh or frozen green peas
6 ounces assorted wild mushrooms, such as morels and stemmed shiitakes, halved or quartered if large
½ teaspoon minced fresh thyme

½ teaspoon minced fresh rosemary
½ cup dried potato flakes
2 tablespoons rice flour or cornstarch
1 large egg
Four 6-ounce skinless cod fillets, about 1½ inches thick

1. In a saucepan of boiling water, blanch the parsley leaves until they are just limp, about 30 seconds. Drain the parsley, rinse it and squeeze it dry, and then transfer the blanched parsley to a blender. Add the ice cubes and 1 tablespoon of the olive oil and blend until smooth. Transfer the parsley mixture to a bowl and whisk in the vinegar, 1½ teaspoons of the lemon juice and the sugar. Whisk in 3 tablespoons of the olive oil and season the vinaigrette with salt and pepper. (**MAKE AHEAD:** The parsley vinaigrette can stand for up to 6 hours.)

2. Heat 1 tablespoon of the olive oil in a nonreactive skillet. Add the carrot sticks and cook over moderately low heat, stirring, until they are soft and caramelized, about 20 minutes. Transfer the carrot sticks to a bowl. Meanwhile, in a saucepan of boiling salted water, cook the peas until they are tender, about 3 minutes for frozen and 10 minutes for fresh; drain.

3. Heat 2 tablespoons of the olive oil in the skillet. Add the mushrooms. Cook over moderately high heat, stirring, until the mushrooms are tender, about 5 minutes. Add the cooked peas and carrots, the remaining 1 teaspoon lemon juice and the minced fresh thyme and rosemary. Season with salt and pepper and cook until the vegetables are just heated through, about 2 minutes; keep warm.

4. In a shallow bowl, combine the dried potato flakes with the rice flour. In another shallow bowl, lightly beat the egg with 2 tablespoons of water. Season the cod fillets with salt and pepper. Dip the tops of the fillets into the egg mixture, then press into the potato-flake mixture. Put the remaining ¼ cup olive oil in a large unheated nonstick skillet. Add the cod fillets, potato-side down, and cook them over high heat until they are golden, about 7 minutes. Carefully turn the cod fillets, lower the heat to moderate and cook until the flesh of the fish flakes easily but is still slightly opaque in the center, about 3 minutes longer.

5. Spoon the mushrooms, peas and carrots onto four plates. Set the cod fillets on top of the vegetable mixture, with the crusted side up. Spoon the parsley vinaigrette around the cod fillets and serve.—MICHAEL SCHLOW

WHEN EVERY MINUTE COUNTS

You get home from work at six and your guests are due at eight. These time-saving tips can help you enjoy your own party.

IN THE DINING ROOM

Since the hours just before dinner will be devoted largely to cooking, take care of everything else the previous night.

- **Set the table. Now is the time to to iron napkins, clean silver and refill salt and pepper shakers.**
- **Put out everything you will need for serving the appetizer and the main course, including bowls, platters, pitchers and utensils.**
- **Set up a dessert tray complete with plates, cups and saucers, utensils, napkins and a coffee or tea service.**
- **Decide where you want each of your guests to sit, and then set out place cards.**
- **Create a simple centerpiece. Group several candlesticks in a variety of heights and finishes. Or place fresh herbs and ivy in a silver bowl. (If you decide to get flowers at the last minute, buy just one type so arranging them will be easy.)**

IN THE KITCHEN

- **When chopping soft-stemmed herbs like cilantro and parsley, don't bother removing the leaves from the stems.**
- **When reducing liquids, try to use a large skillet for maximum surface area.**
- **When searing or sautéing large amounts, use two pans simultaneously instead of working in batches in a single pan.**
- **To minimize chopping, buy ingredients like walnuts already chopped. For chocolate that is going to be melted, use chocolate chips.**
- **When making mashed potatoes, choose large potatoes rather than medium-size ones that take more time to peel. Cut the potatoes to speed cooking.**

CARIBBEAN FISH STEW WITH GREEN BANANAS

6 SERVINGS

2 pounds firm white-fleshed fish steaks, such as halibut, tilefish or cod, 1 to 1½ inches thick
1 tablespoon olive oil
2 large celery ribs, thinly sliced
1 large onion, coarsely chopped
1 medium green bell pepper, coarsely chopped
1 medium tomato, coarsely chopped
2 scallions, coarsely chopped
2 large garlic cloves, minced
Large pinch of saffron threads
Salt and freshly ground pepper
1 to 2 Scotch bonnet chiles, pierced with a knife
4 large fresh thyme sprigs
Three 3-inch strips of lime zest
1 teaspoon allspice berries, coarsely ground
4 large unpeeled green bananas, rinsed and thinly sliced
4 ounces okra, sliced crosswise ⅓ inch thick
1 medium zucchini, halved lengthwise and sliced crosswise ¼ inch thick
2 tablespoons fresh lime juice
Steamed white rice, for serving
Lime wedges, for serving

1. In a large saucepan, cover the fish steaks with 8 cups of water and bring just to a boil over moderately high heat. Reduce the heat to low and simmer, skimming a few times, until the fish steaks are just cooked through, about 8 minutes. Transfer the fish to a plate to cool, then remove and discard the skin and bones. Pour the fish broth into a large bowl.

2. Heat the olive oil in a large heavy saucepan. Add the celery, onion and green pepper and cook over moderately low heat, stirring, until the vegetables are wilted, about 10 minutes. Add the tomato, scallions and garlic and cook over moderately high heat, stirring, for 2 minutes. Add the fish broth and saffron, season with salt and pepper and bring to a simmer. Add the chiles, thyme, lime zest and allspice and simmer over low heat for 10 minutes.

3. In a saucepan of boiling water, simmer the banana slices over moderate heat until tender, about 10 minutes. Transfer the bananas to a plate. Add the okra to the water and simmer until it is tender, about 4 minutes. Drain the okra and add it to the banana slices.

4. Add the zucchini to the stew and simmer until tender, about 4 minutes. Discard the chiles and the lime zest. Add the bananas, okra, lime juice and fish steaks and season the stew with salt and pepper. Serve the stew with the steamed white rice and the lime wedges.—MARCIA KIESEL ➤

Q & A: WINE

Q: What are two surefire wines—one red, one white—that go well with many different foods?

A: For a foolproof white, I'd pick a Sauvignon Blanc from California. My choice: the 1994 Flora Springs Soliloquy. Neither too heavy nor too oaky, it's crisp and citrusy with a herbaceous quality that complements salads, pasta, grilled vegetables and fish.

The red I'd recommend for its range is a Pinot Noir from California or Oregon. It's elegant and fruity, with a silky, satiny texture and a lingering tartness. A top Pinot Noir, such as the 1993 Ponzi Reserve, from Oregon, offers a lot of complexity. Because it's not rich or tannic, it enhances meals that don't have lots of assertive flavors, from grilled salmon to roast chicken to veal stew.—JOHN FREDERICK WALKER

Q: What's your philosophy of pairing food with wine?

A: I base my choice of wine on what I want to drink rather than on the food being served. I think wine should be matched to the person drinking it rather than to the dish on the table. Would I drink red wine with fish? Absolutely. When would I drink a complex, profound, mature Barolo, and when a light, young, juicy Valpolicella? Whenever one or the other is what I feel like having. When would I drink white wine? Outdoors at lunch, when it is hot. What wine would I serve with oysters or smoked salmon or caviar? None. Iced vodka or very cold still water would be more agreeable. And what about dessert wines? Enjoy the wine first—or, even better, keep the wine and send the dessert back.—VICTOR HAZAN

Fish Tacos

FISH TACOS Q

For these sophisticated tacos, it's worth tracking down the delicious organic corn tortillas that are available at health-food stores.

MAKES 12 TACOS

2 tablespoons vegetable oil
1½ pounds skinless meaty fish fillets, such as snapper, bass, tilefish or cod, cut lengthwise into 1-inch strips
1 small onion, finely chopped
2 garlic cloves, minced
Salt and freshly ground pepper
2 tablespoons unsalted butter
12 corn tortillas
Mild salsa, lime wedges, shredded lettuce and diced avocado, tomato and onion, for serving

1. In a large nonreactive skillet, warm the oil over moderately high heat. Add the fish and cook until whitened but still opaque in the center, about 2 minutes per side. Add the onion and garlic, reduce the heat to moderate and cook, stirring, until the onion is wilted and the fish breaks into large flakes. Season with salt and pepper and set aside.
2. In a medium skillet, melt ½ teaspoon of the butter over moderately high heat. Add 1 tortilla and flip it to coat with butter. Cook the tortilla until blistered and lightly toasted, 1 minute per side. Repeat with the remaining butter and tortillas; wrap the tortillas in foil to keep warm.
3. Gently reheat the fish mixture and transfer it to a serving dish. Put the salsa, lime wedges, lettuce, avocado, tomato and onion in small bowls and allow your guests to assemble their own tacos.—MARCIA KIESEL

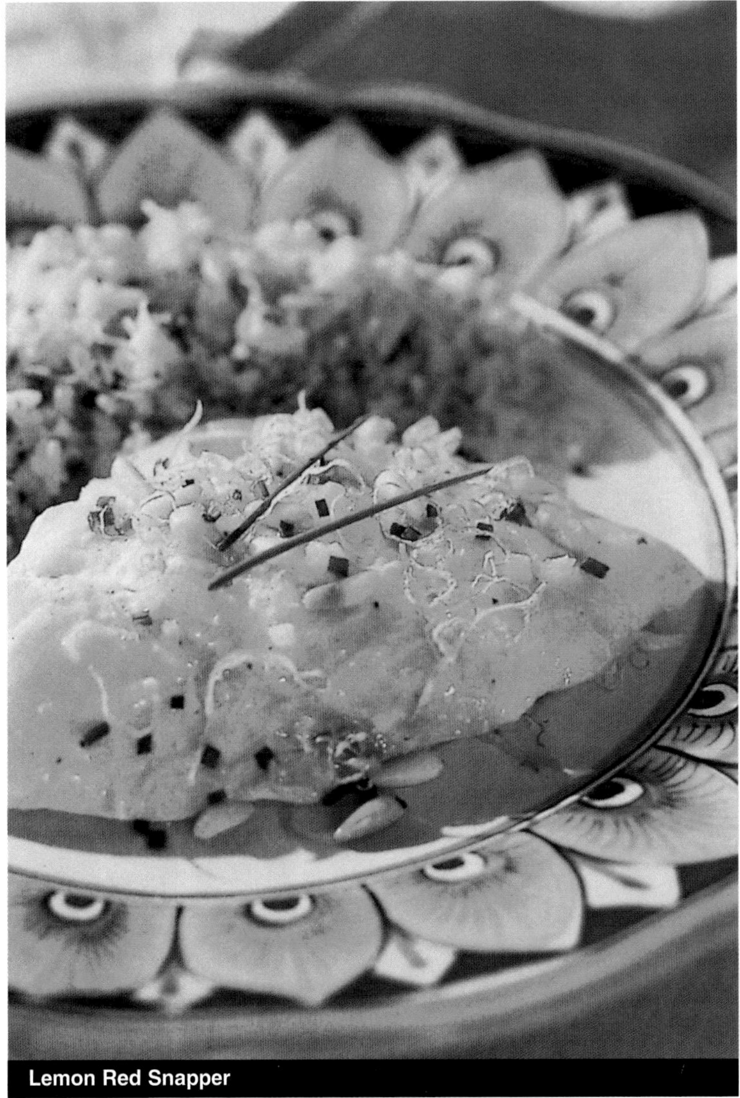
Lemon Red Snapper

CHEF'S LOW-FAT MENU

Liberal use of local citrus and tropical fruits and juices makes it easy for Allen Susser to add bright flavor to both savory and sweet dishes without using lots of fat. His philosophy is simple: Don't try to cut out oil and rich foods altogether; just use small amounts and make sure they're top quality.

Because ginger, lemons and spices can overwhelm dry, subtle wines, look for a simpler aromatic white, such as a West Coast Riesling. The 1994 Hogue Cellars Dry Johannisberg Riesling or the 1993 Trefethen White Riesling are acidic enough to stand up to the tartness and fruity enough to magnify the flavors of the shrimp and the snapper.

SHRIMP ESCABECHE WITH GINGER-GRILLED PINEAPPLE (P. 38)

LEMON RED SNAPPER (P. 147)

BANANA BRÛLÉE WITH CITRUS-FRUIT SALSA (P. 433)

LEMON RED SNAPPER LF

Don't let the length of the ingredient list deter you from making this lemon-scented fish served with coconut rice; it's simple to prepare. You can substitute skinless grouper, tilefish or flounder fillets for the snapper.

6 SERVINGS

COCONUT RICE:

1 tablespoon olive oil
1 medium onion, finely chopped
1½ cups long-grain white rice
2 tablespoons minced fresh seeded jalapeño chile
1 teaspoon minced garlic
1 cup coarsely chopped fresh spinach leaves
¼ cup canned unsweetened coconut milk
1 teaspoon ground cumin
1½ teaspoons coarse salt
½ teaspoon freshly ground pepper
2 tablespoons shredded unsweetened coconut*
2 tablespoons minced fresh cilantro
1½ tablespoons fresh lime juice
1 teaspoon finely julienned lime zest

LEMON SNAPPER:

¼ cup pine nuts
2 tablespoons finely julienned lemon zest
Six 5-ounce red-snapper fillets, with skin
1 small onion, finely chopped
½ cup fresh lemon juice

2 tablespoons dry sherry (see box, opposite page)
1 tablespoon olive oil
½ teaspoon coarse salt
½ teaspoon coarsely ground pepper
2 teaspoons minced fresh chives

*Available at health-food stores

1. Make the coconut rice: Heat the oil in a medium saucepan. Add the onion and cook over moderate heat, stirring occasionally, until translucent, about 5 minutes. Stir in the rice, jalapeño and garlic. Add the spinach, coconut milk, cumin, salt, pepper and 3 cups of water; raise the heat to high and bring to a boil. Reduce the heat to low, cover and cook until the liquid is absorbed and the rice is tender, about 20 minutes. Fluff the rice with a fork, stir in the shredded coconut, cilantro, lime juice and zest and keep warm.

2. Meanwhile, **make the lemon snapper:** Preheat the oven to 350°. In a small ovenproof saucepan, toss the pine nuts with the lemon zest and toast for about 3 minutes, or until the nuts are fragrant and lightly colored.

3. Using a sharp knife, make three ½-inch-deep slashes in each side of the snapper fillets. In a nonreactive baking dish, combine the onion, lemon juice, sherry, oil, salt and pepper. Add the fish, turn to coat and marinate for 5 minutes. Pour half of the marinade into a bowl.

4. Bake the snapper fillets for about 15 minutes, basting with the reserved marinade halfway through cooking, until opaque. Transfer to plates and spoon the pan juices on top. Garnish with the pine nuts and chives and serve with the rice.—ALLEN SUSSER

CHEF'S MENU

🍷 For the spicy flavors of this food, I like Pinot Blanc, a dry, crisp wine with some nice suggestions of fruit, specifically orange and melon, in the nose. It's a little rounder and richer than a Sauvignon Blanc. It also has more body and acidity, which makes it a great foil for the heat of the chiles. The wine exhibits excellent fruit and goes beautifully with the snapper and the squid salad. I recommend the 1994 Wild Horse Pinot Blanc.—LAWRENCE KRETCHMER

🍷 PINEAPPLE RUM COOLERS (P. 460)

GRILLED-SQUID SALAD WITH MANGO (P. 53)

RED SNAPPER GRILLED IN BANANA LEAVES (P. 148)

SAFFRON RICE SALAD (P. 315)

PECAN GRAHAM COOKIES (P. 386)

RED SNAPPER GRILLED IN BANANA LEAVES

Wrapping delicate red-snapper fillets in banana leaves protects them from the direct heat of the grill. If you can't find banana leaves, wrap the fish in foil.

8 SERVINGS

2 banana leaves,* each cut crosswise into 4 rough squares
3 tablespoons olive oil
Eight 6-ounce red-snapper fillets with skin, about ¾ inches thick
Salt and freshly ground pepper
Orange Ancho Relish (recipe follows)

*Available at Latin American and Asian markets

1. Light a charcoal grill or preheat the oven to 450°. Spread the

LOW-FAT TIPS

FROM ALLEN SUSSER

- **Go beyond grilling—try poaching and braising foods in fat-free fruit or vegetable juices.**
- **Punch up taste with top-quality seasonings; fine sea salt and freshly ground peppercorns make a bigger difference than you think.**

FROM HUBERT KELLER

- **Keep a variety of oils in clean, carefully labeled plastic spray bottles, and then use them to lightly coat foods and pans.**
- **Substitute smaller quantities of intensely flavored hard cheeses, such as Romano or Asiago, for fattier varieties. Or try using low-fat cheeses in recipes where texture is important.**

FROM VINCENT GUERITHAULT

- **Use roasted garlic cloves instead of butter to flavor potatoes (especially mashed potatoes) and for spreading on bread.**
- **Replace the heavy cream that is called for in soups and sauces with evaporated skim milk.**

banana leaves on a flat surface and brush lightly with half of the oil. Set a fish fillet, skin-side down, on each leaf and brush with the remaining oil. Season the fish with salt and pepper and fold up the banana leaves like an envelope to enclose the fish.

2. Set the packets, seam-side down, on the grill. Cover the grill and cook for 7 minutes. Alternatively, arrange the fish packets, seam-side down, on a large baking sheet and bake in the oven for 7 minutes. Serve the fish in the banana leaves so each guest can unwrap his own. Pass the relish separately.

Orange Ancho Relish

MAKES ABOUT 2 CUPS

- 3 medium navel oranges
- 1 medium ancho chile, stem and seeds removed
- 3 tablespoons fresh lime juice
- 1 tablespoon olive oil
- 1 tablespoon finely shredded fresh mint
- 1½ teaspoons minced garlic
- 1 teaspoon honey
- Salt and freshly ground pepper

1. Using a sharp paring knife, peel the oranges, removing all the bitter white pith. Cut between the membranes to release the orange segments into a medium bowl.

2. Coarsely grind the chile in a spice grinder or finely chop it with a knife. Transfer the chile to a bowl and add the lime juice, oil, mint, garlic and honey. Gently stir the mixture into the oranges. Let the relish stand at room temperature for 45 minutes. Season with salt and pepper before serving.—BOBBY FLAY

DRY SHERRY

Q: If a recipe calls for dry sherry, which one should I use and why?

A: You can use any brand of dry sherry imported to the United States from Spain. Since sherry is a blended wine, there is remarkably little difference in quality among brands. To be sure a sherry is truly dry, look for the word *fino* or *manzanilla* on the label. Don't use American sherry-style wines; they are inferior to Spanish sherries and somewhat sweet for general cooking.—PENELOPE CASAS

STEAMED FISH WITH GINGER AND SCALLIONS LF

4 SERVINGS

- 2 tablespoons light soy sauce
- 2 tablespoons dry white wine
- 2 teaspoons white-wine vinegar
- 2 teaspoons peanut oil
- ⅛ teaspoon salt
- Generous pinch of freshly ground white pepper
- One 2-pound whole red snapper, striped bass or sea bass, cleaned, head and tail intact
- 2½ tablespoons julienned fresh ginger
- 3 scallions, 2 cut into 2-inch lengths, 1 thinly sliced
- About 8 cups of boiling water
- 1 teaspoon Asian sesame oil
- 1½ tablespoons minced fresh cilantro

1. In a small bowl, stir together the soy sauce, wine, vinegar, peanut oil, salt and white pepper. ➤

Steamed Fish with Ginger and Scallions, and Fried Rice with Asparagus (p. 317)

LOW-FAT MENU

🍷 The peaches-and-pears aroma of Rieslings are ideal for this menu. The wine's fruitiness balances the spicy soup and the ginger flavor of the fish. Consider the 1994 Bonny Doon Pacific Rim Riesling from California or the 1993 Willi Schaefer Wehlener Sonnenuhr Riesling Spätlese from Germany.

VEGETARIAN HOT-AND-SOUR SOUP (P. 80)

STEAMED FISH WITH GINGER AND SCALLIONS (P. 149)

FRIED RICE WITH ASPARAGUS (P. 317)

2. Set the fish in a 10-inch glass or ceramic pie pan and rub the marinade all over the fish, inside and out. Sprinkle ½ tablespoon of the ginger and half of the cut scallions in the cavity; spread the remaining cut scallions and 1 more tablespoon of the ginger under the fish. Sprinkle the remaining 1 tablespoon ginger over the fish.

3. Set a cake rack in a wok and pour in enough boiling water to reach 1 inch below the rack. Set the fish on the cake rack; then cover the wok with a lid and steam the fish over high heat just until the flesh flakes easily and is opaque throughout, about 20 minutes.

4. Using two large metal spatulas, transfer the fish to a platter. Pour the juices in the pie pan over the fish and drizzle with the sesame oil. Garnish with the sliced scallion and cilantro and serve.—EILEEN YIN-FEI LO

STEAMING TIPS

To make the most of steaming, be sure that the rack sits at least one inch above the water in the wok. Have boiling water on hand to replenish any water that evaporates. Steam marinated or sauced items in a pan or on a plate to save the juices. If the lid of the wok is loose, wrap a wet towel around it to seal in the steam.

Seared Black Sea Bass in Roasted-Tomato Broth

SEARED BLACK SEA BASS IN ROASTED-TOMATO BROTH

4 SERVINGS

Four 6-ounce black-sea-bass, striped-bass or red-snapper fillets
Salt and freshly ground pepper
4 roasted-tomato halves from Roasted Tomatoes (p. 362)
12 bay leaves
4 large fresh thyme sprigs, plus 1 tablespoon thyme leaves
2½ tablespoons extra-virgin olive oil, plus more for serving
1½ cups tomato juices from Roasted Tomatoes (p. 362)

1. Put the bass fillets together to form two whole fish; cut each one crosswise to form two pieces of equal weight; the thinner tail pieces will be longer. Separate the fillets and season them with salt and pepper. Lay a roasted tomato on half of the fillet pieces and top with 2 bay leaves and a thyme sprig. Cover with the matching fillets and tie each bundle in three places with kitchen string. Insert a bay leaf under a string in each bundle and season with salt and pepper.

2. In a large skillet, heat the 2½ tablespoons olive oil over moderately high heat. Add the fish bundles to the pan. Cook the fish over moderate heat until the skin is browned and the bottom fillets are just cooked through, about 5 minutes. Turn the bundles, reduce the heat to low and cook the second side; the thinner pieces will be done first.

3. Meanwhile, in a small nonreactive saucepan, gently simmer the tomato juices for 3 minutes. Season with salt and pepper.

4. Spoon the tomato juices onto plates. Set the fish bundles on top. Garnish with thyme leaves and a drizzle of oil. Don't eat the strings or bay leaves.—TOM COLICCHIO

SEA BASS WITH CITRUS COUSCOUS LF

6 SERVINGS

SAUCE:

- 1 tablespoon olive oil
- 1 pound red onions, sliced lengthwise ¼ inch thick
- 2 cups fresh orange juice
- 2 tablespoons finely chopped fresh flat-leaf parsley
- Pinch of ground coriander
- Dash of Tabasco sauce
- Salt and freshly ground pepper

COUSCOUS AND FISH:

- 3 cups vegetable stock or canned low-sodium broth
- Finely grated zest of 1 orange
- Finely grated zest of 1 lemon, plus juice of ½ lemon
- Finely grated zest of 1 lime
- ¼ teaspoon Asian chili paste
- 1 tablespoon plus 1 teaspoon olive oil
- 10 ounces instant couscous
- Salt and freshly ground pepper
- Six 5-ounce skinless, boneless sea-bass fillets, about 1 inch thick
- Flat-leaf parsley sprigs, for garnish

1. Make the sauce: Heat the oil in a nonreactive medium saucepan. Add the onions and cook over moderately low heat, stirring, until softened, about 8 minutes. Add the orange juice and cook over moderately high heat until reduced by half, about 8 minutes. Add the parsley, coriander and Tabasco. Season with salt and pepper; keep warm.

2. Make the couscous and fish: In a nonreactive medium saucepan, combine the stock, citrus zests, chili paste and the 1 tablespoon oil and bring to a boil over high heat. Stir in the couscous, cover and let stand off the heat until the liquid is absorbed, about 10 minutes. Season with salt and pepper and fluff with a fork.

3. Light a grill or preheat the broiler. Rub the sea bass with the remaining 1 teaspoon oil and season on both sides with salt and pepper. Grill or broil for about 2 minutes, or until lightly golden and sizzling. Gently turn the fish, drizzle on the lemon juice and broil for about 3 minutes longer, or until just cooked through.

4. Divide the couscous among six plates. Arrange the fish on top, spoon the sauce over and garnish with parsley.—HANS RÖCKENWAGNER

PAN-ROASTED SEA BASS WITH WILD MUSHROOMS

You need thick, firm-fleshed fillets to take the heat of pan-roasting; sea bass is ideal because the skin crisps up nicely in the hot pan. Tilefish is also good.

4 SERVINGS

- 2 tablespoons olive oil
- 2 pounds assorted fresh mushrooms, such as white, shiitake, oyster or chanterelle, shiitake stems trimmed or discarded, large mushrooms quartered
- 5 tablespoons cold unsalted butter
- Salt and freshly ground pepper
- 3 medium leeks, white and tender green, finely chopped
- ½ cup chicken stock or canned low-sodium broth
- 2 tablespoons vegetable oil
- Four 6-ounce sea-bass fillets with skin, about 1½ inches thick
- ¼ cup finely chopped fresh flat-leaf parsley

1. Heat the oil in a large skillet until almost smoking. Add the mushrooms; cook over moderately high heat, stirring, 2 minutes. Stir in 1 tablespoon butter; reduce the heat to low. Cook until the mushrooms are browned and the pan is dry, about 7 minutes. Season with salt and pepper. Put in a saucepan. ➤

LOW-FAT MENU

🍷 A fruity California Blanc de Noirs has enough flavor to balance the shrimp cocktail and complement the sea bass.

SHRIMP COCKTAIL WITH BLOODY-MARY SORBET (P. 37)

SEA BASS WITH CITRUS COUSCOUS (P. 151)

FRUIT SOUP WITH CHAMPAGNE (P. 422)

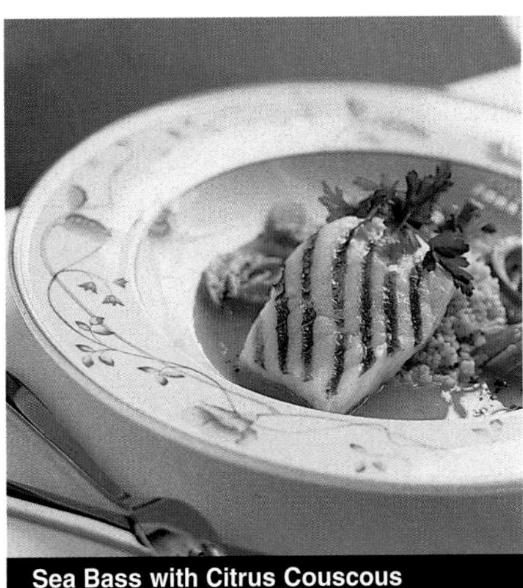

Sea Bass with Citrus Couscous

2. Preheat the oven to 450°. Melt another 2 tablespoons of butter in the skillet. Add the leeks, cover and cook over low heat, stirring a few times, until tender, about 10 minutes. Season with salt and pepper; add to the mushrooms along with the stock. Simmer for 3 minutes. Season with salt and pepper.

3. In a large, heavy-bottomed ovenproof skillet, heat the vegetable oil until almost smoking. Season the fish with salt and pepper. Add to the skillet, skin-side down, and shake to loosen the fillets. Cook over high heat until the skin is crisp and browned, about 5 minutes. Turn the fish. Transfer the skillet to the oven. Roast about 4 minutes, or until just cooked through.

4. Cut the remaining 2 tablespoons butter into pieces and stir into the sauce with the parsley. Divide the sauce among four large plates. Set the fish on top; serve at once.—TRACI DES JARDINS

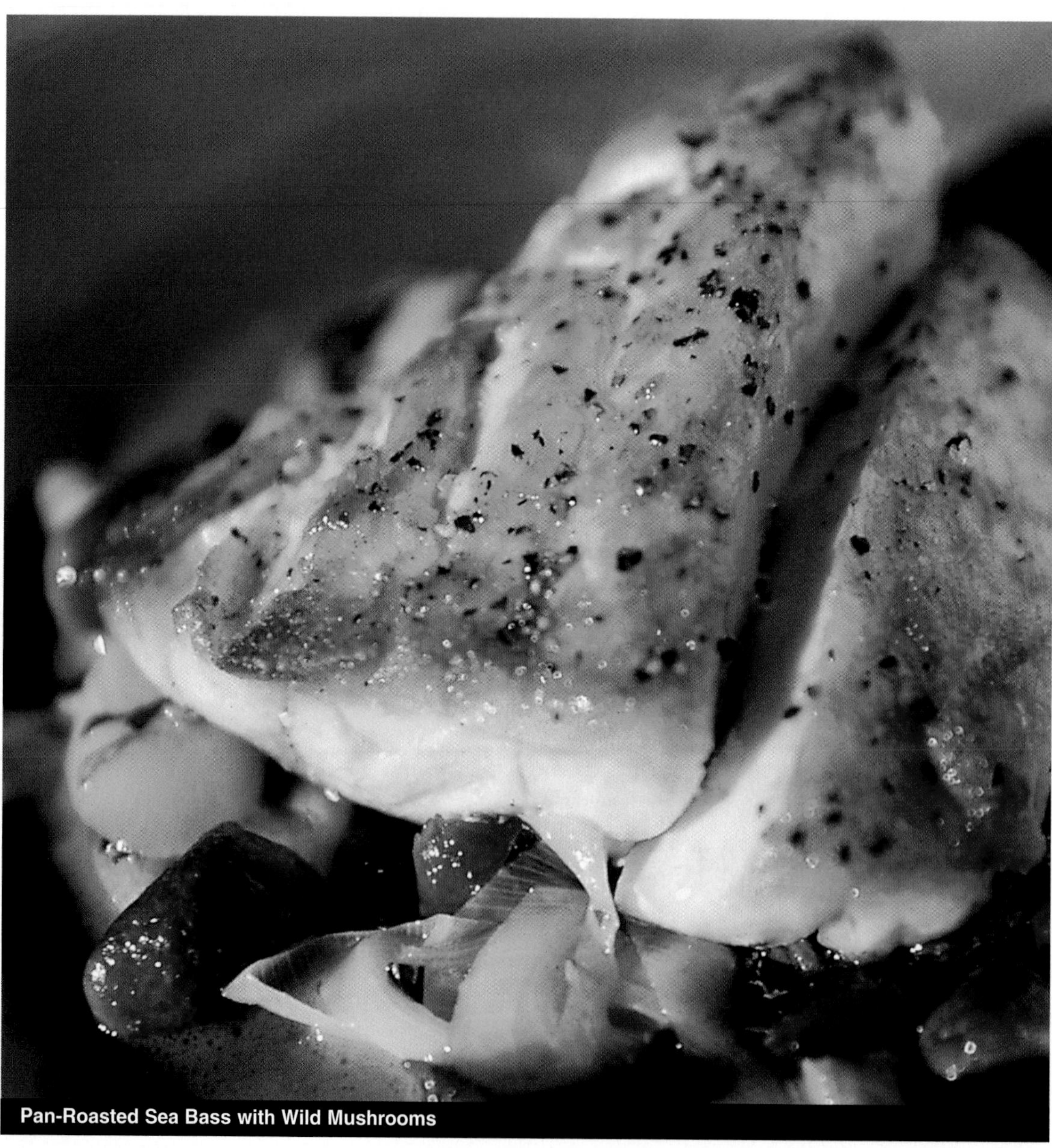

Pan-Roasted Sea Bass with Wild Mushrooms

PAN-ROASTING

Pan-roasting is a simple technique that involves searing food on top of the stove, then completing the cooking in a hot oven. The requirements are basic—a good, heavy ovenproof pan and a little oil—and the execution is easy. Pan-roasting is great for a wide variety of meats, poultry, seafood and vegetables. It's popular with chefs these days partly because it sounds so tempting, partly because it makes cooking for a group as easy as cooking for one.

Some menus use the term loosely, referring to dishes as pan-roasted when in fact they're simply roasted or braised. But I'm a purist: I always start the food in a hot pan on top of the stove to form a crispy browned crust that seals in the juices. Then the pan goes into a preheated oven. I don't crowd the pan with stocks or vegetables, which can keep the main ingredient from cooking properly.

This method produces succulent lamb chops (p. 253), tender chicken breasts (p. 196) and moist tuna steaks (p. 164), dishes where a golden crust and juicy meat are all important. With foods like lobster (p. 168), which don't develop a crust, pan-roasting imparts an appealing smoky flavor that sets off their natural sweetness.—TRACI DES JARDINS

FISH WRAPPED IN RICE PAPER LF

Serve these slightly spicy fish bundles on a bed of steamed spinach. Brush any leftover ginger paste on grilled pork.

4 SERVINGS

- ½ cup candied ginger in heavy syrup,* drained
- 1 chipotle chile packed in adobo,* seeded and minced
- 1 garlic clove, minced
- 1 tablespoon soy sauce
- 1 cup fresh orange juice
- 1 cup fresh carrot juice
- ½ teaspoon cornstarch, dissolved in 1 tablespoon water
- Four 9-inch rice-paper wrappers*
- 1 large egg white, beaten with 2 tablespoons warm water
- Four 4-ounce white-fleshed fish fillets with skin, such as striped bass, about ¾ inch thick
- Salt
- 2 tablespoons fresh cilantro leaves
- Vegetable cooking spray

*Available at specialty-food stores

1. Preheat the oven to 375°. In a mini-processor, process the ginger, chipotle, garlic and soy sauce into a paste. In a nonreactive saucepan, boil the orange juice and the carrot juice over high heat until the liquid is reduced to ¾ cup, about 15 minutes. Stir in the cornstarch and simmer until thickened. Stir in 1 teaspoon of the ginger paste and keep warm.

2. Brush the rice-paper wrappers on both sides with the egg white and let stand until pliable, about 2 minutes. Season the fish fillets lightly with salt, brush the flesh of each with 1 teaspoon of the ginger paste and top with the cilantro. Set the fish, skin-side up, on the wrappers and fold up the sides like an envelope to enclose the fish.

Fish Wrapped in Rice Paper

3. Coat a smooth-bottomed nonstick ovenproof skillet with vegetable cooking spray and heat. Add the fish packets, seam-side down, and cook over moderate heat until golden and crisp, about 3 minutes. Spray the fish packets, turn and cook until golden, about 3 minutes. Turn the fish packets seam-side down and bake them in the oven for 3 to 5 minutes, or until the fish is firm when pressed. Make a pool of carrot sauce on four plates, set a fish packet on each and serve.—GRACE PARISI ➤

Fish Boil

FISH BOIL

This scaled-down but authentic version of Door County, Wisconsin's fish boil is from Clambakes and Fish Fries *(Workman) and features the usual red potatoes and local whitefish, plus onions. Striped bass, lake trout, salmon and bluefish are other good candidates for this recipe.*

4 SERVINGS

1½ pounds medium red potatoes, scrubbed
8 small onions, peeled, stem ends intact
2 tablespoons coarse salt
Four ½-pound whitefish steaks
2 tablespoons finely chopped fresh flat-leaf parsley
Freshly ground pepper
Melted unsalted butter, for serving
Lemon wedges, for serving

1. In a large stockpot, combine the red potatoes and the onions and add about 2 quarts of water, enough to cover the vegetables by 2 inches. Stir in the coarse salt. Bring the water to a boil over high heat. Partially cover the stockpot and cook until the potatoes are almost tender when pierced with a fork, about 15 minutes.

2. Arrange the whitefish steaks in the stockpot in a single layer on top of the onions and red potatoes; don't worry if the fish steaks aren't covered with water. Partially cover the stockpot again, lower the heat to moderate and cook until the whitefish flakes easily with a fork, about 10 minutes longer.

3. Using a slotted spoon, transfer the whitefish steaks from the stockpot to a large, warm platter. Spoon the red potatoes and onions around the fish. Sprinkle with the parsley and a generous amount of pepper. Serve the whitefish and vegetables with the melted unsalted butter and the lemon wedges alongside.—SUSAN HERRMANN LOOMIS

MARINATED FRIED SOLE

In Venice's bacari, *or wine bars,* sfogi in saor*—small sole fried and marinated in vinegar with onions, pine nuts and raisins—is a favorite dish.*

4–6 SERVINGS

¼ cup raisins
1 pound sole fillets
Vegetable oil, for frying
All-purpose flour, for dredging
Salt
2 tablespoons extra-virgin olive oil
1 large onion, very thinly sliced
½ teaspoon sugar
1 cup red-wine vinegar diluted with 1 tablespoon water
3 tablespoons pine nuts

1. In a small bowl, soak the raisins in enough warm water to cover. Cut the sole fillets in half lengthwise, then cut them into 3-inch strips.

2. Pour ½ inch of vegetable oil into a large nonreactive skillet and turn the heat to high. Pat the sole fillets dry with paper towels, then turn them lightly in the flour and shake off the excess. When the vegetable oil is hot, fry the sole fillets until they are deep gold on both sides. Using a slotted spatula, transfer the fried fillets to paper towels; sprinkle them with salt. Discard the vegetable oil and wipe out the skillet.

3. Add the olive oil, onion, sugar and a large pinch of salt to the skillet. Cover and cook over low heat, stirring occasionally from time to time, until the onion is completely limp but still pale, 15 to 20 minutes. Uncover the skillet and cook the onion over moderate heat until the liquid boils off and the onion is a light nut brown, about 3 minutes. Add the diluted red-wine vinegar and boil over high heat for 3 minutes. Remove the skillet from the heat and let cool.

4. Drain the raisins and pat them dry. Place the fried sole fillets in a ceramic or glass dish that will hold them snugly. Using a slotted spoon, spread the onion over the fish. Sprinkle the pine nuts and the raisins on top and then pour the remaining liquid from the skillet over all. Cover the fish with plastic wrap. Set aside at room temperature for up to 12 hours or refrigerate for up to 5 days. Let the fish come to room temperature before serving.—MARCELLA HAZAN

SALMON TROUT TOURNEDOS WITH RED-WINE JUS

The wrapped fillets mimic the shape of classic beef-tenderloin tournedos. If you can find large fillets, serve two tournedos for each serving rather than three smaller ones.

🍷 *A Pinot Noir is light enough to serve with fish and fruity enough to balance the salty bacon. Try the 1993 Beaulieu Vineyard Carneros Reserve or the 1993 Faiveley Mercurey Clos des Myglands.*

4 SERVINGS

- Twelve 4-inch scallion greens
- Six 4- to 5-ounce salmon-trout fillets
- ½ unpeeled medium Golden Delicious apple, cored and cut into 12 thin wedges
- 6 bacon slices, halved crosswise
- 1⅔ cups dry red wine, preferably Pinot Noir
- 3 shallots, coarsely chopped
- 1 fresh rosemary sprig
- 1 cup chicken stock or canned low-sodium broth
- ½ cup veal or duck demiglace
- Salt and freshly ground pepper
- 1½ tablespoons unsalted butter
- ½ pound fresh oyster mushrooms, stems discarded, caps halved
- 1 pound fresh spinach, large stems discarded

1. In a small saucepan of boiling salted water, blanch the scallion greens for 1 minute. Transfer to a bowl of ice water to cool and pat dry.

2. Diagonally cut each of the salmon-trout fillets in half to form two triangular pieces. Top each of the fish pieces with a blanched scallion green and an apple wedge. Starting from the thin end of the fish fillet, roll the salmon trout around the apple wedge and scallion. Wrap a half-slice of bacon around each of the rolls and secure the tournedo with string.

3. Preheat the oven to 350°. In a nonreactive saucepan, boil the red wine, the chopped shallots and the rosemary sprig over high heat until reduced to a thick syrup, about 12 minutes. Add the chicken stock and reduce to ¾ cup, about 5 minutes. Strain the sauce and return it to the pan. Add the demiglace and bring to a simmer. (**MAKE AHEAD:** The sauce can stand at room temperature for 6 hours; refrigerate the tournedos.)

4. Heat a large nonstick skillet. Season the salmon-trout tournedos with salt and pepper and set half of them in the skillet with the bacon side down. Cook the tournedos over moderately high heat, turning once, until the bacon is browned, about 3 minutes per side. Transfer the cooked

Q & A: NONSTICK SAFETY

Q: Do nonstick surfaces present any particular safety hazards?

A: Everyone agrees that nonstick cookware is safe at low to medium temperatures; it is FDA-approved. But manufacturers and consumer advocates emphasize that this cookware should not be exposed to high heat for a long period of time—and never when empty. DuPont warns that nonstick cookware can emit odorless fumes that are toxic to small birds at temperatures above 500° F. An empty lightweight aluminum pan over high heat can get that hot in a bit more than a minute; a heavier bonded pan will take about four minutes. And how about people? Food scientist Harold McGee says that the fumes are dangerous to human health when inhaled. Christa Kaiser, DuPont's worldwide communications manager for Teflon finishes, responds: "Under extremely rare conditions, nonstick cookware can emit fumes. When the heat is too high and there is no ventilation, these fumes can produce a condition called polymer-fume fever. It's flu-like, requires no treatment and has no long-term effects." My advice: use heavy pans and keep the heat low.

Q: Can I use metal utensils with nonstick cooking equipment?

A: Even if the manufacturer says you can, don't! Abrasion shortens the life of any coating. Use plastic, nylon or wooden utensils.

Q: Can I still cook in a pan if its nonstick surface is scratched?

A: Yes. The food you're cooking may stick, but the FDA says that any scraps of coating you may consume accidentally are harmless and pass through the body unchanged.—DEBORAH KRASNER

tournedos to a baking sheet and repeat with the remaining bundles. Discard the strings, cover the tournedos with foil and bake for about 4 minutes, or until the fish is firm.

5. Wipe out the skillet and melt ½ tablespoon of the butter in it. Add the mushrooms, season with salt and pepper and cook over high heat until they are browned on the bottom, about 4 minutes. Stir, then cook until the mushrooms are browned all over, about 2 minutes longer. Transfer the mushrooms to a plate. Add the spinach to the skillet and cook until wilted and the excess liquid is evaporated, 3 to 5 minutes. Season the spinach with salt and pepper and add the mushrooms.

6. To serve, reheat the sauce and whisk in the remaining 1 tablespoon butter. Spoon the spinach and mushroom mixture onto four plates. Set three salmon trout tournedos on each mound of spinach and spoon the red-wine jus around.—CHARLES DALE

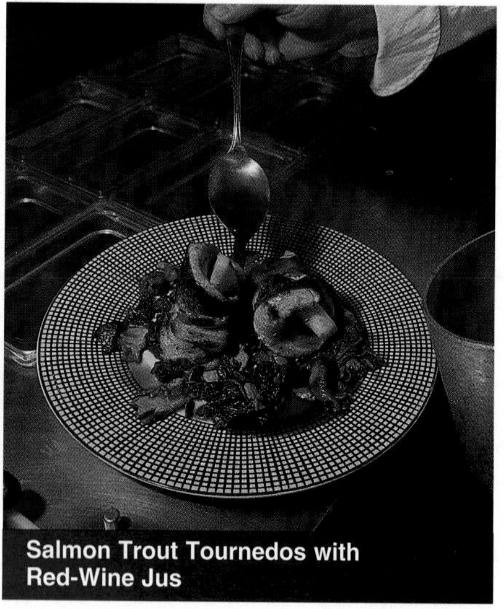

Salmon Trout Tournedos with Red-Wine Jus

MONKFISH WITH SPICY GARLIC VINAIGRETTE

This delicious main dish hails from the Basque province of Vizcaya. It can be made with other fish, such as tuna or red snapper. Serve with scalloped, pureed or mashed potatoes.

1994 Martin Codax Albariño

4 SERVINGS

- ½ cup olive oil
- 2 tablespoons lemon juice
- 1 teaspoon coarse salt
- 1½ pounds cleaned monkfish fillets, cut crosswise into 1-inch medallions
- 2 garlic cloves, thinly sliced
- 1 tablespoon crushed red pepper
- 1 tablespoon sherry vinegar
- 1 tablespoon chopped parsley

1. Combine 2 tablespoons of the olive oil with the lemon juice and salt. Stir to dissolve the salt.

2. Heat a large nonstick skillet over high heat. When the pan is hot, dip half of the monkfish medallions into the oil marinade. Place the medallions in the skillet without touching and sear, turning once, until they are golden brown, about 2 minutes per side. Transfer the cooked medallions to a warm platter. Repeat with the remaining monkfish medallions.

3. Wipe out the skillet. Add the remaining 6 tablespoons oil and warm over moderate heat. Add the garlic and cook until golden, about 2 minutes. Stir in the red pepper and vinegar.

4. Pour the sauce over the fish and sprinkle the parsley on top.—TERESA BARRENECHEA

Catfish with Tomatillo and Garlic Sauce

CATFISH WITH TOMATILLO AND GARLIC SAUCE

Meaty, moist catfish is good for grilling or broiling. Have your fishmonger cut steaks from a whole fish. Or substitute thick catfish fillets or bluefish steaks or fillets. This sauce is also great with skewered grilled scallops.

This dish calls for a medium-weight beer, well-chilled. Try Anchor Steam from San Francisco or Grolsch from the Netherlands.

4 SERVINGS

- Eight 4-ounce catfish steaks, about 1 inch thick
- 2 cups Roasted-Tomatillo Chipotle Salsa (p. 356)
- 2 tablespoons vegetable oil
- 12 unpeeled garlic cloves
- 1 medium onion, thinly sliced
- ¼ to ½ teaspoon ground cumin, preferably freshly ground
- ¼ teaspoon freshly ground pepper
- ⅔ cup fish stock, chicken stock or canned low-sodium chicken broth

Salt
Coarsely chopped fresh cilantro, for garnish

1. Lay the catfish steaks in a large nonreactive baking dish. Mix ¼ cup of the salsa with 1 tablespoon of the oil, then brush the mixture on both sides of the fish. Cover and refrigerate for at least 2 hours or for up to 6 hours.
2. Heat a large nonreactive skillet over moderate heat. Add the garlic cloves and toast, turning occasionally, until softened and blackened in spots, about 15 minutes. Let cool slightly, then peel.
3. Heat the remaining 1 tablespoon oil in the skillet. Add the onion and cook over moderately high heat, stirring occasionally, until beginning to brown, about 5 minutes. Add the remaining 1¾ cups salsa to the skillet along with the cumin, pepper and toasted garlic cloves. Cook, stirring, until slightly thickened, about 3 minutes. Stir in the stock, reduce the heat to low and simmer for 10 minutes. Season with salt.
4. Light a grill or preheat the oven to 450° and heat a large cast-iron grill pan. Remove the fish from the marinade; season lightly with salt. If grilling, cook on a lightly oiled grill, turning once, for 4 to 6 minutes per side, or until nicely seared and cooked through. Alternatively, lightly oil the grill pan and cook over moderately high heat until nicely browned, about 3 minutes. Turn the fish and bake in the oven for about 5 minutes, or until cooked through.
5. Transfer the fish to a serving platter, spoon the sauce over and around and garnish with cilantro. Serve at once.—RICK BAYLESS ➤

Q & A: NONSTICK COOKWARE

Q: What are the different kinds of nonstick surfaces? Are they all basically the same?

A: All nonstick surfaces are various formulations of polytetrafluoroethylene (PTFE) and hardeners, and are nonreactive (that is, they do not react with food) as long as they are undamaged. But they're not all the same. All new nonstick cookware may perform identically, but repeated use reveals enormous differences in durability. Today's newest and toughest reinforced nonstick surfaces are Autograph (made by DuPont) and Excalibur (made by Whitford).

Q: Does it make any difference what kind of metal the pan itself is made of?

A: Yes. The coating is only part of the story. The pan's material, its weight and the way the heat is distributed are also critical. High heat damages the bond between the coating and the pan. Because heavy materials take longer to transmit the heat and thus affect the coating, they are a better base for nonstick coating. HARD ANODIZED ALUMINUM has three advantages: its porous molecular structure (a plus for bonding), good conductivity and hard anodized surface. CAST ALUMINUM has a softer and more vulnerable surface, but it bonds well with a quality nonstick coating. Because the metal is cast, the sides can be made thin and the bottoms thick, for a pan that is lighter in weight and easier to handle. STAINLESS STEEL offers a hard surface for bonding, but it's a poor heat conductor; it should be clad or bonded with a more conductive metal (usually thick aluminum or thinner copper). The best pans have a triple-ply base, with stainless steel protectively sandwiching softer, conductive aluminum or copper. (Magnetized stainless-steel cookware is suitable for electric induction cooking.) ENAMELED STEEL heats up quickly and browns food as well as a comparable-quality stainless-steel pan with an aluminum core. (Because enameled steel pots and pans have an iron-rich core of carbon steel, they are also good for electric induction cooktops.)

Q: Are nonstick pans with textured surfaces, like mottling or fine ridges, better than those with flat surfaces?

A: Assuming that the quality of the coating, the bonding and the basic pan are equivalent, the cooking differences are small, although in my side-by-side tests the food in the flat pan cooked slightly faster. All of these surfaces are equally easy to clean (although food may get stuck in very fine grooves), but textures do make it easier to keep the food above any fat it may release. The coating on textured pans is also more durable, because abrasion can occur only on the highest points of the surface.—DEBORAH KRASNER

CRISP PAN-SEARED SALMON Q

Try an oaky Chardonnay, such as the 1994 Cakebread from California or the 1993 Louis Jadot Puligny-Montrachet from France.

SEARING

Perfect pan-seared salmon depends on a very hot pan. Use a heavy cast-iron skillet, which heats evenly. Warm the pan before you add the oil; this restaurant trick allows the pan to get really hot without burning the oil. A preheated pan also requires less oil. Try this method with other meaty fish or even with sea scallops; they will be golden brown outside and tender inside.

4 SERVINGS

1 teaspoon olive oil
Four 6-ounce skinless center-cut pieces of salmon fillet, about 1¼ inches thick
Scant ¾ teaspoon coarse salt
¼ teaspoon freshly ground pepper

Set a large cast-iron skillet over high heat. When a drop of water skitters on the surface of the pan, after about 3 minutes, add the olive oil. Tilt the pan to coat the bottom evenly and heat until the oil is almost smoking, about 30 seconds. Season the salmon fillets with the salt and pepper and add them to the skillet, skinned-side up. Cook until the salmon fillets are golden brown on the bottom, about 4 minutes. Turn the salmon, lower the heat to moderate and sear until the fillets are just cooked, 3 to 4 minutes longer.—JUDITH SUTTON

SALMON STEAKS TO BRAGG ABOUT

Despite its unappealing name, Bragg Liquid Aminos, a soybean-based sauce, gives the fish a rich, meaty flavor. It's available at health-food stores.

A glass of Duvel or Chimay is the ideal accompaniment to the savory salmon.

4 SERVINGS

⅓ cup Bragg Liquid Aminos sauce
2 tablespoons minced fresh ginger
Four 6-ounce salmon steaks (about ½ inch thick)
2 tablespoons vegetable oil
Freshly ground pepper
Steamed basmati rice, for serving

1. In a shallow baking dish, combine the Bragg sauce and ginger. Add the salmon and turn to coat.

QUICK DINNER

CRISP PAN-SEARED SALMON (P. 158)

GLAZED CUCUMBERS (P. 333)

TABBOULEH (P. 324)

TOASTED-COCONUT CHOCOLATE ICE-CREAM PIE (P. 415)

GAME PLAN:

- **Soak the bulgur. Toast the coconut for the ice-cream pie.**
- **Make the tabbouleh.**
- **Make and freeze the pie crust.**
- **Slice the cucumbers.**
- **Fill and freeze the pie.**
- **Sauté the cucumbers.**
- **Sear the salmon and serve.**

Crisp Pan-Seared Salmon, with Glazed Cucumbers (p. 333) and Tabbouleh (p. 324)

Let marinate in the refrigerator for 15 to 30 minutes.

2. Preheat the oven to 375°. Heat the oil in a large ovenproof skillet. Scrape the ginger from the salmon into the marinade; reserve the marinade. Season the salmon with pepper and cook over moderately high heat until browned on the bottom, about 4 minutes. Turn, transfer the skillet to the oven and bake for about 4 minutes, or until cooked through.

3. Meanwhile, pour the reserved marinade into a small saucepan. Bring to a simmer over moderate heat. Cook until reduced by half.

4. Transfer the salmon steaks to a platter; pour a little of the reduced marinade over them. Serve the remaining sauce spooned over the rice.—CASSANDRA DOOLEY

PISTACHIO-TOPPED SALMON WITH TWO SAUCES

The leftover curry and orange sauces can also be sprinkled on roast lamb, chicken, vegetables and fish.

🍷 *Go for a distinctive white Burgundy, such as the 1993 Bouchard Père et Fils Beaune Clos Saint-Landry, or a well-balanced California Chardonnay, such as the 1994 Robert Mondavi Napa Valley Unfiltered.*

6 SERVINGS

CURRY AND ORANGE SAUCES:

- 2 tablespoons Madras curry powder
- ¾ cup plus 1 tablespoon peanut oil
- 2 tablespoons plus 1 teaspoon minced shallots
- 2 tablespoons plus 1 teaspoon minced fresh ginger
- ¼ cup plus 2 teaspoons rice vinegar
- 1 tablespoon fresh lime juice
- ½ teaspoon soy sauce
- 1 tablespoon honey
- Salt and freshly ground pepper
- 2 cups fresh orange juice
- 2 tablespoons finely chopped fresh jalapeño chiles
- 1 small navel orange
- 2 teaspoons red-wine vinegar
- 2 teaspoons olive oil
- ¼ teaspoon sesame oil

SALMON:

- 3 tablespoons olive oil, plus more for brushing
- Six 6-ounce skinless salmon fillets, preferably center-cut
- Salt and freshly ground pepper
- ½ cup finely chopped unsalted pistachios
- 4 cups fresh baby spinach or torn large spinach leaves
- 2 medium carrots, cut into 1½-by-⅛-inch matchsticks
- 2 medium leeks, white and tender green, cut into 1½-by-⅛-inch matchsticks
- 1 medium red bell pepper, cut into 1½-by-⅛-inch matchsticks
- 1 tablespoon black or white sesame seeds (optional)

1. Make the curry and orange sauces: In a small dry skillet, stir the curry powder over moderate heat until fragrant, about 2 minutes. Transfer to a bowl and stir in the ¾ cup peanut oil. Let stand overnight.

2. In a small bowl, combine the 1 teaspoon shallots, 1 teaspoon ginger and ¼ cup rice vinegar, the lime juice, soy sauce and honey. Whisk in the curry oil in a thin stream until emulsified, then season the sauce with salt and pepper.

STORING GINGER

Ginger takes very little care. Since it isn't highly perishable, it can be left out for a week or so with no ill effects. If you need it to last a bit longer, wrap it, unpeeled, in a brown paper bag or a paper towel inside a plastic bag and store it in the vegetable crisper of the fridge for up to three weeks. The cut part will dry and seal itself and should be sliced off when you use the ginger. Keep in mind, though, that ginger that sits around for more than a week (even if it's refrigerated) loses some of its bite and fragrance. Freezing is an option for ginger that is to be grated, smashed or added to any preparation where firm texture is not important (frozen ginger turns mushy), but since ginger is simple to find and stores well, it's just as easy to buy it when you need it.—LAUREN MUKAMAL CAMP

3. In a nonreactive saucepan, combine the orange juice and the jalapeños with the remaining 2 tablespoons shallots and 2 tablespoons ginger. Boil over moderately high heat until reduced to ½ cup, about 30 minutes; let cool. Meanwhile, peel the orange with a sharp knife, removing all the bitter white pith. Cut between the membranes to release the sections.

4. Add the orange sections, red-wine vinegar and the remaining 2 teaspoons rice vinegar to the orange-juice reduction. Gradually

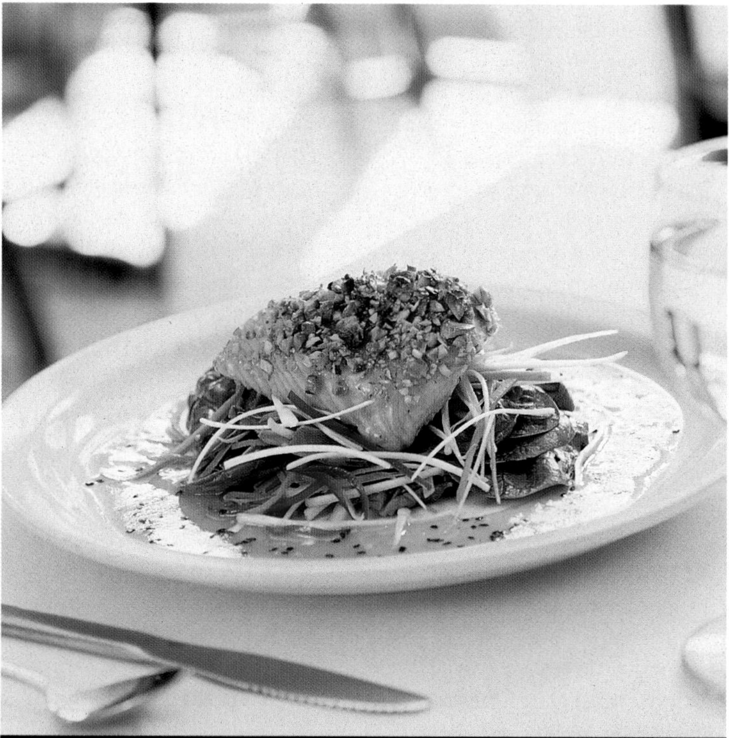
Pistachio-Topped Salmon with Two Sauces

CHEF'S TIP

Some of my favorite dishes allow you to use either prepared or homemade ingredients. When making Pistachio-Topped Salmon with Two Sauces, for example, you can purchase good-quality curry powder, or you can mix your own blend as I do. First toast the spices; I use coriander, cardamom, cumin, mustard and fenugreek seeds, cloves, cinnamon, ginger, turmeric, peppercorns and cayenne. Stir them over moderate heat until they're fragrant and lightly colored. Grind them in a spice grinder or a clean coffee grinder and store them in a tightly covered jar.—MONICA POPE

whisk in the remaining 1 tablespoon peanut oil, the olive oil and the sesame oil and season the sauce with salt and pepper. (**MAKE AHEAD:** The curry sauce and orange sauce can be refrigerated separately for up to 3 days. Allow both of the sauces to return to room temperature before serving.)

5. Make the salmon: Preheat the oven to 350°. Lightly brush a nonstick baking sheet with olive oil. Heat the 3 tablespoons olive oil in a large skillet. Season the salmon fillets with salt and pepper and press one side of the fillets into the chopped pistachios. Add three salmon fillets to the skillet with the pistachio-coated side down. Cook the salmon fillets over high heat until they are lightly golden, about 2 minutes. Carefully transfer the cooked salmon fillets to the baking sheet, pistachio-side up, and repeat the process with the remaining three fillets. Bake for 6 to 8 minutes, or until the flesh of the fish flakes but is still slightly opaque in the center. Let rest on the baking sheet for 5 minutes before serving.

6. In a small, nonreactive saucepan, heat ⅓ cup of the curry sauce. In a large bowl, combine the spinach and the carrot, leek and red-bell-pepper matchsticks. Toss the vegetables with the warm curry sauce and spoon the vegetables onto six plates. Top the vegetables with the salmon fillets. Drizzle each plate with about 1½ tablespoons of the orange sauce and sprinkle with the sesame seeds.—MONICA POPE

HOLLANDAISE-GLAZED SALMON WITH SEAFOOD MOUSSE

Filet de Saumon à la Belle Danoise *is the kind of marvelously delicious old-fashioned dish you dream about but seldom see anymore because people are so afraid of creamy mousses and heavenly hollandaise sauces. But many of these beloved classics are creeping back into favor. This one offers a lovely once-in-a-while binge—one that's not too complicated to produce for those of us who love to cook.*

🍷 *This is the sort of subtle, rich French fish dish that showcases an elegant white Burgundy, such as a Meursault.*

6 SERVINGS

2 pounds skinless, boneless salmon fillet, cut into 6 serving pieces

- 1 tablespoon unsalted butter, softened
- 2 tablespoons minced shallots

Salt and freshly ground pepper

SEAFOOD MOUSSE:

- ¾ pound very fresh lean white fish fillets, such as sole, flounder or halibut, well chilled
- ¼ pound very fresh scallops, washed, drained and well chilled
- 2 egg whites
- 1 cup (more or less) well-chilled heavy cream

Salt and freshly ground white pepper

Freshly grated nutmeg

- 1 teaspoon or so Cognac

¼ to ⅓ cup dry white French vermouth

HOLLANDAISE MOUSSELINE:

- 3 egg yolks

Finely grated zest of 1 lemon

- 1 tablespoon fresh lemon juice
- 1 tablespoon dry white French vermouth

Salt and freshly ground white pepper

- 2 tablespoons cold unsalted butter plus 1 stick (more or less) melted unsalted butter
- ⅓ cup (more or less) well-chilled heavy cream, whipped

1. Carefully go over the salmon with your fingers and pull out any bones with tweezers or pliers. Coat a 9-by-12-inch flameproof baking dish with the butter; the dish should be just large enough to hold the pieces of salmon in a single layer. Sprinkle the shallots in the bottom of the dish. Season the salmon with salt and pepper and arrange it in the dish. Cover with plastic wrap and refrigerate.

2. Make the seafood mousse: Cut the fish for the mousse into 1-inch pieces and place with the scallops in a food processor fitted with the steel blade. Start the machine and add the egg whites, ¼ cup of the chilled cream, ½ teaspoon of salt and pinches of white pepper and nutmeg. Puree until smooth. Lift up a bit of the mousse with the tip of a rubber spatula; it will probably be quite stiff with only this minimum addition of cream.

3. Beat in additional chilled heavy cream by spoonfuls until the mousse holds its shape softly. Taste carefully and add salt and white pepper, if needed, plus the Cognac. Spread the mousse in an even layer over the top of each piece of salmon. (**MAKE AHEAD:** The dish can be prepared to this point up to 4 hours ahead. Cover and refrigerate.)

4. Preheat the oven to 400°. Pour the vermouth around the fish. Cover the dish with buttered wax paper and then with foil and bring just to a simmer on top of the stove. Transfer the dish to the lower third of the preheated oven and bake for 12 to 15 minutes, or until the mousse is set and the salmon is just springy to the touch; do not overcook.

5. Meanwhile, **make the hollandaise mousseline:** In a nonreactive 6-inch saucepan, vigorously beat the egg yolks until thick,

CUTTING CALORIES

Hollandaise-Glazed Salmon with Seafood Mousse is obviously not a diet dish, but there are ways to minimize the calories. I've qualified the amount of each so-called wicked ingredient with "more or less." In other words, I'll let you decide how much cream to process into the fish mousse. The mousse is at its lightest and most delectable when made with as much heavy cream as it will absorb; experiment until you reach the level your taste and your conscience will allow. Do the same with the whipped-cream-enriched hollandaise sauce. As for me, I always prefer a mini (or even a mini-mini) bite of the real thing, to enjoy how it's supposed to taste.—JULIA CHILD

Hollandaise-Glazed Salmon with Seafood Mousse

1 to 2 minutes. Beat in the lemon zest, lemon juice, vermouth, ¼ teaspoon salt and a small pinch of white pepper. Add the 2 tablespoons cold butter.

6. Set the pan over moderately low heat and whisk constantly until the yolks begin to foam and become warm to the touch; soon a wisp of steam will rise from the surface, and in a few seconds the yolks will be creamy and will coat the wires of the whisk. Remove from the heat and beat for several seconds to stop the cooking. Whisk in the melted butter by droplets to make a thick, creamy sauce. Taste the sauce carefully and season it accordingly.

7. When the fish is done, remove it from the oven and preheat the broiler. Drain the fish-cooking juices into a nonreactive saucepan and boil them rapidly down until syrupy, about 3 minutes. Beat the juices into the hollandaise and then fold in the whipped cream.

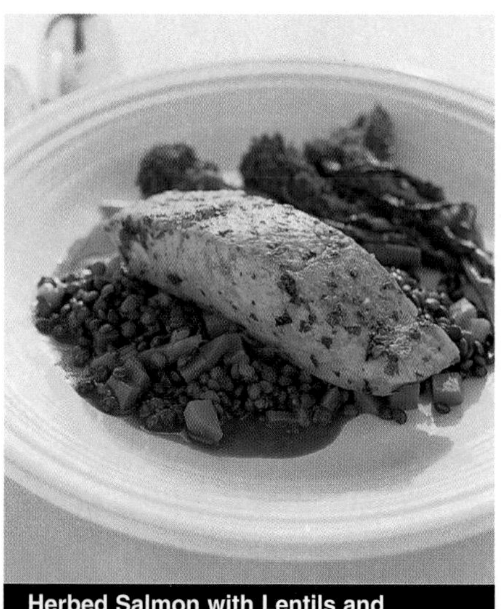

Herbed Salmon with Lentils and Red-Wine Sauce

8. Spoon the sauce over the fish and set under the very hot broiler to brown lightly and unevenly, for 15 to 20 seconds. Serve immediately.—JULIA CHILD

HERBED SALMON WITH LENTILS AND RED-WINE SAUCE

Salmon can pair successfully with light reds as well as rich whites, and the red-wine sauce on this pan-cooked version settles the issue. A light, tart West Coast Pinot Noir, such as the 1993 Ponzi from Oregon or the 1993 Gloria Ferrer from California, served slightly cool, will showcase the fish.

6 SERVINGS

LENTILS:

2 cups French du Puy lentils (about 14 ounces), rinsed and picked over
2 medium carrots, cut into ½-inch dice
2 medium celery ribs, cut into ½-inch dice
1 small onion, finely chopped
2 large garlic cloves, minced
4 fresh thyme sprigs
2 teaspoons coarse salt

SALMON AND RED-WINE SAUCE:

2 fresh tarragon sprigs, leaves finely chopped, stems reserved
2 fresh flat-leaf parsley sprigs, leaves finely chopped, stems reserved
2 fresh chives, finely chopped
3 tablespoons coarse salt
1 tablespoon sugar
Finely grated zest of 1 orange
Freshly ground pepper
Six 7-ounce skinless salmon fillets, about 1 inch thick
1½ cups dry red wine, such as Cabernet Sauvignon
½ cup port
¼ cup red-wine vinegar
2 medium shallots, minced
1 stick (4 ounces) cold unsalted butter, cut into ½-inch dice
Table salt

1. Make the lentils: In a medium saucepan, cover the lentils with 4 cups of water. Bring to a simmer over moderate heat, then reduce the heat to low, cover and simmer for 15 minutes. Stir in the carrots, celery, onion, garlic and thyme sprigs, cover and cook for 15 minutes more. Stir in the coarse salt and cook until the lentils are softened but still slightly firm, 5 to 8 minutes. Let stand for 10 minutes. (**MAKE AHEAD:** The lentils can stand at room temperature for 3 hours or in the refrigerator for up to 1 day; reheat before serving.)

2. Make the salmon and the red-wine sauce: In a small bowl, mix together the chopped tarragon, parsley and chives, the coarse salt, sugar, orange zest and ½ teaspoon pepper. Spread the herb mixture evenly on both sides of the salmon and arrange the fillets in a large baking dish. Let the fish marinate at room temperature for 3 hours.

3. In a nonreactive medium saucepan, combine the red wine, port, vinegar, shallots and the tarragon and parsley stems. Boil over high heat until reduced to a generous ½ cup, about 10 minutes. Strain into a small nonreactive saucepan and bring back to a boil over moderate heat. Lower the heat and gradually whisk in the butter until the sauce is slightly thickened; do not let the sauce boil. Season with table salt and pepper and keep warm.

4. Heat a large, heavy, nonstick skillet. Brush the herbs from the salmon and cook the fillets in two batches over moderate heat, turning once, until they are nicely browned and just opaque throughout, about 4 minutes per side. Transfer the fillets to a plate and keep warm; cook the remaining salmon.
5. Remove the thyme sprigs from the lentils and discard. Make a bed of the lentils on six plates. Set the salmon fillets on top, spoon the red-wine sauce over the fish and the lentils and serve.—AMY SCHERBER AND KERRY HEFFERNAN

Q & A

Q: Does nonstick cookware need special care?

A: Yes. Whatever the surface, follow these steps:

- **After cooking, move empty nonstick pans off of hot burners. Let the pans cool before putting them in water.**
- **Don't put nonstick pans in the dishwasher. Some manufacturers say you can, but dishwasher detergent can damage the coating.**
- **Dry the pans after washing.**
- **If you stack pans for storage, protect the nonstick surfaces with a paper towel.**
- **Some manufacturers suggest periodically wiping nonstick pans with a thin film of oil (I find oil spray a bit too sticky). This is a quick fix for pans that have been damaged by heat.—DEBORAH KRASNER**

GRILLED TUNA AND EGGPLANT WITH TAHINI SAUCE

The eggplant can be cut into three-quarter-inch-thick slices rather than thinly sliced. Either way, be sure to cook it until it's tender. Don't overprocess the Tahini Sauce; it should be the consistency of heavy cream.

6 SERVINGS

- 2 large tomatoes, cut into ½-inch dice
- 1 medium seedless cucumber, peeled and cut into ½-inch dice
- 18 Kalamata olives (about 3½ ounces), pitted and coarsely chopped
- 1 tablespoon minced red onion
- 2 tablespoons fresh lemon juice
- 1 tablespoon extra-virgin olive oil, plus about ¼ cup for brushing
- 1 medium eggplant, peeled and sliced crosswise ¼ inch thick
- Salt and freshly ground pepper
- Six 3-ounce tuna steaks, about ½ inch thick
- Tahini Sauce (recipe follows)
- 1 tablespoon coarsely chopped chives

1. In a medium bowl, combine the tomatoes, cucumber, olives, onion, lemon juice and the 1 tablespoon olive oil. (**MAKE AHEAD:** The salad can stand at room temperature for 4 hours.)
2. Heat a grill pan or preheat the broiler. Brush the eggplant with some of the oil. Season with salt and pepper. Working in batches, grill the eggplant over moderate heat, or broil until very tender and browned, about 2 minutes a side. Transfer to a plate; keep warm.
3. Wipe out the grill pan. Brush the tuna on both sides with oil; season well with salt and pepper, pressing the seasoning into the fish. Grill in the pan over high heat, or broil until nicely browned, about 2 minutes per side.
4. Make a pool of the Tahini Sauce on each of six plates. Fan the eggplant slices out on it. Season the tomato salad with salt and pepper and spoon on top of the eggplant. Set the tuna on the salad; garnish with the chives.

Grilled Tuna and Eggplant

Tahini Sauce

MAKES ABOUT 1 CUP

- ⅓ cup plus 2 tablespoons tahini (see Note)
- 1 small garlic clove, minced
- 2 tablespoons fresh lemon juice
- Salt and freshly ground pepper

In a food processor, combine the tahini, garlic and ½ cup of water and pulse once or twice to blend. Add the lemon juice, salt and pepper and pulse just until combined.
NOTE: Before measuring the tahini (Middle Eastern sesame-seed paste), be sure to stir it to incorporate the oil that has separated from the paste.—LISSA DOUMANI AND HIRO SONE ➤

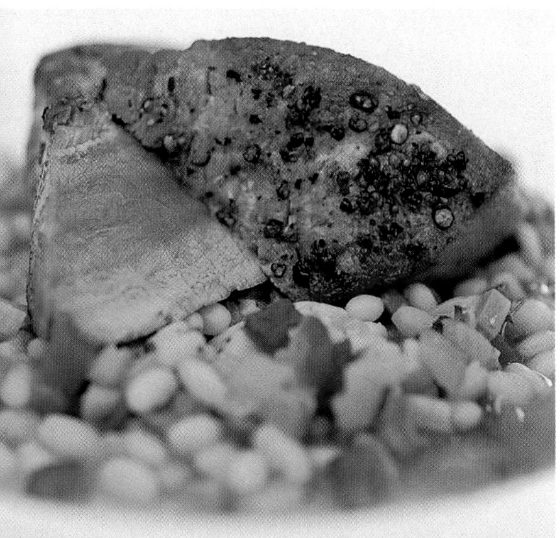
Pan-Roasted Peppered Tuna with White Beans

PAN-ROASTED PEPPERED TUNA WITH WHITE BEANS

The key to this meaty, spice-crusted tuna is to use best-quality fish and to cook it so the center remains rare. I like to buy my tuna in Japanese markets, where it is also sold for sushi.

🍷 *A peppered tuna steak is almost meatlike in texture and flavor, so a rich and fruity red wine with medium body is called for. A great choice is the 1993 Fife Old Vines Merlot. This relatively new Napa Valley winery has already excelled in turning out luscious red wines, such as Zinfandel and Merlot. Equally intense, a shade spicier than the Fife, but perhaps a shade more tannic as well, is the 1993 Liparita Merlot from Napa's Howell Mountain.*

4 SERVINGS

- 1 cup dried small white beans, such as Great Northern, picked over and rinsed
- 2 tablespoons unsalted butter
- 1 medium onion, finely chopped
- 1 medium carrot, cut into ⅓-inch dice
- 1 medium celery rib, cut into ⅓-inch dice
- 1 teaspoon thyme
- ½ teaspoon oregano
- 1 bay leaf
- 4 cups chicken stock or canned low-sodium broth
- 3 medium red or yellow bell peppers or a combination
- 2 tablespoons extra-virgin olive oil
- 2 tablespoons sherry vinegar
- 2 teaspoons finely chopped fresh rosemary
- 2 tablespoons finely chopped fresh flat-leaf parsley
- Salt and freshly ground pepper
- 2 tablespoons vegetable oil
- Four 6-ounce tuna steaks, cut about 2 inches thick
- Coarsely cracked black peppercorns

1. In a medium bowl, cover the beans with 4 cups of water and let soak overnight. Alternatively, cover the beans with water and bring to a boil. Remove from the heat and let stand for 1 hour.

2. Drain and rinse the beans. Melt the butter in a large saucepan. Add the onion, carrot and celery. Cook over moderate heat, stirring, for 4 minutes. Add the beans, thyme, oregano, bay leaf and stock. Cover partially and bring to a boil, then reduce the heat to low and simmer until the beans are tender but not falling apart, about 1 hour; some liquid should remain. (**MAKE AHEAD:** The beans can be refrigerated in their liquid for up to 2 days.)

3. Roast the bell peppers over a gas flame or under the broiler until charred. Transfer to a bowl, cover and let steam for 15 minutes. Peel the peppers, discarding the cores, ribs and seeds. Cut the peppers into ½-inch dice and add them to the beans along with the olive oil and vinegar. Cook over moderate heat until warmed through. Stir in the rosemary and parsley and season with salt and ground pepper.

4. Preheat the oven to 450°. Heat the vegetable oil in a large, heavy-bottomed ovenproof skillet. Season one side of the tuna with salt and a generous amount of the cracked black pepper. Add the tuna to the skillet and cook over high heat until just browned, about 2 minutes per side. Transfer the skillet to the oven and cook for about 6 minutes, or until the tuna feels firm but gives slightly; it should still be pink in the center.

5. Divide the beans among four large plates. Set the tuna steaks on top, peppered-side up, and serve.—TRACI DES JARDINS

TUNA STEAKS WITH BASIL SAUCE LF

6 SERVINGS

- 1 cup plain nonfat yogurt
- ⅓ cup tightly packed fresh basil leaves, plus additional finely chopped basil for garnish
- ¼ cup blanched garlic puree (see box, p. 61)
- Salt and freshly ground pepper
- 12 small red new potatoes
- ⅓ ounce dried porcini mushrooms
- ½ teaspoon fennel seeds
- ½ teaspoon black peppercorns
- Six 5-ounce tuna steaks, at least 1 inch thick
- Vegetable cooking spray

2 pounds fresh spinach, tough stems removed
1 pint cherry tomatoes, halved

1. Spoon the yogurt into a strainer lined with a paper coffee filter or cheesecloth. Set the strainer over a small bowl and refrigerate until most of the liquid has drained off the yogurt, about 3 hours.
2. In a mini-processor or blender, combine the ⅓ cup basil leaves, blanched garlic puree and drained yogurt and season with salt and pepper. Puree the sauce until smooth. Transfer to a bowl. (MAKE AHEAD: The basil sauce can be refrigerated for up to 8 hours. Let return to room temperature before serving.)
3. In a steamer basket set over a pan of simmering water, cook the potatoes until tender, about 17 minutes. Let cool slightly; cut into quarters.
4. Meanwhile, in a spice grinder or mortar, grind the dried porcini, fennel seeds and peppercorns to a fine powder. Pat the tuna steaks dry and season on both sides with salt. Sprinkle the porcini mixture all over the tuna, pressing it into the surface.
5. Lightly coat a large nonstick skillet with vegetable cooking spray and heat. Add the tuna steaks and cook over high heat until browned on the bottom, 2 to 3 minutes. Lightly coat the top of the tuna with vegetable spray, then turn and cook until browned outside but still rare in the center, about 3 minutes longer. Transfer the tuna steaks to a cutting board and cut them into ½-inch-thick slices.
6. Wipe out the skillet and set it over high heat. Add the spinach, season with salt and pepper and cook, stirring occasionally, just until wilted. Add the tomatoes and stir gently until heated through. Mound the spinach and tomatoes in the center of six plates. Arrange the tuna slices and the potatoes around the spinach and drizzle each serving with about 2 tablespoons of the basil sauce. Garnish with the chopped basil and serve at once.—JIM ACKARD

ONE-DISH BLUEFISH Q

A hearty quick-cooking ragout of vegetables and a little dry white wine forms a flavorful bed for pan-poached bluefish fillets. Since the juicy tomatoes and mild sweet potatoes add color and texture as well as good taste, there's no need to make a sauce. Just lay the fish on top of the vegetables, cover the pan and let nature take its course. This recipe works just as well with other fish or with chicken breasts or pork loin.

An oak-aged Chardonnay will have enough edge to provide contrast and enough rich flavor to underscore the fish and ragout. Consider the 1994 Clos du Bois Winemaker's Reserve or the 1994 Napa Ridge Reserve.

4 SERVINGS

1 pound sweet potatoes, peeled and cut into 2-inch chunks
3 tablespoons fruity olive oil
1 large bunch of scallions, white and green, cut into 1-inch pieces (about 4 cups)
2 garlic cloves, finely chopped
½ cup dry white wine
One 15-ounce can peeled tomatoes, drained and coarsely chopped
¾ teaspoon ground cardamom
Salt and freshly ground pepper
4 skin-on bluefish fillets (about 7 ounces each)
2 tablespoons finely chopped fresh flat-leaf parsley

Tuna Steaks with Basil Sauce

LOW-FAT MENU

Tuna is so meaty that it can be paired with substantial whites or lighter reds, but given the additional earthy flavors of the porcini, fennel and basil, red wine is the best choice. A well-aged Rioja Reserva from Spain, such as the 1985 Beronia or the 1988 Bodegas Montecello, would have plenty of flavor to match the dish but enough low-tannin smoothness to keep it from overpowering the tuna. Either one would also complement the garlicky Caesar salad.

GARLIC CAESAR SALAD (P. 61)

TUNA STEAKS WITH BASIL SAUCE (P. 164)

WATERMELON GRANITA (P. 439)

1. Put the sweet potatoes in a food processor and pulse until the largest pieces are about ½ inch and the smallest about ¼ inch. Set the chopped sweet potatoes aside.

2. In a large, deep, nonreactive skillet, heat the olive oil. Add the scallion pieces and cook over moderately high heat until they are just softened, about 3 minutes. Add the chopped garlic and cook until fragrant, about 1 minute. Pour in the white wine, bring to a boil and boil for 1 minute. Add the chopped sweet potatoes, the chopped tomatoes, the ground cardamom, ½ tablespoon salt and ⅛ teaspoon pepper. Reduce the heat to moderate, cover the skillet tightly and cook the vegetables until the sweet potatoes are just tender, about 20 minutes. (**MAKE AHEAD:** The vegetable ragout can be refrigerated for up to 3 hours.)

3. Using a pair of tweezers or pliers, remove the small pin bones that run the length of the bluefish fillets. Season the bluefish fillets with salt and pepper and arrange the fillets, skin-side down, on top of the vegetable ragout, overlapping the fillets slightly if necessary. Sprinkle the bluefish fillets with the chopped parsley, cover the skillet tightly and cook until the bluefish begins to flake, about 15 minutes. Transfer the bluefish fillets and the vegetable ragout onto four serving plates, spoon some of the cooking juices over the bluefish and serve.—PAUL GRIMES

QUICK DINNER

ONE-DISH BLUEFISH
(P. 165)

LEMON THYME ORZO
(P. 108)

RUM SMOOTHIE PARFAITS
(P. 440)

GAME PLAN:

• Freeze the dessert glasses and blender canister. Cut up and cook the vegetables for the bluefish dish; start the orzo water.

• Cook the fish and the orzo. Chop the thyme and the lemon zest. Finish preparing the orzo.

• After clearing the main course, make the ice-cream parfaits.

MACKEREL WITH CITRUS CORIANDER SAUCE

Before adding the orange sections, you can strain the coriander seeds from the sauce—or leave them in for a spicier bite.

🍷 *This relatively acidic, sweetly spiced dish needs a white wine with similar character. Look for a floral-scented but crisp Viognier, such as the 1994 Arrowood, the 1994 Alban from California or the 1993 Horton from Virginia.*

4 SERVINGS

- 1 large navel orange
- 1 cup mirin
- ½ cup fresh lemon juice
- ¼ cup fresh lime juice
- ¼ cup soy sauce

One-Dish Bluefish

CHEF'S TIP

Citrus and fish almost always work well together, but the particularly large amount of acid and the punch of ginger in the Citrus Coriander Sauce makes it best for rich, oily fish, like the mackerel used here. Try bluefish, salmon, tuna or even fresh sardines. Don't use a white-fleshed fish; the sauce will blow it away.

- 1 tablespoon minced fresh ginger
- 1 teaspoon coriander seeds
- 1 tablespoon sesame seeds
- 2 tablespoons extra-virgin olive oil, plus more for brushing
- 2 garlic cloves, thinly sliced
- ½ pound fresh pea shoots,* bok choy or snow peas

Salt and freshly ground pepper
Four 6-ounce Spanish-mackerel or bluefish fillets, with skin
Fresh cilantro sprigs, for garnish

*Available at Asian and farmers' markets and health-food stores

1. Peel the orange with a sharp knife, removing all of the bitter white pith. Cut between the membranes to release the orange sections into a bowl.

2. In a nonreactive saucepan, boil the mirin, lemon juice, lime juice, soy sauce, ginger and coriander seeds over high heat until the liquid is reduced to ¾ cup, about 20 minutes. Add the orange sections and let cool slightly. ➤

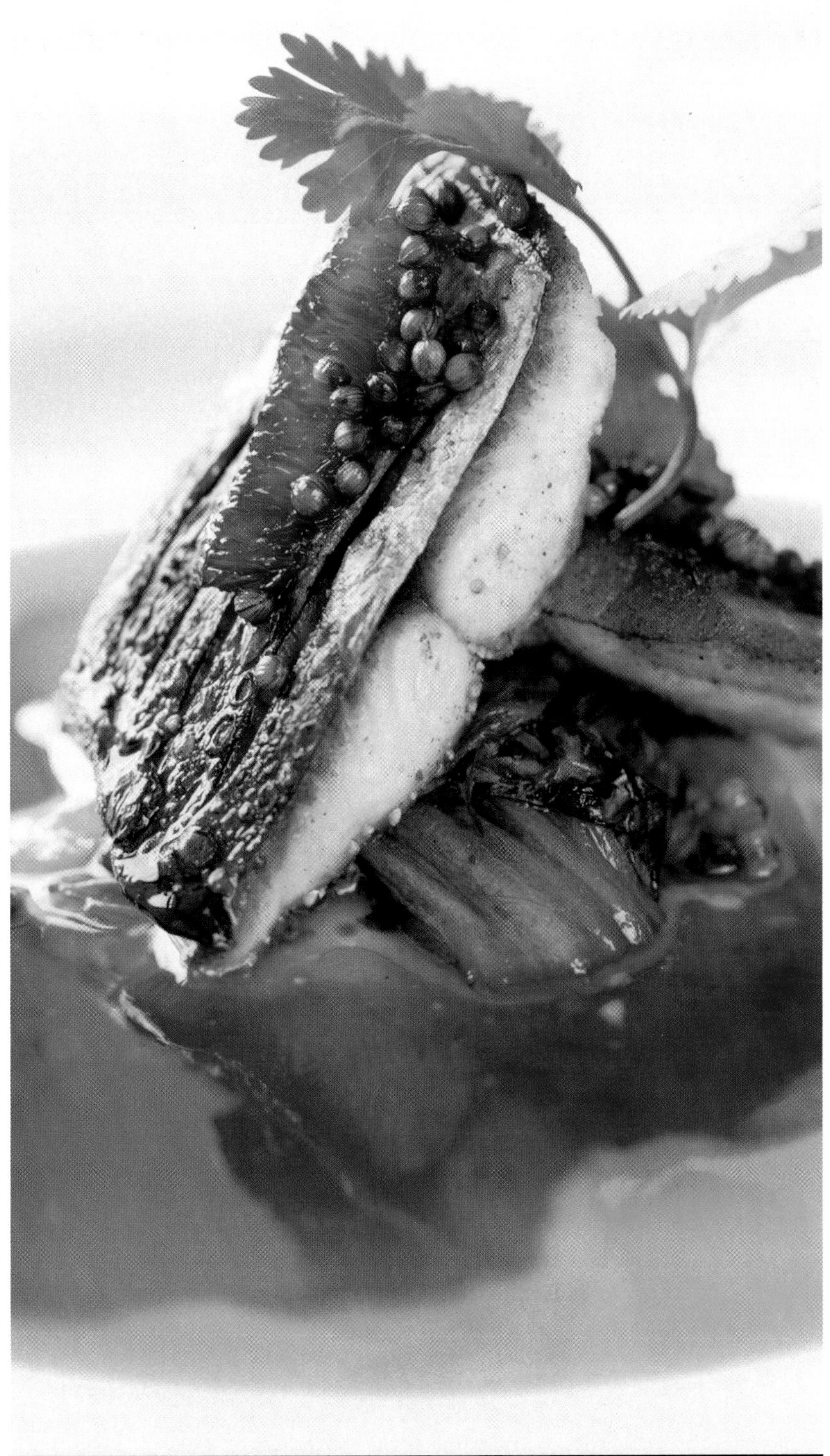

Mackerel with Citrus Coriander Sauce

3. Light a charcoal grill or preheat the broiler. In a small skillet, stir the sesame seeds over low heat until lightly browned, about 1 minute.

4. Heat the 2 tablespoons oil in a large skillet. Add the garlic and cook over moderately high heat, stirring, until just golden, about 3 minutes. Add the pea shoots, season with salt and pepper and cook, stirring, until wilted, about 3 minutes.

5. Cut three or four shallow slashes in the skin of each mackerel fillet. Brush the fillets lightly with olive oil and season them with salt and pepper. Grill or broil the mackerel fillets for about 2 minutes per side, or until the flesh just begins to flake. Sprinkle the fillets with the toasted sesame seeds.

6. Mound the pea shoots in the center of four plates. Set the mackerel fillets on top of the pea shoots and spoon the citrus coriander sauce on top. Garnish with the cilantro sprigs and serve.—SCOTT BRYAN

PAN-ROASTED LOBSTER

Precooking the lobsters for one minute makes the job of cutting them in half easier. Alternatively, have your fishmonger split the live lobsters in half; in that case, you won't have to blanch the lobsters.

4 SERVINGS

Four 1¼-pound live lobsters
- ¼ teaspoon saffron threads, crushed
- ¼ cup dry white wine
- 5 tablespoons olive oil
- 1 medium fennel bulb, trimmed, halved, cored and thinly sliced
- 1 medium onion, thinly sliced
- 4 scallions, white and tender green, thinly sliced
- 1 garlic clove, thinly sliced
- ½ cup chicken stock or canned low-sodium broth

Salt and freshly ground pepper
- 5 tablespoons cold unsalted butter, cut into pieces

1. In a large pot of boiling water, blanch the lobsters until they start to turn pink, about 1 minute. Drain and let the lobsters cool. In a small bowl, cover the crushed saffron threads with the white wine and let steep for at least 30 minutes.

2. Heat 2 tablespoons of the olive oil in a large nonreactive skillet. Add the sliced fennel, onion, scallions and garlic and cook over moderately low heat, stirring, until the vegetables are tender, about 20 minutes. Add the saffron mixture to the vegetables and boil over moderately high heat until the wine evaporates, about 2 minutes. Add the chicken stock and boil until the liquid is reduced by a third, about 5 minutes. Season with salt and pepper and set aside.

3. Meanwhile, preheat the oven to 450°. Halve each of the lobsters lengthwise. Remove the brain sac, sand sac, tomalley and roe if necessary. Crack the claws well all over.

4. In a very large heavy-bottomed roasting pan set over two burners, heat the remaining 3 tablespoons of olive oil until almost smoking. Add the lobsters, cut-side down, and cook over moderately high heat until the lobster meat is browned, about 3 minutes. Transfer the roasting pan to the oven and roast the lobsters for about 5 minutes, or until the lobster meat is cooked through. Transfer the lobsters to a platter, season the meat with salt and pepper and keep warm.

5. Rewarm the fennel mixture. Remove the skillet from the heat and stir in the pieces of butter, a little at a time, until the sauce is thickened. Season with salt and pepper. Divide the fennel mixture among four large plates and arrange two of the roasted lobster halves on each plate.—TRACI DES JARDINS ➤

PAN HANDLING

Six tips that will help you get the most from pan-roasting in your own kitchen.

1. Use a heavy-bottomed ovenproof skillet, preferably cast-iron or copper; a flameproof roasting pan will do for larger quantities.

2. Select the best-quality ingredients—pan-roasting accentuates their flavors.

3. Choose an oil that won't burn in the hot pan, such as vegetable, canola or grapeseed. And don't let the skillet scorch; if you do, you won't be able to use it for the sauce.

4. Do not crowd the ingredients in the pan.

5. Check to make sure the oven is hot enough.

6. Keep plenty of pot holders handy, because pan-roasting really heats up skillet handles.

Pan-Roasted Lobster

Shrimp with Ginger, Garlic and Basil

SHRIMP WITH GINGER, GARLIC AND BASIL

I created this dish one spring Sunday on the way to my Paris market on Rue Poncelet. I wanted to combine giant fresh shrimp with a zesty blend of ginger, garlic and white wine. Here, the wine—a Sauvignon Blanc or a young white Rhône—is slightly reduced, adding depth of flavor to the resulting sauce.

🍷 *A nicely chilled floral wine such as a French or California Viognier or a white Châteauneuf-du-Pape is too expensive for cooking but is a great drinking match.*

4 SERVINGS

- 7 large garlic cloves, finely chopped
- 3 tablespoons freshly grated ginger
- 3 tablespoons extra-virgin olive oil
- Fine sea salt
- 2 cups dry white wine
- 1 pound large shrimp (about 20), shelled, deveined, rinsed and dried
- Steamed basmati rice, for serving
- 2 tablespoons finely shredded fresh basil

1. In a large nonreactive skillet, stir together the chopped garlic, grated ginger, olive oil and a pinch of sea salt. Cook over moderately high heat until the garlic becomes light golden, about 3 minutes. Pour the white wine all over the skillet, bring the wine to a simmer and cook until the liquid is reduced to 1 cup, about 8 minutes.

2. Add the shrimp to the skillet in a single layer and cook, stirring occasionally, until they are pink, about 4 minutes. Serve the shrimp along with the cooking liquid spooned over steamed basmati rice in shallow bowls, with the shredded fresh basil sprinkled on top.—PATRICIA WELLS

PREPARING GINGER

There are many ways to prepare ginger. If it's meant to be eaten, ginger should be shredded or minced: The taste is subtler because there's less of it in each bite, and the texture is more pleasing, too. Crushed or sliced ginger can be tossed into hot oil to add a ginger flavor, and because it's in largish pieces, you can easily fish it out and discard before serving. (You don't want a mouthful of woody ginger.) Either way, a sharp stainless-steel chef's knife or Chinese cleaver and a paring knife are the only tools you need.

TO CRUSH GINGER **Place the flat side of a chef's knife or cleaver over a small piece of ginger and lean on the blade with the heel of your hand.**

TO SLICE GINGER **Cut it across the fibers into coins. Slice it as thin as possible if it is going to be eaten.**

TO SHRED GINGER **Cut it into slices, then stack the slices and cut into fine shreds.**

TO MINCE GINGER **Line up the shreds and cut crosswise into a fine dice. For a rougher cut, crush a piece with the side of a knife and then chop.—LAUREN MUKAMAL CAMP**

PICKLED SHRIMP Q

Be sure to use large shrimp (about twenty to the pound), which won't become too tangy as they marinate overnight in the spicy brine. Serve the shrimp with crusty bread, corn bread or biscuits and a cucumber salad.

4 SERVINGS

- 1 small onion, thickly sliced
- 4 large garlic cloves, chopped
- 1 small red bell pepper, cut into thick strips
- 1 to 2 small dried red chiles, crushed
- 1 tablespoon white-wine vinegar
- 2 teaspoons sugar
- 1 teaspoon whole black peppercorns, crushed
- ½ teaspoon allspice berries, crushed
- 2 pounds large shrimp, shelled and deveined
- Salt
- 1 small lemon, thickly sliced
- ¼ cup extra-virgin olive oil
- 2 tablespoons parsley leaves

1. In a nonreactive saucepan, combine 2 cups of water with the onion, garlic, red bell pepper, chiles, vinegar, sugar, peppercorns and allspice. Boil over high heat for 2 minutes, then stir in the shrimp and cook just until pink and loosely curled. Stir in 2 teaspoons salt and the lemon slices, squeezing them a bit. Transfer the shrimp and marinade to a large bowl or wide 2-quart jar and let cool to room temperature. Cover and refrigerate overnight, stirring a few times.

2. Transfer the shrimp to a clean bowl. Strain ¾ cup of the marinade into a small bowl. Cut four of the red-pepper strips into

Pickled Shrimp

Shrimp Salpicón with Chipotles

small dice. Stir ¾ teaspoon salt into the strained marinade and whisk in the oil. (Discard the remaining marinade.)

3. Pour the dressing over the shrimp and toss well. Spoon the chilled shrimp onto plates and garnish with the red-pepper dice and parsley leaves.—MARCIA KIESEL

SHRIMP SALPICÓN WITH CHIPOTLES

This light main course also works nicely as a starter. If you're using a dried chipotle, soften it in hot water before seeding and slicing it.

The chipotle-fired dressing sharpens the sweetness of the shrimp and the richness of the avocados. To complement these flavors, serve a chilled California Chardonnay with rich, oaky overtones, such as the 1994 Morgan or the 1994 Franciscan.

6 SERVINGS

- 4 medium red potatoes, peeled and cut into ½-inch dice
- 4 medium carrots, cut into ½-inch dice
- 1½ cups Roasted-Tomatillo Chipotle Salsa (p. 356)
- 1½ pounds medium shrimp, shelled and deveined
- 1 large ripe tomato, cut into ½-inch dice
- ¼ cup olive oil
- 1 tablespoon cider vinegar
- Salt and freshly ground pepper
- Boston lettuce leaves, for serving
- 2 ripe avocados, peeled, pitted and cut into ½-inch dice
- Coarsely chopped fresh cilantro
- 1 chipotle chile, seeded and thinly sliced crosswise

THE RIGHT PAN FOR SAUTÉING

Look for a large sauté pan (straight sides) or a skillet (sloping sides) with these features:

HEAVY-GAUGE CONSTRUCTION **Stainless-steel-coated aluminum and copper are best; they conduct heat quickly and evenly. Inexpensive lightweight pans are apt to burn food over the high heat needed for sautéing. (Use pans with untreated surfaces for meat, poultry, vegetables, seafood and meaty fish; use a nonstick surface for delicate fish.) The heavier the pan, the harder it will be to lift. Don't worry. Tossing food in the pan is showy but not always necessary. A good pair of tongs and a spatula will do the job.**

TWELVE-INCH DIAMETER **This size holds a substantial amount of food without being too unwieldy or heavy. A ten-inch pan is fine for small portions.**

OVENPROOF HANDLES **These allow you to finish cooking a dish in the oven in the same pan. A helper handle opposite the long main handle is a boon for turning food out onto a platter.**

1. In two medium saucepans of boiling salted water, cook the diced potatoes and carrots separately until just tender, about 7 minutes each. Drain the vegetables together, rinse with cool water and drain again.

2. In a heavy saucepan, bring the tomatillo salsa to a boil over high heat and cook until slightly reduced, about 5 minutes. Add the shrimp and cook, stirring, until just opaque throughout, about 5 minutes. Transfer the shrimp to a bowl and let cool. Remove the pan from the heat, add the potatoes, carrots and tomato to the salsa and stir gently. Add the olive oil and vinegar, season with salt and pepper and let cool.

3. Arrange the lettuce leaves on a platter. Add the potato mixture and the diced avocados to the shrimp, toss to combine and mound on top of the lettuce. Sprinkle with the chopped cilantro and the sliced chipotle and serve.—RICK BAYLESS

SHRIMP AND SPINACH IN SAFFRON CREAM

This recipe is also excellent for scallops. If you like, substitute large sea scallops for the shrimp and cook in exactly the same way.

4 SERVINGS

- ¼ teaspoon saffron threads
- ¼ cup dry white wine
- 1 pound spinach leaves, washed thoroughly but not dried
- 1 tablespoon unsalted butter
- 1 pound medium shrimp, shelled and deveined
- Salt and freshly ground pepper
- 1 tablespoon olive oil
- 2 large shallots, minced
- 1 large garlic clove, minced
- ⅔ cup heavy cream
- 2 tablespoons shrimp stock or water
- 1 medium tomato or large plum tomato, seeded and cut into ½-inch dice
- 2 teaspoons fresh lemon juice

Shrimp and Spinach in Saffron Cream (*top*), Scallops and Spicy Chorizo (*bottom*)

1. Crush the saffron threads in a small bowl. Pour in the white wine and let the saffron steep while you proceed.

2. Heat a large nonreactive skillet over high heat. Add handfuls of the spinach leaves, with water clinging to them, to the skillet, stirring to wilt the leaves before each addition. Continue until all of the spinach leaves have wilted. Transfer the spinach leaves to a colander to drain well and then chop them coarsely. Wipe out the skillet.

3. Melt the butter in the skillet over moderate heat. When the foam subsides, add the shrimp. Season with salt and pepper and cook, stirring, until the shrimp are pink and beginning to curl, about 3 minutes. Transfer the shrimp and any cooking juices to a plate.

4. Heat the olive oil in the skillet. Add the shallots and cook over moderate heat until softened, about 4 minutes. Add the garlic and cook until fragrant, about 1 minute. Increase the heat to moderately high and add the white wine with the saffron. Boil until the liquid has been reduced by half.

5. Stir in the heavy cream and the shrimp stock (see Note) and bring the mixture to a simmer. Add the spinach leaves and the diced tomato and simmer for 1 minute. Add the shrimp with their juices and cook until just heated through. Season with the lemon juice, salt and pepper and serve at once.

NOTE: After you shell the shrimp for this dish, you can simmer the shells in water to make a simple stock.—MARCIA KIESEL

SHRIMP, SCALLOP AND TOMATO BROCHETTES

Buttered, parsleyed orzo makes a perfect bed for these brochettes.

🍷 *Simple seafood flavors, enlivened by cherry tomatoes, call for a straightforward, crisply acidic dry white. Look for the 1994 Delas Frères Vin de Pays d'Oc Viognier or the 1995 Elk Cove Pinot Gris.*

4 SERVINGS

- 12 large shrimp, shelled and deveined
- 12 sea scallops
- 2 tablespoons olive oil, plus more for brushing
- 8 fresh thyme sprigs, plus additional sprigs tied in a small bundle
- 2 dozen cherry tomatoes
- Salt and freshly ground pepper
- Lemon quarters, for serving

Light a grill or preheat the broiler. In a bowl, toss the shrimp and scallops with the olive oil and the 8 thyme sprigs. Let marinate for 10 minutes. Using wooden skewers, prepare two brochettes per person: one of shrimp and cherry tomatoes, one of scallops and cherry tomatoes. Season the brochettes with salt and pepper. Grill or broil them for about 2 minutes per side or until cooked to your taste, brushing with the fresh thyme bundle dipped in olive oil. Serve with lemon quarters.—NINA ZAGAT

SCALLOPS AND SPICY CHORIZO

This dish was inspired by one at my favorite New York tapas restaurant, El Cid. Serve it with crusty bread to soak up the succulent juices.

4 SERVINGS

- 1 tablespoon extra-virgin olive oil
- Two 3-ounce cured chorizo sausages, quartered lengthwise and sliced crosswise ¼ inch thick
- 1 pound sea scallops
- Salt and freshly ground pepper
- 1 medium leek, white and tender green, quartered lengthwise, cut into 2-by-¼-inch strips and washed
- ½ teaspoon minced garlic
- ⅓ cup dry white wine
- ½ cup clam juice

1. Heat 1 teaspoon of the olive oil in a large nonreactive skillet until it is almost smoking. Add the chorizo pieces to the skillet and cook over high heat, stirring, until browned, about 2 minutes. Transfer to a large plate. Wipe out the skillet, add 1 teaspoon of the oil and heat until almost smoking. Season the scallops with salt and pepper and add them to the skillet in a single layer. Cook over high heat, turning once, until golden, about 3 minutes. Add the scallops to the chorizo.

2. Heat the remaining 1 teaspoon olive oil in the skillet. Add the leek and garlic and sauté over moderately high heat until just softened, about 2 minutes. Pour in the white wine and boil until the liquid is almost evaporated, scraping the bottom of the pan to loosen any browned bits. Pour in the clam juice and boil to reduce by half, about 3 minutes. Return the chorizo and the scallops to the skillet and toss over moderate heat until both are heated through. Serve the dish at once.—GRACE PARISI

Shrimp, Scallop and Tomato Brochettes

Soft-Shell-Crab Sandwiches

SOFT-SHELL-CRAB SANDWICHES

MAKES 6 SANDWICHES

- 6 jumbo soft-shell crabs, cleaned
- 1 cup buttermilk
- 1 cup crushed saltine crackers or ½ cup cornmeal

Salt and freshly ground pepper
¼ cup vegetable oil
3 tablespoons unsalted butter
6 hamburger buns or soft hero rolls
Tomato slices
Curried Pepper Relish (recipe follows)
Lemon wedges

SOFT-SHELL-CRAB POINTERS

• Buy live crabs if possible.

• Choose crabs with soft, moist shells.

• Soft-shells are graded by size, measured across the back, tip to tip: mediums, 3½ to 4 inches; hotels, 4 to 4½; primes, 4½ to 5; jumbos, 5 to 5½; and whales, 5½ inches or more.

• Have the fishmonger clean the crabs, or do it yourself (see "Cleaning Crabs," p. 21).

Pilaf of Mussels

1. In a large shallow glass or ceramic baking dish, cover the soft-shell crabs with the buttermilk and refrigerate for at least 1 and up to 4 hours.

2. On a large plate, blend the cracker crumbs with ½ teaspoon each of salt and pepper. Alternatively, season the cornmeal with 1 teaspoon salt and ½ teaspoon pepper.

3. In a large skillet, heat the vegetable oil over high heat until shimmering. Meanwhile, remove the soft-shell crabs from the buttermilk and shake off the excess. Add the butter to the vegetable oil and, when it stops sizzling, dredge half of the soft-shell crabs at a time in the cracker crumbs or the cornmeal. Set the crabs in the skillet, undersides up, and fry, turning once, until they are cooked through and crisp, about 4 minutes per side; adjust the heat if the oil becomes too smoky.

4. Set a fried soft-shell crab on each bun, top it with the tomato slices and Curried Pepper Relish and serve the sandwiches immediately, with lemon wedges on the side.

Curried Pepper Relish

MAKES ABOUT 1½ CUPS

1 teaspoon curry powder
1½ tablespoons olive oil
¼ cup mayonnaise
1 yellow bell pepper, cut into small dice
1 Anaheim chile or 1 small green bell pepper, cut into small dice
½ to 1 whole small red chile, minced
½ small onion, finely diced
1 small garlic clove, minced
1 tablespoon fresh lime juice
2 teaspoons chopped capers
¼ teaspoon finely grated lime zest
Salt and freshly ground pepper

1. In a small dry skillet, toast the curry powder over moderate heat, stirring, until fragrant, about 30 seconds. Add the olive oil and remove from the heat.

2. Combine the mayonnaise, yellow bell pepper, chiles, onion, garlic, lime juice, capers, and lime zest in a bowl. Season with salt and freshly ground pepper. Scrape the curry oil into the relish and stir it in.—MARCIA KIESEL

PILAF OF MUSSELS

This molded pilaf is one of my favorite mussel dishes. It has a wonderful Provençal flavor and makes a fine impression at the table. If you don't have custard cups or ramekins to mold the rice, you can simply spoon it onto plates in mounds and then form a well in the center. Spoon the warm mussels and their sauce into the wells and garnish with additional parsley before serving.

4 SERVINGS

MUSSELS:

4 pounds mussels, scrubbed and debearded
½ cup finely chopped onion
⅓ cup finely chopped celery
¼ cup finely chopped scallions
2 teaspoons finely chopped garlic
1 tablespoon unsalted butter
1 tablespoon all-purpose flour
½ cup chopped fresh parsley
Salt and freshly ground pepper

RICE PILAF:

- 1 tablespoon unsalted butter
- ½ cup chopped onion
- ½ teaspoon dried thyme
- 1½ cups long-grain white rice
- 3 cups water
- ½ teaspoon salt

1. Make the mussels: Put the mussels in a large nonreactive saucepan, cover the saucepan tightly and bring to a boil over moderately high heat, stirring once in a while. (You don't need to add any liquid; the mussels will release plenty of juices as they cook.) When all of the mussels have opened, after 8 to 10 minutes, remove the pan from the heat.

2. Transfer the mussels to a bowl. Strain the mussel juices into a clean medium saucepan through a sieve lined with a moistened paper towel; you will have about 1⅔ cups of mussel juices. Remove the mussel meat from the shells. If you wish, you can pull off and discard the dark, frilly sinew that encircles each of the mussels (see "Mussels," right).

3. To finish the sauce, add the chopped onion, celery, scallions and garlic to the mussel juices and boil the juices gently for 10 minutes. Meanwhile, knead the butter and the flour until they form a smooth paste. Whisk this paste into the boiling mussel juices. Add the chopped parsley and simmer for 2 to 3 minutes, whisking until the sauce is smooth. Season the sauce to taste with salt and pepper.

4. Make the rice pilaf: Melt the butter in a medium saucepan. Add the onion and thyme, mix

MUSSELS

Mussels are one of the most flavorful and least expensive shellfish. When I first came to the United States, I could rarely find mussels in the markets, although stocks were plentiful all along the coasts of New York and Connecticut. Since then the spots by the ocean where I used to go mussel hunting have become polluted, but the cultivated bivalves are now readily available in fish shops and most supermarkets.

BUYING MUSSELS

When you buy mussels, look for heavy, medium-size specimens; you should get fifteen to eighteen per pound. Freshly harvested mussels are attached to one another in bunches, clinging by hairy, fibrous "beards," which must be removed before cooking. Uncleaned fresh mussels will keep in the refrigerator for about one week. Once the mussels have been separated and cleaned, they should be cooked within three or four days.

Two caveats: If a mussel shell is open, tap it on the counter or immerse in cold water. If the shell closes, the mussel is alive and well—and edible. If not, discard it. If a mussel shell feels unusually heavy for its size, it may be filled with mud instead of meat. Slide the shell apart with your fingers; if you find mud inside, toss the mussel out.

CLEANING MUSSELS

If you have time, soak mussels in cold water with a handful of salt for about an hour to disgorge the sand. Mussels must be washed—rub them against one another, changing the water as necessary. Using a sharp paring knife, pull off the hairy "beards" that protrude from the mussel shells (see photo, bottom left).

Some cooks prefer to remove the frilly black, rubbery sinew that rings each mussel, both for appearance's sake and because it tends to be tough and chewy (see photo, bottom right). This sinew is always left intact, however, when steamed mussels are served in their shells.

You do not need to remove the barnacles that frequently make their home on mussel shells unless you find them unsightly; in fact, there's a good reason to leave them on: They add flavor to the broth when the mussels are steamed.—JACQUES PÉPIN

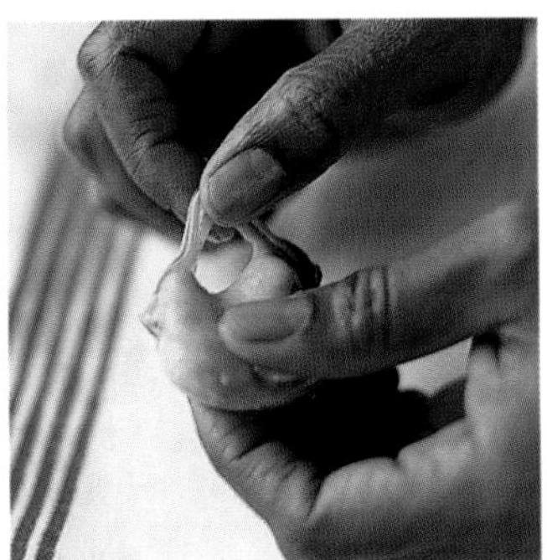

Clams with Garlic Sauce, with Baked Rice with Parsley (p. 317) and Asparagus with Red-Pepper Vinaigrette (p. 334)

QUICK DINNER

The garlicky clams might be paired with a number of whites, but the sharpness of the vinaigrette would diminish the taste of rich, round bottlings. Stick with tart, simple whites, such as those from Spain, notably the 1993 Conde de Valdemar Blanco en Barrica or the 1994 Albariño Lagar de Cerveza.

CLAMS WITH GARLIC SAUCE (P. 178)

BAKED RICE WITH PARSLEY (P. 317)

ASPARAGUS WITH RED-PEPPER VINAIGRETTE (P. 334)

GAME PLAN:

- **Soak the clams. Bring the water for the asparagus to a boil.**
- **Prepare the ingredients for the clams and rice.**
- **Put the rice on to cook.**
- **Blanch the asparagus. Make the vinaigrette, dress the asparagus and let stand at room temperature.**
- **Cook the clams; make the sauce.**

well and cook over moderately high heat for 1 minute. Add the rice and stir to coat the grains of rice with the butter. Add the water and salt and bring to a boil, stirring. Reduce the heat to very low, cover the pan and cook the rice for 20 minutes.

5. Generously butter four 1¼-cup custard dishes, bowls or ramekins. Reheat the mussel sauce and add the cooked mussels to it.

6. Spoon ½ cup of the hot rice pilaf into each of the prepared custard dishes. Using a spoon, press the rice against the side of each dish to make a nest in the center. Spoon ten of the mussels and 3 tablespoons of the sauce into each nest and cover with another ½ cup of the rice pilaf. Press on the rice with the back of the spoon to pack it down slightly, and invert the molded mussel pilaf onto warmed serving plates. Spoon the remaining mussels with the sauce around each serving of the rice pilaf; serve at once.—JACQUES PÉPIN

CLAMS WITH GARLIC SAUCE Q

Just because you're making a Spanish dish with rice and shellfish does not mean it's got to be paella. Unlike that time-consuming old standard, this quick savory main course from the Basque region, home of some of the country's best chefs, makes the succulent clams, not the rice, the main feature. Soaking the clams in water laced with cornmeal helps remove any sand they might contain.

4 SERVINGS

3 dozen littleneck clams, scrubbed
½ cup cornmeal
1 tablespoon coarse salt
4 garlic cloves, minced
¼ cup plus 2 tablespoons minced fresh parsley
A few saffron threads
¼ cup olive oil
1 small onion, minced
½ cup dry white wine
1 tablespoon fresh lemon juice
1 small dried red chile
2 bay leaves
¼ teaspoon hot paprika
Freshly ground black pepper
½ cup fish stock or ¼ cup bottled clam juice diluted with ¼ cup of water

1. In a bowl, cover the clams and cornmeal with water; add the salt. Soak for 45 minutes; drain and rinse.

2. In a blender or mini-processor, puree the garlic with 5 tablespoons of the parsley and the saffron.

3. Heat the olive oil in a nonreactive skillet. Add the onion and cook over moderate heat until translucent. Add the clams, white wine, lemon juice, chile, bay leaves, hot paprika and black pepper. Cover the skillet and cook the clams over high heat, stirring; remove the clams as they open.

4. Add the fish stock and the garlic mixture to the skillet and cook until the sauce is slightly thickened, about 1 minute. Discard the chile and bay leaves. Divide the clams among four soup plates, spoon the garlic sauce on top and garnish with the remaining 1 tablespoon of minced parsley.—PENELOPE CASAS

CHAPTER 7

CHICKEN

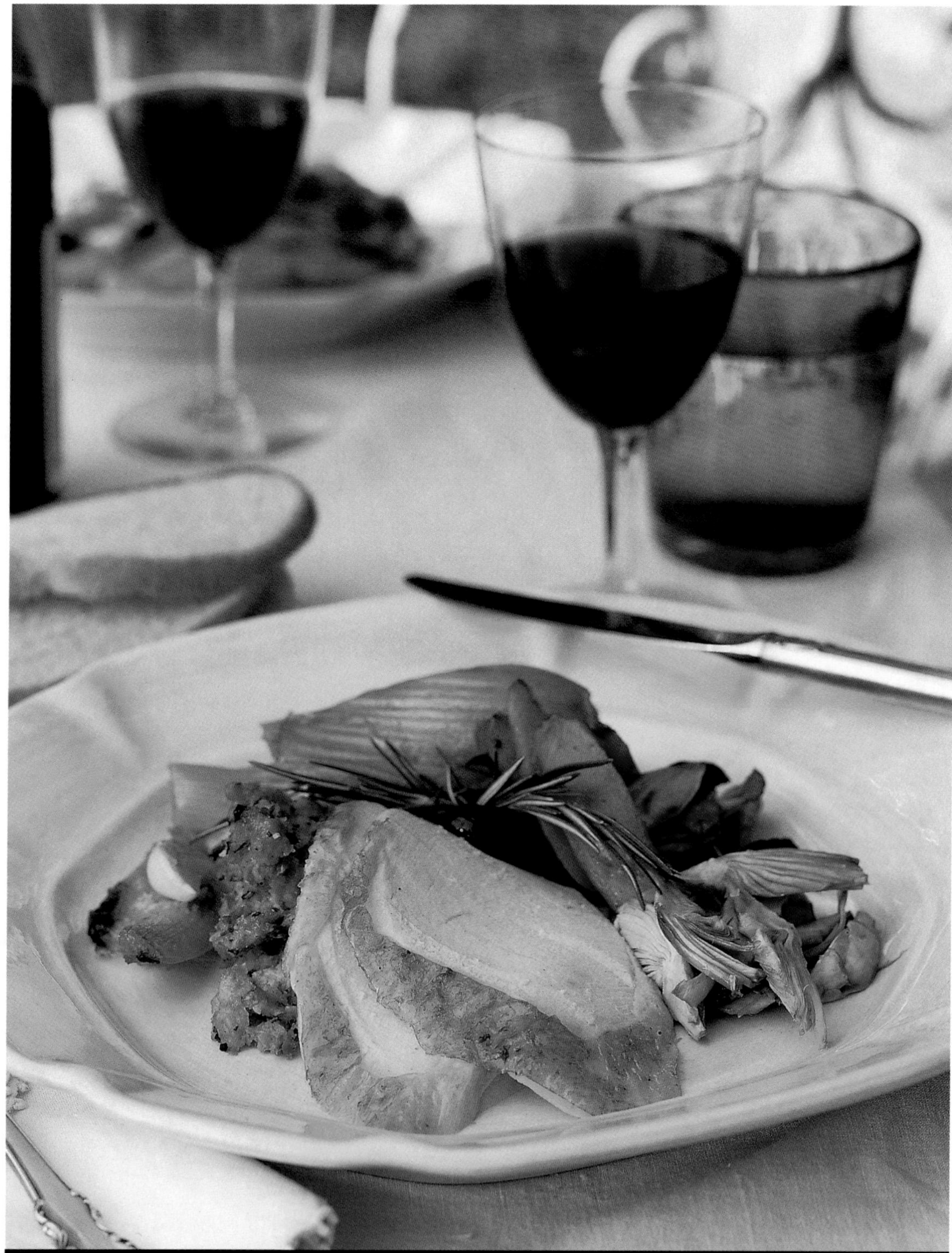

Clockwise from bottom: **Monsieur Henny's Roast Chicken, Gratinéed Fennel (p. 339), Carrots Provençal (p. 338) and Barcelona Artichokes (p. 335)**

MONSIEUR HENNY'S ROAST CHICKEN

If you want extra stuffing, simply increase the ingredients by one-half and bake the additional stuffing in a buttered ovenproof dish at 375° for about forty-five minutes.

🍷 *We always have bottles of our house red, Clos Chanteduc, on hand, but at our last fall celebration, we sampled a rich white Rhône, the 1994 Châteauneuf-du-Pape from Château de Beaucastel. The clean fruity and floral flavors stand up nicely to the dense, rich sausage stuffing.*

8 SERVINGS

STUFFING:

- 1 pound bulk sausage meat
- The reserved heart, liver and peeled gizzard from the chicken (below), cut into bite-size pieces
- 4 ounces coarse dry bread crumbs (1½ cups)
- 2 large eggs, lightly beaten
- 1 tablespoon minced fresh rosemary leaves
- 2 teaspoons fennel seeds
- ¾ teaspoon fine sea salt
- ¼ teaspoon freshly ground pepper

- One 6-pound roasting chicken with the heart, liver, gizzard and neck
- 1½ tablespoons unsalted butter, softened
- Sea salt and freshly ground white pepper

1. Preheat the oven to 425°.

2. Make the stuffing: In a large bowl, using your hands, blend all of the stuffing ingredients thoroughly, breaking up any large pieces of sausage meat. Stuff the cavity and neck of the chicken; don't be afraid to pack the stuffing slightly so there are no air pockets. Tie the legs of the chicken together with kitchen string. Tie the wings together behind the back. Rub the chicken with the butter and season generously with salt and pepper.

3. Place the chicken breast-side up in a shallow flameproof roasting pan. Add the chicken neck to the pan. Loosely tent the chicken with aluminum foil and roast in the center of the oven for 30 minutes. Remove the pan from the oven and gently remove the foil. Baste the chicken thoroughly, re-cover with the foil and roast for 30 minutes longer, basting occasionally. Reduce the oven temperature to 375°. Remove the foil, baste the chicken again and roast about 1½ hours more, or until the juices run clear when a thigh is pierced and the stuffing reaches 165° on an instant-read thermometer.

4. Remove the roasting pan from the oven and immediately season the chicken generously with salt and pepper. Transfer the chicken to a platter and tilt it neck-end down. (This heightens the flavor by allowing the juices to flow down through the breast meat.) Cover the chicken loosely with aluminum foil and allow it to rest for at least 10 minutes or up to 30 minutes.

5. Meanwhile, prepare the sauce: Remove and discard the chicken neck from the roasting pan. Place the pan over moderate heat and cook, scraping and stirring, until the liquid is syrupy, 2 to 3 minutes; do not let it burn. Spoon off and discard any excess fat. Add ½ cup cold water and bring to a boil. Reduce the heat to low and simmer until reduced to ¾ cup, about 5 minutes. Season with salt and white pepper. Strain the sauce through a fine-mesh sieve and pour into a sauceboat.

6. Carve the chicken and arrange the pieces on a warmed platter. Spoon the sausage stuffing into a warmed bowl and serve with the chicken.—PATRICIA WELLS

FRENCH COUNTRY DINNER

SMOKED SALMON TARTARE (P. 25)

WHEAT AND POLENTA BREAD (P. 294)

MONSIEUR HENNY'S ROAST CHICKEN (P. 183)

BARCELONA ARTICHOKES (P. 335)

CARROTS PROVENÇAL (P. 338)

GRATINÉED FENNEL (P. 339)

LEMON LOVER'S TART (P. 397)

ROAST CHICKEN WITH CORN PANCETTA RELISH

Don't be put off by the long ingredient list for this recipe; the luscious, tender chicken and sweet-savory relish are easy to prepare. Serve mashed potatoes with this dish.

🍷 *The tangy and salty accents here call for a full, round and fruity California Chardonnay. Among possible choices: a Carneros district bottling, such as the 1994 Joseph Phelps or the 1994 Saintsbury.*

4 SERVINGS

RELISH:

- 1½ teaspoons finely julienned lime zest
- 1½ teaspoons extra-virgin olive oil
- One 4-ounce piece of pancetta, cut into ½-inch cubes
- 1 medium onion, finely diced
- ½ red bell pepper, finely diced
- ½ green bell pepper, finely diced
- 1½ teaspoons minced garlic
- 1½ teaspoons minced fresh ginger
- Coarse salt and freshly ground black pepper
- ½ cup plus 2 tablespoons fresh lime juice
- ¼ cup dark brown sugar
- ¼ teaspoon cayenne pepper
- ⅛ teaspoon crushed red pepper
- 1 heaping cup fresh corn kernels
- ½ cup coarsely chopped fresh cilantro

CHICKEN:

- One 3-pound chicken, preferably free-range
- 5 garlic cloves
- Zest of 1 lemon, cut into 1-inch strips
- 2 fresh rosemary sprigs
- Coarse salt and freshly ground black pepper
- ¼ cup dry white wine

1. Make the relish: In a small saucepan of boiling water, blanch the lime zest for 1 minute. Drain and set aside. Heat the oil in a nonreactive medium saucepan. Add the pancetta and cook over moderately low heat, stirring, until lightly browned and crisp, about 10 minutes. Using a slotted spoon, transfer to a paper towel to drain.

2. Add the onion to the pan and cook, stirring a few times, until translucent, about 5 minutes. Add the bell peppers, garlic, ginger and a pinch each of salt and

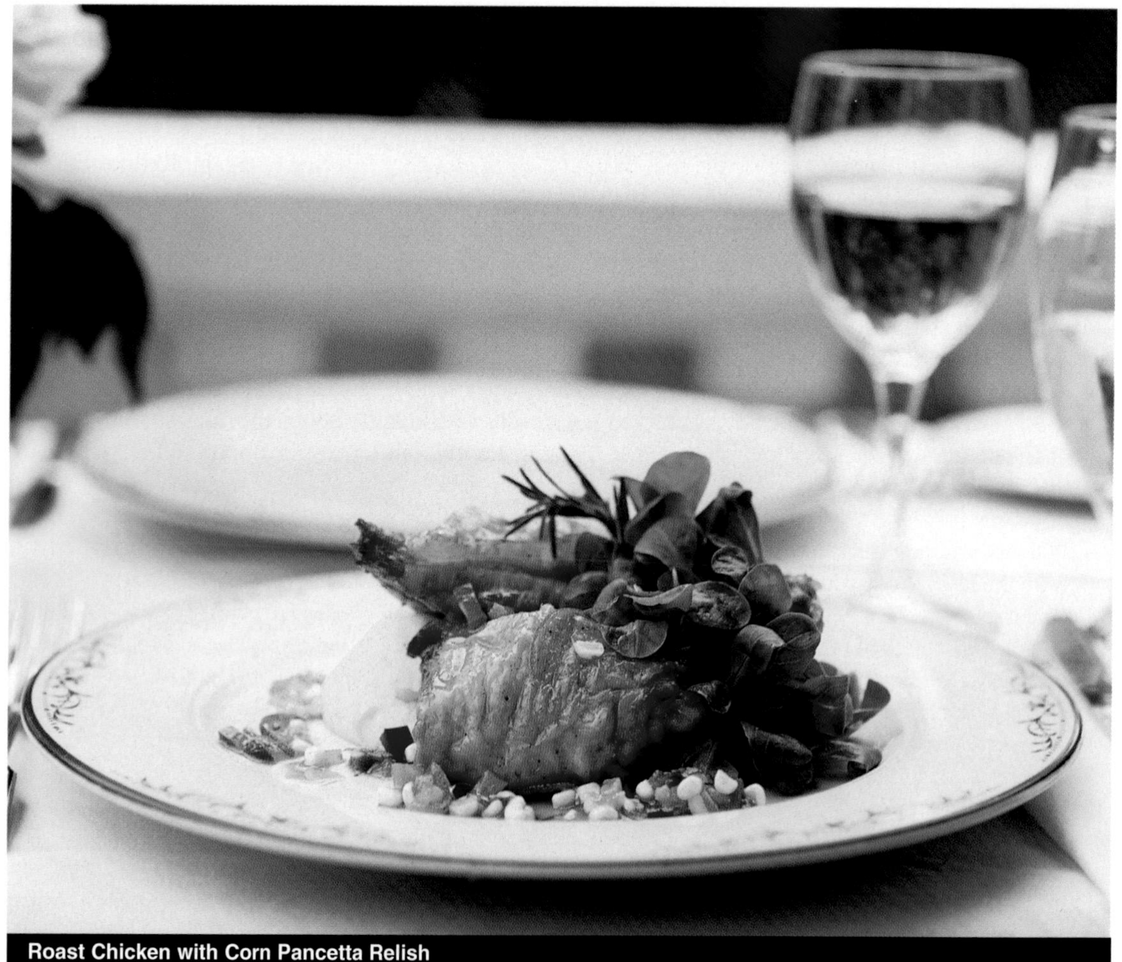

Roast Chicken with Corn Pancetta Relish

black pepper. Raise the heat to moderate and cook, stirring, until fragrant, about 2 minutes. Add the lime juice, brown sugar, cayenne, crushed red pepper and blanched lime zest and bring to a simmer. Add the corn and cook until just tender, about 5 minutes. Stir in the pancetta and transfer to a bowl to cool. Season with salt and pepper. (MAKE AHEAD: The relish can be refrigerated for up to 1 day. Let return to room temperature before serving.) Stir in the cilantro.

3. Make the chicken: Preheat the oven to 475°. Stuff the chicken with the garlic, lemon zest and rosemary and season with salt and pepper. Truss the chicken and set it, breast-side down, on an oiled roasting rack. Roast for 20 minutes. Turn breast-side up and reduce the oven temperature to 400°. Roast the chicken, basting, for about 45 minutes longer, or until the juices from the cavity run clear. Remove the bird and rack from the pan, cover with foil and let stand 10 minutes.

4. Set the roasting pan on two burners over moderately high heat and pour in the wine and ½ cup of water. Simmer over moderately low heat for 5 minutes, scraping up the browned bits. Strain the gravy, skim off the fat and season with salt and pepper.

5. Carve the chicken into four pieces and arrange the pieces on four plates. Spoon the relish over the chicken and serve at once with the pan gravy.—LANCE DEAN VELASQUEZ ➤

Q & A

Q: What do I need to know to make a terrific roast chicken every time?

A: Follow these pointers:

- Know where the chicken comes from. Chickens are sometimes packed in ice, defrosted and then frozen again. If this happens, ice pellets can attach to the breasts of the chickens and make the white meat mushy. Buy freshly killed birds from your butcher if possible.
- Truss the bird with a needle and kitchen string before roasting. The main advantage of trussing is that it holds the bird together, preventing the legs and wings from cooking more quickly than the body.
- Rub the bird with butter before putting it in the oven.
- Cook the chicken, breast-side down, in a preheated 450° oven for fifteen minutes until nicely browned. Then take the bird out of the oven and salt it all over; the salt will cook into the chicken. Place the chicken back in the pan, breast-side up, toss in some sliced onions and carrots, if you wish, and finish cooking.
- When the bird is done, lift it up—use the trussing strings or grasp the ends of the legs with your cooking mitt—and hold it, neck-end down, over the pan; let the juices drain into the pan. They should be yellow. If they have tinges of pink, cook the chicken a little longer.—JULIA CHILD

ENTERTAINING TIPS AND TACTICS

- Develop a few seasonal menus you love to make and can do with your eyes closed. It's great to try new dishes, but when time pressures come into play, you're safest making something familiar.
- Plan menus with flexible cooking times. I often serve roast joints of meat or whole birds when I'm having a big dinner party because they benefit from a long resting time after cooking.
- If you want to experiment with something more exotic, say an organ meat or snails, that might not be a crowd pleaser, serve small quantities as an hors d'oeuvre or an optional side dish.
- Cultivate a look for your table. Mine is crisp white linens, oversized white napkins, antique silverplate and a selection of ochre pottery, both new and old. Since I use all white linens and have tables of several sizes and shapes, I have developed a simple code: I sew a different color of thread on the edge of each cloth—green for the small round table, blue for the large rectangle.
- Put your guests to work. Most people love to pitch in, but they need to be told what to do. I make a mental list of little tasks—opening wine, setting the table—and assign them to the most logical work party.—PATRICIA WELLS

CHICKEN WITH SHALLOTS, THYME AND LEMON

Few dishes are as soothing and welcoming as this—a deliciously moist whole chicken, browned and then braised in wine in a cocotte, a huge cast-iron casserole, with mountains of herbs and an avalanche of perfectly shaped whole shallots. The sauce—which is actually a version of the egg-and-cream-thickened sauce used in a classic blanquette de veau—reminds me of avgolemono, the tangy lemon sauce served in Greek cuisine.

🍷 *You'll need an assertive wine to cut through the richness of the sauce. Any wine with a nicely balanced acidity will be good: a French Riesling, a white Burgundy, a not-too-oaky California Chardonnay. Try a Rhône Valley Viognier or a simple Côtes du Rhône Blanc de Blancs.*

4–6 SERVINGS

One 3-pound free-range roasting chicken, at room temperature
Sea salt and freshly ground pepper
1 small lemon, preferably organic
1 bunch of fresh thyme
3 tablespoons unsalted butter
2 tablespoons extra-virgin olive oil
3 cups dry white wine
20 best-quality large shallots
Bouquet garni made with a generous amount of fresh tarragon, fresh flat-leaf parsley, celery leaves, bay leaves and fresh thyme sprigs tied in cheesecloth
3 large egg yolks
1 tablespoon crème fraîche or heavy cream
1 tablespoon fresh lemon juice
¼ teaspoon freshly grated nutmeg
1 tablespoon fresh thyme leaves
Steamed basmati rice, for serving

1. Generously season the cavity of the chicken with sea salt and pepper. Scrub the lemon and pierce it with a two-pronged fork about a dozen times. Place the lemon and half of the thyme bunch inside the cavity. Truss the chicken.

2. In a large nonreactive flameproof casserole, melt the butter in the olive oil until hot but not smoking. Add the chicken and cook over moderate heat, turning gently with tongs, until it is brown on all sides, about 20 minutes. Transfer the chicken to a platter and season it generously with sea salt and pepper. Discard the fat in the casserole. Pour the white wine into the casserole and cook over moderate heat, scraping the bottom of the casserole with a wooden spoon to loosen the browned bits. Increase the heat to high and boil vigorously until there is no alcohol aroma, about 5 minutes. Return the chicken to the casserole breast-side up. Add the shallots, the bouquet garni and the remaining half bunch of thyme. Cover the casserole and simmer over very low heat until the chicken is cooked through, 40 to 50 minutes.

3. Meanwhile, in a large bowl, stir together the egg yolks, the crème fraîche, the lemon juice and the nutmeg.

Preparing Chicken with Shallots, Thyme and Lemon

COOKING WITH WINE

DO think of wine as a "perfume," to be added at the very last moment: a dash of port to melon, or a splash of white wine to warm potatoes for a salad to prevent them from absorbing too much oil.
DON'T use a great wine, which will lose more than it will give to the dish.
DO add a bit of white wine to a chicken stock or red wine to a beef stock.
DON'T overwhelm the dish. Less is more, at least at first.
DO use wines to deglaze a pan—add a few spoonfuls of white wine to the pan when roasting chicken, or red wine for beef or lamb.
DON'T even think of using anything sold as "cooking sherry" or "cooking wine." These contain salt and are not fit to drink or cook with.
DO lighten cream sauce with a few drops of white wine.
DON'T cook with Champagne. It will lose the very qualities we love it for.
DO save bits of unused red wines in one bottle, whites in another, for up to a week. Try to keep the bottles full so the contents won't turn to vinegar.—PATRICIA WELLS

4. Transfer the chicken and the shallots to a warm serving platter, cover with foil and set aside in a warm oven. Discard the bouquet garni and the thyme. Strain the sauce through a fine-mesh sieve and return it to the casserole. You should have about 1½ cups of sauce; if you have more than that, boil it over high heat until reduced. Whisk the egg mixture into the sauce and cook over low heat, stirring, until the sauce begins to thicken slightly, about 5 minutes; do not allow the sauce to boil. Strain the sauce through a fine-mesh sieve into a bowl.

5. Carve the chicken and arrange the pieces on a large, warm serving platter. Spoon the shallots alongside. Drizzle about half of the sauce over the chicken and the shallots. Sprinkle the fresh thyme leaves on top. Serve the chicken warm with the steamed basmati rice and pass the remaining sauce separately.—PATRICIA WELLS

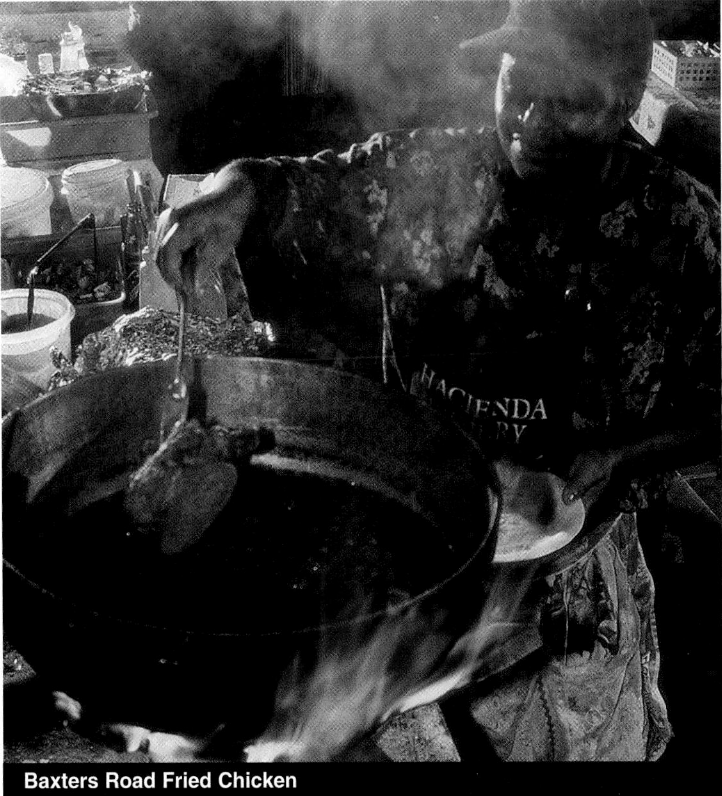

Baxters Road Fried Chicken

BAXTERS ROAD FRIED CHICKEN

In Barbados, enterprising local women bring their own special seasonings and their coal pots and cauldrons into the street and fry chicken and fish.

4 SERVINGS

- 1 medium onion, quartered
- 2 scallions, coarsely chopped
- 1 garlic clove, halved
- ½ Scotch bonnet chile, seeded
- 2 fresh flat-leaf parsley sprigs
- 1 fresh marjoram sprig
- ½ teaspoon fresh thyme
- 2 allspice berries, crushed
- Salt
- One 3-pound chicken, cut into 8 pieces
- 2 cups vegetable oil, for frying
- ½ cup all-purpose flour
- 1 tablespoon cornmeal

2 teaspoons poultry seasoning, such as Bell's
Freshly ground pepper

1. In a mini-processor, puree the onion, scallions, garlic, chile, parsley, marjoram, thyme, allspice and ½ teaspoon salt to a thick paste. (**MAKE AHEAD:** The paste can be refrigerated for up to 10 days.)

2. Score the chicken pieces ½ inch apart and generously fill the slashes with the herb paste. In a large skillet, heat the oil to 375° over moderately high heat. In a paper bag, combine the flour, cornmeal, poultry seasoning, ½ teaspoon of salt and a generous amount of pepper. Add the chicken and shake until coated. Put the chicken in the hot oil and cook, turning, until golden and cooked through, about 25 minutes. Lower the heat if the chicken browns too quickly. Drain the chicken on a rack and serve hot.—JESSICA B. HARRIS

CHICKEN COLOMBO

The curry mixture called colombo *is a legacy of indentured servants who came to the Caribbean island of Guadeloupe from coastal India in the last century. Since then,* colombo *has taken a bit from the French and a bit from the African to become truly Creole.*

4–6 SERVINGS

1½ teaspoons coriander seeds
1½ teaspoons allspice berries
1½ teaspoons cumin seeds
1 teaspoon black peppercorns
¼ teaspoon turmeric
One 4-pound chicken, cut into 8 pieces
2½ tablespoons fresh lime juice
Salt and freshly ground pepper
3 tablespoons unsalted butter
2 tablespoons olive oil
1 onion, coarsely chopped
2 scallions, minced
1 shallot, minced
1 garlic clove, minced
2 tablespoons minced fresh flat-leaf parsley
2 fresh thyme sprigs
2 medium tomatoes, peeled, seeded and coarsely chopped
1 medium chayote, peeled and cut into 1-inch chunks
1 small eggplant, peeled and cut into 1-inch chunks
1 Scotch bonnet chile, pricked with a fork
Boiled white rice, for serving

1. In a small skillet, toast the coriander seeds, allspice berries, cumin seeds and peppercorns over moderately high heat, shaking the pan, until fragrant, about 40 seconds. Transfer to a plate to cool, then finely grind in a spice grinder or mortar. Stir in the turmeric.

2. In a large bowl, toss the chicken with 1½ tablespoons of the lime juice and season with salt and pepper. In a large enameled cast-iron casserole, melt the butter in the oil. Add the chicken and cook over moderately high heat, without turning, until browned, about 3 minutes. Turn the chicken and add the onion, scallions and shallot. Reduce the heat to moderate and cook until the chicken is browned, about 4 minutes. Add the ground spices

Q & A: NONSTICK PANS

Q: Can I use my nonstick pots and pans in the oven?

A: Certainly a baking pan with a nonstick surface is ovenproof. As far as stovetop pots and pans are concerned, the issue is not the coating but the handle. The product information should specify whether the pan and handle are safe for oven use and, if so, to what temperature.

Q: What advantages for low-fat cooking do pans with deep ridges offer?

A: Deep ridges allow fat to drain away from the food. Grill pans and stovetop grills also make food look tempting by marking it with attractive grill lines. One caveat: Grills and grill pans, like woks, are meant to be used for high-heat cooking, which can damage nonstick surfaces.

Q: If I can buy only one piece of nonstick cooking equipment, what should it be?

A: Choose either a large nonstick skillet (flared sides) or sauté pan (straight sides and a cover) of the best quality you can afford. Both are versatile for low-fat cooking because they allow you to cook meat, poultry or fish, then deglaze the pan to make sauces without adding fat. You can also use them to sauté vegetables, caramelize onions and cook down pasta sauces.—DEBORAH KRASNER

and the garlic, parsley and thyme and cook, stirring, until fragrant, about 2 minutes.

3. Add the remaining 1 tablespoon lime juice and 2 cups of water to just cover the chicken. Simmer over very low heat for 30 minutes. Add the tomatoes, chayote, eggplant and Scotch bonnet chile and season with salt and pepper. Cover and simmer until the chicken and vegetables are tender, about 30 minutes. Transfer the chicken to a plate. Boil the stew over moderately high heat until the liquid is slightly reduced, about 4 minutes. Discard the thyme sprigs. Return the chicken to the casserole, season it with salt and pepper and serve with the boiled white rice.—JESSICA B. HARRIS

PAELLA WITH CHICKEN AND SEAFOOD LF

Spanish paella can include a variety of fish, meat and poultry, from eels to snails to duck. This excellent version, chock-full of goodies, uses only ingredients that are easy to find here.

6 SERVINGS

- 1 live lobster (1½ pounds)
- ½ pound medium shrimp, shelled and deveined, shells reserved
- 1 tablespoon tomato paste
- 3 tablespoons brandy
- 1 pound smoked ham hock
- Vegetable cooking spray
- Two ½-pound chicken-breast halves on the bone, skinned and cut into 3 pieces each
- Salt and freshly ground pepper
- 1 medium onion, finely chopped
- 1 large garlic clove, minced
- 1 cup canned peeled tomatoes, drained, seeded and coarsely chopped
- 1½ cups medium-grain rice, such as Valencia or arborio
- ¾ teaspoon sweet paprika
- Scant ¼ teaspoon saffron threads, crumbled
- 6 littleneck clams, scrubbed
- 6 mussels, scrubbed and debearded
- ¼ cup fresh peas or frozen baby lima beans
- 4 ounces small sugar snap peas

1. In a large pot of boiling water, cook the lobster for 2 minutes. Drain and let cool slightly. Remove the meat from the tail and claws; cut the tail meat into four pieces. Reserve the lobster shells.

2. Heat a large saucepan. Add the lobster shells and the reserved shrimp shells and cook over high heat, stirring occasionally, for 5 minutes. Stir in the tomato paste and cook for 2 more minutes. Add the brandy, ignite and cook until the flames subside. Add the ham hock and 8 cups water and bring to a boil. Lower the heat to moderate and cook until the liquid is reduced by half, about 45 minutes. Remove the ham hock and cut ½ cup of lean meat off the bone; reserve the remainder for another use. Strain the broth and skim any fat; keep the broth warm.

3. Preheat the oven to 350°. Coat a smooth-bottomed nonstick ovenproof skillet with vegetable cooking spray and heat. Season the chicken with salt and pepper and cook over high heat, turning once, until golden, about 2 minutes per side; transfer to a plate. Coat the skillet with cooking spray, add the onion and garlic and cook until just translucent, about 4 minutes. Add the tomatoes, rice, paprika and saffron and cook until the liquid is absorbed, about 4 minutes.

Paella with Chicken and Seafood

4. Stir in the broth, ham-hock meat, chicken, 1 teaspoon of salt and ½ teaspoon of pepper. Cover and bring to a boil over high heat. Reduce the heat to low and simmer, shaking the skillet, for 10 minutes. Add the clams, the mussels and the lobster meat; cover and bake until the clams begin to open, about 10 minutes. Add the shrimp, the peas and the sugar snaps and bake covered until the shrimp are cooked through, about 5 minutes. Let the paella rest for 10 minutes, then serve.—GRACE PARISI ➤

Chicken Breasts Glazed with Hot-Pepper Jelly

ASOPAO DE POLLO

Puerto Rico's culinary heritage is a wonderful mix of Spanish, African, Taino and more—all of which have a role in asopao de pollo, *a chicken stew that's a country cousin of Spain's paella.*

6–8 SERVINGS

- 1 teaspoon oregano
- 1 garlic clove, minced
- Salt
- One 3- to 4-pound chicken, cut into 10 pieces
- 2 thick slices bacon
- 1½ ounces smoked ham, chopped
- 2 medium tomatoes, finely chopped
- 1 medium onion, finely chopped
- 1 green bell pepper, chopped
- 1 tablespoon drained capers
- ¼ cup diced pimiento-stuffed olives
- 2 cups medium-grain rice (about 12 ounces), such as Valencia
- 1 cup fresh or frozen green peas
- 4 pimientos, thinly sliced
- ½ cup freshly grated Parmesan cheese

1. In a small bowl, combine the oregano, garlic and salt. Rub the seasonings on the chicken pieces.
2. In a large enameled cast-iron casserole, cook the bacon over moderately low heat until the fat is rendered. Remove the bacon and reserve for another use. Add half of the chicken and cook over moderately high heat, turning, until browned all over, about 7 minutes. Transfer to a plate and brown the remaining chicken. Return all of the chicken to the pan and add the ham, tomatoes, onion and green pepper. Cover and simmer over low heat until

the chicken is cooked through, about 25 minutes. Let cool.

3. Remove the chicken meat from the bones. Discard the skin and bones; return the meat to the pan. Add 6½ cups of water and the capers and olives. Simmer for 5 minutes. Stir in the rice and 1 teaspoon salt and simmer until the rice is tender, about 15 minutes.

4. Meanwhile, in a small saucepan of boiling salted water, cook the peas until tender, about 1 minute for frozen, 4 minutes for fresh.

5. Season the *asopao* with salt. Garnish with the peas and the pimientos and sprinkle with the Parmesan. Serve at once, or the stew will lose its characteristic soupiness.—JESSICA B. HARRIS

SAUTÉING TIPS

Before starting, have all of your ingredients measured and close at hand. You will need to add them in quick succession to cook them evenly.

• Put the skillet over moderate heat for a few minutes. Then add the oil or butter and swirl it around until the palm of your hand feels hot when you hold it close above the pan. If you are using oil, it should shimmer slightly.

• Don't crowd the pan as you add the ingredients. If the pan is too full, the temperature will drop and the food will not brown properly. Instead, the juices will leach out and the food will poach in its own liquid and ultimately overcook. If you have a lot to sauté, cook in batches. Conversely, if the skillet gets too hot and the food starts to brown too quickly, pull it off the heat briefly to cool it down.

• Browning food not only contributes a rich caramelized flavor but also leaves drippings and crusty browned bits that make a wonderful sauce when you deglaze the pan. First, remove the cooked food and pour off the fat (leaving any dark juices). Adjust the heat to prevent the drippings from burning. Pour in a little liquid—wine, stock or water—and stir with a wooden spoon, scraping the bottom of the skillet to loosen the browned bits. Voilà—an instant pan sauce.

• Bear in mind that strong wines and spirits give sauces a quick flavor boost; try sherry, Cognac, Madeira or Marsala.

CHICKEN BREASTS GLAZED WITH HOT-PEPPER JELLY Q

Serve this quick main dish with fragrant rice. To avoid stringy celery, before cutting it, remove the top layer of ribs with a vegetable peeler.

2 SERVINGS

2 tablespoons hot-pepper jelly
½ teaspoon Dijon mustard
Two ½-pound boneless chicken breast halves, pounded lightly to an even thickness
Salt and freshly ground pepper
2 tablespoons unsalted butter
2 medium celery ribs, cut into 2-inch-long matchsticks
1 tablespoon fresh lemon juice
1 tablespoon coarsely chopped celery leaves

1. In a small bowl, combine the pepper jelly and the mustard; set aside. Season the chicken breasts on both sides with salt and pepper. In a large skillet, melt the butter over moderately high heat. When the foam subsides, add the chicken breasts and cook, turning once, until they are browned, about 3 minutes per side.

2. Tilt the skillet and pour off most of the fat. Add 1 tablespoon water and shake the pan to loosen the browned bits on the bottom. Push the chicken to one side, add the celery matchsticks and cook, stirring, for 1 minute. Add the pepper-jelly mixture and the lemon juice to the pan and shake to coat the chicken with the sauce. Cook until the sauce is reduced to a glaze, about 30 seconds. Season with salt and pepper.

3. Transfer the chicken to plates and spoon the celery matchsticks on top. Garnish with the chopped celery leaves and serve at once.—MARCIA KIESEL

MISO-STUFFED CHICKEN

Miso stuffed under the skin of the chicken breast flavors the meat and keeps it moist. A kind of miso demi-glace is also made with the pan juices.

4 SERVINGS

2½ tablespoons dark miso
2 teaspoons minced garlic
¾ teaspoon minced fresh ginger
¼ teaspoon honey
4 large chicken-breast halves on the bone with skin intact (8 to 10 ounces each)
Salt and freshly ground pepper
1 teaspoon vegetable oil
2 medium scallions, white part only, finely chopped
2 cups chicken stock or canned low-sodium broth
1 tablespoon finely chopped fresh basil

1. Preheat the oven to 400°. In a small bowl, combine 1½ tablespoons of the miso with the garlic, the minced fresh ginger and the honey.

2. Pat the chicken breasts dry with paper towels. Using your fingers, make a small opening in each breast between the meat and the skin (be careful not to break the skin). Stuff a quarter of the miso mixture into each opening and press lightly on the skin to work the paste all over the chicken breasts. Lightly season both sides of the chicken with salt and pepper.

3. Heat the oil in a large skillet. Add the chicken breasts to the pan, skin-side down, and cook over moderately high heat until brown and crusty, about 4 minutes. Turn and cook on the other side until brown and crusty, about 3 minutes. Transfer the chicken to a baking sheet and bake for about 15 minutes, or until cooked through.

4. Pour off the fat from the skillet. Add the scallions to the skillet and cook over high heat until fragrant, about 1 minute. Pour in the chicken stock and scrape the bottom of the pan with a wooden spoon to loosen the browned bits. Cook over high heat until the sauce has reduced

CASUAL DINNER

🍷 The smoked salmon needs a tart, dry white to cut its fattiness; the chicken calls for a big, dry white that won't compete with the light meat and rich sauce. Fortunately, a crisp oak-aged Chardonnay goes nicely with both. Consider the 1993 Fetzer Barrel Select from California or the 1992 Louis Latour Mâcon-Lugny Les Genièvres from France.

SMOKED SALMON WITH LEMON-DRESSED MESCLUN (P. 44)

CHICKEN WITH PORTOBELLO-MUSHROOM SAUCE (P. 193)

ROASTED-POTATO AND FENNEL HASH (P. 305)

ICE CREAM WITH STRAWBERRIES AND BALSAMIC GLAZE (P. 421)

GAME PLAN:

- **Start the dessert—macerate the strawberries; toast the walnuts; make the balsamic glaze.**
- **Start the main course—roast and slice the mushrooms; slice and roast the potatoes; slice and sauté the fennel; brown and cook the chicken.**
- **Prep the first course—peel and slice the cucumber and chop the chives; arrange the salmon on plates and make the dressing.**
- **Make the mushroom sauce.**
- **Five minutes before serving the main course, toss the roasted potatoes with the fennel.**

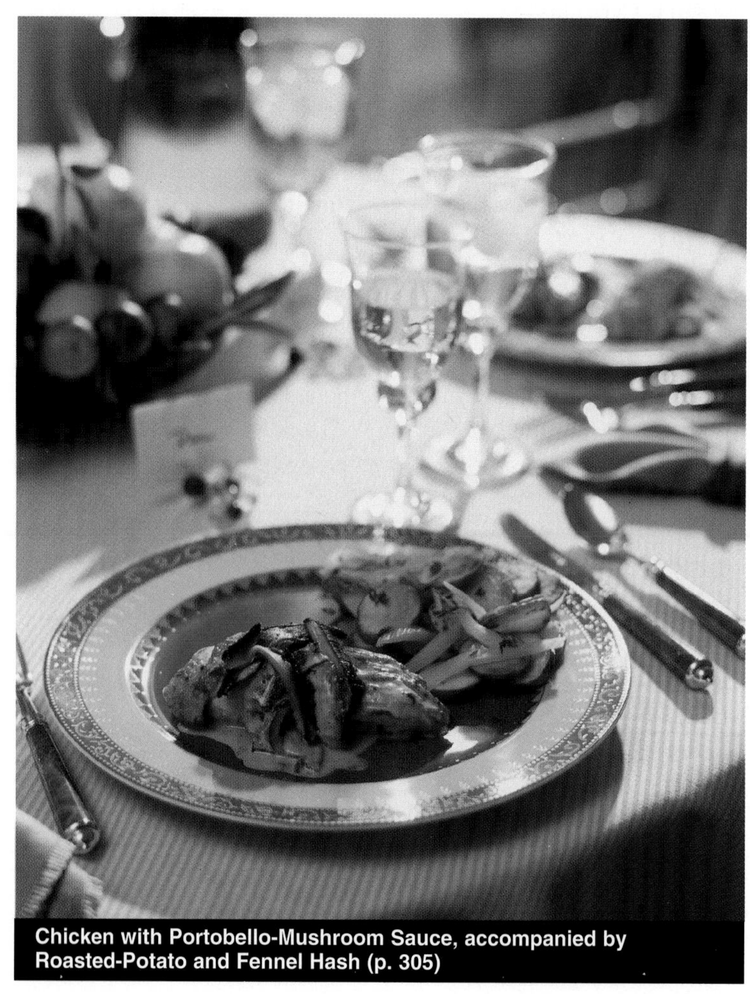

Chicken with Portobello-Mushroom Sauce, accompanied by Roasted-Potato and Fennel Hash (p. 305)

to ½ cup, about 12 minutes. Whisk in the remaining 1 tablespoon of miso. Strain the sauce through a fine-mesh sieve, pressing on the solids. Stir in the basil and season the sauce with salt and pepper.

5. To serve, transfer the chicken breasts to plates and spoon the pan sauce on top.—GRACE PARISI

CHICKEN WITH PORTOBELLO-MUSHROOM SAUCE Q

8 SERVINGS

- 3 large Portobello mushrooms, stems discarded
- 2 tablespoons plus 1 teaspoon olive oil

Salt and freshly ground pepper

- 8 medium boneless chicken-breast halves with skin
- 1 cup dry white wine
- ½ cup chicken stock or canned low-sodium broth
- ½ cup heavy cream

1. Preheat the oven to 425°. Arrange the mushrooms, stemmed-side down, on a baking sheet. Brush the mushrooms with the 1 teaspoon olive oil and season them with salt and pepper. Roast the mushrooms for about 12 minutes, or until tender. Thinly slice the mushrooms and transfer to a plate.

2. Heat the remaining 2 tablespoons olive oil in a large nonreactive skillet. Season the chicken breasts on both sides with salt and pepper and add half the breasts to the skillet, skin-side down. Cook half of the chicken breasts over moderately high heat, turning once, until they are well browned, about 5 minutes. Transfer the cooked breasts to a plate and repeat the process with the remaining breasts. Pour off the fat from the skillet. Return all of the chicken to the skillet, lower the heat to moderate, cover and cook until opaque throughout, about 5 minutes longer. Transfer the chicken to a large plate and keep warm.

3. Add the wine to the skillet and boil over high heat, stirring to scrape up any browned bits, until reduced by half, about 5 minutes. Add the chicken stock and reduce by half, about 3 minutes. Add the cream; continue boiling until reduced by half, about 3 minutes more. Stir in the sliced mushrooms and season with salt and pepper. Set each chicken breast on a large plate, spoon the sauce over it and serve.—NICO MARTIN

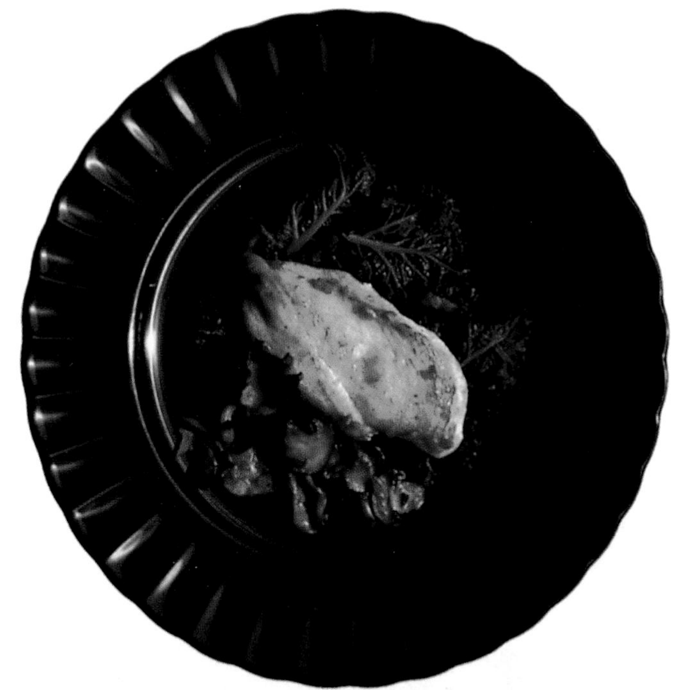

Chicken with Kale and Wild Mushrooms

CHICKEN WITH KALE AND WILD MUSHROOMS

If you prefer, use olive oil for sautéing instead of the rendered bacon fat.

🍷 *A light red with some ripe fruitiness will play off the sharpness of the greens and the meat. A West Coast Pinot Noir, such as the 1993 Erath Willamette Valley from Oregon or the 1993 Sanford Santa Barbara from California, would be an excellent choice.*

4 SERVINGS

- 1 pound kale, tough stems discarded, leaves cut into 2-inch pieces
- 1 tablespoon all-purpose flour
- 2 teaspoons unsalted butter, softened
- 1 tablespoon plus 2 teaspoons extra-virgin olive oil
- 3 ounces slab bacon, cut into 1-by-¼-inch matchsticks

Four 6-ounce skinless, boneless chicken-breast halves, lightly pounded
Salt and freshly ground pepper
½ pound wild mushrooms, such as oyster or chanterelle, sliced ⅓ inch thick
3 medium shallots, minced
⅓ cup dry white wine
⅔ cup chicken stock or canned low-sodium broth
2 teaspoons fresh lemon juice

1. Blanch the kale in a large pot of salted water until it is limp, about 2 minutes. Drain well, pressing on the kale to extract excess water. In a small bowl, blend the flour and the butter until smooth.

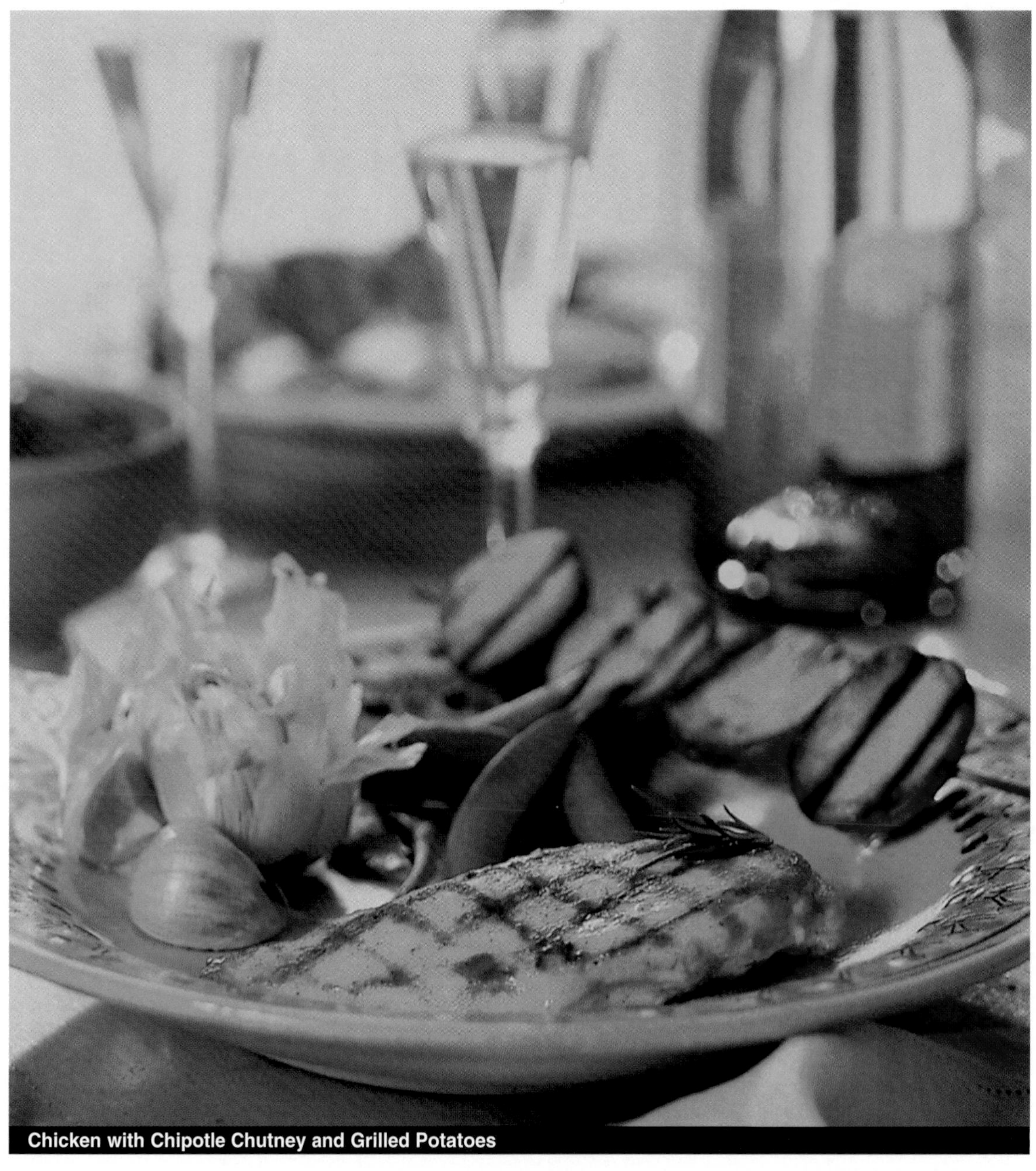
Chicken with Chipotle Chutney and Grilled Potatoes

2. Heat 1 teaspoon of the oil in a large nonreactive skillet. Add the bacon and sauté over high heat until browned and crisp, about 4 minutes. Using a slotted spoon, transfer the bacon to paper towels to drain. Pour the rendered fat into a small bowl.
3. Heat 1 teaspoon of the oil and 1 teaspoon of the bacon fat in the skillet. Separate the tenders from the chicken breasts. Season the chicken with salt and pepper. Add the breasts to the skillet and cook over moderately high heat until brown and crusty on the bottom, about 4 minutes. Turn and cook the other side until lightly browned, about 3 minutes. Brown the tenders in another teaspoon of oil. Transfer the chicken to a platter and cover loosely with foil.
4. Heat 1 teaspoon of the oil and 1 teaspoon of the reserved bacon fat in the skillet. Add the mushrooms, shallots and 2 tablespoons of water, season with salt and pepper and cook over moderate heat, stirring occasionally, until the vegetables are softened and browned, about 6 minutes. Transfer to a bowl and keep warm.
5. Pour the wine into the skillet and cook over high heat, scraping the bottom of the pan to loosen any browned bits, until reduced to a few tablespoons. Add the stock and cook until reduced to ½ cup, about 3 minutes. Whisk in the flour paste and cook until the sauce thickens. Add the mushrooms and cook until warmed through. Transfer the sauce to a small bowl and stir in any accumulated juices from the chicken.
6. Wipe out the skillet. Return it to high heat. Add the remaining 1 teaspoon of oil and an additional teaspoon of bacon fat. Add the kale, season with salt and pepper and sauté until just beginning to brown, about 3 minutes. Stir in the bacon and lemon juice. Arrange the kale on four dinner plates. Top with the chicken and the sauce and serve.—GRACE PARISI

WINE AND LOW-FAT FOOD

Wine and low-fat meals are a good match. The government recently made it official with the announcement that a glass a day (or two, for men) can be part of a healthy diet. And there are other benefits: A five-ounce glass of Chardonnay or Burgundy, at about a hundred calories, gives an impression of richness to a meal without adding fat. Best of all, matching wines to low-fat dishes is easy; it requires only that the wine complement the flavors of the food. Fattier dishes are trickier to match. They need wines that can cut through the unctuousness of the food—a white with an acidic edge, a red with a tannic bite.

CHICKEN WITH CHIPOTLE CHUTNEY AND GRILLED POTATOES LF

Sweet roasted garlic cloves and smoky, fruity chutney spice up these simple grilled chicken breasts. Reserve any leftover garlic for other dishes.

4 SERVINGS

- 4 whole unpeeled heads of garlic
- 8 small unpeeled red potatoes, halved
- 2½ teaspoons olive oil
- ½ teaspoon minced fresh thyme
- Salt and freshly ground pepper
- Four 6-ounce skinless, boneless chicken breasts

LOW-FAT SOUTHWESTERN MENU

Vincent Guerithault's classic French training taught him plenty about the joys of butter and cream but not much about low-fat cooking. Today, at Vincent Guerithault on Camelback in Phoenix, his taste for grilling and for the pungent spices and chiles popular in the Southwest allows him to create dishes that don't need béchamel sauce to be delicious.

🍷 The taco towers are compatible with a number of whites, but the chicken narrows the choice to one with broad flavors that can pull together the chicken, garlic and chutney. Chardonnay has the richness and depth to play such a role. California examples, like the 1994 Kendall-Jackson Grand Reserve or the 1993 Robert Mondavi Carneros, would fit the bill perfectly.

RATATOUILLE TACO TOWERS
(P. 33)

CHICKEN WITH CHIPOTLE CHUTNEY AND GRILLED POTATOES
(P. 195)

STEAMED SUGAR SNAP PEAS

WARM SPICED CHOCOLATE SOUFFLÉ CAKE (P. 376)

4 fresh rosemary sprigs, for garnish
Chipotle Chutney (recipe follows)

1. Light a grill or preheat the oven to 325°. Grill the garlic heads over moderately low heat for about 45 minutes, turning frequently, until they are softened and browned. Alternatively, wrap the garlic heads loosely in foil and roast them in the oven for about 1 hour, until the cloves are tender.
2. If using the oven, increase the temperature to 450°. Bring a medium saucepan of lightly salted water to a boil over high heat. Add the potatoes and cook until just tender, about 5 minutes; drain and pat dry. Brush the potatoes with 1½ teaspoons of the olive oil and thread four potato halves on each of four metal or bamboo skewers.
3. Grill or roast the potatoes for about 10 minutes per side, turning once, until tender. Sprinkle the potatoes with the thyme, season to taste with salt and pepper and set aside.
4. Rub the chicken breasts with the remaining 1 teaspoon olive oil and season with salt and pepper. Grill the chicken for about 12 minutes, turning occasionally, until lightly charred on both sides and cooked through. Alternatively, cook the chicken on the stove in a preheated grill pan over moderately high heat, turning once, for about 4 minutes on each side.
5. Transfer the grilled chicken to four plates and add a roasted head of garlic and a potato skewer to each serving. Garnish each plate with a rosemary sprig and serve with the chutney on the side.

OILS FOR COOKING

Two of oil's primary functions are lubrication and heat transfer. By lubrication I mean coating a food such as a chicken or a leg of lamb before grilling, roasting or baking. The oil prevents the food from sticking to the cooking surface and keeps the texture moist in dry, intense heat. For this purpose, I prefer an inexpensive pure olive oil, which has a high smoking point (that is, it can sustain high temperatures without smoking or burning) and a healthy fatty-acid profile (it is high in "good" monounsaturated fatty acids and low in "bad" saturated fat).

Oil transfers heat in sautéing, frying and deep-frying, when the hot oil itself becomes the cooking medium. For these techniques, an oil must have a smoking point of 375° or higher. Since the taste of an oil is altered when it is heated, there's no reason to use a costly, flavorful oil. An inexpensive oil with a high smoking point and healthy fatty-acid profile is best—olive oil, canola oil, sunflower oil. Avoid generic vegetable oils, which often contain a large percentage of cottonseed oil, an industrial byproduct that must be chemically processed to be edible.—MICHELE ANNA JORDAN

Chipotle Chutney

MAKES ABOUT ¾ CUP

3 fresh Anaheim or poblano chiles
1 medium unpeeled Granny Smith apple, finely chopped
½ cup sherry vinegar
½ cup light brown sugar
¼ cup granulated sugar
1 canned chipotle chile, seeded and minced
1 teaspoon minced garlic

1. Roast the Anaheim or poblano chiles directly over a gas flame or under the broiler as close to the heat as possible, turning, until charred all over. Transfer the chiles to a paper bag and let steam for 10 minutes. Peel off the blackened skins and discard the cores, ribs and seeds. Finely chop the chiles.
2. In a medium nonreactive saucepan, combine the roasted chiles with the apple, vinegar, brown sugar, granulated sugar, chipotle chile and garlic. Cook over moderately low heat, stirring occasionally, until the apple is tender and the liquid is almost completely evaporated, about 25 minutes. Let the chutney cool. (**MAKE AHEAD:** The chutney can be refrigerated for up to 1 week.) —VINCENT GUERITHAULT

PAN-ROASTED CHICKEN WITH POLENTA CAKES

This is comfort food at its best: tender, juicy chicken breasts served with crisp golden polenta.

🍷 *Pinot Noir, a lighter red than Cabernet, has enough fruit and acid to match both the chicken and the fresh tomato sauce. An excellent choice is the 1994 Ponzi Pinot Noir; the Ponzis have made the best of a great vintage for Oregon. Other delicious 1994 Oregon Pinot Noirs to look for are Adelsheim and Panther Creek.*

4 SERVINGS

Coarse salt
1 cup yellow cornmeal, preferably stone-ground
2 tablespoons unsalted butter
3 tablespoons freshly grated Parmesan cheese
Freshly ground pepper
¼ cup vegetable oil
Four 6-ounce boneless chicken-breast halves
2 medium shallots, minced
4 ripe plum tomatoes, cut into ½-inch dice
¼ cup finely shredded fresh basil

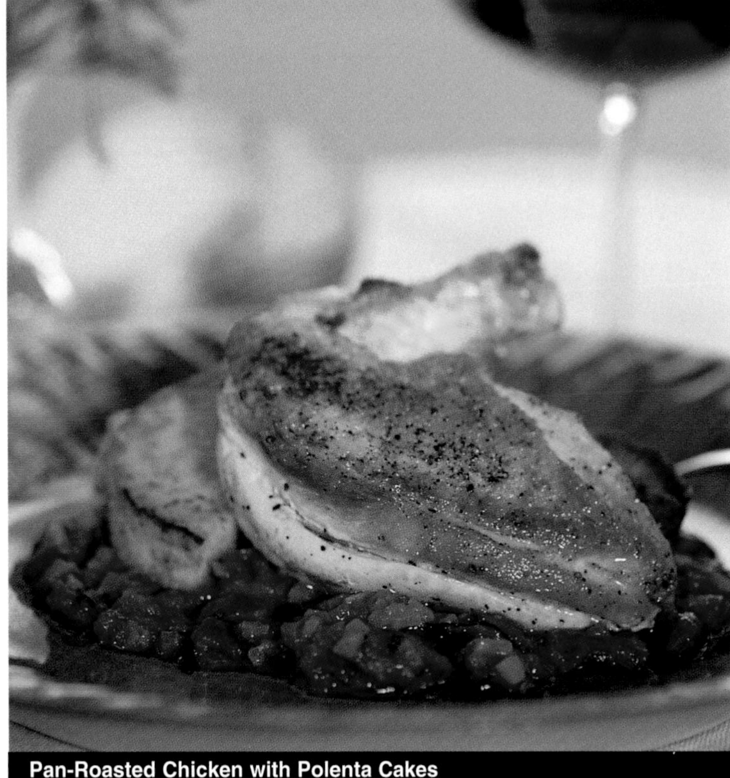

Pan-Roasted Chicken with Polenta Cakes

1. Preheat the oven to 350°. In a medium ovenproof saucepan, bring 2½ cups of water to a boil. Add 1 teaspoon salt, then slowly whisk in the cornmeal over moderate heat until smooth. Simmer, stirring; for 1 minute. Cover and bake in the oven for about 25 minutes, or until thickened; stir the polenta vigorously a few times as it bakes. Stir in the butter and Parmesan and season with salt and pepper.

2. Spoon the polenta into a lightly oiled 10-by-8-inch baking dish and smooth the top. Cover the polenta with plastic and refrigerate until it is firm, at least 2 hours or overnight.

3. Preheat the oven to 450°. Cut the polenta into eight rectangles. Divide the oil between two large, heavy-bottomed ovenproof skillets and heat until almost smoking. Season the chicken with salt and pepper and add to one of the skillets, skin-side down. Arrange the polenta cakes in the second skillet. Cook both over moderately high heat until the chicken and polenta are golden brown on the bottom, about 8 minutes. Turn the chicken and polenta, transfer the skillets to the oven and bake for about 12 minutes, or until the chicken is just cooked through and the polenta is golden brown.

4. Transfer the chicken and the polenta cakes to a platter and keep warm. Set the skillet that the chicken cooked in over low heat and add the minced shallots. Cook, stirring, until softened, about 3 minutes. Add the tomatoes and cook, stirring, for 2 more minutes. Add the basil and season the tomato sauce with salt and pepper.

5. If desired, cut the polenta cakes in half diagonally. Spoon the tomato sauce onto four plates, set the chicken and the polenta cakes on top and serve at once. Leftover polenta cakes can be refrigerated overnight and rewarmed in a 350° oven.—TRACI DES JARDINS

CRISP CHICKEN TENDERS

The long, thin strip of meat attached to each chicken-breast half is known as the tender. Available at supermarkets, tenders are ideal fast-food candidates because they cook quickly and require less trimming than larger pieces of chicken. Spread any leftover dipping sauce on a grilled meat or tomato sandwich.

QUICK DINNER

GINGER-GLAZED CHICKEN (P. 198)

COUSCOUS WITH LEMON AND WATERCRESS (P. 325)

STEAMED SUGAR SNAP PEAS

QUICK STRAWBERRY MINT MOUSSE (P. 449)

GAME PLAN:

• Heat the oven; prepare and marinate the chicken.

• Start baking the chicken. Macerate the strawberries.

• Prepare the couscous.

• Whip the cream and prepare the mousse; refrigerate until time to serve.

• Steam the peas.

Ginger-Glazed Chicken, with Couscous with Lemon and Watercress (p. 325) and steamed sugar snap peas

The ripe, fruity flavors of a California Chardonnay are a perfect foil for this chicken with a garlicky sauce—rich enough to match it but tart enough to provide contrast. Try the 1994 Rodney Strong Chalk Hill or the 1994 Sterling.

4–6 SERVINGS

1½ pounds chicken tenders
2 teaspoons salt
1 teaspoon cayenne pepper
1 teaspoon thyme
½ cup all-purpose flour
2 large eggs, lightly beaten
2 cups fresh bread crumbs
About 8 cups vegetable oil, for frying
Lemon Garlic Dipping Sauce (recipe follows) or lemon wedges, for serving

1. Sprinkle the chicken tenders on both sides with the salt, the cayenne and the thyme. In a paper bag, shake the tenders with the flour. Add the tenders to the eggs in a shallow bowl and stir to coat. Spread the bread crumbs on a plate, add the tenders and turn to coat.

2. Meanwhile, in a deep fryer fitted with a basket or in a heavy medium saucepan, heat 3 inches of oil to 375°; be sure the oil doesn't get any hotter. Quickly add half the tenders, one at a time. Fry until golden and crisp, about 5 minutes. Transfer to paper towels and cook the remaining tenders. Serve with the dipping sauce or lemon wedges.

Lemon Garlic Dipping Sauce

MAKES ABOUT ¾ CUP

1 large garlic clove, minced
¼ teaspoon salt
½ cup mayonnaise
2 scallions, minced
1 tablespoon fresh lemon juice
½ teaspoon cayenne pepper

Using the side of a heavy knife, mash the garlic with the salt. Transfer to a bowl and stir in the mayonnaise, scallions, lemon juice, cayenne and 1 tablespoon of water.—DIANA STURGIS

GINGER-GLAZED CHICKEN Q

This sweet, pungent glaze is as good on chicken breasts as it is on legs. If you're a fan of chicken wings, brush the mixture on wingettes (wings trimmed of the last bony joint, available in supermarkets) and bake for twenty to thirty minutes.

The gingery chicken and lemony couscous suggest a light, not quite dry wine. Try a chilled fruity rosé, such as the 1994 McDowell Grenache Rosé from California or the 1994 Georges Duboeuf Syrah Rosé from France.

4 SERVINGS

4½ to 5 ounces fresh ginger (a piece about 6 inches long)
2 garlic cloves, peeled
2 tablespoons olive oil
¼ cup plus 1 tablespoon teriyaki sauce
4 whole chicken legs (about 3¼ pounds), halved at the joint
Salt and freshly ground pepper

1. Preheat the oven to 450°. Using the side of a teaspoon, scrape the skin from the ginger. Cut the ginger into 1-inch pieces. Put the ginger pieces, the garlic and the olive oil in a food processor or

Chicken Ragout Jeannette

JACQUES PÉPIN'S RUSTIC FOUR-COURSE MENU

🍷 To accompany this menu, I recommend Les Sénanquiés Côtes du Rhône. Look for the 1994 vintage. If you can't find this wine, serve your favorite Côtes du Rhône.

TOASTED-BREAD AND ONION SOUP (P. 88)

CHICKEN RAGOUT JEANNETTE (P. 199)

FRISÉE WITH CROUTONS (P. 59)

MÉMÉ'S APPLE TART (P. 402)

blender and process until the ginger and the garlic are finely chopped. With the machine on, add the teriyaki sauce and process until the mixture is the texture of mustard.

2. In a shallow bowl, slather the ginger glaze over the chicken pieces and let marinate for 10 minutes at room temperature. Arrange the chicken pieces skin-side up on a broiler pan, season them with salt and pepper and bake for about 20 minutes, turning once, until the chicken is cooked through. Set the chicken skin-side up and broil for about 1 minute to crisp the skin.—STEPHANIE LYNESS

CHICKEN RAGOUT JEANNETTE

Similar to lardons in France and pancetta in Italy, salt pork is basically unsmoked bacon. Look for a chunk with as much meat as possible. This recipe is from Jacques Pépin's Table: Cooking with Claudine *(KQED).*

4 SERVINGS

- 1 tablespoon canola or safflower oil
- 4 whole chicken legs (about 2½ pounds), skinned and patted dry
- Salt and freshly ground pepper
- One 4-ounce piece of lean salt pork or bacon, cut into ½-inch-wide strips
- 1 medium bunch of scallions, coarsely chopped
- 1 medium onion, coarsely chopped
- 2 teaspoons all-purpose flour
- ½ cup dry white wine
- 2 large garlic cloves, crushed
- ½ teaspoon thyme
- 2 bay leaves
- 1 pound medium red potatoes, halved
- ¼ teaspoon Tabasco (optional)
- 2 tablespoons coarsely chopped fresh flat-leaf parsley

1. Heat the oil in a large, heavy nonreactive skillet. Add the chicken legs, season with salt and pepper and sauté over moderately high heat, turning occasionally, until browned on both sides, about 8 minutes. Transfer to a plate. ➤

2. Meanwhile, if using salt pork, blanch it by putting the strips in a saucepan with 2 cups of water, bringing to a boil over high heat and boiling for 1 minute. Then drain the salt pork, rinse it with cold water and drain thoroughly.
3. Add the salt pork or the bacon to the drippings in the skillet and cover partially to prevent splattering. Cook over moderately high heat, stirring occasionally, until browned and crisp, about 6 minutes. Add the chopped scallions and onion, mix well, reduce the heat to moderate and continue cooking, stirring occasionally, until just beginning to brown, about 5 minutes. Stir in the flour and continue browning the mixture, stirring occasionally, for 1 minute longer.

4. Add 1¼ cups of water and the white wine to the skillet and bring to a boil over moderate heat, using a wooden spoon to scrape up any browned bits from the bottom of the skillet. Stir in the garlic, the thyme, the bay leaves and ½ teaspoon of salt. Add the halved red potatoes and the chicken legs and bring back to a boil. Cover the skillet and cook over low heat until the potatoes are tender and the chicken is almost falling off the bone, about 30 minutes. Stir in the Tabasco, if using. (**MAKE AHEAD:** The chicken ragout can be refrigerated overnight; rewarm it before serving.) Discard the bay leaves, then sprinkle the chicken ragout with the chopped flat-leaf parsley and serve at once.—JACQUES PÉPIN

Chicken with Many Peppers

CHICKEN WITH MANY PEPPERS

A mixture of hot chile peppers and sweet bell peppers packs this dish with flavor. Serve it with rice, warmed flour tortillas and sliced avocados.

4 SERVINGS

- 2 tablespoons plus 1 teaspoon fresh lime juice
- 2 teaspoons minced garlic
- 1 teaspoon minced chipotle chile in adobo*
- 1 teaspoon sugar
- Salt and freshly ground pepper
- Six 3- to 4-ounce skinless, boneless chicken thighs, lightly pounded
- 2 tablespoons extra-virgin olive oil
- 1 large red bell pepper, cut lengthwise into ⅓-inch strips
- 1 large yellow bell pepper, cut lengthwise into ⅓-inch strips
- 1 small green bell pepper, cut lengthwise into ⅓-inch strips
- 1 large poblano chile, cut lengthwise into ¼-inch strips
- 1 medium red onion, cut lengthwise into ⅓-inch strips
- ½ cup chicken stock or canned low-sodium broth
- 1 tablespoon unsalted butter

*Available at Latin markets and specialty-food markets

1. In a medium bowl, combine the 2 tablespoons lime juice with the garlic, chipotle and sugar; season with salt and pepper. Add the chicken and marinate for 20 minutes.
2. In a large skillet, heat 1 tablespoon of the olive oil until just smoking. Add the red, yellow and green bell peppers and the poblano chile and sauté over

moderately high heat, stirring occasionally, until slightly softened and beginning to brown, about 4 minutes. Add the onion and cook until tender and all the vegetables are slightly charred, about 4 minutes. Transfer the vegetables to a large plate.

3. Heat the remaining 1 tablespoon oil in the skillet. Add the chicken and cook over moderately high heat until brown on the bottom, about 4 minutes. Turn the chicken, reduce the heat to moderate and cook the other side until brown, another 4 minutes. Transfer the chicken to a cutting board and slice it ½ inch thick.

4. Meanwhile, add the chicken stock to the skillet and simmer over moderately high heat, scraping the pan to loosen any browned bits, until the stock is slightly reduced. Strain the sauce through a fine-mesh sieve. Wipe out the skillet and return the sauce to it. Add the butter and the remaining 1 teaspoon lime juice to the sauce in the skillet and swirl over moderately high heat until incorporated. Return the peppers, chicken and any juices that have accumulated to the skillet and heat the sauce through gently. Serve the chicken warm.—GRACE PARISI

CHICKEN POTPIES

8 SERVINGS (2 PIES)

One 4-pound chicken
Coarse salt
5 tablespoons unsalted butter, at room temperature
½ pound small white mushrooms, quartered
Freshly ground pepper
1 large leek, white and tender green, thinly sliced
4 scallions, chopped
2 medium carrots, halved lengthwise, then cut crosswise ½ inch thick
1 pound red potatoes, peeled and cut into 1-inch cubes
¼ cup plus 2 tablespoons flour
¼ cup chopped fresh parsley
1 tablespoon chopped fresh thyme
2 teaspoons fresh lemon juice
Flaky Cornmeal Pastry (recipe follows)

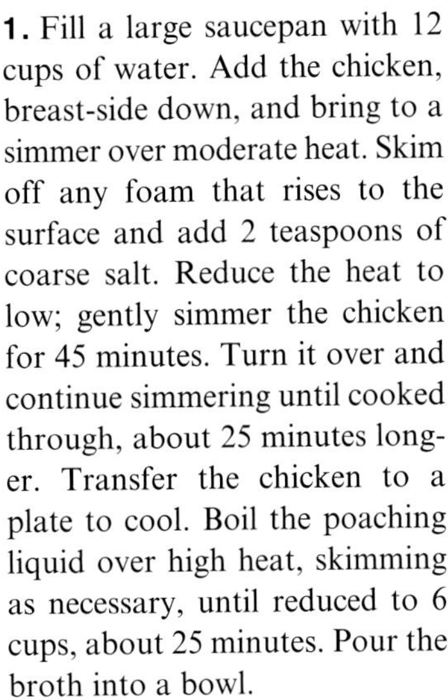

1. Fill a large saucepan with 12 cups of water. Add the chicken, breast-side down, and bring to a simmer over moderate heat. Skim off any foam that rises to the surface and add 2 teaspoons of coarse salt. Reduce the heat to low; gently simmer the chicken for 45 minutes. Turn it over and continue simmering until cooked through, about 25 minutes longer. Transfer the chicken to a plate to cool. Boil the poaching liquid over high heat, skimming as necessary, until reduced to 6 cups, about 25 minutes. Pour the broth into a bowl.

2. Remove all of the meat from the chicken and cut the meat into 2-inch pieces. Cover the chicken pieces and set aside.

3. In the saucepan, melt 1 tablespoon of the butter over high heat. Add the mushrooms, season with coarse salt and freshly ground pepper and cook until lightly browned. Transfer the mushrooms to a plate and add another tablespoon of butter to the pan. Add the leek and scallions and cook over moderately low

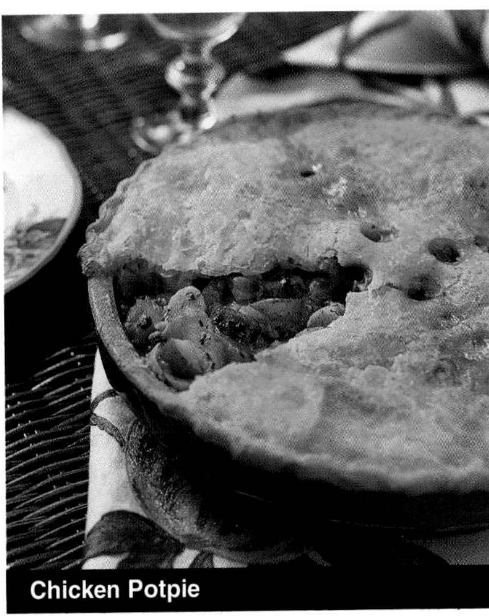

Chicken Potpie

DELECTABLE POTPIE DINNER

Everything on this menu can be prepared and frozen up to a month ahead. Aside from thawing and reheating, you'll need only about ten minutes to put the meal on the table.

🍷 The ripe flavors of a Chardonnay suit the underlying sweetness of the beet soup—accented by the peppery notes in the poblano cream—as well as the creaminess of the chicken potpies. The snappy acidity of the Chardonnay sets off the flavors of the chicken dish, while the wine's full-bodied character replicates its texture. Among possible choices, consider the 1994 Baron Philippe de Rothschild Vin de Pays d'Oc or the 1993 Iron Horse from California.

BEET SOUP WITH ROASTED-POBLANO CREAM (P. 83)

CHICKEN POTPIES (P. 201)

JAM-FILLED CRÊPES WITH ORANGE BOURBON SAUCE (P. 450)

heat, stirring, until translucent, about 5 minutes. Add the chicken broth and bring to a simmer over moderate heat. Add the carrots and potatoes, cover and simmer until tender, about 12 minutes.

4. In a medium bowl, blend the remaining 3 tablespoons butter with the flour. Gradually whisk in 1 cup of the broth from the saucepan until smooth, then whisk the mixture back into the saucepan. Bring the stew to a simmer over moderate heat, whisking occasionally. Simmer for a few minutes, then add the chicken, mushrooms, parsley and thyme and simmer for 5 minutes longer. Season with coarse salt, pepper and the lemon juice. Pour the chicken stew into two 10-inch glass pie plates and refrigerate until chilled.

5. On a lightly floured work surface, roll each disk of pastry into a 13-inch round about ¼ inch thick. Cut a 1-inch-thick ring from the outer edge of each of the rounds; set the pastry rings on the rims of the pie plates. Lightly moisten the pastry rings with water and set the pastry rounds on top; press on the rims to help the pastry adhere. Fold the overhanging pastry under the rims to secure it. (**MAKE AHEAD:** Wrap the pies in a double thickness of plastic wrap, then with foil and freeze for up to 1 month. Thaw in the refrigerator for 2 days before proceeding.)

6. To serve, bake the potpies in a preheated 375° oven for about 1 hour, switching shelves halfway through cooking, until the crust is crisp and golden and the juices are bubbling.

Flaky Cornmeal Pastry

MAKES ENOUGH FOR TWO 10-INCH PIES

- 2 cups all-purpose flour
- ¾ cup cornmeal, preferably stone-ground
- 1 teaspoon salt
- 2 sticks cold unsalted butter (8 ounces), cut into small pieces
- ¾ cup ice water

In a large bowl, whisk together the flour, cornmeal and salt. Using a pastry blender or two knives, cut in the butter until the mixture resembles coarse meal. Drizzle in the ice water and lightly mix the dough with your hands just until it holds together. Divide the dough in half; pat into two disks and wrap well in plastic. Refrigerate or freeze the dough until ready to use. Let stand at room temperature until cool but malleable before rolling the dough out.—MARCIA KIESEL

SPICY CHICKEN STEW IN A CRISP PLANTAIN CRUST

This unusual sweet and savory recipe was given to me by my friend Harry Reillo of Quebradillas, the "town of pirates" on the northwest coast of Puerto Rico.

4–6 SERVINGS

- One 4-pound chicken
- 1 cup plus 2 tablespoons vegetable oil
- Salt and freshly ground pepper
- 1 medium onion, coarsely chopped
- 1 medium red bell pepper, coarsely chopped
- 2 large garlic cloves, minced
- 2 scallions, sliced crosswise
- 2 medium tomatoes, coarsely chopped
- ½ teaspoon fresh thyme leaves
- 2 teaspoons hot or mild pure chile powder
- 2 large very ripe plantains, sliced diagonally 1 inch thick
- 3 ounces feta cheese, crumbled

1. Preheat the oven to 400°. Set the chicken in a roasting pan, rub with 1 tablespoon of the vegetable oil and season with salt and pepper. Roast for about 1½ hours, basting often, until the chicken is golden and cooked through. Transfer the chicken to a platter. Discard any fat from the roasting pan and set the pan over two burners. Add ½ cup of water and simmer over moderate heat for 2 minutes, scraping up the browned bits. Pour the juices into a bowl. Cut the chicken into 1-inch pieces. Discard the skin and bones.

2. Heat 1 tablespoon of the oil in a large skillet. Add the onion and red bell pepper and cook over moderately low heat, stirring, until softened, about 8 minutes. Add the garlic and scallions and cook, stirring, until fragrant, about 3 minutes. Add the tomatoes and simmer over moderate heat until the liquid evaporates, about 5 minutes. Stir in the thyme and the chile powder and cook, stirring, for 3 minutes. Add the chicken and juices and simmer for 2 minutes. Season the mixture with salt and pepper and transfer to a bowl.

3. Preheat the oven to 400°. Wipe out the skillet and heat the remaining 1 cup vegetable oil over moderately high heat until shimmering. Add a single layer of the plantain slices and fry, turning once, until the slices are well browned, about 4 minutes per side; if necessary, lower the heat to cook the plantains all the way through. Transfer the fried plantains to a plate to cool and repeat with the remaining plantain slices. Using a rolling pin or meat pounder, lightly flatten the plantain slices between two pieces of sturdy plastic wrap to a ⅓-inch thickness. Press the flattened plantains into a 9-inch glass pie plate, overlapping them slightly to cover the bottom of the plate.

4. Spoon the chicken stew over the fried plantains in the pie plate. Sprinkle the stew with the crumbled feta cheese and bake for about 45 minutes, or until the stew is heated through and the plantains on the bottom of the pie plate sizzle. Cut into wedges and serve.—MARCIA KIESEL

Chicken-Stuffed Tamal

CHICKEN-STUFFED TAMAL

If you enjoy the tender texture and rich flavor of tamales but you can't imagine taking the time to form, fill and wrap them, then this savory tamal is for you.

MAKES 4–6 MAIN-COURSE OR 8 FIRST-COURSE SERVINGS

- ¾ cup lard or vegetable shortening (about 6 ounces), chilled
- 1½ teaspoons baking powder
- 1½ pounds (about 3 cups) coarse-ground masa for tamales or 3 cups masa harina mixed with 1¾ cups of hot water (see "Masa," next page)
- 1 cup chicken stock or canned low-sodium broth
- Salt
- 1½ cups Roasted-Tomatillo Chipotle Salsa (p. 356)
- 1 cup coarsely shredded cooked skinless chicken meat (about 6 ounces)
- Coarsely chopped fresh cilantro or flat-leaf parsley, for garnish

1. In a large bowl, beat the lard or shortening and the baking powder with an electric mixer until light, about 1 minute. Add the masa in three batches, beating constantly. Slowly add the stock and continue beating until the batter holds its shape in a spoon and a ½-teaspoon dollop floats in a cup of cold water, about 1 minute. Season the batter with salt. In a small bowl, combine ¾ cup of the roasted-tomatillo salsa with the shredded chicken. (**MAKE AHEAD:** The batter and the chicken filling can be refrigerated separately for up to 1 day.)

2. Preheat the oven to 400°. Spoon half of the batter into a greased 10-inch pie plate. Spread the chicken filling over the batter and season it lightly with salt. Cover the filling with the remaining batter. Bake the tamal in the upper third of the oven for 25 minutes. Reduce the oven temperature to 300°. ➤

3. Cover the tamal loosely with foil and bake for about 20 minutes longer, or until the top is golden and the center springs back when lightly pressed. Let the tamal stand for a few minutes, then cut it into wedges. Garnish each serving with cilantro and serve with the remaining tomatillo salsa.—RICK BAYLESS

CHICKEN LIVERS WITH MARSALA AND JICAMA

Serve this sauté with buttered fettuccine or wide egg noodles. If you can't find sweet, crunchy jicama, you can substitute red-radish slivers or mung-bean sprouts.

4 SERVINGS

- 1 tablespoon olive oil
- 1¼ pounds chicken livers, well trimmed and cut into 2-inch pieces
- Salt and freshly ground pepper
- ¼ cup plus 2 tablespoons dry Marsala wine
- 1 tablespoon unsalted butter
- 3 large shallots, thinly sliced
- 2 tablespoons tomato paste dissolved in ½ cup water
- 2 teaspoons chopped fresh tarragon
- 2 teaspoons fresh lemon juice
- 1 cup 1-by-¼-inch jicama sticks

1. Heat ½ tablespoon of the olive oil in a large nonreactive skillet. Add half of the chicken livers in a single layer, season them with salt and pepper and cook over high heat, turning once, until the liver is well browned and medium-rare to medium, about 2 minutes per side. Add 1 tablespoon of the Marsala and cook until reduced to a thin glaze. Reduce the heat to moderately high if the livers start to burn. Transfer the cooked livers to a plate. Repeat the process with the remaining ½ tablespoon oil, the remaining chicken livers and another tablespoon of the Marsala.

2. Melt the butter in the skillet. Add the shallots and cook over moderate heat, stirring, until softened, about 4 minutes. Increase the heat to moderately high, add the remaining ¼ cup Marsala and boil, scraping the skillet to loosen any browned bits, until reduced by half, about 1 minute. Add the tomato paste and boil until slightly thickened, about 2 minutes.

3. Return the chicken livers to the skillet and season with the tarragon, lemon juice, salt and pepper. Simmer to heat through, then transfer to a platter. Scatter the jicama sticks on top and serve.—MARCIA KIESEL

MASA

Masa, or fresh dough, is sold at Latin American markets and—if you're lucky enough to have access to one—at tortilla factories. Ask for coarse-ground masa, made specifically for tamales. Or buy masa harina (powdered dried masa), which is available at Latin American stores and many supermarkets, and mix it with water.

Chicken Livers with Marsala and Jicama

FROZEN-FOOD TIMELINE

Here's the number of months uncooked poultry, meats and other staples can be stored in a freezer at or below zero degrees. Longer storage lowers quality.

POULTRY

Chicken..........4 to 6 months
Game Birds...........6 months
Turkey..........6 to 12 months

MEAT

Bacon ....1 month
Beef (not ground) .....6 to 12 months
Game Meat............6 months
Ground Meats........3 months
Lamb.......................6 months
Pork ....6 months
Smoked Ham ....2 months
Veal.........................6 months

OTHER

Breads ....6 months
Coffee Beans ....1 month
Nuts ....6 months
Seafood ....1 month

CHAPTER 8

~

OTHER BIRDS

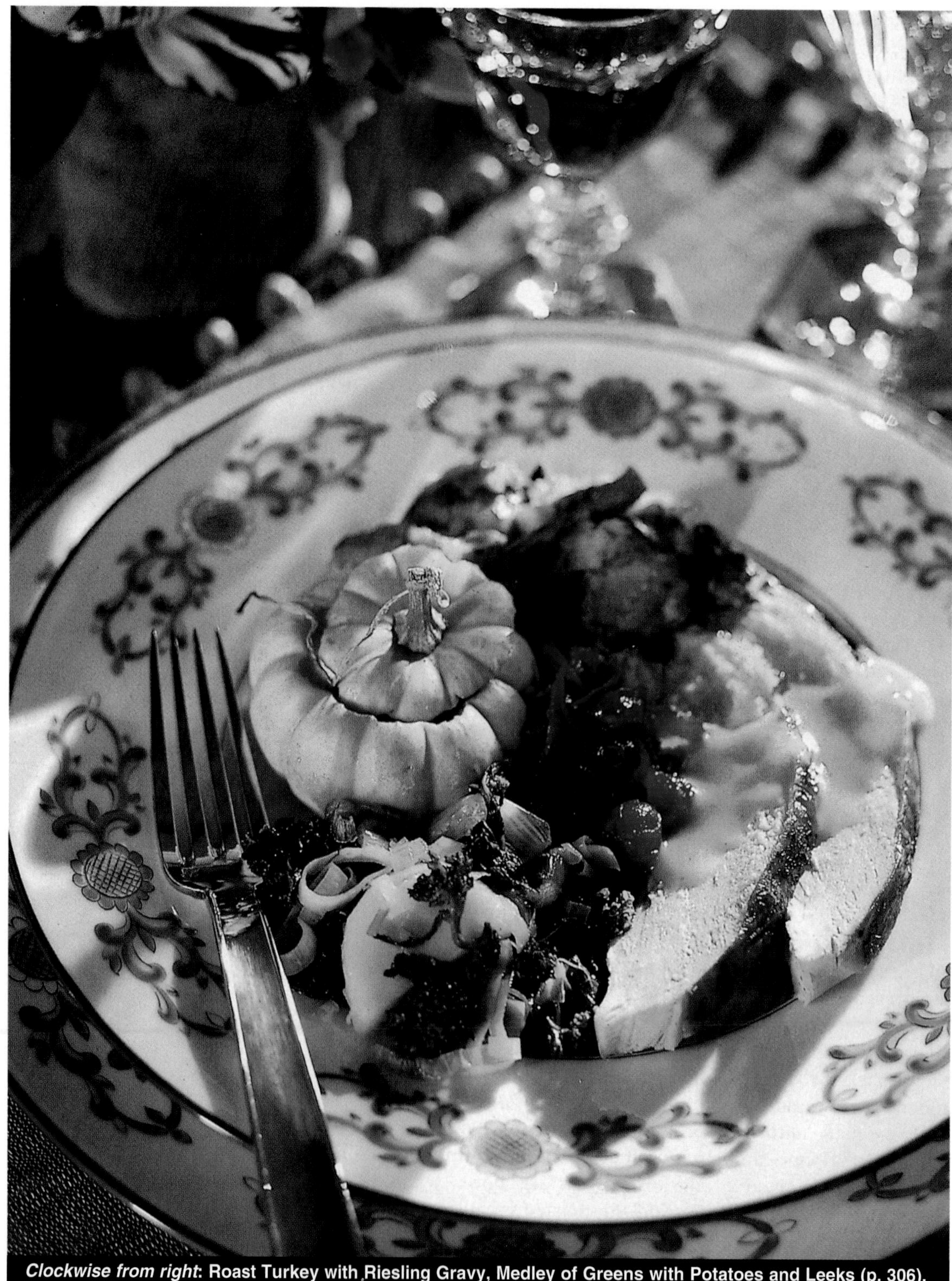

Clockwise from right: Roast Turkey with Riesling Gravy, Medley of Greens with Potatoes and Leeks (p. 306), Roasted Mini Pumpkin (p. 342), Wild-Mushroom Stuffing, Cranberry Citrus Relish (p. 361)

ROAST TURKEY WITH RIESLING GRAVY

12 SERVINGS

One 18-pound turkey, wing tips, neck and giblets reserved
Coarse salt and freshly ground pepper
2 large onions, thinly sliced
2 large carrots, thinly sliced
2 large celery ribs, thinly sliced
4 garlic cloves, thickly sliced
2 large shallots, thickly sliced
12 large fresh sage leaves, plus additional sprigs for garnish
12 large fresh thyme sprigs, plus additional sprigs for garnish
2 bay leaves
5 tablespoons unsalted butter, softened
Turkey Stock and reserved turkey giblets (recipe follows)
5 tablespoons all-purpose flour
½ cup semidry Riesling

1. Preheat the oven to 400°. Season the turkey cavity with salt and pepper. Fill with half the onions, carrots, celery, garlic and shallots, the sage leaves, the 12 thyme sprigs and the bay leaves. Tie the legs together with string; wrap it around the tail to close the cavity.

2. Rub the turkey all over with 2 tablespoons of the butter and season with salt and pepper. Spread the remaining vegetables in a large roasting pan and set the turkey on top. Add 1 cup stock to the pan. Roast for 1½ hours, basting generously and adding one more cup of stock after 1 hour.

3. Add another ½ cup of stock to the pan; cover the breast loosely with foil. Reduce the oven temperature to 325°. Roast for 1½ hours longer, or until an instant-read thermometer inserted in the inner thigh reaches 165°; baste often and add another ½ cup of stock after 1 hour. If the bird isn't nicely browned, remove the foil for the last 30 minutes.

4. Turn the oven off and leave the turkey in for about 1 hour, or until the temperature of the inner thigh reaches 180°. Transfer to a large platter, cover loosely with foil and let rest for up to 1 hour.

5. Meanwhile, strain the roasting juices into a medium saucepan; reserve the vegetables. Add 3 cups of stock and bring to a simmer, skimming as necessary.

6. In a large nonreactive saucepan, melt the remaining 3 tablespoons butter. Add the reserved vegetables and stir in the flour. Cook over moderate heat, stirring

WILD-MUSHROOM STUFFING

12 SERVINGS

6 tablespoons unsalted butter
1½ pounds mixed fresh mushrooms, tough stems removed, mushrooms cut into 1-inch pieces
4 medium shallots, finely chopped
4 large garlic cloves, minced
2 large celery ribs, finely chopped
1 medium onion, chopped
1 tablespoon minced fresh thyme
1 cup dry white wine
5 cups chicken stock or canned low-sodium broth
Salt and freshly ground pepper
One 1-pound loaf of peasant bread, cut into ½-inch dice and toasted until dry
2 cups heavy cream
1 cup finely chopped fresh flat-leaf parsley
3 large eggs, beaten

1. In a large nonreactive skillet, melt 5 tablespoons of the butter. Add the mushrooms and cook over moderately high heat until lightly browned. Stir in the shallots, garlic, celery, onion and 1 teaspoon of the thyme. Cook until all the vegetables are softened slightly. Stir in the wine and simmer until almost evaporated. Add 2 cups of the stock and simmer over moderate heat until the liquid reduces and thickens, about 13 minutes. Season with salt and pepper and transfer the mixture to a large bowl.

2. Add the toasted bread to the bowl along with the remaining 3 cups stock and 1½ teaspoons thyme. Stir in the cream and the parsley. Season with salt and pepper, then stir in the eggs and mix well. Spoon the stuffing into a buttered 9-by-13-inch glass or ceramic baking dish and dot with the remaining 1 tablespoon butter. (**MAKE AHEAD:** The stuffing can be refrigerated overnight. Bring to room temperature before baking.)

3. Preheat the oven to 350°. Cover the stuffing with foil and bake in the middle of the oven for 45 minutes. Uncover and bake about 30 minutes longer, or until the top is golden and crisp and the stuffing is firm. Let rest for at least 15 minutes before serving.—WALDY MALOUF

THANKSGIVING DINNER

🍷 NV Clinton Seyval Naturel
🍷 1995 Millbrook Chardonnay

WINTER WHITE-BEAN SOUP (P. 92)

🍷 1994 Millbrook Tocai Friulano
🍷 1995 Rivendell Riesling

ROAST TURKEY WITH RIESLING GRAVY (P. 209)

WILD-MUSHROOM STUFFING (P. 209)

CRANBERRY CITRUS RELISH (P. 361)

MEDLEY OF GREENS WITH POTATOES AND LEEKS (P. 306)

ROASTED MINI PUMPKINS (P. 342)

ONION WALNUT MUFFINS (P. 300)

ROASTED-GARLIC JAM (P. 359)

MESCLUN AND FRESH-HERB SALAD WITH GOAT CHEESE (P. 62)

INDIAN PUDDING WITH PEARS AND GINGER (P.447)

DEEP-DISH APPLE PIE WITH A CHEDDAR CRUST (P. 401)

PECAN SHORTBREAD COOKIES (P. 390)

TIMETABLE:

ONE WEEK OR MORE AHEAD **Make and freeze the Chicken Stock. Bake and freeze the muffins. Make the cookie dough and the pies and freeze uncooked. Make the relish, garlic jam and butterscotch sauce.**

THREE DAYS AHEAD **Make the soup. Make the corn bread for the pudding.**

ONE DAY AHEAD **Make the Turkey Stock, stuffing and vinaigrette. Make and bake the Indian pudding. Bake the cookies.**

THANKSGIVING DAY **Bake the greens, stuffing and pumpkins. Roast the turkey; make the gravy. Bake the pies. Reheat the soup and side dishes.**

frequently, until very thick and brown, about 5 minutes. Stir in the wine and cook, stirring frequently, until very thick again.

7. Gradually whisk the hot stock and roasting juices into the gravy base. Simmer over low heat for 10 minutes, stirring often. Strain into a medium saucepan and simmer gently over low heat for about 15 minutes, skimming occasionally; you should have about 4 cups. Add more stock if the gravy is too thick. Finely chop the reserved giblets that were cooked in the stock and stir them into the gravy; simmer for 5 more minutes, stirring occasionally. Season with salt and pepper and keep warm.

8. Discard the string and the vegetables from the turkey. Garnish the bird with the sage and thyme sprigs. Carve at the table and pass the gravy alongside.

Turkey Stock

MAKES ABOUT 7 CUPS

4 whole turkey wings or drumsticks
Reserved neck, wing tips and giblets from the turkey (from preceding recipe)
1 large onion, thickly sliced
1 large carrot, thickly sliced
1 large celery rib, thickly sliced
2 garlic cloves, sliced
1 teaspoon coarse salt
Freshly ground pepper

1. Preheat the oven to 400°. Put the wings and wing tips in a flameproof roasting pan. Roast about 1 hour, turning occasionally, until well browned. Put in a large pot.

2. Set the roasting pan over two burners. Add 1 cup of water. Boil over moderately high heat, scraping up the browned bits

Cornish Hens with Creamy Chipotle Sauce

from the bottom of the pan. Add the liquid to the pot.

3. Add the neck, wing tips, gizzard and heart along with the onion, carrot, celery, garlic, salt, generous pinches of pepper and 8 cups of water. Bring to a boil over high heat. Reduce to moderately low and simmer, partially covered, until the meat is falling off the bones and the gizzard is very tender, about 2 hours. Add the liver and poach in the stock until browned outside but still pink in the center, about 6 minutes.

4. Strain the stock. Reserve the liver, heart and gizzard for the gravy. (**MAKE AHEAD:** The stock and giblets can be refrigerated separately for up to 2 days. Skim the fat from the stock before using.) —WALDY MALOUF

CORNISH HENS WITH CREAMY CHIPOTLE SAUCE

A stack of warm tortillas or roasted or baked potatoes will complete the dish.

🍷 *The cream softens the salsa's heat, so a light-bodied red is ideal. Pinot Noir has enough acidity to check the fatty sauce, and enough tart cherry flavor to accent the poultry. Look for California examples such as the 1994 Sterling Winery Lake or the 1994 Gloria Ferrer. Serve slightly chilled.*

4 SERVINGS

Four 1¼-pound Cornish game hens
2½ cups Roasted-Tomatillo Chipotle Salsa (p. 356)
1 pound green beans, trimmed
1 large white onion, sliced ⅜ inch thick
½ cup heavy cream
1 tablespoon vegetable oil or olive oil
Salt, preferably coarse

A SIMPLE HEN

To broil-roast a large (1¾ pound) Cornish hen, cut out the backbone and flatten the bird by pounding down on the breastbone and ribs with your fist. Brush the hen all over with oil and melted butter, season well and set it skin-side down in a baking pan. Broil for several minutes, until lightly browned. Baste again and brush all over with crushed garlic, a squeeze of lemon and a pinch of dried thyme. Turn the bird over and broil it skin-side up until browned. Finish by roasting in a 350° oven for about 20 minutes, or until the legs are tender and the juices run clear. Cut in half lengthwise. Serve with Hash Browns (p. 306), salad, a bit of cheese and a couple of ripe pears for a perfect little dinner for two.—JULIA CHILD

1. Rinse the hens and pat dry. Set in a bowl and coat with the salsa. Cover and let stand at room temperature for 1 hour.

2. In a large pot of boiling salted water, cook the green beans and onion slices until both are crisp-tender, about 4 minutes. Drain and spread out on a tray to cool.

3. Preheat the oven to 450°. Scrape the marinade from the hens back into the bowl and stir in the cream. Set the hens, breast-side up, in a large oiled roasting pan with the legs facing out. Brush the hens with the oil, season with salt and roast in the middle of the oven for 15 minutes. Arrange the beans and onions around the hens, pour the marinade over and roast for about 20 minutes longer, or until the thigh juices run clear when pierced.

4. Transfer the hens and vegetables to a serving platter and cover loosely with foil. Spoon off any fat from the pan sauce. Set the roasting pan over two burners on moderate heat and boil, scraping up any browned bits, for 1 minute. Season with salt. Spoon half of the sauce around the hens and serve with the remaining sauce.—RICK BAYLESS

SKILLET DUCK

Cooking duck like Southern fried chicken—in a covered pan so that steam develops—keeps the meat extremely moist and tender. This recipe is from Jacques Pépin's Kitchen: Cooking with Claudine *(KQED).*

4 SERVINGS

One 4½-pound duck, neck and giblets reserved
½ teaspoon salt

1. Using poultry shears, halve the duck lengthwise: cut along both sides of the backbone and through the breast bone; remove the backbone. Cut each half in two pieces. Or have your butcher do this.

2. Heat a large skillet and add the duck, skin-side down; season with salt. Cook over high heat 5 minutes. Lift the duck to keep it from sticking, but don't turn. Add the neck and gizzard; cover. Turn the heat to low. Cook until the skin is very brown, about 15 minutes. Turn the heat to very low. Cook until tender, about 25 minutes. Add the liver and heart. Cook, covered, 5 minutes more. ➤

3. Transfer the legs, breasts, liver and heart to a large platter; keep warm in a low oven. Discard the neck and gizzard. Pour the rendered fat in a small bowl. Reserve for another use, setting aside 1 tablespoon for the dressing if making Green Salad (see box, below). Add ¼ cup of water to the juices in the skillet and stir to dissolve.

GREEN SALAD

In a large bowl, mix 1 tablespoon red-wine vinegar with 1 teaspoon salt and 1 teaspoon freshly ground pepper. Whisk in 2 tablespoons peanut or canola oil and 1 tablespoon of the rendered fat from Skillet Duck. Add 5 cups mixed salad greens, such as escarole, romaine and Boston lettuce, and toss well. Divide among four plates. Drizzle the reserved duck drippings over the salads and serve immediately.—JACQUES PÉPIN

JACQUES PÉPIN'S MENU

1993 Trimbach Pinot Gris from Alsace

MUSSEL AND POTATO SALAD (P. 54)

1993 Kendall-Jackson Grand Reserve Merlot

SKILLET DUCK (P. 211)

GREEN SALAD (P. 212)

CRÈME AU CHOCOLAT (P. 446)

4. For crisper skin, preheat the broiler. Arrange the duck, skin-side up, on a broiling pan; broil until the skin is crisp. Transfer to plates with the liver and heart. Spoon half the juices over. Reserve the rest for the salad. (**MAKE AHEAD:** Prepare the duck through Step 2 and refrigerate in the rendered fat, which protects it nicely for up to 4 days. To serve, transfer the fat to a jar. Reheat the duck, skin-side down, in a covered skillet over high heat until warmed through; broil to recrisp the skin if needed. Refrigerate the fat for up to 2 months; use it to sauté potatoes.) —JACQUES PÉPIN

ROAST DUCK WITH FIVE-SPICE SAUCE AND RICE NOODLES

This glazed duck is presented in typical Asian fashion: cut into small pieces and served with a host of accompaniments—crisp radishes, chewy noodles, refreshing cilantro and tart lime. You can substitute Nuoc Cham (p. 353) for the five-spice sauce if you like.

6 SERVINGS

MARINATED DUCK:

One 4-pound duck, trimmed of excess fat
2 garlic cloves, minced
2 tablespoons fresh lemon juice
1 tablespoon soy sauce
1 teaspoon vegetable oil
½ teaspoon five-spice powder
½ teaspoon freshly ground black pepper

FIVE-SPICE SAUCE:

2 teaspoons vegetable oil
2 shallots, thinly sliced
2 garlic cloves, minced
¼ teaspoon five-spice powder
¼ teaspoon crushed red pepper
1 tablespoon sugar
2 tablespoons white wine
2 tablespoons soy sauce
1 tablespoon fish sauce (nuoc mam)
¼ teaspoon Asian sesame oil
Salt and freshly ground pepper

¾ pound dried rice vermicelli or rice sticks
1 bunch red radishes, thinly sliced
Lime wedges and fresh cilantro sprigs
Thai or bird chiles, thinly sliced (optional)

1. Marinate the duck: Set the duck in a roasting pan and prick all over with a fork. In a small bowl, combine the garlic, lemon juice, soy sauce, vegetable oil, five-spice powder and pepper. Pour 1 tablespoon of this marinade into the duck cavity and rub the rest all over the skin. Refrigerate uncovered, basting occasionally, at least 8 hours or overnight.

2. Preheat the oven to 375°. Spoon any excess marinade over the duck. Roast about 1½ hours, basting occasionally, until well browned and crisp. If the juices start to burn, add 1 to 2 tablespoons of water. Lift the duck from the pan with two metal spatulas, one in the cavity and the other under the bird. Pour the juices from the bird and the pan into a glass measuring cup. Transfer the duck to a carving board; let stand for up to 30 minutes.

3. Make the five-spice sauce: Skim the fat from the pan juices. Set the roasting pan over two burners on high heat; pour in the pan juices. Add 2 tablespoons of water and scrape up any browned bits. Pour the pan juices back into the measuring cup.

4. Heat the vegetable oil in a small nonreactive saucepan. Add the shallots and cook over moderate heat, stirring, until softened. Add the garlic and cook, stirring, for 1 minute. Stir in the five-spice powder and red pepper and then the sugar. Pour in the wine, soy sauce and reserved pan juices and simmer for 1 minute. Stir in the fish sauce and the sesame oil, season with a little salt and pepper and remove from the heat.

5. Bring a large saucepan of water to a boil. Add the rice vermicelli. Cook over high heat, stirring constantly, until just tender, about 3 minutes. Drain, then return the noodles to the saucepan. Fill the pan with cold water and drain. Fill again with cold water; drain well. Lift the noodles many times to keep them from clumping.

6. Remove the legs and wings from the duck, preferably with a meat cleaver or poultry shears. Cut the legs in half to separate the thighs and drumsticks. Turn the duck on its side; cut along both sides of the backbone to remove it. Cut through the breast bone to halve the duck. Cut the breast halves crosswise into 1-inch-thick slices; each piece should include some meat, skin and bone.

7. Mound the rice vermicelli on a large platter and drizzle with about half of the five-spice sauce. Arrange the duck pieces on top of the noodles and drizzle with a little more sauce, reserving about ¼ cup for passing at the table. Place the radish slices, lime wedges, cilantro sprigs and sliced chiles, if using, around the duck.—MARCIA KIESEL

ELIZABETH'S HAIR-DRYER DUCK

Many years ago, I was preparing a special dinner featuring Elizabeth Schneider's wonderful Aromatic Duck, so rich and tasty that one duck serves three or four people. The recipe involves seasoning the duck with great flavorings for about a day and then drying the skin so that it's as beautiful as that of the finest Peking duck in Chinatown. The problem occurred when my duck was still damp after its requisite drying time in the refrigerator. I called Elizabeth. Her response was, "Mardee, use a hair dryer—whatever it takes to get it dry." God bless her and forgive me, I always use the hair dryer now—for this duck and for other roasted birds.

6–8 SERVINGS

- Two 5-pound Long Island ducks
- 1½ tablespoons whole black peppercorns
- 12 whole cloves
- 4 bay leaves
- 3 juniper berries
- 2 tablespoons coarse salt
- 1 tablespoon dried thyme
- 2 tablespoons light brown sugar
- 3 tablespoons good gin or brandy
- 2 garlic cloves

1. Rinse the ducks inside and out. Pull off any loose clumps of fat. Pat the ducks dry, inside and out.

2. In a spice mill, grind the peppercorns, cloves, bay leaves, juniper berries, salt and thyme until very fine. Pour into a small bowl. Stir in the brown sugar and gin.

3. Rub the spice mixture all over the inside and outside of each duck. Put a garlic clove in each cavity, then put each duck in a snug-fitting sturdy plastic bag and close securely. Refrigerate for 12 to 24 hours; whenever you open the refrigerator, press the bags to work the spices into the skin.

4. Remove the ducks from the refrigerator and let come to room temperature, about 2 hours. ➤

PLUGGED-IN MENU

The recipes in this eclectic menu of bold-flavored dishes use machines in a variety of conventional and unconventional ways.

🍷 The herbal flavors of the focaccia and gazpacho point to a similarly crisp and savory Sauvignon Blanc as the best opening match. Look for a California example with a maximum of flavor, such as the 1994 Preston or the 1994 Flora Springs Soliloquy. Although the duck has an undertone of juniper, the primary consideration in picking a wine is the richness of the meat. For contrast, go for a palate-cleansing red with assertively fruity flavors and enough tannins to check the fattiness of the bird and stand up to the accompaniment, a mustardy remoulade. Try a Syrah-based wine, such as the 1992 Paul Jaboulet Aîné Crozes-Hermitage Les Jalets from France or the 1993 Sean Thackery Orion Old Vines from California.

BREAD-MACHINE FOCACCIA (P. 292)

BLENDER GAZPACHO (P. 78)

ELIZABETH'S HAIR-DRYER DUCK (P. 213)

FOOD-PROCESSOR CELERY-ROOT REMOULADE (P. 66)

TOSSED GREEN SALAD

BOURBON PECAN ICE CREAM WITH MICROWAVE FUDGE SAUCE (P. 440)

Elizabeth's Hair-Dryer Duck, with Food-Processor Celery-Root Remoulade (p. 66) and a tossed green salad

5. Preheat the oven to 350°. Remove the ducks from the bags and pat any moist places with a paper towel. Set a V-shaped roasting rack or a vertical roasting rack in each of two small roasting pans. Get out your hair dryer (the higher the wattage, the better), wipe it clean and using very high heat, begin to dry the ducks; you can stick the nozzle right into the cavities. The drying time will vary but should not be much more than 10 to 15 minutes per duck. Be sure to dry the ducks on all sides, inside and out. Take special care to dry any creased areas.

6. Transfer the ducks to the racks, breast-side up, and roast them for 30 minutes. Reverse the pans front to back and roast for 30 minutes more.

7. Increase the oven temperature to 400°. Using a needle, prick any fatty parts of the duck skin; be careful not to pierce the flesh. If using V-shaped racks, turn the ducks over; you can do this with tongs or by grabbing the hot ducks with a kitchen towel and flipping them. Roast the ducks for 30 minutes, then reverse the roasting pans front to back and roast the ducks for 15 to 30 minutes longer, or until they are golden brown and most of the fat has melted away. Remove the ducks from the oven and let cool for 1 to 3 hours.

8. Using poultry shears or a heavy cleaver, cut each of the ducks into twelve to fourteen serving pieces, taking care that each piece of duck has its own covering of the delicious browned skin. Serve the duck at room temperature.—MARDEE HAIDIN REGAN

DUCK IN COCONUT CURRY

Succulent sliced duck breasts provide an excellent base for the sweet, hot and tangy curry sauce. Though the chile-paste recipe makes more than enough for the duck, it's worth preparing this relatively large amount because the paste keeps for a month and is delicious in coconut-milk-based sauces, soups and stews.

🍷 *Red wine is the classic choice for duck; choose one with a fruity spiciness to match the coconut accents, like the 1994 Alderbrook Zinfandel from California or the 1994 Clarendon Hills Grenache from Australia.*

4 SERVINGS

Four 5-ounce duck-breast halves, skin on
2 teaspoons soy sauce
1 teaspoon vegetable oil
Coarse salt
1½ cups thick unsweetened coconut milk*
3 tablespoons Panaeng Chile Paste (recipe follows)

THAI GLOSSARY

You'll find these Thai ingredients at Asian markets, and many are found at well-stocked supermarkets and specialty-food stores as well. All but the coriander root can be mail-ordered from The Oriental Pantry (1-800-828-0368).

CORIANDER ROOT **The root end of the coriander, or cilantro, plant. Wash well before using. If you do not have the root, substitute an equal measure of coriander stems.**

GALANGAL **A root that resembles ginger, with a subtle, spicy flavor. Available fresh or dried; soften the dried in hot water before using.**

KAFFIR LIME LEAVES **Glossy, thick leaves of the kaffir tree that have a very strong citrus flavor. Use fresh, frozen or dried, or substitute one teaspoon of finely grated lime zest for each leaf.**

LEMONGRASS **A fragrant lemony grass. Use the white bulb end, peeling off the tough outer leaves to reach the tender core. A teaspoon of finely grated lemon zest may be substituted for each tablespoon of minced lemongrass.**

PALM SUGAR **Creamy tan-colored sugar that is made from the sap of the coconut, sugar or palmyra palm. You can substitute an equal amount of maple sugar or light brown sugar.**

SHRIMP PASTE **A strong-smelling salty paste that's made from fermented shrimp and imparts a briny flavor.**

TAMARIND CONCENTRATE **A jelly-like reduction of strained tamarind pulp that's tart and fruity.**

THAI CHILES **Small, skinny, very hot chiles that ripen from green to red. Refrigerate the green ones; store the red at room temperature.**

UNSWEETENED COCONUT MILK **Made from grated coconut soaked in water. To get thick and thin coconut milk, chill an opened can in the refrigerator. The thick milk, which is used to enrich dishes, will rise to the top; the thin milk, often used as a cooking liquid, will settle. A thirteen-and-a-half-ounce can yields about one-half cup of thick and one cup of thin coconut milk.**

2 cups thin unsweetened coconut milk*
1 tablespoon tamarind concentrate* dissolved in 1 tablespoon boiling water
2 tablespoons Thai fish sauce (nam pla)*
2 teaspoons palm sugar*
8 canned lychees, drained
2 teaspoons fresh lime juice
1 fresh red Thai chile,* thinly sliced crosswise
1 fresh or frozen kaffir lime leaf,* thinly sliced
4 fresh basil leaves, thinly sliced
Steamed jasmine rice, for serving

*Available at Asian markets

1. Preheat the broiler. Deeply score the duck in a crosshatch pattern. Rub the soy sauce and oil

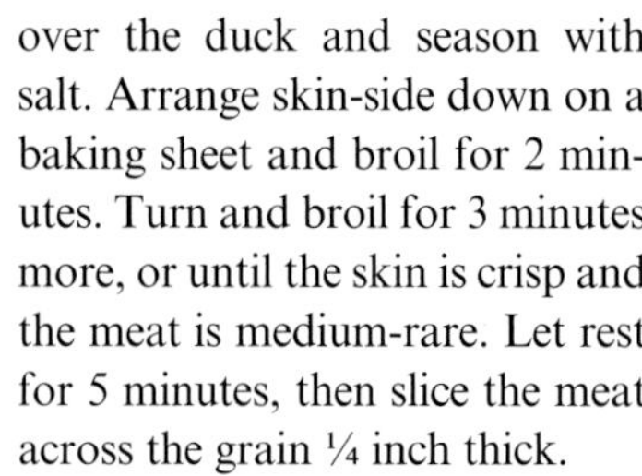

over the duck and season with salt. Arrange skin-side down on a baking sheet and broil for 2 minutes. Turn and broil for 3 minutes more, or until the skin is crisp and the meat is medium-rare. Let rest for 5 minutes, then slice the meat across the grain ¼ inch thick.

2. In a large saucepan, bring the thick coconut milk to a simmer over high heat. Stir in the chile paste, reduce the heat to low and cook, stirring, for 5 minutes. Add the thin coconut milk, raise the heat to moderate and simmer until thickened, about 5 minutes. Stir in the tamarind liquid, fish sauce and palm sugar.

3. In a small bowl, combine the lychees, lime juice and a pinch of salt. Add the duck to the curry. Cook over moderate heat just until warmed through. Transfer the curry to a shallow bowl. Garnish with the lychees, Thai chile, lime leaf and basil. Serve with rice.

Duck Breasts with Broccoli Rabe

Panaeng Chile Paste

MAKES ABOUT 1 CUP

11 large dried semi-hot chiles, such as guajillo, pasilla or New Mexico, stems and seeds discarded
Boiling water
1½ tablespoons vegetable oil
13 garlic cloves—6 coarsely chopped, 7 halved
4 shallots—2 thinly sliced, 2 coarsely chopped
¼ cup unsalted peanuts
3 tablespoons coarsely chopped fresh coriander (cilantro) root*
2 tablespoons minced fresh lemongrass,* white bulb only
2 quarter-size slices of peeled fresh galangal*
½ teaspoon coarse salt
2 fresh, frozen or dried kaffir lime leaves,* minced
1 teaspoon shrimp paste*
½ teaspoon cinnamon
½ teaspoon ground cumin

*Available at Asian markets

1. In a bowl, cover the chiles with boiling water. Let soak until softened, about 20 minutes. Drain and coarsely chop.

2. Heat the oil in a small skillet. Add the chopped garlic and sliced shallots. Cook over moderate heat, stirring, until lightly browned, about 4 minutes. Using a slotted spoon, transfer the garlic and shallots to a plate. Add the peanuts to the skillet, reduce the heat to low and cook, shaking the pan, until the nuts are toasted and browned, about 3 minutes. Add to the plate.

3. In a large mortar or mini-processor, grind the coriander, lemongrass, galangal and salt to a paste. Work in the halved garlic and chopped shallots. Add the chiles, garlic mixture and lime leaves; pound to a coarse puree. Stir in the shrimp paste, cinnamon and cumin. (**MAKE AHEAD:** The paste can be refrigerated up to 1 month in a covered jar.) —THAI COOKING SCHOOL, THE ORIENTAL HOTEL, BANGKOK

DUCK BREASTS WITH BROCCOLI RABE

For extra kick, sprinkle some crushed red pepper into the garlic in the skillet.

The intensity of duck, garlic, onion and sherry add up to a strong sweet savoriness. A Rhône, such as the 1993 Domaine Raspail Gigondas or the 1992 Guigal Côtes du Rhône, can provide a contrasting fruity note.

4 SERVINGS

Four 6-ounce boneless duck breasts, skin scored in a crosshatch pattern
- 1 tablespoon soy sauce
- ¼ cup medium dry sherry, such as amontillado
- 2 pounds broccoli rabe, tender stems and flowery stalks only

Salt and freshly ground pepper
- 2 tablespoons plus 1 teaspoon olive oil
- 1 medium red onion, thinly sliced
- ½ red bell pepper, thinly sliced
- 2 medium garlic cloves, minced
- ½ teaspoon anchovy paste (optional)
- 1 tablespoon unsalted butter

1. Rub the duck breasts all over with the soy sauce and 1 tablespoon of the sherry. Let marinate at room temperature for up to 1 hour.

2. Cook the broccoli rabe in boiling salted water until bright green, about 2 minutes. Drain in a colander. Let the broccoli rabe cool, chop coarsely and set aside.

3. Season the duck breasts on both sides with salt and pepper. Heat a large nonreactive skillet over high heat. Add the 1 teaspoon olive oil and when it is almost smoking, add the duck breasts, skin-side down. Reduce the heat to moderate and cook until the skin is brown and crisp, about 4 minutes. Turn the breasts over and cook them on the other side until browned, about 3 minutes for medium-rare. Transfer the duck breasts to a plate and pour the fat from the skillet.

4. Heat the remaining 2 tablespoons oil in the skillet. Add the onion and bell pepper and cook over moderate heat, stirring, until softened, about 5 minutes. Stir in the garlic and the anchovy paste and cook for 1 minute. Stir in the broccoli rabe and season with salt and pepper. Add the remaining 3 tablespoons sherry and simmer over moderately high heat for 2 minutes. Stir in the butter; season with salt and pepper.

5. Return the duck breasts, skin-side up, to the skillet to reheat briefly. Transfer the broccoli rabe to four plates. Arrange the duck breasts on the plates alongside the broccoli rabe and serve at once.—MARCIA KIESEL

ROASTED DUCK BREASTS WITH GRAPEFRUIT SAUCE

🍷 *Red is usually a good choice for duck, but the acidity in the grapefruit sauce will challenge most reds. Go for one with plenty of acidity of its own, such as a Barbera d'Alba from Italy. Look for the 1994 Prunotto Fiulot or the 1993 Bruno Giacosa.*

4 SERVINGS

- ½ tablespoon honey
- 1 teaspoon sugar
- 2 grapefruits, 1 squeezed (⅔ cup juice), 1 peeled and sectioned
- 4 duck-breast halves (5 to 6 ounces each), skin scored in a crosshatch pattern
- 1 cup chicken stock or canned low-sodium broth
- ¼ cup heavy cream
- 2 fresh thyme sprigs
- 1 tablespoon unsalted butter

Salt and freshly ground pepper

Sweet-Potato Pancakes (recipe follows)

Roasted Duck Breasts with Grapefruit Sauce

1. Preheat the oven to 350°. Mix ¼ teaspoon each of the honey and sugar with 2 tablespoons of the grapefruit juice. Brush on the duck breasts.

2. Heat an ovenproof large skillet. When the pan is hot, add the duck breasts, skin-side down, and sear over low heat until browned, about 6 minutes. Turn the breasts and cook for 2 minutes, then roast in the oven for 5 minutes. Let the duck rest on a cutting board for 4 minutes, covered loosely with foil.

3. Meanwhile, in a small nonreactive saucepan, mix the remaining ¾ teaspoon sugar and 1¼ teaspoons honey with 1 tablespoon of the duck fat from the pan. Cook until the mixture is light brown, then add the stock, cream, thyme and the remaining ½ cup grapefruit juice. Simmer over moderate heat until reduced to ½ cup. Stir in the butter and the grapefruit sections and season with salt and pepper. Remove from the heat. ➤

4. Thinly slice the duck breasts and arrange on warmed plates with the pancakes. Top with the grapefruit sauce and serve.

Sweet-Potato Pancakes

4 SERVINGS

- 1 sweet potato (¾ pound), peeled and cut into 1½-inch chunks
- 2 tablespoons all-purpose flour
- 2 large eggs
- 2 tablespoons milk
- Salt and freshly ground pepper
- Vegetable oil or reserved duck fat, for frying

1. In a saucepan, cover the sweet potato with cold water and boil until tender, about 10 minutes. Drain and mash until smooth. Stir in the flour, eggs and milk and season with salt and pepper.
2. In a large nonstick skillet, heat about 2 tablespoons oil or duck fat. Spoon twelve rounded tablespoons of the pancake batter into the skillet and cook over low heat until browned; flip the pancakes and brown on the other side.—MARCUS SAMUELSSON

PHEASANT WITH CHORIZO-AND-CORN-BREAD STUFFING

You'll need a little more than half of the corn bread for the pheasant. Serve the rest warm for snacks or breakfast.

4–6 SERVINGS

STUFFING:

- ¾ pound dried chorizo sausage, crumbled
- 4 tablespoons unsalted butter
- ¾ cup finely chopped onion
- 2 tablespoons finely diced celery
- 5 serrano chiles, seeded and minced
- 1 medium garlic clove, minced
- 3 cups crumbled Blue-Corn Bread (recipe follows)
- 2 teaspoons finely chopped thyme
- ½ teaspoon crumbled dried sage
- ½ cup finely chopped cilantro
- 3 tablespoons half-and-half
- 1 large egg, lightly beaten
- ¼ teaspoon freshly ground pepper

- 1 tablespoon vegetable oil
- Two 2½-pound pheasants
- 4 slices of bacon

1. **Make the stuffing:** In a heavy medium skillet, cook the chorizo over moderately high heat until browned, about 5 minutes. Transfer the chorizo to a large bowl. Discard the fat.
2. Melt 2 tablespoons of the butter in the skillet. Add the onion, celery, chiles and garlic. Cook until slightly softened, about 3 minutes. Toss with the chorizo. Mix in the corn bread, thyme, sage and cilantro. Stir in the half-and-half and egg. Season with the pepper and mix thoroughly.
3. Preheat the oven to 400°. In a large heavy skillet, melt the remaining 2 tablespoons butter in the oil. Add the pheasants and sear over moderately high heat, turning with tongs, until golden all over, about 6 minutes. Transfer to a plate to cool.
4. Stuff each of the pheasants with about half of the stuffing and reserve the rest. Place the pheasants in a roasting pan, breast-side up, so that they do not touch. Crisscross two bacon strips over each bird. Roast until the juices run clear when the thighs are pierced with a small knife, about 45 minutes. Cover loosely with foil and let rest for 20 minutes before carving.
5. Meanwhile, shape the remaining stuffing into twelve 2-inch-round patties. Preheat a cast-iron skillet over moderate heat, add the patties and cook, turning, until lightly browned, 4 to 6 minutes.
6. Carve the birds and serve with the patties and cavity stuffing.

Blue-Corn Bread

MAKES ONE 8-INCH SQUARE CORN BREAD OR ABOUT 5½ CUPS CRUMBS

- 1 stick (4 ounces) unsalted butter, melted
- 1 large egg, lightly beaten
- 1 cup blue cornmeal*
- ¾ cup all-purpose flour
- ¼ cup whole-wheat flour
- 2 teaspoons baking powder
- ¾ teaspoon salt
- ½ teaspoon baking soda
- 1½ cups buttermilk

*Available at specialty-food stores

1. Preheat the oven to 425°. Butter an 8-inch square cake pan. Put the butter, egg, cornmeal, all-purpose flour, whole-wheat flour, baking powder, salt and baking soda in a food processor and pulse to combine. Add the buttermilk and process for 5 seconds, or just until smooth.
2. Scrape the batter into the pan and bake for 25 minutes, or until the center is firm. Transfer the bread to a rack to cool a bit, then turn out and let cool completely. (**MAKE AHEAD:** The bread can be made up to 1 day ahead. Wrap in plastic and keep at room temperature.)—MARK MILLER

ROSES BY MAIL

These mail-order sources sell roses suitable for cooking:

- **Epicurean Specialty, 2888 Lynn Road, Sebastopol, CA 95472; 707-829-3881.**
- **Quail Mountain Herbs, P.O. Box 1049, Watsonville, CA 95077-1049; 408-722-8456.**
- **White Flower Farm, Rte. 63, Box 50, Litchfield, CT 06759; 203-496-9600 (for roses to plant in your own garden).**

Roasted Squab with Rose Petals

ROASTED SQUAB WITH ROSE PETALS

Inspired by the quail with rose-petal sauce in the book and movie Like Water for Chocolate, *this is a simplified version. Magic transformed that recipe into an aphrodisiac. Here I like to think it's the sensuality of the dish that puts people under a romantic spell.*

🍷 *The sweetness of the Madeira and the aromatic qualities of the rose petals call for a scented red with ripe berry flavors and a hint of roses, such as a West Coast Pinot Noir. The 1993 Jekel Gravelstone from California or the 1993 Ponzi Reserve from Oregon would make a harmonious pairing.*

2 SERVINGS

3 tablespoons unsalted butter, 2 room-temperature, 1 chilled
Two 1-pound squabs
Salt and freshly ground pepper
2 tablespoons Malmsey Madeira or ruby port
1 cup fragrant edible rose petals (see "Roses by Mail," above)

1. Preheat the oven to 450°. In a large ovenproof skillet, melt the 2 tablespoons room-temperature butter over high heat. Season the squabs with salt and pepper. When the butter is very hot, add the squabs, breast-side down, and brown well on all sides, about 9 minutes. Turn breast-side up and roast in the upper third of the oven, basting a few times, for about 15 minutes, or until the breast meat is medium rare. Transfer to a warm plate.

2. Pour off the fat in the skillet. Add the Madeira. Simmer 2 minutes over moderate heat, scraping the bottom of the pan with a wooden spoon to loosen browned bits. Remove from the heat.

3. Using a boning knife, cut along the breast bone and around the legs to halve and partially bone each squab. Arrange two halves on each plate. Pour the carving juices into the pan sauce and simmer for 1 minute over moderately high heat. Remove from the heat. Swirl in the 1 tablespoon chilled butter. Season the sauce with salt and pepper and pour over the squab. Scatter the rose petals on top and serve.—MARCIA KIESEL

CHAPTER 9

~

PORK & VEAL

Pork Crown Roast

PORK CROWN ROAST

This dramatic roast is formed by tying the rib section of a pork loin into a circle, with the ribs up. The hollow center of the roast is filled with Boudin, a spicy blend of rice, ground pork and vegetables. Ask your butcher to make a half-inch-deep cut between each of the ribs, "french" the bones (this means scraping clean the bones that protrude beyond the meat) and tie up the roast.

12 SERVINGS

One 16-rib crown roast of pork (about 8½ pounds), tied
Salt and freshly ground pepper
Boudin (recipe follows)

1. Preheat the oven to 450°. Season the pork generously with salt and pepper. Put it in a large flameproof roasting pan and roast in the upper third of the oven for 20 minutes. Reduce the oven temperature to 325° and roast for another 45 minutes. Cover the outside of the meaty part of the pork with foil and cook for 20 minutes longer. Meanwhile, in a large skillet, stir 2 cups of the Boudin over moderately high heat until hot, about 5 minutes. Spoon the remaining Boudin into a large, shallow ovenproof dish.

2. Remove the pork from the oven and spoon the hot Boudin into the cavity. Increase the oven temperature to 450° and set the pork in the upper third of the oven. Roast for about 45 minutes longer, about 2¼ hours total, or until the stuffing is brown and crisp on top and the internal temperature of the meat reads 160° on an instant-read thermometer. While the pork roasts, set the dish of Boudin on the bottom shelf and bake it for about 25 minutes, or until the Boudin is very hot and slightly crisp on top. Transfer the pork to a carving board, cover loosely with foil and let rest for 15 minutes.

3. Pour the pan juices into a small bowl and skim off the fat. Set the roasting pan over two burners on moderately high heat. Pour in 1½ cups of water and cook, scraping up any browned bits from the bottom of the pan. Reduce the heat to low and simmer the liquid until flavorful, about 4 minutes. Strain the liquid into a small saucepan and add the reserved pan juices. Season with salt and pepper. Reheat and pour into a sauceboat before serving.

4. Present the stuffed roast to the table, then scoop the stuffing into a serving dish. Carve the roast, cutting down between the ribs; serve one chop per person. Pass the Boudin and the pan juices separately.

Boudin

MAKES ABOUT 12 CUPS

- 2 sticks unsalted butter (½ pound)
- 1 pound ground pork
- 4 large celery ribs, finely chopped (2 cups)
- 2 medium onions, finely chopped (2 cups)
- 2 medium bell peppers, 1 green and 1 red, finely chopped (2 cups)
- 6 large garlic cloves, minced (2 tablespoons)
- ¼ cup fresh thyme leaves
- 4 bay leaves
- 1 tablespoon freshly ground black pepper
- 1 tablespoon crushed red pepper, or to taste
- 2 cups long-grain rice
- 4 cups chicken stock or canned low-sodium broth
- 2 pounds chicken or duck livers, trimmed and finely chopped
- 8 large scallions, chopped (2 cups)
- Coarse salt
- Louisiana hot sauce

1. In a large dutch oven, melt the butter over moderately high heat. Add the pork and cook, stirring to break up the meat, until lightly browned and cooked through, about 5 minutes. Add the celery, onions, bell peppers, garlic, thyme, bay leaves, ground pepper and crushed red pepper. Reduce the heat to moderately low and cook, stirring occasionally, until the vegetables are tender, about 12 minutes. Add the rice and cook, stirring occasionally, for 5 minutes longer.

2. Add the stock to the pot; stir well. Bring to a simmer. Reduce

CHRISTMAS BUFFET

🍷 When a variety of dishes are served as a buffet, it makes sense to offer a variety of wines. The Shrimp Remoulade, Golden Roasted Oysters, Oyster Patties and Seafood Gumbo with Okra need a flavorsome white, such as a Chardonnay, which can bridge the spicy-savory richness of the dishes. Look for California examples such as the 1994 Fess Parker or the 1994 Sinskey Los Carneros. The Pork Crown Roast with its Boudin stuffing and the Creole Ratatouille call for a red wine with enough flavor to enhance the meat and enough tart fruitiness to stand up to the spice. One good option: a Pinot Noir, such as the 1994 Alderbrook or the 1994 Morgan Monterey Reserve.

🍷 MINT JULEP (P. 461)

🍷 BOURBON MILK PUNCH (P. 462)

GOLDEN ROASTED OYSTERS (P. 22)

SHRIMP REMOULADE (P. 19)

OYSTER PATTIES (P. 23)

SEAFOOD GUMBO WITH OKRA (P. 96)

PORK CROWN ROAST (P. 222)

BOUDIN (P. 223)

CREOLE RATATOUILLE (P. 332)

SWEET-POTATO CHOCOLATE PIE (P. 412)

FIG TART (P. 413)

COFFEE

PRALINES (P. 452)

—COMMANDER'S PALACE, NEW ORLEANS

Roast Pork with Garlic and Sage, with Buttered Leeks (p. 340)

the heat to low, cover and cook until the rice is tender, about 15 minutes. Stir the rice a few times while it cooks to prevent sticking. When the rice is tender, stir in the chicken livers and scallions. Cover and cook until the livers are pink inside, about 5 minutes. Season with coarse salt and hot sauce. (**MAKE AHEAD:** The Boudin can be refrigerated for up to 2 days.) —JAMIE SHANNON

ROAST PORK WITH GARLIC AND SAGE

For this recipe, have the butcher cut the loin off the rack and then tie it back in place. Serve the pork with baby new potatoes roasted with olive oil and rosemary.

🍷 *Pork, like veal or chicken, is mild enough to be paired with full-flavored whites or light reds. Here, the garlic adds a richness that says red—a Pinot Noir. California bottlings, such as the 1994 Iron Horse or the 1993 Raymond Napa Valley Reserve, have just the right intensity for the occasion.*

4 SERVINGS

One 3¾-pound pork loin (bone-in weight)
20 fresh sage leaves
3 large garlic cloves, cut into small pieces
Salt and freshly ground pepper

1. Preheat the oven to 475°. Make twelve small cuts along the pork loin. With the point of a sharp knife, insert a sage leaf and a piece of garlic into each cut. Tuck the remaining garlic and sage between the meat and the bones. Season the roast with salt and pepper.
2. Set the meat in a heavy pan and roast in the upper third of the oven for about 50 minutes, basting occasionally after the first 10 minutes. The roast is done when the juices have only a tinge of pink and an instant-read thermometer inserted in the center reads 135°. Cover the roast loosely with foil and let stand for at least 10 minutes before carving to allow the juices to settle and the internal temperature to rise to 145°. —NINA ZAGAT

PAN-ROASTED PORK LOIN WITH APPLES

4 SERVINGS

1 pound medium sweet potatoes
7 tablespoons unsalted butter
2 medium Golden Delicious apples, peeled, quartered and cored
1 medium onion, quartered
1 pound sturdy greens, such as kale or collard greens, tough stems discarded, leaves cut into 2-inch pieces
2 tablespoons vegetable oil
1½ pounds boneless pork loin
Salt and freshly ground pepper
2 large shallots, minced
¼ cup dry white wine
1 cup chicken stock or canned low-sodium broth
1 tablespoon grainy mustard
1 tablespoon minced fresh flat-leaf parsley
2 teaspoons minced fresh thyme

1. Preheat the oven to 350°. Roast the sweet potatoes for about 30 minutes, or until slightly tender. Let cool, then peel and slice the potatoes crosswise ⅓ inch thick.
2. In a large enameled cast-iron casserole, melt 2 tablespoons of the butter over moderate heat. Add the apples and onion and stir to coat. Cover and bake until tender, about 15 minutes, stirring a few times. Transfer to a plate.
3. Add ⅓ cup of water and 2 tablespoons of the butter to the casserole and bring to a boil over moderately high heat. Add the greens, cover and steam until tender, about 5 minutes. Remove

Pan-Roasted Pork Loin

from the heat and add the sweet potatoes, apples and onion.

4. Raise the oven temperature to 425°. In a large, heavy-bottomed ovenproof skillet, heat the oil until shimmering. Season the pork generously with salt and pepper, add to the skillet fat-side down and cook over high heat until golden brown on three sides, about 5 minutes. Turn the pork so the uncooked side is down and roast in the oven for about 15 minutes, or until an instant-read thermometer inserted in the center registers 145°. Transfer to a platter, cover with foil and let stand for 10 minutes.

5. Melt 1 tablespoon of the butter in the skillet. Add the shallots and cook over low heat, stirring to scrape up any bits, until translucent, about 4 minutes. Raise the heat to moderate, add the wine and boil until almost completely evaporated, about 2 minutes. Add the stock and boil until reduced by half, about 5 minutes. Whisk in the mustard, parsley and thyme. Remove from the heat, whisk in the remaining 2 tablespoons butter and season with salt and pepper.

6. Gently rewarm the vegetable mixture over moderately high heat, season with salt and pepper and divide among four plates. Slice the pork loin about ½ inch thick and arrange the meat over the vegetable mixture. Spoon the mustard sauce over the pork and serve.—TRACI DES JARDINS

PORK WITH GINGER SAUCE AND APPLE ONION FLANS

The pickled ginger usually served with sushi turns up in the sweet tangy sauce for these pork medallions.

🍷 *The sweet, spicy, tart and fruity flavors surrounding a mild tenderloin call for a dry white wine that can cut through the fat and won't be diminished by the ginger notes or the creamy flan. A Gewürztraminer, such as the 1994 Bouchaine from California or the 1992 Domaine Weinback Cuvée Théo from Alsace, has just the aromatic spiciness to pull all these flavors together.*

4 SERVINGS

- 2½ tablespoons sugar
- 2 tablespoons cider vinegar
- 2 tablespoons fresh lemon juice
- 1 tablespoon plus ½ teaspoon olive oil
- ½ tablespoon finely chopped onion or shallot
- ½ tablespoon finely chopped carrot
- ¾ teaspoon finely chopped fresh ginger
- 1 cup chicken stock or canned low-sodium broth
- ½ teaspoon julienned pickled ginger
- ⅛ teaspoon finely grated lime zest
- 1½ pounds pork tenderloin, trimmed and cut into 12 medallions
- Salt and freshly ground pepper
- 1 lime, cut into 8 wedges
- Apple Onion Flans (recipe follows)

1. In a small nonreactive saucepan, bring the sugar, vinegar and lemon juice to a boil over high heat. Cook until golden and reduced to 1½ tablespoons, about 3 minutes.

2. In another small saucepan, heat the ½ teaspoon oil. Add the onion and carrot and cook over moderate heat, stirring, until softened, about 4 minutes. Add the vinegar syrup, the fresh ginger and the

Pork with Ginger Sauce and Apple Onion Flans

stock and boil over high heat until reduced to about ½ cup, about 15 minutes. Strain the sauce into a small bowl. Stir in the julienned pickled ginger and lime zest.

3. Heat the remaining 1 tablespoon olive oil in a large, heavy, nonreactive skillet. Season the pork on both sides with salt and pepper. Add the medallions to the skillet, in batches if necessary, and cook over high heat until browned and crisp, about 3 minutes per side for medium. Arrange the pork on four plates and keep warm.

4. Add the ginger sauce to the skillet and bring to a simmer over high heat, scraping up any browned bits. Spoon the sauce over the pork and garnish with the lime wedges. Unmold a flan onto each plate and serve at once.

Apple Onion Flans

4 SERVINGS

- 1 tablespoon olive oil
- 1 medium onion, finely chopped
- 1 large egg
- ¼ cup heavy cream
- ¼ cup half-and-half

1 tablespoon unsalted butter
1 medium Granny Smith apple, peeled, cored and cut into ¼-inch dice
Salt and freshly ground pepper

1. Preheat the oven to 350°. Butter four ⅓-cup ramekins.
2. Heat the oil in a small skillet. Add the onion and cook over moderate heat, stirring, until softened and lightly browned, about 8 minutes. Transfer to a food processor and puree. Let cool, then add the egg, cream and half-and-half and process until combined. Strain the custard into a bowl.
3. Melt the butter in a small skillet. Add the apple and cook over high heat, stirring, until browned and just tender, about 3 minutes. Let cool. Stir the apple into the custard and season with salt and pepper. Pour into the ramekins. (**MAKE AHEAD:** The flans can be prepared to this point and refrigerated overnight.)

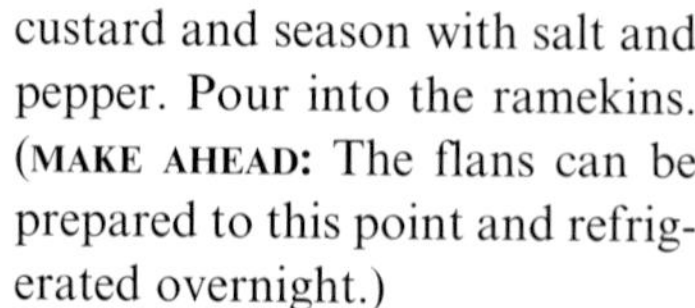

4. Set the ramekins in a small baking dish and add enough hot water to the dish to reach two-thirds of the way up the sides of the ramekins. Bake for about 25 minutes, or until the flans are firm. Remove from the water bath and let stand for 10 minutes. Run a small knife around the flans and unmold them onto plates.—MARY BETH AND ROLAND LICCIONI

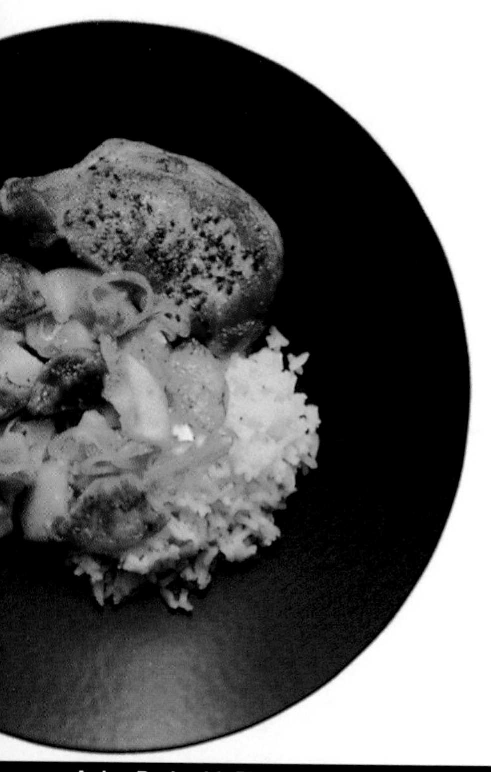

Anise Pork with Figs and Apples

PORK MEDALLIONS WITH CURRY HONEY GLAZE LF

Steamed basmati rice and sautéed chayote or cucumber slices make ideal accompaniments to this dish.

4 SERVINGS

2 teaspoons curry powder
2 tablespoons honey
2 tablespoons Worcestershire sauce
1 garlic clove, minced
Two 10-ounce pork tenderloins, trimmed and cut crosswise into 1¼-inch medallions
Vegetable cooking spray
½ cup chicken stock or canned low-sodium broth
3 tablespoons whole milk
1 teaspoon all-purpose flour
Lime wedges, for serving

1. In a small skillet, stir the curry powder over high heat until fragrant, about 2 minutes. Transfer to a shallow bowl and stir in the honey, Worcestershire sauce and garlic. Add the pork, turn to coat and let marinate for at least 1 hour or up to 3 hours.
2. Coat a large nonstick skillet, preferably with a textured bottom, with vegetable cooking spray and heat. Add the pork, reserving the marinade, and cook over moderately high heat, turning once, until browned and just cooked through, about 3 minutes per side. Transfer to a plate and keep warm.
3. Add the stock and the reserved marinade to the skillet and cook over moderately high heat, scraping up any browned bits. In a bowl, gradually stir the

PICKING PANS

These days you can't walk through a cookware store without bumping into a new line of low-fat cookware. How much difference could all those bumps and ridges really make? To find out, we tested more than a dozen pans. All were versatile, but three proved especially suitable for our recipes:
CIRCULON **for recipes like Pork Medallions with Curry Honey Glaze. The shallow concentric ridges trap bits of food, an advantage for sautéing meat and poultry and making rich pan sauces.**
CUISINART **has a smooth, heavy bottom that's great for omelets, as well as Fish Wrapped in Rice Paper (p. 153).**
ALL-CLAD LTD **for such recipes as Paella with Chicken and Seafood (p. 189). Actually, the smooth, very sturdy bottom and sides of this pan suit almost any dish.**

milk into the flour until smooth. Add to the skillet and cook, stirring, until thickened, about 2 minutes. Strain the sauce and serve with the pork medallions and lime wedges.—GRACE PARISI

ANISE PORK WITH FIGS AND APPLES

The sweet licorice taste of aniseed or fennel seeds adds depth of flavor to pork. For the sauce, look for dried figs that are soft and moist. If they seem very dry, soften them in hot water before cutting.

4 SERVINGS

- ¾ teaspoon crushed aniseed or fennel seeds
- Four 6-ounce boneless pork loin steaks
- Salt and freshly ground pepper
- 1 tablespoon olive oil
- 2 tablespoons unsalted butter
- 2 large shallots, thinly sliced
- 1 large garlic clove, minced
- 1 cup ¼-inch-thick tart apple slices
- ½ cup fresh orange juice
- 4 dried Calimyrna figs, quartered
- 1 tablespoon red-wine vinegar

1. Sprinkle the aniseed on both sides of the pork steaks and season with salt and pepper. In a large nonreactive skillet, heat the oil until almost smoking. Add the pork steaks and cook over moderately high heat, turning once, until well browned, about 3 minutes per side. Reduce the heat to moderate and cook the pork until firm and barely pink inside, about 4 minutes longer. Transfer the meat to a plate.

2. Melt 1 tablespoon of the butter in the skillet. Add the shallots and cook over moderate heat until softened, about 4 minutes. Add the garlic and cook until fragrant, about 1 minute. Add the apple slices and cook, turning, until lightly browned, about 2 minutes. Add 2 tablespoons of the orange juice and cook until the apple slices are just tender, about 1 minute. Add the figs and the remaining 6 tablespoons orange juice, increase the heat to moderately high and simmer to blend flavors, 1 to 2 minutes.

3. Season the sauce with the red-wine vinegar, salt and pepper. Swirl in the remaining 1 tablespoon butter. Return the pork and any juices that have accumulated; reheat briefly. Serve at once.—MARCIA KIESEL

HONEY-GLAZED PORK CHOPS Q

An Alsace Gewürztraminer, such as the 1992 Trimbach or the 1992 Léon Beyer, has a dry, aromatic spiciness that accents the chops and a pleasantly bitter finish that contrasts with the honeyed sweetness of the glaze.

4 SERVINGS

- 1 tablespoon honey
- 1 tablespoon red-wine vinegar
- 1 teaspoon dry mustard
- Four 1-inch-thick pork loin chops, preferably boneless, trimmed of excess fat
- ½ tablespoon vegetable oil
- Salt and freshly ground pepper

1. In a shallow nonreactive baking dish, blend the honey, vinegar and mustard. Add the pork chops, turn to coat and let marinate for at least 10 minutes.

2. Preheat the oven to 450°. Heat a large, heavy ovenproof skillet. Add the oil and heat until almost smoking. Season the pork chops with salt and pepper, add them to the skillet and cook over high heat until well browned on the bottom, about 2 minutes. Turn the chops, put the skillet in the oven and bake for about 12 minutes, or until the meat is just cooked through but still juicy. Transfer the chops to plates and serve.—MARCIA KIESEL

QUICK DINNER

HONEY-GLAZED PORK CHOPS (P. 227)

ANTHONY'S HOME FRIES (P. 305)

SAUTÉED WATERCRESS (P. 337)

APPLE PIZZA (P. 401)

GAME PLAN:

- **Put the water for the potatoes on to boil; cover the pan to speed up the process.**
- **Marinate the pork chops.**
- **Boil the potatoes for the home fries.**
- **Assemble and chill the apple pizza.**
- **Pan-fry and bake the chops.**
- **Prepare the home fries.**
- **Sauté the watercress.**
- **Bake the apple pizza.**

GRILLED APRICOT-AND-SAGE-GLAZED PORK CHOPS

An uncomplicated Beaujolais, such as the 1995 Georges Duboeuf Régnié, or a California equivalent, such as the 1995 Beringer Gamay Beaujolais, is fruity enough to match the sweet glaze here.

4 SERVINGS

- 2 tablespoons plus 1 teaspoon extra-virgin olive oil

- 1 medium shallot, finely chopped
- 8 fresh apricots, pitted and thinly sliced, or 16 dried California apricots, coarsely chopped
- 2 tablespoons light brown sugar
- 2 tablespoons soy sauce
- 1 tablespoon minced fresh sage
- ½ cup dry white wine
- Four 8-ounce pork loin chops, about 1 inch thick
- 2 pounds small red potatoes, halved
- 1 large head of garlic, cloves separated and peeled
- 2 teaspoons minced fresh rosemary
- Salt and freshly ground pepper

1. Heat the 1 teaspoon oil in a nonreactive saucepan. Add the shallot and cook over moderately high heat, stirring, until golden, about 3 minutes. Add the apricots, brown sugar, soy sauce, sage, wine and ½ cup of water and bring to a boil. Reduce the heat to moderately low and simmer, stirring, until the glaze is thick and glossy, about 25 minutes. Let cool. Rub half of the apricot glaze all over the pork and let marinate in the refrigerator for 4 hours.

2. Preheat the oven to 400°. In a roasting pan, combine the potatoes, garlic, rosemary and the remaining 2 tablespoons oil. Season with salt and pepper and roast for about 1 hour, or until brown and tender.

3. Light a grill or preheat the broiler. Season the pork chops with salt and pepper and grill or broil them about 6 inches from the heat, turning once, for 7 to 8 minutes per side, or until just cooked through.

4. Reheat the remaining apricot glaze. Divide the roasted potatoes and garlic among four large plates. Set a pork chop on each plate and serve with the remaining apricot glaze.—MARIA HELM

Grilled Apricot-and-Sage-Glazed Pork Chops

PORK WITH CLOUD-EAR MUSHROOMS

The mildness of pork allows it to pair with either substantial whites or light reds, but the soy, ginger and oyster sauce in this recipe suggest a full-bodied white with enough ripe, fruity flavors to balance the savory elements of the dish. The hints of melon and vanilla in an oak-aged California Chardonnay, such as the 1994 Zaca Mesa or the 1994 Beringer Private Reserve, would be ideal.

4 SERVINGS

- ¾ pound boneless pork loin, sliced crosswise ⅛ inch thick
- ½ ounce small dried cloud-ear mushrooms* (about ½ cup)
- ½ ounce dried lily buds* (about 50)

CHEF'S TIP

I like to pair pork with sweet fruit. Apricots are my favorite, but cherries and Mission figs are great too. Both might require a little more liquid for cooking than the apricots in the recipe for Grilled Apricot-and-Sage-Glazed Pork Chops. And be sure to use ripe fresh fruit so that you get plenty of juice.—MARIA HELM

2 tablespoons finely grated fresh ginger
2 tablespoons Shao-Hsing wine* or dry sherry
1½ tablespoons oyster sauce*
1 tablespoon low-sodium soy sauce
1 tablespoon peanut oil
1 tablespoon cornstarch dissolved in 6 tablespoons cold water
1 teaspoon Asian sesame oil
1 teaspoon sugar
¼ teaspoon salt
Freshly ground white pepper
6 cups boiling water
8 fresh cilantro sprigs, for garnish
Steamed white rice, preferably jasmine, for serving

*Available at Asian markets

1. Cut the sliced pork into 2-by-1-inch strips. Soak the cloud-ears and lily buds separately in hot water until softened, about 20 minutes. Rinse the cloud-ears in fresh water and drain well. Rinse the lily buds in fresh water, drain well and cut off the tough ends; cut each bud in half.
2. Mash the ginger through a fine-mesh strainer or garlic press. Set aside 1 teaspoon of the ginger juice.
3. In a medium bowl, combine the pork, cloud-ears, lily buds, ginger juice, wine, oyster sauce, soy sauce, peanut oil, dissolved cornstarch, sesame oil, sugar, salt and a pinch of white pepper. Let marinate at room temperature for 30 minutes.
4. Transfer the pork mixture to an 8-inch cake pan and set the pan in a bamboo steamer. Pour the boiling water into a large wok. Place the bamboo steamer in the wok. Cover and cook over high heat, stirring halfway through, until the pork is no longer pink, 10 to 12 minutes.
5. Transfer the pork to a serving platter, garnish with the cilantro and serve with the rice.—EILEEN YIN-FEI LO

EASY PORK STEW WITH GARLIC AND ESCAROLE Q

To save cooking time when making stews, use tender cuts of meat like the pork tenderloin here.

4 SERVINGS

1¼ pounds pork tenderloin, trimmed and sliced crosswise ½ inch thick
Salt and freshly ground pepper
2 tablespoons olive oil
5 garlic cloves, crushed
2 medium onions, chopped
½ teaspoon rosemary, crumbled
¼ cup dry white wine
1¼ pounds red potatoes, cut into ¾-inch chunks
2½ cups chicken stock or canned low-sodium broth
½ head of escarole, torn into 1-inch pieces (5 cups)

1. Season the pork slices with salt and pepper. In a large heavy nonreactive skillet, heat 1 tablespoon of the oil. Brown the pork in two batches over high heat, about 2 minutes per side; transfer to a plate.
2. Add the remaining 1 tablespoon oil to the pan; reduce the heat. Add the garlic and cook, mashing and stirring it, until soft and golden, about 4 minutes. Add the onions and rosemary. Cook, stirring, until the onions soften, about 5 minutes. Add the wine; simmer until almost evaporated, about 4 minutes. Add the potatoes and stock; season with salt and pepper. Bring to a boil, cover and boil gently until the potatoes are tender, about 20 minutes.
3. Add the pork to the stew; simmer for 2 minutes. Add the escarole in two parts and cook, stirring, until wilted but still bright green and the pork is cooked through, about 2 minutes. (**MAKE AHEAD:** The pork stew can be made a day ahead; be careful not to overcook when reheating.) Serve hot.—JUDITH SUTTON

Pork with Cloud-Ear Mushrooms

PORK STEW IN RED CHILE SAUCE

This is one of those simple but delicious stews, Asado de Chile Colorado, *typical of the cooking from the north of Mexico. It's usually made with the chile colorado from Chihuahua, which is also known as* chile seco del norte *or dried California chile. Either pork or beef can be used, although pork lends a fuller flavor. Serve the stew with white rice or warm flour or corn tortillas.*

4 SERVINGS

- 1½ pounds boneless pork shoulder, trimmed of some but not all of its fat, cut into ¾-inch cubes
- Salt
- 15 seco del norte chiles
- Boiling water
- 2 garlic cloves, coarsely chopped
- ½ inch cinnamon stick
- 1 bay leaf, preferably Mexican
- 1 heaped teaspoon crumbled dried oregano

1. Arrange the pork in one or two layers in a wide, heavy, flameproof casserole. Barely cover with water, and season with salt. Cover and cook over moderate heat until almost tender, about 30 minutes. Drain off most of the broth and reserve, adding enough water to make 2½ cups. Continue to cook the pork uncovered until the fat has been rendered and the meat is slightly browned, about 5 minutes longer.

2. Meanwhile, using a small sharp knife, slit the chiles lengthwise and remove the stems, seeds and veins. Cover with boiling water and set aside to soak for 15 minutes. Drain.

3. Pour ⅓ cup of the reserved pork broth into a blender. Add the garlic, cinnamon, bay leaf and oregano and blend until smooth. Add the mixture to the pork in the casserole; fry for a few seconds.

4. Add one more cup of the reserved broth and the drained chiles, a few at a time, to the blender and puree. Strain the chiles over the pork through a fine-mesh sieve, pressing to extract as much of the flesh and juice as possible. Fry the pork, scraping the bottom of the pan to prevent sticking, about 5 minutes longer.

5. Add the remaining pork broth to the casserole and cook over low heat until the meat is tender and the sauce is thick enough to coat the back of a wooden spoon, about 1 hour. Season with salt. (**MAKE AHEAD:** The stew can be refrigerated for up to 1 day. Rewarm over moderately low heat.) —DIANA KENNEDY

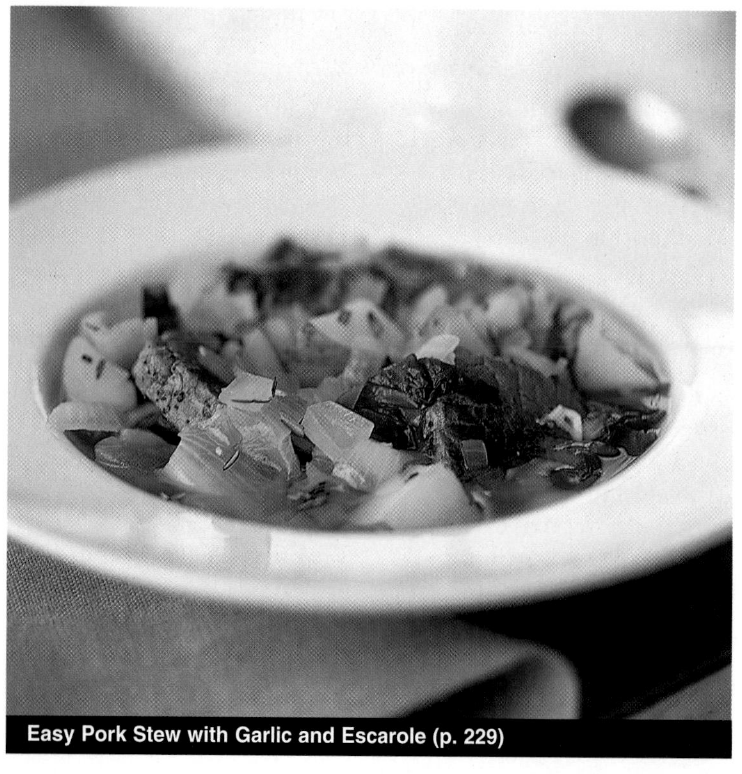

Easy Pork Stew with Garlic and Escarole (p. 229)

TOMATILLO-CHIPOTLE-GLAZED COUNTRY RIBS

To me, a perfectly balanced plate is these hot and tangy ribs, a green salad and a spoonful of Mexican beans. I love meaty country ribs—which are not really ribs, but chops from the loin. You can use spareribs or baby back ribs if you prefer.

🍷 *Go for an Australian red with lots of up-front flavor. Consider the 1994 Tyrrell Long Flat Red or the 1993 Geoff Merrill Owen's Estate Shiraz.*

4–6 SERVINGS

- 6 dried guajillo or Anaheim chiles, stemmed and seeded
- 2 cups Roasted-Tomatillo Chipotle Salsa (p. 356)
- 3 pounds pork country ribs
- 2 tablespoons honey
- Romaine lettuce leaves, for serving
- Sliced radishes and fresh cilantro sprigs, for garnish

1. Heat a dry griddle or heavy skillet over moderate heat. Add two of the chiles, opening them

Tomatillo-Chipotle-Glazed Country Ribs

Pork Stew in Red Chile Sauce

flat on the hot surface. Toast, pressing down, until they start to crackle. Turn and toast the other side, then transfer to a blender. Toast the remaining chiles; add them to the blender along with the salsa. Blend until smooth, scraping the sides. Pass the puree through a medium strainer into a bowl. (MAKE AHEAD: The chile mixture can be refrigerated for up to 1 week.)

2. In a large bowl, smear the ribs with half the chile mixture, then cover and refrigerate 6 hours or overnight. In another bowl, mix the remaining chile mixture with the honey; cover and refrigerate.

3. Preheat the oven to 325° and spread the ribs and the marinade in a single layer in a baking dish. Drizzle ¼ cup of water around them, cover with foil and roast for 1½ hours. Uncover and bake for about 15 minutes longer, or until tender. Discard the pan juices.

4. Raise the oven temperature to 350°. Brush the ribs generously with the chile-and-honey sauce. Bake for about 15 minutes or until glazed and a little crusty.

5. Line a serving platter with the romaine and pile the ribs on top. Garnish with the radishes and cilantro; pass around any remaining sauce.—RICK BAYLESS

HEARTY STUFFED CABBAGE

8 SERVINGS

1 cup dried Polish mushrooms or porcini (1 ounce)
One 3½- to 4-pound head of green cabbage
Ice water
14 ounces to 1 pound skinless kielbasa, cut into chunks
1 large onion, finely chopped
1 pound lean ground beef
1½ cups fresh bread crumbs
1 tablespoon sweet paprika
2 teaspoons dried dill
2½ teaspoons salt
2 large eggs, lightly beaten
1 Granny Smith apple
1½ cups dry white wine
Two 15-ounce cans of tomato sauce (3½ cups)
1 imported bay leaf
Basmati rice or steamed potatoes, for serving

1. In a small bowl, cover the mushrooms with 1 cup of hot water and let soak for 30 minutes. Drain the mushrooms, reserving the liquid. Rinse the mushrooms to remove any grit, then chop them. Strain the soaking liquid

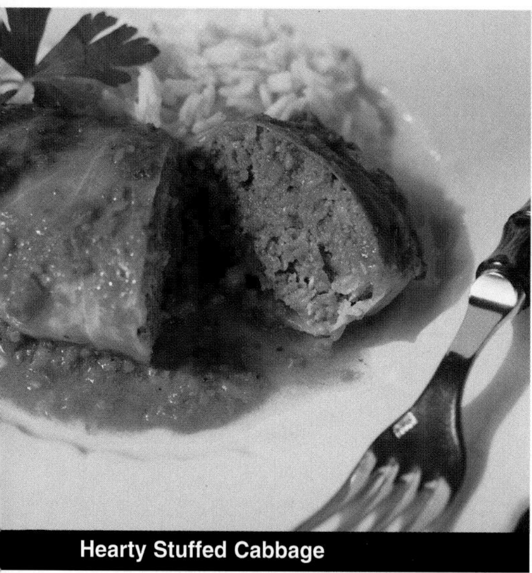

Hearty Stuffed Cabbage

HEARTY STUFFED-CABBAGE SUPPER

All that this menu requires in terms of last-minute labor is putting together the salad.

🍷 Although the main dish uses white wine, a substantial red is better suited to the porcini and kielbasa in the stuffed cabbage—and the acidity of tomato sauce calls for a red with some tartness of its own. A Chianti Classico Riserva, such as the 1991 Villa Antinori or the 1988 Castello di Gabbiano, would be ideal. Don't worry about the acidity of the salad flattening the flavor of the wine; the pecans, goat cheese and pepperoni are all wine-friendly ingredients.

MIXED GREENS WITH GOAT CHEESE AND PECANS (P. 62)

HEARTY STUFFED CABBAGE (P. 231)

ROSY APPLE CRISP (P. 427)

through a sieve lined with a moistened paper towel and reserve.

2. Meanwhile, bring a large saucepan of water to a boil. Remove any damaged outer leaves from the cabbage. With a sharp knife, core the cabbage, cutting a hole at least 1 inch wide and deep. Place the cabbage in the saucepan, cored-end down, and boil for 12 minutes. With two large spoons, transfer the cabbage to a large bowl of ice water and let cool slightly. Carefully peel off as many softened leaves as you can without tearing them. Return the cabbage to the saucepan and repeat the process, if necessary, until you have sixteen whole leaves.

3. Quarter the remaining cabbage and transfer to a food processor; chop fine. Measure out two packed cups and place in a large, heavy enameled casserole; reserve the rest for another use.

4. Add the kielbasa to the food processor and grind fine. In a large nonstick skillet, cook the kielbasa over moderately high heat until lightly browned; transfer to a large bowl. Add the onion to the skillet and cook over moderate heat until softened. Spoon half of the onion into the bowl with the kielbasa and the other half into the casserole.

5. Crumble the ground beef over the kielbasa and add the chopped mushrooms, bread crumbs, paprika, dill and 1½ teaspoons of the salt; mix well. Blend in the eggs and half of the reserved mushroom liquid.

6. Using a sharp knife, shave the raised thick rib from each of the cabbage leaves so that it is level with the leaf. Spread out the cabbage leaves and fill each one with a rounded ¼ cup of the meat stuffing. Fold the rib end of each leaf up over the stuffing and fold the top of the leaf down over it. Using both index fingers, tuck in the ends of each cabbage roll to form a neat tubular package.

7. Preheat the oven to 350°. Peel the apple and grate it into the casserole; discard the core. Add the wine and simmer over moderate heat for 10 minutes. Stir in the remaining mushroom-soaking liquid, 2 cups of water, the tomato sauce, the bay leaf and the remaining 1 teaspoon salt and bring to a boil. Carefully add the cabbage rolls and bring to a simmer. Cover the casserole, transfer it to the oven and cook for 1¼ hours. (**MAKE AHEAD:** The stuffed cabbage can be refrigerated for up to 4 days. Add ¼ cup of water to the sauce and reheat in a 350° oven for about 1 hour.) Discard the bay leaf. Serve two rolls per person, with the rice or potatoes.—DIANA STURGIS

VEAL SCALOPPINE WITH CELERY AND ORANGE

This is a variation on the classic scaloppine al limone. *Instead of lemon, I have used orange—freshly squeezed juice for its refreshing aroma and zest paired with strips of celery for its penetrating flavor and interesting texture. The combination of veal and citrus is a sprightly one I never tire of.*

4 SERVINGS

- 4 tablespoons unsalted butter
- 1 tablespoon vegetable oil
- 1 pound veal scaloppine, thinly sliced from the top round and pounded very thin
- 1 cup all-purpose flour

1 cup celery, stalks peeled, stripped of their strings and cut into 1½-by-¼-inch strips
Salt
¼ cup fresh orange juice
1 tablespoon very fine strips of orange zest
Freshly ground pepper

1. In a large skillet, melt 3 tablespoons of the butter in the oil over high heat. When the fat is very hot, dredge the scaloppine one by one in the flour, shake off any excess and add them to the pan without crowding. Brown the scaloppine quickly on both sides, about 1½ minutes; transfer them to a platter.

2. Add the celery to the pan and turn the heat down to very low. Add the remaining tablespoon of butter, a little salt and all the juices released by the meat. Stir once or twice, cover and cook until the celery is crisp-tender, about 10 minutes.

3. Add the orange juice and zest and increase the heat to moderate. Stir with a wooden spoon to loosen all the cooking residues from the bottom of the pan.

4. Season the scaloppine with salt and pepper and return them to the pan. Turn them two or three times in the sauce until heated through. Transfer the scaloppine to a warmed platter. Pour the pan sauce and the celery over the meat and serve at once.—MARCELLA HAZAN

BRAISED VEAL À L'ORANGE

Tendrons of veal are cut from the cartilaginous portion of the breast (where the ribs meet). They become meltingly tender when braised for a long time. If tendrons are not available at the butcher shop, veal ribs from the upper part of the rib cage can be used instead.

8 SERVINGS

3 tablespoons vegetable oil
8 tendrons of veal (about 6 ounces each)
Salt and freshly ground pepper
Flour, for dusting
2 medium carrots, finely chopped

VEAL FOR SCALOPPINE

To achieve the brilliantly fresh taste that makes scaloppine so irresistible, the bond between the meat and its accompanying flavors must occur very quickly. The veal scallops, therefore, must be cut and pounded thin enough for you to cook them in a few bats of an eyelash. But mere thinness gets you only halfway. A slice of scaloppine must be tender and juicy, and it must lie perfectly flat in the pan so that, during its brief time there, it cooks evenly and becomes uniformly browned. Whether or not this actually happens depends on how the butcher cuts the meat.

Like all the meat we consume, scallops are cut from a muscle. Muscles are stacked in layers which, seen in cross section, form a finely hatched grain. The muscle layers, like so many bands of elastic, can stretch or contract. If the butcher cuts through those layers, the scallops will always lie flat. If, however, he slices in the same direction in which the muscle layers are stacked, the scallop will tighten and contract the moment it is put in the hot pan. Instead of a flat slice, you will get a wavy one; instead of a relaxed, tender piece of meat, you will have a stringy, chewy one.

Unfortunately, the scaloppine in the supermarket are almost invariably cut the wrong way. You must make friends with the butcher and explain that you want scallops from the top round, cut across, or perpendicular to, the muscle's grain rather than parallel to it.—MARCELLA HAZAN

Veal Scaloppine with Celery and Orange

SKI-PARTY MENU

- 2 celery ribs, thinly sliced
- 1 medium onion, thinly sliced
- 4 garlic cloves, finely chopped
- 1 cup dry white wine
- 4 cups chicken stock or canned low-sodium broth
- 2 medium tomatoes, finely chopped (about 2 cups)
- 2 fresh thyme sprigs
- 1 bay leaf
- 1 tablespoon tomato paste
- ¾ cup fresh orange juice
- Zest from 2 navel oranges, cut into fine julienne strips

1. Heat the oil in a large enameled cast-iron casserole. Season the tendrons of veal with ½ teaspoon each of salt and pepper. Flour the veal and shake off any excess. Add the veal to the casserole and cook over moderately high heat, turning often with tongs, until the meat is golden brown on all sides. Remove the veal to a platter.

2. Add the carrots, celery, onion and garlic to the casserole and cook, stirring often, until softened, about 5 minutes. Set the veal on top of the vegetables and pour in the wine. Increase the heat to high and boil until almost all of the wine has evaporated. Add the chicken stock, tomatoes, thyme and bay leaf. In a small bowl, mix the tomato paste with 2 tablespoons of the cooking liquid. Add to the casserole along with the orange juice and bring to a boil. Reduce the heat to moderate, cover and simmer until the veal is very tender, about 1½ hours.

3. Meanwhile, in a small saucepan, blanch the orange zest for 3 minutes to remove its bitterness.

4. Remove the meat to a large deep serving dish and cover with foil to keep warm. Increase the heat to high and boil the sauce until it is reduced by half and very flavorful, 20 to 30 minutes. Strain the sauce through a fine sieve into a medium saucepan, pressing gently on the vegetables; discard the solids.

5. Bring the sauce to a boil and stir in the orange zest. Season the sauce with salt and pepper, pour it over the meat and serve at once.—CATHERINE ALEXANDROU AND MICHEL BOURDEAUX

GREEN-HEARTED MEATBALL

Similar to a meat loaf—but unlike any meat loaf your grandmother might have made—this meatball has a delicate texture and subtle flavor that come from an astute combination of simple ingredients.

4 SERVINGS

- ½ pound finely ground very lean veal or a half-and-half mixture of ground pork and lean ground beef
- 1 cup plus 3 tablespoons dry bread crumbs
- 1 cup freshly grated Pecorino or Parmigiano-Reggiano cheese
- 3 large eggs
- ½ teaspoon salt
- 1 teaspoon freshly ground pepper
- 6 young green chard leaves, stemmed
- 1 large carrot
- 3 tablespoons unbleached flour
- 1½ ounces very thinly sliced caciocavallo or Provolone cheese
- 6 tablespoons extra-virgin olive oil
- 2 fresh rosemary sprigs
- 1½ cups dry white wine

1. In a large bowl, combine the ground veal with the 1 cup bread crumbs, the grated cheese, the eggs, salt and pepper. Combine the ingredients thoroughly with your hands.

2. Bring a large pot of water to a rolling boil. Add the chard leaves and cook until just wilted, about 1 minute. Rinse the chard under cold water until cool. Squeeze out any excess moisture and set aside. Add the carrot to the boiling water and cook until al dente, about 10 minutes. Drain and rinse under cold water. Cut the carrot lengthwise in six ⅛-inch-thick slices.

3. Combine the flour with the remaining 3 tablespoons bread crumbs and heavily dust a large work surface with the mixture.

On the work surface, pat the ground veal into an 8-by-12-inch rectangle, about ½ inch thick. Arrange the chard leaves over the meat, leaving a border of about 1 inch at the top and bottom. Layer the carrot slices evenly over the chard leaves, then top the carrots with the sliced cheese.

4. Beginning with a long side, roll up the meat jelly-roll fashion into a long thin cylinder with the vegetables and cheese inside, packing the meat. As you roll the cylinder, it will lengthen to approximately 16 inches. Pack this with your hands to make it as firm and tight as you can. Cut the cylinder in half crosswise. Seal the ends thoroughly with the meat mixture to prevent the cheese from oozing out during cooking. The outsides should be thoroughly dusted with the flour mixture; if necessary, sprinkle a little more flour on the work surface and roll the cylinders in it.

5. In a large, heavy, nonreactive skillet, heat the oil. Add the rosemary sprigs to the pan. Add the cylinders and brown well on all sides over moderately low heat, turning carefully with two wooden spoons or metal spatulas. When the meat is thoroughly browned, carefully pour off as much oil from the pan as possible.

6. Pour half of the wine over the cylinders. Turn the heat to low, cover the pan and cook for 15 minutes. Turn the cylinders and add the remaining wine. Cover and cook for 15 minutes longer; if the pan begins to look dry at any point during cooking, add a little water.

7. Transfer the cylinders to a cutting board. Return the skillet to moderately high heat and add ½ cup of water. Boil the sauce, scraping up any brown bits, until it has reduced to 3 tablespoons. Strain the sauce to remove the rosemary sprigs. Serve the meat hot, in slices, or let cool to room temperature and slice it as thin as possible. Drizzle the reduced sauce over the slices.—NANCY HARMON JENKINS

CHAPTER 10

~

BEEF, LAMB & GAME

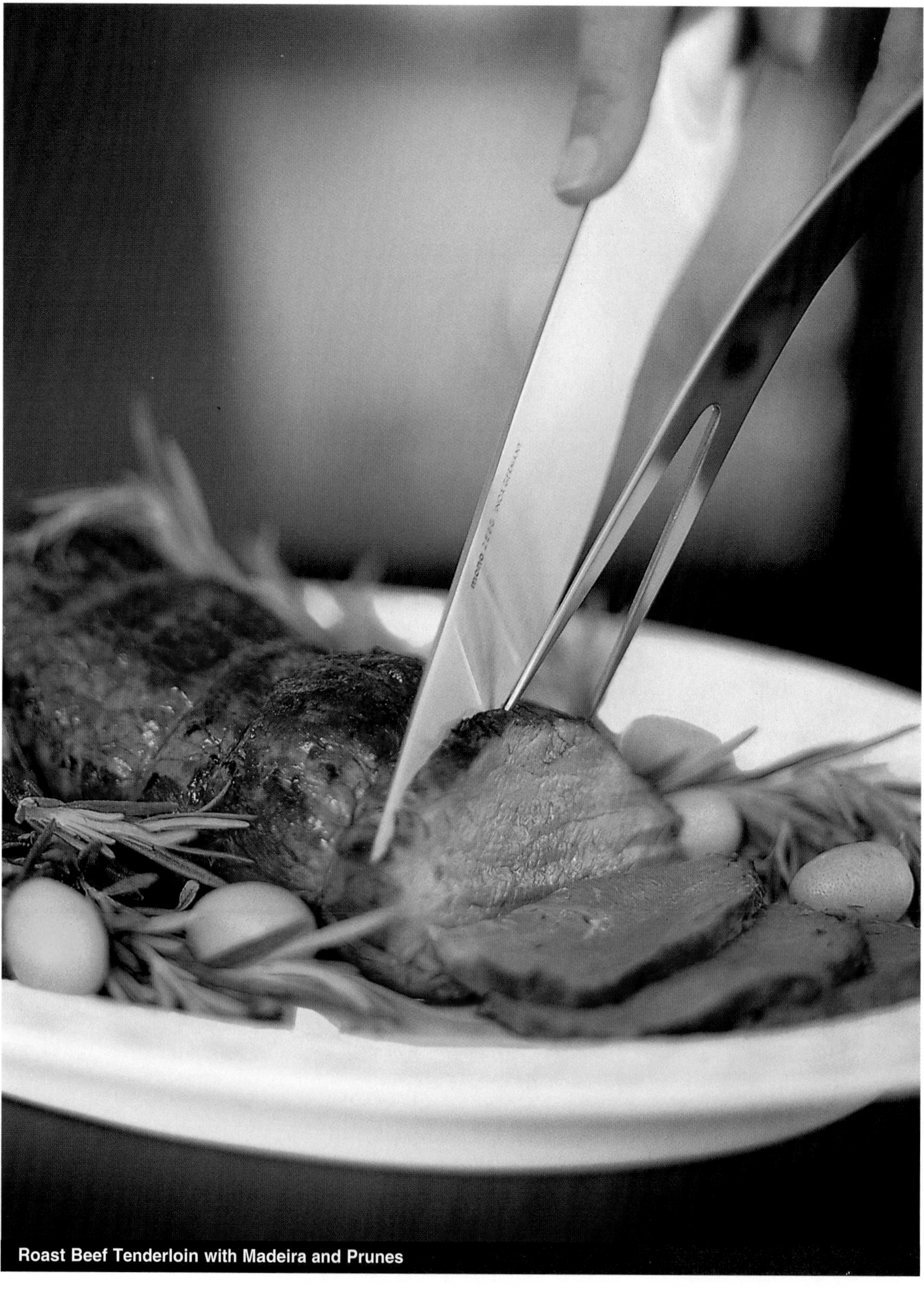

Roast Beef Tenderloin with Madeira and Prunes

ROAST BEEF TENDERLOIN WITH MADEIRA AND PRUNES

Plumping the prunes in Madeira takes a day or two, but preparing the roast is quick and easy.

8 SERVINGS

24 pitted prunes
1½ cups Malmsey Madeira
3 tablespoons vegetable oil
One 4-pound trimmed and tied beef tenderloin roast
Salt and freshly ground pepper
2 large shallots, minced
1 cup red wine
2 cups chicken stock or canned low-sodium broth
2 tablespoons cold unsalted butter

1. One to two days ahead, put the prunes in a nonreactive bowl and cover with the Madeira; set aside at room temperature to plump.
2. Preheat the oven to 450°. In a large, heavy flameproof roasting pan set over two burners, heat the oil over moderately high heat. Season the beef with salt and pepper. When the oil is hot but not smoking, add the meat to the pan and brown it well on all sides.
3. Transfer the roasting pan to the oven; roast the meat for about 20 minutes, or until an instant-read thermometer inserted in the thickest part registers 125° for medium rare. Set the roast on a large warmed platter, cover loosely with foil and keep warm.
4. Discard the fat in the roasting pan. Set the pan over two burners, add the shallots and red wine and simmer over moderately low heat until the wine is reduced by half, about 8 minutes. Increase the heat to moderately high, add 1½ cups of the stock and boil until reduced by half, about 5 minutes. Add the prune soaking liquid and boil until reduced to 1½ cups, about 7 minutes. Pour the sauce into a nonreactive medium saucepan. Add the soaked prunes and the remaining ½ cup stock and simmer over low heat, stirring occasionally; the sauce will thicken slightly.
5. Cut the beef into sixteen slices. Pour any meat juices into the sauce and stir in the butter, 1 tablespoon at a time. Season with salt and pepper and serve alongside the beef.—MARCIA KIESEL

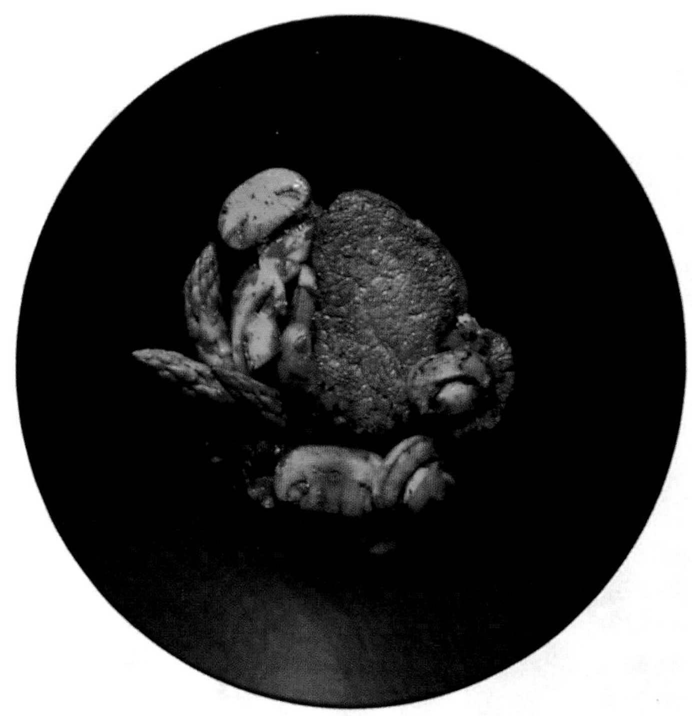

Medallions of Beef with Mushrooms

MEDALLIONS OF BEEF WITH MUSHROOMS

In this recipe, glazing beef with Cognac gives it a rich flavor and seals in juices. Serve the meat over orzo or egg noodles.

4 SERVINGS

1 cup asparagus tips (from about 1 pound asparagus)
Four 6-ounce beef tenderloin steaks
Salt and freshly ground pepper
1½ teaspoons olive oil
2½ tablespoons unsalted butter
2 tablespoons Cognac or brandy
¾ pound mushrooms, stemmed and caps thickly sliced
2 large shallots, minced
⅓ cup Madeira
1 teaspoon Dijon mustard

1. In a large nonreactive skillet, bring 1 cup of water to a boil. Add the asparagus tips and boil over high heat until just tender, about 3 minutes. Drain in a colander and rinse under cold water to refresh. ➤

2. Season the steaks with salt and pepper. Heat the oil in the skillet over moderately high heat until almost smoking. Add ½ tablespoon of the butter and when the foam subsides, add the steaks and cook, turning once, until well browned, about 6 minutes for medium-rare.

3. Remove the skillet from the heat and pour in the Cognac; stand back in case it ignites. Return the skillet to moderately high heat and turn the steaks to coat. Cook until the sauce is slightly reduced, about 2 minutes. Transfer the steaks to a plate.

4. Melt ½ tablespoon of the butter in the skillet. Add the mushrooms and sauté over moderately high heat, stirring occasionally, until browned and tender, about 6 minutes. Add 1 tablespoon butter and the shallots and cook over moderate heat, stirring, until the shallots soften, about 4 minutes. Increase the heat to moderately high and add the asparagus tips. Pour in the Madeira and boil until reduced by one-third, about 2 minutes. Season with salt and pepper. Stir in the mustard and the remaining ½ tablespoon butter.

5. Reduce the heat to moderate and add the steaks. Turn to coat with sauce and simmer to heat through, about 1 minute. Transfer the steaks to plates, spoon the sauce and vegetables on top and serve.—MARCIA KIESEL

STEAK WITH LEMON BUTTER Q

Serve any leftover lemon butter with roasted chicken or baked potatoes.

4 SERVINGS

- 6 anchovy fillets, minced
- 6 tablespoons unsalted butter, softened
- 1 small shallot, minced
- 1 tablespoon minced fresh parsley
- 1½ teaspoons finely grated lemon zest
- 1½ teaspoons fresh lemon juice
- Freshly ground pepper
- Four 1-inch-thick steaks (about 11 ounces each for bone-in steaks, 8 ounces for boneless)
- Salt

1. In a bowl, combine the anchovies, butter, shallot, parsley, lemon zest, lemon juice and ¼ teaspoon pepper. Wrap the butter in a piece of plastic wrap, shape into a 1-inch-thick log and freeze until firm.

2. Preheat the broiler. Arrange the steaks on a broiler pan, season with salt and pepper and broil for about 2 to 3 minutes per side for medium-rare. Transfer the steaks to plates, top each one with a ¾-inch pat of the butter and serve immediately.—PAUL GRIMES

Steak with Lemon Butter

SPICE-CRUSTED STEAK Q

4 SERVINGS

- 2 teaspoons cumin seeds
- 2 teaspoons fennel seeds
- 2 teaspoons minced garlic
- 1 teaspoon freshly ground pepper
- Four 1-inch-thick steaks (about 11 ounces each for bone-in steaks, 8 ounces for boneless)
- Salt

1. In a spice grinder or mortar, coarsely grind the cumin and fennel seeds. Work in the garlic and pepper. Press the mixture on both sides of the steaks. Let stand for 30 minutes.

2. Preheat the broiler. Season the steaks on both sides with salt. Broil for 2 to 3 minutes per side for medium-rare.—PAUL GRIMES

Smoky Beef Fajitas

SMOKY BEEF FAJITAS

For an even quicker version, sauté the peppers and onions together for two minutes instead of charring them. Chipotle chiles packed in adobo are available at specialty-food stores and Latin American markets.

🍷 *The sharp flavors here—tangy beef, chipotles, sweet roasted peppers and onions—all point to beer. Pick a light brew like Carta Blanca or Lone Star.*

4 SERVINGS

- 2 canned chipotle chiles in adobo, seeded and minced
- 2 large garlic cloves, minced
- 1/4 cup plus 1 tablespoon olive oil
- 2 tablespoons fresh lime juice
- 1 pound skirt steak, sliced against the grain 1/4 inch thick
- 8 flour tortillas
- 1 medium red bell pepper, cut into 1/3-inch-thick strips
- 1 medium yellow bell pepper, cut into 1/3-inch-thick strips
- 2 medium red onions, halved and sliced lengthwise 1/3 inch thick
- Salt and freshly ground black pepper
- 1 large Hass avocado, coarsely chopped, for serving
- Sour cream, for serving
- Pico de Gallo (recipe follows), for serving
- 1/4 cup loosely packed fresh cilantro leaves, for serving

1. In a large, sturdy plastic bag, combine the chipotles, garlic, 2 tablespoons of the oil and the lime juice. Add the steak and marinate for 30 minutes.

2. Preheat the oven to 250°. Heat a large cast-iron skillet. Working with one at a time, add the tortillas to the skillet and warm them quickly over high heat, turning once, until softened and heated through, about 15 seconds per side. Wrap the tortillas in foil and keep warm in the oven.

3. Heat 2 tablespoons of the oil in the skillet until almost smoking. Add the red and yellow peppers and cook over high heat, stirring, until starting to brown, about 3 minutes. Add the onions and cook, stirring, until tender and lightly charred, about 5 minutes. Season with salt and pepper, transfer to a large plate and keep warm in the oven.

4. Add the remaining 1 tablespoon olive oil to the skillet and heat just until smoking. Pat the steak strips dry with paper towels. Add half the strips to the skillet in a single layer, season with salt and pepper and cook, turning once, until browned, about 2 minutes per side. Transfer to a plate and cook the remaining steak. Return all the meat to the skillet and cook, stirring, for 1 minute.

5. Mound the steak on a plate and serve it with the tortillas, onions and peppers, avocado, sour cream, Pico de Gallo and cilantro. Let everyone assemble his own fajita.

Q & A

Q: How should I store tortillas?

A: Commercially made flour and corn tortillas usually come in convenient resealable plastic bags and can be refrigerated for four days. When I buy a large package of thirty-six, I keep them frozen for up to one month and peel the tortillas off as I need them. When I make my own, I store corn tortillas in a plastic bag as well, but I wrap flour ones in aluminum foil. Both types should stay fresh for up to a week in the refrigerator.—ZARELA MARTINEZ

Pico de Gallo

MAKES ABOUT 1 CUP

½ pound ripe plum tomatoes, seeded and finely chopped
2 tablespoons minced red onion
1 garlic clove, minced
1 canned chipotle chile, seeded and minced
1 tablespoon fresh lime juice
1 tablespoon minced fresh cilantro
Salt and freshly ground pepper

Combine all the ingredients in a medium bowl. Let stand at room temperature for at least 30 minutes or up to 2 hours.—GRACE PARISI

POT ROAST

Nothing says home like pot roast. This version of the family favorite is from photographer Richard Avedon, who says, "This pot roast has been lovingly eaten by four generations of Avedons."

12 SERVINGS

¼ cup vegetable oil
7 pounds beef brisket
Salt and freshly ground pepper
3 pounds onions, coarsely chopped
2 bay leaves
Two 16-ounce cans whole tomatoes, drained and crushed
Two 8-ounce cans tomato sauce

1. Preheat the oven to 325°. In a nonreactive roasting pan set over two burners, warm the oil over moderately high heat. Season the brisket with salt and pepper and sear it well, about 8 minutes; transfer to a plate.

2. Add the onions to the pan and cook until browned. Set the brisket on top, add ½ cup water and the bay leaves; season with salt and pepper. Cover the pan with foil and bake for 1½ hours. Turn the brisket and bake 1½ hours longer.

3. Remove the brisket and slice ¼ inch thick. Stir the tomatoes and tomato sauce into the onions. Return the meat to the pan, cover with foil and bake for 30 minutes. Season with salt and pepper.—RICHARD AVEDON

BEEF STEW

Preparing beef stew is so simple: All that's involved is marinating, browning and braising, which you can easily do in a single day. Or you may start and stop along the way, taking three or more days to complete the dish. In fact, it does a stew good to wait around in its aromatic brew while the flavors blend and intensify. All this makes a good beef stew a grand fuss-free dish for an informal party.

Here's one scenario: Let's say today is **Tuesday**, and you have decided to have six friends over for a beef stew after work on Friday. You'll need about 3 pounds of trimmed boneless stewing beef. If you are in a hurry, you can buy it cut into chunks and ready to cook. However, I always prefer to do the trimming and cutting myself, so I buy a 4-pound chuck steak (pot roast) a good

2½ to 3 inches thick. I remove all the surrounding fat with a boning knife, then cut the meat into pieces according to its natural muscle separations, trimming as I go. Finally, I cut the pieces into 1½-inch chunks.

When the meat is ready, toss it in an enameled or stainless casserole with 1 tablespoon salt blended with 1 teaspoon crushed black peppercorns and 2 fresh thyme sprigs or ½ teaspoon dried thyme. Add 3 cups thinly sliced onions (can't have too many onions!), 1½ cups thinly sliced carrots, several smashed and peeled large garlic cloves and ¼ cup olive oil or vegetable oil. Toss thoroughly, then toss again with 3 tablespoons red-wine vinegar. Cover and refrigerate overnight.

Now it is **Wednesday**. Dry the beef chunks in paper towels. In a medium frying pan, cook the marinade vegetables and any accumulated liquid over moderate heat until the onions are translucent. Meanwhile, set a large heavy frying pan over moderately high heat and add 1 tablespoon of oil. Add the beef in batches and cook until the chunks are well browned all over. Return the meat to the casserole and strew the cooked marinade vegetables on top, along with 4 chopped fresh Italian plum tomatoes and 2 imported bay leaves.

Discard the fat from the pan in which the meat was browned. Deglaze the pan by pouring in ¼ cup of water and simmering it for a moment. With a wooden spoon, scrape all the flavorful brown bits from the bottom of the pan into the liquid and pour over the beef. At this point, I pour in 1 cup of strong beef stock or broth and enough good young red wine (such as Chianti or Zinfandel) to almost submerge the ingredients. Then I cover and refrigerate the stew; the wine marinade will only improve the flavor. It is still Wednesday, and the main work is already done. The only thing that remains is several hours of unattended stewing.

BEEF-STEW TIPS

• Choose flavorful cuts, such as chuck and round, that benefit from long, slow, moist cooking and won't fall apart.

• Don't try to rush when you're browning meat for a stew. It's a very important step that will take at least ten to fifteen minutes to do right. Make sure you dry the meat thoroughly on paper towels before browning it, and don't crowd the pan. Damp meat won't brown, nor will pieces that are too close together in the pan.

• If you're tight on time, simply ladle the beef stew over noodles and accompany it with a fresh green salad. When you've got more time—or friendly help—you can finish the stew by adding two dozen small braised onions, several large spoonfuls of sautéed mushrooms and two cups or so of braised cut carrots and turnips, plus fresh peas and green beans, and simmering them all together briefly.—JULIA CHILD

Beef Stew

Thursday, at your leisure, you bring the stew to a simmer on top of the stove, then set it, covered, in a 300° oven so that it barely bubbles. You can stop the cooking at any point and continue the following day. It will take about 2½ hours for the meat to become fork-tender; take an occasional small bite to be sure. Let the stew cool, then cover it and refrigerate overnight.

Some time on **Friday**, you need to finish the stew. Using a spoon, skim all the solidified fat from the surface. Reheat the stew, then strain the hot cooking liquid into a large nonreactive saucepan, pressing on the cooking vegetables, which will have disintegrated considerably by this point. Taste the sauce very carefully for strength and seasoning, and boil down rapidly if it seems weak; you should have about 2½ delicious cups. If the sauce seems too liquid, thicken it with a slurry: for each cup of sauce, you'll need 1 tablespoon all-purpose flour blended in a bowl with 1½ tablespoons cold beef stock. Whisk dribbles of hot sauce into the slurry, then whisk the slurry mixture into the sauce. Simmer for several minutes, then pour the hot sauce over the warm stew and simmer it for several minutes before serving.

Once you've checked the seasoning one more time, the stew is done. You can keep it warm in its covered casserole on a hot plate for about half an hour. If dinnertime is still some hours away, let the stew cool, then press a piece of plastic wrap over its surface and put it in the refrigerator. To serve, remove the plastic wrap and rewarm the stew slowly.—JULIA CHILD

INFORMAL DINNER

🍷 A round, rich California Chardonnay, such as the 1994 Chateau de Baun or the 1993 Pine Ridge Knollside, would nicely complement the tastes in the salad. Although the beef could be paired with many full-bodied reds, the sauce suggests a deep 1990 Barolo, such as Elio Altare or Fontanafredda.

GRILLED-SCALLOP SALAD (P. 52)

BEEF IN BAROLO (P. 244)

SOFT POLENTA WITH THYME (P. 320)

ROASTED FENNEL WITH ROSEMARY (P. 339)

LEMON TARTLETS (P. 397)

TIMETABLE:

TWO DAYS AHEAD **Braise the brisket.**

ONE DAY AHEAD **Make the tartlet filling; bake the pastry. Roast the fennel.**

FOUR HOURS AHEAD **Bake the tartlets. Make the dressing and the tomato garnish for the scallop salad. Make the polenta. Carve the brisket and return it to the casserole.**

SHORTLY BEFORE SERVING **Rewarm the brisket. Rewarm the fennel and polenta. Cook the onions; grill the scallops. Assemble the salads.**

BEEF IN BAROLO

This classic Italian dish is traditionally made with round or rump roast. I started making it with brisket years ago in England because I didn't know how to ask for rump, and I've made it this way ever since. The sauce is rich and unctuous—the essence of Barolo. Like most braised dishes, this improves in flavor as it sits, so try to make it a day or two ahead.

6 SERVINGS

- 3 pounds trimmed beef brisket
- 3 slices bacon, cut crosswise into ¼-inch strips
- 3 garlic cloves, finely chopped
- 3 tablespoons finely chopped fresh parsley
- 2 tablespoons finely chopped fresh rosemary
- 1 teaspoon finely chopped fresh sage
- ⅓ cup plus 2 tablespoons all-purpose flour
- 1 teaspoon paprika
- Salt and freshly ground pepper
- 2 tablespoons unsalted butter

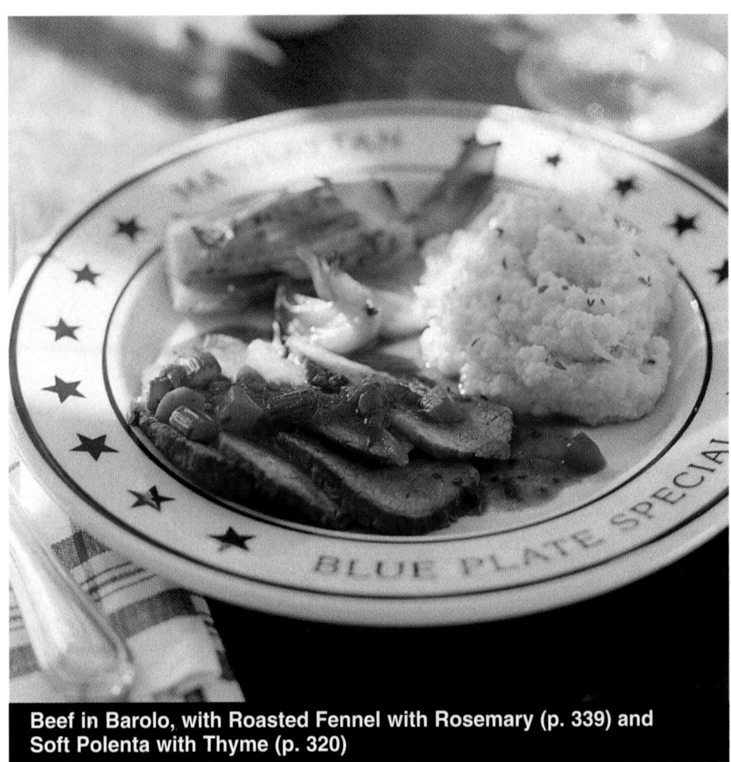

Beef in Barolo, with Roasted Fennel with Rosemary (p. 339) and Soft Polenta with Thyme (p. 320)

1 tablespoon olive oil
1 small onion, thinly sliced
2 bay leaves
2 medium carrots, cut into ¼-inch dice
2 celery ribs, cut into ¼-inch dice
1 bottle (750 ml) Barolo

1. Using a small sharp knife, make ½-inch-deep slits all over the brisket. Push a strip of bacon into each slit using the end of a teaspoon.

2. In a small bowl, combine the garlic, parsley, rosemary and sage; set aside. On a large plate, mix the ⅓ cup flour with the paprika, 1 teaspoon salt and ½ teaspoon pepper. Dredge the brisket in the flour; shake off the excess.

3. In a large enameled cast-iron casserole, melt the butter in the oil over moderate heat. Add the onion and cook, stirring, until softened, about 4 minutes. Raise the heat to moderately high and push the onion to one side. Add the brisket and cook undisturbed until well browned on the bottom, about 5 minutes. Turn the brisket over and scatter the herb mixture, bay leaves, carrots and celery around it; cook until well browned on the second side, about 5 minutes longer. Transfer the meat to a platter.

4. Preheat the oven to 300°. Return the casserole to the heat and add the remaining 2 tablespoons flour. Cook, stirring, for 1 minute. Add 1 cup of the wine and boil over high heat until reduced by half, stirring occasionally. Stir in the remaining wine and bring to a simmer. Return the brisket to the casserole and season with salt and pepper.

5. Tightly cover the casserole and braise the meat in the oven until very tender, about 4 hours. Turn the meat every 45 minutes and add a little water to the casserole if the sauce looks very thick or the brisket begins to stick. (**MAKE AHEAD:** Allow the brisket to cool, then cover and refrigerate the meat in its sauce for up to 2 days.)

6. Skim the fat from the surface of the sauce and rewarm the brisket. Transfer the meat to a cutting board. Slice it across the grain, then return it to the sauce. Continue to reheat gently until hot. Discard the bay leaves before serving.—BRIGIT LEGERE BINNS

BEEF AND WHITE-WINE DAUBE

In this fragrant stew, thin slices of beef are cooked with white wine, capers, anchovies, garlic, onions and tomatoes. The high acidity of these ingredients helps tenderize the beef as well as lighten the dish. The recipe, known as Broufado *and* Boeuf aux Câpres, *is an ancient one. It's a dish that takes especially well to reheating; it tastes even better the second or third day.*

🍷 *Serve the white wine used in the recipe. Otherwise, serve a young red, such as a Côtes du Rhône.*

4–6 SERVINGS

4 anchovy fillets, rinsed
¼ cup whole milk
2 tablespoons drained capers
One 28-ounce can Italian peeled tomatoes, drained
2 medium onions, halved lengthwise and thinly sliced
8 to 10 large garlic cloves, thickly sliced
6 French cornichons or small gherkin pickles, thinly sliced
Fine sea salt
1 bottle (750 ml) white wine, preferably a Rhône Valley Sablet
1 dried imported or fresh bay leaf
1 huge fresh thyme sprig
2 pounds boneless braising beef in 1 piece (such as beef shoulder, chuck, blade, neck, rump or brisket), cut against the grain into six 1½-inch-thick slices
Freshly ground pepper
Cheesy Semolina with Bay Leaf (p. 323), for serving

1. Soak the anchovy fillets in the milk for 10 minutes to soften and

ENTERTAINING, KITCHEN-STYLE

The dining room isn't the only place for a dinner party. For an informal meal and intimate conversation, the kitchen is often the preferred spot. Here are some tips for entertaining in everyone's favorite room.

- **Avoid recipes that require you to use a noisy blender, deep fryer or food processor at the last minute.**
- **Set the table before your guests arrive.**
- **Have early arrivals open the wine and slice the bread, but don't let them near the stove.**
- **Keep the china—and the mood—casual.**
- **Be inventive. When there's soup on the menu, serve it from a pitcher.**

to remove excess salt. Soak the capers in cold water for 10 minutes to remove excess salt.

2. In a large bowl, combine the tomatoes, onions, garlic and cornichons. Drain and rinse the anchovies and capers; add to the bowl. Add 1 teaspoon salt. Toss with a wooden spoon to blend, lightly breaking up the tomatoes.

3. In a large nonreactive saucepan, simmer the wine to cook off the alcohol, about 10 minutes. Meanwhile, spread about a third of the tomato mixture in a large, heavy, nonreactive flameproof casserole. Add the bay leaf and the thyme sprig and set two pieces of beef on top. Season lightly with sea salt and pepper. Repeat with the remaining tomato mixture and the beef to make two more layers. Pour in the simmered wine.

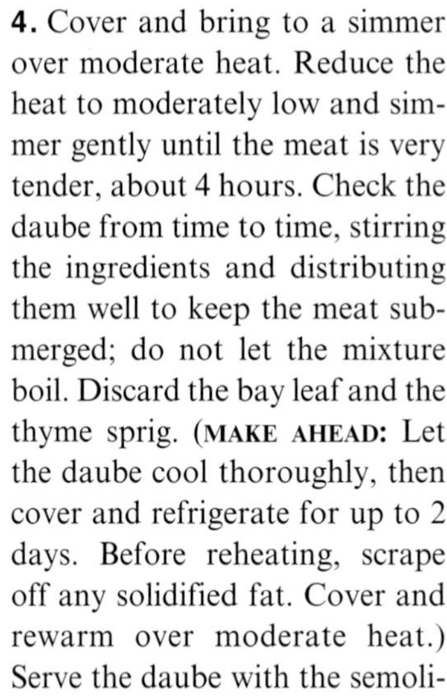

4. Cover and bring to a simmer over moderate heat. Reduce the heat to moderately low and simmer gently until the meat is very tender, about 4 hours. Check the daube from time to time, stirring the ingredients and distributing them well to keep the meat submerged; do not let the mixture boil. Discard the bay leaf and the thyme sprig. (**MAKE AHEAD:** Let the daube cool thoroughly, then cover and refrigerate for up to 2 days. Before reheating, scrape off any solidified fat. Cover and rewarm over moderate heat.) Serve the daube with the semolina.—PATRICIA WELLS

BEEF CARBONADE WITH RODENBACH

For this flavorful Belgian beef-and-beer stew, you can substitute another Belgian ale, such as Duvel.

6 SERVINGS

- 1 tablespoon unsalted butter
- ¼ cup vegetable oil
- 10 medium shallots, finely chopped
- 1 medium onion, minced
- 2 garlic cloves, minced
- 2 tablespoons all-purpose flour
- Salt and freshly ground pepper
- 2 pounds beef sirloin, cut into 1½-inch cubes
- Large pinch of ground coriander
- 2½ cups Rodenbach red ale
- 2 fresh thyme sprigs
- 2 tablespoons minced fresh parsley
- 2 bay leaves
- 1 tablespoon Dijon mustard
- Boiled red potatoes, for serving

1. In a large nonreactive saucepan, melt the butter in 1 tablespoon of the oil. Add the shallots, onion and garlic and cook over moderately low heat, stirring occasionally, until softened, about 7 minutes. Transfer the vegetables to a plate.

2. Heat 1½ tablespoons of the oil in the saucepan. In a shallow bowl, combine the flour with ½ teaspoon salt and ¼ teaspoon pepper. Add half of the meat cubes and toss to coat. Add the floured beef to the pan and sear over moderately high heat, turning, until well browned all over. Transfer to a plate. Flour the remaining beef and sear it in the remaining 1½ tablespoons oil.

3. Return all of the beef to the pan and stir in the ground coriander. Add the ale, thyme, parsley and bay leaves. Bring the stew to a boil, scraping up any browned bits. Reduce the heat to low, cover and cook, stirring,

Beef and White-Wine Daube

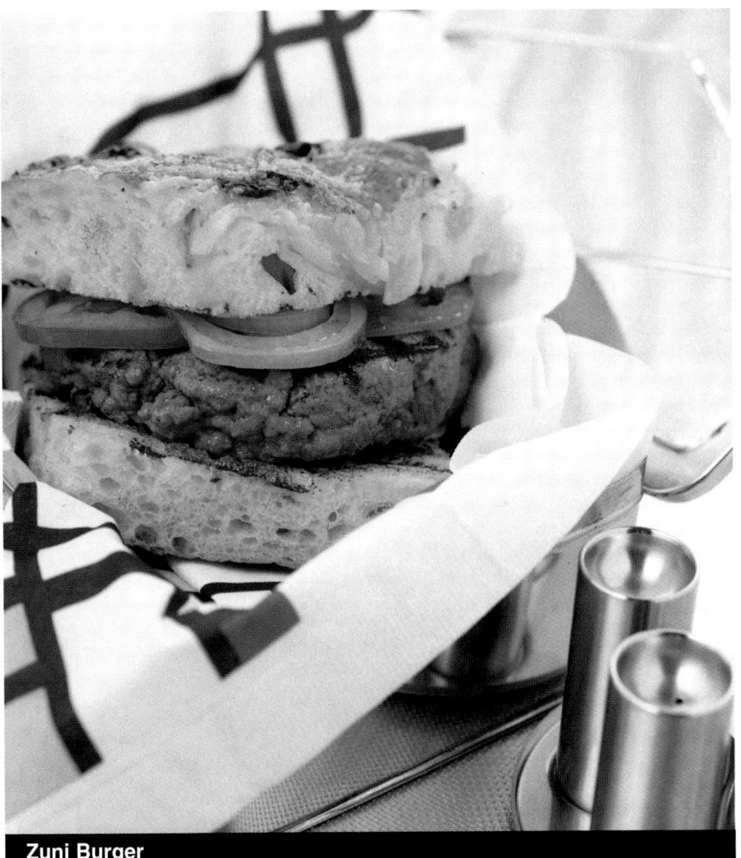
Zuni Burger

until the beef is tender, 1¼ to 1½ hours. Remove from the heat and discard the bay leaves and thyme sprigs. Stir in the mustard and season with salt and pepper. Serve with the potatoes.—CASSANDRA DOOLEY

ZUNI BURGERS

The taste of freshly ground chuck in these burgers is accentuated by the light salt cure given to the meat before it is ground.

🍷 *Burgers call for a red wine with plenty of fruitiness to wrap around the meaty taste. Look for a lusty young Australian Shiraz, such as the 1993 Rosemount or the 1992 Penfolds Kalimna Bin 28.*

4 SERVINGS

1¾ pounds boneless beef chuck, cut into 3-by-1-inch strips
Fine sea salt
Freshly ground pepper
4 squares of focaccia, split
Slices of tomato and red onion

1. In a bowl, toss the meat with ½ teaspoon salt. Cover with plastic and refrigerate overnight.
2. Coarsely grind the meat in a grinder and shape into 1¼-inch-thick patties; work quickly so that the meat remains chilled.
3. Light a grill or heat a grill pan or a cast-iron skillet. Season the burgers with salt and pepper and grill or pan-fry over moderately high heat, turning once, about 4 minutes per side for medium-rare or until done to your liking. Let rest for 2 minutes, then serve on the focaccia with the tomato and red onion.—JUDY RODGERS

Q & A

Q: How can I prevent flare-ups when I'm cooking food on my outdoor grill?

A: A clean grill is the key. Here are a few tips for getting it clean and keeping it that way.
- **Scrub the rack thoroughly on both sides with a wire brush. Then, using a cloth, wipe on a very small amount of canola or vegetable oil.**
- **Before grilling pieces of food, brush them with just enough oil to prevent the food from sticking to the rack but not enough to drip into the flames. (You can also smooth on the oil with clean hands.)**
- **Don't let your fire get so hot that any oil that does drip sets off a major conflagration. However, you do want the fire to heat up properly, so you should get rid of old ashes, which might smother new briquets.—DEAN FEARING**

BANANAS STUFFED WITH CURRIED BEEF

6 SERVINGS

2 tablespoons vegetable oil
1 pound ground beef chuck
1 medium onion, finely chopped
1 large garlic clove, minced

2 tablespoons curry powder
1 tablespoon tomato paste dissolved in 3 tablespoons water
1 teaspoon fresh lemon juice
Salt and freshly ground pepper
6 semiripe medium unpeeled bananas
1 small red bell pepper, minced

1. Preheat the oven to 400°. Heat the oil in a nonreactive skillet. Add the beef and brown over high heat, breaking it up with a wooden spoon, until cooked through. Add the onion, garlic and curry powder and cook, stirring, until fragrant, about 4 minutes. Stir in the tomato paste and lemon juice and season with salt and pepper.

2. Using a small knife, cut each banana lengthwise just through the top skin. Pull the skin apart slightly and stuff each banana with the curried beef. Arrange the bananas in a roasting pan, cover with foil and bake for about 25 minutes, or until the bananas are tender and heated through. Sprinkle with the red pepper and serve.—MARCIA KIESEL

PRESSURE-COOKER PINTO-BEAN AND BEEF CHILI

For a vegetarian chili, just leave out the meat. Don't omit the oil, though; it's needed to subdue the foam created as the beans cook under pressure.

6 SERVINGS

2 cups pinto beans, picked over, rinsed and soaked overnight in water to cover, or speed-soaked (see "Beans in a Flash," below)
3 tablespoons vegetable oil
1 pound trimmed boneless beef chuck or shoulder, cut into 1-inch cubes
2 cups coarsely chopped onion
1 red bell pepper, diced
1 green bell pepper, diced
1½ tablespoons minced garlic
2 jalapeño chiles, seeded and minced
2½ teaspoons whole cumin seeds
2 tablespoons mild chili powder
2 teaspoons dried oregano

Bananas Stuffed with Curried Beef

BEANS IN A FLASH

The speed of pressure cooking is a big advantage when it comes to beans. Dishes that are based on freshly cooked dried beans can easily become part of your regular diet when the cooking time is cut by seventy-five percent.

You can even speed-soak beans in the new-style pressure cookers. Place three parts water to one part beans in the cooker. Bring to high pressure. For small beans, turn off the heat and allow the pressure to come down naturally. For medium and large beans, cook for one minute or three minutes, respectively, then turn off the heat and allow the pressure to come down naturally. Drain and rinse.—LORNA J. SASS

⅛ teaspoon cinnamon
2 large bay leaves
2 cups boiling water
3 tablespoons tomato paste
Salt and freshly ground black pepper
¼ cup finely chopped fresh cilantro

1. Drain the pinto beans. Heat 1 tablespoon of the oil in a pressure cooker. Add half of the cubed meat and cook over moderately high heat until well browned all over; transfer to a plate. Repeat with the remaining meat and another tablespoon of the oil. Set the meat aside.
2. Add the remaining 1 tablespoon oil to the cooker, along with the onion, red and green bell peppers, garlic, jalapeños and cumin seeds. Cook over moderately high heat, stirring frequently, until the vegetables soften, about 2 minutes; scrape up any browned bits sticking to the bottom of the cooker. Stir in the chili powder, oregano, cinnamon and bay leaves, then add the drained pinto beans, the browned meat and the boiling water.
3. Lock the lid in place and bring to high pressure over high heat. Lower the heat just enough to maintain high pressure and cook for 15 minutes. Turn off the heat and allow the pressure to come down naturally; do not quick-release, or the meat will toughen. Remove the lid, tilting it away from you to allow any excess steam to escape.
4. Remove and discard the bay leaves. Stir the tomato paste into the chili and season with salt and black pepper. Simmer for a few minutes to blend the flavors. If the chili seems too soupy, set it aside for a few hours at room temperature, or puree about a cupful of the beans and stir them back in. Stir in the cilantro just before serving.—LORNA J. SASS

ROASTED LOIN OF LAMB

Ask your butcher for boneless saddles of lamb with the flanks attached for enclosing the walnut stuffing.

8 SERVINGS

4 ounces bacon, cut into ½-inch dice
1 large onion, chopped
1 garlic clove, minced
¾ cup finely chopped walnuts (about 5 ounces), toasted
½ of a 1-pound loaf of whole-wheat bread, crumbled into coarse crumbs (about 4 cups)
1 large egg, beaten
¼ cup milk
½ tablespoon finely chopped fresh rosemary, plus more for garnish
Salt and freshly ground pepper
2 lamb loin roasts (3 pounds each on the bone or 2½ pounds boneless), flank flaps attached and intact
1 cup rich beef stock or demiglace*
Reserved compote juices (see Step 3 of the compote recipe)
Tomato, Onion and Rosemary Compote (recipe follows)

*Available at specialty-food stores

1. In a medium skillet, cook the bacon over moderately high heat for 3 minutes. Add the onion and garlic and cook over moderate heat until softened, about 7 minutes. Transfer to a bowl and let cool. Add the walnuts, bread crumbs, egg, milk, rosemary, ¾ teaspoon salt and ½ teaspoon pepper.
2. Trim any excess fat from the lamb, being sure to leave the loins and flaps attached and intact. Place the meat on a work surface, fat-side down, and season with salt and pepper. Pack half of the stuffing along the length of each loin, in a loose sausage shape. Roll up the flaps, covering the stuffing, and tie each loin securely with kitchen string. ➤

HOW TO RELEASE STEAM

Pressure-cooker recipes often lapse into shorthand when telling you how to release the steam. Here are translations for two common instructions.

USE A QUICK-RELEASE METHOD: **One way to release steam quickly is to place the cooker in the sink under cold running water until the pressure drops completely. Or, if your cooker offers the option of stovetop pressure release, pulse the appropriate button or lever to release the pressure. When using this method, point the vent away from you and out into the kitchen (if the steam hits a wall, it will condense into droplets).**

ALLOW THE PRESSURE TO COME DOWN NATURALLY: **Turn off the heat and let the cooker sit until the pressure drops of its own accord. If you are using an electric stove, move the pressure cooker to a cool burner.**—LORNA J. SASS

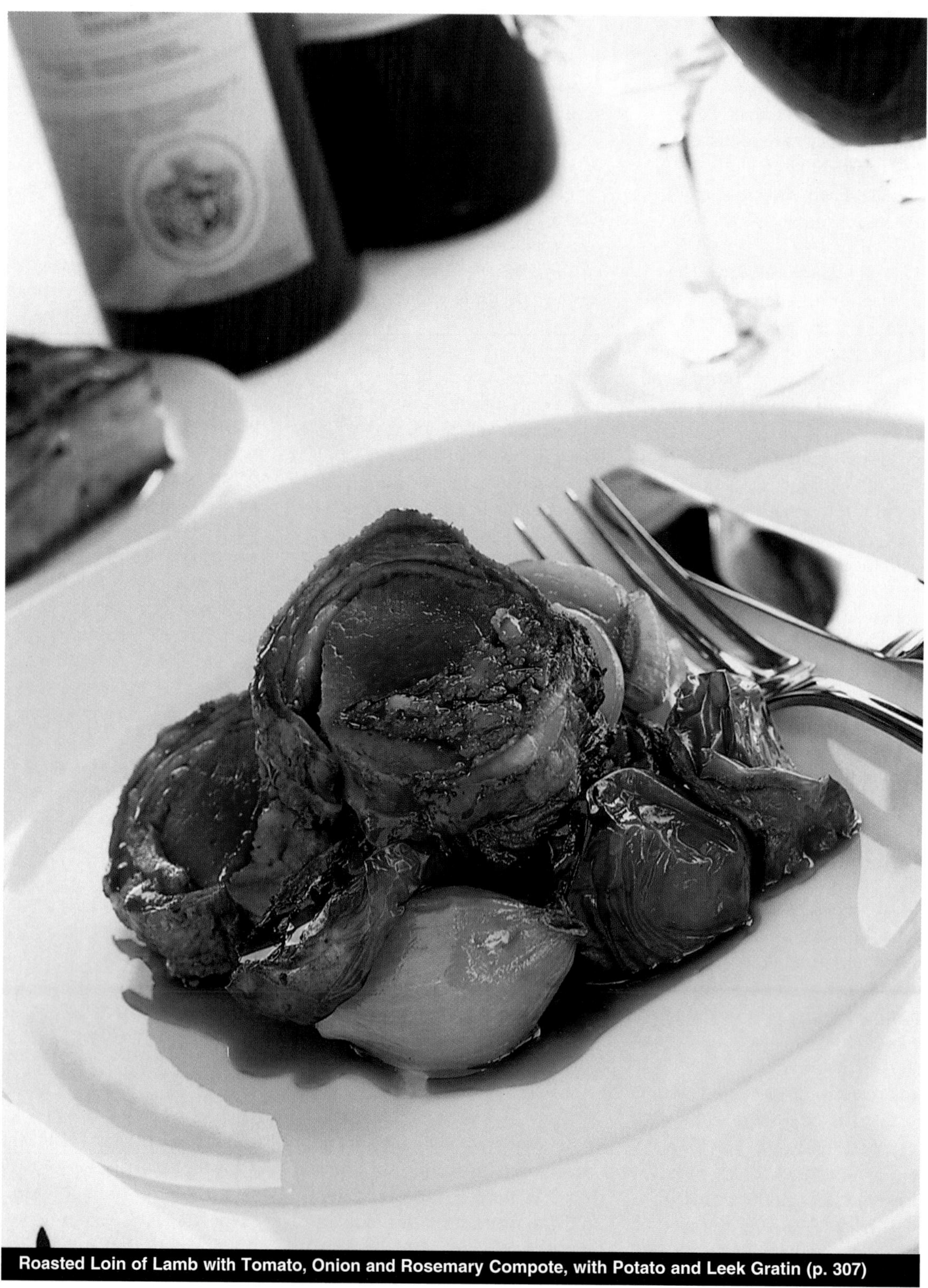

Roasted Loin of Lamb with Tomato, Onion and Rosemary Compote, with Potato and Leek Gratin (p. 307)

3. Preheat the oven to 500°. Heat a large heavy nonreactive skillet. Add the lamb loin roasts and cook over high heat, turning occasionally, until the roasts are browned and crusty on all sides. Pour off any fat as it accumulates in the pan.

4. Transfer the lamb to a roasting pan and roast for 20 to 25 minutes, or until an instant-read thermometer inserted in the center of the meat registers 130° (for medium rare). Transfer the lamb roasts to a cutting board, cover them loosely with foil and allow them to rest for 10 minutes before carving.

5. Meanwhile, add the beef stock and the reserved compote juices to the skillet and bring to a boil, scraping up any browned bits that cling to the skillet. Cook until the liquid is slightly thickened and reduced to ¾ cup, about 5 minutes.

6. Using a sharp knife, cut off the strings from the roasts. Cut each loin into eight slices and arrange two slices on each of eight warmed dinner plates. Spoon some of the sauce over the lamb, sprinkle with chopped rosemary and serve with the compote.

Tomato, Onion and Rosemary Compote

8 SERVINGS

- 3 pounds Spanish onions (about 4), peeled and quartered lengthwise with root ends intact
- 6 tablespoons extra-virgin olive oil
- Salt and freshly ground pepper
- 1 pound shallots, unpeeled
- 16 ripe plum tomatoes, halved lengthwise and cored
- 2 tablespoons balsamic vinegar
- Finely chopped rosemary, for garnish

1. Preheat the oven to 400°. Position one rack in the middle of the oven and one in the lower third. Put the onions on a rimmed baking sheet, drizzle with 2 tablespoons of the oil and season with salt and pepper. Put the shallots in a large roasting pan and drizzle with 2 tablespoons of the oil. Season with salt and pepper. Roast the onions and shallots for about 50 minutes, tossing occasionally, until soft and lightly browned. Let the shallots cool slightly, then peel them. Pour any juices from the onions and shallots into a bowl and reserve. Return the shallots to the roasting pan and add the onions.

2. Place the tomatoes, cut-side down, on a large rimmed baking sheet. Drizzle with the remaining 2 tablespoons oil and the balsamic vinegar and season with salt and pepper. Roast the tomatoes for 40 minutes, or until their skins are wrinkled and lightly browned. Let cool slightly, then remove the skins.

3. Pour any accumulated tomato juices into the bowl with the reserved onion and shallot juices and save them for making the sauce. Add the tomatoes to the roasting pan and toss the vegetables. Cover loosely with foil and keep warm. Garnish the compote with rosemary before serving. (**MAKE AHEAD:** The compote can be refrigerated for up to 2 days.) —ALI SEEDSMAN ➤

WINEMAKER'S DINNER

This meal was designed by chef Ali Seedsman and winemaker John Duval to showcase the food-friendly nature of Penfolds wines.

🍷 1995 Old Vine Barossa Valley Sémillon

BEET, BASIL AND WATERCRESS SALAD (P. 63)

WINEMAKER'S COMMENT: The rich, concentrated flavors of the wine work beautifully with the equally rich, concentrated flavors of the vinaigrette and the beets.

🍷 1995 South Australia Koonunga Hill Chardonnay

TROUT IN GINGERED DASHI WITH SUSHI RICE (P. 96)

WINEMAKER'S COMMENT: The subtlety of the dish complements the peachy Chardonnay. The wine isn't over-oaked, so there's no clash of flavors.

🍷 1993 South Australia Bin 389 Cabernet-Shiraz and the 1993 South Australia Bin 707 Cabernet Sauvignon

ROASTED LOIN OF LAMB (P. 249)

POTATO AND LEEK GRATIN (P. 307)

WINEMAKER'S COMMENT: It's the Cabernet component of the 389 that makes it work so well here; as the wine ages, the shiraz component will come forward. The 707 is a big, rich wine for a big, rich dish.

🍷 Grandfather's Port

ICE-CREAM SANDWICHES (P. 441)

WINEMAKER'S COMMENT: Chocolate and liqueur-style fortified wines are made for each other.

VIENNA SHORTCAKES (P. 386)

RACK OF LAMB WITH CHIMICHURRI SAUCE

Your butcher can french the racks—scrape the rib bones clean of meat, fat and gristle—for you. The pungent South American sauce is excellent with any grilled or roasted meat or with shrimp.

4 SERVINGS

- 2½ tablespoons unsalted butter
- ¼ cup finely chopped onion
- 1 teaspoon minced fresh thyme
- 1 cup Thai black rice or wild rice (about 6 ounces)
- 2½ cups chicken stock or canned low-sodium broth
- Table salt and freshly ground pepper
- 2 cups coarse salt
- 12 unpeeled shallots
- 2 frenched racks of lamb with 8 bones each
- Chimichurri Sauce (recipe follows)
- 2 tablespoons olive oil

1. Melt 1 tablespoon of the butter in a saucepan. Add the onion and thyme and cook over moderate heat, stirring, until the onion is translucent. Stir in the rice and cook for 2 minutes. Add the chicken stock and bring to a simmer. Reduce the heat to low, cover and cook, stirring, until tender, about 30 minutes for black rice and 45 minutes for wild rice. Season with salt and pepper.

2. Preheat the oven to 350°. Spread the coarse salt in a roasting pan and set the shallots on top. Bake for about 45 minutes, or until tender. Let cool, then peel the shallots and trim the root ends. Raise the oven temperature to 450°.

3. Cut the lamb racks in half to form 4-chop racks. Season with salt and pepper and coat each rack with ½ tablespoon of the Chimichurri Sauce. Melt 1 tablespoon of the butter in the oil in an ovenproof skillet. Add the lamb racks, fat-side down, and sear over high heat, turning once, until well browned all over, about 2½ minutes per side. (**MAKE AHEAD:** The lamb, shallots and rice can stand at room temperature for 1 hour.)

4. Transfer the skillet to the oven with the racks fat-side up and roast for about 10 minutes for medium-rare meat. Let rest for 5 minutes. Meanwhile, in a small skillet, melt the remaining ½ tablespoon butter. Add the roasted shallots and toss over moderately high heat until warmed through. Season with salt and pepper. Rewarm the rice.

5. Mound the rice on four large plates. Carve the racks and arrange the chops on the rice, garnishing each plate with the shallots and a drizzle of Chimichurri Sauce. Pass the remaining sauce separately.

Chimichurri Sauce

MAKES ABOUT 1 CUP

- 1½ cups fresh parsley
- 6 garlic cloves, quartered
- 1 tablespoon oregano
- ¾ cup olive oil
- 3 tablespoons white-wine vinegar
- 1 tablespoon coarse salt
- 1 teaspoon freshly ground pepper

In a food processor, finely chop the parsley, garlic and oregano. Transfer the mixture to a small bowl and stir in the olive oil, vinegar, salt and pepper. (**MAKE AHEAD:** The chimichurri can be refrigerated for 1 week.) —GEORGE MAHAFFEY

CHEF'S MENU

The pistachio dressing and grilled vegetables are best paired with a crisply acidic white with herbaceous flavors. Try a Sauvignon Blanc, such as the 1994 Matanzas Creek or the 1993 Grgich Hills Fumé Blanc. The tangy, garlicky Chimichurri Sauce on the lamb suggests the intense flavors of a Syrah-based wine, such as the 1992 Domaine Jamet Côte Rôtie or the 1993 Domaine Belle Crozes-Hermitage Cuvée Louis Belle.

GRILLED-VEGETABLE SALAD WITH PISTACHIO VINAIGRETTE (P. 63)

RACK OF LAMB WITH CHIMICHURRI SAUCE (P. 252)

PLUM AND ALMOND POTSTICKERS (P. 420)

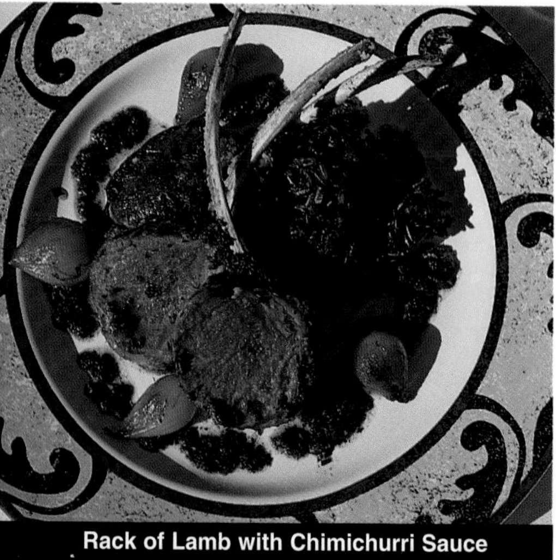

Rack of Lamb with Chimichurri Sauce

PAN-ROASTED LAMB CHOPS WITH MASHED-POTATO CAKE

🍷 *The assertive combination of the lamb and the olive-and-tomato relish needs a robust red wine that can stand up to and complement those strong flavors. The 1993 Alejandro Fernandez Tinto Pesquera from Spain is ideal. It is full-bodied, supple, yet complex and spicy, with a slight black-olive note in the background. A solid alternative to this wine that comes from closer to home is the 1993 Dalla Valle Cabernet Sauvignon from the Napa Valley.*

4 SERVINGS

- 2 tablespoons extra-virgin olive oil
- 2 teaspoons finely chopped fresh thyme
- Salt and freshly ground pepper
- 2 pounds plum tomatoes, peeled, quartered lengthwise and seeded
- ½ cup small green olives, such as Picholine (about 3 ounces), pitted and coarsely chopped
- ½ cup brine-cured black olives, such as Gaeta (about 2½ ounces), pitted and coarsely chopped
- 1 garlic clove, minced
- 1 teaspoon finely grated lemon zest
- ¼ cup coarsely chopped fresh basil
- 2 tablespoons vegetable oil
- Eight 6-ounce bone-in lamb loin chops
- Mashed-Potato Cake (recipe follows)

1. Preheat the oven to 200°. Spread the olive oil on a rimmed baking sheet and sprinkle with the thyme and a large pinch each of salt and pepper. Arrange the tomatoes in a single layer on top and bake for about 2 hours, or until slightly dried and firm. Transfer the tomatoes to a bowl and stir in the olives, garlic, lemon zest and basil.

2. Raise the oven temperature to 450°. Divide the vegetable oil between two large heavy-bottomed ovenproof skillets and heat until almost smoking. Season the lamb chops with salt and pepper and cook over moderately high heat until well browned on the bottom, about 3 minutes. Turn the chops and cook for 1 minute. Transfer the skillets to the oven and roast the chops for about 6 minutes for medium rare. Arrange the chops on plates and serve with the tomato relish and a wedge of potato cake.

Mashed-Potato Cake

4 SERVINGS

- 2 pounds waxy potatoes, such as Yukon Gold, peeled and quartered
- Coarse salt
- ½ cup olive oil
- Freshly ground pepper

1. In a medium saucepan, cover the potatoes with cold water and bring to a boil over moderately high heat. Add 1 teaspoon of salt

FREEZING TIPS FROM THE EXPERTS

The pros agree that when freezing meat, poultry and fish, it's best to wrap it in plastic, then in foil, and seal it in a sturdy plastic bag, pressing out as much air as you can.

MEAT **Freeze fresh meat only; don't try to save meat that's days old by freezing it. Wrap in serving portions and freeze in a single layer; stack when frozen solid. Thaw the meat in the refrigerator; submerge the airtight bag in a bowl of cold water if you're in a hurry.**—JACK UBALDI, *JACK UBALDI'S MEAT BOOK*

CHICKEN **Freeze skinless, boneless breasts uncovered in a single layer, then wrap them individually and stack in plastic bags. Thaw as directed above.**—JIM FOBEL, *THE WHOLE CHICKEN COOKBOOK*

SOUPS **Don't freeze soups made with milk, cream or coconut milk, which can separate or curdle.**—JAMES PETERSON, *SPLENDID SOUPS*

SEAFOOD **Fish with a relatively high fat content, like salmon and trout, freeze best. Thaw, without unwrapping, at room temperature in a bowl of cold water or in the refrigerator.**—JAMES PETERSON, *FISH & SHELLFISH*

CAKES **Freeze frosted cakes uncovered until solid, then wrap tightly in plastic and foil. Wrap unfrosted cakes or cheesecakes with plastic and freeze. Thaw all cakes wrapped to minimize condensation.**—MAIDA HEATTER, *MAIDA HEATTER'S BOOK OF GREAT DESSERTS*

BREAD **Loaves freeze better than slices and small breads freeze best. Freeze the bread uncovered until solid, then store in plastic bags; thaw in the bag.**—BERNARD CLAYTON, JR., *BERNARD CLAYTON'S NEW COMPLETE BOOK OF BREADS*

and boil until the potatoes are tender, about 20 minutes; drain. Return the potatoes to the pan and shake over high heat to dry them out. Using a potato masher, mash the potatoes well. Add ¼ cup of the olive oil and season the potatoes with salt and pepper. (**MAKE AHEAD:** The mashed potatoes can be refrigerated for up to 2 days.)

2. Preheat the oven to 400°. In a 9-inch heavy-bottomed ovenproof skillet, heat 2 tablespoons of the oil. Add the mashed potatoes and smooth the top. Cook over high heat until a crust starts to form, about 3 minutes. Transfer the skillet to the oven and bake for about 20 minutes, or until the potato cake is browned and crusty on the bottom.

3. Set the skillet over high heat and shake the pan to loosen the potato cake from the sides. Invert the potato cake onto a large cookie sheet. Heat the remaining 2 tablespoons oil in the skillet. Slide the potato cake into the skillet, crusty-side up, and cook over high heat for 2 minutes. Return the skillet to the oven and cook for about 10 minutes, or until the bottom is browned and crusty. Cut the cake into quarters; serve hot.—TRACI DES JARDINS

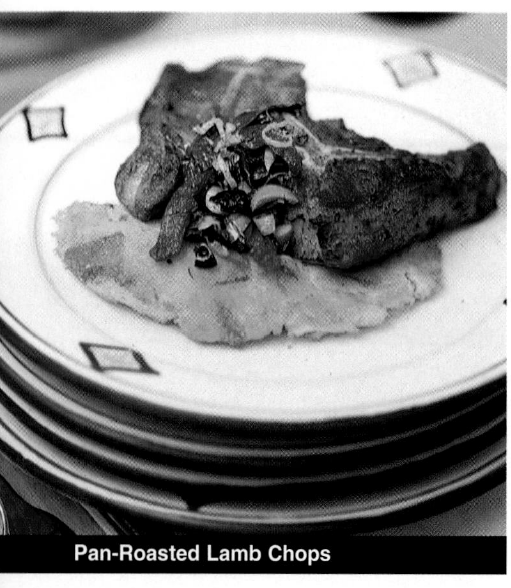

Pan-Roasted Lamb Chops

SPICED LAMB CHOPS WITH COUSCOUS Q

8 SERVINGS

- 1 tablespoon plus 1 teaspoon ground coriander
- 1 tablespoon plus 1 teaspoon cinnamon
- 1 tablespoon plus 1 teaspoon ground cumin
- 1 teaspoon ground cloves
- Salt and freshly ground pepper
- 16 loin lamb chops (about 5 ounces each), about ¾ inch thick
- 3 tablespoons olive oil
- 1 tablespoon unsalted butter
- 1½ cups instant couscous

1. In a small bowl, combine the coriander, cinnamon, cumin, cloves, 2 teaspoons salt and 1 tablespoon plus 1 teaspoon pepper. Coat the lamb on both sides with the spice mixture.

2. Heat 1½ tablespoons of the oil in each of two large skillets. Add half of the chops to each skillet; if necessary, cook them in batches. Sear the chops over high heat, turning once, until browned, about 4 minutes. Transfer the chops to a large rimmed baking sheet; reserve the pan juices. (**MAKE AHEAD:** The lamb chops can stand at room temperature for up to 1 hour.)

3. Preheat the oven to 400°. In a medium saucepan, bring 3 cups of water to a boil with the butter and ½ teaspoon salt. Stir in the couscous and remove the pan from the heat. Cover and let the couscous stand until tender, at least 5 minutes.

4. Bake the lamb chops for about 10 minutes, or until they are firm to the touch. Fluff the couscous with a fork. Divide the couscous among eight plates, set the lamb chops on top of the couscous and spoon any pan juices over.—PEGGY RYAN

COCONUT LAMB CURRY WITH POTATOES AND CAULIFLOWER

The juicy meat from lamb rib chops suits this quick curry. If you don't want to bone the meat yourself, ask your butcher to do it. Alternatively, you can use ten ounces of trimmed, boneless lamb loin. Serve the curry with nan, *an Indian flat bread that is similar to pita; it is available at some supermarkets.*

🍷 *This spicy-sweet hearty dish would overwhelm reds usually served with lamb. Go for a soft and fruity red that stays in the background: an Australian Shiraz, such as the 1993 Mitchelton or the 1993 Wyndham Estate Bin 555.*

4 SERVINGS

- 4 medium new red potatoes, cut into ½-inch dice
- ¼ medium head of cauliflower, cut into 1-inch florets (2 cups)
- 1½ pounds lamb rib chops
- Salt and freshly ground pepper
- 1 tablespoon plus 2 teaspoons extra-virgin olive oil
- 2 small onions, halved and thinly sliced
- 2 medium jalapeño chiles, seeded and minced
- 2 medium garlic cloves, minced

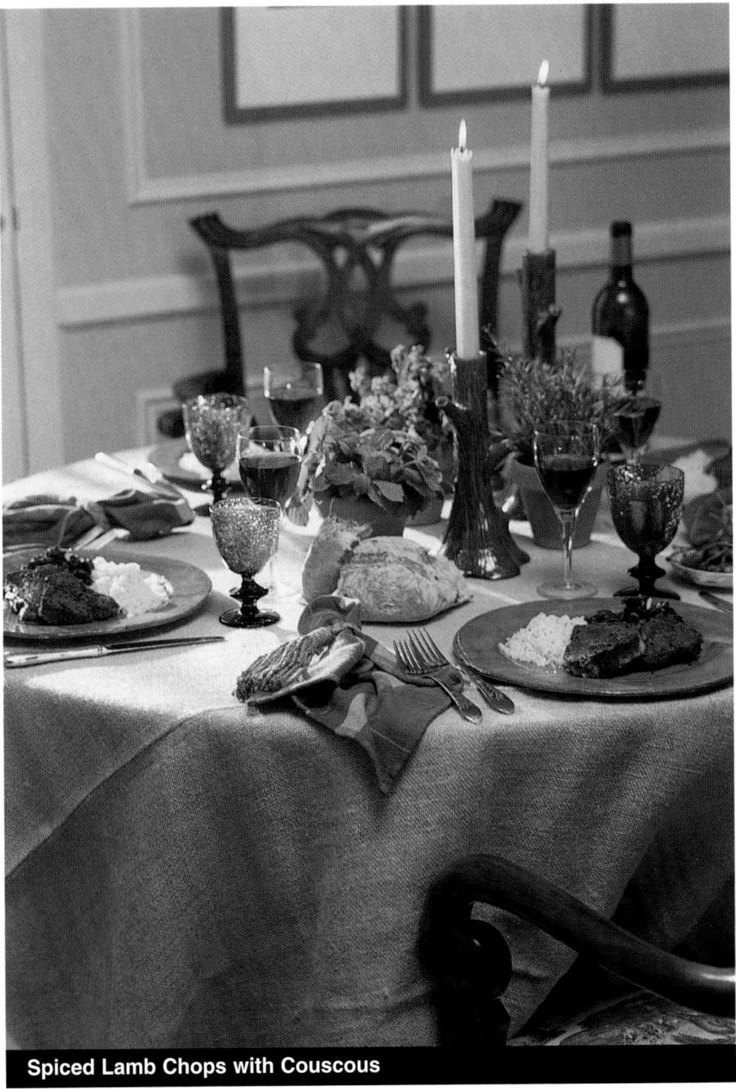

Spiced Lamb Chops with Couscous

- 3 tablespoons Madras curry powder
- ¾ cup chicken stock or canned low-sodium broth
- 1 cup unsweetened coconut milk
- ¼ cup heavy cream
- ¼ cup dried currants
- 1 tablespoon honey
- 2 tablespoons finely chopped fresh cilantro

1. Bring a medium pot of salted water to a boil. Add the potatoes and the cauliflower; cook the vegetables until they are just tender, about 7 minutes. Drain.

2. Using a boning knife, trim off excess fat from the lamb chops and scrape the lamb off of the bones. Cut the meat into 3-by-1-by-¼-inch strips. Season the lamb strips with salt and pepper. Heat 1 teaspoon of the olive oil in a large, straight-sided, nonreactive skillet. Add half of the lamb in a single layer and cook

SIMPLY ELEGANT DINNER

🍷 The Parmesan makes the salad wine friendly, and the spicy lamb chops practically demand a rich red as an accompaniment. But given the pine nuts and sweet raisins in the spinach, your best bet would be a fruity red with emphatic flavors, such as the 1994 Georges Duboeuf Côtes du Rhône Domaine des Moulins from France or the 1992 Swanson Syrah from California.

RADICCHIO SALAD WITH PARMESAN PEPPER CROSTINI (P. 61)

SPICED LAMB CHOPS WITH COUSCOUS (P. 254)

SPINACH WITH PINE NUTS (P. 337)

ORANGE GRATIN WITH SABAYON (P. 432)

GAME PLAN:

- **Start the main course—soak the raisins, clean the spinach.**
- **Prep the first course—tear the radicchio and cut the endives, slice the bread, make the Parmesan butter and spread it on the bread.**
- **Start the dessert—section the oranges, make the sabayon.**
- **Cook the main course—coat the chops with spices and sear them, make the couscous, cook the spinach.**
- **Ten minutes before serving the first course, bake the crostini. Make the dressing and toss the salad.**
- **Ten minutes before serving the main course, bake the lamb.**
- **Just before serving the dessert, brown the gratin under the broiler.**

over moderately high heat, turning once, until browned and crusty, about 2 minutes. Transfer to a platter. Repeat with the remaining lamb and another teaspoon oil.

3. Heat 2 teaspoons of the oil in the skillet. Add the onions, jalapeños and garlic and sauté over moderately high heat until just softened, about 3 minutes. Add the potatoes and cauliflower and sauté until lightly browned, about 2 minutes. Add the vegetables to the lamb.

4. Heat the remaining 1 teaspoon oil in the skillet. Add the curry powder and cook over moderately high heat, stirring, until fragrant, about 30 seconds. Pour in the chicken stock, scraping the bottom of the pan to loosen any browned bits, and cook until reduced by two-thirds, about 3 minutes. Stir in the coconut milk, heavy cream, currants and honey and simmer until slightly reduced and thickened, about 3 minutes.

5. Return the lamb, potatoes, cauliflower and any accumulated juices to the sauce and simmer until heated through. Season the curry with salt and pepper. (**MAKE AHEAD:** The curry can be made up to 1 day ahead. Rewarm over low heat.) Stir in the cilantro and serve.—GRACE PARISI

Coconut Lamb Curry with Potatoes and Cauliflower

STUFFED LEG OF SPRING LAMB

For carving tableside, leg of lamb looks best if the shank bone is left in. Use country-style white bread or an Italian loaf with a light crumb for the stuffing, or it will be too heavy.

8–12 SERVINGS

- 3¾ cups cubed day-old bread
- 3 tablespoons olive oil
- 1 large shallot
- 2 ounces pancetta, finely diced
- 2 ounces mortadella, finely diced
- 8 fresh sage leaves, finely chopped
- 1 cup lamb broth (see Note)
- ¾ cup freshly grated Parmigiano-Reggiano cheese
- Freshly ground pepper
- One 4½- to 5-pound leg of spring lamb, butterflied, with the shank bone left in
- Coarse salt

1. Preheat the oven to 400°. Toss the bread with 1½ tablespoons of the oil. Spread the bread on a baking sheet and toast in the oven for 12 to 15 minutes, until dry and brown.

2. In a small skillet, warm the remaining 1½ tablespoons oil. Add the shallot, pancetta, mortadella and sage and stir over moderate heat until the shallot is soft, about 5 minutes.

3. In a bowl, combine the toasted bread with the lamb broth and let stand for 5 minutes. Add the pancetta mixture along with the cheese and mix well. Season the stuffing liberally with pepper.

4. Open the leg of lamb and season the meat with salt and pepper. Spread the stuffing over the meat and then re-form the leg, patting it into an even cylindrical shape. Tie the roast at 1-inch intervals and place in a small roasting pan. Season with salt and pepper.

5. Roast the leg of lamb on the top shelf of the oven for 1 hour and 10 minutes, basting with the pan juices every 20 minutes. The meat is medium-rare when the internal temperature reaches 125°. Let the roast rest for about 10 minutes, then carve and serve with the pan juices. (If the pan is dry, deglaze it by stirring in approximately 1 cup of water and boiling until the juices are well reduced and flavorful.)

NOTE: You can make lamb broth with the bones and trimmings from the leg. Or you can use dry white wine or an easy mushroom broth made by soaking a small handful of dried porcini mushrooms in 1¼ cups of hot water for about 30 minutes.—PAUL BERTOLLI

MOROCCAN SPICE-RUBBED LEG OF LAMB

This spice-crusted roast can be served with any or all of the intensely flavored Middle Eastern-style dipping sauces that follow. The next day, serve leftover lamb, slathered with any one of the sauces, in pita sandwiches.

8–10 SERVINGS

- Zest from 2 lemons, finely julienned
- ½ cup fresh lemon juice
- ¼ cup honey
- 2 teaspoons coriander seeds, coarsely cracked
- 1 teaspoon ground cardamom
- 1 teaspoon ground cumin
- 1 teaspoon cinnamon
- 1 teaspoon sweet paprika
- 1 teaspoon turmeric
- ¼ teaspoon cayenne pepper
- One 7½-pound boneless leg of lamb, rolled and tied
- 1 whole unpeeled head of garlic, halved horizontally
- Coarse salt and freshly ground black pepper
- 2 tablespoons olive oil

1. Preheat the oven to 375°. In a small saucepan of boiling water, blanch the lemon zest until softened and pale, about 10 minutes. Drain and transfer to a small bowl. Stir in the lemon juice and the honey.

2. In a small skillet, combine the coriander, cardamom, cumin, cinnamon, paprika, turmeric and cayenne. Toast the spices over high heat, stirring frequently, until fragrant, about 1 minute.

3. Light a charcoal grill or heat a grill pan. Rub the lamb all over with the cut sides of the garlic. Coat well with the toasted spices. Season with salt and pepper and brush with the oil. Grill the lamb over moderate heat until well browned all over, about 5 minutes per side.

4. Transfer the leg of lamb to a roasting pan and roast in the oven for 1¼ hours. Brush the lamb liberally with the honey-lemon sauce and roast for about 15 minutes longer, or until an instant-read thermometer inserted in the thickest part of the leg registers 140° (for medium-rare).

5. Transfer the lamb to a cutting board, cover loosely with foil and let rest for 15 minutes before carving. Pour the pan juices into a sauceboat and serve alongside.

Yogurt Cucumber Sauce

MAKES ABOUT 3 CUPS

- 1 large seedless cucumber, peeled and finely diced
- 2 cups plain low-fat yogurt
- 2 tablespoons honey
- 2 teaspoons finely shredded fresh mint
- 2 garlic cloves, minced
- 1 teaspoon olive oil
- Pinch of cayenne pepper
- Coarse salt

In a medium bowl, combine the cucumber, yogurt, honey, mint, garlic, oil and cayenne. Refrigerate for at least 1 hour or overnight. Season with salt just before serving.

Fresh-Mint Chutney

MAKES ABOUT ¾ CUP

- 1 quart fresh orange juice
- Pinch of cayenne pepper
- ⅓ cup sliced almonds (about 1 ounce)
- ½ cup finely chopped fresh mint
- 2 tablespoons pure maple syrup

SPRING MENU

🍷 1994 Monte Volpe Pinot Bianco

POACHED-SALMON SALAD (P. 51)

🍷 1994 Bruno Giacosa Roero Arneis

SPRING VEGETABLE SOUP (P. 85)

🍷 1985 Badia a Coltibuono Chianti Classico

STUFFED LEG OF SPRING LAMB (P. 256)

ARTICHOKES WITH GARLIC AND THYME (P. 336)

ROASTED POTATOES WITH OLIVES (P. 309)

🍷 1991 Topaz Special Select Late Harvest Sauvignon Blanc-Sémillon

FRESH CHERRY CROSTATA (P. 399)

Moroccan Spice-Rubbed Leg of Lamb

SUMMER MENU

🍷 A dry California rosé is the ultimate warm-weather wine. My choice is the 1993 McDowell Grenache Rosé. This wine has a beautiful deep-pink color and lots of fresh fruit flavors, but it is dry, not sweet. The wine is tasty and lots of fun.—LAURENCE KRETCHMER

MOROCCAN SPICE-RUBBED LEG OF LAMB (P. 257)

FOUR DIPPING SAUCES:
YOGURT CUCUMBER SAUCE (P. 257)
FRESH-MINT CHUTNEY (P. 257)
TOMATO JAM (P. 258)
HAZELNUT SAUCE (P. 258)

TUNISIAN COUSCOUS SALAD (P. 71)

BULGUR WITH FAVA BEANS (P. 324)

GRILLED CARDAMOM NAN BREAD (P. 295)

HONEY ORANGE ICE (P. 439)
WALNUT COOKIE STICKS (P. 390)

—MATTHEW KENNEY

1 teaspoon fresh lemon juice
Salt and freshly ground black pepper

1. Preheat the oven to 350°. In a medium nonreactive saucepan, bring the orange juice to a boil over high heat. Boil until reduced to ⅓ cup, about 30 minutes. Transfer the orange syrup to a medium bowl, add the cayenne and let cool.
2. Meanwhile, toast the almonds on a small baking sheet in the oven for about 5 minutes, or until golden. Let cool. Transfer the almonds to a mini-processor and pulse until finely ground, or mince with a knife. Add the almonds to the orange syrup along with the mint, maple syrup and lemon juice. Season with salt and pepper. (**MAKE AHEAD:** The chutney can be refrigerated overnight. Let return to room temperature before serving.)

Tomato Jam

MAKES ABOUT 1⅔ CUPS

1 tablespoon unsalted butter
2 tablespoons minced fresh ginger
2 garlic cloves, minced
¼ cup cider vinegar
1 cinnamon stick
2½ pounds fresh plum tomatoes, peeled, seeded and coarsely chopped, or 2 cups drained canned Italian tomatoes, seeded and coarsely chopped
¼ cup (packed) light brown sugar
1 teaspoon ground cumin
⅛ teaspoon ground cloves
¼ teaspoon cayenne pepper
¼ cup honey
Salt and freshly ground black pepper

Melt the butter in a heavy medium saucepan. Add the ginger and the garlic and cook over moderately high heat, stirring frequently, until fragrant, about 1 minute. Add the vinegar and the cinnamon stick and cook until the liquid is reduced to a glaze, about 1 minute. Stir in the tomatoes, brown sugar, cumin, cloves and cayenne. Reduce the heat to low and cook, stirring occasionally, until the liquid is completely evaporated, about 1½ hours. Stir in the honey and season with salt and pepper. (**MAKE AHEAD:** The Tomato Jam can be refrigerated for up to 4 days.) Discard the cinnamon stick and serve the jam at room temperature.

Hazelnut Sauce

MAKES ABOUT 1¾ CUPS

1½ cups hazelnuts (about 7 ounces)
2 garlic cloves, crushed
1 teaspoon ground ginger
1 teaspoon minced lemon zest
1 teaspoon coriander seeds
2 tablespoons pomegranate molasses* diluted with 2 tablespoons warm water (see Note)
2 tablespoons olive oil
Pinch of cayenne pepper
Pinch of saffron threads
Salt

*Available at Middle Eastern markets

1. Preheat the oven to 350°. Toast the hazelnuts in a pan for about 10 minutes, or until the nuts are fragrant and the skins blister. Transfer to a kitchen towel and rub the nuts together to remove the skins. Let the nuts cool.

2. In a blender, combine the hazelnuts, garlic, ginger, lemon zest and coriander seeds and coarsely chop. In a bowl, combine the diluted pomegranate molasses with the oil, cayenne, saffron and ¾ cup of warm water. With the machine on, gradually add the liquid to the blender and blend until smooth. Refrigerate for at least 30 minutes. (**MAKE AHEAD:** The sauce can be refrigerated for up to 2 days.) Season with salt and serve slightly chilled.

NOTE: Pomegranate molasses adds a tart, exotic flavor to this sauce, but you can substitute 3 tablespoons of unsweetened cranberry juice for the diluted molasses if you like.—MATTHEW KENNEY

BRAISED LAMB SHANKS WITH PEARL ONIONS

Start the shanks the day before you serve them so that there will be time to chill and degrease the cooking liquid.

🍷 *A low-tannin but flavorful California Cabernet Sauvignon, such as the 1992 Cain Cuvée or the 1993 Chateau Montelena Calistoga Cuvée, would frame and contrast the flavors here.*

6 SERVINGS

- 3 tablespoons olive oil
- 6 meaty lamb shanks, trimmed
- Salt and freshly ground pepper
- 2 cups dry white wine
- 15 unpeeled garlic cloves
- 2 cups chicken stock or canned low-sodium broth
- 1 tablespoon finely chopped fresh rosemary, plus 6 tiny fresh rosemary sprigs for garnish
- ½ pound pearl onions

1. Preheat the oven to 325°. Heat the oil in a large enameled cast-iron casserole. Sprinkle the lamb shanks generously with salt and pepper and add three of them to the casserole. Cook over moderately high heat until the lamb shanks are well browned on all sides, about 10 minutes. Transfer to a plate. Repeat with the remaining lamb shanks.

2. Drain the fat from the casserole and return the lamb shanks to it. Add the wine and boil for 5 minutes, then add the garlic, chicken stock and chopped rosemary and bring to a boil. Cover tightly and braise in the oven for 1½ hours, turning the lamb shanks occasionally. Transfer the lamb shanks to a plate and pour the cooking juices and garlic into a heatproof bowl. (**MAKE AHEAD:** Cover the lamb shanks and refrigerate overnight. Skim all the fat from the liquid before proceeding.)

3. In a small saucepan of boiling water, blanch the pearl onions for 1½ minutes. Drain the onions and let them cool slightly, then slip off their skins.

4. Preheat the oven to 325°. Rewarm the cooking juices and the garlic in a small saucepan. Return the lamb shanks to the casserole and strain the cooking juices over them; press on the garlic cloves to squeeze the pulp from the skins through the sieve. Bring to a simmer over moderate heat. Add the onions, cover and braise in the oven for about 1 hour, turning the shanks occasionally, until the meat is meltingly tender.

5. Transfer the lamb shanks and the onions to warmed plates or a

INFORMAL DINNER

FRESH-SAGE AND GOAT-CHEESE RAVIOLI (P. 122)

BRAISED LAMB SHANKS WITH PEARL ONIONS (P. 259)

GARLICKY SPINACH (P. 337)

VICHY CARROTS (P. 338)

ANCHOVY MASHED POTATOES (P. 309)

PEARS POACHED IN WHITE WINE WITH STAR ANISE (P. 429)

Braised Lamb Shanks with Pearl Onions, with Garlicky Spinach (p. 337), Vichy Carrots (p. 338) and Anchovy Mashed Potatoes (p. 309)

platter. Reduce the cooking liquid, if necessary, to concentrate the flavor and spoon over the shanks and onions. Garnish with rosemary sprigs.—BRIGIT LEGERE BINNS

BRAISED LAMB SHANKS WITH ROASTED TOMATOES

Be sure to ask the butcher to saw the lamb shanks in half for you.

🍷 *This is one of those dishes that cries out for a deep-flavored red. The lamb shanks, tarragon and rosemary would harmonize equally well with Cabernet Sauvignon or Merlot, but the sweet savoriness of the roasted garlic favors a velvety-textured California Merlot or Merlot blend. Try the 1993 Matanzas Creek or the 1992 Duckhorn Howell Mountain Red.*

Braised Lamb Shanks with Roasted Tomatoes

4 SERVINGS

- 2 tablespoons canola oil
- 4 well-trimmed lamb shanks, cut in half crosswise
- Salt and freshly ground pepper
- 1 small leek, white and tender green, halved lengthwise and cut into 2-inch pieces
- 1 small onion, coarsely chopped
- 1 small carrot, coarsely chopped
- 1 small celery rib, coarsely chopped
- 3 garlic cloves, chopped
- 2 fresh thyme sprigs
- 8 cups chicken stock, preferably homemade
- 8 roasted-tomato halves from Roasted Tomatoes (p. 362)
- 8 roasted garlic cloves from Roasted Tomatoes (p. 362)
- 4 fresh tarragon sprigs
- 4 cups packed arugula leaves
- Cannellini Beans (recipe follows)

1. In a large enameled cast-iron casserole or Dutch oven, heat the canola oil until almost smoking. Season the lamb shanks with salt and pepper. Add them to the casserole and cook over moderately high heat, turning, until well browned all over.

2. Add the leek, onion, carrot, celery, garlic and thyme and stir for 2 minutes. Add the stock and bring to a simmer. Cover partially, reduce the heat to low and continue to simmer, turning occasionally, until the lamb is tender, about 2 hours. Remove the shanks to a plate.

3. Strain the cooking liquid and return it to the casserole along with the lamb shanks. Add the roasted tomatoes and garlic and simmer over low heat, basting the lamb shanks occasionally, until the liquid is very flavorful, about 25 minutes. Ten minutes before the lamb shanks are done, add the tarragon sprigs. Season the lamb with salt and pepper. (MAKE AHEAD: The lamb shanks can be cooled and refrigerated for up to 3 days. Reheat gently before proceeding.)

4. Discard the tarragon sprigs. Stir the arugula into the hot braising juices until wilted. Put two pieces of lamb shank, two tomato halves and two garlic cloves in each of four shallow bowls or soup plates. Spoon the cannellini beans into the bowls and ladle the arugula and braising juices over all.

Cannellini Beans

MAKES ABOUT 5 CUPS

- 2 cups dried cannellini beans (about 14 ounces), soaked overnight in cold water to cover
- 1 onion, quartered
- 1 carrot, halved
- 1 celery rib, halved
- 1 fresh tarragon sprig
- 1 fresh thyme sprig

Salt and freshly ground pepper

1. Drain the beans and rinse them in cold water. In a medium saucepan, combine the beans with the onion, carrot, celery and 8 cups cold water and bring to a boil over high heat. Reduce the heat to low and simmer gently, stirring occasionally, until the cannellini beans are almost tender, about 1 hour and 10 minutes; add more cold water if necessary to keep the beans covered.

2. Add the tarragon and thyme sprigs. Simmer until the beans are very tender, about 20 minutes longer. (**MAKE AHEAD:** The cannellini beans can be cooked up to 2 days ahead and refrigerated in their cooking liquid. Reheat before proceeding.) Remove and discard the tarragon and thyme sprigs. Drain the beans and season with salt and pepper before serving.—TOM COLICCHIO

Lamb Shanks with Summer Salad

LAMB SHANKS WITH SUMMER SALAD

🍷 *The meaty lamb needs a red with plenty of flavor but not too much tannin. A sturdy Syrah-based wine, such as the 1993 Fess Parker Reserve Syrah from California or the 1993 Château Routas Mistral from Provence, is a good option.*

4 SERVINGS

LAMB:

- 1½ tablespoons olive oil
- 4 lamb shanks (about 1 pound each), trimmed

Salt and freshly ground pepper

- 2 medium onions, coarsely chopped
- 2 medium carrots, coarsely chopped
- 2 medium celery ribs, coarsely chopped
- 1 head of garlic, cloves peeled and coarsely chopped
- 4 medium tomatoes, coarsely chopped
- 1 bottle (750 ml) full-bodied red wine, such as Côtes du Rhône
- 2 cups chicken stock or canned low-sodium broth
- 5 sprigs fresh flat-leaf parsley
- 5 sprigs thyme
- 5 sprigs marjoram

One 2-inch-wide strip of orange zest

SUMMER SALAD:

- 2 cups large dried white beans (about 12 ounces), such as Emergo* or cannellini, picked over, rinsed and soaked overnight in cold water to cover
- 2 medium celery ribs, 1 coarsely chopped and 1 thinly sliced
- 1 medium onion, coarsely chopped
- 1 medium carrot, coarsely chopped
- 6 fresh marjoram sprigs
- 3 bay leaves
- 6 whole black peppercorns
- ¼ cup fresh orange juice

3 tablespoons extra-virgin olive oil
1 teaspoon finely grated orange zest
Salt and freshly ground pepper
4 ounces baby mustard greens or mesclun mix

*Available at specialty-food stores

1. Make the lamb: Preheat the oven to 300°. Heat the olive oil in a large enameled cast-iron casserole. Season the lamb shanks with salt and pepper, add them to the casserole and sear over moderately high heat until well browned all over, about 20 minutes. Transfer the lamb shanks to a plate.

2. Add the onions, carrots, celery and garlic to the casserole and cook over low heat, stirring, until the vegetables start to brown, about 8 minutes. Raise the heat to high, add the tomatoes and boil until the juices evaporate, about 4 minutes. Add the wine and boil for 3 minutes. Add the stock, parsley, thyme, marjoram and orange zest and bring to a simmer. Return the lamb to the casserole, cover and bake for about 4 hours, or until the meat is very tender and falling off the bone.

3. Transfer the lamb to a platter and discard the herbs and zest. In a food mill or food processor, puree the vegetables and sauce. Transfer to a bowl and let stand for 10 minutes, then skim the fat from the surface. Season the sauce with salt and pepper and return it to the casserole along with the lamb. (**MAKE AHEAD:** The lamb can be refrigerated for up to 2 days.)

4. Make the summer salad: Drain and rinse the beans. Transfer them to a saucepan and add 2 quarts of water. Put the chopped celery, the onion, carrot, marjoram, bay leaves and peppercorns in a large square of cheesecloth and tie with string. Add the bundle to the beans and bring to a boil over high heat. Reduce the heat to low and simmer until the beans are tender, about 2 hours.

5. Rewarm the lamb in the sauce. Drain the beans, discarding the cheesecloth bundle, and transfer to a bowl. Add the orange juice, olive oil and orange zest to the beans, season with salt and pepper and stir in the salad greens and the sliced celery. Spoon the lamb sauce into four shallow bowls and mound the bean salad in the center. Top each salad with a lamb shank and serve at once.—JIM MOFFAT

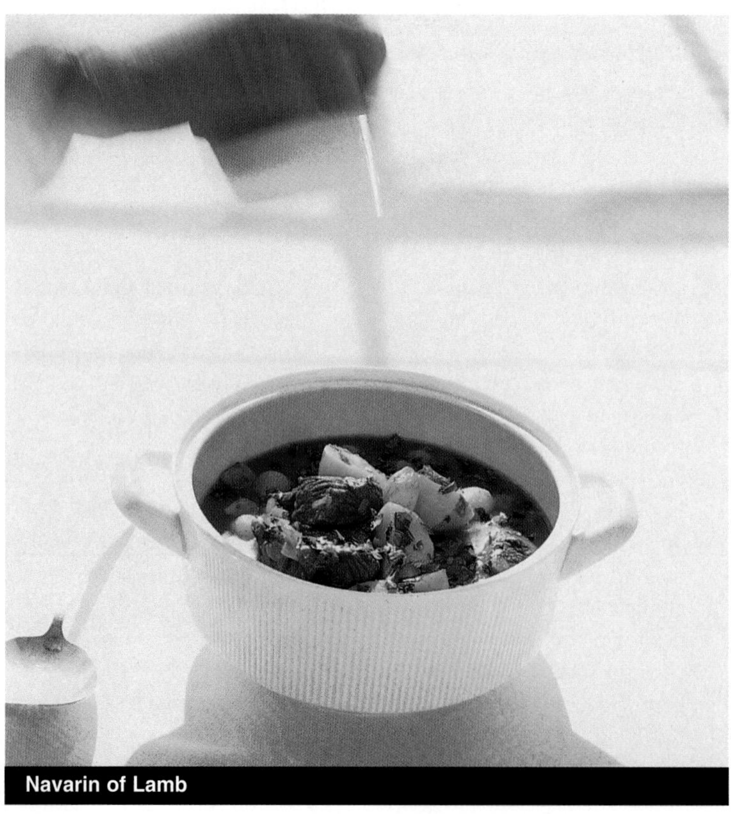

Navarin of Lamb

NAVARIN OF LAMB

All this homey, satisfying lamb stew needs for a wine partner is a fruity, dry red that can harmonize with the rich but mild meat flavor and the sweetness of the caramelized onions. One choice: a California Zinfandel, such as the 1992 Storybook Mountain or the 1991 Haywood Los Chamizai Vineyard.

8–10 SERVINGS

¼ cup plus 2 tablespoons olive oil
6 pounds lamb shoulder, trimmed and cut into 1½-inch cubes

Salt and freshly ground pepper
3 medium yellow onions, coarsely chopped
4 large garlic cloves, minced
3 tablespoons all-purpose flour
3 tablespoons tomato paste
Bouquet garni made with 1 fresh thyme sprig, 1 fresh rosemary sprig, 1 bay leaf and 3 fresh parsley sprigs tied in cheesecloth
3 pounds red potatoes, halved or quartered if large
1 tablespoon unsalted butter
1 pound pearl onions, peeled (see Note)
1 tablespoon finely chopped fresh flat-leaf parsley

1. Heat 1 tablespoon of the oil in a large enameled cast-iron casserole. Season the lamb cubes with salt and pepper and add one-quarter to the casserole. Sear the lamb over moderately high heat until browned all over, about 7 minutes. Transfer to a platter. Brown the remaining meat in three more tablespoons of the oil and transfer to the platter. Add the chopped onions and garlic to the casserole and cook, stirring occasionally, until just softened, about 4 minutes. Add one more tablespoon oil and the flour to the casserole, stirring to coat the onions. Stir in the tomato paste.

2. Return the lamb to the casserole. Add 5 cups of water and the bouquet garni, season with salt and pepper and bring to a boil over moderately high heat. Reduce the heat, cover and cook, stirring occasionally, until the meat is tender but not falling apart, about 1½ hours.

3. Bring a saucepan of salted water to a boil. Add the potatoes and boil over moderately high heat for 5 minutes. Drain and add to the stew. Continue cooking until the potatoes are tender and the lamb is very tender, about 15 more minutes. Discard the bouquet garni.

4. Meanwhile, in a medium skillet, melt the butter in the remaining 1 tablespoon oil. Add the pearl onions and cook over moderate heat, stirring often, until lightly browned, about 8 minutes. Season with salt and pepper. Add ¼ cup of lamb-stew liquid and ½ cup of water and cook, stirring occasionally, until tender and well glazed, about 15 minutes. If necessary, add a little more water to the skillet during cooking.

5. Stir the pearl onions into the navarin and season with salt and pepper. Garnish with the parsley and serve.

NOTE: To peel pearl onions, trim the root ends. Soak the onions in very hot water for 2 to 3 minutes. Drain and rinse with cold water. The skins will slip right off.—PHILIPPE AND SUSAN BOULOT

Preparing Rabbit Braised in Red Wine

RABBIT BRAISED IN RED WINE

This makes an exquisite platter of tender rabbit in a thick sauce made from Barolo, sweet red peppers, cloves and cinnamon. For best results, be certain to use a rather high-alcohol wine (about thirteen percent). Marinating serves to tenderize the meat without denaturing it.

4–6 SERVINGS

1 whole fresh rabbit (about 3 pounds), cut into serving pieces
2 cups tannic red wine, such as Barolo, Barbera or Côtes du Rhône
1 onion, halved lengthwise and studded with 3 whole cloves

3 tablespoons extra-virgin olive oil
Bouquet garni made with 2 fresh bay leaves and a large bunch of thyme tied with kitchen string
1 cinnamon stick, halved
2 large red bell peppers
Sea salt and black pepper

1. Combine the rabbit, wine, onion, 2 tablespoons of the oil, the bouquet garni and the cinnamon. Let marinate at room temperature for 2 hours, turning the rabbit occasionally.
2. Meanwhile, roast the bell peppers directly over a gas flame or under the broiler as close to the heat as possible, turning often, until charred all over. Transfer the roasted peppers to a paper bag and set them aside to steam for 10 minutes. Scrape off the blackened skins and remove the stems, seeds and ribs from the peppers. Cut the peppers lengthwise into ¼-inch-wide strips.
3. In a large nonreactive flameproof casserole, heat the remaining 1 tablespoon oil until hot but not smoking. Remove the rabbit pieces from the marinade, pat dry and season lightly with sea salt and black pepper. Add the rabbit and its marinade to the casserole and bring just to a simmer over moderately high heat. Add the roasted bell-pepper strips and reduce the heat to very low. Cover and simmer gently, turning occasionally, until the rabbit is fork-tender, about 2 hours.
4. Using a slotted spoon, transfer the rabbit and the pepper strips to a platter and cover to keep warm. Strain the sauce and wipe out the casserole. Return the sauce to the casserole and boil over high heat until thick and glossy. Return the rabbit and peppers to the casserole, cover and cook over low heat, turning once or twice, until heated through, about 5 minutes. (MAKE AHEAD: The rabbit can be cooled, covered and refrigerated for up to 1 day. Reheat before serving.) —PATRICIA WELLS

CHEF'S MENU

Venison has a tendency to overpower light reds. Choose a red with a meatiness of its own, such as a 1991 Arrowood Cabernet Sauvignon from California.

PAN-ROASTED GNOCCHI SALAD WITH PANCETTA (P. 69)

VENISON MEDALLIONS WITH WILTED SPINACH SALAD (P. 264)

INDIVIDUAL POACHED-PEAR CHEESECAKES (P. 455)

VENISON MEDALLIONS WITH WILTED-SPINACH SALAD

8 SERVINGS

VENISON:
½ cup dry red wine
¼ cup red-wine vinegar
¼ cup olive oil
3 tablespoons unsulphured molasses
2 medium shallots, thinly sliced
1 tablespoon minced fresh sage
1 tablespoon crushed black peppercorns
3 pounds venison tenderloin or boneless loin, trimmed

COOKING WINE

If you don't have odds and ends of leftover wine, here are some inexpensive candidates to use in the kitchen.
YOUNG, ROBUST, DEEPLY COLORED REDS: **a Côtes du Rhône, a Bordeaux, a Rioja or a California Zinfandel.**
YOUNG, LIGHT, ACIDIC WHITES: **any inexpensive wine made from the Pinot Blanc grape, such as a Muscadet or a California Pinot Blanc; an Aligoté from Burgundy.**
FRAGRANT WHITES: **an Alsatian Riesling, or one from California or Australia; a Côtes du Rhône Blanc de Blancs.**

LENTILS:
2 tablespoons olive oil
1 small onion, finely chopped
1 small carrot, finely chopped
4 large garlic cloves, minced
1 teaspoon ground cumin
1 pound black lentils or French du Puy lentils (about 2 cups)
4 cups chicken stock or canned low-sodium broth
½ teaspoon thyme
¼ cup red-wine vinegar
Salt and freshly ground pepper

FINISH:
¼ cup olive oil
1 pound fresh spinach leaves, large leaves torn in half
2 shallots, thinly sliced
1 teaspoon minced fresh sage
1 tablespoon red-wine vinegar
Salt and freshly ground pepper

1. Marinate the venison: In a shallow nonreactive baking dish, combine the wine, vinegar, oil, molasses, shallots, sage and peppercorns. Add the venison and turn to coat. Cover and refrigerate for at least 8 hours or overnight.

2. Make the lentils: Heat the oil in a nonreactive saucepan. Add the onion and carrot and cook over moderately high heat, stirring, until the onion is softened. Stir in the garlic and cumin and cook for 2 minutes. Add the lentils, chicken stock and thyme and bring to a simmer. Cover and simmer over low heat, stirring, until tender, about 40 minutes. Stir in the vinegar and season with salt and pepper. Reserve ¼ cup of the cooking liquid. Cover the lentils and keep warm.

3. Finish the dish: Heat 1 teaspoon of the oil in a large nonreactive skillet. Add the spinach by handfuls and stir over high heat until wilted before adding more. Transfer to a bowl, discarding any liquid.

4. Heat 1 tablespoon plus 2 teaspoons of the olive oil in the skillet. Add the shallots and cook, stirring, until lightly browned. Add the sage and vinegar. Stir in the spinach. Add the reserved lentil-cooking liquid and season with salt and pepper. Return to the bowl and keep warm.

5. Pat the venison dry with paper towels and cut the meat into 24 medallions; they should be about ¾ inch thick for tenderloin and ½ inch thick for loin. Season with salt and pepper. Divide the remaining 2 tablespoons oil between two large skillets and heat until smoking. Add the medallions and sear over high heat, turning once, until well browned but still rare inside, 3 to 5 minutes.

6. Drain the lentils and mound them on eight plates. Arrange the venison medallions over the lentils, top with the spinach salad and serve at once.—NICK MORFOGEN

MAIL-ORDER SOURCES

Can't find black lentils or venison in your local supermarket? These companies are good sources for hard-to-find ingredients.

- **A Southern Season (1-800-253-3663) is the place to find black lentils, demiglace and truffle-flavored oil.**
- **Kalustyan's (212-685-3451) has Asian ingredients, such as Thai black rice.**
- **Broken Arrow Ranch (1-800-962-4263) has American venison and many other types of game, like antelope and boar.**
- **Penzeys Ltd. (414-574-0277) specializes in unusual spices of excellent quality; they'll send customers such rarities as Vietnamese cinnamon and Kashmir saffron.**

CHAPTER 11

~

OTHER MAIN DISHES

Lobster Lo Mein Salad

LOBSTER LO MEIN SALAD

Asian wheat noodles have a tender texture that befits this delicate salad. Look for dried Chinese lo mein or Japanese somen *or* hiyamugi *noodles. The noodles and fish sauce are available at well-stocked supermarkets and Asian markets, and the seaweed at Asian markets and health-food stores.*

🍷 *A straightforward Riesling with a hint of sweetness will underscore the richness of the lobster and balance the Asian flavors. Consider the 1994 Sichel Piesporter Goldtröpfchen Riesling Spätlese from Germany or the 1993 Columbia Winery Cellarmaster's Reserve Johannisberg Riesling from Washington State.*

4 SERVINGS

Four 1- to 1¼-pound live lobsters or 1 to 1¼ pounds cooked lobster meat
1 tablespoon dried Japanese *hijiki* seaweed
½ cup boiling water
2 teaspoons soy sauce
2 tablespoons plus 1 teaspoon sugar
1¼ teaspoons Asian sesame oil
¾ pound snow peas
Ice water
2 garlic cloves, minced
1 teaspoon finely grated fresh ginger
½ teaspoon crushed red pepper, or more to taste
5 tablespoons Asian fish sauce
2½ tablespoons fresh lime juice
1 pound dried Chinese lo mein noodles
¼ cup fresh cilantro leaves
Freshly ground pepper
¼ cup salted peanuts

1. If using live lobsters, plunge them head first into a large saucepan of boiling water and cook until they are bright red all over, about 8 minutes. Using tongs, remove the lobsters to a bowl. When they are cool enough to handle, crack the claws and tail and remove all the meat. Slice the tail and claw meat ¼ inch thick and refrigerate until ready to use.

2. Put the *hijiki* in a small bowl. Add the boiling water; set aside until softened, about 15 minutes. In a small bowl, combine the soy sauce, the 1 teaspoon sugar and ¼ teaspoon of the sesame oil. Drain the *hijiki* and add to the bowl. Set aside for at least 10 minutes.

3. In a medium saucepan of boiling water, blanch the snow peas until bright green, about 1 minute. Using a slotted spoon, transfer them to the ice water to stop the cooking. Drain and pat dry. Slice lengthwise into thin strips.

4. In a bowl, combine the garlic, ginger, red pepper, fish sauce, lime juice and the remaining 2 tablespoons sugar and 1 teaspoon sesame oil. Stir in 5 tablespoons water.

5. Bring a large saucepan of water to a boil. Add the noodles and cook, stirring, until al dente, about 4 minutes. Drain in a colander and return to the saucepan. Fill the pan with cold water; swirl the noodles around, then drain. Repeat the process one more time. Drain well.

6. In a large bowl, combine the noodles with the lobster meat, snow peas and the *hijiki* and its marinade. Toss well, using clean hands or tongs. Add the fish-sauce dressing and the cilantro leaves, season with pepper and toss well. Turn out onto a large platter, sprinkle the peanuts on top and serve.—MARCIA KIESEL

SHRIMP-AND-BARLEY SALAD WITH GREEN BEANS

4 SERVINGS

¾ cup pearl barley (6½ ounces), rinsed
1 pound medium shrimp, shelled and deveined
Salt and freshly ground black pepper
1 pound thin green beans or *haricots verts*
¼ cup olive oil
3 tablespoons fresh lemon juice
¼ cup minced shallots
2 teaspoons finely grated lemon zest
1 cup diced celery (⅓ inch)
1 large red bell pepper, finely diced
1 large green bell pepper, finely diced
¼ cup chopped fresh basil
3 tablespoons chopped fresh cilantro

1. In a medium saucepan, cover the barley with 6 cups of cold water and bring to a boil over high heat. Reduce the heat and

Shrimp-and-Barley Salad

simmer until the barley is tender, about 1 hour. Drain the barley and let cool. (**MAKE AHEAD:** The barley can be refrigerated for up to 1 day. Let it return to room temperature before proceeding.)
2. Bring a medium saucepan of water to a boil over high heat. Add the shrimp and cook for 30 seconds after the water returns to a boil. Drain and let cool. Season with salt and black pepper.
3. Fill the saucepan with fresh water and bring to a boil. Add 1 teaspoon of salt and the beans and boil until just tender, about 5 minutes. Drain the beans and rinse them under cold running water. Drain and pat dry.
4. In a medium bowl, whisk the oil with the lemon juice, 1½ teaspoons salt and ¾ teaspoon black pepper. Stir in the shallots and lemon zest. In a large bowl, toss the barley with the shrimp, celery, red and green bell peppers, basil and cilantro. Add the dressing to the salad and toss.
5. Mound the shrimp-and-barley salad on plates or a platter. Toss the beans in the dressing that clings to the bowl and season them with salt and black pepper. Garnish the salad with the beans and serve at room temperature.—DIANA STURGIS

OCTOPUS-AND-POTATO SALAD

When tomatoes are at their peak of ripeness, they can be sliced and added to the salad just before serving.

4 SERVINGS

1 pound waxy (boiling) potatoes
1 pound cooked tender octopus tentacles, whole or sliced crosswise ¼ to ⅓ inch thick
3 scallions, white and green, thinly sliced
2 tablespoons chopped fresh flat-leaf parsley
½ cup extra-virgin olive oil
3 tablespoons fresh lemon juice
1 garlic clove, finely chopped
Salt and freshly ground pepper

1. Cook the potatoes in a pan of rapidly boiling lightly salted water until completely tender but not falling apart, 15 to 20 minutes. Drain well. As soon as the potatoes are cool enough to handle, peel and slice them ⅓ inch thick.
2. Arrange the potato slices on a small platter and mound the octopus on top. Sprinkle with the scallions and parsley.
3. In a small bowl, combine the oil, lemon juice, garlic and salt and pepper to taste. Pour the dressing over the octopus and potatoes. Cover; let marinate in a cool place for several hours before serving.—NANCY HARMON JENKINS

SEARED FRESH TUNA WITH ROASTED-TOMATO AND FENNEL SALAD

4 SERVINGS

Four 6-ounce trimmed fresh tuna steaks, cut 1 inch thick
2 tablespoons coarsely ground pepper
Salt
3 tablespoons extra-virgin olive oil

Seared Fresh Tuna with Roasted-Tomato and Fennel Salad

- 1 large fennel bulb, quartered, cored and thinly sliced lengthwise, some feathery fronds reserved
- 1 small red onion, thinly sliced
- 2 tablespoons fresh chives in 1-inch lengths
- 4 roasted-tomato halves from Roasted Tomatoes (p. 362)

Finely ground pepper
Roasted-Tomato Vinaigrette (recipe follows)
Fresh chive blossoms, for garnish

1. Coat both sides of the tuna steaks with the coarsely ground pepper and season with salt. In a large heavy skillet, heat 2 tablespoons of the oil over high heat until almost smoking. Add the tuna and cook until well seared, about 2 minutes per side; the tuna should be rare inside. Let the fish rest for a few minutes.

2. Meanwhile, in a large bowl, combine the fennel, onion, chives and tomato halves. Add the remaining 1 tablespoon olive oil, season with salt and finely ground pepper and toss well. Mound the salad on four large plates.

3. Using a very sharp knife, slice the tuna across the grain ¼ inch thick and arrange it on the salads. Drizzle the vinaigrette all around and garnish with the fennel fronds and chive blossoms.

TOMATO TIPS

- **Buy tomatoes from farmers' markets or farm stands.**
- **Try some heirloom varieties. My favorites include Striped Germans, Cherokee Purples, Amish Brandywines and Moskviches from Russia.**
- **For salads, mix varieties of tomatoes for a balance of flavors, textures and colors.**
- **For eating raw, the low-acid varieties—usually those that aren't the classic bright red—have the best flavor.**
- **To ripen slightly underripe tomatoes, leave them out on the counter, stem-end down.**
- **Never refrigerate fresh tomatoes.—TOM COLICCHIO**

Roasted-Tomato Vinaigrette

MAKES ABOUT 1 CUP

- 2 roasted-tomato halves from Roasted Tomatoes (p. 362)
- ¼ cup tomato juices from Roasted Tomatoes (p. 362)
- 2 tablespoons red-wine vinegar
- ½ cup extra-virgin olive oil

Salt and freshly ground pepper

In a blender, puree the tomato halves with the tomato juices and the vinegar. With the machine running, gradually add the oil. Season the dressing with salt and pepper.—TOM COLICCHIO

GRILLED-TUNA SALAD WITH WASABI DRESSING

This Japanese-style salad gets its kick from wasabi. Or you could use an equal amount of powdered dry mustard.

4 SERVINGS

- 1 tablespoon plus 2 teaspoons soy sauce
- 1 tablespoon plus 2 teaspoons olive oil
- 1¼ pounds fresh tuna steak
- 4 teaspoons wasabi powder*
- 2 tablespoons tahini* (sesame paste)
- 2 tablespoons rice vinegar
- 1 teaspoon Dijon mustard
- 1 teaspoon sugar
- 2 small garlic cloves, minced

Salt and freshly ground pepper

- 7 ounces alfalfa sprouts (4 cups)
- 7 ounces trimmed enoki mushrooms* (2 cups)
- ½ pound young spinach, stemmed
- 2 tablespoons slivered Japanese pickled ginger*

*Available at Asian markets and health-food stores

1. In a shallow glass dish, combine 1 tablespoon of the soy sauce and 1 teaspoon of the oil. Add the tuna; coat well. Refrigerate 15 minutes, turning the fish twice.

2. Light a grill or preheat the broiler. In a small bowl, mix the wasabi with 4 teaspoons hot water. Cover; set aside 5 minutes.

3. In another bowl, stir 2 tablespoons warm water into the tahini. Stir in the wasabi paste, the vinegar, mustard, sugar, garlic and the remaining 2 teaspoons soy sauce and 4 teaspoons oil. Season with salt and pepper.

4. Season the tuna with salt and pepper; grill or broil until crusty on the outside and rare within, about 4 minutes per side. Transfer the fish to a plate to rest for a few minutes, then slice it against the grain ⅓ inch thick.

5. In a large bowl, toss the alfalfa sprouts with the mushrooms and all but 2 tablespoons of the dressing; loosen the sprouts to evenly distribute the dressing. Scatter the spinach on four plates; arrange the tuna on top. Drizzle on the remaining dressing. Mound the salad on the tuna, scatter the ginger on top and serve.—MARCIA KIESEL ➤

Russian-Style Salade Niçoise

AVOCADO AND CURRIED-TUNA SALAD

4 SERVINGS

- ¾ teaspoon curry powder
- ½ cup plus 2 tablespoons mayonnaise
- 1 cup finely diced peeled tart apple
- 2 tablespoons finely chopped dill
- 1 small onion, finely diced
- 2 celery ribs, finely diced
- 1 large scallion, thinly sliced
- 2 teaspoons freshly squeezed lemon juice
- Two 6-ounce cans water-packed albacore tuna, drained
- Salt and freshly ground pepper
- 2 cups arugula leaves (lightly packed)
- 2 medium tomatoes, cut into 1-inch dice
- 2 ripe avocados, preferably Hass, halved, peeled and pitted

1. In a small skillet, toast the curry powder over moderate heat, stirring, until it is fragrant, about 30 seconds. Scrape the toasted curry powder into a large bowl.

2. Add the mayonnaise, diced apple, chopped dill, diced onion and celery, sliced scallion and freshly squeezed lemon juice. Flake the tuna into the bowl and mix well. Season the tuna-salad mixture with salt and pepper. Cover the salad and refrigerate it for at least 30 minutes. To serve the salad, mound the arugula leaves and the diced tomatoes on four plates. Set an avocado half on top and fill it with the tuna salad.—MARCIA KIESEL

RUSSIAN-STYLE SALADE NIÇOISE

Smoked trout and a horseradish dressing stand in for the classic tuna and vinaigrette in this composed salad. Rather than serve the dressing on the side, you can dress the vegetables separately before arranging them on plates.

4 SERVINGS

- 1 pound small beets (about 8)
- ¼ pound *haricots verts* or thin green beans
- 1 pound small new potatoes, scrubbed
- 2 tablespoons minced shallots
- 2 tablespoons prepared horseradish
- 2 tablespoons sherry vinegar
- 2 tablespoons sour cream
- 1 teaspoon Dijon mustard
- ¼ cup extra-virgin olive oil
- 3 tablespoons heavy cream
- Salt and freshly ground pepper
- 1 tablespoon chopped fresh dill
- 2 whole smoked trout (about 1 pound each), skinned and boned, flesh flaked
- 6 hard-boiled eggs, quartered lengthwise
- 1 cup cherry tomatoes, halved

1. Preheat the oven to 425°. Wrap the beets in foil and bake for about 1 hour, or until tender when pierced. When cool enough to handle, peel the beets and cut them into 2-by-½-inch matchsticks or small wedges.

2. Bring a medium saucepan of lightly salted water to a boil. Add the *haricots verts* and cook until tender, about 4 minutes. Using a slotted spoon, transfer the beans to a colander and rinse under cool running water; pat dry. Pour off all but 2 inches of water from the saucepan and set a

IMPROVISING A MAIN-DISH SALAD

"Salads afford considerable scope for the exercise of individual taste," opined Mrs. Beeton, Victorian England's gift to the world of fine cooking. She was right, of course. There are few rules for the creation of a salad except that the greens be fresh and crisp. When inventing your own salads, it's easy to be inspired by fresh summer produce—and hard to make mistakes if you follow a few rules:

- **Match assertive greens (arugula, dandelion, chicory, endive, frisée and radicchio) with strong-flavored dressings and hearty ingredients, such as beef or sausage.**
- **Coat milder greens (romaine, Boston, Bibb and red-leaf lettuces, plus mung-bean, alfalfa and sunflower sprouts) with subtle dressings that won't overpower them.**
- **Play with textures and temperatures—cool, lacy greens with warm goat cheese in crisp phyllo dough, or just-grilled beef with room-temperature citrus.**
- **For tossed salads, use ingredients of similar size and weight; heavy items will fall to the bottom as you toss.**
- **Serve starch-based salads —pasta, rice, potatoes, bread or grains—at room temperature, not chilled.**
- **Don't be afraid to use meat, seafood or poultry straight from the grill.**

steamer basket inside. Add the potatoes and steam until tender, about 18 minutes. Let cool slightly, then quarter the potatoes.

3. In a medium bowl, combine the shallots, horseradish, vinegar, sour cream and mustard. Whisk in the oil, 1 tablespoon at a time, until emulsified. Whisk in the heavy cream and season with salt and pepper. (**MAKE AHEAD:** The vegetables and dressing can be refrigerated overnight.)

4. Just before serving, stir the dill into the dressing. In a bowl, toss the flaked trout with ¼ cup of the dressing and mound on four large dinner plates. Garnish each serving with the beets, *haricots verts*, potatoes, eggs and tomatoes. Pass the remaining dressing separately.—GRACE PARISI

FRISÉE SALAD WITH BEANS AND WARM-BACON DRESSING

This salad offers a plethora of contrasting flavors and textures: tangy goat cheese and slightly bitter frisée, creamy beans, juicy tomatoes and crisp croutons—all in a warm bacon dressing. The tender white leaves from the center of a head of chicory or escarole are a good substitute for the frisée.

🍷 *The garlicky, smoky flavors suggest a dry white, and the goat cheese narrows the choice to a tart, crisp Sauvignon Blanc. Look for the 1994 Flora Springs Soliloquy or the 1993 Grgich Hills Fumé Blanc, both from California.*

4 SERVINGS

- 1 cup dried navy beans, picked over, rinsed and soaked overnight in 4 cups of cold water
- 1 bay leaf
- 2 garlic cloves, lightly crushed
- Salt
- 2 cups cubed crustless peasant bread (¾ inch)
- 2 tablespoons plus 2 teaspoons extra-virgin olive oil
- ¼ pound thick-sliced bacon, cut crosswise into ¾-inch strips
- 3 large shallots, thinly sliced
- 3 tablespoons Champagne vinegar or white-wine vinegar
- Freshly ground pepper
- ½ pound frisée, torn into 2-inch pieces
- ½ cup yellow cherry tomatoes, halved
- ¼ pound mild goat cheese, crumbled into 1-inch pieces

1. Drain and rinse the beans. In a medium saucepan, combine the beans with the bay leaf, garlic and 4 cups of water and bring to a boil over high heat. Reduce the heat to moderately low, cover partially and simmer the beans until tender but not mushy, about 1 hour; add ½ teaspoon salt 10 minutes before the beans are done. Drain the beans and let cool to room temperature. Discard the bay leaf and garlic.

2. Meanwhile, preheat the oven to 350°. Toss the bread cubes with 2 teaspoons of the olive oil and arrange in a single layer in a baking dish. Bake for about 8 minutes, or until golden but not dry.

3. In a nonreactive medium skillet, fry the bacon over moderately high heat until crisp. Transfer to paper towels to drain. Add the remaining 2 tablespoons olive oil to the fat in the skillet. Add the shallots and cook over moderate heat, stirring occasionally, until they are just beginning to brown, about 7 minutes. Stir in the vinegar, season with salt and pepper and keep warm.

4. In a large bowl, toss the frisée with the beans, bacon, croutons and tomatoes. Add the dressing and toss. Add the goat cheese and toss gently but thoroughly. Serve immediately.—GRACE PARISI

PARSLEY POBLANO SALAD WITH ORANGE-GLAZED BEEF

Flat-leaf parsley makes a refreshing and nutritious salad, especially when paired with spicy poblano chiles and sweet oranges.

🍷 *Pick a red wine with enough brisk acidity to cope with the raw citrus and sharp parsley. One option is an Italian Barbera, perhaps the 1994 Michele Chiarlo Barbera d'Asti or the 1993 Bruno Giacosa Barbera d'Alba.*

4 SERVINGS

BEEF:

- 1 teaspoon balsamic vinegar
- 1 teaspoon olive oil
- 1 garlic clove, minced
- ¼ teaspoon finely grated orange zest
- Pinch of sugar
- Four 5- to 6-ounce beef tenderloin steaks
- Salt and freshly ground pepper

SALAD:

- 2 poblano chiles
- 2 garlic cloves, lightly smashed
- ¼ cup fresh orange juice
- 2 tablespoons olive oil
- 2 teaspoons balsamic vinegar
- ½ teaspoon sugar
- ½ teaspoon finely grated orange zest
- ½ teaspoon ground cumin
- Salt and freshly ground pepper

Frisée Salad with Beans and Warm-Bacon Dressing

2 large navel oranges
4 cups firmly packed fresh flat-leaf parsley (small sprigs)
1 medium red onion, thinly sliced

1. Make the beef: In a shallow glass or ceramic dish, combine the vinegar, oil, garlic, orange zest and sugar. Rub the mixture over both sides of the steaks and let marinate at room temperature for at least 15 minutes or up to 2 hours.

2. Make the salad: Roast the poblano chiles directly over a gas flame or under the broiler, turning, until lightly charred all over; be careful not to burn off too much of their thin skins. Put the chiles in a small bowl, cover with plastic wrap and let steam for 5 minutes. Working over the bowl, peel off all the charred skins and remove the stems and seeds. Strain any accumulated poblano juices into a clean small bowl. Cut the chiles into thin 2-inch strips.

3. In a large bowl, combine the chile strips with the garlic, orange juice, oil, vinegar, sugar, orange zest, cumin and ½ teaspoon each of salt and pepper. Stir in any reserved poblano juices and set the mixture aside for 15 minutes.

4. Light a grill or preheat the broiler. Peel the oranges with a sharp knife, taking care to remove all the bitter white pith. Cut in between the membranes to release the orange sections.

5. Season the meat with salt and pepper. Grill or broil the steaks for about 3 minutes per side, or until nicely browned, crusty and medium-rare. Let the steaks rest for 5 minutes.

6. Remove the garlic from the dressing in the bowl. Add the parsley and onion and toss well. Mound the salad on four large plates. Cut the steaks into thin slices and arrange alongside. Garnish with the orange sections and serve.—MARCIA KIESEL

MARINATED-STEAK SALAD Q

4 SERVINGS

1 medium shallot, minced
½ teaspoon minced fresh rosemary
Salt and freshly ground pepper
3 tablespoons sherry wine vinegar
2 tablespoons Dijon mustard
¼ cup walnut oil
¼ cup plus 1 tablespoon vegetable oil
Four 1-inch-thick boneless steaks (about 7 ounces each)
½ cup coarsely chopped walnuts
2 Belgian endives, cut crosswise into 1-inch pieces
1 pound escarole, torn into bite-size pieces
4 ounces Roquefort cheese, crumbled (about 1 cup)

Marinated-Steak Salad

1. In a small nonreactive saucepan, combine the shallot, rosemary and ½ teaspoon each of salt and pepper. Stir in the vinegar and mustard. Whisk in the walnut oil and the vegetable oil. Arrange the steaks on a nonreactive baking sheet, pour ¼ cup of the dressing on top and turn to coat. Let marinate for 30 minutes.

2. Meanwhile, preheat the oven to 350°. Toast the walnuts for about 3 minutes, or until fragrant.

3. Preheat the broiler. Warm the remaining dressing over low heat; keep warm. Broil the steaks for about 2 minutes per side for medium-rare. Let rest 2 minutes.

4. Toss the endives, escarole, Roquefort and walnuts with the warm dressing and mound on four plates. Cut each steak diagonally across the grain into five slices and arrange the slices on the salads.—PAUL GRIMES

NAPA-CABBAGE, HAM AND APPLE SALAD

Mild Napa cabbage is the ideal foil for the crisp, sweet apple and smoky ham. If you prefer, substitute smoked turkey or chicken.

Salty ham, sweet apples, rich walnuts and pungent onions can be matched successfully with a variety of wines—but not necessarily with the same ones. The overt fruitiness of a California Pinot Noir, such as the 1994 Morgan or the 1993 Robert Stemmler, will work with all these tastes. Serve the wine cool to accentuate its cherrylike tartness.

4 SERVINGS

PARMESAN CROÛTES:
16 to 20 thin slices cut from a narrow baguette

Napa-Cabbage, Ham and Apple Salad

2 tablespoons olive oil
¼ cup freshly grated Parmesan cheese

SALAD:

1 cup walnut pieces
⅓ cup olive oil
¼ cup plus 1 teaspoon white-wine vinegar
3 tablespoons grainy mustard
Salt and freshly ground pepper
¼ cup dried currants
1 Red Delicious apple
1½ pounds Napa cabbage, quartered lengthwise, cored and coarsely chopped
¾ pound smoked ham, cut into 1-by-¼-inch strips
1 medium red onion, halved lengthwise and thinly sliced crosswise
2 teaspoons caraway seeds

1. Make the Parmesan croûtes: Preheat the oven to 375°. Lightly brush one side of each bread slice with the oil and sprinkle with the Parmesan. Bake for about 10 minutes, or until lightly browned.

2. Make the salad: Spread the walnuts in a small pan and bake for 4 to 5 minutes, or until fragrant and lightly toasted. In a small bowl, whisk the oil with the ¼ cup vinegar, the mustard and ½ teaspoon each of salt and pepper. Stir in the currants and set the dressing aside.

3. Quarter and core the apple; thinly slice the quarters crosswise. Toss the apple with the remaining 1 teaspoon vinegar to prevent discoloring.

4. In a large bowl, toss together the cabbage, ham, onion, walnuts, apple and caraway seeds. Whisk the dressing, then pour it over the salad and toss thoroughly. Serve at once on large plates, with the croûtes on the side.—DIANA STURGIS

GRATIN OF EGGS LOUTE

The eggs, mushrooms and soubise, *a white sauce (béchamel) flavored with onion, can all be prepared ahead of time; the dish can even be assembled in advance—either in individual gratin dishes or in a large one—and reheated in the oven just before it is served. The gratin makes a wonderful main course for brunch, lunch or a light supper.*

8 SERVINGS

8 large eggs, pierced (see "Cooking Eggs," next page)
3 tablespoons unsalted butter
3 medium scallions, thinly sliced
¾ pound white or cremini mushrooms, coarsely chopped
1 anchovy fillet, minced
Salt and freshly ground pepper
½ pound onions, thinly sliced
1 tablespoon all-purpose flour
1 cup milk
½ cup heavy cream
½ cup grated Gruyère cheese

1. Put the eggs in a medium saucepan and cover with hot tap water. Bring to a boil over high heat, then lower the heat to moderate and simmer for 10 minutes. Drain off the water and shake the pan to lightly crack the eggs. Add ice and cold water to the pan and let stand until the eggs are cold. Drain and peel the eggs.

2. Meanwhile, in a medium skillet, melt 1 tablespoon of the butter over moderately high heat. When the foam subsides, add the scallions; cook until just wilted. Add the mushrooms and cook, stirring occasionally, until all the liquid is evaporated and the mushrooms begin to brown, about 10 minutes. Stir in the anchovy fillet and season with salt and pepper. Spread the mushroom mixture on the bottom of a

A GOOD EGG

Although the nutritional value of eggs has never been in question, in recent years concerns about cholesterol have prompted many people, myself included, to cut back. Now, however, nutritionists and dietitians alike are recognizing that eggs are not as bad for you as they were once thought to be, and egg dishes are gaining in favor once again as part of a balanced diet. I like to buy my eggs from a local farm or from health-food stores that stock farm-fresh eggs. They may cost a bit more, but they have a lot more flavor.—JACQUES PÉPIN

6-cup gratin dish. Slice the eggs with an egg slicer, arrange them over the mushrooms in an even layer and season lightly with salt and pepper.

3. Preheat the broiler. Wipe out the skillet and melt 1 teaspoon of the butter. Add the onions and ½ cup of water and cook over moderately low heat until the onions are tender and the water is almost evaporated, about 12 minutes. Transfer the onions to a food processor and puree.

4. In a medium saucepan, melt the remaining butter. Whisk in the flour until blended and cook for 15 seconds. Add the milk and bring to a boil, whisking frequently. When the mixture is thickened, add the cream and the onion puree, season with salt and pepper and bring to a boil. Pour the sauce over the eggs, shaking the dish gently to let the sauce seep down. Sprinkle the cheese on top and broil for 3 to 4 minutes, until browned and bubbling.—JACQUES PÉPIN

COOKING EGGS

Hard-cooking eggs properly is a simple yet delicate process. Often, the eggs served in restaurants and cafeterias have rubbery whites, green-tinged yolks and a strong sulfur smell—all clear signs that the eggs were cooked for too long a time over too high a heat. For perfect hard-cooked eggs:

1. Begin by piercing raw eggs at their rounded ends, where there is an air space, using either a little device designed for the purpose or a push pin; this will make it easier to peel the eggs once they are cooked.

2. Gently lower the eggs into a pan of hot tap water and bring to a light boil; for large eggs, count ten minutes from the time the water boils, keeping the water at a gentle boil at all times.

3. As soon as the eggs are done, pour off the water and shake the pan to crack the egg shells.

4. Immediately add ice and cold water to the pan and let the eggs stand until cold. At this point the eggs can be shelled.—JACQUES PÉPIN

BEET-GREEN FRITTATA

The leafy tops of beets lend color and nutrition to this egg dish.

4 SERVINGS

- ½ pound beet greens, stemmed
- 1 tablespoon unsalted butter
- 2 tablespoons olive oil
- 1 small onion, finely chopped
- 1 garlic clove, minced
- Salt and freshly ground black pepper
- 8 large eggs
- 1 tablespoon of freshly grated Parmesan cheese

1. Preheat the oven to 375°. In a saucepan of boiling salted water, blanch the beet greens for 2 minutes. Drain and let cool slightly, then squeeze out some water,

Gratin of Eggs Loute

leaving the greens moist. Coarsely chop the greens.

2. In a 9-inch nonstick ovenproof skillet, melt the butter in 1 tablespoon of the oil. Add the onion and cook over moderate heat, stirring, until translucent, about 3 minutes. Add the garlic and cook, stirring, until fragrant, about 2 minutes. Add the remaining 1 tablespoon oil and the beet greens and continue cooking just until they are heated through, stirring to break up any clumps. Season the greens with salt and pepper.

3. In a bowl, lightly beat the eggs with a large pinch each of salt and pepper. Pour the eggs over the greens and cook over moderate heat, stirring and lifting the cooked portions, until the eggs are partially set, about 2 minutes. Bake in the top third of the oven for about 8 minutes, or until firm. Loosen the sides of the frittata and slide onto a large plate. Dust the top with the Parmesan, cut into wedges and serve hot or warm.—F&W TEST KITCHEN

ASPARAGUS POTATO FRITTATA Q

Choose asparagus spears of similar size so that they will cook evenly. Serve the frittata with a salad and crusty bread.

4 SERVINGS

- ½ pound unpeeled red new potatoes, cut into ⅓-inch chunks
- ½ pound asparagus, peeled and cut into ¾-inch lengths
- 3 tablespoons extra-virgin olive oil
- 1 medium onion, minced

Asparagus Potato Frittata

1 teaspoon salt
¼ teaspoon freshly ground pepper
8 large eggs
¼ cup heavy cream

1. Steam the potatoes until they are barely tender, about 5 minutes; set aside. Steam the asparagus until bright green but still crisp, about 2 minutes.
2. In a 10- to 12-inch nonstick skillet, heat 1½ tablespoons of the olive oil over high heat. Add the steamed potatoes and sauté until browned and crisp, about 7 minutes. Add the steamed asparagus and the onion, season with the salt and pepper and cook until tender, about 3 minutes; transfer to a plate.
3. Wipe out the skillet, set it over moderate heat and add 1 tablespoon of the oil. Beat the eggs with the heavy cream until smooth. Stir in the vegetables and pour the mixture into the skillet. Reduce the heat to low and cook until the edges just begin to set. Lift the sides of the frittata with a rubber spatula, tilting the skillet to allow the uncooked eggs to seep under. Continue cooking until the bottom is set and the top is barely runny, about 7 minutes.
4. Set a large flat plate over the skillet and invert the frittata onto the plate. Add the remaining ½ tablespoon olive oil to the skillet and slide the frittata back in. Cook until the bottom of the frittata is golden, about 3 minutes. Slide the frittata onto a large plate and cut into wedges. Serve warm or at room temperature.—GRACE PARISI

CHEESE FRITTATA WITH PICO DE GALLO

4 SERVINGS

PICO DE GALLO:
¾ pound ripe tomatoes, halved
1 small jalapeño, minced
2 tablespoons finely chopped fresh cilantro
1 teaspoon ground cumin
½ teaspoon salt

FRITTATA:
2 teaspoons unsalted butter
8 large eggs
½ cup milk
Salt and freshly ground pepper
⅓ cup grated Port Salut or Fontina cheese (about 2 ounces)
2 tablespoons finely chopped scallions

1. Make the *pico de gallo*: Working over a strainer set over a bowl, seed the tomatoes, reserving the juices. Coarsely chop the tomatoes.
2. In a blender or mini-processor, pulse the tomatoes, jalapeño, cilantro and cumin until finely chopped but not pureed. Transfer to a bowl and stir in 2 tablespoons of the reserved tomato juices. (**MAKE AHEAD:** The *pico de gallo* can be refrigerated overnight. Let return to room temperature before proceeding.) Stir in the salt.
3. Make the frittata: Preheat the broiler. In a 10-inch omelet pan, preferably nonstick, melt the butter until the foam subsides. In a medium bowl, combine the eggs and milk and season with salt and pepper. Add the eggs to the pan and cook over high heat without stirring until the edges set. Lower the heat to moderate and lift the sides of the eggs, tilting the skillet to let the uncooked eggs spread underneath. Cook until the bottom is golden and the top is still slightly runny, about 3 minutes.
4. Spoon ½ cup of the *pico de gallo* on top of the eggs and sprinkle with the cheese and scallions. Set the pan under the broiler and broil until the top is set and the cheese is melted. Slide the frittata onto a large plate and cut into wedges. Serve the remaining *pico de gallo* alongside.—SARDY HOUSE HOTEL & RESTAURANT, ASPEN, COLORADO

PUERTO RICAN VEGETABLE OMELET

If you like, you can use a seven-inch pan to make individual omelets. If you're doubling the recipe, cook two large or four small omelets rather than trying to assemble one very big one.

2 SERVINGS

1 small red potato, peeled and cut into ¼-inch dice
⅓ small chayote, peeled and cut into ¼-by-1½-inch matchsticks
1 teaspoon extra-virgin olive oil
¼ small red onion, thinly sliced
¼ small red bell pepper, cut into ¼-by-1½-inch matchsticks
1 garlic clove, minced
Salt and freshly ground pepper
1 teaspoon finely chopped fresh flat-leaf parsley
1 teaspoon minced fresh cilantro
2 teaspoons unsalted butter

4 large eggs, lightly beaten
¼ cup heavy cream

1. In a small pan of boiling water, cook the potato and chayote until just tender, about 4 minutes. Drain and transfer to a plate.
2. Heat the oil in a small skillet. Add the onion and red pepper and cook over moderately high heat, stirring, until wilted, about 2 minutes. Add the potato, chayote and garlic, season with salt and pepper and cook for 1 minute. Stir in the parsley and cilantro, cover and keep warm.
3. In a 10-inch omelet pan, preferably nonstick, melt the butter until the foam subsides; tilt the pan to coat the bottom and sides. In a bowl, combine the eggs and cream, and season with salt and pepper. Add the eggs to the pan and cook over high heat without stirring just until the edges set. Lower the heat to moderate and lift the sides of the eggs, tilting the pan to let the uncooked eggs spread underneath. Cook until the bottom is browned and the top is still slightly runny, about 2 minutes.
4. Spread the vegetables on top of the eggs. Tilt the pan and fold over one-third of the omelet to partially cover the vegetables. Roll the omelet onto a cutting board, flipping it over itself. Cut the omelet in half and serve on warmed plates.—HORNED DORSET PRIMAVERA HOTEL, PUERTO RICO

POTATO PIE

The rich pastry, chock-full of bacon, eggs and potatoes, makes a satisfying main course when served with a green salad. Allow enough time to refrigerate the pastry overnight.

This hearty pie needs only a light, fruity tart red for contrast. Beaujolais would be perfect; look for the 1994 Château de la Chaize Brouilly or 1995 Georges Duboeuf Beaujolais Nouveau.

6 SERVINGS

PASTRY:

1¾ cups all-purpose flour, sifted
¾ teaspoon salt
1 stick plus 1 tablespoon (4½ ounces) unsalted butter, cut into pieces
1 large egg yolk, beaten with enough water to make ¼ cup

FILLING:

8 slices of bacon (5 ounces), cut crosswise into ¼-inch pieces
1¼ pounds all-purpose potatoes
¼ cup finely chopped fresh flat-leaf parsley
Salt and freshly ground pepper
5 hard-cooked eggs, thinly sliced
½ cup crème fraîche or heavy cream
1 large egg beaten with 2 tablespoons cold water, for egg wash

1. Make the pastry: In a medium bowl, combine the flour and salt. Using your fingertips, rub the butter into the flour until it resembles coarse meal. Make a well in the center, pour in the beaten yolk mixture and stir until just moistened. Gather the dough into a ball. Working quickly, roll out the dough on a lightly floured surface into a 12-by-6-inch rectangle. Starting at a short end, fold the dough in thirds, forming a 4-by-6-inch rectangle. Wrap the rectangle in plastic and refrigerate it overnight. Remove the dough from the

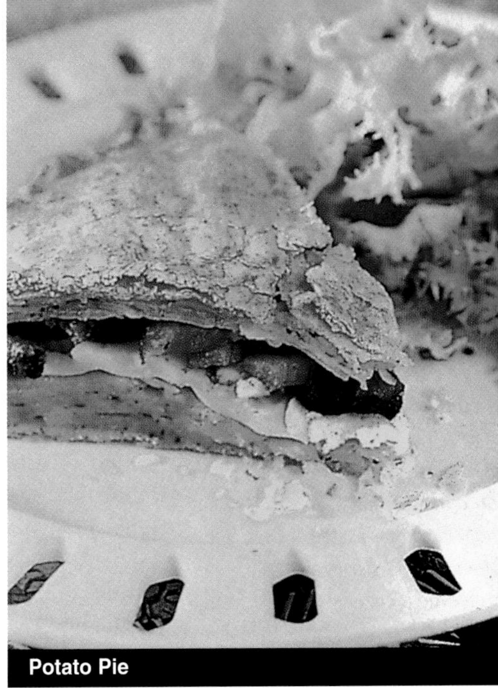
Potato Pie

refrigerator 15 minutes before rolling it out to soften slightly.
2. Halve the dough. On a lightly floured surface, roll out one piece into a 12-inch round. Place the dough in a 9-inch pie plate without stretching. Do not trim the overhanging pastry. Roll out the second piece of dough into a 10-inch round and transfer the round to a parchment-lined baking sheet. Refrigerate the pastry for 10 minutes.
3. Make the filling: Preheat the oven to 400°. In a small skillet, cook the bacon over moderately high heat until softened and just beginning to brown, about 2 minutes. Transfer the bacon to paper towels to drain.
4. Peel the potatoes and slice them ⅛ inch thick. Rinse the potato slices in cold water, drain and pat dry. In a medium bowl, toss the potato slices with the

parsley; season the potatoes with salt and pepper.

5. Arrange half the potato slices in an even layer in the bottom of the prepared pie shell. Sprinkle the bacon on top and cover with the sliced eggs. Spread the crème fraîche over the eggs. Top with the remaining potato slices.

6. Brush the overhanging edge of pastry with some of the egg wash. Place the top crust over the filling. Trim the pastry so it's even all around, then crimp the edges together to seal. Pierce the top crust to make three or four small vents. Brush the pie with some of the egg wash.

7. Bake the pie in the middle of the oven for 20 minutes. Lower the temperature to 350° and bake the pie for 1 hour, covering the edges with foil when brown. Lower the oven temperature to 300°, remove the foil and bake the pie for 10 minutes longer. Allow the pie to rest for 10 minutes before serving. (**MAKE AHEAD:** The potato pie can be baked up to 1 day ahead; reheat in a warm oven.) —ANDRÉ SOLTNER

WILD-MUSHROOM MATZO BREI

The Lobster Club in Manhattan serves this traditional Passover dish year-round.

4–6 SERVINGS

- 1 stick unsalted butter
- 1 pound Spanish onions, minced
- ¾ pound wild mushrooms, sliced
- 2 tablespoons vegetable oil
- Salt and pepper
- 6 unsalted matzos
- 6 large eggs, beaten with ½ cup milk
- ¼ cup chopped parsley

1. Melt half the butter in a large skillet. Add the onions and cook slowly until caramelized, about 20 minutes. Remove the onions. Sauté the mushrooms in the oil and season with salt and pepper; add them to the onions.

2. Soak the matzos in warm water for 30 seconds, then crumble them into the egg mixture. Add the onions and mushrooms. Season with salt and pepper.

3. Heat the remaining butter in the skillet. Add the matzo mixture and stir over moderately high heat until the eggs set, about 5 minutes. Sprinkle with the parsley and serve.—THE LOBSTER CLUB, NEW YORK CITY

TORTILLA TOMATILLO CASSEROLE WITH CHEESE

8 SERVINGS

- 1 tablespoon olive oil
- ½ pound fresh shiitake mushrooms, stemmed and sliced ¼ inch thick
- 1½ cups fresh or thawed frozen corn kernels
- 10 ounces fresh small spinach leaves, washed but not dried
- Salt
- ½ cup vegetable oil
- 16 corn tortillas, preferably slightly stale, halved
- 5 cups Roasted-Tomatillo Chipotle Salsa (p. 356)

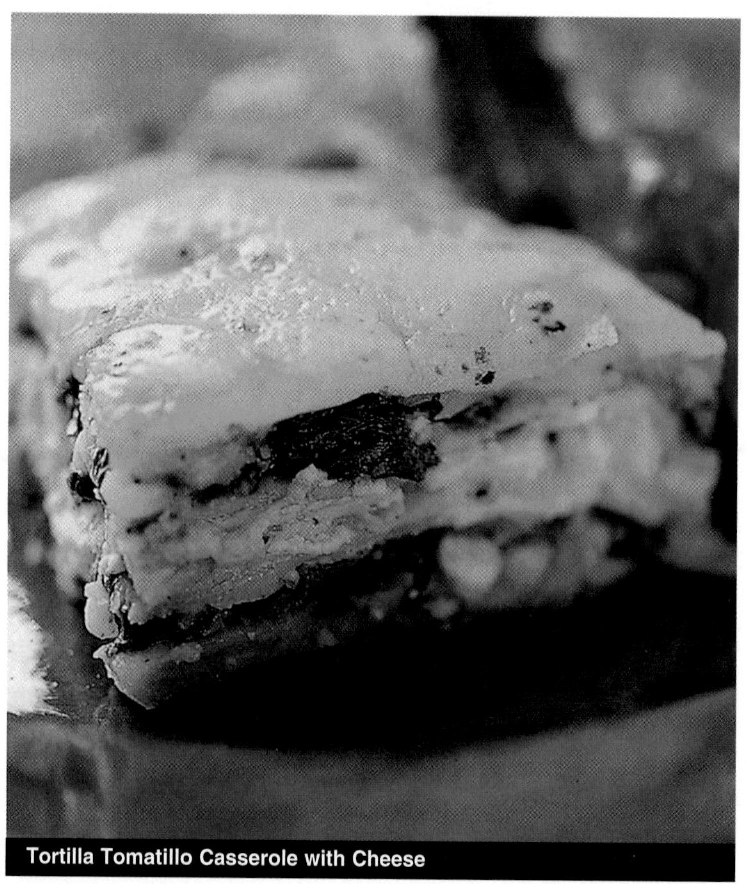

Tortilla Tomatillo Casserole with Cheese

1 cup heavy cream or plain yogurt
¾ pound shredded mild melting cheese, such as Monterey Jack (about 3 cups)
15 to 16 ounces ricotta cheese
About ⅓ cup coarsely chopped fresh cilantro, for garnish

1. Heat the olive oil in a large skillet or enameled cast-iron casserole. Add the mushrooms; sauté over moderate heat until almost tender, about 3 minutes. Add the corn and sauté for 2 minutes. Transfer to a large plate to cool.
2. Add the spinach, with the water that clings to the leaves, to the skillet and cook over moderate heat, stirring constantly, until wilted, 1 to 2 minutes. Transfer to a colander and press out the extra liquid, then add to the mushrooms and corn. Season with salt.
3. In a small skillet, heat the vegetable oil over moderate heat. Fry the tortillas one at a time, turning once, just until softened, a few seconds per side. Drain in a single layer on a paper-towel-lined baking sheet, blotting dry with additional paper towels.
4. Preheat the oven to 350°. Lightly butter a 13-by-9-inch nonreactive baking dish. Mix the salsa with the cream in a bowl and spread 1 scant cup in the prepared dish. Arrange 8 tortilla halves in a single layer on the salsa. Top with half of the vegetables, 1½ cups of the salsa mixture, 1 cup of the melting cheese and eight tortilla halves. Spread the ricotta on the tortillas and cover with 1½ cups of the salsa mixture. Top with eight tortilla halves, the remaining vegetables, 1½ cups of the salsa mixture and 1 cup of the cheese. Finish with the remaining eight tortilla halves, salsa and cheese.
5. Cover the dish loosely with foil and bake for 25 minutes. Uncover and bake for about 25 minutes longer, or until bubbling and lightly browned. Let stand for at least 10 minutes. (MAKE AHEAD: The casserole can be refrigerated for up to 1 day. Rewarm in a 350° oven before serving.) Sprinkle with the cilantro and serve.—RICK BAYLESS

TOMATILLOS

Small, round and pale green, tomatillos look like cherry tomatoes in a parchment wrapping. They're widely available fresh. Choose little tomatillos, which are sweeter than the larger, golf-ball-size ones. They keep well for several weeks in the vegetable bin of your refrigerator. If canned ones are all you can find, an eleven-ounce can equals one pound of fresh.

GRILLED HERBED VEGETABLES WITH GOAT-CHEESE SAUCE Q

Here's a light supper of grilled vegetables and country bread with a creamy goat-cheese sauce. For a more substantial meal, add some spicy sausages to the grill. A bowl of fresh cherries makes the perfect dessert.

To echo the dominant flavors of vegetables and goat cheese, look for a Sauvignon Blanc with strong varietal character, such as the 1994 Sterling or Silverado, both from California.

Grilled Herbed Vegetables with Goat-Cheese Sauce

4 SERVINGS

1 small eggplant, sliced lengthwise ¼ inch thick
2 medium zucchini, sliced lengthwise ¼ inch thick
2 medium yellow squash, sliced lengthwise ¼ inch thick
3 tablespoons olive oil, plus more for brushing
Salt and freshly ground pepper
2 tablespoons minced fresh basil
2 teaspoons minced fresh oregano
1 teaspoon minced fresh tarragon
4 small tomatoes, halved crosswise
1 medium red onion, cut crosswise into 4 slices
3 medium bell peppers, preferably 1 each red, yellow and purple, quartered lengthwise and seeded
4 thick slices of country bread
⅔ cup heavy cream
1 medium garlic clove, finely chopped
4½ ounces mild goat cheese, crumbled

1. Light a grill or preheat the broiler. Combine the eggplant, zucchini and yellow squash in a large shallow bowl. Add the 3 tablespoons oil and toss to coat, then season the vegetables with salt and pepper. In a small bowl, mix the basil with the oregano and tarragon and toss all but 1½ teaspoons with the vegetables. Brush the cut sides of the tomatoes and the red onion with oil and season with salt and pepper.

2. Grill the peppers, skin-side down, for about 12 minutes, or until charred. Grill the eggplant, zucchini, yellow squash and onion, turning once or twice, until tender: about 5 minutes for the zucchini and squash, about 6 minutes for the onion and 8 to 10 minutes for the eggplant. Grill the tomatoes, starting cut-side down and turning once, for about 5 minutes, until slightly softened. Lightly brush the bread with oil and grill until toasted. Peel the peppers. Arrange all the grilled vegetables on a platter or large plates. Keep warm in a low oven.

3. In a small nonreactive saucepan, bring the cream and garlic to a simmer over low heat; simmer the mixture for 5 minutes. Whisk in the goat cheese until the sauce is smooth and season with pepper. Spoon the sauce over the grilled vegetables, sprinkle with the remaining 1½ teaspoons minced herbs and serve with the grilled bread.—JUDITH SUTTON

ROASTED-VEGETABLE TARTS Q

Whether your supermarket resembles a chichi gourmet shop or a corner deli, you can easily find what you need for this dish: It uses ordinary items, but in a not-so-ordinary way. The ready-to-use pie crusts called for here are so buttery and flaky that nearly everyone on our staff thought they were homemade.

Match the earthy tastes here with an herbal Australian Cabernet Sauvignon like the 1993 Hardys Coonawarra or the 1992 Chateau Tahbilk.

6 SERVINGS

- 1 medium eggplant (about 12 ounces), sliced ¼ inch thick
- 2 medium Portobello mushrooms, caps only, sliced ¼ inch thick
- 2 medium shallots, thinly sliced
- 1 medium red bell pepper, cut into ½-inch dice
- 1 medium zucchini, sliced crosswise ¼ inch thick
- 2 tablespoons olive oil
- Salt and freshly ground pepper
- 4 ounces Roquefort or other blue cheese, crumbled
- 3 ounces cream cheese, softened
- 1 large egg
- 1 tablespoon freshly grated Parmesan cheese
- 2 prepared pie crusts, not in tins (15-ounce package)

1. Place racks in the upper and lower thirds of the oven and preheat to 450°. Line two baking sheets with foil.

2. In a large roasting pan, toss the eggplant, mushrooms, shallots, red bell pepper and zucchini with the olive oil and salt and pepper to taste. Roast the vegetables for 12 to 14 minutes, stirring once or twice, until softened.

3. Using a handheld electric mixer, beat the Roquefort and the cream cheese together until smooth. Add the egg and Parmesan; beat until blended.

Roasted-Vegetable Tart

4. Place one pie crust on each baking sheet, unfold and pinch together any tears. Divide the cheese mixture between the crusts and spread it out, leaving a 2-inch border of dough. Arrange the roasted vegetables on top. Fold the dough up to partially cover the filling, crimping to seal the edges. Bake for 20 to 25 minutes, or until golden, reversing the pans halfway through cooking. Serve warm.—GRACE PARISI

FRIED TOFU WITH MUSHROOM GRAVY

Mushrooms marry well with tofu, and oyster sauce provides a mellow base to this dish. Serve it as part of a vegetarian meal with sautéed greens and steamed medium-grain rice.

4 SERVINGS

- 1½ tablespoons peanut oil
- 12 ounces fresh shiitake mushrooms, stems discarded and caps thinly sliced
- 2 tablespoons soy sauce
- 2 large garlic cloves, thinly sliced
- 1 small onion, finely chopped
- 2 tablespoons dry white wine
- ¼ cup oyster sauce
- 1 teaspoon cornstarch
- ¼ teaspoon Asian sesame oil
- Freshly ground pepper
- 2 cups vegetable oil, for frying
- 1½ pounds soft tofu, cut crosswise into 12 slices

1. In a large nonreactive skillet, heat 1 tablespoon of the peanut oil over high heat. Add the mushrooms in an even layer and cook, turning once, until browned, about 3 minutes on each side. Add 1 tablespoon of the soy sauce, toss to coat and cook for 2 minutes longer. Transfer the mushrooms to a plate.

2. Reduce the heat to low and add the remaining ½ tablespoon peanut oil to the skillet. Add the garlic slices in an even layer and cook until golden brown, about 3 minutes. Increase the heat to moderate, add the onion and cook, stirring, until wilted, about 3 minutes.

3. Add the wine and scrape the bottom of the pan to loosen the browned bits. Add the oyster sauce and the remaining 1 tablespoon soy sauce and bring to a simmer.

4. Meanwhile, dissolve the cornstarch in 1 cup of water and stir it into the sauce in the skillet. Return the mushrooms to the skillet and simmer the sauce until it is thickened, about 4 minutes. Stir in the sesame oil and season the sauce with freshly ground pepper. Remove from the heat.

5. In a medium saucepan, heat the vegetable oil over moderately high heat until it registers 360° on a deep-fry thermometer. Gently pat the tofu dry with paper towels and carefully lower four slices into the hot oil. Stand back—the oil may spatter. Fry the tofu until golden brown, gently scraping it off the bottom of the pan with a slotted spatula if it seems to be sticking, about 4 minutes. Using the spatula, transfer the tofu to a baking sheet. Pat with paper towels to remove excess oil, and keep warm in a low oven. Repeat with the remaining tofu slices.

6. Rewarm the mushroom gravy over moderately high heat, stirring. Pour the gravy onto a platter, arrange the tofu slices on top and serve at once.—MARCIA KIESEL

QUICK DINNER

ROASTED-VEGETABLE TARTS (P. 284)

MESCLUN WITH SUN-DRIED-TOMATO VINAIGRETTE (P. 58)

ITALIAN PLUM BETTY (P. 420)

GAME PLAN:

- **Preheat the oven.**
- **Cut up the vegetables and roast them while you prepare the tarts.**
- **While the tarts bake, make the dressing. Assemble the dessert.**
- **Put the dessert in the oven when the vegetable tarts are done.**

CHAPTER 12

~

YEAST BREADS, QUICK BREADS & SANDWICHES

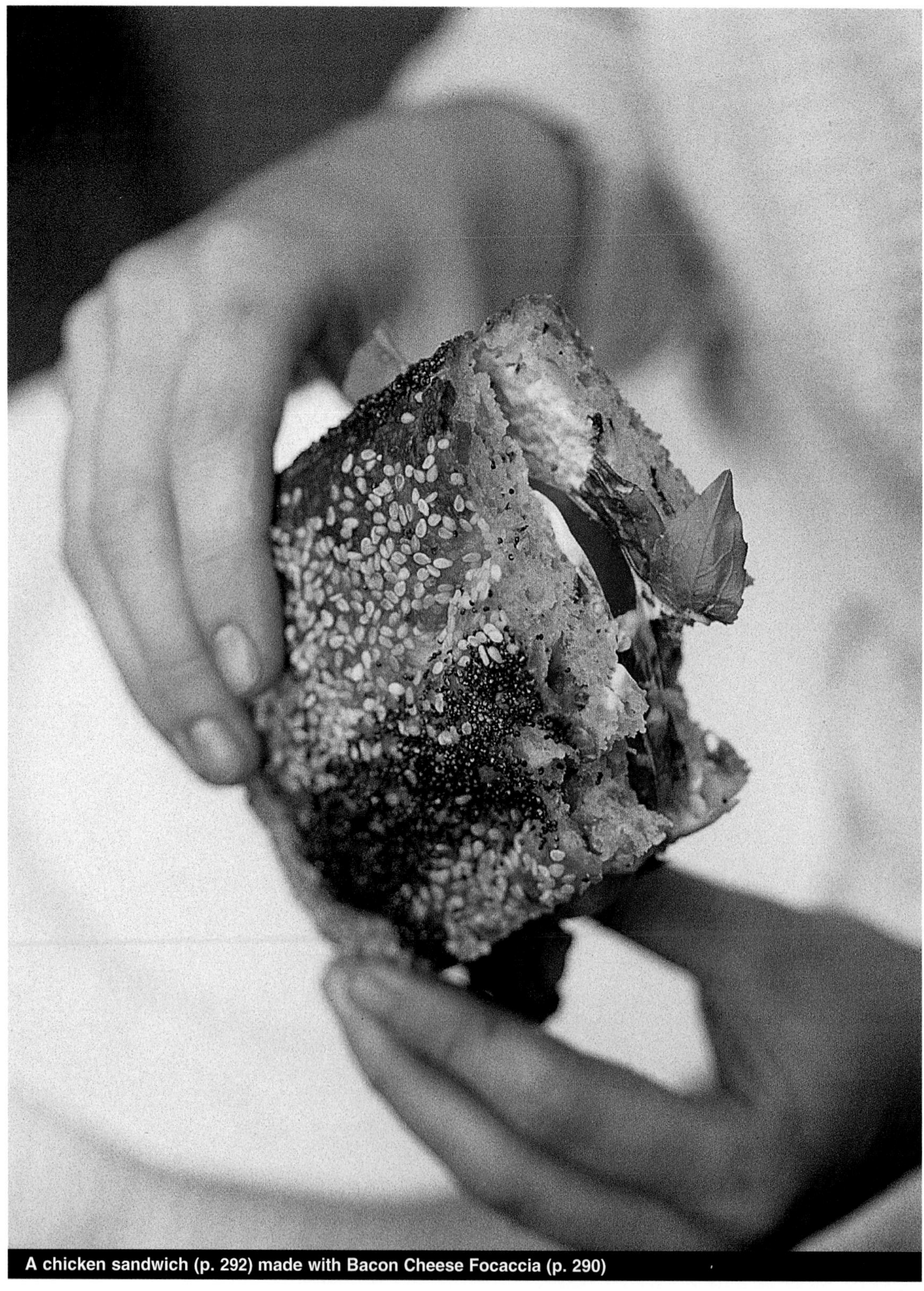

A chicken sandwich (p. 292) made with Bacon Cheese Focaccia (p. 290)

BASIC HERB FOCACCIA

Focaccia, the rustic Italian flat bread that's crusty outside and chewy inside, has taken America by storm. The best news is that it's easy and fun to make at home. All you need is a willingness to dig your hands into the dough and the patience to let it rise. Here's one basic dough with three variations.

MAKES A 17-BY-13-INCH FOCACCIA

- 3 tablespoons extra-virgin olive oil, plus more for brushing
- 1 cup (packed) minced yellow onion
- 2 medium garlic cloves, minced
- ¼ cup finely chopped fresh basil
- 1 tablespoon minced fresh thyme
- 2 teaspoons minced fresh rosemary
- Freshly ground pepper
- 1½ cups lukewarm water (105° to 115°)
- 1 cup lukewarm milk (105° to 115°)
- 1 scant tablespoon table salt
- 2 teaspoons plus a pinch of sugar
- One ¼-ounce envelope active dry yeast
- About 6½ cups bread flour
- Cornmeal, for dusting
- Coarse salt, for sprinkling
- ¼ cup ice water

***Clockwise from left*: Olive Onion Focaccia (p. 290), Bacon Cheese Focaccia (p. 290) and Parmesan Pine-Nut Focaccia (p. 291)**

1. Heat the oil in a medium skillet over moderate heat. Stir in the onion and garlic, reduce the heat to low and cook until softened and fragrant, about 3 minutes. Add the herbs and a generous amount of pepper and cook for 1 minute. Transfer the mixture to a large bowl. Stir in 1 cup of the water, then the milk, table salt and 2 teaspoons sugar.

2. In a small bowl, dissolve the yeast and the pinch of sugar in the remaining ½ cup lukewarm water until creamy and starting to bubble. Add to the onion mixture. Stir in the flour, 1 cup at a time, just until the dough becomes too stiff to stir. Turn out the dough onto a lightly floured work surface. With the help of a dough scraper, knead in only as much additional flour as is necessary to keep the dough from sticking. Knead the dough until smooth, supple and elastic, about 5 minutes.

3. Generously grease a clean large bowl with olive oil. Transfer the dough to the bowl and turn to coat with oil. Cover the bowl with plastic wrap and a kitchen towel. If desired, label the bowl to remind you when to punch down and shape the dough. Set aside in a warm draft-free spot until the dough is doubled in bulk, about 2 hours.

4. Punch down the dough. Recover the bowl and let the dough rise again until doubled in bulk, about 1 hour.

5. Brush olive oil over the bottom and sides of a 17-by-13-by-1-inch black steel or heavy aluminum baking sheet. Sprinkle cornmeal on the baking sheet, then tap out any excess.

6. Punch down the dough and turn it out onto a cornmeal-dusted work surface. Turn the dough over and over to coat lightly with cornmeal and shape into a rough rectangle. Lift the dough and place in the prepared baking sheet. Gently pull, push and pat the dough so that it fills the baking sheet. Let the dough rise uncovered in a draft-free spot until billowy, 45 minutes to 1 hour.

7. Preheat the oven to 450° and position a rack in the bottom third. If using a baking stone or tiles, place on the rack and heat for 30 minutes.

8. Dip your fingers in flour and make many deep indentations in the dough. Brush lightly with oil and sprinkle with coarse salt.

9. Place the baking sheet in the oven, toss the ice water on the oven floor and bake the focaccia for about 30 minutes, until the edges are crisp and a deep golden color. Using a long metal spatula, slide the focaccia onto a large rack to cool. To serve, cut into pieces with a serrated knife.

Olive Onion Focaccia

FOR THE DOUGH:

- 1/3 cup chopped pitted black oil-cured olives (about 24)

FOR THE TOPPING:

- 1/4 cup extra-virgin olive oil
- 1 large or 2 medium yellow onions, cut into thin wedges and separated into strips (3 cups)
- 2 large garlic cloves, thinly sliced
- 1 tablespoon finely chopped mixed fresh herbs
- Coarse salt and freshly ground pepper
- 12 oil-cured olives, halved and pitted

1. Make the dough: Follow the recipe for Basic Herb Focaccia through Step 7, with this change: Stir in the olives when you add the herbs in Step 1.

2. Meanwhile, **for the topping:** Heat a large, deep skillet over moderate heat. Add the oil and onions, reduce the heat to low and cook until the onions are slightly softened, about 3 minutes. Add the garlic and cook until softened but not brown, about 3 minutes more. Add the mixed herbs, season with coarse salt and pepper and cook for 1 minute. Set aside to cool.

3. Spread the onion topping over the dough, leaving a 1-inch border. Dip your fingers in flour and make many indentations through the topping. Arrange the olive halves decoratively on the dough and sprinkle coarse salt evenly all over the top. Bake according to Step 9 above.

Bacon Cheese Focaccia

FOR THE DOUGH:

- 1 pound 1/4-inch-thick lean bacon slices, cut into 1/4-inch dice
- 1 1/2 cups finely shredded Jarlsberg cheese (about 6 ounces)
- Olive oil and cornmeal, for the baking sheet

FOR THE TOPPING:

- 1 large egg white, lightly beaten with 1 teaspoon water
- 2 tablespoons poppy seeds or sesame seeds or a combination
- Melted unsalted butter or olive oil, for brushing
- Coarse salt, for sprinkling

1. Make the dough: Follow the recipe for Basic Herb Focaccia through Step 3. While the dough rises, cook the diced bacon in a

Q & A: STORING FOCACCIA

Q: How should I store and reheat baked focaccia?

A: Because the focaccia here contain ingredients like onions, bacon and cheese, which can spoil, I refrigerate or freeze them.

• To refrigerate focaccia, make sure it's completely cool, then wrap it snugly in foil or plastic wrap. Place the bread in a plastic bag and seal and refrigerate for up to two days.

• You can freeze baked focaccia for up to one month. For extra protection, place the wrapped bread in a heavy-duty freezer bag before placing it in the freezer. To thaw the bread, let it sit in its wrapping at room temperature overnight.

• Whether refrigerated or frozen, focaccia should be reheated to refresh it and restore its crisp exterior. Toast pieces in a toaster oven or place the focaccia whole on a wire rack in a shallow baking sheet and heat it in a 400° oven for five minutes. Then turn off the heat and let the bread sit for about ten minutes until it's crisp but not dry.—LAUREN GROVEMAN

medium saucepan over moderately high heat, stirring, until crisp, about 10 minutes. Using a slotted spoon, transfer the bacon to paper towels to drain. Let the bacon cool.

2. Punch down the dough, turn out onto a work surface and knead in the bacon and cheese, distributing them evenly. Return the dough to the bowl, re-cover and let rise again until doubled, about 1 hour.

3. Brush olive oil over the bottom and sides of a 17-by-13-by-1-inch black steel or heavy aluminum baking sheet. Line the bottom of the baking sheet with parchment paper. Brush the paper with more olive oil and sprinkle the baking sheet with cornmeal, tapping out any excess.

4. For the topping: Proceed with Step 6 of the Basic Herb Focaccia recipe, but before you set aside the dough to rise, gently brush the top with the egg white and sprinkle with the seeds.

5. Preheat the oven as directed in Step 7 above. Gently brush the risen dough with enough melted butter or olive oil to coat lightly. Dip your fingers in flour and make many indentations in the dough. Sprinkle the coarse salt on top. Bake according to Step 9.

Parmesan Pine-Nut Focaccia

FOR THE DOUGH:

½ cup pine nuts (about 3 ounces)
1 cup freshly grated Parmesan cheese

FOR THE TOPPING:

¼ cup olive oil, plus more for brushing
2 cups finely chopped onion
4 large garlic cloves, minced
½ teaspoon dried oregano
Freshly ground pepper
Coarse salt, for sprinkling
½ cup freshly grated Parmesan cheese

1. Make the dough: Follow the recipe for Basic Herb Focaccia through Step 3. While the dough rises, preheat the oven to 350°. Toast the pine nuts on a baking sheet for about 7 minutes, until golden. Let cool.

2. Punch down the dough, turn it out onto a work surface and knead in the nuts and the Parmesan, distributing them evenly. Return the dough to the bowl, re-cover and let rise again until doubled, about 1 hour.

3. Meanwhile, **for the topping**: In a medium skillet, heat the ¼ cup olive oil. Add the onion and the garlic and cook over moderately high heat for about 5 minutes. Season with the oregano and the pepper. Let cool.

4. Proceed with Steps 5 and 6 of the Basic Herb Focaccia recipe, but before you let the dough rise, gently brush it with enough olive oil to coat lightly. Spread the onion mixture on top, leaving a 1-inch border.

5. Preheat the oven as directed in Step 7 of the Basic Herb Focaccia recipe. Dip your fingers in flour and make many indentations in the dough. Sprinkle pepper and coarse salt on top. Proceed with Step 9, but bake the dough for 25 minutes; sprinkle the Parmesan on top and bake the focaccia until it is golden, about 10 minutes longer.—LAUREN GROVEMAN ➤

Q & A: BAKING FOCACCIA

Q: What's the best pan to use for baking focaccia?

A: A shallow baking sheet, preferably one made of black steel, which encourages good browning. Very heavy aluminum also works well. If you use a more reflective material, such as stainless steel, you may need to bake the bread longer to achieve the desired color and crispness. Because focaccias are baked at high temperatures, avoid using nonstick or flimsy baking sheets, which are weaker and could buckle in a very hot oven.

Q: Will using baking tiles or a baking stone in the oven make a significant difference?

A: Yes, it will make a difference. The crust of the focaccia will be especially crisp if it is baked in a baking sheet that sits on baking tiles or a baking stone. Baking tiles are unglazed terracotta squares that fit into a baking sheet, which is then placed on a rack in the oven. A baking, or pizza, stone is a heavy unglazed slab that rests on a rack or on the floor of the oven. I prefer baking tiles for all of my breads because their dark color encourages heat retention, which in turn promotes a crisper exterior.—LAUREN GROVEMAN

BREAD-MACHINE FOCACCIA

I started making this rosemary focaccia years ago at the beginning of the bread-machine craze. Since I don't like the feeling of flour on my hands—too powdery and drying—making the focaccia dough in a bread machine set me free.

MAKES TWO 9-INCH ROUNDS

One ¼-ounce envelope active dry yeast
3 cups bread flour
1 teaspoon sugar
¾ teaspoon salt
1 cup plus 3 tablespoons lukewarm water (105° to 115°)
3 tablespoons extra-virgin olive oil
1 tablespoon coarse salt
Leaves from 2 fresh rosemary sprigs

SANDWICHES

Focaccia is perfect for toppings and fillings. Here are three tasty alternatives.

• Chicken, tomato, arugula, basil and mayonnaise on Bacon Cheese Focaccia (p. 290).

• Broiled Portobello mushrooms, oven-dried tomatoes, fresh mozzarella (melted under the broiler), basil and freshly ground black pepper on Parmesan Pine-Nut Focaccia (p. 291).

• Oil-marinated roasted yellow, green and red bell peppers with capers, basil and Parmesan cheese on Parmesan Pine-Nut Focaccia (p. 291).—LAUREN GROVEMAN

1. In the order suggested by your bread-machine manufacturer, combine the yeast, flour, sugar, salt and lukewarm water in the container of your machine. Set the machine on the dough cycle and, if you have the capability, the French-bread or white-bread mode. Close the cover and let the machine do its thing.

2. When the dough is ready and the machine signals the end of the cycle, transfer the dough to a lightly floured surface and divide it in half. Shape each half into a rounded disk and transfer the disks to one large or two small baking sheets. Cover with plastic wrap and set aside to rise until doubled in bulk, usually 45 minutes to 1 hour. (Don't worry if it takes as long as 2 hours.)

3. Punch down the disks and spread out each one into an 8- to 9-inch round about ½ inch thick. Use your knuckles to dimple the top of the dough. Cover and set aside until the dough is risen and puffy, about 45 minutes; again, up to 2 hours is fine.

4. Preheat the oven to 425°. Just before baking, use your knuckles to dimple the surface of each focaccia again. Drizzle the oil over the rounds and spread it into the dimples with the back of a spoon. Sprinkle the focaccia with the coarse salt, and scatter the rosemary leaves on top.

5. Bake the focaccia in the top third of the oven for about 18 minutes, or until the tops are golden and the bottoms are lightly browned and crisp. Transfer to a wire rack. Cut into wedges and serve at once, or let cool and wrap for later.—MARDEE HAIDIN REGAN

PERFECT SANDWICH BREAD

It's just about impossible where I live to buy a loaf of sturdy white sandwich bread that will hold a filling without disintegrating. When I want white bread for eating, toasting or making fancy sandwiches, I bake my own, and I start it out in the bread machine. Using the machine as a tool to make the dough is the way to go, I think, because the mixing and initial kneading are so easily and neatly done. My machine calls for loading the liquids first, followed by the dry ingredients. Adapt the procedures for your own machine.

MAKES ONE 10-BY-4½-BY-4-INCH LOAF

1½ cups cold milk
4 tablespoons unsalted butter (sliced thin)
½ cup Optional Starter (recipe follows)
2 teaspoons salt
½ teaspoon sugar
3½ cups unbleached bread flour or unbleached all-purpose flour, plus more if needed
1 teaspoon active dry yeast if using the starter and 2 teaspoons if not

Optional starter: I like to include a bit of starter (also known as a sponge, *poulish* or *biga*) in my white sandwich-bread dough since I think it gives a superior flavor and texture and improves the loaf's keeping qualities. This is a simple batter of flour, water and yeast that has been allowed to rise and bubble for several hours. To make it, whisk ½ cup of tepid water (105° to 110°) with ½ teaspoon active dry yeast and 1 cup all-purpose flour or bread flour in a bowl. Cover with plastic wrap and leave it at cool room temperature for several hours or overnight. It will rise and form big bubbles and then sink down, at which time it is ready to use. You can also cover the starter and refrigerate it for several days.

The bread pan: An ideal loaf of sandwich bread is a perfect rectangle. You must pack the dough into a covered pan to prevent it from humping up in the usual loaf shape. I use an almost straight-sided 2-quart loaf pan, 10-by-4½-by-4 inches. You'll need to butter or spray the inside of the bread pan and the shiny side of a 12-by-8-inch piece of aluminum foil. I top the bread pan with a baking sheet held down with a 5-pound ovenproof weight of some sort, like a brick or a stone—it's always surprising how much push is in a yeast-powered dough!

Mixing the dough: Remove the container from the bread machine. Pour ½ cup of the milk into a small saucepan and add the butter. Swirl the pan over moderate heat only until the butter has almost melted. Remove from the heat and cool the liquid by pouring in the remaining 1 cup of milk. If you are using the starter, stir ½ cup of it into the liquid; it will not break up completely. Pour the liquid (with or without the starter) into the container and, without stirring, add the salt, sugar and flour. Then make an indentation the size of a soup spoon in the flour and add the yeast. Replace the container securely and set the machine at least 1 foot from the edge of the counter. (Machines can walk when the kneading is vigorous—mine did.) Program for "dough" and start the machine. After 10 minutes of kneading, check the dough. If it feels wet and sticky, keep the machine running and sprinkle in a tablespoon or two of flour; if dry, add drops of water. When the cycle ends, after about 1 hour and 45 minutes, the risen dough will have been deflated by the machine.

Second kneading and rise: Remove the dough from the container and give it a vigorous 1 minute of kneading on a lightly floured work surface. You should have a smooth, supple dough. Return the dough to the machine for its second rise. In 1 to 1½ hours, it should have risen to the top of the container again; a slight overrise will not hurt it.

Forming the dough: Transfer the risen dough to your lightly floured work surface. With lightly floured hands, firmly press and pat the dough into a 10-inch rectangle with the ends to your left and right. With the side of your hand, firmly press a lengthwise trench along the center of the dough and fold it in half, bringing the top long edge down to meet the bottom. Press firmly to seal the edges. Rotate the dough, seal-side up, and repeat the process. Transfer the dough, seal-side down, to the prepared bread pan.

Final rise: Drape a lightly floured towel over the pan. Let the dough rise at 72° to 75° until the pan is four-fifths filled; this should take no more than an hour. Meanwhile, preheat your oven to 425° and set a rack in the lower third of it.

For baking: Lay the aluminum foil, buttered side down, over the bread pan and place the baking sheet on top of it. Set the bread pan in the oven and center the weight on the baking sheet. Bake for about 35 minutes, checking several times to be sure that the

VARIATIONS

Here are three ways to make Perfect Sandwich Bread.

BY-HAND VARIATION. You can, of course, make the bread entirely by hand, or you can use a heavy-duty mixer to mix and knead the dough. If you are doing it by hand, let the dough double in bulk at both the first and second risings.

OPEN-PAN VARIATION. For a traditional humped American loaf of white bread, let the dough fill the pan completely during the final rise. Bake the bread uncovered in the preheated 425° oven for about twenty minutes, or until puffed and browned. Cover the loaf loosely with foil, reduce the heat to 375° and bake for twenty to thirty minutes.

CURRANT-BREAD VARIATION. This recipe for sandwich bread also makes delicious currant bread, and I particularly like it baked in a closed pan. Follow the same procedure, but knead one-and-a-half cups of currants into the dough by hand, following the first rise. The second rise will go a little faster because of the sugar content of the currants.—JULIA CHILD

rising dough has not dislodged the weight.

When is it done?: To test, rapidly remove the pan and close the oven door. Turn the loaf out onto your work surface. The bread should come out of the pan easily and be lightly browned all over. It's very important to note that the thump method is not a dependable test. Poke an instant-read thermometer into the center of the loaf through the underside and let the mercury climb. If it reaches just over 200° to about 210°, the bread is done. If not, return the bread to the pan and bake another 10 minutes or so.

Cooling and storing: Set the loaf on a rack on its side and let cool thoroughly, about 2 hours. Bag it in plastic. Its flavor and texture will improve after 24 hours, and if you plan to slice it very thin, give it a 2-day wait. Freeze the bread for longer storage.—JULIA CHILD

BUTTER

A thick slice of freshly baked crusty bread just begs to be spread with delicious butter. Whether mass-produced or hand-crafted, butter appears in several forms at the market. Here is a rundown of common types.

SALTED BUTTER, the most popular kind in the United States, is made from milk, cream or both with no less than eighty percent butterfat. Sometimes only the ingredient list, not the label, reveals that the butter is salted.

UNSALTED or SWEET BUTTER is the same as the above, without salt.

CULTURED BUTTER is made from cream to which lactic-acid cultures have been added. The mild fermentation that results produces a richer, more developed flavor. Imported brands of butter are usually cultured.—FLORENCE FABRICANT

WHEAT AND POLENTA BREAD

I am always searching for new flavors for my breads. One day I had polenta on my mind and created this loaf, which is pleasantly corn-rich but not heavy, as many corn breads can be.

MAKES TWO 2-POUND LOAVES

1 teaspoon active dry yeast
1 teaspoon sugar
¾ cup lukewarm milk (105° to 115°)
1 tablespoon plus 1 teaspoon fine sea salt
1 tablespoon extra-virgin olive oil
2¼ cups lukewarm water (105° to 115°)
About 6 cups bread flour
2 cups polenta (not instant)
Coarsely ground cornmeal, for sprinkling

1. In the bowl of a standing mixer fitted with the paddle, combine the yeast, sugar and milk. Let stand until foamy, about 5 minutes.

2. Add the salt, oil and water and mix at low speed for 1 minute. Gradually add about two-thirds of the flour to the bowl, beating constantly. Gradually mix in the polenta. Mix in as much of the remaining flour as needed to make the dough begin to form a ball. Continue to knead for 5 minutes at low speed. Scrape the paddle clean, cover the bowl with plastic wrap and refrigerate the dough until doubled in bulk, about 8 hours or overnight.

3. Remove the dough from the refrigerator, punch it down and cover with plastic wrap. Let rise at room temperature until it has doubled in bulk, 2 to 3 hours.

4. Punch down the dough. Knead it on a lightly floured work surface for 30 seconds. Divide it in half and shape it into two round loaves. Cover a baking sheet or two round baskets of the same size with kitchen towels and sprinkle generously with flour and cornmeal. Place the loaves on the towels; cover loosely with more kitchen towels. Let the dough rise at room temperature until doubled in bulk, about 1 hour.

5. At least 40 minutes before baking, preheat the oven to 475°.

6. Lightly flour a baking sheet and turn the loaves over onto it. Slash the tops of the loaves several times with a razor blade and place in the oven. Using a plant mister filled with water, generously spray the oven roof and walls, then shut the oven door. Spray the oven three more times during the first 10 minutes of baking.

7. After 10 minutes, reduce the oven temperature to 400° and bake the loaves of bread for 20 to 25 minutes more, or until the loaves are dark golden brown. Rotate the loaves as necessary during baking so that they

Q & A: BREAD BAKING

Q: Is there a proper technique for kneading?

A: Here are three tips for kneading yeast dough. Remember, you're the boss, so don't be afraid to be pushy and aggressive.

• Use a dough scraper when you start. It helps you handle the dough easily at the beginning of the kneading process, when the dough is at its stickiest. Here's the drill: Turn out the shapeless mass of dough onto a lightly floured work surface. Flour one hand and grasp the dough scraper with the other. Begin to knead by sliding the scraper under the far side of the dough and folding it toward you to the center. Continue to scrape and fold until the dough is evenly dusted with flour.

• Knead firmly and quickly. Drive the palms and heels of your hands into the center of the dough. Use your fingertips to pull the dough from the far side to the center. Reflour your hands and then fold another side of the dough into the center. Give the dough a quarter turn. Continue pushing, pulling, folding and turning the dough until it is smooth, supple and bounces back into shape after it's squeezed between your hands. Don't delay: The longer you rest your hands on the dough, the greater the possibility that it will stick, tearing the elastic structure you are trying to create.

• Dust with flour. Whenever the dough begins to stick, lightly reflour your hands, the work surface and any wet-looking areas of the dough. To flour the work surface beneath the dough, scrape up the dough cleanly and hold it in one hand while you lightly dust the surface with flour.

Q: Can I freeze unbaked dough?

A: Plain yeast dough can be frozen for up to two weeks. After that, the dough develops an off-scent and an off-taste because the fermented yeast converts to alcohol. To freeze the dough, generously grease the interior of a plastic bag, place the dough inside and seal the bag securely so that it's airtight. Label and date the bag for easy identification.

Q: I've heard that you can refrigerate unbaked yeast dough overnight. Does this yield successful results?

A: Definitely. Chilling the dough encourages it to settle down and behave. In effect, it retards, or relaxes, the rubbery web of elasticity that develops when you knead. Here's what you do: After the first full rise, punch down the dough, cover and refrigerate it overnight; then proceed with the shaping and the final rise. You should let the dough return to room temperature before shaping it. If you don't, it will lose quite a bit of height and have a heavier texture when baked. Allow plenty of time; it can take chilled dough almost four hours to reach room temperature.—LAUREN GROVEMAN

brown evenly. Cool the loaves on a rack for at least 1 hour before slicing them. (MAKE AHEAD: The wheat bread can be stored in a sturdy plastic bag for 3 to 4 days.)—PATRICIA WELLS

GRILLED CARDAMOM NAN BREAD

MAKES 8 NAN

- 1 envelope active dry yeast
- 1¼ cups lukewarm water (110° to 115°)
- 1 tablespoon honey
- 1 tablespoon olive oil, plus more for brushing
- 3½ cups bread flour
- 1 tablespoon salt
- 1 tablespoon ground cardamom

1. In a large bowl, dissolve the yeast in the lukewarm water and stir in the honey. Allow the mixture to stand until foamy, about 10 minutes. Add the 1 tablespoon oil, the bread flour, salt and cardamom and stir until the dough forms a cohesive mass.

2. Turn the dough out onto a lightly floured surface and knead until it is smooth and elastic, about 6 minutes. Divide the dough into eight pieces and shape each of the pieces into a ball. Set the balls of dough on an oiled baking sheet and brush with oil. Cover the dough loosely with plastic and let rise in a warm place until doubled in bulk, 1 to 2 hours. (MAKE AHEAD: The dough can be refrigerated overnight. Punch down the balls before proceeding.) ➤

3. On a lightly floured surface, roll out each of the balls of dough into an 8-inch disk. Arrange the disks on three oiled baking sheets and allow the dough to rest for 20 minutes.
4. Light a grill or heat a grill pan or cast-iron skillet. Brush each nan lightly with olive oil and grill for about 1 minute, until the nan is golden on the bottom and light bubbles form on the top. Turn the nan and cook until it is golden all over, about 1 minute. Keep the nan warm while you cook the remaining nan.—WAYNE BRACHMAN

GRILLED-PORTOBELLO AND SMOKY-TOMATO SANDWICHES

Grilled Portobellos and tomatoes combine with creamy ricotta and crisp tangy arugula in a satisfying sandwich.

8 SERVINGS

- 1/4 cup balsamic vinegar
- 1/4 cup plus 2 tablespoons olive oil
- 1 garlic clove, minced
- Coarse salt and freshly ground pepper
- 3 large Portobello mushrooms, stems removed
- 8 ripe plum tomatoes, halved lengthwise and seeded
- 1 large French baguette, halved lengthwise
- 1/4 cup ricotta cheese, preferably fresh
- 16 arugula leaves

1. In a small bowl, whisk 3 tablespoons of the balsamic vinegar with 3 tablespoons of the oil, the garlic and a pinch each of salt and pepper. Pour the vinaigrette over the mushroom caps and let them marinate at room temperature for 1 hour.
2. Light a grill or heat a lightly oiled grill pan or cast-iron skillet. Drizzle the cut sides of the tomatoes with 1 tablespoon of

PICNIC IN THE PARK

A dry sparkling wine—perhaps an Italian spumante, like the nonvintage Ca' del Bosco Brut Nuova Cuvée—would give a lift to any picnic.

RED-PEPPER AND FENNEL SOUP (P. 79)

GRILLED-PORTOBELLO AND SMOKY-TOMATO SANDWICHES (P. 296)

BARLEY-AND-CORN SALAD (P. 70)

FLAVORS' ROASTED POTATO SALAD (P. 67)

RASPBERRY-DRESSED COLESLAW (P. 64)

PEACHES IN BLUEBERRY SYRUP (P. 419)

CHOCOLATE PEANUT COOKIES (P. 386)

Grilled-Portobello and Smoky-Tomato Sandwiches

the oil and season with a pinch each of salt and pepper. Grill the tomatoes over high heat, skin-side down, for about 3 minutes, or until softened and lightly charred. Transfer to a plate.

3. Grill the mushrooms, turning once, for about 5 minutes per side, or until tender and charred. Transfer to paper towels to drain. Slice each mushroom cap into four to five pieces.

4. Brush the cut sides of the baguette with 1 tablespoon of the oil and grill or toast until lightly browned. In a small bowl, combine the ricotta with a large pinch each of salt and pepper. Spread the ricotta on the bottom half of the grilled baguette and layer the tomatoes, arugula and Portobellos on top. Drizzle with the remaining 1 tablespoon oil and 1 tablespoon balsamic vinegar and cover with the top half of the baguette. Cut into eight pieces and serve.—PAMELA MORGAN

TEMPEH SANDWICHES

Tempeh, a chewy mixture of soybeans and grains with a subtle smoky flavor, makes a terrific-tasting sandwich. Use a round, crusty loaf of coarse peasant bread. If you are serving hungry eaters, this recipe will serve two people nicely.

4 SERVINGS

- 1 medium garlic clove, minced
- Salt
- ¼ cup mayonnaise
- 1 tablespoon finely chopped fresh flat-leaf parsley
- One 8-ounce package of tempeh
- 1 tablespoon balsamic vinegar
- Freshly ground pepper
- 1 medium red onion, thinly sliced crosswise
- 4 teaspoons olive oil
- 4 large ½-inch-thick slices of peasant bread, halved crosswise
- 4 ripe plum tomatoes, thinly sliced crosswise
- Half a small bunch of arugula, stems trimmed

1. On a work surface, using the flat side of a large knife, crush the garlic with ¼ teaspoon salt until almost pureed. In a small bowl, stir together the garlic, mayonnaise and parsley.

2. Using a thin sharp knife, cut the block of tempeh crosswise on an angle into twelve slices about ¼ inch thick. Brush the tempeh slices on both sides with the vinegar and season lightly with salt and pepper.

3. In a large nonstick skillet, cook the onion in 1 teaspoon of the oil over moderate heat, stirring occasionally and separating the onion into rings, until slightly softened, about 5 minutes. Transfer the cooked onion rings to a plate.

4. Add 2 teaspoons of the oil to the skillet and swirl the pan to coat. Add half the tempeh in a single layer and cook over moderate heat, pressing lightly with a spatula and turning once, until lightly browned, 1½ to 2 minutes per side. Transfer the tempeh to a plate and repeat the process with the remaining 1 teaspoon oil and tempeh.

5. Toast the slices of peasant bread and spread each one with the prepared mayonnaise. Place the tempeh on four pieces of toast and top with the onion rings, tomatoes and arugula. Sandwich together with the other pieces of toast and serve at once.—DIANA STURGIS ➤

Tempeh Sandwich

GORGONZOLA AND MÂCHE SANDWICHES

8 SERVINGS

¼ pound Italian Gorgonzola cheese, at room temperature
3 tablespoons extra-virgin olive oil
¼ pound mâche, roots trimmed, leaves washed and dried
8 slices firm-textured white bread, crusts trimmed

1. Put the Gorgonzola in a small bowl and break it into small pieces with a fork. Add the olive oil and mash until creamy.
2. Put the mâche in a bowl. Add the creamed Gorgonzola, a little at a time, turning the leaves gently with a fork until they are evenly coated.
3. Mound one-fourth of the mâche and Gorgonzola filling in the center of each of four slices of bread; top with the other slices. Position a sharp knife diagonally across the slice of bread; hold the bread down with your other hand so as not to flatten the filling and quickly slice the sandwich to produce two *tramezzini*.—MARCELLA HAZAN

HARD-BOILED-EGG SANDWICHES WITH ANCHOVIES AND CAPERS

8 SERVINGS

2 hard-boiled eggs
10 flat anchovy fillets
2 tablespoons drained capers
3 tablespoons mayonnaise
2 cups very finely shredded Romaine lettuce
Freshly ground pepper
8 slices firm-textured white bread, crusts trimmed

In a food processor, pulse the eggs with the anchovies and capers until coarsely chopped. Transfer to a bowl. Fold in the mayonnaise, shredded lettuce and pepper until uniformly combined. Mound the filling in the center of half of the bread slices. Top with the remaining bread and slice the sandwiches on the diagonal with a sharp knife.—MARCELLA HAZAN

VENETIAN SANDWICHES

***Tramezzino*, which translates as "a little something held in between," is a term that was coined in Venice to replace the foreign word "sandwich." But a *tramezzino* is a particular kind of sandwich whose most distinctive characteristic is that it is soft: soft is the bread that is used to make them, and soft are the fillings, which are often bound with mayonnaise.**

Each *tramezzino* is actually a triangular half of a diagonally cut overstuffed sandwich. At the smart parties in the palazzi, they're arranged in stacks, cut sides facing outward to spare guests the unpredictability of a blind choice.

The filling varies with the fancy of the maker. It can be meat (such as Celery and Ham Sandwiches), cheese (Gorgonzola and Mâche Sandwiches), hard-boiled eggs (Hard-Boiled-Egg Sandwiches with Anchovies and Capers) or fried eggplant. But whatever else a *tramezzino* contains, it is almost certain to include one or more of the wonderful greens that are grown on the farm islands in the Venetian lagoon.—MARCELLA HAZAN

BROILED-WHITEFISH SANDWICHES

It's the simple combination of fresh fish, homemade tartar sauce and a soft semolina roll that makes this sandwich so good. You can also use trout or flounder.

4 SERVINGS

½ cup mayonnaise
3 tablespoons minced dill pickle
2 tablespoons minced red onion
1 teaspoon fresh lemon juice
1 teaspoon finely chopped fresh tarragon
Salt and freshly ground pepper
Four 7-ounce skinless whitefish fillets
1 tablespoon unsalted butter, melted
½ teaspoon dill
½ teaspoon sweet paprika
4 semolina rolls, split
4 romaine lettuce leaves
4 tomato slices

1. Combine the mayonnaise, pickle, onion, lemon juice and tarragon. Season with salt and pepper.
2. Preheat the broiler. Arrange the fish fillets on a broiler pan and brush with the butter. Sprinkle with the dill, paprika, salt and pepper. Broil until the fish is golden and cooked through, about 4 minutes.

3. Spread the tartar sauce on the tops and bottoms of the rolls. Set a fish fillet on each roll, top with a lettuce leaf and tomato slice and serve.—THE SHORELINE RESTAURANT, GILLS ROCK, WISCONSIN

GRILLED-CHICKEN CAESAR-SALAD SANDWICHES

4 SERVINGS

- ¼ cup plus 1 tablespoon mayonnaise
- ¼ cup plus 2 tablespoons freshly grated Parmesan cheese
- 3 anchovy fillets, minced
- 1 garlic clove, minced
- 1 teaspoon Dijon mustard
- 1 tablespoon fresh lemon juice
- Freshly ground pepper
- 1 tablespoon olive oil
- 4 medium skinless, boneless chicken-breast halves, breasts flattened slightly, tenders reserved separately
- Salt
- 4 sandwich rolls, split
- 1 large bunch of arugula, large stems removed

1. In a mini-processor, blend the mayonnaise, Parmesan, anchovies, garlic, mustard, lemon juice and ¼ teaspoon pepper; alternatively, combine these ingredients in a bowl.

2. Brush a grill pan or a cast-iron skillet with 1 teaspoon of the oil and heat. Brush the chicken breasts and tenders on both sides with the remaining 2 teaspoons oil and season with salt and pepper. Pan-grill over high heat, turning once, until browned and cooked through, about 3 minutes per side. Let rest for 5 minutes.

3. Add the tenders to the pan. Grill, turning once, until browned and cooked through, about 2 minutes per side. Cut the tenders in half lengthwise. Slice each breast diagonally ½ inch thick.

4. Spread the mayonnaise mixture on the top and bottom half of each roll. Arrange a sliced chicken breast and tender on the bottom half of each roll, cover with arugula and close the sandwiches.—GRACE PARISI

CELERY AND HAM SANDWICHES

MAKES 6 SERVINGS

- 1 cup chopped celery (not too fine)
- ¼ pound boiled ham, chopped (not too fine)
- 3 tablespoons mayonnaise
- 2 teaspoons mustard or more to taste
- 6 slices firm-textured white bread, crusts removed

In a bowl, combine the celery, ham, mayonnaise and mustard. Mound the mixture in the center of three slices of bread and top with the other slices. Using a large sharp knife, slice the sandwiches on the diagonal.—MARCELLA HAZAN

FRENCH TOAST SARDY

The sweet creamy flavor of vanilla ice cream enriches this breakfast specialty.

4–8 SERVINGS

- 1 medium French baguette, ends discarded, cut diagonally into twenty-four ¾-inch-thick slices
- 4 large eggs
- ½ cup premium vanilla ice cream, softened
- ¼ cup fresh orange juice
- 1 tablespoon pure vanilla extract
- 1 tablespoon cinnamon
- Pinch of freshly grated nutmeg
- 2 tablespoons unsalted butter
- Pure maple syrup, for serving
- Assorted fresh berries, halved if large, for serving

1. In a large nonreactive baking dish, spread out half of the bread slices. In a medium bowl, combine the eggs, ice cream, orange juice, vanilla, cinnamon and nutmeg and pour over the bread. Turn the slices and soak until saturated, about 5 minutes.

2. Melt 1 tablespoon of the butter in a large cast-iron skillet. Add the soaked bread slices and cook in a single layer over moderately low heat, turning once, until they are golden brown and heated through, about 2 minutes per side. Transfer to a platter and keep warm. Soak the remaining bread slices and cook them in the remaining 1 tablespoon butter. Serve with syrup and fresh berries.—SARDY HOUSE HOTEL AND RESTAURANT, ASPEN, COLORADO ➤

French Toast Sardy

ONION WALNUT MUFFINS

MAKES 2 DOZEN MUFFINS

Vegetable cooking spray
4 medium onions, peeled and quartered
2 sticks (½ pound) unsalted butter, melted and cooled
¾ cup sugar
4 extra-large eggs, lightly beaten
1 tablespoon coarse salt
1 tablespoon baking powder
3 cups walnuts, coarsely chopped (¾ pound)
3 cups all-purpose flour

Onion Walnut Muffins

Citrus Bread

1. Preheat the oven to 425° and spray two 12-cup muffin tins with nonstick vegetable cooking spray.
2. In a food processor, pulse the onions until pureed. Transfer 2 cups of the puree to a bowl and stir in the butter, sugar and eggs. One at a time, stir in the salt, baking powder, nuts and flour; mix thoroughly. Spoon the batter into the prepared tins and bake for 20 minutes, or until the muffins are brown and a toothpick inserted in the center comes out clean.
3. Let the muffins cool in the pan for 10 minutes, then unmold them on a wire rack and let cool. (**MAKE AHEAD:** The muffins can be frozen for up to 1 week. Thaw completely and rewarm before serving.) —WALDY MALOUF

NORMA'S SCONES

MAKES 8 SCONES

⅓ cup hazelnuts (about 1½ ounces)
1¾ cups unbleached all-purpose flour
¼ cup sugar
1 teaspoon baking powder
½ teaspoon baking soda
½ teaspoon salt
⅔ cup buttermilk
⅓ cup unsalted butter, melted
¾ cup fresh raspberries

1. Preheat the oven to 350°. Lightly butter a large baking sheet. Toast the hazelnuts in a small cake pan for about 12 minutes, or until the nuts are fragrant and the skins blister. Transfer to a kitchen towel and rub the nuts together to remove the skins. Coarsely chop the nuts and let cool. Raise the oven temperature to 400°.
2. In a large bowl, stir together the flour, sugar, baking powder, baking soda, salt and the hazelnuts. In a large measuring cup, combine the buttermilk and butter. Stir in the raspberries. Stir the liquid mixture into the dry ingredients just until combined. Scoop eight equal spoonfuls of the dough onto the prepared baking sheet and bake for about 20 minutes, or until the scones are golden. Let cool slightly before serving.—BELTANE RANCH, GLEN ELLEN, CALIFORNIA

CITRUS BREAD

Buttery citrus bread is a delicious accompaniment to morning coffee.

MAKES ONE 5-BY-8-INCH LOAF

2 cups all-purpose flour
¼ cup plus 2 tablespoons self-rising flour
4 large eggs, lightly beaten
1½ cups sugar
2 teaspoons finely grated orange zest
2 sticks unsalted butter (½ pound), softened
½ cup fresh orange juice

1. Preheat the oven to 350°. Lightly butter a 5-by-8-inch loaf pan. In a medium bowl, sift together the all-purpose and self-rising flours. In a large bowl, combine the eggs, sugar and orange zest. Add the butter and stir until combined. Add the orange juice. Stir in the dry ingredients and spoon into the prepared pan.

2. Bake the citrus bread for about 1¼ hours, or until the top of the loaf is golden and cracked and a few crumbs cling to a skewer inserted in the center; cover the loaf with foil halfway through baking. Let cool in the pan for 10 minutes, then transfer the loaf to a rack and allow it to cool completely. (MAKE AHEAD: The loaf of citrus bread can be wrapped and kept at room temperature for 1 day or frozen for up to 1 month.) —HORNED DORSET PRIMAVERA HOTEL, PUERTO RICO

THE BEST BUTTERMILK PANCAKES

Ripe raspberries serve as both a base for the fruity syrup and as a garnish for the pancakes.

4–6 SERVINGS

- 1½ cups unbleached all-purpose flour
- 2 teaspoons baking soda
- ¾ teaspoon salt
- 2 cups buttermilk
- 6 tablespoons unsalted butter, melted
- 2 large eggs, at room temperature, separated
- Fresh raspberries, for garnish
- Beltane Ranch Raspberry Syrup (recipe follows)

1. In a medium bowl, stir together the unbleached all-purpose flour, baking soda and salt. In a large bowl, combine the buttermilk, the melted butter and the egg yolks.

2. In another medium bowl, beat the egg whites until stiff peaks form. Add the dry ingredients to the buttermilk mixture and stir just until combined. Using a rubber spatula, gently fold the beaten egg whites into the batter just until combined.

3. Heat a lightly buttered griddle or a cast-iron skillet. For each pancake, gently spread ¼ cup of the batter on the hot surface to form a 4-inch circle. Cook over moderately low heat until the top is set, about 2 minutes. Flip the pancake and continue cooking until golden, about 1 minute longer. Transfer to a large plate and keep warm while you cook the remaining pancakes. Divide the pancakes among plates, garnish with fresh raspberries and serve with the syrup.

Beltane Ranch Raspberry Syrup

MAKES 1½ CUPS

- 5 cups fresh raspberries
- 1½ cups sugar

In a medium nonreactive saucepan, combine the raspberries and ¼ cup water. Lightly crush the raspberries against the side of the pan, then cover and bring to a boil over high heat. Strain the raspberries into a bowl, pressing down on the berries. Wipe out the pan and pour in the raspberry puree. Stir in the sugar, bring to a boil over high heat and cook, skimming, until the sugar dissolves, about 1 minute. (MAKE AHEAD: The raspberry sauce can be refrigerated for up to 1 week or frozen for up to 1 month.) Serve the syrup warm.—BELTANE RANCH, GLEN ELLEN, CALIFORNIA

The Best Buttermilk Pancakes

MAPLE PEAR PANCAKE

4–6 SERVINGS

- 3 tablespoons butter
- 1 cup milk
- 1 egg
- 1 cup flour
- 2 teaspoons baking powder
- 2 tablespoons sugar
- ½ teaspoon salt
- 2 pears, peeled and sliced
- ½ cup maple syrup
- 2 teaspoons lemon juice

1. Heat the oven to 350°. Melt 2 tablespoons butter. Mix together the milk, egg, and melted butter. In a bowl, sift the flour, baking powder, sugar and salt. Stir in the egg mixture; let stand 10 minutes.

2. In a nonreactive ovenproof skillet, cook the pears in the remaining 1 tablespoon butter and ¼ cup of the syrup over high heat until caramelized. Remove from the heat. Add the lemon juice and the remaining syrup.

3. Pour the batter over the pears. Bake 12 minutes, or until a tester inserted in the center comes out clean. Invert the pancake onto a platter and serve with additional maple syrup.—GRACE PARISI

CHAPTER 13

~

POTATOES

Crisp French Fries

CRISP FRENCH FRIES

The secret to making good french fries is to cook them twice: the first time to cook the potatoes through, the second time, at a higher temperature, to brown and crisp them. If you don't have a frying basket, remove the fries from the oil with a large slotted spoon.

4 SERVINGS

2 pounds unpeeled russet potatoes, cut lengthwise into ⅓-inch-thick sticks
About 8 cups vegetable oil, for frying
Fine sea salt

1. In a large bowl, cover the potatoes with water. In a deep fryer fitted with a basket or in a heavy medium saucepan, heat 3 inches of the vegetable oil to 340°. Drain the potatoes and pat dry with paper towels. Add half the potatoes to the oil and cook until they begin to blister and turn golden, about 15 minutes. Spread the french fries on paper towels to drain and cool. Repeat with the remaining fries. (**MAKE AHEAD:** The fries can stand at room temperature for up to 4 hours.)
2. Heat the oil to 375°. Add a quarter of the fries and cook until browned and crisp, 1 to 2 minutes. Drain on paper towels and repeat with the remaining fries. Sprinkle with salt.—DIANA STURGIS

ROASTED-POTATO AND FENNEL HASH Q

8 SERVINGS

2 pounds small unpeeled red potatoes, sliced ½ inch thick
1 tablespoon olive oil
Salt and freshly ground pepper
3 tablespoons unsalted butter
3 medium fennel bulbs, trimmed, cored and thinly sliced crosswise
1 tablespoon finely chopped fresh thyme
2 tablespoons coarsely chopped fresh parsley

1. Preheat the oven to 425°. Spread the potato slices in a single layer on two lightly oiled baking sheets. Drizzle the oil over the potatoes and season with salt and pepper. Roast for about 45 minutes, turning occasionally, until browned and crisp.
2. Meanwhile, melt the butter in a large skillet. Add the fennel and cook over moderate heat, stirring often, until tender, about 15 minutes. Stir in the thyme.
3. Just before serving, add the potatoes and parsley to the fennel and stir quickly over high heat until warmed through. Season the hash with salt and pepper and serve.—NICO MARTIN

ANTHONY'S HOME FRIES Q

A former colleague, the late Anthony Delgado, gave me this delicious recipe.

4 SERVINGS

4 large Idaho potatoes, peeled and quartered
2 tablespoons unsalted butter
1 tablespoon vegetable oil
1 medium onion, coarsely chopped
½ medium red bell pepper, coarsely chopped
½ medium green bell pepper, coarsely chopped
Salt and freshly ground black pepper
Hot pepper sauce, for serving

***Clockwise from bottom*: Anthony's Home Fries, with Honey-Glazed Pork Chops (p. 227) and Sautéed Watercress (p. 337)**

1. Bring a large saucepan of salted water to a boil and add the potatoes. Cook until just tender, about 15 minutes. Drain the potatoes and coarsely chop them.
2. In a large heavy skillet, preferably cast iron, melt 1 tablespoon of the butter in the oil. Add the onion and red and green peppers and cook over moderately high heat, stirring, until wilted, about 4 minutes. Mix in the potatoes and press into an even layer in the skillet. Cook over moderate heat until browned and crusty on the bottom, about 5 minutes. Season with salt and pepper. Turn the potatoes, adding the remaining 1 tablespoon butter to the skillet as you turn, and cook until well browned, about 5 minutes more. Season the potatoes with salt and pepper and serve with hot sauce.—MARCIA KIESEL ➤

HASH BROWNS

During a fast noontime grocery shopping at my local market, I was drawn to a batch of Yukon Gold potatoes. "Hash browns!" I said to myself, scooping up a half-dozen. Only the day before, my appetite for those crusty pan fries had been whetted by a vivid description in the legendary James Beard's seminal tome, American Cookery. *His hash browns were the crisp informal kind made famous in the days of short-order cooks. They'd grab a handful of boiled potatoes and toss them into a pan of fresh bacon fat, dribble over them a little butter, brown on the other side and turn out a crunchy brown cake on a nicely warmed platter.*

2 SERVINGS

1 pound Yukon Gold potatoes, peeled and cut into ½-inch pieces
Salt
2 tablespoons vegetable oil
2 tablespoons unsalted butter
Freshly ground pepper

1. Put the potatoes in a medium saucepan, add 4 cups of water and 1 teaspoon salt and bring to a boil. Simmer, partially covered, until the potatoes are almost tender. Drain and pat dry.

2. Heat a 10-inch nonstick skillet. Add the vegetable oil and 1 tablespoon of the butter. When the foam subsides, add the potatoes and cook, tossing, until lightly golden. Season with salt and pepper and roughly mash the potatoes with a spatula. Dot the remaining 1 tablespoon butter over the potatoes, cover and cook until crusty on the bottom, about 3 minutes. Slide the potatoes onto a plate and invert them back into the pan. Cook until the underside is nice and crusty. Slide the potatoes onto a platter and serve.—JULIA CHILD

MEDLEY OF GREENS WITH POTATOES AND LEEKS

12 SERVINGS

Kosher salt
5½ pounds mixed bitter greens, such as Swiss chard, escarole, turnip or mustard greens, chicory, broccoli rabe, kale and spinach, tough stems discarded
1 stick unsalted butter (4 ounces)
4 large leeks, white and tender green, thinly sliced crosswise
2 garlic cloves, thinly sliced
3 cups chicken stock or canned low-sodium broth
Freshly ground pepper
3 pounds Yukon Gold potatoes

1. Bring a large pot of water to a boil and add salt. Cut the greens into 1-inch pieces and wash them thoroughly. Add the greens to the pot and cover. As soon as the water returns to a boil, drain the greens in a colander; pat dry.

2. Preheat the oven to 375°. In a large skillet, melt 4 tablespoons of the butter. Add the leeks and garlic and cook over moderate heat until just beginning to brown, about 10 minutes. Add the stock and bring to a boil. Season generously with salt and pepper and remove from the heat.

3. Peel and halve the potatoes and slice them ¼ inch thick. In a

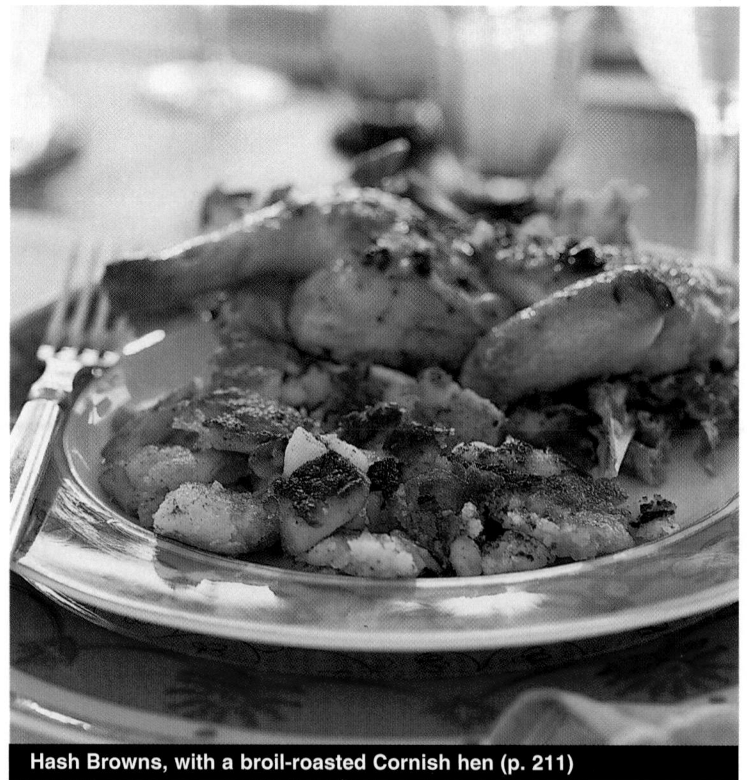

Hash Browns, with a broil-roasted Cornish hen (p. 211)

large bowl, toss the potatoes with the greens and leeks. Season with salt and pepper. Transfer the mixture to a large nonreactive baking dish and press the vegetables down firmly. Dot with the remaining 4 tablespoons of butter. Cover the pan tightly with foil and bake for 1 hour. Uncover and bake for about 15 minutes longer, or until the potatoes are very tender. (**MAKE AHEAD:** The dish can be prepared early in the day and reheated in the oven before serving.)—WALDY MALOUF

POTATO AND LEEK GRATIN

8 SERVINGS

- 3 pounds waxy potatoes, such as Yukon Gold, peeled and thinly sliced
- 1 pound leeks, white part only, thinly sliced
- ⅔ cup olive oil
- Salt and freshly ground pepper

1. Preheat the oven to 350°. In a medium bowl, gently toss the potatoes with the leeks, oil, 1½ teaspoons salt and ½ teaspoon pepper. Transfer to a 9-by-13-inch glass or ceramic baking dish and pat into an even layer. Cover with foil and bake for about 1½ hours, or until the potatoes are tender. Let cool completely, then cover with plastic wrap and refrigerate until chilled. (**MAKE AHEAD:** The potatoes can be refrigerated overnight.)

2. Preheat the oven to 450°. Cut the gratin into eight squares. Using a metal spatula, transfer the squares to a rimmed nonstick baking sheet. Bake for 30 minutes, or until the tops are brown. Serve immediately.—ALI SEEDSMAN

MARIE'S POTATO GRATIN LF

This rich-tasting dish was inspired by my colleague Bernadette Pochat's mother, Marie, who continued to make gratins during the Second World War in France, even when luxuries like cream were in short supply.

8 SERVINGS

- 2½ cups chicken stock or canned low-sodium broth, skimmed of fat
- ⅔ cup thinly sliced shallots (about 4 ounces)
- 2½ pounds medium Idaho potatoes, peeled and sliced crosswise ⅛ inch thick
- Salt and freshly ground pepper
- ¼ cup freshly grated Parmesan cheese
- ¼ cup finely chopped fresh chives
- ½ cup grated Gruyère cheese (about 2 ounces)

1. Preheat the oven to 400°. Bring the stock to a boil in a medium saucepan. Add the shallots, cover partially and cook over low heat until tender, about 5 minutes. Strain the stock and spread the shallots in a large oval gratin dish. Keep the stock warm.

2. Arrange a quarter of the potato slices in a slightly overlapping layer over the shallots and season with salt and pepper. Spread another quarter of the potato slices on top, sprinkle with half each of the Parmesan and the chives and season with salt and pepper. Make two more layers with the remaining potatoes, seasoning each layer with salt and pepper. Add enough stock so that the top layer of potatoes is just above the liquid. Sprinkle with the remaining Parmesan

Marie's Potato Gratin

and chopped chives and the Gruyère. Bake the gratin for about 1¼ hours, or until the potatoes are tender and the top is browned. Let the gratin rest for 10 minutes, then serve.—BOB CHAMBERS

ROASTED-CHILE AND POTATO GRATIN

There's nothing like chiles to pep up potatoes.

4 SERVINGS

- 2 large mild fresh red chiles, such as Hungarian wax or New Mexico, or red bell peppers
- 1 small garlic clove, minced
- ½ cup heavy cream
- 1 teaspoon salt
- ¼ teaspoon freshly ground pepper
- 2 large Idaho potatoes, peeled and very thinly sliced crosswise

1. Roast the chiles over a gas flame or under a broiler, turning, until charred all over. Put the chiles in a bowl, cover with plastic wrap and let steam for 5 minutes. Working over the bowl, remove the charred skins, ribs, stems and seeds from the chiles; strain and reserve any juices that have collected in the bowl. Cut the chiles into ½-inch pieces and put them in the bowl with the reserved juices.

2. Preheat the oven to 400°. In a small bowl, combine the garlic, cream, salt, pepper and 1¼ cups of water. Spread the sliced potatoes in a nonreactive 9-by-13-inch baking dish and tuck the chile pieces between the slices; drizzle with the chile juices. Pour the cream mixture over all, shaking the dish to settle the potatoes and cream in an even layer. Bake in the upper third of the oven for about 35 minutes, or until bubbling and browned on top. Serve hot.—MARCIA KIESEL

SALT

Empires have been founded on salt and have foundered without it. Besides preserving everything from fish to olives, it has been the cause of wars, a valuable monopoly and a medium of exchange. Part of a Roman soldier's pay was salt, *salarium*, hence our word salary. The Greeks traded it for slaves—a good slave was "worth his salt." Centuries later, during Napoléon's retreat from Moscow, many of his troops died because they were deprived of salt and their wounds would not heal.—SHIRLEY CORRIHER

HORSERADISH SCALLOPED POTATOES

This heavenly gratin makes a creamy accompaniment to a beef roast. If you are using prepared horseradish, drain it well before adding.

8 SERVINGS

- 3½ cups heavy cream
- 2 garlic cloves, minced
- 1¾ teaspoons salt
- ½ teaspoon freshly ground pepper
- About 6 tablespoons grated peeled fresh horseradish root
- 2½ pounds Idaho potatoes (about 5), peeled and thinly sliced
- ½ large tart apple, such as Granny Smith, peeled, halved, cored and thinly sliced
- ¼ cup freshly grated Parmesan cheese

1. In a medium bowl, combine the heavy cream, garlic, salt and pepper. Gradually stir in the horseradish, tasting for strength.

2. Preheat the oven to 400°. In a 13-by-9-inch nonreactive baking dish, layer the potatoes and apple. Pour the horseradish cream over the potatoes. (**MAKE AHEAD:** The potatoes can be prepared to this point up to 2 hours ahead. Do not refrigerate.) Bake the gratin in the upper third of the oven for about 30 minutes, or until bubbling. Sprinkle the Parmesan cheese over the top and bake for about 15 minutes longer, or until the potatoes are tender and the top is nicely browned. Cover the gratin with foil and let stand in a warm place for 10 to 30 minutes before serving. Cut the gratin into eight squares with a pie server.—MARCIA KIESEL

ROASTED POTATO STICKS LF

There isn't a drop of oil in this recipe. Salt, pepper, potato starch and thyme form a tasty crust on the baked potato wedges.

6 SERVINGS

- ¼ cup potato starch
- 4 teaspoons thyme
- 4 teaspoons salt
- 2 teaspoons freshly ground pepper
- 4 large baking potatoes, scrubbed, each potato cut lengthwise into 12 wedges

Preheat the oven to 450°. Line a baking sheet with parchment paper. In a bowl, blend the potato starch, thyme, salt and pepper. In a large sturdy plastic bag, shake one-third of the potato sticks with one-third of the seasonings until the potatoes are coated. Set the potatoes, skin-side down, on the baking sheet.

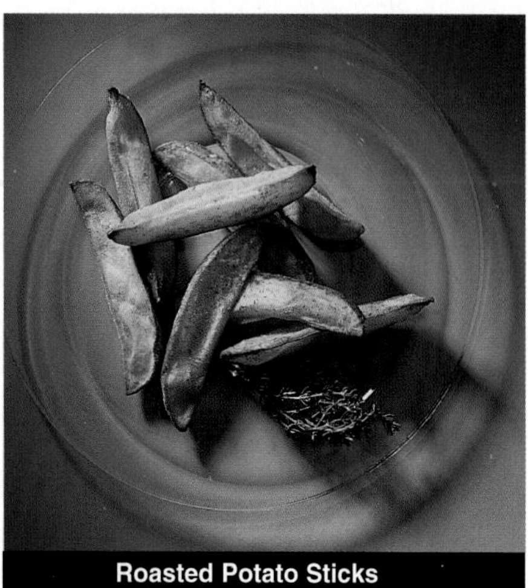

Roasted Potato Sticks

Repeat with the remaining potatoes and seasonings. Bake the potatoes for about 45 minutes, or until browned.—BOB CHAMBERS

BOB'S ROASTED POTATOES

Charred lemon slices make a tasty addition to these simple herb-roasted potatoes. Serve them for breakfast with scrambled eggs.

4 SERVINGS

- 4 medium red potatoes, cut into 1-inch chunks
- 1 medium lemon, thinly sliced crosswise and seeded
- 5 fresh rosemary sprigs
- ¾ teaspoon coarse salt
- 2 tablespoons olive oil

Preheat the oven to 425°. Spread the red potatoes in a single layer in a baking dish. Add the lemon slices and rosemary sprigs, sprinkle with the salt and drizzle with the olive oil. Bake for about 40 minutes, or until the potatoes are tender. Serve at once.—BELTANE RANCH, GLEN ELLEN, CALIFORNIA

ROASTED POTATOES WITH OLIVES

Parboiling the potatoes before roasting makes for a fluffy interior and a crisp golden brown surface. Olives and garlic are added at the end of roasting so that their flavors remain vibrant.

8 SERVINGS

- 4 pounds boiling potatoes, such as Yukon Gold, Red Rose or Finnish, peeled and cut into 1-inch chunks
- 1 tablespoon plus ½ teaspoon coarse salt
- ½ cup olive oil
- ½ cup picholine olives
- 1 tablespoon finely chopped garlic
- Freshly ground pepper

1. Preheat the oven to 400°. In a large saucepan, cover the potatoes with 2 quarts of water. Add the 1 tablespoon salt and bring to a boil, then reduce the heat and simmer until the potatoes are almost tender, about 20 minutes. Drain the potatoes in a colander and let them dry in their own steam for 10 minutes.

2. Transfer the potatoes to a rimmed baking sheet and gently toss them with the oil. Roast the potatoes in the oven for about 1 hour, turning them every so often with a flat spatula, until they are golden brown.

3. Pour off any excess oil in the pan. Scatter the olives and garlic over the potatoes and toss. Lower the oven temperature to 350° and bake the potatoes for 10 minutes longer. Sprinkle them with the remaining ½ teaspoon salt and a little fresh pepper and serve piping hot.—PAUL BERTOLLI

CHARRED-ONION MASHED POTATOES **Q**

These creamy mashed potatoes go particularly well with steak.

4 SERVINGS

- 1½ pounds unpeeled all-purpose potatoes, cut into 1-inch cubes
- Salt
- 6 tablespoons unsalted butter
- 1 onion, minced
- ¾ cup hot milk
- Freshly ground pepper

1. Put the potatoes in a medium saucepan and cover them with water. Add 1 teaspoon salt and boil over moderate heat until tender, about 15 minutes. Drain, return to the pan and keep warm.

2. Melt 4 tablespoons of the butter in a skillet. Add the onion and cook over moderately low heat, stirring, until well browned, about 20 minutes.

3. Mash the potatoes with the hot milk and the remaining 2 tablespoons butter. Stir in the onion and season with salt and pepper.—PAUL GRIMES

Clockwise from top left: **Roasted Potatoes with Olives, with Artichokes with Garlic and Thyme (p. 336) and Stuffed Leg of Spring Lamb (p. 256)**

ANCHOVY MASHED POTATOES

6 SERVINGS

- 3 large russet potatoes
- 6 tablespoons unsalted butter

½ medium onion, finely chopped
6 flat anchovy fillets, rinsed, dried and minced
½ cup milk
3 tablespoons heavy cream
Salt and freshly ground pepper
3 tablespoons minced scallion greens

1. Peel the potatoes and cut them into 1-inch chunks. Steam the potatoes, covered, until very tender, about 20 minutes. Press the potatoes through a ricer or the medium disk of a food mill set over a bowl.
2. In a large nonreactive saucepan, melt 4 tablespoons of the butter. Add the onion and cook over moderately low heat, stirring, until softened. Add the anchovies and stir until melted. Stir in the milk and the heavy cream, season with salt and pepper and bring to a simmer. Add the potato puree and stir until smooth and warmed through. (**MAKE AHEAD:** The potatoes can stand at room temperature for up to 4 hours.) Stir in the scallion greens and the remaining 2 tablespoons of butter and serve hot.—BRIGIT LEGERE BINNS

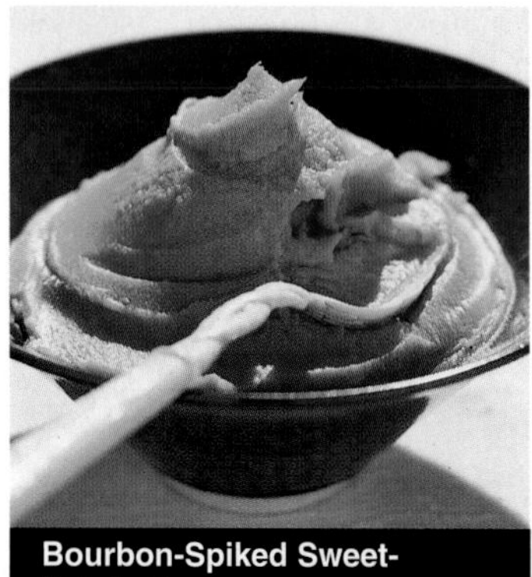
Bourbon-Spiked Sweet-Potato Puree

PASILLA CHILES STUFFED WITH POTATO

Pasilla chiles are stuffed with a mashed-potato and cheese filling, then fried and covered with a slightly sweet tomatillo sauce. Serve the chiles with corn tortillas.

6 SERVINGS

1 pound new potatoes
12 pasilla chiles
6 ounces *queso fresco*, feta cheese or cream cheese, crumbled
Salt
⅓ cup vegetable oil

TOMATILLO SAUCE:
2 pounds tomatillos, husked and rinsed
2 tablespoons coarsely chopped white onion
2 garlic cloves, finely chopped
1 heaped tablespoon dark brown sugar
Salt
½ cup chicken stock or water

1. In a large saucepan of boiling water, cook the potatoes until fork-tender, about 20 minutes. Drain, cool the potatoes slightly and peel. Transfer the potatoes to a large bowl and mash them roughly.
2. Using a small sharp knife, slit the chiles lengthwise, leaving the stems intact. Carefully remove the seeds and veins. Place the chiles in a bowl, cover with hot water and let soak until just beginning to soften, about 20 minutes (depending on how dry they were in the first place). Drain.
3. Add the cheese to the potatoes, season with salt and mash together well. Stuff the chiles fully with the filling, but leave enough room so that the seams almost close.
4. Heat the oil in a large nonreactive skillet. Gently fry the chiles in batches, rolling them over from time to time so that they cook evenly without browning too much, about 5 minutes. Transfer to paper towels to drain. Reserve the oil in the skillet.
5. Make the tomatillo sauce: In a large nonreactive saucepan, cover the tomatillos with water and simmer until soft, about 10 minutes. Drain and transfer to a blender. Add the onion and garlic and blend until almost smooth (but still textured).
6. Preheat the oven to 350°. Heat the reserved oil in the skillet. Add the brown sugar and fry for a few seconds. Add the tomatillo sauce, season with salt and cook over high heat until reduced, about 5 minutes. Stir in the chicken stock.
7. In a baking dish large enough to hold them in one layer, arrange the chiles side by side. Pour the sauce over the chiles and bake until heated through, about 15 minutes. Serve warm.—DIANA KENNEDY

BOURBON-SPIKED SWEET-POTATO PUREE LF

8 SERVINGS

5 pounds medium unpeeled sweet potatoes or yams
1 tablespoon fresh lemon juice
½ teaspoon finely grated lemon zest
Salt and freshly ground pepper
¼ cup good-quality bourbon
¼ cup dark brown sugar

1. Preheat the oven to 450°. Pierce the sweet potatoes a few times and roast them in a large nonstick roasting pan for about 1 hour, or until soft and browned on the bottom. Let cool for 15 minutes. Remove the skin, leaving as much caramelized flesh as possible. Cut the potatoes into large chunks and transfer to a food processor. Add the lemon juice and zest, season with salt and pepper and process until the potatoes are smooth.

2. In a large nonreactive saucepan, combine the bourbon and brown sugar and bring just to a boil. Add the sweet potatoes and stir until blended. (MAKE AHEAD: The puree can be refrigerated for up to 1 day.) Warm the sweet-potato puree over low heat, then transfer it to a large bowl and serve.—BOB CHAMBERS

GRILLED SWEET-POTATO WEDGES Q

A hinged grilling basket makes cooking the potato wedges easier.

4 SERVINGS

- 2 pounds medium sweet potatoes, cut lengthwise into 6 wedges each
- 2 tablespoons olive oil
- Salt and freshly ground black pepper
- Large pinch of cayenne pepper

Light the grill. In a large saucepan of boiling, salted water, simmer the sweet potatoes until almost tender, about 5 minutes. Drain, transfer the potatoes to a large bowl and toss with the oil, salt, black pepper and cayenne. Grill over moderate heat for about 15 minutes, turning, until tender and lightly charred. Serve warm.—SUSAN LANTZIUS

Grilled Sweet-Potato Wedges accompanying chicken topped with Black-Bean Mango Salsa (p. 358)

CHAPTER 14

~

RICE & GRAINS

Saffron Rice Salad accompanying Red Snapper Grilled in Banana Leaves (p. 148)

SAFFRON RICE SALAD

8–10 SERVINGS

- 2 tablespoons unsalted butter
- 1 small onion, finely chopped
- 2 tablespoons minced garlic
- 2 cups long-grain rice
- ½ teaspoon saffron threads
- Salt
- 3 medium red bell peppers
- 3 medium yellow bell peppers
- 1 pound thin asparagus, cut into 2-inch pieces
- ⅓ cup fresh lime juice
- 1 tablespoon red-wine vinegar
- 2 tablespoons honey
- 2 chipotle chiles in adobo,* seeded and minced
- ¼ cup olive oil
- Freshly ground black pepper
- ¼ cup coarsely chopped fresh cilantro

*Available at Latin American markets

1. Melt the butter in a medium saucepan. Add the onion and garlic and cook over moderately high heat, stirring occasionally, until translucent, about 4 minutes. Stir in the rice and saffron threads. Add 4 cups of water and 2 teaspoons salt and bring to a boil, stirring occasionally. Cover the pan, reduce the heat to low and cook until the rice is tender, about 20 minutes. Transfer the rice to a large bowl and let cool completely.

2. Meanwhile, roast the red and yellow bell peppers over a gas flame or under a broiler, turning occasionally, until charred all over. Transfer to a paper bag and let steam for 15 minutes. Remove the skin, seeds, cores and ribs and coarsely chop. (**MAKE AHEAD:** The rice and peppers can be refrigerated separately for up to 1 day; let return to room temperature before proceeding.)

3. In a medium saucepan of boiling salted water, cook the asparagus until just tender, about 2 minutes. Drain, rinse with cold water and drain again. Add the asparagus to the rice with the chopped peppers.

4. In a small bowl, combine the lime juice, vinegar, honey and chipotles. Whisk in the olive oil and season with salt and pepper. Pour the dressing over the rice and toss to combine. Stir in the cilantro and serve.—BOBBY FLAY

ROASTED-TOMATO RISOTTO

4 SERVINGS

- 6 cups chicken stock, preferably homemade
- 1½ tablespoons extra-virgin olive oil
- 1 onion, cut into ⅓-inch dice
- 1½ cups arborio rice (10 ounces)
- 3 roasted-tomato halves from Roasted Tomatoes (p. 362), coarsely chopped
- 4 roasted garlic cloves from Roasted Tomatoes (p. 362)
- 1 tablespoon unsalted butter
- ¼ cup freshly grated Parmesan cheese
- Salt and freshly ground pepper

1. In a medium saucepan, bring the stock to a simmer; keep it at a bare simmer over low heat.

2. In a medium saucepan, warm the oil. Add the onion and stir over moderate heat until softened. Add the rice and cook for 1 minute, stirring to coat with oil.

3. Add 1 cup of the hot stock to the rice and cook, stirring constantly, until almost all the stock has been absorbed. Add the tomato halves, garlic and another cup of stock and cook, stirring,

MAKING RISOTTO

To make perfect risotto:

• Use the right-size pot. A two-quart heavy-bottomed stainless-steel saucepan will do just fine for one cup of rice. If your pot is too large, the rice and stock mixture will spread out and boil dry too quickly. This requires you to add stock continually to keep the dish from burning. The result: a risotto that's too rich.

• Chop the onion fine (use one medium onion per cup of rice) so it won't overpower the risotto.

• Sweat the onion slowly without browning for about five minutes before adding it to the rice. This drives off the excess water in the onion and also helps to concentrate its flavor.

• Sauté the rice in the onion and oil for a minute, or until the rice is pearl-colored. This softens the rice so that it's ready to absorb the stock.

• Use a high-quality stock—preferably homemade.

• Stir, stir, stir.

• Use an aged Parmigiano-Reggiano cheese (called *stravecchio*). If you're trying to reduce fat, you can cut the amount of cheese in half without sacrificing any flavor.—MICHAEL CHIARELLO

until the stock is absorbed. Continue to add hot stock, 1 cup at a time, stirring until it is absorbed before adding more. The risotto is done when the grains are just tender and bound with a creamy sauce, about 25 minutes in all. Stir in the butter and Parmesan, season with salt and pepper and serve.—TOM COLICCHIO

GARLIC RISOTTO WITH TOMATO SAUCE

A Barolo, such as the 1990 Vietti Riserva Villero or the 1990 Prunotto Bussia, has enough character to handle the garlicky, salty and cheesy flavors in this rich risotto.

> **CHEF'S TIP**
>
> **I like to tell people that if they're not sweating when the risotto's done, they haven't made it the right way. There's no shortcut. To have perfect risotto, you have to stir the rice constantly.—NICK MORFOGEN**

Garlic Risotto with Tomato Sauce

4 SERVINGS

TOMATO SAUCE:

- ¼ cup olive oil
- 1 teaspoon minced garlic
- 4 pounds vine-ripened tomatoes, peeled, seeded and coarsely chopped
- ¼ cup vegetable stock or canned broth
- 1½ teaspoons honey
- 6 fresh basil leaves
- Salt and freshly ground pepper

RISOTTO:

- 5 large unpeeled garlic cloves
- ¼ cup plus 1 tablespoon olive oil
- 4 anchovy fillets, mashed
- 1 teaspoon minced fresh flat-leaf parsley
- 1 teaspoon minced fresh basil
- 1 teaspoon minced fresh oregano
- 3¾ cups vegetable stock or canned broth
- ¼ fennel bulb, finely chopped
- 1 cup arborio rice (about 7 ounces)
- 2 bay leaves
- ⅓ cup dry white wine
- 3 tablespoons unsalted butter, softened
- 1¼ cups freshly grated Parmesan cheese (about 4 ounces)
- Salt and freshly ground pepper

FRIED OLIVES:

- Peanut oil, for frying
- 24 Kalamata olives (about 5 ounces), halved and pitted
- ¼ cup buttermilk
- 1 cup all-purpose flour

1. Make the tomato sauce: Heat the oil in a large nonreactive saucepan. Add the garlic and cook over moderately high heat until lightly browned, about 1 minute. Add the tomatoes, stock, honey and basil and bring to a boil. Lower the heat to moderate and simmer, stirring, until the tomatoes break apart and the sauce thickens, about 20 minutes. Strain the sauce, pressing down on the solids, and season with salt and pepper. (**MAKE AHEAD:** The sauce can be refrigerated for up to 2 days; rewarm before serving.)

2. Make the risotto: Preheat the oven to 325°. Toss the garlic with the 1 tablespoon oil, wrap in foil and roast for about 45 minutes, or until tender; let cool. Slip the garlic cloves from their skins and mash with the anchovies, parsley, basil and oregano.

3. In a medium saucepan, heat the stock over moderate heat; keep warm. Heat the remaining ¼ cup oil in a heavy nonreactive medium saucepan. Add the fennel and cook over low heat, stirring, until tender, about 5 minutes. Add the rice and bay leaves and stir to coat with the oil; try not to break up the bay leaves. Stir in the wine and simmer until absorbed, about 2 minutes.

4. Add one-quarter of the warm stock to the rice and cook, stirring constantly, until absorbed, about 5 minutes. Add the remaining stock in three batches; cook, stirring constantly until the stock is absorbed before adding more. The rice is done when it is just cooked through and lightly bound with creamy liquid, about 25 minutes altogether. Stir in the garlic paste with the last batch of stock. When the risotto is done, add the butter and Parmesan and season with salt and pepper.

5. Make the fried olives: Heat 1 inch of peanut oil in a medium skillet. Coat the olives with buttermilk and dredge them in the flour. Fry over high heat until crisp and golden, about 2 minutes. Transfer to paper towels; drain and keep warm.

6. Rewarm the tomato sauce and pour it into four shallow bowls. Mound the risotto in the center, garnish with the fried olives and serve at once.—NICK MORFOGEN

PRESSURE-COOKER SAFFRON RISOTTO

The cooking time for this recipe and the amount of stock needed will vary slightly, depending upon the type of short-grain Italian rice you use. I find that arborio rice works well with three-and-a-half cups of stock, while Vialone Nano and Carnaroli usually require a half-cup more stock and about a minute of additional cooking in an uncovered pressure cooker.

SUREFIRE RISOTTO

A pressure cooker allows you to create superb risotto in five minutes with almost no stirring. The texture is just right; the grains of rice are cooked through but still slightly chewy and bound with a creamy, silky liquid. Pressure-cooker risotto is so simple and reliable that it has become my standard company dish. After tasting my latest risotto, a friend told me, "I'm buying a cooker on the way home. If I make nothing else in that pot, it's still a bargain."—LORNA J. SASS

6 SERVINGS

- 1 tablespoon olive oil
- 3 large shallots, finely chopped
- 1½ cups Italian short-grain rice (10 ounces)
- ½ cup dry white wine or vermouth
- 3½ to 4 cups chicken stock or vegetable stock
- 1 teaspoon salt
- Scant ¼ teaspoon saffron threads, crumbled
- ½ cup freshly grated Parmesan cheese (2 ounces)
- 3 tablespoons minced fresh parsley
- Freshly ground pepper

1. Heat the olive oil in a pressure cooker. Add the chopped shallots and cook over high heat until just translucent, about 30 seconds. Add the rice and stir to coat thoroughly with oil. Add the wine and stir constantly until it has evaporated, about 1 minute. Stir in 3½ cups of the stock along with the salt and saffron.

2. Lock the lid of the pressure cooker in place and bring to high pressure over high heat. Lower the heat just enough to maintain high pressure and cook for 5 minutes. Reduce the pressure with a quick-release method. Remove the lid, tilting it away from you to allow any excess steam to escape.

3. Give the risotto a vigorous stir. If the rice is still a bit too hard or the risotto too soupy, cook it over moderately high heat, stirring constantly, until the desired texture and consistency are reached. Add the remaining ½ cup of stock if necessary. Stir in the Parmesan and parsley and season with pepper. Serve immediately in shallow bowls.—LORNA J. SASS

BAKED RICE WITH PARSLEY Q

4 SERVINGS

- 2 tablespoons unsalted butter
- ½ small onion, minced
- 1 cup medium-grain rice, such as Valencia or arborio
- 2¼ cups fish stock or 1¼ cups bottled clam juice diluted with 1 cup of water
- 2 tablespoons minced fresh parsley
- Salt

Preheat the oven to 400°. Melt the butter in an ovenproof saucepan. Add the onion and cook over high heat, stirring, until translucent, about 2 minutes. Add the rice and stir until the grains are coated. Add the fish stock, parsley and a large pinch of salt and bring to a boil. Stir the rice, cover and bake for 18 minutes. Remove from the oven and let stand, covered, for 10 minutes. Stir the rice and season with salt.—PENELOPE CASAS

FRIED RICE WITH ASPARAGUS LF

Rinsing and soaking the rice ensures perfectly cooked grains. If you have leftover cooked long-grain white rice, use it here; you'll need four cups.

4 SERVINGS

- 1½ cups extra-long-grain rice
- 1 large egg
- 1 large egg white
- 1 tablespoon peanut oil
- ¼ cup chicken stock or canned low-sodium broth
- 2 tablespoons oyster sauce
- 1½ teaspoons light soy sauce
- 2 teaspoons white wine
- 1 teaspoon sugar

½ teaspoon Asian sesame oil
Freshly ground white pepper
1½ teaspoons minced garlic
12 asparagus spears, trimmed and cut into ½-inch pieces
6 canned water chestnuts, rinsed, drained and cut into ¼-inch dice
3 scallions, thinly sliced
3 tablespoons minced fresh cilantro

1. In a saucepan, rinse the rice with water, rubbing the grains between your palms. Drain and rinse the rice two more times. Drain and return the rice to the saucepan. Add 1½ cups of water and let stand for 1 hour.
2. Bring the rice to a boil over high heat. Stir, then cook until most of the water has evaporated, about 5 minutes. Reduce the heat to low and stir again. Cover and simmer for 7 minutes. Remove from the heat, fluff the rice with a fork and let stand, covered, until tender, about 20 minutes. Fluff the rice to separate the grains, transfer to a plate and let cool completely. (MAKE AHEAD: The rice can be refrigerated for up to 2 days.)
3. In a small bowl, beat the egg with the egg white and mix in 1 teaspoon of the peanut oil. Heat a wok over moderately high heat for 20 seconds. Add the eggs and scramble until cooked through. Transfer the eggs to a work surface and coarsely chop them.
4. In a bowl, combine half of the chicken stock with the oyster sauce, soy sauce, wine, sugar, sesame oil and pepper. Set the wok over high heat for 30 seconds. Add the remaining 2 teaspoons peanut oil and swirl to coat the wok. Add the garlic and stir-fry until fragrant, about 30 seconds. Add the asparagus and stir-fry for 1 minute. Add the water chestnuts and the remaining chicken stock and stir-fry for 2 minutes. Add the rice and stir to separate the grains. Add the eggs and toss to combine. Stir in the oyster-sauce mixture and stir-fry for 2 minutes more. Stir in the scallions and cilantro and serve.—EILEEN YIN-FEI LO

CREAMY WILD RICE WITH MUSHROOMS LF

8 SERVINGS

1¾ cups wild rice (¾ pound)
½ tablespoon unsalted butter
½ tablespoon vegetable oil
½ cup minced shallots
1 tablespoon minced fresh thyme
Salt and freshly ground pepper
1 pound white mushrooms, trimmed and sliced ¼ inch thick
¾ pound fresh shiitake mushrooms, stemmed, caps sliced ¼ inch thick
1½ cups skim milk
1½ cups whole milk
2 tablespoons arrowroot
2 tablespoons minced fresh flat-leaf parsley
1 tablespoon minced fresh chives

1. In a saucepan of salted boiling water, cook the rice until very tender, about 45 minutes; drain.
2. Preheat the oven to 475°. Melt the butter in the oil in an enameled cast-iron casserole. Add the shallots and thyme, season with salt and pepper and cook over high heat, stirring, for 2 minutes. Stir in the white and shiitake mushrooms. Bake for about 15 minutes, or until the mushrooms are just wilted. Stir and bake for about 10 minutes more, or until the mushrooms are dry.
3. In a large measuring cup, combine the skim milk and the whole milk. In a small bowl, gradually whisk ¼ cup of the milk mixture into the arrowroot until smooth.
4. Set the casserole over high heat. Add the remaining milk and bring to a boil. Stir in the arrowroot mixture and cook until thickened, about 1 minute. Add the rice and cook, stirring, until heated through. Add the parsley and chives; season with salt and pepper.—BOB CHAMBERS

CORN PILAF LF

Before serving, remove the cinnamon stick and cardamom pods—or leave them in as a garnish, but warn your guests not to eat them.

4 SERVINGS

2 teaspoons olive oil
½ teaspoon cumin seeds
2-inch cinnamon stick
4 to 5 whole cardamom pods (optional)
1 cup basmati or long-grain white rice, rinsed and drained
2¼ cups vegetable stock or canned broth or chicken stock, skimmed of fat
¾ cup thawed frozen corn kernels
Salt

Heat the oil in a medium saucepan. Add the cumin seeds, cinnamon stick and cardamom pods and cook over moderate heat, stirring often, until the cumin is browned, about 1 minute. Add

QUICK TIP

Precooked cornmeal, ground from cooked corn kernels, is the key to quick tamales. This is not to be confused with standard cornmeal, which is made from dried uncooked corn kernels. Goya's precooked cornmeal, also called *masarepa*, is the most widely available. P.A.N., from Venezuela, is another good brand. For information on stores near you, call 1-800-275-4692.

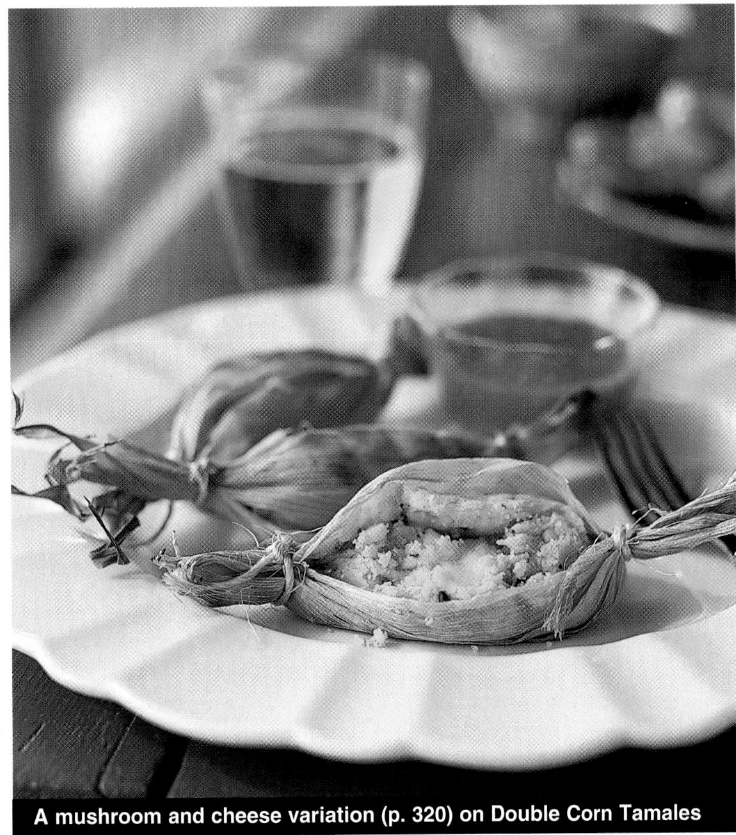

A mushroom and cheese variation (p. 320) on Double Corn Tamales

the rice and stock, cover and bring to a boil. Reduce the heat to low and simmer, covered, until all the liquid is absorbed and the rice is tender, about 15 minutes. Add the corn, cover and cook until heated through, about 2 minutes more. Season with salt, fluff with a fork and serve.—BHARTI KIRCHNER

DOUBLE CORN TAMALES

MAKES ABOUT 14 TAMALES

- 4 large ears of corn, husks carefully removed and kept whole, silk discarded
- 2 cups precooked cornmeal (about 11 ounces; see "Quick Tip," above)
- 1 teaspoon salt
- 5 tablespoons unsalted butter, softened
- 1 teaspoon hot pepper sauce
- Tomatillo Sauce and Fresh Tomato Sauce, for serving (recipes follow)

1. Cut the corn kernels from the cobs; you should have about 2 cups. Cook the corn kernels in 4 cups of boiling salted water until tender, about 4 minutes. Drain the kernels in a colander set over a bowl and let the corn and liquid cool completely.

2. In a large skillet, toast the cornmeal over moderate heat, stirring occasionally, until fragrant, about 3 minutes. Transfer to a plate to cool.

3. In a large bowl, combine the cornmeal with the salt. Blend in the butter with your hands. Stir in the corn kernels and hot sauce. Using a wooden spoon, beat in about 2 cups of the reserved corn liquid, ½ cup at a time, beating well to incorporate as much air as possible; the dough should be very moist and light.

4. Separate the corn husks. Overlap two to three of the husks to make a 6-inch-wide wrapper for each tamale. Mound ⅓ cup of the dough in the center of each set of husks and pat down slightly, leaving a 1½-inch border all around. Wrap the husks around the filling to completely enclose it; allow room for the tamale dough to expand during cooking. Pinch the ends and tie tightly with string, leaving 1 inch of husk sticking out at each end.

5. Light a grill or preheat the oven to 500°. Grill the tamales over moderate heat, turning often, for about 8 minutes, or until browned and crisp outside and heated through. Alternatively, roast them in the oven for about

MAKING TAMALES

Beat the tamale dough to incorporate as much air as possible; the dough should be light, not heavy.

Carefully fold the corn husks up and over the mounded tamale filling to enclose it completely.

Secure each end of the tamale with string, leaving a little space for the dough to expand.

Grill the tamales for four to five minutes per side, until they are heated through and firm when pressed.

10 minutes. In either case the cooked tamales should feel firm and the husks should puff. Serve at once with the sauces.

Tomatillo Sauce

MAKES ABOUT 1 CUP

- 10 medium tomatillos, husked and cored
- ½ small onion, finely chopped
- 1 small garlic clove, minced
- ¼ cup minced fresh cilantro
- Salt

1. In a small saucepan of boiling water, cook the tomatillos until just tender, about 3 minutes. Drain and cool. Coarsely chop the tomatillos.
2. In a food processor, process the tomatillos for 5 seconds. Add the onion and process to a coarse puree. Transfer the sauce to a bowl and stir in the garlic and cilantro. Just before serving, season with salt.

TAMALE VARIATIONS

Here are four easy variations on the Double Corn Tamales. For each one, add the ingredients to the tamale dough with the corn kernels.

MUSHROOM AND CHEESE TAMALES **Stem and dice ½ pound fresh shiitake mushrooms. Sauté in 1 tablespoon olive oil until tender; use in place of 1 cup of the corn kernels. Cut fourteen ½-inch cubes of Monterey Jack cheese and push one into each tamale before wrapping in the husks.**

CHICKEN TAMALES **Replace 1 cup of the corn kernels with 1 cup of diced cooked chicken; add a few tablespoons of roast-chicken pan drippings, if you have any.**

CHORIZO TAMALES **Replace 1 cup of the corn kernels with a boiled, diced 4-ounce chorizo sausage.**

SWEET-POTATO TAMALES **Replace 1 cup corn kernels with 1 cup cooked, diced sweet potato.**

Fresh Tomato Sauce

MAKES ABOUT 1 CUP

- 1 large ripe tomato, coarsely chopped
- 2 garlic cloves, smashed
- 1 tablespoon extra-virgin olive oil
- Salt

In a mini-processor, process the tomato to a coarse puree. Transfer to a bowl and stir in the garlic and oil. Let stand for at least 20 minutes or up to 2 hours. Before serving, discard the garlic. Season with salt.—MARCIA KIESEL

SOFT POLENTA WITH THYME

Polenta is available at specialty-food shops and at health-food stores, where it is often labeled coarsely ground cornmeal. Don't try to make polenta with finely ground cornmeal; you'll be disappointed.

6 SERVINGS

- 2 tablespoons extra-virgin olive oil
- 1 medium onion, finely chopped
- 3 garlic cloves, minced
- 4½ cups chicken stock or canned low-sodium broth
- Coarse sea salt

1½ cups polenta or coarsely ground cornmeal
4 tablespoons unsalted butter
1 teaspoon finely chopped fresh thyme
½ cup freshly grated Parmesan cheese (about 1½ ounces)
Freshly ground pepper

1. Heat the oil in a large heavy saucepan. Add the onion and garlic and cook over moderate heat, stirring occasionally, until softened, about 6 minutes.
2. Add the stock, 1½ cups of water and 1 teaspoon coarse sea salt and bring to a simmer over moderately high heat. Whisk in the polenta in a slow, thin stream, whisking constantly so that no lumps form. Cook, stirring frequently in the same direction with a flat wooden paddle, until the polenta is fairly thick, 25 to 30 minutes. Stir in the butter, thyme and Parmesan. Season with salt and pepper and remove from the heat. (MAKE AHEAD: The polenta can be covered and kept warm for up to 4 hours in a metal bowl set over a pan of simmering water. Stir it occasionally, and if it becomes too thick, stir in a few tablespoons of boiling water.) Serve hot.—BRIGIT LEGERE BINNS

PEPPERY POLENTA WITH WILD MUSHROOMS LF

This rich-tasting, cheesy yet low-fat dish can be made with regular as well as coarse cornmeal; just don't use fine cornmeal, or the polenta will be gluey.

4 SERVINGS

3 large red bell peppers
1 tablespoon plus 1 teaspoon olive oil
1 small onion, minced
3 large tomatoes, peeled, seeded and finely chopped
2 garlic cloves, minced
1 teaspoon honey
1 tablespoon minced fresh basil
¼ teaspoon minced fresh thyme
Salt and freshly ground pepper
1 large fennel bulb, trimmed, halved, cored and sliced lengthwise ⅓ inch thick
1½ pounds assorted fresh wild mushrooms, such as cremini, chanterelles and shiitakes, stems discarded from the shiitakes
About 7 cups vegetable stock or canned broth
1½ cups coarse cornmeal*
½ cup 2% milk
¼ cup freshly grated Romano cheese
2 tablespoons thinly sliced scallions

*Available at specialty-food stores

1. Roast the peppers directly over a gas flame or under the broiler as close to the heat as possible, turning often, until charred all over. Transfer to a paper bag and let steam for 10 minutes. Peel off the blackened skins and discard the cores, ribs and seeds. Finely chop the peppers.
2. Heat 2 teaspoons of the oil in a nonreactive saucepan. Add the onion and cook over moderately high heat, stirring, until translucent, about 5 minutes. Add the roasted peppers, tomatoes, garlic, honey, basil and thyme and season with salt and pepper. Cook, stirring, until thickened, about 15 minutes. Working in batches, puree in a blender or food processor. (MAKE AHEAD: The sauce can be refrigerated up to 2 days. Thin it with a little stock before rewarming.)
3. Preheat the oven to 400°. Arrange the fennel slices in a small baking dish, season with salt and pepper and roast for about 20 minutes, or until tender and lightly browned.
4. Heat the remaining 2 teaspoons oil in a large nonstick skillet. Add the mushrooms, season with salt and pepper and cook over moderately high heat, stirring occasionally, until softened,

CHEF'S MENU

For Hubert Keller, the intense flavors of roasted vegetables are the secret to tasty, satisfying low-fat dishes. For this menu, he strips most of the fat but none of the flavor from smoky eggplant with crisp croutons and soft polenta with fennel and wild mushrooms.

The peppers and tomatoes in the eggplant appetizer point to a light, crisp, herbaceous Sauvignon Blanc. Try the 1994 Château Bonnet Entre-Deux-Mers or the 1994 Jean Sauvion Sancerre Les Fondettes. The deeper flavors of the polenta with wild mushrooms call for a medium-bodied red, such as the 1992 Podere Il Palazzino or the 1992 Castello di Ama Chianti Classico.

EGGPLANT CAVIAR (P. 15)

PEPPERY POLENTA WITH WILD MUSHROOMS (P. 321)

FROZEN RASPBERRY YOGURT (P. 439)

CHOCOLATE MERINGUES (P. 445)

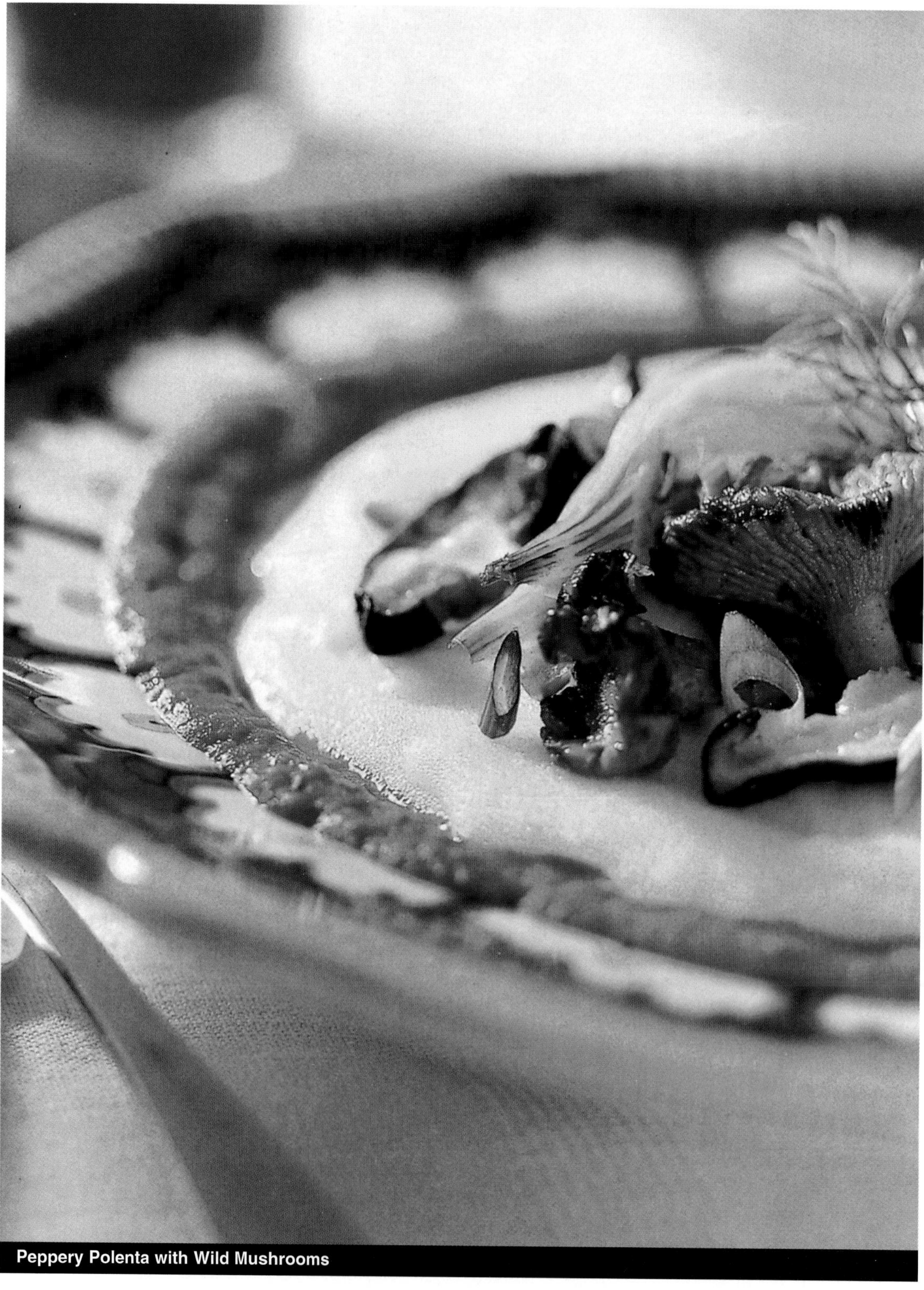

Peppery Polenta with Wild Mushrooms

about 10 minutes. Add a little stock if the mushrooms seem dry.

5. In a heavy medium saucepan, bring 6½ cups of the vegetable stock to a boil. Gradually whisk in the cornmeal. Simmer over moderate heat, stirring constantly, until thickened, about 25 minutes depending on the coarseness of the cornmeal. Stir in the milk and cook, stirring frequently, until the cornmeal is creamy, about 10 minutes longer. Remove from the heat, stir in the cheese and season well with pepper.

6. Rewarm the red-pepper sauce, fennel and mushrooms. Divide the polenta among four plates. Spoon a little sauce around the polenta and arrange the fennel and wild mushrooms on top. Garnish with the scallions and serve the remaining sauce alongside.—HUBERT KELLER

SWEET-POTATO POLENTA GALETTES

These galettes resemble crisp-fried polenta, but they have a creamier texture and a lovely sweet-potato flavor.

MAKES ABOUT 30 GALETTES

- 2 cups cornmeal
- 2 large sweet potatoes, peeled and quartered
- 4 tablespoons unsalted butter
- Salt and freshly ground black pepper
- ⅓ cup freshly grated Parmesan cheese

1. Lightly oil a jelly-roll pan or other shallow-rimmed baking sheet. In a bowl, combine the cornmeal with 2 cups cold water and set aside to soak.

2. Put the potatoes in a medium saucepan, cover with cold water and bring to a boil. Boil the potatoes until very soft, about 20 minutes. Drain well and pass through the fine disk of a food mill. Alternatively, mash the potatoes by hand until smooth. (You should have about 1¼ cups.)

3. In another medium saucepan, bring 2 cups of water to a boil. Add 2 tablespoons of the butter, 1 teaspoon salt, ½ teaspoon pepper and the cornmeal mixture. Bring to a boil, reduce the heat to moderately high and cook, stirring often, until the mixture is very thick, 6 to 8 minutes. Remove from the heat and stir in the sweet-potato puree. Season with salt and pepper. Spread the mixture on the prepared baking sheet in an even ¾-inch-thick layer and cover with wax paper. Refrigerate until firm, at least 1 hour.

4. Using a round or oval 2- to 3-inch fluted cookie cutter, stamp out the galettes. Alternatively, the sweet-potato mixture can be cut into 2-inch squares with a knife.

5. Preheat the broiler. In a large skillet, melt the remaining 2 tablespoons butter over moderately high heat. Fry the galettes in batches until lightly browned on both sides. As they are done, transfer them to cookie sheets. Sprinkle with the cheese and broil 4 to 6 inches from the heat for about 3 minutes, or until they are lightly browned around the edges and heated through. Serve the galettes immediately.—CATHERINE ALEXANDROU AND MICHEL BOURDEAUX

Sweet-Potato Polenta Galettes accompanying Braised Veal à l'Orange (p. 233) and buttered broccoli

CHEESY SEMOLINA WITH BAY LEAF

Delicate grains of semolina—coarsely ground durum wheat—are cooked in much the same manner as polenta, but for far less time. You can use either fine semolina or what is sold as semolina flour for making pasta. If you can't spare the time to infuse the milk with bay leaves, simply add the leaves to the semolina as it is simmering in Step 2 and remove them before serving.

6–8 SERVINGS

- 1 quart whole milk
- 2 dried imported or fresh bay leaves
- 2 teaspoons fine sea salt
- 1 cup fine semolina
- ½ cup freshly grated Parmigiano-Reggiano cheese (2 ounces)
- Freshly grated nutmeg

1. In a large nonreactive saucepan, bring the milk and the bay leaves to a boil over moderate heat. Remove the saucepan from the heat and let the milk steep for 1 hour.

2. Bring the milk to a simmer over moderate heat. Add the sea salt and gradually add the semolina in a thin, steady stream, stirring constantly with a wooden spoon to prevent lumping. (If any lumps form, press them against the side of the pot and they will disappear.) Adjust the heat to maintain a simmer and cook, stirring constantly, until the semolina becomes a soft mass that cleanly pulls away from the sides of the pan, 3 to 5 minutes.

3. Stir in the cheese and a sprinkling of freshly grated nutmeg. Discard the bay leaves and serve at once.—PATRICIA WELLS

TABBOULEH Q

4 SERVINGS

- ¾ cup bulgur (about 4 ounces), rinsed
- ¾ cup finely chopped fresh flat-leaf parsley (1 large bunch)
- ¼ cup finely chopped fresh mint
- 6 scallions, white and tender green, finely chopped
- 3 tablespoons olive oil
- 2 tablespoons fresh lemon juice
- Salt and freshly ground black pepper
- Generous pinch of cayenne pepper

1. Put the bulgur in a medium bowl and add hot water to cover by at least 2 inches. Let soak for 15 minutes. Drain in a fine sieve, pressing on the grains to extract excess water. Transfer to a bowl.

2. Add the parsley, mint, scallions, oil and lemon juice and toss. Season with salt, black pepper and cayenne and toss. Cover and let stand at room temperature for at least 30 minutes. (MAKE AHEAD: The tabbouleh can be refrigerated for 1 day. Let return to room temperature before serving.) —JUDITH SUTTON

LEFTOVERS

If you want to serve Cheesy Semolina with Bay Leaf a second night, smooth the leftovers into a gratin dish, dot with butter and more cheese, and place under a broiler to brown.—PATRICIA WELLS

BEET TABBOULEH

Beets make this tabbouleh colorful and sweet, while the allspice dressing adds a spicy note.

6–8 SERVINGS

- 2 pounds medium beets, stems trimmed
- ¼ cup plus 3 tablespoons olive oil
- 1½ cups medium bulgur (9 ounces)
- 5 cups boiling water
- ½ teaspoon allspice berries
- ½ teaspoon cumin seeds
- ¼ cup plus 1 tablespoon fresh lemon juice
- Salt and freshly ground pepper
- 1 medium sweet onion, such as Vidalia, finely chopped
- 3 tablespoons finely chopped fresh spearmint

1. Preheat the oven to 350°. Put the beets in a baking dish and toss with 2 tablespoons of the oil. Cover with foil and bake for about 1½ hours, or until tender when pierced with a knife. Let cool slightly, then slip off the skins. Cut into 1-inch cubes.

2. Meanwhile, put the bulgur in a medium bowl and pour the boiling water over it. Cover with a plate and let stand until the water is absorbed and the bulgur is tender, about 1 hour. Drain the bulgur, rinse with cold water and squeeze dry in handfuls, fluffing it with your fingers as you transfer it to a large bowl.

3. In a small skillet, toast the allspice and cumin over moderately high heat until fragrant, about 1 minute. Let cool. Grind in a spice grinder or mortar, or finely chop with a knife. Transfer to a bowl. Add the remaining ¼ cup plus 1 tablespoon olive oil, the lemon juice, ½ teaspoon salt and a generous pinch of pepper.

4. Add the dressing and the onion to the bulgur, toss well and season with salt and pepper. Add the beets; toss again. (MAKE AHEAD: The tabbouleh can be refrigerated for up to 1 day.) Stir in the spearmint and serve chilled or at room temperature.—MARCIA KIESEL

BULGUR WITH FAVA BEANS

8 SERVINGS

- 1⅓ cups bulgur (about ½ pound)
- ½ cup pine nuts (about 3 ounces)
- 1 pound young fresh fava beans, shelled, or 1 cup frozen baby lima beans, thawed
- ½ cup finely diced seeded tomato
- 2 garlic cloves, minced
- ¼ cup chopped dates
- ½ cup fresh lemon juice
- ½ cup olive oil

Salt and freshly ground pepper
2 tablespoons finely chopped fresh cilantro

1. In a medium saucepan, bring 4 cups of water to a boil. Add the bulgur and cook for 2 minutes. Remove from the heat and let stand uncovered until softened and chewy, about 30 minutes.
2. Meanwhile, preheat the oven to 350°. Toast the pine nuts for about 7 minutes, or until golden. If using fava beans, blanch them in a small saucepan of boiling water until just tender, about 5 minutes. Peel off the tough skins. If using lima beans, blanch them in a saucepan of boiling water until tender, about 2 minutes.
3. Drain the bulgur in a fine sieve, pressing lightly to extract as much water as possible. Transfer to a bowl and stir in the beans, tomato, garlic, dates, lemon juice and oil. Season with salt and pepper. Let stand at room temperature for at least 1 hour or up to 3 hours to allow the flavors to blend. Stir in the cilantro and pine nuts.—MATTHEW KENNEY

COUSCOUS WITH LEMON AND WATERCRESS Q

4 SERVINGS

1 tablespoon unsalted butter
Salt
1 cup instant couscous (about 7 ounces)
1 large bunch watercress, 3 inches of stems removed, cut crosswise into ½-inch pieces
1 medium scallion, finely chopped
1 garlic clove, crushed through a press
¼ cup fresh lemon juice
2 tablespoons olive oil
2 tablespoons coarsely chopped fresh flat-leaf parsley
Freshly ground pepper

1. In a medium saucepan, combine 1½ cups of water with the butter and ½ teaspoon salt and bring to a boil over high heat. Stir in the couscous. Cover the pan. Remove from the heat. Let stand until tender, about 5 minutes.
2. Fluff the couscous with a fork. Stir in the watercress, cover and let stand until wilted, about 15 minutes. Stir in the scallion, garlic, lemon juice, oil and parsley; season with salt and pepper. Serve the couscous at room temperature.—STEPHANIE LYNESS

BAKED MUSHROOM POLENTA WITH MOZZARELLA LF

8 SERVINGS

Vegetable cooking spray
1 pound medium mushrooms, thickly sliced
4 cups chicken stock or canned low-sodium broth, skimmed of fat
1½ cups yellow cornmeal
¼ cup plus 2 tablespoons freshly grated Parmesan cheese
Salt and freshly ground pepper
3 large shallots, finely chopped
2 large garlic cloves, minced
1 cup dry white wine
One 28-ounce can crushed tomatoes, with their liquid
2 tablespoons minced fresh flat-leaf parsley
1 teaspoon minced fresh thyme
Pinch of sugar
2 medium red bell peppers, roasted, peeled, cored and seeded
2 medium yellow bell peppers, roasted, peeled, cored and seeded
½ pound part-skim mozzarella, grated (about 1½ cups)

1. Coat a large nonstick skillet with cooking spray. Warm over moderately high heat. Add the mushrooms; cook, stirring, until browned, about 10 minutes.
2. In a heavy saucepan, bring the stock and 1½ cups of water to a boil over moderately high heat. Whisk in the cornmeal until smooth and cook, stirring, until tender and pulling away from the sides of the pan, about 30 minutes. Stir in the mushrooms, the 2 tablespoons Parmesan, 1½ teaspoons salt and ½ teaspoon pepper. Spread the polenta about ½ inch thick in a jelly-roll pan and let cool until set. Cut the polenta into 3-by-1-inch rectangles.
3. In a nonreactive saucepan, simmer the shallots and garlic in the wine until almost all of the liquid has evaporated, about 4 minutes. Add the tomatoes, parsley, thyme and sugar, season with salt and pepper and cook, stirring, until thickened, about 10 minutes.
4. Preheat the oven to 375°. Cut the peppers into 1-by-¼-inch strips. Spread one-third of the tomato sauce in a large nonreactive baking dish. Arrange half the polenta on top, overlapping if necessary. Sprinkle with half of the mozzarella and peppers and half of the remaining sauce and Parmesan. Arrange the rest of the polenta on top; cover with the rest of the mozzarella, peppers, sauce and Parmesan. Bake about 30 minutes, or until bubbling and just browned on top.—BOB CHAMBERS

CHAPTER 15

~

VEGETABLES

Corn with Smoky Bacon in Foil

CORN WITH SMOKY BACON IN FOIL

4 SERVINGS

- 4 large ears of corn, kernels cut from the cobs
- 2 ounces smoked bacon, cut into 3 pieces
- 1 scallion, white and tender green, thinly sliced

1. Light a grill or preheat the oven to 475°. In a medium saucepan of boiling water, blanch the corn kernels for 1 minute and then drain.

2. Mound the corn on half of a 2-foot piece of foil, leaving a 1-inch border around the sides. Tuck the bacon pieces among the kernels. Fold the other half of the foil over the corn and make small folds around the edges to seal. Grill for 6 to 8 minutes, or until the packet is puffed. Alternatively, set the packet on a baking sheet and bake on the bottom of the oven for about 10 minutes. Open the packet and stir in the scallion rounds.—MARCIA KIESEL

GRILLED CORN WITH THYME BUTTER Q

4 SERVINGS

4 large ears of corn, husks pulled back but not removed, corn silk discarded and husks replaced
4 tablespoons unsalted butter, softened
2 teaspoons minced fresh thyme
Salt and freshly ground pepper

1. Light the grill. Soak the corn in a large bowl of cold water for 15 minutes, then drain. Grill over moderately high heat for about 20 minutes, turning often, until tender; the corn husks will blacken.

2. Combine the butter and thyme. Serve the corn with the butter, salt and pepper.—SUSAN LANTZIUS

HOW TO BUY AND STORE EGGPLANT

- **Look for glossy skin that is stretched tautly over full, firm curves.**
- **Pick out an eggplant that is relatively light for its size, whatever the variety and shape. Overripe eggplants, which feel heavier in the hand, have bigger seeds and are less sweet.**
- **Store eggplant in the vegetable drawer of the refrigerator for not more than two or three days.—MARCELLA HAZAN**

CHICKPEA AND RED-PEPPER MEDLEY LF

The garlic here is cooked whole and treated as a vegetable, not a seasoning.

4 SERVINGS

3 cups canned chickpeas in their liquid
1 tablespoon olive oil
1 large onion, finely chopped
6 whole garlic cloves, peeled
1 teaspoon turmeric
2 large red bell peppers, cut into 2-by-⅛-inch strips
2 medium jalapeños, seeded and minced
Salt

1. Drain the chickpeas, reserving about 1 cup of the liquid. In a blender or food processor, puree 1 cup of the chickpeas along with the reserved liquid until smooth.

2. Heat the oil in a large skillet. Add the onion and garlic. Cook over moderately high heat, stirring frequently, until the onion is translucent and the garlic is golden, 2 to 3 minutes. Stir in the turmeric. Add the chickpea puree, bell peppers and jalapeños and season with 1 teaspoon salt. Reduce the heat to low and simmer, covered, for 5 minutes. Add the remaining chickpeas, cover and simmer until the bell peppers are just tender, about 5 minutes more. If the stew is too thick, stir in a little water. (MAKE AHEAD: The stew can be refrigerated for up to 1 day. Rewarm before serving, stirring in a small amount of water to thin it.) Season with salt and serve.—BHARTI KIRCHNER

Clockwise from top: **Chickpea and Red-Pepper Medley, Corn Pilaf (p. 318) and Roasted Eggplant in Smoky Tomato Sauce (p. 331)**

SWISS-CHARD TIMBALES WITH EGGPLANT AND RED PEPPER

8 SERVINGS

3 large slender eggplants (about 5 pounds total)
1 large red bell pepper
Ice water
16 medium Swiss-chard leaves
2 tablespoons extra-virgin olive oil
1 large shallot, minced
3 garlic cloves, minced
1 large scallion, minced
2 large plum tomatoes, peeled, seeded and diced
2 teaspoons fresh lemon juice
½ teaspoon fresh rosemary, finely chopped
¼ teaspoon thyme
Salt and freshly ground black pepper
Pinch of cayenne pepper

1. Preheat the oven to 500°. Using a paring knife, pierce the eggplants in several places. Put them on a large baking sheet along with the red pepper and roast the vegetables until tender and the skins darken, about 25 minutes.

2. Remove the roasted vegetables from the oven. Working over a bowl, peel the red pepper as soon as it is cool enough to handle. Remove the stem and seeds and discard them, but allow any pepper juices to fall into the bowl. Cut the red pepper into eight rough squares of equal size. Peel the eggplants and remove as many seeds as possible from the flesh; keep the flesh in thick strips. Drain in a colander set over a plate for about 10 minutes, then cut the eggplants into coarse chunks.

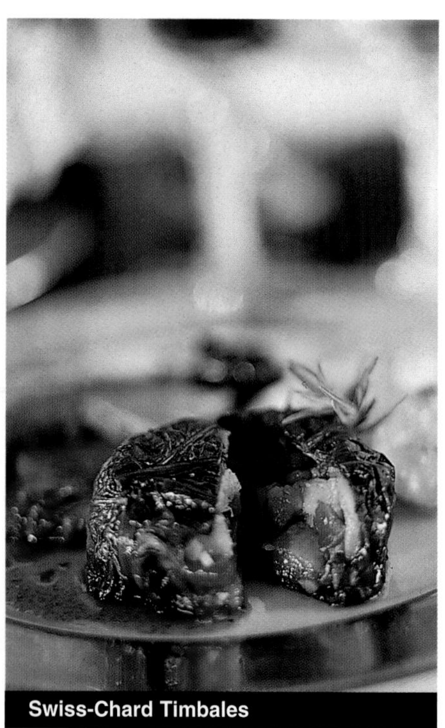
Swiss-Chard Timbales

3. Bring a large saucepan of water to a boil. Have ready a large bowl of ice water. Working with three or four Swiss-chard leaves at a time, hold them by their stems and dip them into the boiling water for about 30 seconds, just until they wilt. Plunge the wilted chard leaves into the ice water. Repeat with the remaining chard leaves. Remove all of the leaves from the ice water and drain on paper towels. Cut off the stems and reserve for another use.

4. In a large nonreactive skillet, heat the olive oil over low heat. When hot, add the shallot and cook, stirring, until softened, about 4 minutes. Add the garlic and scallion and cook, stirring, until fragrant, about 1 minute. Add the tomatoes and increase the heat to moderate. Cook the tomatoes, stirring, until most of the liquid has evaporated, about 3 minutes. Stir in the reserved pepper juices, the eggplant strips, the lemon juice, rosemary and thyme. Season with salt, black pepper and cayenne. Transfer the vegetables to a large plate and let cool.

5. Generously butter eight ½-cup ramekins. Cut any tough veins from the Swiss chard and halve the leaves lengthwise. Thickly line the ramekins with the chard leaves, allowing about 1 inch of overhang. Put about 3 tablespoons of the tomato-and-eggplant mixture into each ramekin and then top with a red-pepper square, pressing lightly. Cover with another 3 tablespoons of the tomato-and-eggplant mixture, using up the remainder. Fold the overhanging chard leaves over the tomato-and-eggplant mixture and press lightly. (MAKE AHEAD: The timbales can be refrigerated for up to 1 day.)

6. Preheat the oven to 350°. Set the ramekins in a roasting pan. Pour enough hot water into the pan to reach halfway up the sides of the ramekins. Cover the pan with foil and bake the timbales for about 20 minutes, or until a knife tip inserted in the center of a timbale comes out hot. The timbales can be kept in their water bath for up to 20 minutes after baking. To serve, wipe the ramekins dry and gently invert them onto dinner plates; the timbales should fall out easily.—MARCIA KIESEL

COOKING EGGPLANT

A way of preparing eggplant that is popular in many cuisines from Provence to Turkey is to cook it whole in its skin and then chop or puree the flesh and combine it with any number of other ingredients. The eggplant can be cooked in the oven, although I have found that if it's roasted—always in its skin—over the flame of a stove-top burner or an outdoor grill, the flesh acquires an exciting smoky tang. After the eggplant is done, I like to pull the flesh away in strips with my fingers, but you can certainly use a knife. The important thing is not to cut it up too fine, which would make its texture uninteresting.—MARCELLA HAZAN

ROASTED EGGPLANT WITH PEPPERS AND CUCUMBER

6 SERVINGS

One 1½-pound eggplant
- ½ teaspoon minced garlic
- ½ cup diced red bell pepper (about ⅓ inch)
- ¼ cup diced yellow bell pepper (about ⅓ inch)
- ½ cup diced cucumber (about ⅓ inch)
- 1 tablespoon chopped fresh parsley
- 2 tablespoons extra-virgin olive oil

1½ to 2 tablespoons fresh lemon juice
Freshly ground black pepper
Salt

1. Roast the eggplant directly over a charcoal grill or a gas burner, or under the broiler; when the side nearest the heat is blackened and the eggplant has become soft, turn it with tongs. Repeat until the eggplant is evenly charred and softened throughout. Set it aside to cool.
2. Pick off as much of the eggplant skin as you can. Cut the flesh into strips less than 1 inch wide. If there are many blackish seeds, remove them. Transfer the eggplant strips to a colander set over a deep dish to drain for at least 30 minutes, or until no more liquid is being released.
3. Transfer the eggplant to a medium bowl. Add the remaining ingredients except for the salt and toss well. Season the eggplant mixture with salt before serving.—MARCELLA HAZAN

TOASTING SPICES

Indian spices, such as cumin and coriander, are at their most flavorful when they're freshly toasted and ground. To toast spices, cook the seeds in a dry skillet over moderate heat, shaking the pan, until they are nicely browned and fragrant, about one minute. Transfer to a spice grinder or mortar and grind to a powder. One tablespoon of whole seeds will yield about one tablespoon of ground spice.

ROASTED EGGPLANT IN SMOKY TOMATO SAUCE LF

4 SERVINGS

- 2 large eggplants, halved lengthwise
- 1½ pounds plum tomatoes, halved lengthwise
- 1 tablespoon olive oil
- 1 large onion, finely chopped
- 1 tablespoon plus 1 teaspoon freshly ground cumin (see "Toasting Spices," left)
- 1 teaspoon turmeric
- 1 teaspoon sugar

Salt
Cayenne pepper
Coarsely chopped cilantro
Lemon wedges

1. Preheat the broiler. Line a large baking sheet with foil. Arrange the eggplant and tomato halves, cut-side down, on the baking sheet. Roast in the middle of the oven for 8 to 10 minutes, or until the tomato skins shrivel and crack. Transfer the tomatoes to a plate as they are done. Continue cooking the eggplant for about 15 minutes longer, or until the flesh softens and the skins char; don't overcook, or the flesh will dry out. Allow the vegetables to cool slightly.
2. Peel the tomatoes and puree them in a blender or food processor. Remove the eggplant flesh from the skin with a fork; discard the skin and coarsely chop the flesh.
3. Heat the oil in a large nonreactive skillet. Add the onion and cook over high heat, stirring frequently, until softened and lightly browned around the edges, 3 to 5 minutes. Stir in the cumin and turmeric to lightly coat the onion. Add the tomato puree, reduce the heat to low and simmer, covered, until slightly thickened, 12 to 15 minutes. Stir in a

Roasted Eggplant with Peppers and Cucumber

LOW-FAT MENU

🍷 A Sauvignon Blanc-Sémillon blend would complement the red peppers, tomatoes and eggplant and balance the spices. Consider such California bottlings as the 1992 Murrieta's Well Vendimia or the 1993 Lakewood Chevriot.

ROASTED EGGPLANT IN SMOKY TOMATO SAUCE (P. 331)

CHICKPEA AND RED-PEPPER MEDLEY (P. 329)

CORN PILAF (P. 318)

little water if the sauce is too thick. Add the eggplant, sugar, 1 teaspoon salt and a pinch of cayenne. Cover and cook over low heat for 10 minutes more. (**MAKE AHEAD:** The eggplant can be refrigerated for up to 1 day. Rewarm before serving.) Season the roasted eggplant with salt and cayenne, garnish with chopped cilantro and serve with lemon wedges.—BHARTI KIRCHNER

ASIAN GLAZED EGGPLANT

4 SERVINGS

- 3 tablespoons peanut oil
- 2 large garlic cloves, thinly sliced
- 2 pounds thin Japanese eggplant, peeled and sliced crosswise ¼ inch thick
- 2 tablespoons dry white wine
- 2 tablespoons oyster sauce
- 2 tablespoons soy sauce
- 2 teaspoons Asian sesame oil
- 2 teaspoons sugar

Salt and freshly ground pepper

1. Heat 1 tablespoon of the peanut oil in a wok. Add the garlic and cook over moderate heat, stirring occasionally, until softened and lightly browned, about 3 minutes. Transfer the garlic to a small bowl.

2. Add one more tablespoon of the peanut oil to the wok, tilting to coat with oil, and raise the heat to high. Add half of the eggplant slices in a single layer around the bottom and sides. Cook without stirring until the eggplant is browned on the bottom, about 3 minutes. Turn and cook until browned on the other side, about 1 minute more. Drizzle 1 tablespoon of the wine all over the eggplant and cook until evaporated. Transfer the eggplant to a dish. Add the remaining 1 tablespoon peanut oil to the wok and repeat the process with the remaining eggplant and wine.

3. Meanwhile, add the oyster sauce, soy sauce, sesame oil and sugar to the cooked garlic. Return all of the eggplant to the wok, add the garlic sauce and stir over high heat until the sauce boils. Season the eggplant with salt and pepper, transfer to a platter and serve.—MARCIA KIESEL

CREOLE RATATOUILLE

12 SERVINGS

- 1 cup olive oil
- 1 tablespoon crushed red pepper
- ¼ cup minced garlic
- 2 medium zucchini, cut into ¾-inch dice
- 2 medium yellow squash, cut into ¾-inch dice
- 2 medium tomatoes, seeded and cut into ¾-inch dice
- 1 medium onion, cut into ¾-inch dice
- 1 medium eggplant, cut into ¾-inch dice
- 3 medium bell peppers, 1 red, 1 green and 1 yellow, cut into ¾-inch dice

Coarse salt

- ½ tablespoon chopped fresh basil
- ½ tablespoon fresh thyme leaves
- ½ tablespoon chopped fresh rosemary leaves
- 1 tablespoon chopped fresh chives
- 2 tablespoons balsamic vinegar

1. In a large nonreactive bowl, mix together the oil, crushed red pepper and garlic. Add the zucchini, yellow squash, tomatoes, onion, eggplant and bell peppers and marinate for 2 hours at room temperature.

2. Preheat the oven to 450°. With a slotted spoon, place the vegetables in two large shallow roasting pans in an even layer. Season with salt. Roast, stirring twice, for 30 minutes, or until tender and beginning to brown.

Asian Glazed Eggplant

3. In a small nonreactive bowl, combine the basil, thyme, rosemary, chives and balsamic vinegar and toss with the vegetables. (**MAKE AHEAD:** The ratatouille can be refrigerated for up to 1 day. Serve reheated or at room temperature.) —JAMIE SHANNON

FRYING TIPS

• Use a neutral-tasting vegetable oil unless you specifically want to impart the flavor of olive oil to the food you are frying.

• The oil should reach at least one inch—better an inch and a half—up the side of the pan.

• The oil should be very hot before you put in any food. If using *pastella* (see Fried Zucchini, below) test the temperature by spooning in a small dollop of batter: It should rise instantly to the surface. If using breading, carefully dip a little corner of the breaded food in the pan; the oil should sizzle around it immediately.

• When you begin to fry, do not add any more pieces to the pan than will occupy just half the pan's surface. After about thirty seconds, fill the pan loosely with more of the food you are frying. When the edges of the first pieces become a tawny gold color, turn them. When you finish turning them, turn the batch you added later. Remove the first batch with a slotted spoon and add new pieces to take its place. Remove the second batch, and repeat.

• Have ready a wire rack set over a rimmed baking sheet or tray. The moment you remove a piece of fried food from the hot oil, place it on the rack to drain.

• When all the food is fried, salt it. Do not add salt to the batter or while frying because salt retains excess moisture instead of allowing it to be vaporized quickly by the hot oil.—MARCELLA HAZAN

ZUCCHINI AND SUMMER SQUASH WITH OREGANO Q

4 SERVINGS

2 tablespoons olive oil
1 pound zucchini, cut into ½-by-2-inch sticks
1 pound yellow summer squash, cut into ½-by-2-inch sticks
Salt and freshly ground pepper
1 garlic clove, minced
1½ teaspoons minced fresh oregano

Heat the oil in a skillet. Add the zucchini, summer squash and salt and pepper to taste. Cook over moderately high heat, stirring, until brown and almost tender, about 5 minutes. Add the garlic and stir for 1 minute. Stir in the oregano.—JACKIE BOBROW

FRIED ZUCCHINI

The zucchini is covered with a simple flour and water batter Italians call pastella. *It produces a marvelously thin, crackling crust that does not fall off. You can use it on onion rings, asparagus, fresh sage leaves, squash blossoms and blanched cauliflower florets.*

4 SERVINGS

⅔ cup all-purpose flour
Vegetable oil
¾ pound very fresh medium zucchini, sliced lengthwise ⅛ inch thick
Salt

1. Put 1 cup water in a shallow bowl; gradually sift in the flour, stirring with a fork until the batter is smooth. It should have the consistency of sour cream. Add more flour or water if necessary.
2. Pour 1½ inches of oil into a large skillet and place over high heat. When the oil is very hot but not smoking, drop five slices of zucchini into the batter. Slip a fork under the zucchini, one slice at a time, and slide it into the skillet; the oil must always be hot enough to sizzle on contact.
3. Cook until a fine golden crust forms on one side, then turn and cook on the other side. With tongs, transfer to a wire rack set over a baking sheet to drain. Repeat until all of the zucchini is fried. Sprinkle with salt and serve piping hot.—MARCELLA HAZAN

GLAZED CUCUMBERS Q

4 SERVINGS

2 medium cucumbers, peeled, halved lengthwise and seeded
1 tablespoon unsalted butter
Salt and freshly ground pepper

Slice the cucumbers ¼ inch thick, cutting on the diagonal. Melt the butter in a large skillet. Add the cucumber slices, season with salt and freshly ground pepper and cook over moderately high heat, stirring occasionally, until tender, 5 to 7 minutes. (**MAKE AHEAD:** The glazed cucumber slices can stand at room temperature for 3 hours. Rewarm them before serving.) —JUDITH SUTTON ➤

Thai-Style Haricots Verts

are softened and browned, about 3 minutes. Add the shiitakes to the beans.

3. Heat the remaining 1 teaspoon oil in the skillet. Add the garlic and cook over high heat, stirring, until fragrant but not browned, about 30 seconds. Add the Swiss-chard leaves and 2 tablespoons of water and cook until wilted and tender, about 2 minutes. Return all of the vegetables to the skillet and sauté until they are heated through. Stir in the chicken broth and the fish sauce and heat through. Serve warm.—GRACE PARISI

THAI-STYLE HARICOTS VERTS

This recipe works best with the thin green beans commonly called haricots verts, *but tender young green beans will do. Sautéing* haricots verts *gives them a melt-in-your-mouth texture and nutty flavor. Serve with Jasmine rice or sticky rice or as an accompaniment to chicken, pork or fish.*

4 SERVINGS

- 2 tablespoons peanut oil
- 2 small dried red chiles
- ¾ pound *haricots verts,* trimmed
- ¾ pound red Swiss chard, stems cut into 3-by-¼-inch matchsticks and leaves into 2-inch pieces
- ½ pound shiitake mushrooms, stems discarded and caps sliced ¼ inch thick
- 2 medium garlic cloves, minced
- ½ cup chicken stock or canned low-sodium broth
- 2 tablespoons fish sauce,* preferably Squid brand, or 2 tablespoons soy sauce mixed with a pinch of sugar

*Available at Asian markets

1. Heat 1 tablespoon of the oil in a large nonreactive skillet until almost smoking. Add the chiles and cook over moderately high heat until just brown, about 30 seconds. Add the beans and the Swiss-chard stems and sauté until tender and charred, about 6 minutes. Transfer to a platter and discard the chiles.

2. Heat 2 teaspoons of the oil in the skillet. Add the shiitakes and sauté over high heat until they

ASPARAGUS WITH RED-PEPPER VINAIGRETTE Q

Spoon the leftover dressing over steamed broccoli or toss with a crisp green salad. Bottled roasted peppers that are deep red have the best flavor.

4 SERVINGS

- 1¼ pounds asparagus, trimmed
- ½ cup olive oil
- 3 tablespoons red-wine vinegar
- 2 tablespoons coarsely chopped drained bottled roasted red bell pepper (pimiento)
- 1 garlic clove, smashed
- ½ teaspoon Dijon mustard
- ¾ teaspoon minced fresh thyme

Pinch of sugar
Salt and freshly ground pepper

1. In a skillet of boiling, salted water, cook the asparagus over high heat until just tender, about 3 minutes. Drain well and transfer to four plates.

2. In a blender or mini-processor, combine the olive oil, vinegar, red pepper, garlic, mustard, thyme and sugar and season with salt and pepper to taste. Blend until smooth. Drizzle a third of the red-pepper vinaigrette over the cooked asparagus and serve.—PENELOPE CASAS

BARCELONA ARTICHOKES

Serve this versatile dish as a particularly complementary accompaniment to roast poultry or fish, or as an appetizer or luncheon dish.

8 SERVINGS

- 2 tablespoons fresh lemon juice
- 6 tablespoons extra-virgin olive oil
- 4 garlic cloves, minced
- Fine sea salt
- 8 firm, fresh globe artichokes or 16 baby artichokes

1. In a large nonreactive bowl, whisk together the lemon juice, the olive oil and the garlic. Season with salt.
2. Trim the artichoke stems to 1 inch and peel off the tough, fibrous skin. Pull off and discard all the outer leaves of the artichokes until you reach the tender inner yellow leaves. Using a stainless-steel knife, cut 1 inch off the tops of the artichokes. Cut the artichokes in half lengthwise. Using a grapefruit spoon or a melon baller, scrape out and discard the fuzzy chokes. Cut the artichokes lengthwise into very thin slices. Add the artichoke slices to the dressing and toss. (**MAKE AHEAD:** The artichokes can stand at room temperature for up to 2 hours.)
3. Preheat the broiler. Spread the artichoke slices in a single layer on a rimmed nonstick baking sheet and pour the dressing on top. Broil the artichokes about 3 inches from the heat, stirring occasionally, for 5 or 6 minutes, or until golden and sizzling. Transfer the artichokes with the dressing to a serving bowl. Season the artichokes with salt, toss well and serve.—PATRICIA WELLS ➤

Barcelona Artichokes

ARTICHOKES WITH GARLIC AND THYME

Choose the smallest artichokes you can find for this dish; the truly small ones have no choke to speak of and can be served whole.

8 SERVINGS

3 dozen small artichokes or 8 medium globe artichokes
2 lemons
5 tablespoons extra-virgin olive oil
1 small head of garlic, cloves peeled and halved
1 teaspoon coarse salt
Freshly ground pepper
8 fresh thyme sprigs

1. Pull off the outer leaves of the artichokes until you reach the pale green hearts. Cut off the top third of each of the small artichokes; cut off the top two-thirds if using larger ones. Cut off the stems and trim the leaves around the base. Leave the small artichokes whole; scoop out the chokes from the larger artichokes and halve or quarter the trimmed bottoms. Transfer them to a bowl of cold water mixed with the juice of one of the lemons to prevent browning.
2. Warm 3 tablespoons of the olive oil in a large nonreactive saucepan. Add the artichokes, garlic, salt, pepper, thyme sprigs and the juice of the remaining lemon. Pour in ¾ cup of water and bring to a boil. Reduce the heat to low, cover tightly and braise gently until all the water has evaporated and the artichokes are tender, 15 to 20 minutes. Season with the remaining 2 tablespoons olive oil and serve warm.—PAUL BERTOLLI

JUNE VEGETABLE RAGOUT

Inspired by the extraordinary array of fresh vegetables in the market in June, I combined young garlic, purple-tipped artichokes, plump fava beans, last-of-season peas and asparagus for this dish. (I've also had terrific results with thawed, frozen artichoke hearts, as well as thawed, frozen lima beans instead of fava beans.) The fruit and acid of the wine bridge the flavors of the vegetables.

🍷 *Select a delicate, not too floral white. My choice would be a wine made from Sauvignon Blanc, a grape that loves garlic.*

4 SERVINGS

1 lemon, halved
8 large artichokes
2 pounds fresh peas in their pods, shelled (2 cups)
20 asparagus tips
Ice water
¼ cup plus 2 tablespoons extra-virgin olive oil
2 medium onions, halved lengthwise and thinly sliced crosswise
1 large head of garlic, cloves peeled and thickly sliced
Bouquet garni made with a small bunch of fresh summer savory or thyme and fresh flat-leaf parsley tied with kitchen string
Salt
2 pounds fresh fava beans in their pods, shelled and skinned (2 cups)
3 tomatoes, peeled, cored, seeded and coarsely chopped
1½ cups dry white wine
Garden Pesto (recipe follows), for serving
Crusty bread, for serving

1. Squeeze the lemon juice into a large bowl of cold water and add the lemon halves. Break off or cut the stem from the base of the artichokes. Using your hands, snap off the tough outer leaves near the base. Continue snapping off leaves until only the central cone of yellow leaves with pale green tips remain. Using a large sharp knife, trim the top cone of leaves to just below the green tips. Trim any dark green areas from the base with a small sharp knife. Using a small spoon or a melon baller, scrape out and discard the hairy choke. Quarter the artichoke hearts and place them in the acidulated water.
2. In a large saucepan of boiling salted water, blanch the peas and the asparagus tips for 2 minutes.

PESTO

Each summer I make sure that my basil crop is abundant, and then I bottle that summertime flavor in the form of *pistou*, or pesto, an olive oil, basil and garlic sauce. If you like, you can add ground pine nuts and freshly grated Parmigiano-Reggiano cheese to the recipe for Garden Pesto. Even if you make this pesto in the food processor, it is better to mince the garlic by hand. In addition to flavoring the June Vegetable Ragout, Garden Pesto is great tossed with pasta, stirred into vegetable soups, dolloped on fish or spread on toasted pieces of baguette.—PATRICIA WELLS

Drain and then plunge the peas and asparagus into a bowl of ice water. Drain again thoroughly.
3. In a large nonreactive skillet, combine the oil, onions, garlic and bouquet garni; season with salt. Cover and cook over low heat until partially softened, about 10 minutes.
4. Add the artichoke hearts, fava beans and tomatoes. Stir in the white wine and simmer until the vegetables are tender, about 10 minutes longer. Add the blanched peas and asparagus and cook for 1 minute longer. Transfer the vegetables to a platter, drizzle the pesto all over and serve at once with plenty of crusty bread.

Garden Pesto

MAKES ½–¾ CUP

4 large garlic cloves, minced
Fine sea salt
2 cups loosely packed fresh basil leaves and flowers
½ cup extra-virgin olive oil

Place the garlic in a mortar, add sea salt to taste and mash to a paste with a pestle. Add the basil, little by little, pounding with the pestle until thoroughly ground. Then stir in the olive oil until incorporated. (Alternatively, grind the garlic, salt and basil into a paste in a food processor. With the machine on, drizzle in the olive oil and process to a paste.) Stir the pesto just before serving. (**MAKE AHEAD:** Cover the pesto and refrigerate for up to 1 day or freeze for up to 6 months. Bring the pesto to room temperature before stirring and stir again.)—PATRICIA WELLS

GARLICKY SPINACH

Nothing could be simpler than this side dish of spinach sautéed with shallots and garlic.

6 SERVINGS

2 tablespoons extra-virgin olive oil
2 garlic cloves, minced
1 large shallot, finely chopped
4 pounds fresh spinach, large stems discarded, leaves well washed and drained
Salt and freshly ground pepper

Heat the oil in a large nonreactive saucepan. Add the garlic and shallot and cook over moderate heat, stirring, until softened. Add the spinach and season with salt and pepper. Cover and cook for 2 minutes, then turn the spinach, cover and cook until all the leaves are wilted. (**MAKE AHEAD:** The spinach can stand at room temperature up to 4 hours.) Season the spinach with salt and pepper, drain well and serve.—BRIGIT LEGERE BINNS

SPINACH WITH PINE NUTS **Q**

8 SERVINGS

½ cup golden raisins
2 tablespoons olive oil
3 pounds fresh spinach, large stems discarded
⅓ cup pine nuts (about 2 ounces)
Salt and freshly ground pepper

1. In a small bowl, cover the raisins with warm water and let stand until plumped, about 10 minutes; drain.
2. Heat the oil in a large skillet. Add the spinach, raisins and pine nuts and cook over moderately high heat, stirring, until just wilted, about 5 minutes. Press the spinach to discard any excess liquid, season with salt and pepper and serve.—PEGGY RYAN

SAUTÉED WATERCRESS **Q**

4 SERVINGS

½ tablespoon vegetable oil
2 large bunches of watercress, large stems trimmed
Salt and freshly ground pepper

Heat the oil in a medium skillet. Add the watercress and stir constantly until wilted, about 1 minute. Season with salt and pepper and serve.—MARCIA KIESEL

BAKED RADICCHIO

6 SERVINGS

2 pounds radicchio, preferably the long variety called Treviso, or a mixture of radicchio and Belgian endive
Salt and freshly ground pepper
⅓ cup extra-virgin olive oil

1. Preheat the oven to 400°. If using round radicchio, cut it into four wedges. If using Treviso or Belgian endive, halve lengthwise. Make three parallel lengthwise incisions in the cores. Rinse the vegetables and shake off the excess water. Arrange the vegetables, cut-side down, in a baking dish in which they fit snugly in a single layer. Season with salt and pepper and evenly pour the olive oil all over.
2. Bake the vegetables for 10 minutes. Turn them over and bake for 7 minutes longer. Turn them once again and bake, and

turn each head over. Bake for about 7 minutes and turn them once again. Continue baking for about 10 minutes longer, or until the vegetables are tender at the core ends. Allow the dish to settle for a few minutes before serving hot, or serve at room temperature.—MARCELLA HAZAN

PAN-FRIED OKRA

Late spring through early fall is the best time to find fresh okra—unless you're in the South, where it's available throughout the year.

2 SERVINGS

- ½ teaspoon cumin seeds
- 1 tablespoon vegetable oil
- ½ pound small okra, stem ends trimmed
- ½ tablespoon tomato paste
- 1 teaspoon fresh lemon juice
- Salt and freshly ground pepper

Carrots Provençal (*top*) and Gratinéed Fennel

1. In a large nonreactive skillet, toast the cumin seeds over moderately high heat, stirring, until fragrant, about 30 seconds. Let cool, then grind in a spice grinder or mortar or finely chop with a knife.
2. Heat the oil in the skillet until shimmering. Add the okra and cook over moderately high heat, shaking the pan occasionally, until beginning to brown, about 3 minutes. Add the tomato paste, lemon juice and ground cumin and stir well to coat the okra. Continue cooking until the okra is tender but firm and nicely glazed, about 1 minute more. Season with salt and pepper and serve at once.—MARCIA KIESEL

CARROTS PROVENÇAL

This is a beautiful dish, with its colorful contrast of black and orange. The carrots can be served warm or at room temperature, so you can make them in advance. If baby carrots are available, halve them lengthwise.

8 SERVINGS

- 2 tablespoons extra-virgin olive oil
- 2 pounds carrots, peeled and sliced ¼ inch thick on the diagonal
- 1 head of garlic, cloves peeled and halved lengthwise
- Sea salt
- About ½ cup brine-cured black olives, pitted and halved lengthwise (3½ ounces)

1. In a large skillet, heat the oil over moderately high heat until hot but not smoking. Add the carrots; stir to coat with oil. Reduce the heat to moderate, cover and cook, stirring frequently, until the carrots are almost tender, about 20 minutes.
2. Add the garlic and season with salt. Reduce the heat to low; cook, uncovered, stirring, until the carrots are almost caramelized and the garlic is soft and tender, about 15 minutes more. (**MAKE AHEAD:** The carrots can stand at room temperature up to 2 hours. Reheat gently if serving hot.)
3. Stir in the olives and season with salt. Serve hot or at room temperature.—PATRICIA WELLS

VICHY CARROTS

This French classic was traditionally prepared with the mineral-rich water for which the town of Vichy is famous.

6 SERVINGS

- 1 tablespoon unsalted butter
- 1 tablespoon olive oil
- 1½ pounds young carrots, sliced ¼ inch thick on the diagonal
- 1 tablespoon vermouth
- Salt and white pepper
- 2 teaspoons dark brown sugar
- 1 tablespoon finely chopped fresh parsley

1. In a large heavy saucepan, melt the butter in the olive oil. Add the carrots and cook over moderately high heat until beginning to soften. Add the vermouth, 1 tablespoon water, salt and white pepper. Reduce the heat, cover partially and cook, stirring occasionally, until the carrots are tender, about 5 minutes; add more water if necessary.
2. Increase the heat to high and add the brown sugar. Toss constantly until the carrots are slightly browned and glazed, 3 to 4 minutes. Sprinkle the parsley on top and serve.—BRIGIT LEGERE BINNS

ROASTED FENNEL WITH ROSEMARY

6 SERVINGS

- 2 large heads of fennel, trimmed and cut through the cores into 8 wedges each
- 6 medium shallots, peeled and halved lengthwise
- 1½ tablespoons unsalted butter, cut into small pieces
- 1½ tablespoons olive oil
- 2 teaspoons finely chopped fresh rosemary
- 1 teaspoon sugar
- Salt and freshly ground pepper
- 1 lemon wedge

1. Preheat the oven to 350°. In a heavy medium casserole, toss the fennel with the shallots, butter, oil, rosemary and sugar. Season with salt and pepper. Cover tightly and roast in the oven for about 50 minutes, or until the fennel is tender, stirring the mixture two or three times. (**MAKE AHEAD:** The cooked fennel can be refrigerated, covered, for up to 1 day and gently reheated.)

2. Squeeze the lemon over the fennel, toss well, transfer to a platter or six plates and serve.—BRIGIT LEGERE BINNS

ROASTED FENNEL WITH OLIVES LF

8 SERVINGS

- Vegetable cooking spray
- 4 medium fennel bulbs, trimmed and cut lengthwise into eighths
- Coarse salt and freshly ground pepper
- 15 sun-dried-tomato halves (not oil-packed)
- 1 tablespoon unsalted butter

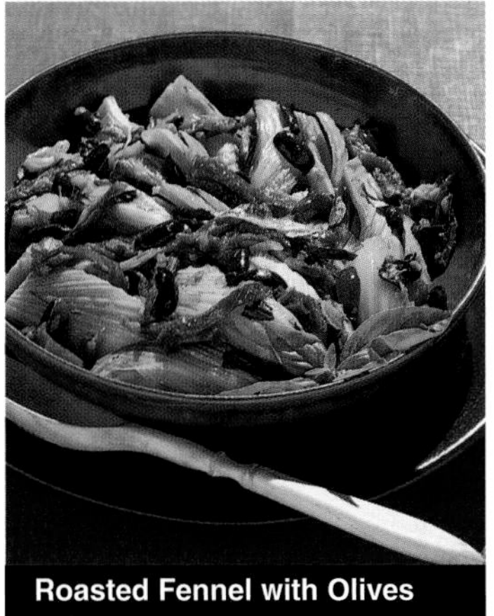

Roasted Fennel with Olives

- 1 large onion, sliced crosswise ⅛ inch thick
- 1 cup chicken stock or canned low-sodium broth, skimmed of fat
- 15 Kalamata olives, pitted and quartered
- ¼ cup shredded fresh basil

1. Preheat the oven to 450°. Coat a large nonstick baking sheet with vegetable cooking spray. Arrange the fennel on the baking sheet, season it with salt and pepper and roast for 20 minutes. Transfer the fennel to a large baking dish. Lower the oven temperature to 375°.

2. In a bowl, cover the sun-dried tomatoes with hot water and let soak until softened, about 20 minutes. Drain the tomatoes and slice them ¼ inch thick.

3. Melt the butter in a nonstick skillet. Add the onion and cook over moderately high heat, stirring, until browned, about 7 minutes. Add the stock; bring to a simmer. Pour over the fennel, cover tightly with foil and bake for 10 minutes. Uncover and bake for about 30 minutes longer, or until the fennel is tender. Mix in the olives, the sun-dried tomatoes and the basil and serve.—BOB CHAMBERS

GRATINÉED FENNEL

Since fennel is one of my favorite vegetables, no one need coax me to prepare this dish. Anything that comes bubbling from the oven with a nice coating of cheese wins my appetite! Much of the work can be done in advance. The fennel is lightly browned in olive oil, then braised in a touch of broth. The drained fennel is gratinéed at the last minute under the broiler.

8 SERVINGS

- ½ cup extra-virgin olive oil
- 4½ pounds fennel bulbs, quartered lengthwise
- Sea salt
- 3 cups vegetable stock, chicken stock or canned low-sodium broth
- ½ cup freshly grated Parmigiano-Reggiano cheese (3½ ounces)

1. In a large skillet, heat the oil over moderately high heat until hot but not smoking. Reduce the heat to moderate, add the fennel and season with salt. Cook, stirring, until the fennel browns lightly and absorbs the oil, about 5 minutes. Add the stock, cover and cook over moderately low heat until the fennel is meltingly tender throughout, about 30 minutes. If any stock remains in the skillet, remove the fennel and reduce the liquid over high heat until just a few tablespoons of thick sauce remain. If the fennel was removed, return it to the skillet. Cover and set aside. (**MAKE AHEAD:** The fennel can be refrigerated for up to 2 hours.) ➤

2. Preheat the broiler. Arrange the fennel, slightly overlapping, in a large gratin dish. Sprinkle the cheese evenly over the top. Broil about 3 inches from the heat for 3 to 5 minutes, or until the cheese melts and the fennel sizzles. Serve hot.—PATRICIA WELLS

BREADED FRIED FINOCCHIO

When carefully executed—and that is a most significant "when"—frying is the ideal way to cook (see "Frying Tips," p. 333). It flatters surfaces with a crisp, light crust, seals in sweet juices and is simple and quick. Fried need not mean greasy, either; properly fried food ought always to be perfectly dry and clean tasting. Of the great variety of coatings and batters used in frying, this one—an egg and bread-crumb coating—is one of my favorites.

6 SERVINGS

- 3 large fennel bulbs, tops trimmed
- 2 large eggs
- 1½ cups toasted fine plain bread crumbs
- Vegetable oil
- Salt

1. Discard any bruised or discolored portions of the fennel bulbs. Slice off ¼ inch from the root ends. Stand the bulbs upright and slice them lengthwise ½ inch thick. Wash the fennel well in cold water.
2. Cook the fennel in 3 quarts of boiling water until the core is tender yet firm when prodded with a fork, about 7 minutes. Drain and let cool.
3. Beat the eggs in a small bowl and place the bread crumbs in a shallow plate. Dip the fennel slices in the eggs, letting the excess egg flow back into the bowl, then turn the slices in the bread crumbs, coating both sides. Press the bread crumbs onto each slice with your palm until your hand feels dry and the crumbs are sticking firmly.
4. Pour 1½ inches of oil into a large skillet and set it over moderately high heat. Test the temperature by dipping in the edge of a slice of fennel; if it sizzles, the oil is ready.
5. Slip as many slices of fennel into the pan as will fit loosely without crowding. Cook over moderately high heat until a crisp, golden-brown crust forms on one side; then turn and fry the other side. Using a slotted spoon or tongs, transfer the fennel to a wire rack set over a baking sheet to drain. Continue frying the remaining fennel in batches. Sprinkle with salt and serve immediately.—MARCELLA HAZAN

Breaded Fried Finocchio (*top*) and Fried Zucchini (p. 333)

A CLASSIC COAT

The egg and bread-crumb coating I love is the one you would use for meat or eggplant cutlets, mushroom caps and fresh artichoke hearts cut into wedges. Here are my tips for achieving a thin, crisp bread-crumb coating that doesn't fall off.

- **Begin with fine, very dry bread crumbs made from stale good-quality bread.**
- **The egg coating must be as thin as possible. Dip a piece of the food to be fried into the beaten egg, pull it up quickly and allow all the excess egg to drip back into the bowl.**
- **Turn the food in the bread crumbs; when both sides are well coated, press the food down against the crumbs in the plate with your palm, then turn it and press down on the other side. The breading can be done one to two hours before frying.—MARCELLA HAZAN**

BUTTERED LEEKS

4 SERVINGS

- 8 medium leeks, white and tender green, thinly sliced crosswise
- Coarse salt
- Freshly ground pepper
- 1 tablespoon unsalted butter

Rinse the sliced leeks thoroughly. In a saucepan of boiling salted water, cook the leeks until tender, about 5 minutes. Drain well. Spread the leeks in a baking dish, season with salt and pepper and dot with the butter. Cover and keep warm until ready to serve.—NINA ZAGAT

CAULIFLOWER GRATIN

10–12 SERVINGS

2 heads of cauliflower (about 3 pounds each)
1 quart milk
1 imported bay leaf
4 tablespoons unsalted butter
½ cup all-purpose flour
1 tablespoon Dijon mustard
½ teaspoon freshly ground white pepper
Freshly grated nutmeg (optional)
1 pound Gruyère cheese, grated
Salt
1 cup coarse bread crumbs

1. Preheat the oven to 350°. Bring two large saucepans of salted water to a boil. Cut the cauliflower into 2½-inch florets. Add the florets to the saucepans, cover and cook over moderate heat until just tender when pierced, about 6 minutes. Drain well. Arrange the cauliflower in a 9-by-13 inch (3 quart) baking dish.
2. Meanwhile, in a medium saucepan, combine the milk and bay leaf and bring just to a simmer over moderately low heat.
3. In another medium saucepan, melt the butter over moderate heat. Add the flour and cook, stirring, for 2 minutes. Whisk in one-third of the hot milk until smooth. Gradually whisk in the remaining milk and boil for 2 minutes, whisking frequently. Remove the bay leaf.
4. Whisk the mustard into the sauce. Season with the white pepper and a few gratings of nutmeg. Set aside 1½ cups of the grated Gruyère and add the remainder to the sauce. Remove from the heat and stir to melt the cheese. Season with salt.
5. Pour the cheese sauce over the cauliflower. Toss the reserved cheese with the bread crumbs and sprinkle the mixture evenly over the top. Bake for about 45 minutes, until the gratin is bubbling and golden.—DIANA STURGIS

SAUTÉED CABBAGE WITH PROSCIUTTO LF

8 SERVINGS

1 tablespoon unsalted butter
2 large carrots, cut into ⅓-inch pieces
1 large onion, finely chopped
Two 1½ pound Savoy cabbages, shredded ⅓ inch thick
1 cup chicken stock or canned low-sodium broth, skimmed of fat
2 teaspoons sugar
Coarse salt and freshly ground pepper
4 ounces thinly sliced prosciutto, trimmed of all visible fat, cut into ⅓ inch strips
2 tablespoons minced fresh flat-leaf parsley
½ teaspoon minced fresh thyme

Melt the butter in an enameled cast-iron casserole. Add the carrots and onion and cook over moderately high heat, stirring, until the onion is lightly browned, about 8 minutes. Add the cabbages, stock and sugar, season with salt and pepper and toss to coat. Cover and cook over low heat, stirring, until tender, about 15 minutes. Uncover, raise the heat to high and cook, stirring, until most of liquid has evaporated, about 5 minutes. Stir in the prosciutto, parsley and thyme, cook for 1 minute more and serve.—BOB CHAMBERS

MASHED ACORN SQUASH WITH APPLES LF

8 SERVINGS

Vegetable cooking spray
Four 1½-pound acorn squash, halved lengthwise, seeds removed
Coarse salt and freshly ground pepper
4 large Golden Delicious apples
2 tablespoons sugar
Scant ¼ teaspoon cinnamon
3 to 4 tablespoons honey
2 tablespoons unsalted butter

1. Preheat the oven to 450°. Coat a nonstick baking sheet with vegetable cooking spray. Season the cut sides of the squash with salt and pepper and set them, cut-side down, on the baking sheet. Bake for about 1 hour, or until the flesh is tender and caramelized on the bottom. Let cool on the baking sheet.
2. Meanwhile, peel and core the apples and cut them lengthwise into eighths. Slice each piece crosswise ¼ inch thick. Transfer to a bowl and toss with the sugar and cinnamon. Coat another large nonstick baking sheet with cooking spray and spread the apples on it. Bake for about 30 minutes, or until the apples are tender and brown.
3. Peel the baked squash and transfer it to a bowl along with

Squash with Pan-Roasted Root Vegetables

any caramelized bits from the baking sheet. Mash the squash coarsely. Add the apple pieces with any caramelized bits.

4. In a large saucepan, bring the honey and the butter just to a boil. Add the squash, stir well and season with salt and pepper. (**MAKE AHEAD:** The squash can be refrigerated for up to 1 day.) Warm the squash over moderate heat. Transfer to a large bowl and serve.—BOB CHAMBERS

SQUASH WITH PAN-ROASTED ROOT VEGETABLES

This Asian-flavored dish can become the centerpiece of a vegetarian meal; use vegetable stock in place of the chicken stock and serve with sautéed greens and rice. For meat eaters, roast chicken is the perfect partner.

4 SERVINGS

Two 2-pound acorn squash, halved lengthwise and seeded
Salt and freshly ground pepper
- 2 tablespoons vegetable oil
- 2 medium turnips, peeled and cut into 1-inch cubes
- 3 medium parsnips, peeled and cut into 1-inch pieces
- 2 medium carrots, peeled and cut into 1-inch pieces
- 1 medium celery root, peeled and cut into 1-inch cubes
- 1 medium onion, cut into 1-inch pieces
- ½ cup chicken stock or canned low-sodium broth
- 2 tablespoons soy sauce
- 1 tablespoon mirin or medium dry sherry

1. Preheat the oven to 400°. Lightly oil a baking sheet. Season the squash with salt and pepper and set them cut-side down on the baking sheet. Roast for about 40 minutes, or until tender and browned.

2. Heat the oil in a large, heavy-bottomed flameproof roasting pan set over two burners. Add the turnips, parsnips, carrots, celery root and onion and cook over moderately high heat, stirring, until starting to brown, about 12 minutes. Transfer to the oven and roast for about 35 minutes, or until the vegetables are tender.

3. In a small bowl, combine the stock, soy sauce and mirin. Set the roasting pan back on two burners over moderately high heat, add the stock mixture and cook, stirring, until the vegetables are nicely glazed, about 2 minutes. Season with salt and pepper. Set each squash half on a plate, spoon the pan-roasted vegetables into the cavities and serve.—TRACI DES JARDINS

ROASTED MINI PUMPKINS

12 SERVINGS

- 12 mini pumpkins
- ¼ teaspoon cinnamon
- ⅛ teaspoon freshly grated nutmeg
- ⅛ teaspoon ground allspice
- 6 tablespoons unsalted butter
- ¼ cup pure maple syrup

Salt and freshly ground pepper

1. Preheat the oven to 400°. With a grapefruit knife or sharp paring knife, cut a ring around the stem of each pumpkin to form a

TO ROAST A PUMPKIN

Halve a large pumpkin lengthwise and scoop out the seeds and membranes; cut it into wedges. If you are using a small pumpkin, slice it crosswise into rings. Brush with olive oil and season with salt and pepper. Cover with foil and roast at 400° for about 50 minutes, or until tender. Brush with one of the following, then serve.

MAPLE CHILE BUTTER

In a small dry skillet, toast 1 tablespoon pure chile powder for 30 seconds, stirring. Mix with 4 tablespoons unsalted butter, 1 tablespoon pure maple syrup, and ½ teaspoon salt.

MUSTARD CURRY OIL

Combine 1 tablespoon each of olive oil, curry powder, white wine and Dijon mustard. Season with salt and pepper.

lid; remove the pumpkin lids and set aside. With a small spoon, scrape out the seeds and any membranes from the pumpkins.

2. In a small bowl, combine the cinnamon, nutmeg and allspice and sprinkle the spices inside the pumpkins. Add ½ tablespoon of the butter and 1 teaspoon of the maple syrup to each of the pumpkins and season with salt and pepper.

3. Set the pumpkins in a baking dish and add ½ inch of water. Replace the pumpkin lids and roast the pumpkins for about 30 minutes, or until tender. Serve hot.—WALDY MALOUF

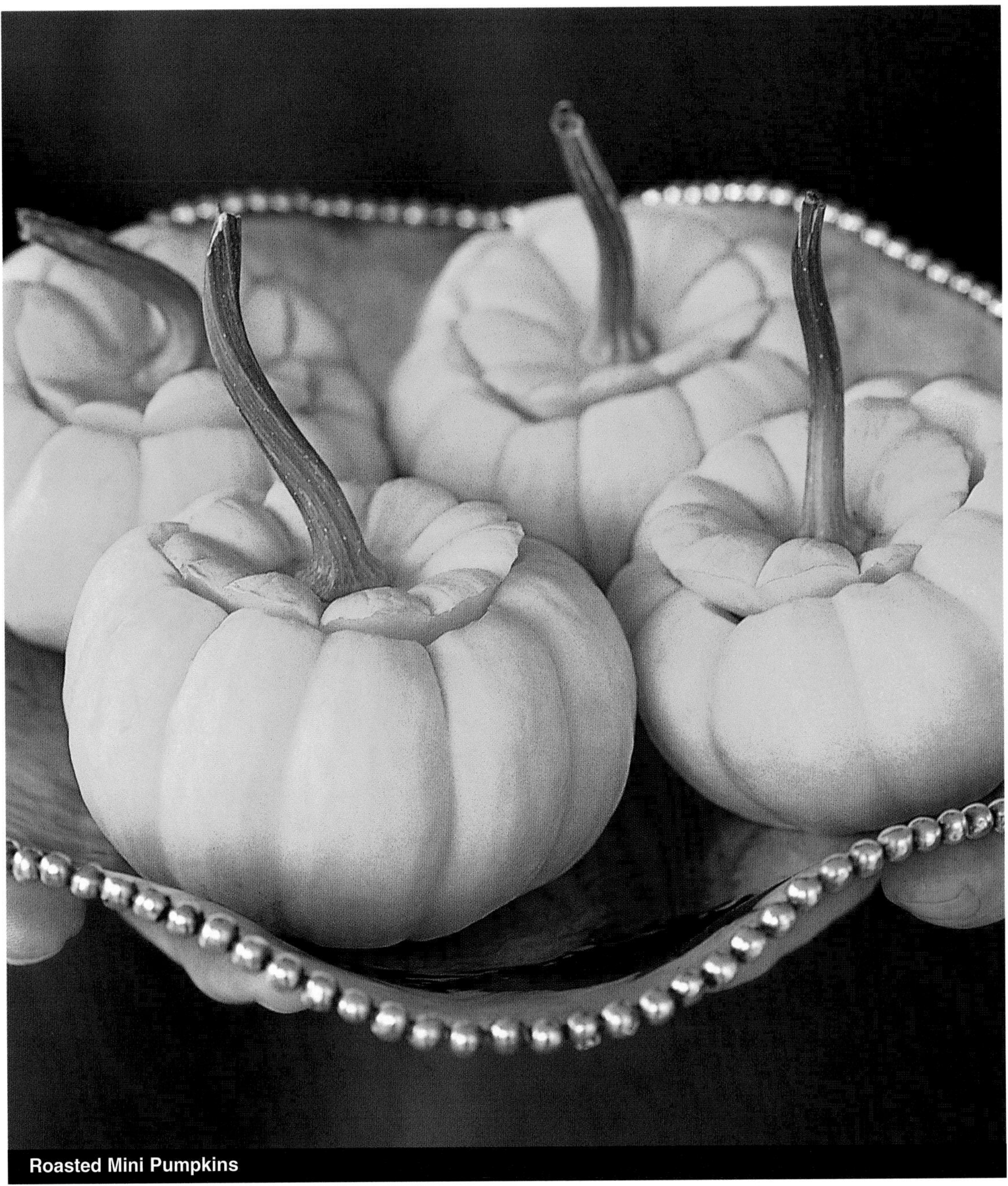

Roasted Mini Pumpkins

CHAPTER 16

~

MARINADES, SAUCES & CONDIMENTS

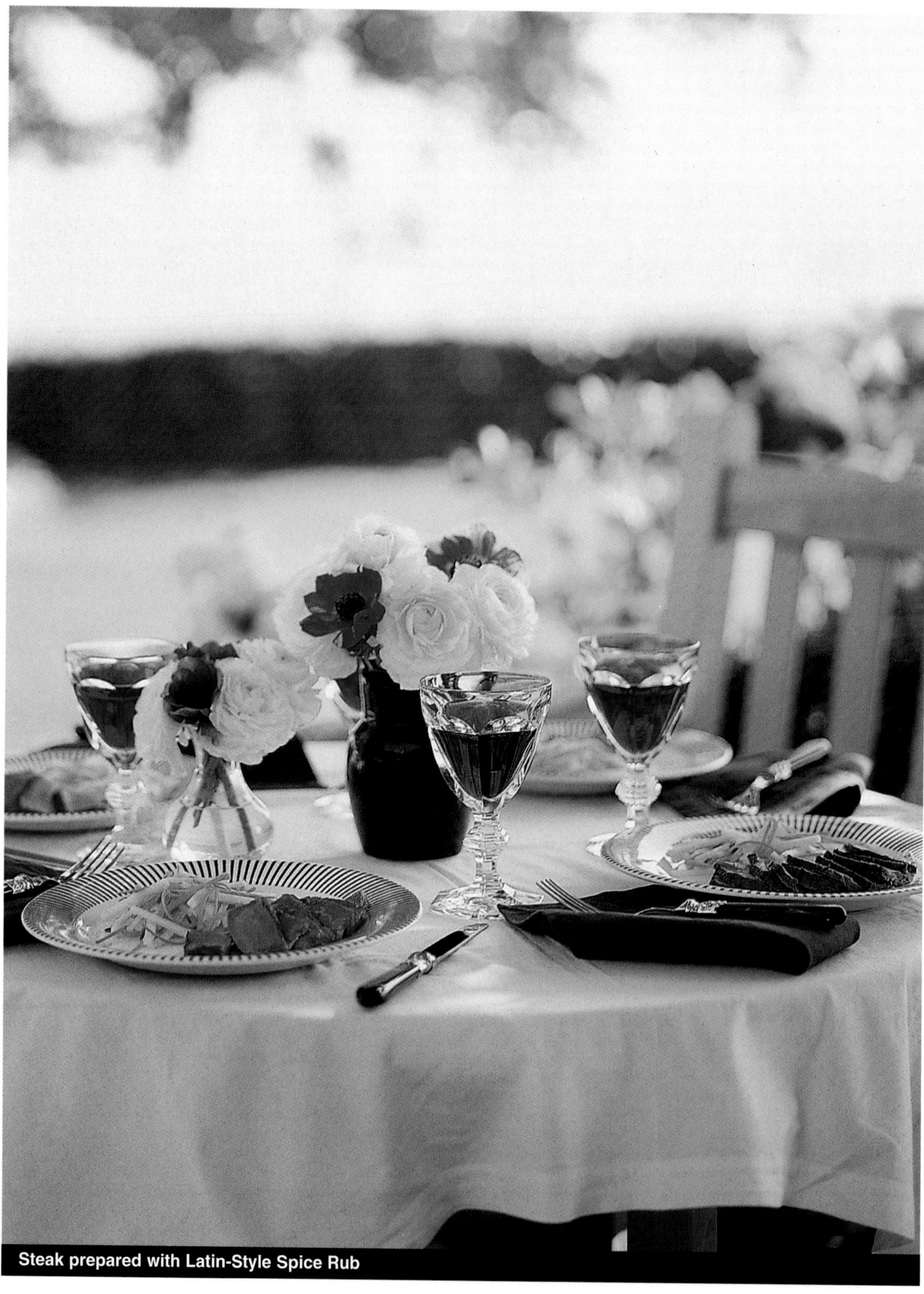

Steak prepared with Latin-Style Spice Rub

LATIN-STYLE SPICE RUB

Rub skirt steak, pork, chicken legs or any oily fish with this combination just before grilling.

MAKES ABOUT 1 CUP

- ¼ cup cumin seeds
- 2 tablespoons coriander seeds
- 2 tablespoons chili powder
- 1 tablespoon light brown sugar
- 2 tablespoons coarse salt
- 1 teaspoon cinnamon
- 1 teaspoon cayenne pepper
- 2 tablespoons freshly ground black pepper

In a small dry skillet, toast the cumin and coriander seeds over moderately low heat, shaking the pan, until fragrant, about 2 minutes. Transfer to a spice grinder or mortar, add the remaining ingredients and grind to a fine powder. (**MAKE AHEAD:** The spice rub will keep at room temperature for up to 1 month.)—CHRIS SCHLESINGER AND JOHN WILLOUGHBY

FIVE-SPICE RUB

Rub this on pork or chicken six to nine hours before grilling, or on firm white-fleshed fish two to three hours ahead.

MAKES 1 CUP

- ½ teaspoon fennel seeds
- ½ teaspoon aniseed
- ½ teaspoon coriander seeds
- ½ teaspoon cumin seeds
- ½ teaspoon dill seeds
- 1 cup olive oil

In a small dry skillet, toast the spices over moderately low heat, shaking the pan, until fragrant, about 2 minutes. Transfer to a spice grinder or mortar and finely grind. Transfer to a bowl; stir in the oil.—SCOTT COHEN

BALSAMIC SHALLOT MARINADE

This marinade works well with any kind of beefsteak, pork, lamb or chicken. Marinate two to four hours.

MAKES ABOUT 1½ CUPS

- ½ cup balsamic vinegar
- 2 tablespoons coarsely chopped shallots
- 1 tablespoon coarsely chopped fresh sage
- 1 tablespoon coarsely chopped fresh rosemary
- 1 teaspoon freshly ground pepper
- 1 cup olive oil

In a blender or food processor, combine the vinegar, shallots, sage, rosemary and pepper. With the machine on, add the oil in a slow, steady stream and blend until emulsified.—JIM COHEN ➤

HOW TO ADD FLAVOR BEFORE GRILLING

How much marinade do you need? Too much and the food will be overwhelmed; too little and you won't know it's there. Here are some guidelines for getting the balance right.

- **For marinades or rubs based on mild liquids, such as coconut milk or oil (see Coconut Marinade, p. 349, and Five-Spice Rub), you'll need about one cup for two to three pounds of meat, poultry, fish or shellfish.**
- **If there's a high proportion of sugar or a pungent ingredient in the marinade (as in Tamarind Ketchup Marinade, p. 350, and Hunan Marinade, p. 350), lightly brush the food you're grilling.**
- **For dry rubs, allow one to two teaspoons for each serving of meat, fish or poultry.**

WINE WITH GRILLED FOODS

To make your choice, consider the flavor spin that the marinade or sauce gives the food you're grilling.

SPICE RUBS **Balance the penetrating spicy bite on fish, chicken and pork with fruity whites from Germany and Alsace, particularly Gewürztraminer. For beef, go for soft, low-tannin reds, such as California Merlot and French Côtes du Rhône.**

CITRUSY MARINADES **Match the tanginess with a crisp, herbal white, such as a West Coast Sauvignon Blanc or a French Sancerre.**

SWEET MARINADES AND GLAZES **Balance the sweetness with round, rich whites; try California and Australian Chardonnays.**

FRUITY SAUCES AND SALSAS **For fish and poultry, go for whites of matching sweetness, such as West Coast Rieslings and Chenin Blancs. Steak needs a red with maximum grapiness, like Beaujolais or Gamay.**

SPICY SAUCES AND SALSAS **Very fruity wines can take the heat. For fish, serve Vouvray or Chenin Blanc; for meat, California Zinfandel. Poultry and pork will go with either.**

MORE MACHO FISH MARINADE

Cut up rinds from the juiced citrus fruits for an attractive and flavorful addition to this robust and tangy marinade. Use it on any meaty fish; marinate two to three hours

MAKES ABOUT 2 CUPS

¾ cup olive oil
½ cup fresh orange juice
⅓ cup fresh lemon juice
¼ cup light soy sauce
2 tablespoons fresh lime juice
½ medium fennel bulb, trimmed, cored and thinly sliced crosswise
½ medium red onion, thinly sliced
6 garlic cloves, thinly sliced
1-inch piece of fresh ginger, peeled and thinly sliced
2 fresh thyme sprigs
2 bay leaves
¼ teaspoon crushed peppercorns

In a large bowl, stir together the olive oil, the orange and lemon juices, the soy sauce and the lime juice. Add the thinly sliced fennel, onion, garlic and ginger, the thyme sprigs, the bay leaves and the crushed peppercorns and mix them until combined.—NORMAN VAN AKEN

TYPES OF GINGER

Besides being found in marinades, sauces and condiments, ginger is often a condiment in itself—as well as a snack, a spice and a sweet.

PRESERVED GINGER is a popular Chinese snack that is often flavored with lemon and salt.

BENI-SHOGA, a ginger pickle, is packaged in slices, chunks and slivers. Japanese chefs serve it with cold rice and noodle dishes.

GARI—slices of ginger pickled in rice vinegar—refreshes the palate between bites of sushi.

DRIED GINGER, as with any spice, is best freshly ground. Buy pieces of it and grind it yourself.

POWDERED GINGER adds a sweet fieriness to Southeast Asian curries, Chinese five-spice powder and, of course, gingerbread.

SHREDDED FRESH GINGER and scallions are used by Cantonese cooks to garnish steamed fish.

CRYSTALLIZED GINGER is enjoyed as is, dipped in chocolate, or folded into more elaborate desserts.—LAUREN MUKAMAL CAMP

BUYING GINGER

Ginger grows best in tropical conditions—high temperatures and humidity and very heavy rainfall. It grows along the equator, from Asia and the Pacific Rim to Africa and South and Central America. India and China produce the bulk of the crop, but we see little of their agricultural efforts in U.S. grocery stores. Most of the ginger available here comes from Hawaii and Fiji.

Almost all of it is mature ginger, with its fibrous texture and full, hot flavor. American recipes don't even bother to specify fresh *mature* ginger; it's understood. But if you are prowling around Asian groceries in the early summer to early fall, you'll see young ginger, also known as baby, stem, spring or summer ginger. Young ginger is cream-colored with rosy tips and translucent skin. Because it's not at all woody and has a delicate flavor, the Chinese cook it as a vegetable. It can also be pickled, preserved in syrup or candied, though to some tastes young ginger treated in these ways doesn't deliver enough zing.

There are several things to keep in mind when choosing fresh, mature ginger. Skin color, which ranges naturally from light beige to tan, is not an indicator of either quality or age; heaviness and firmness are. You want to pick ginger in the same way you select carrots or potatoes: a rock-hard piece is destined for great things; a wrinkled, puckery one, however, is past its prime. In terms of sheer convenience in peeling and cutting, the larger the "hand" of ginger (a piece that resembles a small human hand), the better.

Mature ginger is available pretty much year-round. Given a choice, opt for Hawaiian ginger, which comes in big, fat, heavy hands and is generally in the stores winter to late spring. Ginger from Fiji is at its best from the late summer to fall.—LAUREN MUKAMAL CAMP

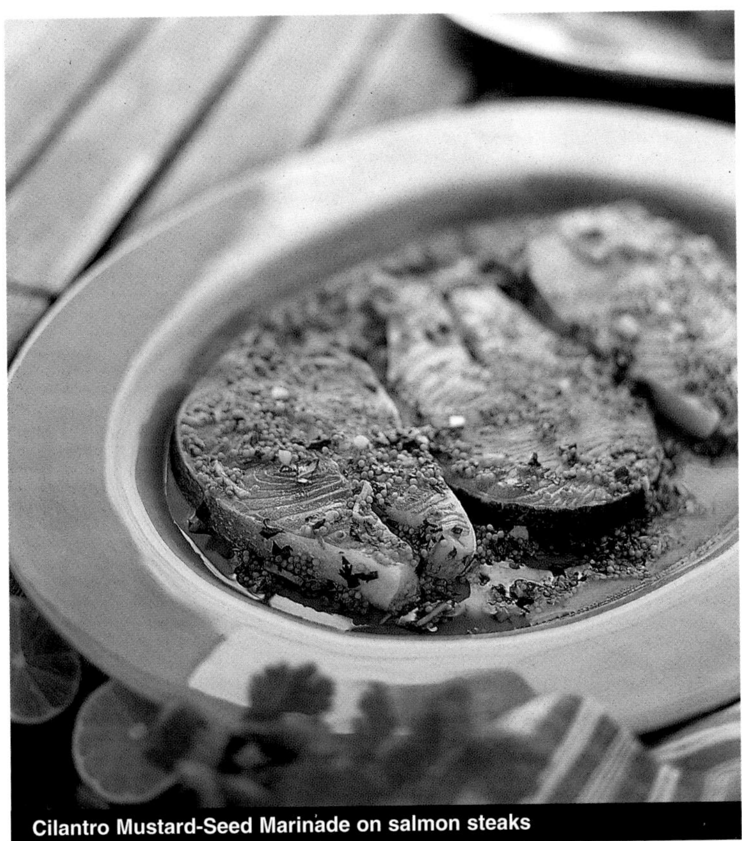
Cilantro Mustard-Seed Marinade on salmon steaks

CILANTRO MUSTARD-SEED MARINADE

Here's a marinade that can also double as a zesty dipping sauce for grilled fish, shellfish or poultry. If you want to use the marinade both before and after grilling, be sure to set aside about half a cup prior to marinating to serve as a sauce. Marinate chicken and any meaty fish for six to twelve hours; marinate shrimp for two to three hours

MAKES ABOUT 1½ CUPS

- 3 tablespoons mustard seeds
- ¼ cup fresh lime juice
- 2 tablespoons minced fresh ginger
- 1 tablespoon minced garlic
- 2 teaspoons finely grated lime zest
- Pinch each of salt and freshly ground pepper
- ½ cup peanut oil
- 1 cup coarsely chopped fresh cilantro

1. In a small dry skillet, toast the mustard seeds over moderate heat, shaking the pan, until lightly browned, about 2 minutes. Let cool.
2. In a medium bowl, combine the toasted mustard seeds, the lime juice, ginger, garlic, lime zest, salt and pepper. Stir in the peanut oil, then the chopped cilantro, and let the marinade stand at room temperature for 30 minutes. Scrape off most of the marinade from the meat before grilling.—TOM DOUGLAS

CURRIED YOGURT MARINADE

This spicy, smoky-flavored marinade tenderizes poultry and meat while contributing a subtle curry flavor. It's good with any kind of beefsteak, lamb or chicken. Marinate them for eight to twelve hours.

MAKES ABOUT 2 CUPS

- 1 dried ancho chile
- 2 garlic cloves, peeled
- 1 tablespoon Madras curry powder
- ½ tablespoon olive oil
- 2 cups plain yogurt
- 1 small red onion, finely chopped

1. In a small bowl, cover the ancho chile with hot water. Let the ancho soak until softened, about 20 minutes. Drain, reserving 2 tablespoons of the ancho-soaking liquid. Halve, stem and seed the chile.
2. In a blender, combine the garlic and the ancho and blend until finely chopped. Add the curry powder, olive oil and the reserved ancho-soaking liquid and blend until smooth. Blend in the yogurt. Transfer to a bowl and stir in the onion.—JIM COHEN

COCONUT MARINADE

If using this marinade with chicken or firm white-fleshed fish, marinate for eight to twelve hours; with shrimp, four to six hours.

MAKES ABOUT 2½ CUPS

- 1 cup canned unsweetened coconut milk
- 1 medium onion, quartered
- 1 small green bell pepper, cut into 2-inch pieces
- 6 garlic cloves, peeled

2 tablespoons olive oil
1 teaspoon salt
1 teaspoon freshly ground pepper
¼ cup coarsely chopped fresh flat-leaf parsley

In a blender or food processor, combine the coconut milk, onion, green bell pepper, garlic, olive oil, salt and freshly ground pepper and puree. Add the chopped parsley and blend until smooth.—STEVEN RAICHLEN

GRILLING TIP

Score the skin of chicken and fish to allow the flavor of spice rubs and marinades to permeate the flesh.

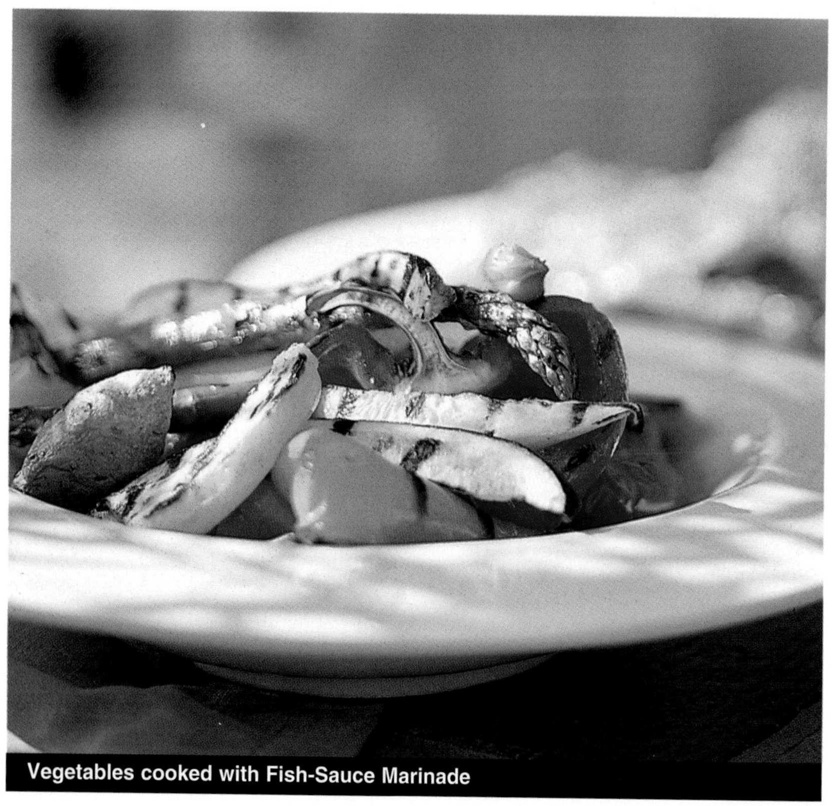

Vegetables cooked with Fish-Sauce Marinade

HUNAN MARINADE

Use this Asian-inspired mix with any kind of beefsteak, lamb or duck; marinate the meat for one to three hours

MAKES ABOUT 1 CUP

¼ cup plus 1 tablespoon good-quality hoisin sauce
3 tablespoons honey
2 tablespoons soy sauce
2 tablespoons dry sherry
2 tablespoons sesame seeds
1 jalapeño chile, seeded and minced
1 tablespoon sesame oil
1 tablespoon curry powder
1 tablespoon finely grated orange zest
1 tablespoon fermented black beans*

*Available at Asian markets

Combine all of the ingredients in a medium bowl.—HARLAN PETERSON

TAMARIND KETCHUP MARINADE

Marinate any kind of beefsteak or chicken with this glaze for one hour, or brush it over shrimp just before grilling.

MAKES ABOUT 1½ CUPS

1 cup tamarind paste*
2 tablespoons fish sauce*
2 tablespoons soy sauce
2 tablespoons rice-wine vinegar
2 tablespoons sugar
2 garlic cloves, minced
2 teaspoons finely chopped jalapeño chile

*Available at Asian markets

Combine all of the ingredients in a small bowl.—JEAN-GEORGES VONGERICHTEN

FISH-SAUCE MARINADE

This pungent mixture is especially good with sweet vegetables, such as red and yellow bell-pepper wedges and quartered red onions, or with kale. Just before grilling, lightly brush the vegetables or dip them in the marinade so that the salty fish sauce won't overpower them. To use with kale, dilute with an equal amount of water before dipping.

MAKES ABOUT 1½ CUPS

1 cup fish sauce*
½ cup extra-virgin olive oil
4 garlic cloves, minced
Freshly ground pepper

*Available at Asian markets

Combine all of the ingredients in a medium bowl.—NAOMI DUGUID AND JEFFREY ALFORD

MAPLE GLAZE

Because this sweet, peppery glaze is made with a high proportion of maple syrup, be sure to grill the meat or poultry slowly over moderately low heat so that it cooks evenly without burning. The marinade works best with pork, chicken, duck breasts or squab; brush it on before and during grilling.

MAKES ABOUT ½ CUP

¼ cup olive oil
3 tablespoons pure maple syrup
1 garlic clove, crushed
4 fresh thyme sprigs
1 teaspoon freshly ground pepper

In a small saucepan, combine all of the ingredients and simmer over low heat until slightly thickened, about 3 minutes. Let the marinade stand for 2 hours before using. (**MAKE AHEAD:** The glaze can be refrigerated for up to 3 days.) —JIM COHEN

Grilled chicken prepared with Maple Glaze

TWO-MUSTARD HONEY GLAZE

Brush this over pork before grilling, or chicken and salmon during grilling.

MAKES 2 CUPS

1 cup honey
½ cup Dijon mustard
½ cup grainy mustard
Salt and freshly ground pepper

Combine all of the ingredients in a medium bowl.—SCOTT COHEN

BLUEBERRY BARBECUE SAUCE

A robust sauce will pick up almost any plain grilled food. Try this one on any kind of beefsteak, hamburgers, pork chops or chicken.

MAKES ABOUT 1½ CUPS

2 teaspoons vegetable oil
¼ cup minced onion
1 tablespoon minced fresh jalapeño chile, seeded
¼ cup ketchup
¼ cup rice-wine vinegar
3 tablespoons light brown sugar
3 tablespoons Dijon mustard
1 teaspoon Tabasco
2 cups fresh or frozen blueberries
Salt and freshly ground pepper

1. Heat the vegetable oil in a nonreactive saucepan. Add the onion and jalapeño and cook over moderate heat, stirring, until wilted, about 3 minutes. Add the ketchup, vinegar, sugar, mustard and Tabasco and bring to a simmer. Add the blueberries and simmer over low heat, stirring, until thickened, about 10 minutes.

2. Puree the sauce in a blender or food processor until smooth. Pass the sauce through a strainer and season with salt and pepper. (**MAKE AHEAD:** The sauce can be refrigerated for up to 1 day.) Serve the sauce at room temperature.—ROBERT MCGRATH

BANANA MANGO KETCHUP

Use this sauce with any kind of beefsteak, pork, Italian sausage, kielbasa or chicken.

MAKES ABOUT 3 CUPS

1 tablespoon vegetable oil
1 medium onion, finely chopped

Clockwise from left: Spicy Grilled-Onion Relish (p. 359), Blueberry Barbecue Sauce (p. 351) and Green Corn Sauce

HOW TO ADD FLAVOR AFTER GRILLING

When the steak or the chops come off the grill, the amount of sauce you'll want to serve alongside them depends on how potent the condiment is. But texture counts, too: A thick sauce or salsa will go further than a less concentrated one.

SALSA **Allow about a quarter to a third of a cup for each person.**

SAUCES, RELISHES AND KETCHUPS **If the sauce is intensely flavored, allow just two to three tablespoons per serving. For condiments that pack less of a punch, count on about a third of a cup per person**

- 1 pound very ripe bananas, broken into 1-inch pieces
- 1 ripe mango, peeled and cut into ¼-inch dice
- ¼ cup fresh orange juice
- 1 tablespoon light brown sugar
- 1½ teaspoons curry powder
- Salt and freshly ground pepper
- 1 tablespoon white-wine vinegar
- About ⅓ cup fresh lime juice

Heat the vegetable oil in a nonreactive medium saucepan. Add the chopped onion and cook over moderate heat, stirring, until the onion is translucent, about 7 minutes. Add the bananas and cook, stirring occasionally, for 5 minutes. Add the mango, orange juice, brown sugar and curry powder and season with salt and pepper. Cook, stirring, until the fruit mixture is thickened, about 5 minutes more. Remove the mixture from the heat and stir in the white-wine vinegar and ⅓ cup of the lime juice, adding more of each to taste. (**MAKE AHEAD:** The ketchup can be refrigerated for up to 2 days.) Serve warm or at room temperature.—CHRIS SCHLESINGER AND JOHN WILLOUGHBY

GREEN CORN SAUCE

This creamy sauce gets its appealing color and wonderful flavor from roasted Anaheim and poblano chiles, and its texture from sweet corn kernels. Serve it with any kind of beefsteak, pork, lamb, chicken, salmon or lobster tails.

MAKES ABOUT 1½ CUPS

- 2 fresh Anaheim or Slim Jim chiles
- 1 fresh poblano chile
- 2 teaspoons olive oil
- ¾ cup fresh or thawed frozen corn kernels
- ¼ cup finely chopped onion
- 1 cup chicken stock or canned low-sodium broth
- 2 tablespoons minced fresh cilantro
- Salt and freshly ground pepper
- 2 tablespoons cold unsalted butter, cut into small pieces

1. Roast the Anaheim and poblano chiles over a gas flame or under a broiler, turning often, until charred all over. Put the chiles in a bowl, cover with plastic wrap and let steam for 5 minutes. Peel the charred skin, allowing the juices to fall into the bowl. Discard the cores, ribs and seeds, coarsely chop the chiles and transfer them to a small bowl. Strain the chile juices over the chopped chiles.

2. Heat the oil in a medium nonreactive saucepan. Add ½ cup of the corn kernels and the chopped onion and cook over moderate heat, stirring occasionally, until the onion is wilted, about 4 minutes. Add the stock to the pan and raise the heat to high. Boil until the liquid is reduced by half, about 5 minutes. Stir in the chopped chiles with their juices and the cilantro and season with salt and pepper.

3. Transfer the mixture to a blender or food processor and puree until smooth. Return the sauce to the saucepan and add the remaining ¼ cup corn kernels. (**MAKE AHEAD:** The sauce can be refrigerated for up to 1 day.) Bring the corn sauce to a simmer over low heat and whisk in the butter until incorporated; do not allow the sauce to boil. Remove the corn sauce from the heat and season it with salt and pepper before serving.—ROBERT MCGRATH

NUOC CHAM

The principal ingredient in this classic Vietnamese dipping sauce is a pungent, vitamin-B-rich fish sauce, which is a beautiful balance of sugar, chiles and lime juice. The sauce is an ideal accompaniment to any Asian fried snack or dumpling; it also goes well with grilled chicken or pork and with steamed rice.

MAKES ABOUT 1 CUP

- 2 large garlic cloves, halved
- ½ to 1 teaspoon crushed red pepper
- 1 tablespoon sugar
- ¼ cup plus 2 tablespoons fish sauce (nuoc mam)
- ¼ cup plus 1 tablespoon fresh lime juice

In a mortar or a mini-chopper, pulverize the halved garlic cloves with the crushed red pepper. Add the sugar and pound the mixture to a glossy paste. Pour the paste into a bowl and stir in the fish sauce, the fresh lime juice and ¼ cup of water. (**MAKE AHEAD:** The Nuoc Cham can be refrigerated for up to 5 days. Allow it to return to room temperature before serving.)—MARCIA KIESEL

BLACK-EYED-PEA CHILI

Top any kind of beefsteak, pork, chicken, shrimp or any kind of meaty fish with this chili sauce.

MAKES ABOUT 3 CUPS

- 2 tablespoons peanut oil
- ¼ cup finely diced green bell pepper
- 1 tablespoon chili powder
- One 15-ounce can black-eyed peas, drained and rinsed, or 1⅔ cups thawed frozen
- 1½ pounds ripe tomatoes, seeded and finely diced
- ¼ cup finely chopped scallions
- Salt and freshly ground pepper

Heat the peanut oil in a large nonreactive skillet. Add the green bell pepper and the chili powder and cook over high heat, stirring, until fragrant, about 1 minute. Add the black-eyed peas and ¼ cup of water, lower the heat to moderate and simmer the mixture for 5 minutes. Add the diced tomatoes and the chopped scallions and season the chili with salt and pepper. Transfer the chili to a bowl and allow it to cool.—ELIZABETH TERRY ➤

NOT JUST PLAIN BUTTER

Butter is used in innumerable ways, sometimes straight from the package, sometimes in classic preparations of its own. Here are several that frequently crop up in recipes.

CLARIFIED BUTTER is made by slowly melting butter so that the pure butterfat separates from the milk solids and water; any foam on the surface is also skimmed. The resulting clear liquid is poured off for use. Because clarifying removes the proteins, it raises the smoking point of the butter, making it ideal for sautéing. Ghee, a type of clarified butter with a strong, nutty, somewhat fermented taste, is used in India and countries in the vicinity of the Himalayas. Smen, an herb-flavored butter used for cooking in Morocco, is often made from clarified sweet butter with salt and seasonings added.

DRAWN BUTTER is a melted version to which an acid, such as lemon juice or vinegar, or a flour thickener is added. The term is sometimes used interchangeably with clarified butter.

BEURRE BLANC, literally "white butter," is a delicate sauce made with a reduction of white wine and vinegar into which bits of cold butter are gradually beaten until a thick, creamy emulsion forms. A variation, *beurre rouge* ("red butter"), is made with red instead of white wine.

BROWN BUTTER (*beurre noisette*) is made by cooking butter over low heat until it turns light brown, the color of hazelnuts. If allowed to darken further it becomes black butter (*beurre noir*). Both black butter, which is often seasoned with lemon and capers, and brown butter are used as sauces.

BEURRE MANIÉ is a paste made of soft butter kneaded with flour. It is used to thicken sauces.

MAÎTRE D'HÔTEL BUTTER is made by melting butter with lemon juice or vinegar along with parsley, salt and pepper. It is typically used to top meat and fish.—FLORENCE FABRICANT

HOT SAUCES

ASIAN-STYLE SAUCES

These sauces rely on small, hot red chiles, such as Thai chiles. Labeling and distribution are very erratic, so look for them by type, not brand.

• Chinese black-bean chile sauce is chunky and richly flavored with fermented black beans, bits of red chile and lots of garlic. Vegetable oil or sesame oil is sometimes added to the sauce.

• Chinese chile garlic sauce, which is a blend of red chiles and garlic, has a coarse texture and refreshing taste.

• Sriracha is a smoothly textured all-purpose sauce with a sharp vinegar-and-garlic edge. Made from red jalapeños or Thai chiles, it hails from Thailand and China and is also produced in California.

CARIBBEAN-STYLE SAUCES

These tend to be on the thick side and flavored with mustard or fruit. The predominant chiles here—Scotch bonnets and habaneros—combine remarkable heat with a fruity flavor.

• Busha Browne's Pukka Hot Pepper Sauce, a mix of Scotch bonnets, vinegar and salt, will blow your head off with its heat.

• Inner Beauty Real Hot Sauce is a tangy brew full of tropical fruit juices, habaneros and mustard.

• "Original" Smoked Habanero, which is produced in Costa Rica, blends habaneros, pasilla chiles and lemon.

• Matouk's is a Trinidadian blend of Scotch bonnets and mustard.

• Bello Special Pepper Sauce, made in Dominica from Scotch bonnets and papaya, is deliciously fruity.

• Evadney's All-Purpose Jamaican Hot Sauce is thick and intensely flavored, full of tomatoes and Jamaican flavorings—Scotch bonnets, ginger, allspice.

MEXICAN AND SOUTHWESTERN SAUCES

They use a range of chiles, from the milder poblano to the hot jalapeño, chipotle and pequin. The sauces are usually smooth, with few other ingredients in the mix.

• Santa Fe Olé 3 Pepper Sauce blends smoked chipotle chiles, New Mexico red chiles and red jalapeños.

• El Yucateco Sauce, from the Yucatan peninsula, gets its surreal green color from unripe habanero chiles.

• Poblano Mexican Green Jalapeño sauce, which is made from jalapeños, not poblanos, is bright green, lively and sharp. Cholula Hot Sauce is a smooth, red variation made from pequin chiles.

NORTH AMERICAN-STYLE SAUCES

These sauces are as varied as our regional cuisine.

• Lowcountry Lemon Hot Sauce, made in South Carolina from tabasco and green chiles, is bracing and citrusy.

• Scorned Woman, from Georgia, is a blend of habanero and tabasco chiles, vinegar and lemon.

• Endorphinator Mango BBQ Sauce, which hails from Texas, combines smoky chipotles with sweet mango.

• Dat'l Do-It, from Florida, home of the datil chile, is thick, slightly sweet and wonderfully rich.

• Tabasco, the old reliable, uses tabasco chiles aged according to a method developed by a Louisiana company. Tabasco Jalapeño is a pleasing new addition.

• Frank's Original Redhot is a mild, smooth Louisiana-style aged cayenne sauce that will satisfy timid palates.

• Vermont Piquant gets a slight apple flavor from cider vinegar.

USING HOT SAUCE

Collecting these small bottles of fire opens a window onto cuisines from all over the world. The dishes for which they were originally developed show them off best. Still, there's plenty of room for cross-cultural experimentation. Here are some suggestions.

• Top tacos and burritos, fried chicken, fried oysters and crab cakes with Bello Special Pepper, Cholula, Frank's Original Redhot, Poblano Mexican Green Jalapeño or Tabasco sauce.

• Add sriracha to noodle dishes and soups or mix it with hoisin sauce and use it as a dip.

• Serve Chinese black-bean chile sauce or chile garlic sauce with steamed clams and shrimp, or as a dumpling dipping sauce.

• Busha Browne's Pukka Hot Pepper, El Yucateco, Inner Beauty, Lowcountry Lemon, Santa Fe Olé 3 Pepper, Scorned Woman and Vermont Piquant fire up soups, stews, meat loaves and other rich, hearty dishes.

• Mix Dat'l Do-It, Evadney's All Purpose Jamaican or "Original" Smoked Habanero into marinades and mayonnaise-based dips.

• Put Endorphinator Mango BBQ Sauce or Mantouk's on Caribbean-spiced grilled seafood and meats or rice and bean dishes.

TWO-TOMATO SALSA WITH POBLANOS

MAKES ABOUT 2 CUPS

- 4 poblano chiles (4 ounces each)
- 1 small jalapeño chile
- 2 small tomatoes, halved crosswise
- 10 oil-packed sun-dried-tomato halves, well drained and finely chopped
- 1 tablespoon finely chopped flat-leaf parsley
- 2 tablespoons minced cilantro
- 1 small garlic clove, minced
- 2 tablespoons minced red onion
- 1½ teaspoons fresh lime juice
- Salt

Roast the chiles directly over a gas flame until charred all over. Transfer to a bowl and cover with plastic for 15 minutes to loosen the skins. Rub off the charred skins with your fingers and remove the seeds and ribs. Finely chop the poblanos and mince the jalapeño. Working over a strainer set in a bowl, seed the tomatoes; press on the seeds to release the juices. Finely chop the tomatoes and add to the juices with the chiles. Stir in the sun-dried-tomatoes, parsley, cilantro, garlic, onion and lime juice. Season with salt. Let stand at room temperature for 3 hours before serving.—BOB CHAMBERS

HEAT BY MAIL

To order or to learn more about hot sauces, contact:

- **Chile Pepper, P.O. Box 769, Mt. Morris, IL 61054-0769; 1-800-959-5468. Bimonthly magazine.**
- **Chile Today-Hot Tamale, 919 Highway 33, Suite 47, Freehold, NJ 07728; 1-800-468-7377. Catalog.**
- **Hot Sauce Club of America, P.O. Box 5784, Baltimore, MD 21224; 1-800-728-2328. Catalog; newsletter for club members.**
- **Mo Hotta-Mo Betta, P.O. Box 4136, San Luis Obispo, CA 93403; 1-800-462-3220. Catalog.**

ROASTED-TOMATO SALSA LF

MAKES ABOUT 2½ CUPS

- 4 ripe plum tomatoes (about 1 pound)
- 1 red bell pepper
- 2 medium unpeeled garlic cloves
- 1 jalapeño chile
- 2 medium shallots, chopped
- 1 chipotle chile in adobo,* chopped
- ½ teaspoon dried oregano
- 1 teaspoon fresh lime juice
- Salt
- ½ teaspoon cumin seeds
- ⅓ to ½ cup tomato juice

*Available at specialty-food stores and many supermarkets

1. Preheat the broiler. Position a broiler rack 8 inches from the heat. Broil the tomatoes, bell pepper, garlic and jalapeño until blackened all over. Transfer to a bowl and cover with plastic wrap for 20 minutes to loosen the skins. Peel the bell pepper and jalapeño and remove the seeds and ribs. Peel the garlic. Leave most of the blackened skin on the tomatoes. Place with all the ingredients except the cumin seeds and tomato juice in a food processor and pulse until coarsely chopped.

2. In a small dry skillet, toast the cumin seeds over high heat, shaking the pan, until fragrant, about 2 minutes. Grind to a fine powder in a spice grinder. Stir the cumin into the salsa and add tomato juice as needed to moisten. Refrigerate for up to 4 hours before serving. (MAKE AHEAD: The salsa will keep 4 days in the refrigerator.) —BOB CHAMBERS ➤

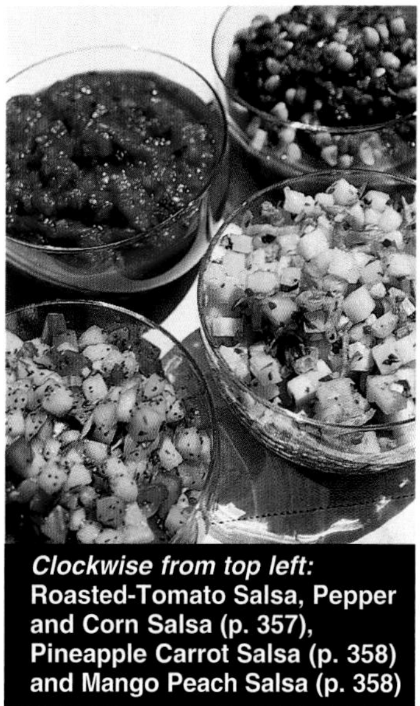

Clockwise from top left: **Roasted-Tomato Salsa, Pepper and Corn Salsa (p. 357), Pineapple Carrot Salsa (p. 358) and Mango Peach Salsa (p. 358)**

SALSA PARTNERS

- **Roasted-Tomato Salsa: Pasta, burritos, chips.**
- **Pepper and Corn Salsa (p. 357): Chips, chicken and pork.**
- **Mango Peach Salsa (p. 358): Poultry, salads, salmon and snapper.**
- **Pineapple-Carrot Salsa (p. 358): Pork, chicken and veal.**
- **Two-Tomato Salsa with Poblanos: Chips, tacos, burritos.**

ROASTED-TOMATILLO CHIPOTLE SALSA

This very simple building-block recipe from Rick Bayless's Mexican Kitchen *(Scribner) needs only three basic ingredients. Add anything more than salt and sugar and you're gilding the lily. Chipotles, both dried and packed in adobo, are available in most supermarkets and at any Latin American market.*

MAKES ABOUT 2½ CUPS

- 4 to 6 dried chipotle chiles, stems discarded, or 4 to 5 chipotles in adobo
- 6 large unpeeled garlic cloves
- 1 pound tomatillos, husked and rinsed
- Salt
- Sugar (optional)

1. If using dried chiles, heat a dry griddle or a heavy skillet over moderate heat. Toast half of the chiles, pressing down on them with a metal spatula, until they start to crackle. Turn and toast the other side. Transfer to a bowl and repeat with the remaining chiles. Cover the chiles with hot water and let soften for 30 minutes, stirring occasionally. Drain the chiles. If using canned chiles, simply wipe off the adobo.

2. Heat a dry griddle or heavy skillet over moderate heat. Toast the garlic, turning occasionally, until softened and blackened in spots, about 15 minutes. Let cool, then peel and roughly chop.

3. Meanwhile, preheat the broiler. Spread the tomatillos on a rimmed baking sheet and broil for about 8 minutes, turning once, or until blackened in spots and softened. Let cool on the baking sheet.

4. Scrape the tomatillos and any accumulated juices into a food processor or blender and add the chiles and roasted garlic. Puree until thickened and smooth. (For a chunkier salsa, pulse the tomatillos and roasted garlic until coarsely pureed; finely chop the chiles and add them to the tomatillo mixture.) Transfer the salsa to a bowl and stir in 6 to 8 tablespoons of water, so the salsa has a spoonable consistency. Season with salt, plus a little sugar, if you want to soften the tangy edge. (**MAKE AHEAD:** The salsa can be refrigerated for up to 2 days.) —RICK BAYLESS

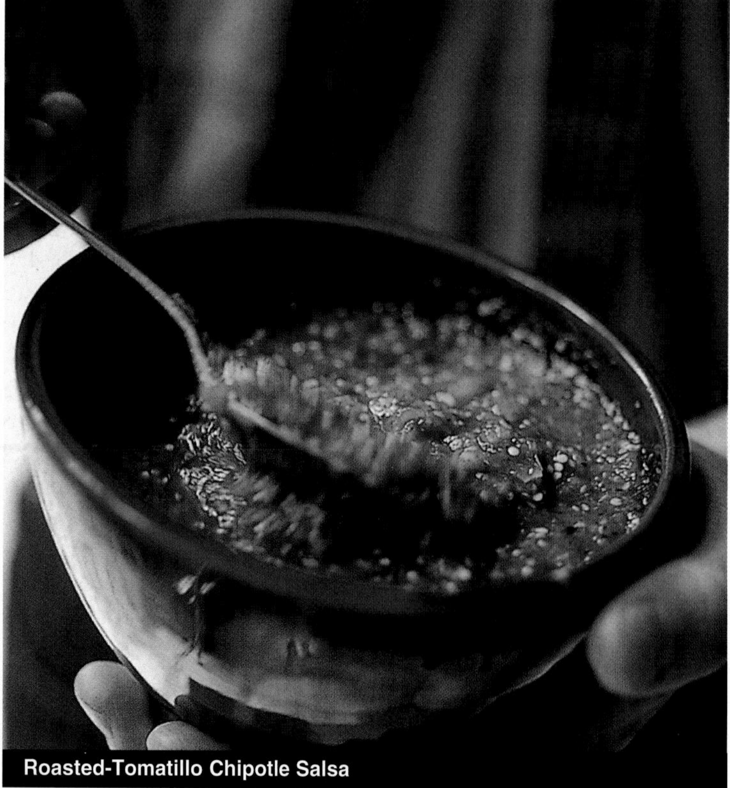

Roasted-Tomatillo Chipotle Salsa

FIESTA FOOD

Roasted-Tomatillo Chipotle Salsa is a central ingredient in all of these main dishes. Just add a salad and some warm tortillas, and you're ready for a party.

- **Catfish with Tomatillo and Garlic Sauce (p. 156)**
- **Shrimp Salpicón with Chipotles (p. 173)**
- **Chicken-Stuffed Tamal (p. 203)**
- **Cornish Hens with Creamy Chipotle Sauce (p. 211)**
- **Tomatillo-Chipotle-Glazed Country Ribs (p. 230)**
- **Tortilla Tomatillo Casserole with Cheese (p. 282)**

FRESH SALSA MEXICANA FROM JEREZ

You can vary this salsa according to what is available in your market. Do not remove the seeds of small chiles like serranos. Serve the salsa as a condiment.

MAKES ABOUT 1¾ CUPS

- 1 poblano chile, stems, seeds and veins removed and flesh finely chopped
- 1 red jalapeño chile, stems, seeds and veins removed and flesh finely chopped
- 2 yellow chiles, stems, seeds and veins removed and flesh finely chopped
- 2 serrano chiles, finely chopped
- 3 tablespoons finely chopped white onion
- 1 ripe medium tomato (about 4 ounces), finely chopped
- ½ cup water
- 3 tablespoons fresh lime juice
- ½ teaspoon crumbled dried oregano

Salt

Mix the chiles, onion, tomato, water, lime juice and oregano together in a bowl; season with salt to taste. Set aside to macerate for about 1 hour.—DIANA KENNEDY

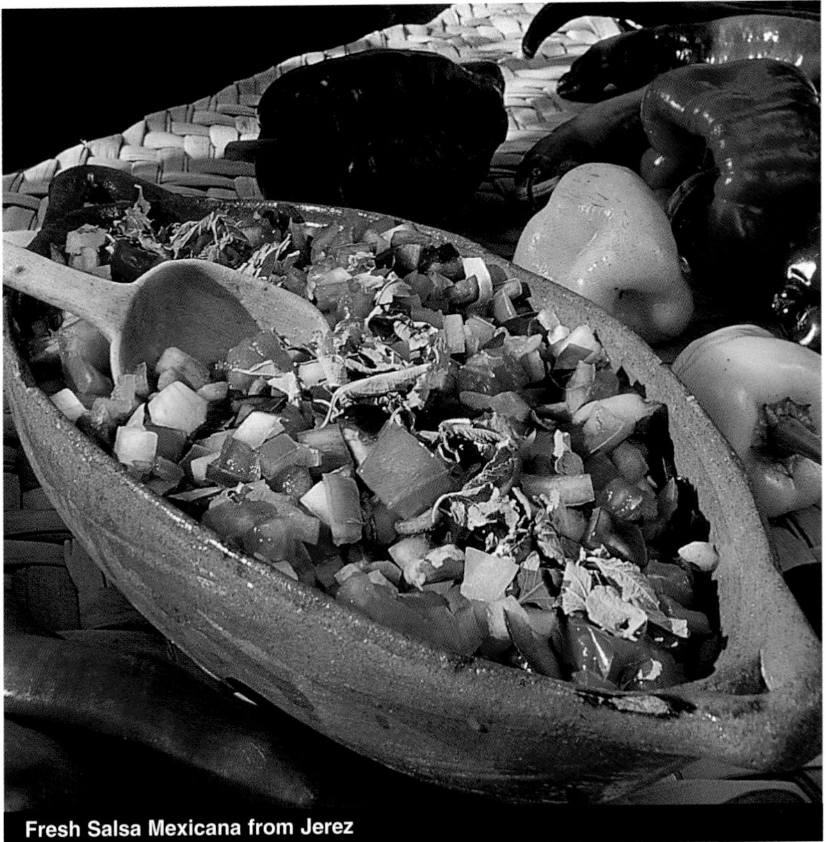

Fresh Salsa Mexicana from Jerez

PEPPER AND CORN SALSA LF

MAKES ABOUT 2¾ CUPS

- 2 large red bell peppers
- 2 large yellow bell peppers
- 1 medium green bell pepper
- 3 jalapeño chiles
- ¾ cup fresh corn kernels (from 2 ears)
- ½ teaspoon fennel seeds
- ½ teaspoon cumin seeds
- 1 tablespoon fresh lemon juice

2 to 3 tablespoons finely shredded fresh basil leaves

Salt and freshly ground black pepper

1. Preheat the broiler and position a rack 8 inches from the heat. Broil the red, yellow and green bell peppers and the jalapeños until they are blackened all over. Transfer the bell peppers and jalapeños to a bowl and cover them with plastic wrap for 20 minutes to loosen the skins. Peel the bell peppers and jalapeños, then remove the seeds and ribs and transfer to a food processor. Pulse until finely chopped but not pureed, then scrape into a bowl.

2. In a saucepan of lightly salted boiling water, blanch the corn kernels for 1 minute. Drain and let cool.

3. In a small dry skillet, toast the fennel seeds and cumin seeds over moderately high heat, shaking the skillet frequently, until the spices are fragrant, 2 to 3 minutes. In a spice grinder, grind the toasted seeds to a fine powder. Add the blanched corn kernels, the lemon juice, the shredded basil leaves and the ground fennel and cumin seeds to the bowl with the chopped bell peppers and jalapeños. Season the salsa with salt and black pepper and let stand for 2 hours.—BOB CHAMBERS ➤

FUNKY NEW ORLEANS SALSA

Serve this salsa with pork, Italian sausage, chicken, shrimp or any meaty or firm, white-fleshed fish.

MAKES ABOUT 2½ CUPS

1 medium red bell pepper
½ cup diced pineapple (½ inch)
½ cup diced mango (½ inch)
½ cup diced papaya (½ inch)
1 small starfruit, sliced ¼ inch thick
1 medium jalapeño chile, seeded and minced
¼ cup fresh lemon juice
2 tablespoons fresh lime juice
Salt and freshly ground white pepper
2 tablespoons minced fresh cilantro

1. Roast the bell pepper over a gas flame or under a broiler, turning often, until charred. Transfer to a paper bag and let steam for 5 minutes. Peel the charred skin and discard the core, ribs and seeds. Finely chop the pepper.
2. Combine all the ingredients except the cilantro in a medium bowl. (MAKE AHEAD: The salsa can be refrigerated for up to 6 hours.) Stir in the cilantro and serve chilled or at room temperature.—EMERIL LAGASSE

BLACK-BEAN MANGO SALSA

This topping goes well with any kind of beefsteak, pork, lamb, chicken, duck breasts or any firm, white-fleshed fish.

MAKES ABOUT 2½ CUPS

1 cup drained canned black beans, rinsed
1 ripe medium mango, peeled and cut into ½-inch dice
½ medium red bell pepper, cut into ½-inch dice
1 medium jalapeño chile, seeded and finely chopped
1 medium scallion, minced
1½ tablespoons fresh lime juice
1 tablespoon olive oil
1½ teaspoons rice-wine vinegar
1½ teaspoons minced fresh ginger
½ teaspoon sugar
½ teaspoon coarse salt
Pinch of cayenne pepper
1 tablespoon minced fresh cilantro

In a bowl, combine the black beans, mango, red bell pepper, jalapeño and scallion. In a small bowl, combine the lime juice, oil, vinegar, ginger, sugar, salt and cayenne. Fold the mixture into the beans. (MAKE AHEAD: The salsa can be refrigerated for up to 6 hours.) Stir in the cilantro and serve chilled or at room temperature.—HARLAN PETERSON

PINEAPPLE CARROT SALSA LF

MAKES ABOUT 3 CUPS

2 cups diced fresh pineapple (¼ inch)
½ cup finely grated carrots
¼ cup golden raisins, plumped in boiling water and drained
½ small red onion, finely diced
2 tablespoons minced red bell pepper
½ tablespoon minced fresh tarragon
1 tablespoon minced fresh cilantro
½ jalapeño chile, seeded and minced
1 tablespoon fresh lemon juice
Salt
¼ cup pine nuts, toasted

Combine all the ingredients except the pine nuts in a bowl and let stand for 1 hour. Just before serving, stir in the pine nuts.—BOB CHAMBERS

MANGO PEACH SALSA LF

MAKES ABOUT 2½ CUPS

1 large mango, peeled and cut into ¼-inch dice
1 large peach, peeled and cut into ¼-inch dice
½ small red onion, finely chopped
2 small plum tomatoes, seeded and diced
½ serrano chile, minced
½ tablespoon fresh lime juice
2 tablespoons fresh orange juice
¼ teaspoon finely grated orange zest
1 tablespoon minced cilantro
Salt and freshly ground pepper
Pinch of sugar (optional)
2¼ teaspoons poppy seeds

Combine all of the ingredients in a bowl and let stand for 1 hour.—BOB CHAMBERS

GUACAMOLE

The avocados must be ripe, yielding easily to a squeeze; if they're too firm, let them ripen in a paper bag on the counter for a few days.

MAKES ABOUT 4 CUPS

1 large ripe tomato, finely diced
2 serrano chiles, minced
1 large garlic clove, minced
3 tablespoons coarsely chopped fresh cilantro

1 medium white onion, finely diced
3 large ripe avocados
2 to 3 tablespoons fresh lime juice
Salt
Radish slices, for garnish

1. In a medium bowl, mix the tomato, chiles, garlic and cilantro. Stir in the diced onion.
2. Peel and seed the avocados. Scoop the flesh into a medium bowl. Mash against the side of the bowl, leaving some chunks. Add the tomato mixture and lime juice; season with salt. Let sit for a few minutes, garnish with radish slices and serve.—RICK BAYLESS

SUN-DRIED-TOMATO COMPOTE

Spoon this compote over any meaty or firm white-fleshed fish, scallops or chicken.

MAKES ABOUT 1½ CUPS

3 garlic cloves, minced
½ cup olive oil
⅔ cup drained oil-packed sun-dried-tomato halves (about 4 ounces)
¾ cup pitted halved Kalamata olives
2 tablespoons balsamic vinegar
Salt and freshly ground pepper
¼ cup minced fresh mint

In a small saucepan, cook the garlic in the oil over low heat until fragrant and just golden, about 15 minutes. Let cool. In a bowl, combine the tomatoes, olives and garlic with its cooking oil. Stir in the vinegar; season with salt and pepper. (**MAKE AHEAD:** The compote can be refrigerated up to 1 day.) Stir in the mint. Serve at room temperature.—GORDON HAMERSLEY

Guacamole

ROASTED-GARLIC JAM

MAKES ABOUT 1 CUP

6 large heads of garlic, unpeeled
¾ cup extra-virgin olive oil

1. Preheat the oven to 300°. Halve the heads of garlic crosswise. In a saucepan of boiling salted water, blanch the garlic for 5 minutes; drain well. Trim off the roots.
2. Pour the oil into a 9-by-13-inch baking pan. Add the garlic, cut-side down, and roast for 1 hour, or until the garlic is soft.
3. Squeeze the garlic from the skins into a coarse strainer set over a bowl and press the garlic through the strainer with a spatula. Whisk the puree until creamy. (**MAKE AHEAD:** The jam can be refrigerated for up to 10 days.) Save the garlicky oil to use in cooking.—WALDY MALOUF

SPICY GRILLED-ONION RELISH

Use this to top any kind of beefsteak, pork, Italian sausages or chicken.

MAKES ABOUT 2½ CUPS

2 pounds Spanish onions, sliced crosswise ½ inch thick

Sun-Dried-Tomato Compote over scallops

¼ cup olive oil
3 tablespoons balsamic vinegar
2 tablespoons light brown sugar
¼ teaspoon cayenne pepper
Salt and freshly ground black pepper

1. Light a grill. Brush the slices of onion on both sides with 2 tablespoons of the oil. Grill over low heat for about 20 minutes, turning only once or twice to keep the slices intact, until charred and tender. Brush the onion slices with the remaining 2 tablespoons oil during grilling. Let cool slightly. Cut the onions into ½-inch dice and transfer to a large bowl.
2. In a small nonreactive saucepan, simmer the vinegar and brown sugar over low heat, stirring occasionally, until the sugar has dissolved, about 3 minutes. Pour the mixture over the onions and stir in the cayenne. Season with salt and black pepper. (**MAKE AHEAD:** The relish can be refrigerated for up to 2 days.) Serve warm or at room temperature.—JOHANNE KILLEEN AND GEORGE GERMON ➤

CHILES

FRESH CHILES

• CHILACA chiles, long and narrow (about 7 inches by 1 inch) and dark to blackish green, have a shiny surface with undulating vertical ridges. Their slightly sweet flavor varies from mildly hot to hot. Dried chilacas are called pasillas.

• HABANERO chiles are squat with a slightly tapering lantern shape, about 1¾ inches long and 1¼ inches across. Their pale to medium green color ripens to yellow and then to orange. There are cultivars that ripen to a pale apricot color and others to a chocolate brown. The surface of a habanero is very shiny, almost translucent, and undulating. Habaneros are often rated as the hottest chiles in Mexico, with a lingering flavor and aroma when charred.

• JALAPEÑO chiles are without a doubt the best known outside of Mexico because they are pickled, canned and widely distributed. There are many cultivars, but they are all unmistakable: a smooth blunt-nosed elongated triangle, about 2½ inches long and 1 inch wide, whose color is a shiny medium to dark green that ripens to a bright red. Some have dark patches; others have a brown vertical striping, or corking. They are very fiery. Ripened and smoke-dried, jalapeños are called chipotles.

• POBLANO chiles are large, fleshy and triangle-shaped with a shiny, green to blackish green color that ripens to a deep red. An average poblano is 4½ inches long and 2½ inches across the top; it is distinguished by a deep ridge around the base of the stalk. It has a delicious mild to hot flavor. With rare exceptions, the poblano is charred and peeled before using. Dried, it is called ancho. This chile is erroneously referred to as pasilla in many California markets (or even fresh pasilla, a contradictory term since pasilla refers to something dried and wrinkled).

• SERRANO chiles are the ones most commonly used throughout Mexico for making sauces. Generally speaking, serranos are small (2 inches long and ½ inch wide) and slightly pointed at the tip. They are medium to dark green with occasional dark patches; they ripen to a bright red. Their heat varies from hot to very hot. These chiles are never skinned, nor are the seeds removed.

• VERDE DEL NORTE chiles are long, skinny and bright green. They are similar to Anaheim chiles, which are available in California. Their smooth, slightly undulating surface ripens to bright orange and then to red. Compared with other chiles, they do not have a very distinct flavor; it varies from mild to fairly hot. These chiles are always charred and peeled before using since they have a tough skin.

DRIED CHILES

• ANCHO chiles are the most commonly used dried chiles throughout Mexico. They are in fact poblanos ripened to a deep red and then dried. A good ancho (which means wide), about 4½ inches long and 3 inches wide, has flexible, reddish brown wrinkled skin that still has some shine. Its heat ranges from almost mild to hot. As it dries out, the color becomes increasingly dark and more difficult to distinguish from that of the mulato. To accurately identify the ancho, slit it open and hold it up to the light: it should be a reddish color; the mulato will be a brownish color. The ancho is decidedly fruitier and sharper than the mulato.

• CASCABEL chiles are small and round, about 1 inch long and 1¼ inches in diameter. They have reddish brown skin. The name derives from *cascabel*, or rattlesnake, because the chile's seeds rattle inside if you shake it. Cascabels are quite hot, and have a rich earthy flavor when toasted.

• CHIPOTLE (sometimes written *chilpotle* or *chipocle*) chiles are jalapeños that have been ripened and smoke-dried. Relatively small (about 2¼ inches long and ¾ inch wide), the chiles have a tough, leathery, wrinkled, light-brown skin the surface of which appears to be covered with a golden webbing. Chipotles are extremely hot and have a fruity-smoky flavor.

• The CHIPOTLE MORA is another type of dried and smoked jalapeño. About 2 inches by ¾ inches, it is mulberry-colored with a matte, very wrinkled skin. It is close to the chipotle in flavor and piquancy.

• The smallest of the smoked chiles is the MORITA, a triangular, smooth and mulberry-colored chile, about 1 inch long and ½ inch wide. It is probably a late-harvested ripe jalapeño and is therefore considered a chipotle.

• DE ARBOL chiles are long and skinny (about 3 inches by ⅜ inch) with smooth skin. They are exceedingly hot. The fresh chile is a bright green that ripens to bright red, a color that it retains when it is dried with care.

• GUAHILLO chiles have a smooth, tough, dark-red skin with purplish tones. These chiles are long (about 5 inches) and narrow (about 1½ inches across the widest part), tapering to a point. They can range from fairly hot to hot with a pleasant sharp flavor. A narrower guajillo, called puya, is considered more piquant.

• MULATO chiles, rarely used in their fresh state and among the most expensive dried chiles, are essentially the same as poblanos (anchos), but with slightly different genes that give them a darker, shinier and smoother skin and a sweeter, almost chocolatey taste. A top-quality mulato is 5 inches long and 3 inches wide on the average and can range from quite mild to rather hot.

• PASILLA chiles—chilacas ripened and dried—are about 6 inches long and 1 inch wide. Their shiny, black, wrinkled surface has vertical ridges. Their flavor is rich but sharp.

• SECO DEL NORTE chiles are verde del nortes ripened and dried. An average one is about 5 inches long and almost 2 inches wide. It is very full at the top and either tapers to a point or is blunt-nosed. It is burgundy-colored with a smooth, matte finish. The flavor is sharp and slightly acidic and can range from mild to hot.

BUYING CHILES

• When selecting fresh chiles, look for ones that are firm to the touch, with smooth skin. Once they are wrinkled, their crisp texture and fresh flavor are gone, and they develop an earthy taste.

• Choose serranos, jalapeños, poblanos and verdes that are still green, unless the recipe specifies otherwise.

• Whenever possible, buy dried chiles loose, rather than packaged, so that you can examine them closely. Besides, they are much cheaper.

• Accustom yourself to the shape of dried chiles so that you can be sure you are getting the correct ones. Packaged chiles in particular are often mislabeled.

• Select dried chiles that are still a little flexible and not dried to a crisp. If only crisp ones are available, place them on a warm pan before using; as they heat through they will become pliable.

• On the other hand, do not buy damp dried chiles, for it means that either the chiles have been incorrectly stored or the vendor has dampened the chiles so that they will weigh more. Chances are good that the moisture will cause mold to form.

STORING CHILES

• Use fresh chiles as soon after purchasing them as possible. If you have to store them, wrap in a dry terry-cloth towel inside a paper bag in the refrigerator or a cool dark place.

• Store dried chiles in a cool, dry place, or freeze them in a freezer bag. Check them to make sure the fruit moth has not damaged them. If it has, the chiles' skin will be translucent, and there will be dark eggs just visible that will hatch greedy caterpillars.—DIANA KENNEDY

CRANBERRY CITRUS RELISH

MAKES ABOUT 3⅓ CUPS

- 1 navel orange
- 1 lemon
- 1 lime
- 1 cup sugar
- 3 cups fresh cranberries
- ¼ cup Grand Marnier

1. Using a vegetable peeler, strip the zest from the orange, lemon and lime. Cut the zests into very thin 1½-inch-long strips. Peel the citrus fruits using a sharp paring knife, making sure to remove all the bitter white pith. Working over a bowl, cut in between the membranes to release the sections; squeeze the juice from the membranes into the bowl.

2. Put the sugar in a nonreactive medium saucepan and cook over moderate heat, stirring with a wooden spoon, until a clear amber syrup forms, 3 to 4 minutes. Immediately add the citrus zests and stir constantly for 30 seconds, then stir in the citrus fruits and juices and cook for 30 seconds more. Add the cranberries and bring to a gentle boil. Cook, stirring occasionally, until the relish is jamlike, about 12 minutes. Remove from the heat and stir in the Grand Marnier. Let cool completely, then refrigerate. (**MAKE AHEAD:** The relish can be refrigerated for up to 1 week.) Serve the relish at room temperature.—WALDY MALOUF

CHIPOTLES EN ADOBO

Adobo, a paste made of ground chiles, spices, herbs and vinegar, is often used to season meat. These chipotle chiles can be served as a condiment, sprinkled with a little olive oil and

crumbled queso fresco, or they can be ground, with peanuts for example, in a cooked sauce.

MAKES ABOUT 3 CUPS

4 ounces chipotle mora chiles (about 60)
3 ancho chiles, seeds and veins removed
4 garlic cloves, coarsely chopped
Leaves of 2 fresh marjoram sprigs, or ⅛ teaspoon dried marjoram
Leaves of 2 fresh thyme sprigs, or ⅛ teaspoon dried thyme
Pinch of cumin seeds, crushed
1 bay leaf, torn into small pieces
2 tablespoons olive oil
¾ cup mild vinegar
¾ cup strong vinegar
¼ cup tightly packed dark brown sugar
1 tablespoon sea salt

1. Rinse the chipotle mora chiles and drain. Pierce each one all the way through with a sharp fork or skewer. Place the chipotles in a pressure cooker with water to cover and cook at low pressure for about 15 minutes; the chipotles should be soft but not mushy. (Alternatively, cook the chipotles with water to cover in a tightly covered nonreactive medium saucepan over low heat for 30 to 40 minutes.)

2. Drain the chipotles, remove the stems and wipe off any stray seeds clinging to the outside. Set the chipotles aside.

3. Meanwhile, in a medium nonreactive saucepan, cover the anchos with hot water and simmer for 5 minutes. Drain the anchos and transfer them to a blender. Add 1 cup of water plus the garlic, marjoram, thyme, cumin seeds, bay leaf and four of the cooked chipotles and blend until almost smooth.

4. Heat the oil in a shallow nonreactive skillet. Add the blended ingredients. Fry over moderately high heat for about 3 minutes, scraping the bottom of the pan to prevent sticking. Add the vinegars, brown sugar, salt and ½ cup of water and cook for 5 minutes longer. Then add the remaining chipotles and cook over moderate heat, scraping the bottom of the pan from time to time to prevent sticking, until the sauce has reduced and thickened, about 15 minutes. (MAKE AHEAD: The Chipotles en Adobo can be refrigerated in an airtight container for up to 1 month. Before using, place in a medium saucepan, moisten with a little vinegar and bring to a boil. Let boil for a few minutes.) —DIANA KENNEDY

VARIATIONS

If you prefer a less pungent version of Chipotles en Adobo, boil the chiles first for about five minutes. Drain, slit them open and remove the seeds and what remains of the veins. Discard the water and start at the beginning of the recipe, reducing the cooking time by five minutes. If you wish to have a lighter sauce, simply add six ounces of broiled tomatoes to the adobo.

ROASTED TOMATOES

Tomatoes are slowly roasted in the oven with olive oil, fresh thyme and garlic cloves. The flavorful juices should be drained off as they are released to prevent the tomatoes from stewing. This almost effortless process yields three versatile components—intensely flavored tomatoes, creamy roasted garlic and delicious cooking juices—that will keep in the refrigerator for up to three weeks and can be used alone or in combination in a wide variety of easy-to-assemble dishes (see "Using Roasted Tomatoes," below).

USING ROASTED TOMATOES

Restaurant chefs always make their own ingredients, which become the foundations of dishes ranging from soups and sauces to main courses. My Roasted Tomatoes appear year-round on the menu at Manhattan's Gramercy Tavern, in one seasonal guise or another. I've adapted this technique for you to use at home to make these dishes:

- **Tomato Ravioli with Roasted-Tomato Sauce (p. 33)**
- **Clam Ragout with Bacon and Roasted Tomatoes (p. 40)**
- **Seared Black Sea Bass in Roasted-Tomato Broth (p. 150)**
- **Braised Lamb Shanks with Roasted Tomatoes (p. 260)**
- **Seared Fresh Tuna with Roasted-Tomato and Fennel Salad (p. 270)**
- **Roasted-Tomato Risotto (p. 315)**

—TOM COLICCHIO

MAKES 40 ROASTED-TOMATO HALVES, ABOUT 20 ROASTED GARLIC CLOVES AND 3 CUPS TOMATO JUICES

- 20 ripe tomatoes (10 pounds), rinsed, stemmed and halved crosswise
- 2 large heads of garlic, separated into unpeeled cloves
- 8 large fresh thyme sprigs
- ½ cup extra-virgin olive oil
- Coarse salt and freshly ground pepper

1. Preheat the oven to 350°. Line two large rimmed baking sheets with parchment paper. Put the tomato halves on the prepared baking sheets, cut-side down, and scatter the garlic cloves and thyme sprigs on top of them. Drizzle the mixture evenly with the olive oil, rubbing it over the tomatoes, and season with salt and pepper.

2. Roast the tomato halves for 20 minutes, or until the skins are wrinkled. Remove the baking sheets from the oven. Pull the skins off the tomatoes and discard. Tilt the baking sheets over a large bowl and pour off the tomato juices. Return the tomato halves to the oven and roast them for 2½ hours longer; pour off the juices every 20 minutes or as necessary. Allow the tomatoes to cool completely on the baking sheets. Discard the thyme sprigs.

3. To store, use a fork or tongs to pack the roasted tomatoes and the garlic cloves in glass jars. Strain the tomato juices into the jars and refrigerate for up to 3 weeks.—TOM COLICCHIO

HOW TO ROAST TOMATOES

Halve the tomatoes crosswise. Put on a parchment-lined sheet and top with aromatics, seasonings and oil.

Roast tomatoes for twenty minutes. Pull off the tomato skins. Pour off and save the accumulated juices.

Using a fork or tongs, transfer the roasted tomatoes and garlic cloves to a bowl or glass jar.

CHAPTER 17

~

CAKES & COOKIES

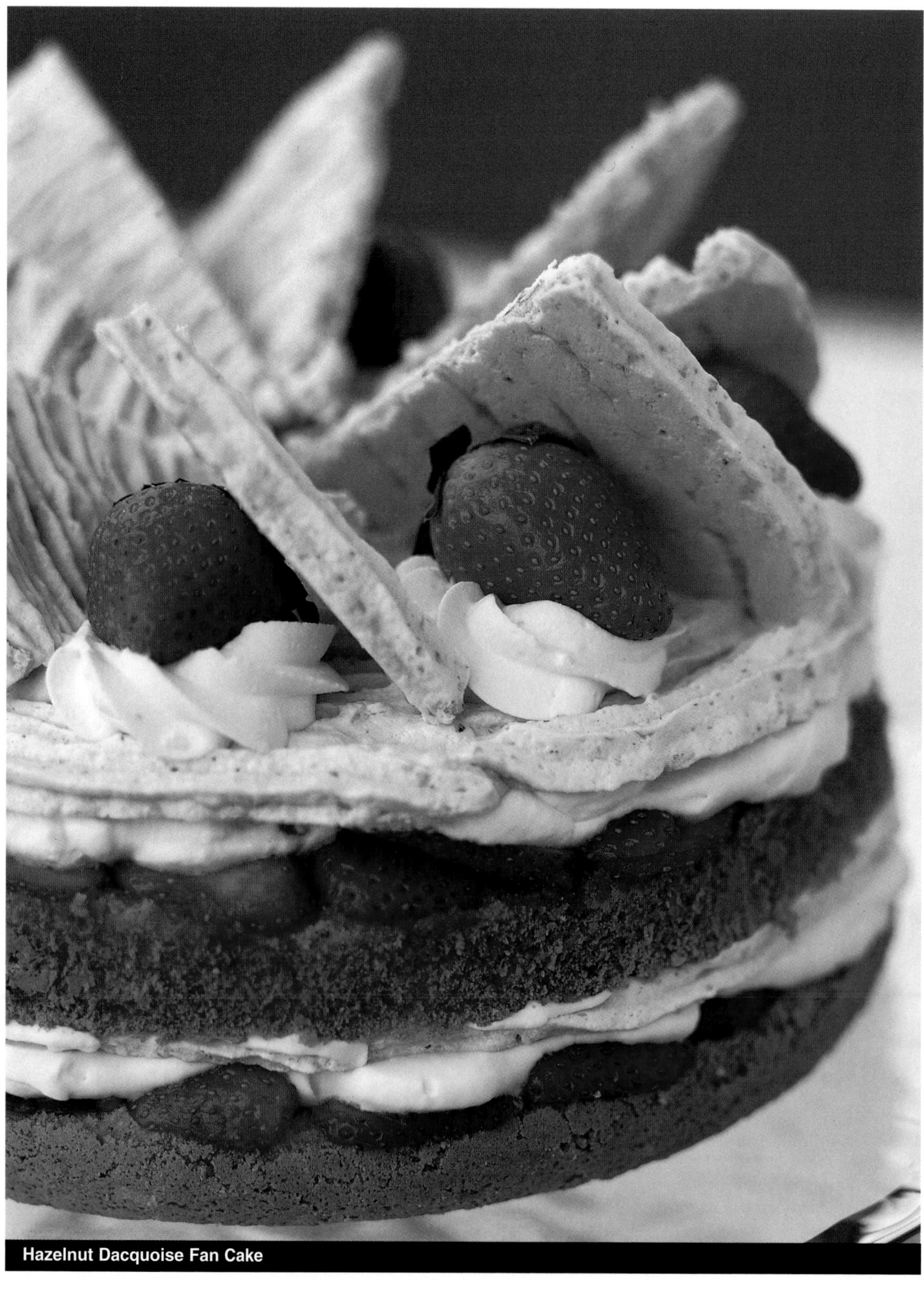

Hazelnut Dacquoise Fan Cake

HAZELNUT DACQUOISE FAN CAKE

In this dramatic-looking dessert, crisp disks of hazelnut meringue alternate with sponge cake, vanilla-flavored strawberries and whipped cream.

MAKES ONE 9-INCH CAKE

SPONGE CAKE:

- ⅔ cup cake flour
- ¾ teaspoon baking powder
- ¼ teaspoon salt
- 2 large eggs
- 4 large egg yolks
- ¾ cup granulated sugar
- 1 teaspoon pure vanilla extract
- 1½ tablespoons unsalted butter
- 3 tablespoons milk

HAZELNUT DACQUOISE:

- ⅔ cup hazelnuts (3 to 3½ ounces)
- ½ cup confectioners' sugar
- 1 tablespoon cornstarch
- 4 large egg whites
- ¼ teaspoon cream of tartar
- ¾ cup superfine sugar

STRAWBERRIES AND CREAM:

- About 2½ pints strawberries
- 2 tablespoons superfine sugar
- 1½ teaspoons pure vanilla extract
- 2 cups cold heavy cream
- ¼ cup confectioners' sugar

1. Make the sponge cake: Preheat the oven to 350°. Butter and flour a 9-by-2-inch round cake pan. In a small bowl, sift together the flour, baking powder and salt. Whisk to combine.

2. In the bowl of a standing electric mixer, whisk together the eggs, egg yolks and granulated sugar. Set the bowl over a saucepan of barely simmering water; don't let the bottom of the bowl touch the water. Whisk vigorously until the mixture is warm to the touch. Return the bowl to the mixer. Beat at medium high speed for 2 minutes. Add the vanilla. Continue beating until the mixture is the consistency of whipped cream, 2 to 3 minutes longer.

3. Meanwhile, in a small saucepan, melt the butter in the milk; do not boil. Remove from the heat and whisk.

4. Sift one-third of the dry ingredients over the whipped eggs and gently fold in. Repeat this procedure twice. Pour the warm milk mixture into the batter in a slow stream and continue folding until just incorporated.

5. Scrape the batter into the prepared pan and bake for about 30 minutes, or until a tester inserted in the center of the cake comes out clean. Cool in the pan on a rack for 2 minutes, then turn the cake out to cool completely. (**MAKE AHEAD:** The cake can be made up to 1 day ahead; wrap and store at room temperature.)

6. Make the hazelnut dacquoise: Preheat the oven to 425°. Spread the hazelnuts on a baking sheet and toast in the oven for about 8 minutes, or until fragrant. Wrap the hot nuts in a kitchen towel and vigorously rub them together to remove most of the skins. Let the nuts cool completely. Lower the oven temperature to 225°.

7. Line two large cookie sheets with parchment paper. Using the bottom of the 9-inch cake pan as a guide, trace two circles on one sheet of parchment paper and a third on the other.

8. In a food processor, finely grind the hazelnuts with the confectioners' sugar and cornstarch.

9. Put the egg whites in the large bowl of a standing electric mixer and set it over a saucepan of barely simmering water; don't allow the bottom of the bowl to touch the water. Whisk the egg whites vigorously until warm to the touch; don't stop for even a few seconds or the whites will cook. Then beat the egg whites with the mixer at high speed until foamy. Add the cream of tartar and beat until soft peaks form. Add the superfine sugar, 1 tablespoon at a time, beating for 10 seconds between each addition. The meringue will be stiff and glossy. Using a large rubber spatula, gently fold the nut mixture into the meringue.

10. Scoop the meringue into a pastry bag fitted with a #5 open star tip (about ½ inch). Pipe a ring of meringue on one of the outlined circles on the cookie sheets, ¼ inch in from the perimeter. Then, starting in the center of the circle, pipe a continuous spiral to meet the outer ring. Fill in any holes with more meringue. It doesn't have to be perfect. Repeat to fill in the other two circles. Bake the meringues for 2 hours, or until dry and firm. (**MAKE AHEAD:** If the weather is dry, the dacquoise can be made up to 1 day ahead; keep, unwrapped, in a cool dry place.)

11. Prepare the strawberries and cream: Set aside eight perfect strawberries. Slice the remaining berries ¼ inch thick. Toss the berries in a bowl with the superfine sugar and vanilla. Set aside, stirring occasionally.

12. In a small chilled bowl, whip the heavy cream with the confectioners' sugar until slightly firmer than soft peaks. Refrigerate until ready to use.

13. No more than 3 hours before serving, **assemble the cake:** Split the sponge cake into two even layers. Invert the top layer onto a 9-inch cardboard cake round or serving platter.

14. Drain the strawberries, reserving the juice. Using a pastry brush, dab half of the strawberry juice on the cake layer. Evenly distribute half of the sliced strawberries on the cake and spread 1 heaping cup of the whipped cream on top. Place a dacquoise disk over the whipped cream and spread with an additional ½ cup of the whipped cream. Repeat the layering with the second cake layer, the remaining strawberry juice and strawberries, another heaping cup of whipped cream and a second dacquoise disk.

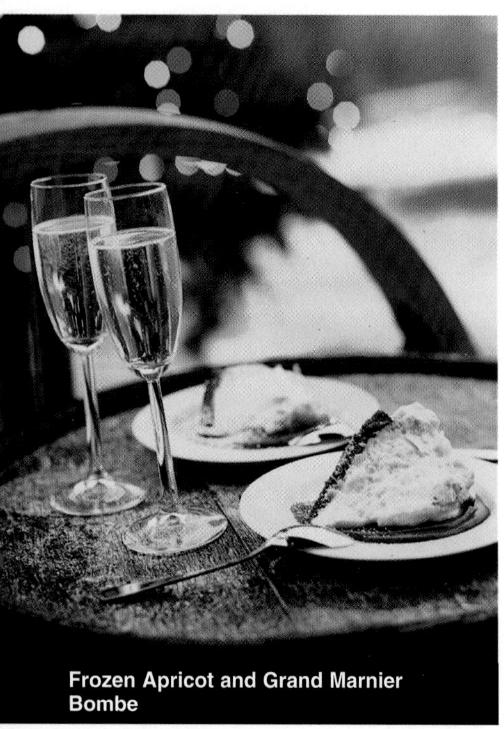
Frozen Apricot and Grand Marnier Bombe

15. Using a serrated knife, quarter the remaining dacquoise disk, and then cut each quarter in half to get eight wedges. If a wedge breaks, just glue it with a little whipped cream. Whisk the remaining whipped cream until it's stiff and transfer to a pastry bag fitted with the #5 star tip. Pipe eight evenly spaced rosettes of whipped cream about ½ inch from the edge of the cake. Lay a reserved strawberry on each rosette and lean a wedge of the dacquoise against each berry with the point toward the center of the cake. To serve, slice with a serrated knife.—PEGGY CULLEN

FROZEN APRICOT AND GRAND MARNIER BOMBE

A variation of baked Alaska, this bombe combines rich orange ice cream with moist chocolate almond cake and fluffy apricot meringue. Though composed of many elements, it is really quite simple to prepare. Assemble the bombe in advance and then slide it under the broiler just before serving. The cake is also delicious served on its own with a dusting of confectioners' sugar and a dollop of whipped cream.

MAKES ONE 8-INCH BOMBE

ICE CREAM:

- Zest of 1 orange, cut into very fine strips
- ½ cup Grand Marnier
- ½ cup sugar
- ½ cup water
- 4 large egg yolks
- 1 cup heavy cream

MERINGUE:

- ½ cup dried apricots (about 4 ounces)
- 4 large egg whites
- ¼ teaspoon cream of tartar
- ¼ cup sugar

Chocolate Almond Cake (recipe follows)

Hot Chocolate Sauce (recipe follows)

1. Make the ice cream: Line a 2-quart round ice-cream mold or bowl with plastic wrap. In a medium saucepan of boiling water, blanch the orange zest for 2 minutes; drain. In a small bowl, cover the blanched zest with the Grand Marnier.

2. In a small saucepan, combine the sugar and water and bring to a boil over high heat. Boil for 5 minutes. Meanwhile, in a large heatproof bowl, beat the egg yolks with an electric mixer until frothy. Gradually add the boiling sugar syrup, beating constantly to prevent the egg yolks from scrambling. Set the bowl over a pot of simmering water and beat until the yolk mixture is thick, about 10 minutes. Then place the bowl over a larger bowl of ice and water and beat the yolk mixture until chilled. Beat in the orange zest and ¼ cup of the Grand Marnier; reserve the rest. Stir occasionally until the mixture is thoroughly chilled.

3. Beat the cream until stiff and fold it into the chilled yolk mixture. Spoon into the prepared mold and cover with plastic wrap. Freeze for at least 12 hours.

4. Make the meringue: In a small saucepan, cover the apricots with ¾ cup water and simmer over moderate heat until completely softened, 6 to 8 minutes. (Add more water if the apricots absorb it all before softening.) Transfer to a food processor or blender and puree until smooth. Scrape the puree into a bowl.

5. Using an electric mixer, beat the egg whites with the cream of tartar until just barely stiff. Add the sugar and continue beating until stiff but not dry. Fold one-fourth of the egg whites into the apricot puree, then fold in the remaining whites.

6. To assemble the bombe, set the cake on a round heatproof platter and sprinkle it with the reserved Grand Marnier. (Trim the cake, if necessary; the ice cream should rest neatly on top.) Unmold the ice cream onto the cake; peel off the plastic wrap. With a large spatula, spread the apricot meringue all over the ice cream and cake, right down to the platter. Swirl decoratively. (MAKE AHEAD: The bombe can be frozen for up to 12 hours. Cover it with plastic wrap as soon as it's frozen solid.)

7. To serve, preheat the broiler. Set the bombe about 8 inches from the heat and broil for 5 to 10 minutes, turning to brown evenly. Slice the bombe into wedges and serve with the chocolate sauce.

Chocolate Almond Cake

MAKES ONE 8-INCH CAKE

- 7 ounces pure almond paste
- ¾ cup granulated sugar
- 1 stick unsalted butter (4 ounces)
- 1 large egg
- ½ cup unsweetened cocoa powder
- ⅔ cup cake flour
- ¼ cup milk

1. Preheat the oven to 375°. Butter and flour a shallow 8-inch cake pan.

2. In a medium bowl, using an electric mixer, beat the almond paste with the sugar until blended. Beat in the butter and then the egg. Sift the cocoa powder with the cake flour. Add to the batter alternately with the milk.

3. Scrape the batter into the prepared pan; bake for 25 minutes, or until a toothpick inserted in the center comes out clean. Let cool in the pan for 10 minutes, then unmold onto a rack to cool completely.

Hot Chocolate Sauce

MAKES ABOUT 1½ CUPS

- 1 cup heavy cream
- ½ pound imported bittersweet chocolate, cut into small pieces

In a small saucepan, bring the cream to a simmer over moderate heat. Add the chocolate, turn off the heat and cover. Let stand for 10 minutes, then whisk to blend. Rewarm just before serving.—PRISCILLA MARTEL

KEY LIME MERINGUE TORTE

This delicate cake combines sweet and tart, tender and crisp. The meringue bakes right on top of the cake batter for an effect as impressive as it is easy.

MAKES ONE 8-INCH TORTE

MERINGUE CAKE:

- 1 cup cake flour
- 1 teaspoon baking powder
- ⅛ teaspoon salt
- 1 stick unsalted butter (4 ounces), at room temperature
- 1¼ cups plus 2 teaspoons sugar
- 4 large eggs, separated, at room temperature
- 3 tablespoons milk
- 1 teaspoon pure vanilla extract
- ⅓ cup sliced almonds (about 1 ounce)

LIME CURD:

- 2 large eggs
- 1 large egg yolk
- ⅓ cup Key lime juice (see box, above) or fresh lime or lemon juice
- ¾ cup sugar
- 1 teaspoon cornstarch
- Pinch of salt
- 4 tablespoons cold unsalted butter, cut into 4 pieces

1. Preheat the oven to 350°. Line the bottoms of two 8-by-2-inch round cake pans with wax paper and grease the paper. ➤

Key Lime Meringue Torte

KEY LIME JUICE

If you're lucky enough to find fresh Key limes, use them. Otherwise, you can purchase bottled Key lime juice from specialty-food stores or The King Arthur Flour Baker's Catalogue, 1-800-827-6836.

2. **Make the meringue cake**: Sift together the flour, baking powder and salt. In a large bowl, using an electric mixer, cream the butter with ½ cup of the sugar until fluffy. Add the egg yolks and beat for 2 minutes. In a measuring cup, stir together the milk and vanilla; beat into the butter mixture in two batches, alternating with the dry ingredients, until just incorporated. Scrape into the prepared pans (the batter will barely reach up the sides of the pan).

MORE THAN A SWEETENER

Sugar does much more than make food taste good.

• It aids in browning through a chemical reaction with amino acids, peptides or proteins contained in foods.

• It feeds yeast fermentation, which helps raise breads and most other baked goods.

• It lightens batters when it is creamed with butter or shortening by breaking up the fat and letting it hold more air.

• It tenderizes doughs by slowing the development of gluten, the protein substance in flour that forms strong elastic bonds when moistened.

• It retards the growth of bacteria, extending the life of baked goods and preserves.

• It creates a smooth, creamy or grainy texture in candies, depending on the degree to which it crystallizes.

• It holds in moisture, prolonging shelf life.—CAROLE BLOOM

3. In another large bowl, using clean beaters, beat the egg whites at medium speed until they hold soft peaks. With the mixer on, gradually sprinkle in ¾ cup of the sugar and beat until the whites are glossy, 3 to 4 minutes. Gently spread the meringue over the cake batter in the pans; do not smooth the tops. Sprinkle the almonds, then the remaining 2 teaspoons sugar, on the meringue.

4. Bake the cakes in the bottom third of the oven for 25 minutes, or until the meringue is puffed and lightly browned. Transfer the pans to racks and let the cakes cool completely; the tops will sink considerably.

5. Meanwhile, **make the lime curd:** Place the whole eggs and the egg yolk in a heatproof bowl and whisk. In a medium nonreactive saucepan, bring the lime juice, sugar, cornstarch and salt to a boil over moderate heat, whisking. Gradually whisk the mixture into the eggs. Scrape the lime curd into the saucepan and cook over moderate heat, stirring with a wooden spoon, until thick enough to coat the spoon, about 5 minutes; do not boil. Remove from the heat and stir in the butter.

6. Strain the curd into a clean bowl. Let cool at room temperature briefly, whisking occasionally; then press a piece of wax paper directly on the surface and refrigerate until chilled, at least 2 hours or overnight.

7. Assemble the cake: Run a knife around the sides of the cake layers to loosen them from the pans. Carefully invert the layers onto baking sheets; remove the wax paper. Invert one layer onto a cake platter. Spread all the lime curd on top. Cover with the other cake layer, meringue side up. To serve, slice gently with a serrated cake knife. (**MAKE AHEAD:** The cake can be refrigerated for up to 1 day; loosely cover with plastic wrap.) —TRACEY SEAMAN

PECAN COCONUT CAKE

This cake was inspired by Boston cream pie, a yellow cake with custard filling and chocolate frosting. The cake's moist pecan layers are filled with coconut pastry cream and glazed with chocolate.

MAKES ONE 8-INCH CAKE

PECAN SPONGE CAKE:

1½ cups pecan halves (5½ ounces)
1 cup sugar
1 cup all-purpose flour
1 teaspoon baking powder
6 large eggs, at room temperature
5 tablespoons unsalted butter, melted

COCONUT PASTRY CREAM:

6 tablespoons sugar
2 tablespoons cornstarch
Pinch of salt
1 large egg
1 large egg yolk
1 cup canned unsweetened coconut milk
⅓ cup heavy cream
1½ tablespoons unsalted butter
1 teaspoon pure vanilla extract
⅓ cup lightly packed sweetened flake coconut (about 1 ounce)

CHOCOLATE GLAZE:

3 ounces bittersweet chocolate
4 tablespoons unsalted butter
1 tablespoon corn syrup

1. Preheat the oven to 350°. Lightly butter two 8-by-2-inch round cake pans and line the bottom of each pan with wax paper. Lightly butter and flour the wax paper.

2. Make the pecan sponge cake: In a food processor, pulse the pecans with ¼ cup of the sugar until very finely ground; transfer to a medium bowl. Sift together the flour and baking powder and add to the nuts. Whisk to blend.

3. Combine the eggs and the remaining ¾ cup sugar in the large bowl of a standing electric mixer. Set the bowl over a saucepan of simmering water; do not let the bowl touch the water. Whisk the eggs and sugar until warm and the sugar is dissolved, about 4 minutes. Remove from the heat and beat at medium high speed until cool, pale and tripled in volume, 5 to 8 minutes.

4. Sprinkle the dry ingredients over the eggs, about ½ cup at a time, gently folding in each addition with a rubber spatula. Drizzle the melted butter down the side of the bowl in two additions and gently fold in.

5. Scrape the batter into the prepared pans and smooth the top. Bake in the bottom third of the oven for 25 to 30 minutes, or until the center springs back when touched and the edges are golden. Let the cakes cool in the pans for 20 minutes. Then run a knife around the cakes and invert onto racks to cool completely. (**MAKE AHEAD:** The cakes can be baked 1 day ahead; wrap in plastic and store at room temperature.)

6. Make the coconut pastry cream: In a medium heatproof bowl, whisk together the sugar, cornstarch and salt. Whisk in the whole egg and the egg yolk until smooth. In a saucepan, bring the coconut milk and the heavy cream just to a boil over moderate heat. Gradually whisk this hot liquid into the egg mixture. Pour the pastry cream into the saucepan and cook over moderate heat, stirring, until it is very thick and close to a boil, about 5 minutes. Remove the pan from the heat and stir in the butter and vanilla, then add the coconut. Let cool briefly, whisking occasionally. Press a piece of wax paper directly on the surface of the pastry cream and refrigerate until chilled, at least 3 hours or overnight.

7. Assemble the cake: Using a large serrated knife, split each of the cakes into two layers (see "Slicing the Layers," next page). Invert the top layer of one cake onto a cake platter and spread ½ cup of the coconut pastry cream on top. Invert the bottom layer on top of the first layer and peel off the wax paper. Spread another ½ cup of pastry cream on top. Continue with the remaining cake layers and pastry cream. Cover the cake with plastic wrap and refrigerate.

8. Make the chocolate glaze: In a small bowl set over a pan of barely simmering water, melt the bittersweet chocolate, butter and corn syrup, stirring occasionally. Remove the glaze from the heat and set it aside until it is cool to the touch.

9. Slowly pour the chocolate glaze onto the top of the cake and, using a small metal icing spatula, spread it evenly over the surface. Spread the glaze just to the edge, or let a little drip down the sides of the cake. To serve the cake, slice it gently using a serrated cake knife. (**MAKE AHEAD:** The cake can be refrigerated for up to 8 hours; allow it to stand for 30 minutes before serving.) —TRACEY SEAMAN ➤

Pecan Coconut Cake

SLICING THE LAYERS

Put the cake on a cardboard cake round, then on a cake-decorating turntable. With a serrated cake knife, using an even sawing motion, slice the cake into layers; turn it as you proceed. Before you remove the top layer, place toothpicks in a vertical line down the side of the cake, one in each layer, so you will be able to realign the layers after you have spread the filling on them.

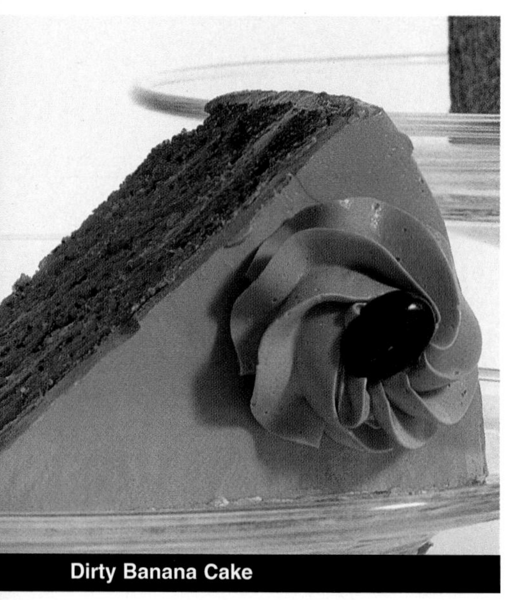

Dirty Banana Cake

DIRTY BANANA CAKE

This rich cake was inspired by the Dirty Banana, a blender drink I enjoyed more than once during a college break. It combines the creamy sweetness of bananas with coffee's slightly bitter taste.

MAKES ONE 9-INCH CAKE

BANANA CAKE:

- 2 cups all-purpose flour
- 2 teaspoons baking soda
- 1 teaspoon baking powder
- ¼ teaspoon salt
- 1 stick unsalted butter (4 ounces), at room temperature
- 1⅓ cups sugar
- 4 large eggs, at room temperature
- 3 overripe medium bananas, mashed (about 1¼ cups)
- ½ cup buttermilk or plain yogurt

BANANA BUTTERCREAM FILLING:

- 2 large egg yolks
- ¾ cup confectioners' sugar
- ¼ cup milk
- ¼ cup mashed overripe banana
- 2 sticks unsalted butter (8 ounces), at room temperature
- 1 tablespoon instant espresso powder dissolved in 2 teaspoons hot water

COFFEE FROSTING:

- 1 cup sugar
- ½ cup egg whites (from 4 to 5 large eggs)
- 2½ sticks cold unsalted butter (10 ounces), cut into tablespoons
- 2 tablespoons instant espresso powder dissolved in 1 tablespoon hot water
- 1 teaspoon pure vanilla extract
- Chocolate-covered espresso beans

1. Preheat the oven to 350°. Line a 9-by-3-inch round cake pan or springform pan with wax paper and grease the paper. (If using a springform pan that doesn't seal tightly, wrap the bottom in foil to prevent leakage.)

2. Make the banana cake: Sift together the flour, baking soda, baking powder and salt. In the large bowl of a standing electric mixer, cream the butter and sugar at medium speed until smooth. Add the eggs one at a time, beating for 1 minute after each addition. In a bowl, mash the bananas with the buttermilk. Beat the dry ingredients into the butter at medium speed in two additions, alternating with the bananas. (The batter may appear slightly curdled.)

3. Scrape the batter into the prepared pan and smooth the top. Bake in the bottom third of the oven for about 1 hour or until a cake tester inserted in the center comes out clean. (**MAKE AHEAD:** The cake can be baked 1 day ahead; wrap in plastic and store at room temperature.)

4. Make the banana buttercream filling: In a large bowl, using an electric mixer, beat the egg yolks and confectioners' sugar at high speed until pale and thick. Meanwhile, in a medium saucepan, bring the milk and banana to a boil over moderate heat, whisking occasionally. Slowly whisk the hot milk into the egg yolks. Pour the mixture into the saucepan and cook over moderately low heat, stirring, until thick, about 5 minutes; do not boil. Transfer the custard to a medium bowl and let cool briefly, whisking occasionally; then press a piece of wax paper directly on the surface and refrigerate until chilled, at least 3 hours or overnight.

5. In a bowl, using an electric mixer, beat the butter at high speed until fluffy. Reduce the speed to low and gradually mix in the cold banana custard. Beat at medium speed until fluffy. Then beat in the espresso.

6. Assemble the cake: Split the cake into three layers (see "Slicing the Layers," opposite page). Place one layer on a cake platter and cover with half of the buttercream filling. Top with a second layer and the remaining filling. Place the third layer on top, cover with plastic wrap and refrigerate.

7. Make the coffee frosting: In a large heatproof bowl, using an electric mixer, beat the sugar and egg whites until mixed. Place the bowl over a large saucepan of simmering water; do not let the bowl touch the water. Heat the mixture, whisking occasionally, until the sugar is dissolved, about 5 minutes. Remove from the heat and beat at high speed until fluffy, about 3 minutes. Beat the meringue at medium speed until cool to the touch, about 5 minutes. Beat in the butter several pieces at a time, waiting until the butter is incorporated before adding more. Whip the frosting until fluffy. (If the frosting appears lumpy, beat at high speed until smooth. If the mixture is soft and runny, refrigerate for 5 minutes, then beat again.) Beat in the espresso and vanilla until blended.

8. Frost the cake: Set aside ½ cup of the frosting for decorating. Spread the remaining frosting on the sides and top of the cake (see "Frosting the Cake," right). With the reserved frosting, using a pastry bag fitted with a star tip, pipe eight rosettes on the top edge of the cake. Place a chocolate-covered espresso bean in the center of each rosette. To serve, slice gently with a serrated cake knife. (**MAKE AHEAD:** The cake can be refrigerated for up to 1 day; let stand at room temperature for 1 hour before serving.)—TRACEY SEAMAN

MAPLE SPICE CAKE WITH CARAMEL CREAM

The spices in this cake remind me of apple pie and mulled cider. If you want a final flourish, serve the cake with sliced peeled apples sautéed in a little butter with lemon juice and cinnamon-sugar.

MAKES ONE 8-INCH CAKE

SPICE CAKE:

- 1 stick unsalted butter (4 ounces), at room temperature
- 1⅓ cups packed light brown sugar
- 2 large eggs, at room temperature
- ⅓ cup pure maple syrup
- 2½ cups cake flour
- 1½ teaspoons cinnamon
- 1 teaspoon baking powder
- 1 teaspoon baking soda
- 1 teaspoon ground allspice
- ¾ teaspoon ground ginger
- ½ teaspoon salt
- 1 cup buttermilk

CARAMEL CREAM:

- ⅔ cup sugar
- 2½ cups cold heavy cream
- 2 tablespoons confectioners' sugar

1. Preheat the oven to 350°. Line the bottom of two 8-by-2-inch round cake pans with wax paper and grease the paper thoroughly.

2. Make the spice cake: In a large bowl, using an electric mixer, cream the butter with the brown sugar until fluffy. Add the eggs one at a time, beating well after each addition. Beat in the maple syrup.

3. In a medium bowl, whisk the flour with the cinnamon, baking powder, baking soda, allspice, ginger and salt. Mix the dry ingredients into the batter in three additions, alternating with the buttermilk.

4. Scrape the batter into the prepared cake pans and smooth the

FROSTING THE CAKE

Spoon the frosting into a pastry bag fitted with a wide star or plain tip. Pipe the frosting in zigzags around the sides of the cake. Then pipe a spiral on top of the cake, beginning at the edge. Using an icing spatula, spread the frosting on the sides as you turn the cake. Then, holding the spatula at a slight angle, smooth the top from the edge to the center.

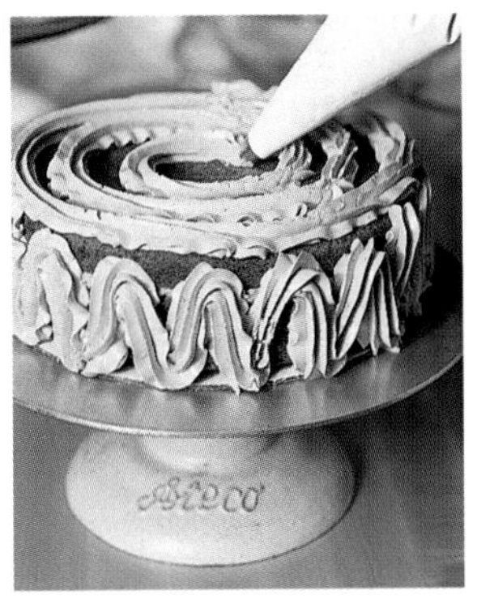

top. Bake the cakes in the bottom third of the oven for about 35 minutes, or until a cake tester inserted in the center comes out clean. Let the cakes cool for 15 minutes, then remove the cakes from the pans, peel off the wax paper and place right-side up on racks to cool completely. (**MAKE AHEAD:** The cakes can be baked 1 day ahead; wrap them in plastic and store at room temperature.)

5. Make the caramel cream: In a medium saucepan, combine the sugar and 3 tablespoons of water. Bring to a boil over moderately high heat, brushing down the sides of the pan with a wet pastry brush. Let the syrup boil until it turns a medium amber color, about 5 minutes; swirl the pan gently to blend the color. Remove from the heat and carefully pour in ½ cup of the heavy cream; stand back to avoid spatters. Stir with a wooden spoon until blended and smooth. Let cool completely. (**MAKE AHEAD:** The caramel can be kept at room temperature for up to 4 hours.)

Maple Spice Cake with Caramel Cream

6. Beat the remaining 2 cups heavy cream with the confectioners' sugar until firm. Fold ½ cup of the caramel into the cream in two additions.

7. Assemble the cake: Place one cake layer right-side up on a cake platter. Spread 1 cup of the caramel cream on top. Cover with the second cake layer, bottom-side up. Spread the sides and top of the cake with the remaining caramel cream. Drizzle the remaining caramel in zigzags over the top of the cake. To serve, slice gently with a serrated cake knife. (**MAKE AHEAD:** The cake can be refrigerated for up to 3 hours.) —TRACEY SEAMAN

CHOCOLATE CLOUD CAKE

MAKES ONE 9-INCH CAKE

CHOCOLATE CAKE:

- 2 cups cake flour
- 1 teaspoon baking soda
- 1 teaspoon baking powder
- ½ teaspoon salt
- 1 cup light brown sugar
- 1 cup granulated sugar
- 3 ounces unsweetened chocolate, coarsely chopped
- 1 stick unsalted butter (4 ounces), at room temperature
- 3 large eggs, separated, at room temperature
- ¾ cup milk, at room temperature
- 1 teaspoon pure vanilla extract

GANACHE:

- 8 ounces bittersweet chocolate, coarsely chopped, plus 2 ounces bittersweet chocolate, coarsely grated or shaved, for decorating
- 2 cups heavy cream
- 1 teaspoon pure vanilla extract

1. Preheat the oven to 350°. Line two 9-by-2-inch round cake pans with wax paper; grease the paper.

2. Make the chocolate cake: In a large bowl, sift together the flour, baking soda, baking powder and salt. In a medium saucepan, combine the brown sugar, granulated sugar, chocolate and ½ cup of water and cook over moderately low heat, stirring, until smooth. Let cool slightly, stirring occasionally.

3. Using an electric mixer, beat the butter and egg yolks until blended. Gradually beat in the chocolate mixture. Beat in the dry ingredients in two batches, alternating with the milk, until smooth. Beat in the vanilla. (The batter will be rather thin.)

4. In a medium bowl, using clean beaters, beat the egg whites until barely firm. Stir one-third of the whites into the batter. Fold in the remaining whites until incorporated.

5. Scrape the batter into the two prepared pans. Bake the cakes in the bottom third of the oven for 25 to 30 minutes, or until a cake tester inserted in the center comes out clean. Let the cakes cool for 15 minutes, then remove from the pans and place right-side up on racks to cool completely. (**MAKE AHEAD:** The cakes can be baked 1 day ahead; wrap in plastic and store at room temperature.)

6. Make the ganache: In a saucepan, melt half of the chopped chocolate in the heavy cream over moderately low heat, stirring. Remove from the heat and stir in the vanilla and remaining chopped chocolate until smooth. Scrape the ganache into a bowl and refrigerate until chilled, at least 3 hours or overnight.

7. Using an electric mixer, briefly beat the ganache until it is thick enough to hold its shape. Do not overbeat or the ganache will become grainy; if it does, melt it again over low heat and then beat it once more.

8. Assemble the cake: Peel off the paper from the cake layers. Place one layer right-side up on a cake platter and spread one scant cup of the whipped ganache on top. Place the second cake layer upside down on top of the filling. Spread the sides and top of the cake evenly with the remaining whipped ganache. If desired, reserve about ½ cup of the ganache for decorating as follows: Using a pastry bag fitted with a star tip, pipe simple stars or a scallop trim around the top or the base of the cake. Sprinkle the grated chocolate all over the top of the cake. To serve, slice gently with a serrated cake knife. (**MAKE AHEAD:** The cake can be refrigerated for up to 1 day.) —TRACEY SEAMAN

Chocolate Cloud Cake

GERMAN CHOCOLATE CAKE

If you are not comfortable using a pastry bag, simply spread half of the ganache on the second cake layer and half around the side of the cake.

MAKES ONE 8-INCH CAKE

CAKE:

- 1 cup sugar
- ¾ cup all-purpose flour
- ½ cup unsweetened cocoa powder, preferably Dutch process
- 1 teaspoon baking soda
- ½ teaspoon baking powder
- Pinch of salt
- 2 large eggs
- ½ cup cold strong brewed coffee
- ½ cup buttermilk
- ½ teaspoon pure vanilla extract
- 4 tablespoons unsalted butter, melted

GANACHE:

- 1 cup heavy cream
- ½ pound imported semisweet chocolate, finely chopped

NUT FILLING:

- 2 large egg yolks
- ¾ cup sugar
- ¾ cup evaporated whole milk
- 3 tablespoons unsalted butter, cut into small pieces
- 1 cup coarsely shredded unsweetened coconut* (about 2½ ounces)
- 1 cup coarsely chopped pecans (about 4 ounces)
- ¾ teaspoon pure vanilla extract

*Available at specialty-food stores and health-food stores

1. Make the cake: Preheat the oven to 350°. Butter an 8-by-2-inch round cake pan and line the bottom with parchment paper. In a bowl, sift together the sugar, flour, cocoa, baking soda, baking powder and salt. In another bowl, whisk together the eggs, coffee, buttermilk and vanilla.

2. Beat the coffee mixture into the dry ingredients in two batches with an electric mixer on low speed. Beat in the butter. Pour the batter into the prepared pan and bake for about 50 minutes, or until a cake tester inserted in the center comes out clean. Let the cake cool in the pan on a rack.

3. Make the ganache: In a small saucepan, bring the cream to a boil over moderately high heat. Remove from the heat and stir in the chocolate. Let stand for 1 minute, then whisk until smooth. Transfer the ganache to a bowl and refrigerate, stirring occasionally, until chilled and thickened, about 2 hours.

4. Make the nut filling: In a heavy medium saucepan, whisk together the egg yolks and sugar. Whisk in the evaporated milk and then the butter. Cook over moderate heat, stirring constantly, until the mixture thickens and lightly coats a spoon, about 10 minutes; do not let it boil. Remove from the heat and stir in the coconut, pecans and vanilla. Transfer to a bowl and let cool completely. (**MAKE AHEAD:** The recipe can be prepared to this point up to 1 day ahead. Let the cake stand at room temperature; refrigerate the ganache and the nut filling separately. If the cold ganache is too thick to spread, stir it briefly.)

5. Invert the cake onto a work surface and peel off the paper. Using a serrated knife, slice the cake horizontally into three even layers (see "Slicing the Layers," p. 372). Set a layer on a large plate and spread on half of the nut filling. Top with the second cake layer and cover with a ¼-inch-thick layer of ganache. Set the third cake layer on top and cover with the remaining nut filling. Spread half of the remaining ganache on the sides. Transfer the rest of the ganache to a pastry bag fitted with a medium star tip. Pipe a border of rosettes around the top of the cake and serve.—MICHELLE AND BILL BRACKEN

German Chocolate Cake

WARM SPICED CHOCOLATE SOUFFLÉ CAKE LF

4 SERVINGS

Vegetable cooking spray
- 2 ounces bittersweet chocolate, coarsely chopped
- ¼ cup plain nonfat yogurt
- 1 tablespoon pure vanilla extract
- 2 teaspoons instant espresso powder dissolved in 1 tablespoon hot water
- ½ teaspoon sweet paprika
- ½ teaspoon cinnamon
- 1 tablespoon unsweetened cocoa powder
- 1 tablespoon all-purpose flour
- 4 large egg whites
- ½ cup granulated sugar
- ½ teaspoon confectioners' sugar

1. Preheat the oven to 375°. Lightly coat a 4-cup soufflé dish with cooking spray. In a small bowl set over a pan of simmering water, stir the chocolate until melted; alternatively, melt the chocolate in a microwave oven. Let cool to tepid.

2. In a small bowl, combine the yogurt, vanilla, espresso, paprika and cinnamon. In another bowl, stir together the cocoa and flour.

3. In a large bowl, beat the egg whites until they form soft peaks. Gradually beat in the granulated sugar until stiff peaks form. Using a rubber spatula, lightly fold in the melted chocolate. Fold in the yogurt mixture and then the dry ingredients just until combined. Scrape the batter into the prepared dish. Bake the cake in the lower third of the oven for about 30 minutes, or until the top is just set and moist crumbs cling to a toothpick inserted in the center. Dust the soufflé cake with confectioners' sugar and serve.—VINCENT GUERITHAULT

CHOCOLATE ANGEL FOOD CAKE WITH MARSHMALLOW FROSTING LF

Except for a minuscule amount of fat in the cocoa powder in the cake and in the chocolate shavings on top, this is a totally fat-free dessert. An extra-thick layer of fluffy marshmallow frosting is the perfect topping for this light yet rich-tasting cake.

MAKES 1 ANGEL FOOD CAKE

CHOCOLATE ANGEL FOOD CAKE:
- 1 cup superfine sugar
- ½ cup unsweetened cocoa powder
- ⅓ cup cake flour
- ¼ teaspoon salt
- 8 large egg whites, at room temperature
- ½ teaspoon cream of tartar

MARSHMALLOW FROSTING:

3 large egg whites, at room temperature
¾ cup granulated sugar
¼ teaspoon cream of tartar
1 teaspoon pure vanilla extract
Chocolate shavings, for decorating

1. Make the chocolate angel food cake: Preheat the oven to 350°. Sift ⅔ cup of the superfine sugar onto a piece of wax paper or parchment; set aside. Sift the remaining ⅓ cup superfine sugar with the cocoa powder, cake flour and salt; set aside.

2. In the large bowl of a standing electric mixer, beat the egg whites at medium speed until foamy. Add the cream of tartar and beat until the foam is white and holds the lines from the beater. Increase the speed to medium high and add the sifted superfine sugar, 1 tablespoon at a time, until completely incorporated. Beat for 30 seconds longer until soft peaks form.

3. Remove the bowl from the mixer. Sift and fold the dry ingredients into the beaten whites, folding them in with a large rubber spatula. (It may be easier to have someone else sift while you fold). Pour the batter into a 10-cup angel food cake pan or bundt pan and gently smooth the top without deflating the mixture. Bang the pan once (not too hard) on your work surface to release any large air pockets.

4. Bake the cake in the bottom third of the oven for about 35 minutes, or until a tester inserted in the center of the cake comes out clean. Invert the cake pan onto its feet, if it has them, or over a narrow-necked bottle. Let the cake cool completely in the pan, about 1 hour.

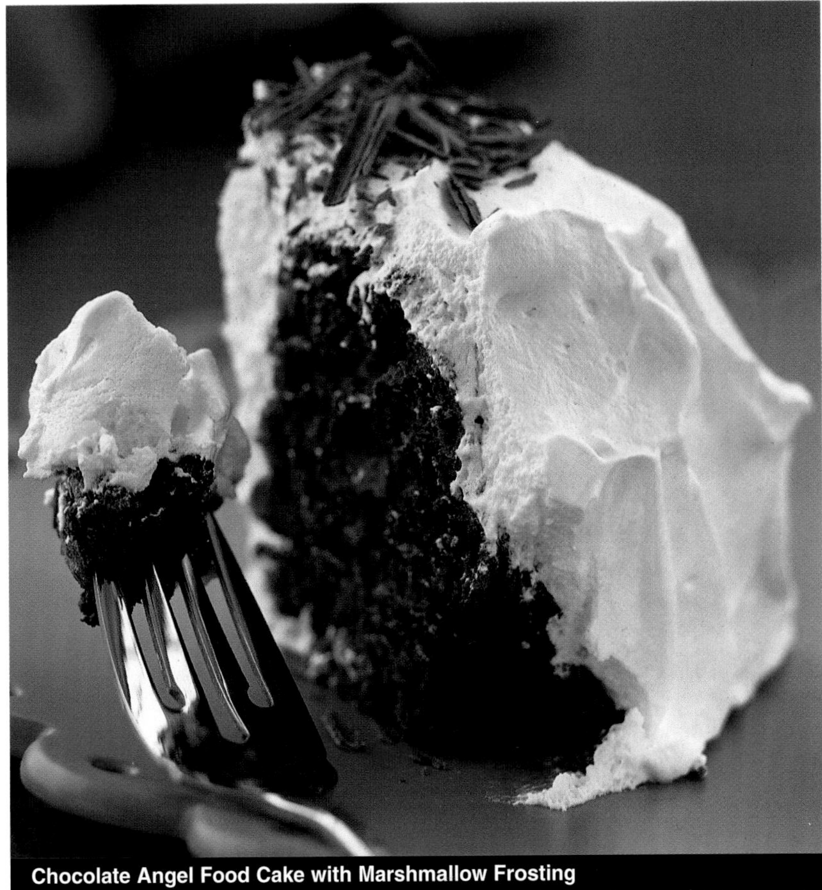

Chocolate Angel Food Cake with Marshmallow Frosting

5. Run a thin flexible metal spatula or knife between the cake and the sides and center tube of the pan to loosen (you may need to jiggle the pan to completely release the cake). Invert the cake onto a cardboard cake circle or serving platter. (MAKE AHEAD: The cake can be made up to 1 day ahead; wrap loosely in plastic and store at room temperature.)

6. Make the marshmallow frosting: Put the egg whites in the large bowl of a standing electric mixer. In a small heavy saucepan, stir together the granulated sugar and ⅓ cup of water. Bring to a boil over moderately high heat, washing down the saucepan with a wet pastry brush.

7. When the sugar syrup comes to a boil, begin beating the egg whites at medium high speed. When they become foamy, add the cream of tartar. Beat at medium speed until stiff peaks form.

8. Insert a candy thermometer into the sugar syrup (be sure the bulb is completely submerged). Cook until the syrup reaches 242°. Remove from the heat. With the mixer still on, beat the sugar syrup into the whites in a slow stream until completely incorporated. Increase the speed to high and beat for 5 minutes, scraping down the sides of the bowl once with a rubber spatula. Add the vanilla and beat for 1 more minute. The icing will still be a little warm.

9. Frost the cake: Using a metal icing spatula, first spread a thin layer of frosting all over the cake, including the inside of the center opening, to glue down the crumbs. Then coat the cake with the remaining frosting. Decorate the top of the cake with the chocolate shavings. To serve, gently slice the cake with a serrated knife or an angel food comb.—PEGGY CULLEN

HOW SUGAR IS PROCESSED

• First, sugarcane stems or sugar-beet roots are cut, crushed and washed with hot water. Their juice is extracted and clarified or filtered.

• The resulting liquid is put in a centrifuge, which separates molasses from concentrated crystals. (The molasses you find in the market is from sugarcane; molasses from sugar beets is unpalatable.) The crystals formed at this stage are sometimes partially refined and sold as raw sugar.

• The sugar then goes through a process of liquefaction and crystallization until equal-size crystals of pure white sugar (99.8 percent sucrose) are produced and mechanically sorted into various sizes.

• Light or dark brown sugar is made by adding varying amounts of molasses back into the white sugar crystals (from sugarcane, not sugar beets); the molasses contributes the characteristic flavor and color.—CAROLE BLOOM

ROSE-PETAL CAKE WITH WHITE-CHOCOLATE GLAZE

This single-layer tea cake is buttery and rich. An undercoat of pretty pink jam shows through a transparent glaze of white-chocolate frosting. You can split the cake and fill it with the jam, but this simpler version is equally delicious.

MAKES ONE 8-INCH CAKE

CAKE:

1 cup all-purpose flour
1 teaspoon baking powder
¼ teaspoon salt
5 tablespoons unsalted butter, softened
½ cup superfine sugar
1 large egg, beaten
½ teaspoon pure vanilla extract
¼ cup milk

TOPPING:

Rose-Petal Jam (recipe follows)
6 ounces white chocolate, broken into small pieces
2 tablespoons unsalted butter
½ tablespoon canola oil
½ teaspoon fresh lemon juice

1. Make the cake: Preheat the oven to 350°. Butter and flour an 8-inch-square cake pan. In a bowl, sift the flour, baking powder and salt.

2. In a bowl, using a hand-held electric mixer, beat the butter and sugar until light and fluffy, about 3 minutes. Beat in the egg and vanilla until smooth. On low speed, beat in the dry ingredients alternately with the milk in three parts, beginning and ending with the dry ingredients.

3. Scrape the batter into the prepared pan; smooth with a rubber spatula. Bake in the middle of the oven for about 25 minutes, or until a cake tester inserted in the center comes out clean. Let the cake cool slightly on a rack set over a baking sheet. Run a knife around the edge to loosen it. Unmold it and place right-side up on the rack.

4. Make the topping: Mix the jam well to loosen it. Using a metal icing spatula, spread the jam on the top of the cake.

5. In a small heatproof bowl set over a saucepan of barely simmering water, melt the chocolate and the butter; don't let the chocolate get too hot. Remove from the heat; stir to blend. Stir in the oil and lemon juice until smooth.

6. Pour the glaze over the cake, covering the top and sides. Use the icing spatula to smooth it over the top and sides. Transfer the cake to a platter and refrigerate until the glaze is set, about 20 minutes. Cut into squares and serve. (**MAKE AHEAD:** The cake can be made 1 day ahead; cover and store at room temperature.)

Rose-Petal Jam

MAKES ABOUT ⅓ CUP

½ cup sugar
2 cups (tightly packed) fragrant edible rose petals (see "Roses by Mail," p. 219)

1. In a small saucepan, bring the sugar and ½ cup of water to a simmer over moderate heat, stirring until the sugar is dissolved.

Set aside until slightly cooled but still very warm to the touch. Stir in the roses, packing them into the syrup as they wilt. Using a rubber spatula, scrape into a glass measure or small heatproof glass bowl. Cover with plastic wrap; let steep at room temperature at least 6 hours, or refrigerate overnight.

2. Pass the syrup through a coarse strainer, reserving the rose petals. Pour the syrup into a small saucepan and boil over high heat until reduced by half, about 4 minutes. Set aside to cool slightly.

3. In a food processor, combine the syrup with the reserved petals; process until the petals are coarsely ground. Scrape into a glass jar and let cool. (**MAKE AHEAD:** The jam will keep refrigerated for up to 6 months.) —MARCIA KIESEL

CHOCOLATE SOUFFLÉ YULE LOG

This light flourless roll filled with vanilla cream melts in your mouth.

MAKES ONE 17-INCH LOG

- 1¾ cups heavy cream
- 1 vanilla bean, split lengthwise
- 2 teaspoons pure vanilla extract
- 4 ounces best-quality semisweet chocolate, chopped

Chocolate Soufflé Yule Log

8 large eggs, at room temperature
1⅓ cups superfine sugar
⅛ teaspoon cream of tartar
Confectioners' sugar

1. The day before baking the cake, flavor the filling: In a small saucepan, scald the heavy cream; remove from the heat just before it boils. Pour the cream into a bowl. Add the vanilla bean and the vanilla extract. Let cool, then cover and refrigerate overnight.
2. Preheat the oven to 325°. Grease a 17-by-11-inch rimmed sheet pan; line it with wax paper.
3. Melt the chocolate in a small bowl set over a pot of simmering water. Alternatively, melt the chocolate in a microwave oven. Set aside to cool slightly.
4. Meanwhile, separate the eggs into two large bowls; the bowl for the whites must be completely free of grease. Beat the yolks on medium high speed and gradually add ⅔ cup of the superfine sugar. Beat the yolks at high speed until thick, stiff and pale in color, about 5 minutes. Stir in the melted chocolate with a large rubber spatula.
5. Wash and dry the beaters. Beat the whites on medium high speed until they are foamy. Add the cream of tartar and beat until the mixture whitens. Add the remaining ⅔ cup superfine sugar, 1 tablespoon at a time. Continue beating until the whites hold soft peaks.
6. Using a large rubber spatula, fold one-fourth of the beaten whites into the yolk mixture. Fold in the remaining whites in two additions. Pour the batter into the prepared pan. Use the spatula to gently level the batter and nudge it into the corners. Bake in the middle of the oven for 30 minutes. Transfer the pan to a rack and let the cake cool completely.
7. Meanwhile, remove the vanilla bean from the chilled cream. Scrape the seeds from the pod into the cream; discard the pod. Add 3 tablespoons confectioners' sugar and beat the cream until stiff.
8. Spread a dishcloth on a work surface and sift confectioners' sugar over it. Invert the sheet pan onto the cloth. Remove the pan and peel the wax paper off the cake. Spread the whipped cream evenly over the cake. Starting at a long edge and using the cloth to help, roll the cake as tightly as possible. Roll the log onto a serving dish, seam-side down. Refrigerate the cake for 1 to 6 hours.
9. Lightly sift confectioners' sugar over the yule log in a few spots so that it resembles a dusting of snow. Before serving, slice off the uneven ends of the log with a sharp serrated knife.—PEGGY CULLEN

YULE-LOG BASICS

- **Roll the logs as tightly as possible.**
- **Make sure that your eggs are at room temperature before you begin.**
- **For perfect cakes, use the exact pan size called for in the recipes.**
- **Before lining the pan with wax paper, use a pastry brush to grease an "X" on the bottom of the pan and to thoroughly grease the sides and corners.**
- **Press the wax paper into the corners and against the sides of the pan. Trim any overhanging paper to one inch.**—PEGGY CULLEN

GINGERBREAD YULE LOG WITH COFFEE CREAM

The café-au-lait-colored filling for this spicy cake is shingled onto the outside of the log for a barklike effect.

MAKES ONE 15-INCH LOG

GINGERBREAD CAKE:

½ cup all-purpose flour
1 tablespoon ground ginger
1½ teaspoons cinnamon
1 teaspoon unsweetened cocoa
½ teaspoon freshly grated nutmeg
¼ teaspoon ground cloves
1 teaspoon instant espresso granules
1 teaspoon pure vanilla extract
4 eggs, at room temperature
⅔ cup superfine sugar
½ cup unsulphured molasses
Pinch of cream of tartar

COFFEE CREAM FILLING:

4 teaspoons instant espresso granules
1 tablespoon pure vanilla extract
8 ounces cream cheese
1 cup confectioners' sugar
1½ cups heavy cream

1. Preheat the oven to 350°. Grease a 15-by-10-inch jelly-roll pan and line it with wax paper.
2. Make the gingerbread cake: In a small bowl, sift together the flour, ginger, cinnamon, cocoa,

nutmeg and cloves. Whisk well. In a cup, dissolve the instant espresso granules in the vanilla.

3. Separate the eggs into two bowls; the bowl for the whites must be completely free of grease. Beat the yolks on medium high speed and gradually add ⅓ cup of the superfine sugar. Increase the speed to high and beat, scraping down the bowl once, until the mixture is thick, stiff and pale, about 4 minutes. Using a large rubber spatula, stir in the molasses, the dissolved espresso and the flour mixture.

4. Wash and dry the beaters. Beat the whites on medium high speed until foamy. Add the cream of tartar and beat until the mixture whitens. Beat in the remaining ⅓ cup superfine sugar, 1 tablespoon at a time. Continue beating until the whites are stiff but not dry.

5. Using a large rubber spatula, fold the beaten whites into the yolk mixture in three additions. Pour the batter into the prepared pan; use the spatula to gently level the batter and nudge it into the corners. Bake for 15 to 17 minutes, or until the cake springs back when lightly touched. Let cool on a rack.

6. Meanwhile, **make the coffee cream filling:** In a medium bowl, dissolve the instant espresso in the vanilla. Beat in the cream cheese and confectioners' sugar. In another bowl, beat the heavy cream until it holds soft peaks; fold it into the coffee cream.

7. Turn the cake out onto a sheet of wax paper; peel the wax paper off the cake. Place a piece of plastic wrap over the cake and flip it so it is right-side up again. Remove the wax paper. Evenly spread 2¼ cups of the coffee cream on the cake and roll it up tightly, starting at a long edge; roll the plastic wrap around it. Chill the cake, seam-side down, for at least 10 minutes. Chill the extra cream as well.

8. Transfer the cake to a platter and remove the plastic wrap. Spread a thin layer of coffee cream over the entire log. Apply the remaining cream with a palette knife in thick strokes to resemble bark. Refrigerate for at least 2 and up to 6 hours before serving.—PEGGY CULLEN

COCONUT LEMON ROULADE

Toasted coconut chips—fantasy birch bark—cover this classic sponge roll, which is spread with a thin layer of tangy lemon curd and lots of fluffy marshmallow frosting.

MAKES ONE 15-INCH ROULADE

LEMON CURD:

- 3 large egg yolks
- ¼ cup sugar
- ¼ cup strained fresh lemon juice

SUGAR-TOASTED COCONUT:

- 2⅓ cups unsweetened coconut chips* (3½ ounces)
- 2 tablespoons sugar
- 1 tablespoon boiling water

SPONGE CAKE:

- ⅔ cup all-purpose flour
- ½ teaspoon baking powder
- 4 large eggs
- 1 large egg yolk
- ¾ cup sugar
- 2 tablespoons unsalted butter, cut into small pieces
- ¼ cup milk

DECORATING YULE LOGS

To give yule logs a festive touch, try these trimmings:

SUGARED CRANBERRIES **Roll fresh cranberries in lightly beaten egg white and then in granulated sugar.**

MARZIPAN HOLLY LEAVES **Tint marzipan using food coloring in liquid, powder or paste form. Roll the marzipan into a rope. Cut it into one-inch pieces. Form ovals, flatten and roll out between plastic wrap. Make the leaf points by cutting out semicircles with the back of a small piping tip. Score the leaves with a knife. Drape over egg cartons and let dry for six hours.**

MARZIPAN BERRIES **Tint marzipan red and roll into small balls. Moisten; roll in sugar.**

MARSHMALLOW FROSTING:

- 4 large egg whites
- 1 cup sugar
- ⅛ teaspoon cream of tartar
- 1 teaspoon pure vanilla extract

*Available at health-food shops and specialty-food stores

1. Make the lemon curd: In a small nonreactive saucepan, whisk the egg yolks with the sugar and lemon juice. Cook over low heat, stirring constantly, until the mixture just begins to thicken; do not let it boil. Immediately strain the curd into a bowl. Place plastic wrap directly on the surface of the curd and refrigerate until cold. ➤

2. Make the sugar-toasted coconut: Preheat the oven to 350°. Line a baking sheet with parchment or wax paper. Put the coconut in a medium bowl. In a cup, combine the sugar and boiling water; stir to dissolve the sugar. Add the sugared water to the coconut and toss until thoroughly coated. Spread the coconut evenly on the baking sheet and toast it in the oven for 6 to 10 minutes, stirring occasionally, until golden. Watch the coconut carefully so that it does not burn. Transfer to a plate.

3. Make the sponge cake: Preheat the oven to 400°. Grease a 15-by-10-inch jelly-roll pan and line it with wax paper.

4. Sift the flour and baking powder onto a sheet of wax paper. In a large heatproof bowl, whisk together the eggs, egg yolk and sugar. Set the bowl over (but not in) a pot of simmering water and whisk constantly until the mixture is warm to the touch. Remove the bowl from the heat and beat the mixture on high speed until it is pale in color and as thick as whipped cream.

5. Meanwhile, in a small saucepan, melt the butter in the milk over low heat. Turn off the heat but leave the pan on the stove.

6. Sift one-third of the sifted flour over the egg mixture and gently fold it in with a large spatula; repeat in two more additions. Stir the milk mixture and pour half of it in a circle on the batter; fold it in. Repeat with the remaining milk and fold gently until incorporated. Pour the batter into the prepared jelly-roll pan and gently smooth the surface. Bake for 10 minutes, or until the cake springs back when gently pressed. Let the cake cool completely on a rack.

Coconut Lemon Roulade

7. Make the marshmallow frosting: Put the egg whites in a grease-free metal bowl. In a small saucepan, stir the sugar with ⅓ cup of water and bring to a boil, wiping down the sides of the pan with a wet pastry brush. Boil the syrup until it reaches 236° on a candy thermometer, about 5 minutes.

8. Start beating the whites on medium speed until foamy, then add the cream of tartar and continue beating. When the sugar syrup reaches 242°, pour it onto the whites in a slow stream and continue to beat the frosting for 3 minutes, or until it is thick and fluffy. Add the vanilla when almost finished. The frosting will still be slightly warm.

9. Turn the cooled cake out onto a piece of foil and peel off the wax paper. Place a piece of plastic wrap over the cake and flip it so that it is right-side up again. Remove the foil.

10. Evenly spread the lemon curd over the cake. Spread about

2¼ cups of the marshmallow frosting over the curd. Starting at a long edge, roll the cake as tightly as possible and wrap it in plastic. Let the log stand at room temperature for about 5 minutes, seam-side down.

11. Transfer the log to a platter and unwrap it. Spread the remaining frosting in a thick layer over the entire log. Scatter the toasted coconut over the log. Press with your hands to help the coconut adhere to the frosting. The cake can stand at room temperature for up to 4 hours. With a hot knife, slice about ½ inch off each end before serving.—PEGGY CULLEN

FRESH PINEAPPLE UPSIDE-DOWN CAKE

Fresh fruit gives a lift to this favorite from the Twenties, when supersweet canned pineapple and Maraschino cherries were chic. Use a juicy, ripe pineapple that yields to thumb pressure and has a sweet perfume.

MAKES ONE 9-INCH CAKE

- 1 ripe medium pineapple
- 1 cup unbleached all-purpose flour
- 1 teaspoon baking powder
- 1 stick plus 3 tablespoons unsalted butter (5½ ounces), softened
- ½ cup granulated sugar
- 2 large eggs, at room temperature
- 2 tablespoons Cognac or other brandy
- ⅔ cup light brown sugar
- 9 fresh cherries, pitted (optional)

Vanilla ice cream, for serving

1. Using a sharp knife, peel the pineapple and remove the eyes. Halve the pineapple lengthwise and cut out the center core. Cut each pineapple half crosswise into five ⅔-inch-thick semicircles. Cut one of the semicircles into three pieces.

2. Preheat the oven to 375°. In a small bowl, stir together the flour and baking powder. In a medium bowl, beat the stick of butter until pale and creamy. Gradually beat the granulated sugar into the butter until the mixture is fluffy. Beat in the eggs one at a time, beating well after each addition. Stir in the flour mixture in three batches just until smooth. Stir in the Cognac and set aside.

3. Melt the remaining 3 tablespoons butter in a 9-inch cast-iron skillet; if the handle isn't ovenproof, wrap it in foil. Stir in the brown sugar and cook over moderate heat until melted and bubbling, about 3 minutes. Remove the pan from the heat. Arrange the nine pineapple semicircles in a tight concentric ring in the skillet and fit the three small pieces in the center. Cook over moderately high heat for 10 minutes. Turn the pineapple slices and lower the heat so that the mixture simmers vigorously. Cook until the fruit is tender when pierced, about 10 minutes longer. Insert a cherry in the hollow of each semicircle.

4. Remove the skillet from the heat and spread the cake batter evenly over the hot pineapple; the batter may not completely cover the fruit, but it will spread as it cooks. Bake in the middle of the oven for about 20 minutes, or until the cake springs back when pressed. Let the cake cool for 10 minutes, then invert the cake onto a large platter. Serve the cake warm with vanilla ice cream.—DIANA STURGIS

FRESH APPLE CAKE WITH MAPLE SAUCE

MAKES ONE 9-BY-13-INCH CAKE

CAKE:

- 3 cups all-purpose flour
- 1½ teaspoons baking soda
- 1 teaspoon cinnamon
- ½ teaspoon salt
- ¼ teaspoon ground nutmeg
- 1 stick unsalted butter (4 ounces), softened
- ½ cup vegetable oil
- 2 cups sugar
- 3 large eggs
- 2 teaspoons pure vanilla extract
- 3 large tart apples, such as Granny Smith, peeled, cored and cut into 1-inch pieces

MAPLE SAUCE:

- 1 cup pure maple syrup
- 1 stick unsalted butter (4 ounces)
- ½ cup heavy cream
- ¼ teaspoon salt

Vanilla ice cream, for serving

1. Make the cake: Preheat the oven to 350°. Lightly butter a 9-by-13-inch baking dish. In a bowl, sift together the flour, baking soda, cinnamon, salt and nutmeg.

2. Using a standing electric mixer fitted with a paddle or a hand-held electric mixer, beat the butter, oil and sugar on high speed until thoroughly combined. Add the eggs one at a time, beating well after each addition. Add the vanilla and beat until light and fluffy, 3 to 4 minutes.

3. Beat in the dry ingredients on medium speed just until blended. Fold in the apples. Spread the batter in the prepared dish and bake for about 50 minutes, or until golden and a cake tester inserted in the center comes out clean. If the top of the cake browns too quickly, cover loosely with foil during the last 20 minutes. Let the cake cool slightly on a rack.

4. Meanwhile, **make the maple sauce:** In a saucepan, bring the maple syrup, butter, cream and salt to a boil over moderate heat. Boil rapidly for 1 minute. Allow the sauce to cool slightly. (MAKE AHEAD: The cake and sauce can be refrigerated separately for 2 days. Rewarm the cake in the oven and the sauce on top of the stove before serving.) Cut the apple cake into pieces and serve warm with the maple sauce and vanilla ice cream.—BRUCE AND SUSAN MOLZAN

STORING OILS

Store cooking oils in the coolest and darkest part of the pantry, and try to use them within three months of opening. Walnut and hazelnut oils, both highly perishable, can be stored in the refrigerator. Never refrigerate olive oil, however; the cold will destroy its delicate flavor.—MICHELE ANNA JORDAN

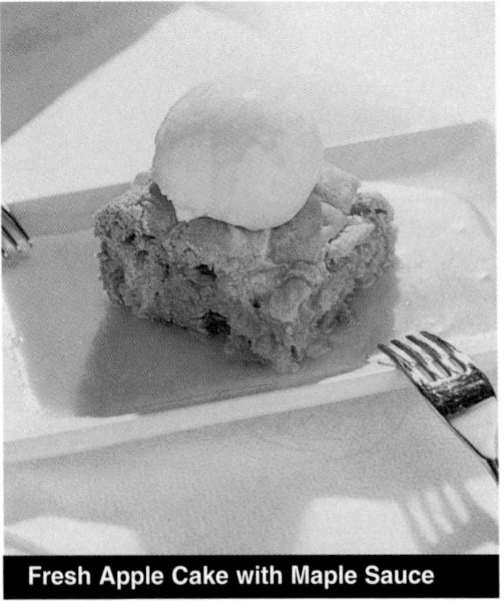

Fresh Apple Cake with Maple Sauce

CINNAMON LEMON POUND CAKE

With its mild citrus flavor and tight texture, this almond-coated pound cake makes an ideal partner for stewed or poached fruit. Try it with Red-Fruit Compote (p. 426).

MAKES ONE 9-INCH CAKE

- ½ cup sliced almonds
- 2 sticks (8 ounces) plus 1 tablespoon unsalted butter, softened
- 2 cups granulated sugar
- 3 tablespoons finely grated lemon zest (from 3 to 4 large lemons)
- 1 tablespoon fresh lemon juice
- ½ teaspoon cinnamon
- 5 large eggs, at room temperature
- 3 cups cake flour
- 2 teaspoons baking powder
- ¾ cup milk

1. Preheat the oven to 325°. Generously butter a 9-by-2½-inch springform pan. Press the almonds evenly over the base and sides of the pan.

2. In a large bowl, combine the butter, sugar, lemon zest, lemon juice and cinnamon and beat until the mixture is light and fluffy, about 3 minutes. Beat in the eggs one at a time.

3. Sift together the flour and the baking powder. Stir one-third of the milk into the egg mixture, then add one-third of the flour mixture. Repeat twice more, stirring just until the ingredients are incorporated and the batter is smooth; do not overmix.

4. Scrape the batter into the prepared pan and bake for about 1 hour and 25 minutes, or until the cake is well browned and a tester inserted in the center comes out clean. Let the pound cake cool on a rack for 20 minutes before unmolding. Serve the cake upside down to show the almond crust.—JACQUES PÉPIN

HUNGARIAN COFFEE CAKE

Chocolate, spice and prunes swirl through this moist sour-cream cake.

MAKES ONE 10-INCH CAKE

- 2 sticks unsalted butter (8 ounces)
- 1 tablespoon finely grated orange zest
- 2 cups sugar
- 2 teaspoons pure vanilla extract
- ¼ teaspoon salt
- 2 cups sour cream
- 3 large eggs
- 1½ teaspoons baking soda
- 1 teaspoon baking powder
- 3 cups all-purpose flour
- ½ cup prune puree (see Note)
- 1 tablespoon cinnamon
- 2 tablespoons cocoa powder
- ½ cup chopped walnuts

1. Preheat the oven to 350°. Grease a heavy nonstick 10-inch Bundt pan. In a large saucepan, melt the butter over moderate heat, adding the orange zest halfway through. Remove from the heat.

2. Using a wooden spoon, stir in the sugar, vanilla, salt, sour cream and eggs until smooth. Add the baking soda and baking powder in pinches, breaking up any lumps with your fingers; mix in. Vigorously mix in the flour. Spoon the prune puree over the batter; sprinkle the cinnamon, cocoa and walnuts evenly on top. Swirl in these ingredients.

3. Pour the batter into the prepared pan and bake for 50 to 55 minutes, or until a tester inserted in the center comes out with a crumb or two clinging to it. Let the cake cool in its pan on a rack for 10 minutes; then invert it onto the rack and allow it to cool completely. (**MAKE AHEAD:** The coffee cake can be wrapped and refrigerated for up to 5 days.)

NOTE: Prune puree, also known as prune pastry filling or lekvar, is available at most supermarkets.—ANDREW SCHLOSS

Q & A

Q: What are the advantages of nonstick bakeware? Do you need to grease or spray it?

A: Nonstick coatings provide "release insurance," especially for Bundt pans and other pans with complicated shapes. Be sure to cool the cake in the pan before turning it out. Nonstick pans are also easy to clean with a nonabrasive pad. Finally, although you do need to lightly grease nonstick baking pans, you never need to flour them, and that contributes to a smoother crust.—DEBORAH KRASNER

COCOA CUPCAKES WITH WHITE ICING LF

These moist cupcakes are guaranteed to satisfy even the most serious chocoholics.

MAKES 12 CUPCAKES

CUPCAKES:

1¼ cups all-purpose flour
¼ cup plus 1 tablespoon unsweetened cocoa powder
1 teaspoon baking soda
½ teaspoon baking powder
Pinch of salt
⅓ cup light brown sugar
2 tablespoons unsalted butter, softened
1 large egg
½ cup light corn syrup
¼ cup unsweetened applesauce
1 teaspoon pure vanilla extract
1 cup low-fat (1.5%) buttermilk

WHITE ICING:

1 cup granulated sugar
1 large egg white
Pinch of salt
½ teaspoon pure vanilla extract

1. Make the cupcakes: Preheat the oven to 350°. Line a 12-cup muffin tin with paper liners. In a bowl, sift together the flour, cocoa, baking soda, baking powder and salt.

2. In another bowl, cream the brown sugar and butter. Beat in the egg until it is incorporated. Add the corn syrup, applesauce and vanilla and beat well. Add the dry ingredients in three batches, alternating with the buttermilk, and mix just until blended.

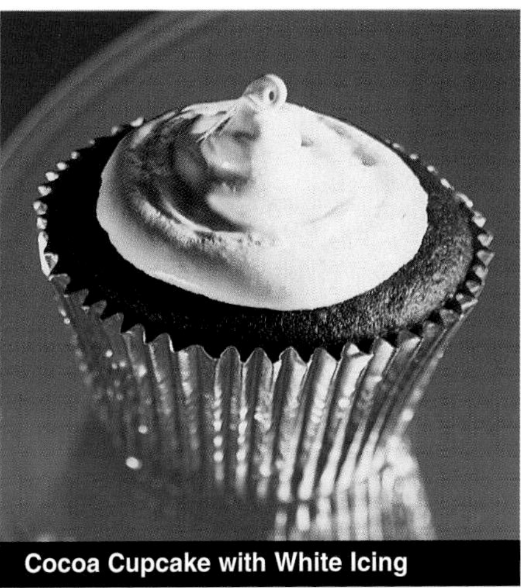
Cocoa Cupcake with White Icing

3. Spoon the batter into the muffin cups. Bake for about 18 minutes, or until a cake tester inserted in the center comes out clean. Let cool. (**MAKE AHEAD:** The cupcakes can be frozen for 1 month or kept in an airtight container for 2 days.)

4. Make the white icing: In a small saucepan, combine the sugar with ½ cup of water. Bring to a boil and cook until the syrup reaches 240° on a candy thermometer.

5. Meanwhile, using a standing mixer or handheld electric mixer, beat the egg white with the salt until foamy. While beating, add the hot syrup in a thin steady stream. Add the vanilla and beat until the icing is thickened and cooled. Spread the icing on the cupcakes; let them stand for up to 1 hour to allow the icing to set.—BOB CHAMBERS ➤

VIENNA SHORTCAKES

Serve these buttery, luscious, melt-in-your-mouth cakes after dessert for an elegant final touch.

MAKES 2 DOZEN SHORTCAKES

- 1⅓ cups cake flour
- ¾ cup confectioners' sugar, plus about 2 tablespoons for dusting
- ½ cup cornstarch
- 2 sticks unsalted butter (½ pound), softened
- ½ cup store-bought lemon curd

1. Preheat the oven to 350°. In a small bowl, stir together the flour, ¾ cup confectioners' sugar and the cornstarch.

2. In a medium bowl, cream the butter. Stir in the dry ingredients. Spoon the dough into nonstick mini muffin pans with cups about 1 inch deep. Bake for about 20 minutes, or until golden. Let the shortcakes stand for 10 minutes, then make a ½-inch indentation in the center of each cake with the handle of a wooden spoon. Carefully turn the cakes out onto a rack and let cool completely.

3. Dust the cakes lightly with confectioners' sugar, then fill each one with 1 teaspoon lemon curd.—THE BATHERS PAVILION, SYDNEY, AUSTRALIA

Vienna Shortcakes

CHOCOLATE PEANUT COOKIES

Peanuts lend a salty crispness to these chocolate cookies, and peanut-butter chips add a sweet creaminess. If you like, you can use two additional cups of peanuts in place of the peanut-butter chips.

MAKES 2 DOZEN COOKIES

- ½ pound good-quality semisweet chocolate, coarsely chopped
- 1¾ cups all-purpose flour
- ⅓ cup unsweetened cocoa powder
- 1 teaspoon baking soda
- ½ teaspoon salt
- ½ pound unsalted butter (2 sticks), softened
- 1 cup light brown sugar
- ½ cup granulated sugar
- 2 teaspoons pure vanilla extract
- 2 large eggs
- 2 large egg whites
- 1 cup unsalted peanuts (about 6 ounces)
- 1 cup peanut-butter chips (about 6 ounces)

1. Preheat the oven to 375°. Lightly butter two large baking sheets. In a small bowl, melt the chocolate over a pan of simmering water; let cool.

2. In another small bowl, combine the all-purpose flour, cocoa powder, baking soda and salt. In a large bowl, beat the butter until it is light and fluffy. Add the brown sugar, the granulated sugar and the vanilla to the butter and blend until smooth. Add the melted semisweet chocolate, the whole eggs and the egg whites and mix until incorporated. Stir in the dry ingredients just until combined; then add the unsalted peanuts and the peanut-butter chips.

3. For each cookie, scoop a scant ¼ cup of the dough onto the prepared baking sheets, leaving about 2 inches between each of the cookies. Bake the cookies for 10 to 12 minutes, or until they are just set in the middle; bake them for about 3 minutes longer if you want crisper cookies. Transfer the cookies to a wire rack to cool. (**MAKE AHEAD:** The cookies can be stored in an airtight container for up to 3 days.) —PAMELA MORGAN

PECAN GRAHAM COOKIES

These cookies are good on their own or delicious as the base for about twenty gooey s'mores. To make the s'mores, you'll need about twenty toasted marshmallows as well as twenty one-inch squares of bittersweet or semisweet chocolate.

MAKES ABOUT 40 COOKIES

- ¾ cup coarsely chopped pecans (about 3 ounces)
- 1¼ cups whole-wheat flour
- ½ cup rye flour
- 1½ teaspoons baking powder
- 1 teaspoon baking soda
- ¾ teaspoon ground cinnamon
- ½ teaspoon salt

- 1 stick unsalted butter (4 ounces), softened
- 1 cup sugar
- 1 large egg
- 1 tablespoon unsulphured molasses
- 1 tablespoon honey
- ½ teaspoon pure vanilla extract

1. Preheat the oven to 350°. Toast the chopped pecans on a baking sheet for about 10 minutes, or until fragrant. Let the pecans cool. Increase the oven heat to 375°.

2. In a medium bowl, combine the whole-wheat and rye flours with the baking powder, baking soda, cinnamon and salt. In another bowl, cream the butter and sugar with an electric mixer on high speed. Add the egg and beat until fluffy. On low speed, beat half of the dry ingredients into the egg mixture until just combined. Beat in the unsulphured molasses, honey and vanilla, then the toasted pecans and the remaining dry ingredients until just combined.

3. Roll scant tablespoons of the cookie dough into walnut-size balls and arrange the balls about 2½ inches apart on two nonstick baking sheets. With lightly moistened fingers, flatten each of the balls into a 2-inch round. Bake the cookies for about 12 minutes, or until they are golden and lightly cracked on top. Let the cookies cool for 5 minutes on the baking sheets, then transfer them to a wire rack to cool. (MAKE AHEAD: The cookies can be stored in an airtight container for 3 days or frozen for up to one month.) —WAYNE BRACHMAN ➤

TYPES OF SUGAR

WHITE SUGAR

• Granulated sugar is the most common form of sugar and the type most frequently used in recipes. Its distinguishing characteristics are a paper-white color and fine crystals.

• Sugar cubes, made from moist granulated sugar that is pressed into molds and dried, can be crushed and used like granulated.

• Superfine sugar is similar to granulated except that it has very tiny crystals. Since it dissolves quickly and completely, leaving no grainy texture, it's perfect for caramel, meringues, drinks, cold desserts and fine-textured cakes. If you can't find it, you can approximate it by grinding granulated sugar for one minute in a food processor.

• Confectioner's sugar is the granulated variety ground to a powder and sifted. Because powdered sugar tends to hold moisture and is prone to clumping, it is blended with about three percent cornstarch during processing. Always sift it before using. Confectioners' sugar is ideal for uncooked icings and frostings because it leaves no graininess. It also looks pretty dusted over the top of a dessert.

• Coarse sugar is shaped into small pearl-like balls that are several times as big as granulated sugar crystals. It is used to decorate and garnish confections and baked goods. Because its large crystals do not dissolve easily, it is not used as a sweetener.

• Crystal sugar is similar to coarse except that it is cylindrical, not round. It, too, is used for decorating and garnishing, and is often tinted with food coloring and sold as "rainbow sugar."

BROWN SUGAR

• Dark and light brown sugar are made up of sugar crystals coated with molasses, which lends a slightly grainy, moist texture. This moisture creates small pockets of air, so the sugar must be tightly packed when measuring. Dark brown sugar (about 6.5 percent molasses) has a stronger, more full-bodied flavor than light brown sugar (about 3.5 percent), though they're often interchangeable. Use them instead of white sugar when you want a distinct, rich flavor.

• Muscovado sugar is a dark and sticky variety noted for its deep molasses flavor. Its crystals tend to be a little larger than those of the regular brown sugars.

• Demerara sugar has crystals that are slightly larger than muscovado's. It has less molasses, and thus a lighter taste and color.

RAW SUGAR

• Raw sugar is essentially the product at the point before the molasses is removed. True raw sugar is unrefined and contains various molds and bacteria considered unsafe for human consumption. What we buy as raw sugar is partially refined: It is washed with steam to purify it. With crystals about the size of coarse sugar, it can be used in place of brown sugar.

• Turbinado is a form of raw sugar with light amber cylindrical crystals and a mild brown sugar flavor.—CAROLE BLOOME

BROWN-SUGAR ICEBOX COOKIES

This basic sugar-cookie dough can be flavored in myriad ways (see "Icebox-Cookie Variations," below). Or pair it with the dough for Chocolate Icebox Cookies to make Combination Icebox Cookies, like pinwheels and checkerboards.

MAKES ABOUT 5 DOZEN COOKIES

- 1 stick unsalted butter (4 ounces), softened
- ½ cup (packed) light brown sugar
- ¼ cup granulated sugar
- 1 large egg
- 1½ teaspoons pure vanilla extract
- 1⅔ cups all-purpose flour
- ½ teaspoon baking soda
- ⅛ teaspoon salt

1. In a bowl, beat the butter with an electric mixer until fluffy. Add the brown sugar and granulated sugar and beat until well blended. Beat in the egg and the vanilla until thickened. Beat in ⅔ cup of the flour along with the baking soda and salt. Stir in the remaining 1 cup flour; the dough will be soft.

2. Divide the dough in half. Wrap each half in wax or parchment paper or plastic wrap and shape it into a 6-inch log. Refrigerate until firm. (**MAKE AHEAD:** The logs can be stored in a plastic bag and refrigerated for up to 1 week or frozen for up to 2 months.)

3. Preheat the oven to 350°. Using a thin knife, slice each log ⅛ to ¼ inch thick. Arrange the cookies 1 inch apart on buttered cookie sheets and bake 10 to 15 minutes, or until lightly golden.—JIM FOBEL

ICEBOX-COOKIE VARIATIONS

Add these extras to the dough for Brown-Sugar Icebox Cookies.

GINGER ALMOND **Add ½ cup finely chopped crystallized ginger to the dough with the final portion of flour. Roll each log in ⅓ cup finely chopped blanched almonds before chilling.**

LEMON POPPYSEED **Add 3 tablespoons poppyseeds and 1 tablespoon grated lemon zest to the dough with the final portion of flour. Roll each log in 1 tablespoon poppyseeds before chilling.**

SPICE **Add 1 teaspoon freshly ground nutmeg, 1 teaspoon cinnamon and ¼ teaspoon ground cloves to the dough with the final portion of flour. Roll each log in ⅓ cup finely chopped walnuts before chilling.**

COFFEE-EDGED **Roll each log in 1½ tablespoons very finely ground French-roast coffee before chilling.**

PECAN **Add 1 cup finely chopped toasted pecans to the dough with the final portion of flour. Roll each log in ⅓ cup finely chopped toasted pecans before chilling.**

Make Chocolate Icebox Cookies even better with these additions.

CHOCOLATE MINT **Add 1 teaspoon of pure peppermint extract to the dough along with the vanilla.**

DOUBLE CHOCOLATE **Add 2 ounces chopped semisweet chocolate to the dough along with the final portion of flour.**

CHOCOLATE MACADAMIA **Add ⅔ cup finely chopped unsalted macadamia nuts to the dough with the final portion of flour. Roll each of the logs in ⅓ cup of finely chopped macadamia nuts before chilling.**

CHOCOLATE HAZELNUT **Add 1 cup of finely chopped toasted and peeled hazelnuts to the dough along with the final portion of flour. Roll each of the logs in ⅓ cup finely chopped hazelnuts before chilling.**

CHOCOLATE PEANUT **Add 1 cup finely chopped unsalted roasted peanuts to the dough with the final portion of flour. Roll each of the logs in ⅓ cup finely chopped peanuts before chilling.**

CHOCOLATE ICEBOX COOKIES

Chocolate gives these addictively delicious cookies a delicate texture.

MAKES ABOUT 5 DOZEN COOKIES

- 1 stick unsalted butter (4 ounces), softened
- ½ cup (packed) light brown sugar
- ⅓ cup granulated sugar
- 1 large egg
- 1 teaspoon pure vanilla extract
- 2 ounces unsweetened chocolate, melted and cooled
- 1¾ cups all-purpose flour
- ½ teaspoon baking soda
- ⅛ teaspoon salt

1. In a large bowl, beat the butter until it is fluffy. Add the brown sugar and the granulated sugar to the butter and beat until well blended. Add the egg and the vanilla and beat until thickened. Beat in the melted chocolate, then add ¾ cup of the all-purpose flour along with the baking soda and salt. Stir in the remaining 1 cup flour to make a soft dough.

2. Divide the cookie dough in half. Wrap each half in wax or parchment paper or plastic wrap and shape the dough into a 6-inch log. Refrigerate the logs until firm. (**MAKE AHEAD:** The cookie-dough logs can be stored in a plastic bag and refrigerated for up to 1 week or frozen for up to 2 months.)

3. Preheat the oven to 350°. Using a thin knife, slice each log of cookie dough ⅛ to ¼ inch thick. Arrange the cookie-dough slices 1 inch apart on buttered cookie sheets and bake for 10 to 15 minutes, or until the cookies are lightly golden.—JIM FOBEL

COMBINATION ICEBOX COOKIES

These fanciful cookies are made by rolling two types of icebox-cookie dough together into logs. If the doughs get too soft as you work with them, chill before proceeding.

MAKES ABOUT 5 DOZEN COOKIES

- ½ recipe Brown-Sugar Icebox Cookies, prepared through Step 1 only
- ½ recipe Chocolate Icebox Cookies, prepared through Step 1 only

Checkerboards

Shape each half-batch of dough into a 6-inch rectangle. Slice each of the rectangles lengthwise ½

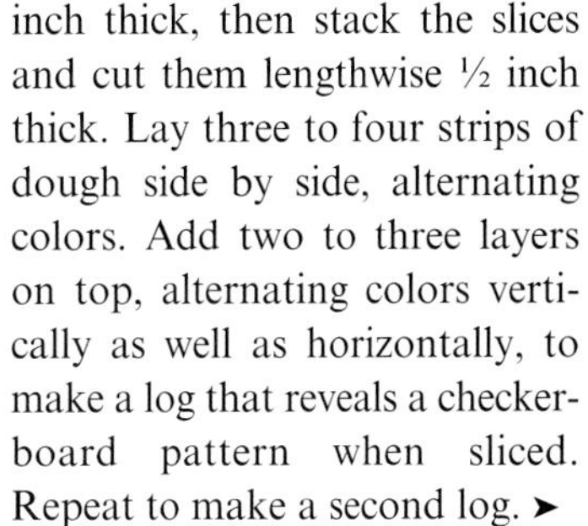

inch thick, then stack the slices and cut them lengthwise ½ inch thick. Lay three to four strips of dough side by side, alternating colors. Add two to three layers on top, alternating colors vertically as well as horizontally, to make a log that reveals a checkerboard pattern when sliced. Repeat to make a second log. ➤

Combination Icebox Cookies

ICEBOX-COOKIE TIPS

Making icebox cookies is easy. Start by preparing the dough—Chocolate, Brown-Sugar or both—and flavoring it with additions ranging from more chocolate to nuts to spices. Shape the dough into logs and roll them up in wax or parchment paper or plastic wrap. Chilling, which is essential to icebox cookies, firms up the dough so it's easy to slice before baking. When you have a log or two on hand, mouthwatering cookies are only minutes away. A few tips:

- **Add flavor, texture and a pretty edge to each cookie by rolling the logs in ingredients like chopped nuts or very finely ground coffee beans. Or try shredded sweetened coconut or coarse colored-sugar granules.**
- **If the dough is too soft to shape into a log, chill briefly until it begins to firm.**
- **As you slice cookies, give the log an occasional quarter-turn to prevent flattening on one side.**

Marbled

Shape each half-batch of dough into a 6-inch log. Quarter each log lengthwise. Stack four strips of dough, alternating colors, then lightly twist to combine and reshape into a log. Repeat to make a second log.

Pinwheels

Pat each half-batch of dough out to a 6-inch square between sheets of wax or parchment paper or plastic wrap. Remove the top sheets and put the doughs together, paper sides out. Roll the doughs up tightly, peeling off the paper as you roll.—JIM FOBEL

WALNUT COOKIE STICKS

MAKES ABOUT 3 DOZEN COOKIES

- ½ cup walnuts (about 2 ounces)
- ½ cup plus 2 tablespoons sugar
- 1¼ cups all-purpose flour
- ¼ cup yellow cornmeal
- ¼ teaspoon baking powder
- ⅛ teaspoon salt
- 4 tablespoons unsalted butter, softened
- 1 large egg
- 2 tablespoons maple syrup

1. In a food processor, pulse the walnuts with the 2 tablespoons sugar until finely ground. Transfer to the bowl of a standing electric mixer fitted with a paddle. Add the remaining ½ cup sugar and the flour, cornmeal, baking powder and salt. Mix on low speed until combined. Add the butter and mix until a coarse meal forms. Add the egg and maple syrup and mix until combined.

2. Divide the cookie dough in half. Roll out each piece of dough to make a 7-inch log, about 1½ inches thick. Wrap each log in plastic and refrigerate for at least 2 hours or overnight.

3. Preheat the oven to 350°. Slice each cookie-dough log ⅓ inch thick. Using your hands, roll each slice of dough out to an 8-inch stick and arrange the sticks about 1 inch apart on two nonstick baking sheets. Twist and turn one end of each stick of dough to make a little squiggle. Bake the cookies for about 18 minutes, or until they are browned and crisp. Let the cookies cool on the baking sheet before serving.—WAYNE BRACHMAN

STORING SUGAR

All forms of white sugar will last practically indefinitely if stored in airtight containers in a cool, dry place. A tightly sealed glass jar in the pantry works well. When brown sugar is exposed to air, it becomes hard because its moisture evaporates. Store it in a thick plastic bag or an airtight container. If it dries out, try one of these remedies.

- **Add a slice of fresh apple to the sugar and set aside for about three days.**
- **Heat the sugar in a microwave oven at high power for thirty seconds to a minute.**
- **Warm the sugar in a shallow baking pan in a conventional oven at 250° for about five minutes.—CAROLE BLOOM**

PECAN SHORTBREAD COOKIES

MAKES ABOUT 6 DOZEN COOKIES

- 1½ cups cake flour
- 1 cup finely chopped pecans
- 1½ sticks unsalted butter (6 ounces), at room temperature
- ¼ cup confectioners' sugar
- ¼ cup granulated sugar
- ½ teaspoon pure vanilla extract
- ¼ teaspoon salt

1. Combine the flour and the pecans in a bowl. In another bowl, beat the butter with the sugars, vanilla and salt until light and fluffy. Add the flour and the pecans and mix on low speed just until combined. Divide the cookie dough into thirds.

2. On a lightly floured surface, roll each portion of dough into a 12-inch log. Wrap each log in plastic and refrigerate until firm. (**MAKE AHEAD:** The logs can be frozen for up to 1 month. Defrost before slicing and baking.)

3. Preheat the oven to 350°. Slice the logs ¼ inch thick and bake on cookie sheets for 10 minutes, or until golden. Let the cookies cool on the sheets for 10 minutes, then transfer them to racks to cool completely. (**MAKE AHEAD:** The cookies can be stored in an airtight container for up to 4 days.)—WALDY MALOUF

PINE-NUT ALMOND MACAROONS

These are classic southern Italian cookies—chewy almond macaroons covered with pine nuts. In this case, they are not cloyingly sweet. They evoke a Mediterranean Easter and, being flourless, are an ideal Passover

cookie. If you can, buy Mediterranean, or Italian, pine nuts. They have a more delicate flavor than the Chinese pine nuts.

MAKES ABOUT 3 DOZEN MACAROONS

- 7 ounces almond paste
- ½ cup superfine sugar
- 3 tablespoons egg whites (from 2 lightly beaten whites), at room temperature
- ⅔ cup pine nuts (3 ounces)

1. Preheat the oven to 350°. Line two cookie sheets with parchment paper.
2. In a standing electric mixer, beat the almond paste and the superfine sugar for 1 minute. Scrape down the bowl and beat for 30 seconds longer. Beat in the egg whites, 1 tablespoon at a time, until blended. Scrape down the bowl and beat for a few seconds; the batter will be soft but not runny.
3. Scrape the batter into a pastry bag fitted with a #5 round tip (about ½ inch). Pipe 1¼-inch rounds about 1½ inches apart on the prepared cookie sheets and sprinkle the pine nuts all over the tops and sides of the mounds. Bake the macaroons for 20 minutes, turning the cookie sheets once, until the cookies are golden brown. Slide the parchment paper onto a rack and allow the macaroons to cool completely. Remove the macaroons from the parchment paper and serve. (**MAKE AHEAD:** The macaroons will keep in an airtight container for 1 week; or you can freeze them for up to 1 month.)—PEGGY CULLEN

Christmas Cookies

CHRISTMAS COOKIES

MAKES ABOUT 4 DOZEN COOKIES

- 2½ sticks unsalted butter (10 ounces), at room temperature
- 1 cup sugar
- Pinch of salt
- 4 large egg yolks, at room temperature
- 1 teaspoon finely grated lemon zest
- 1 teaspoon pure vanilla extract
- 3 cups all-purpose flour
- Small silver dragées,* for decorating
- Apricot or seedless raspberry jam

*Available at pastry-supply shops

1. In an electric mixer, beat the butter with the sugar and salt until creamy. Beat in the egg yolks, lemon zest and vanilla. On low speed, beat in the flour, 1 cup at a time, until just combined. Divide the dough into four equal pieces; flatten into smooth disks. Wrap separately in wax paper; refrigerate until firm, at least 30 minutes. (**MAKE AHEAD:** The dough can be refrigerated up to 2 days, or frozen for up to 1 month.)
2. Preheat the oven to 350°. On a lightly floured surface, roll one

disk of the dough ⅛ inch thick. Using cookie cutters, cut it into star and moon shapes. Use mini cutters to stamp out patterns in half of the cookies and decorate with dragées. With a metal spatula, transfer the cookies to a large cookie sheet lined with parchment paper. Bake for 15 to 20 minutes, until pale golden. Let cool on the parchment, then transfer to a rack to cool completely. Repeat with the remaining disks.

3. Spread a rounded teaspoon of jam on each of the solid cookies; top with a decorated cookie. (**MAKE AHEAD:** The cookies can be stored up to 3 days in an airtight container.) —SUSAN LANTZIUS

CHEWY CHERRY FRUIT BARS LF

MAKES 32 BARS

- 1 cup dried sour cherries (about 4 ounces), coarsely chopped
- 3-inch strip of orange zest
- ½ cup unsweetened apple juice
- 1½ tablespoons honey
- 1 cup all-purpose flour
- ½ cup whole-wheat flour
- 1 teaspoon baking powder
- ¼ teaspoon salt
- ¼ teaspoon cinnamon
- ⅔ cup light brown sugar
- 2 tablespoons unsalted butter, softened
- 1 large egg
- 2 tablespoons unsweetened applesauce
- 1 large egg white, lightly beaten
- 1 tablespoon coarse sugar (optional)

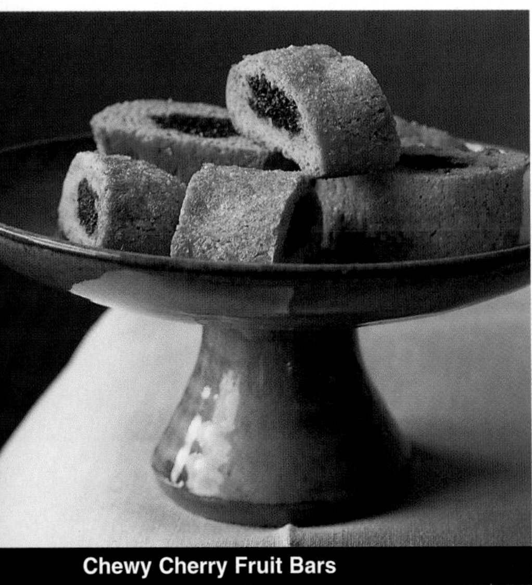
Chewy Cherry Fruit Bars

1. Preheat the oven to 325°. Combine the dried cherries, orange zest, apple juice and honey in a small nonreactive ovenproof saucepan and bring to a boil over moderate heat. Cook, stirring, for 5 minutes. Put the pan in the oven and bake for about 30 minutes, stirring, until the liquid is absorbed. Let cool slightly, then pulse in a food processor until finely chopped. Refrigerate until chilled, or for up to 4 days.

2. In a medium bowl, stir together the all-purpose and whole-wheat flours, the baking powder, salt and cinnamon. Using an electric mixer, beat the brown sugar and butter until combined. Add the egg and beat on high speed until thick and pale, about 5 minutes. Add the applesauce and the dry ingredients and beat on low speed until combined; the dough will be sticky. Divide the dough in half and wrap each piece in plastic. Shape each half into a 12-inch log and refrigerate until firm.

3. Preheat the oven to 350°. Unwrap one log and set it between two pieces of plastic wrap. Roll out the dough to a 13-by-5-inch rectangle, about ¼ inch thick. Remove the top piece of plastic. Spoon half of the cherry filling in a 1-inch-thick stripe down the center of the length of the dough, leaving a ½-inch border at each end. Using the plastic wrap, fold up one side of the dough to partially cover the filling and flatten slightly. Lift the other side to cover the filling, slightly overlapping the first piece of dough, and pinch the sides together to seal. Tuck in the ends. Repeat the process with the remaining dough and filling.

4. Put the filled logs onto a baking sheet, seam-side down, and flatten so that they are about 12 inches by 2 inches. Brush each log lightly with the egg white and sprinkle with coarse sugar. Bake for about 20 minutes, or until golden and the tops begin to crack. Let cool on the baking sheet for 5 minutes. Using a serrated knife, trim the ends and slice each log into sixteen 1-inch bars.—GRACE PARISI

CHEWY CHOCOLATE PECAN MACAROONS

These flourless cookies have a thin, crusty, cracked exterior and a moist, chewy center. Be careful not to overbake, which will make them too dry.

MAKES 3 DOZEN MACAROONS

- 1¼ cups pecans (5 ounces)
- ⅓ cup unsweetened Dutch process cocoa powder, sifted
- 2 large egg whites, at room temperature
- Pinch of salt

BUTTER: SELECTION AND STORAGE

There are times when nothing but good butter will do—like when you're baking cookies. But before you bake, be sure the butter's not bad. Butter keeps few secrets. Look at it; it should be free of moisture at room temperature. Sniff it, and you should detect a faint, clean aroma. Then taste it. The flavor must be fresh, not too greasy, perhaps slightly nutty-sweet and seductively rich. Because butter readily picks up odors, keep it in its original wrapper, which is designed to protect it. Store it in the coldest spot in your refrigerator—the temperature should be maintained at no more than 38°—for up to one month. You can freeze butter for up to six months; enclose the original package in foil or an airtight freezer bag.—FLORENCE FABRICANT

1¾ cups confectioners' sugar, sifted

1. Preheat the oven to 350°. Line two cookie sheets with parchment paper. In a food processor, pulse the pecans until finely ground. In a small bowl, combine the pecans and cocoa.
2. In the large bowl of a standing electric mixer, beat the egg whites at high speed until foamy. Add the salt; beat until stiff. Lower the speed to medium. Add the confectioners' sugar ½ cup at a time. Scrape down the bowl with a large rubber spatula. Beat at high speed 30 seconds longer. Using the spatula, fold in the nut mixture.
3. Spoon the cookie batter onto the prepared cookie sheets in ½-tablespoon mounds. Bake for 10 minutes, or until the tops crack slightly (the cookies may appear a little moist). Slide the paper onto a rack and let cool completely. Remove the cookies from the paper and serve. (MAKE AHEAD: The cookies will keep in an airtight container for up to 1 week, or you can freeze them for up to 1 month.) —PEGGY CULLEN

FUDGY CHOCOLATE BROWNIES LF

MAKES 16 BROWNIES

3 tablespoons unsalted butter, softened
¾ cup sifted all-purpose flour
⅓ cup unsweetened cocoa, preferably Dutch process
½ teaspoon baking powder
½ teaspoon salt
1 cup dark brown sugar
1 large egg
1 teaspoon pure vanilla extract
1 ounce semisweet chocolate, melted
¼ cup unsweetened applesauce

1. Preheat the oven to 350°. Butter a 9-inch square baking pan with ½ teaspoon of the butter. Sift together the flour, cocoa, baking powder and salt.
2. Using an electric mixer, beat the brown sugar and the remaining butter. Add the egg and vanilla and beat until fluffy. Beat in the chocolate, then the applesauce. Beat in the dry ingredients on low speed until combined. Spread the brownie batter in the prepared pan. Bake for about 25 minutes, or until a toothpick inserted in the center comes out clean. Let cool; cut the brownies into squares.—GRACE PARISI

CHAPTER 18

~

PIES

Lemon Lover's Tart

LEMON LOVER'S TART

Lemon is one of my preferred winter flavors, and this rich, creamy tart is the perfect ending to a festive family dinner. The lemon-curd filling thickens slowly; you may find the hand-beating a bit tedious, but the results are well worth it. The tart can be prepared several hours in advance and requires no last-minute fussing, making it ideal for entertaining.

MAKES ONE 9-INCH TART

2 large eggs, at room temperature
3 large egg yolks, at room temperature
1 cup sugar
1 stick unsalted butter (4 ounces), at room temperature, cut into 8 tablespoons
Finely grated zest of 2 lemons, blanched and refreshed (see "Blanching Lemon Zest" below)
½ cup fresh lemon juice, strained
Lemon Pastry Shell (recipe follows)
Fine strips of lemon zest, blanched and refreshed, for garnish (optional)

1. In the top of a nonreactive double boiler set over but not touching simmering water, combine the eggs, the egg yolks and the sugar. Whisk frequently until the mixture is thick and pale yellow, about 10 minutes.

2. Whisk in the butter, piece by piece, allowing each piece to melt before adding the next. Add the grated zest and the lemon juice and whisk frequently until the mixture is thick and the first bubbles appear, about 10 minutes longer; do not let it boil.

3. Pour the filling into the pastry shell. Smooth the top with a spatula and set the tart aside at room temperature until the filling firms up, about 30 minutes, before unmolding and serving. Garnish with the strips of lemon zest, if desired.

BLANCHING LEMON ZEST

To blanch lemon zest, boil it in water for three minutes; drain, rinse in cold water to refresh it and drain again.

Lemon Pastry Shell

MAKES ONE 9-INCH SHELL

1 stick unsalted butter (4 ounces), melted and cooled
¼ teaspoon pure vanilla extract
⅛ teaspoon pure almond extract
Grated zest of 1 lemon, blanched and refreshed (see "Blanching Lemon Zest," below)
¼ cup confectioners' sugar
Pinch of fine sea salt
1¼ cups plus 1 tablespoon unbleached all-purpose flour

1. Preheat the oven to 350°. Butter a 9-inch fluted tart pan with a removable bottom.

2. In a medium bowl, using a wooden spoon, stir together the melted butter, vanilla, almond extract, lemon zest, confectioners' sugar and salt. Gradually stir in the flour to form a smooth, soft dough. Place the dough in the center of the prepared pan. Using the tips of your fingers, evenly press the dough along the bottom and up the sides of the pan; it will be quite thin.

3. Bake the pastry shell in the center of the oven for 12 to 15 minutes, or just until the dough is firm and lightly browned. Let the shell cool completely before filling. Do not remove from the pan before the tart is filled and set.—PATRICIA WELLS

LEMON TARTLETS

These tartlets are high on the pucker scale; if you prefer a gentler lemon flavor, add another tablespoon or two of sugar to the filling. The pastry is buttery and quite delicate; if it breaks when you are putting it in the tartlet pans, patch it with your fingers.

MAKES SIX 4½-INCH TARTLETS

PASTRY:

1¾ cups all-purpose flour
⅓ cup superfine sugar
1½ teaspoons finely grated lemon zest
Pinch of salt
1 stick plus 6 tablespoons cold unsalted butter (7 ounces), cut into tablespoons
2 large egg yolks
¼ teaspoon pure vanilla extract
1 tablespoon fresh orange juice
1 teaspoon dark rum

FILLING:

⅔ cup fresh lemon juice
½ cup plus 1 tablespoon granulated sugar
1 tablespoon finely grated lemon zest
1½ tablespoons cornstarch blended with 1 tablespoon water
4 tablespoons unsalted butter, softened
4 large egg yolks
Vegetable cooking spray

1. Make the pastry: In a food processor, combine the flour, superfine sugar, grated lemon zest and salt and pulse to blend. Add the cut-up butter, the egg yolks, vanilla extract, orange juice and dark rum and pulse until the pastry dough begins to clump together. Transfer the dough to a work surface, gather it up and roll it into a thick cylinder. Cover the cylinder of dough well with plastic wrap and refrigerate for at least 4 hours.

2. Make the filling: In a small nonreactive saucepan, combine the lemon juice, granulated sugar, lemon zest and ⅓ cup of water. Bring to a boil over moderate heat, stirring occasionally to dissolve the sugar. Whisk in the cornstarch; continue whisking until the mixture is bubbling and thickened, about 1 minute. Remove the saucepan from the heat and whisk in the softened butter and the egg yolks. Strain the lemon filling through a fine stainless-steel sieve into a glass or ceramic bowl. Allow the filling to cool to room temperature, and then cover and refrigerate. (**MAKE AHEAD:** The pastry and the lemon filling can be refrigerated overnight.)

Lemon Tartlet

3. Preheat the oven to 400° and set a heavy baking sheet on the middle rack. Lightly spray six 4- or 4½-inch tartlet shells with vegetable cooking spray. Cut the cylinder of pastry dough into six equal pieces. On a lightly floured work surface, roll one piece of the pastry dough into a 6-inch round and carefully fit it into one of the tartlet shells, smoothing out any cracks. Repeat the process with the remaining pastry. Trim the overhanging pastry dough so that it is flush with the rims of the tartlet pans.

4. Prick the bottoms of the tartlet shells all over with a fork and line each one with foil. Fill each tartlet shell with dried beans, rice or pie weights and then bake the shells on the baking sheet for 15 minutes, or until the edges of the shells are golden. Remove the foil and the dried beans and bake the shells for about 8 minutes longer, or until they are golden brown and beginning to pull away from the sides of the pans. Transfer the baked tartlet shells to a rack and let them cool slightly. (**MAKE AHEAD:** The tartlet shells can be stored overnight at room temperature in an airtight tin.)

5. Turn the heat in the oven down to 350°. Spoon the lemon filling into the tartlet shells and bake for 5 minutes. Allow the lemon tartlets to cool at room temperature for a few hours until the lemon filling firms up, or refrigerate them for up to 4 hours before serving.—BRIGIT LEGERE BINNS

Fresh Cherry Crostata

FRESH CHERRY CROSTATA

MAKES ONE 12-INCH CROSTATA

- 2 cups plus 1 tablespoon all-purpose flour
- ¼ cup granulated sugar
- ½ teaspoon salt
- 1½ sticks cold unsalted butter (6 ounces), cut into ¼-inch dice, plus 1 tablespoon melted butter
- ½ cup ice water
- 2 tablespoons slivered blanched almonds, very finely chopped
- 3 pounds fresh sweet cherries, pitted

1. In a bowl, mix the 2 cups flour with 1 tablespoon of the sugar and the salt. Add the cold butter and cut it in briefly using a pastry blender. Add the ice water and stir just until the dough begins to come together.

2. Gather up the dough and knead briefly on a lightly floured surface until it forms a smooth, cohesive mass. Pat into a disk, wrap in plastic and refrigerate for at least 1 hour before rolling out.

3. Mix the chopped blanched almonds with the remaining 1 tablespoon flour and 1 tablespoon of the sugar.

4. Preheat the oven to 400°. On a lightly floured surface, roll out the dough to a 15-inch round and transfer the round to a baking sheet. Sprinkle the almond mixture all over the dough to within 1½ inches of the edge. Arrange the cherries on top. Fold the edge of the dough up and over the fruit.

5. Brush the melted butter over the pastry border and sprinkle the remaining 2 tablespoons sugar over the whole crostata. Bake for 50 minutes to 1 hour, or until the crostata is deeply browned. Let cool on a rack for 10 minutes. Dip a brush into the crostata and glaze the cherries with some of their juices. Serve warm.—PAUL BERTOLLI ➤

JESSIE'S SOUR-CHERRY PIE

Frozen sour cherries are available all year by mail order from Orchard Harvest, 1-800-286-7209.

MAKES ONE 8-INCH PIE

1¼ cups sugar
¼ cup cornstarch, sifted
1¼ pounds fresh or frozen pitted sour cherries
3 tablespoons unsalted butter
1 teaspoon almond extract

Jessie's Sour-Cherry Pie

Pear "Toasts"

2 cups all-purpose flour
½ teaspoon salt
¾ cup vegetable shortening or lard
4 to 5 tablespoons ice water

1. In a nonreactive saucepan, combine the sugar and cornstarch. Stir in the cherries; let stand until soupy, about 15 minutes. Cook over moderate heat, stirring, until thickened, 8 to 10 minutes. Stir in the butter and almond extract. Let cool.
2. Preheat the oven to 450°. In a bowl, mix the flour and salt. Cut in the shortening until the mixture resembles small peas. Stir in the ice water until the dough forms a ball. Divide the dough in half and pat each half out to a 6-inch disk.
3. Lightly flour the disks and place each between two sheets of wax paper. Roll out one disk to a 10-inch round. Peel off the top sheet of paper; invert the dough into an 8-inch pie dish. Peel off the paper and fit the dough into the dish. Roll out the remaining disk, remove the paper and cut a few slits in the center to vent steam.
4. Pour the filling in the pie dish. Wet the rim of the bottom crust; top with the vented crust. Trim and crimp the edge. Bake for 15 minutes. Lower the temperature to 400°. Bake for about 40 minutes more, or until the crust is golden; let cool.—JESSIE CROMWELL

PEAR "TOASTS"

These tartlets are called "toasts" because they're shaped like, well, toast.

MAKES FOUR 5-INCH TARTLETS

4 ripe Comice pears, peeled, halved lengthwise and cored
32 ounces bottled pear juice
3 tablespoons sugar
1 vanilla bean, split lengthwise
½ pound chilled puff-pastry dough

1. In a medium nonreactive saucepan, combine the pears and pear juice and bring to a simmer over moderate heat. Cook, stirring occasionally, until the pears are tender when pierced, about 30 minutes. Drain the pears (you can save the juice to drink) and refrigerate them until cool, about 1 hour or overnight.
2. Preheat the oven to 425° and line a baking sheet with parchment paper.
3. Pour the sugar into a medium bowl. Using the back of a table knife, scrape the seeds from the vanilla bean and mix them into the sugar. Chop one of the cooled pears into a chunky paste and toss with 1 tablespoon of the vanilla sugar.
4. On a lightly floured work surface, roll the puff-pastry dough into a 10-inch square. Cut the dough into four 5-inch squares. Slightly round off two corners of each square to resemble bread slices. Transfer the "toasts" to the prepared baking sheet and refrigerate until chilled, about 10 minutes. Divide the pear paste among the toasts and spread almost to the edges. Cut the remaining pears crosswise into ⅛-inch slices and arrange, overlapping, on the toasts. Sprinkle evenly with the remaining vanilla sugar.
5. Bake for about 15 minutes, or until golden brown on the bottom and edges. Remove the toasts immediately to a rack and let cool before serving.—MAURY RUBIN

Apple Pizza

APPLE PIZZA Q

MAKES TWO 15-BY-10½-INCH PIES

14 ounces thawed frozen puff-pastry dough, chilled
2 medium Granny Smith apples, peeled, cored and very thinly sliced
2 tablespoons unsalted butter, softened
1 tablespoon sugar
Vanilla ice cream, for serving

1. Preheat the oven to 450°. On a lightly floured surface, roll out the puff-pastry dough to a 16-by-10-inch rectangle. Transfer the rectangle to a 15-by-10½-inch baking sheet, trimming the excess. Arrange the apple slices in crosswise rows on the pastry. Spread the butter over the apples and sprinkle with the sugar. Refrigerate the pizza until the pastry is firm, at least 15 minutes.
2. Bake the apple pizza for about 15 minutes, or until the pastry is puffed and golden and the apples are glazed. Serve the apple pizza warm with vanilla ice cream.—MARCIA KIESEL

DEEP-DISH APPLE PIE WITH A CHEDDAR CRUST

MAKES TWO 9-INCH PIES

PASTRY:
3 cups all-purpose flour
½ pound sharp cheddar cheese, grated
½ teaspoon coarse salt
2 sticks cold unsalted butter (½ pound), cut into tablespoons
2 eggs, lightly beaten

FILLING:
5 pounds Golden Delicious apples (about 12), peeled, cored and sliced ¼ inch thick
Juice of 1 large lemon
1½ cups light brown sugar
¼ cup all-purpose flour
1 teaspoon coarse salt

1. Make the pastry: In a food processor, pulse the flour, cheese and salt to mix. Add the butter and pulse until the mixture resembles coarse meal. Transfer the mixture to a large bowl and make a well in the center. Stir in the eggs and work the dough into a ball.
2. Divide the dough into quarters and flatten the quarters into disks. Roll out each disk to an 11-inch round between two sheets of wax paper. Remove the wax paper and line each of two 9-inch pie pans with a dough round. Refrigerate the lined pans and the two dough rounds, covered, until they are thoroughly chilled.
3. Make the filling: Preheat the oven to 375°. In a large bowl, toss the apples with the lemon juice. Sprinkle on the brown sugar, flour and salt and toss well. Divide the apples between the lined pie pans. Moisten the pie-shell rims with water and cover with the dough rounds. Trim any overhang and crimp the edges to seal. Cut four steam vents in the top of each pie. (**MAKE AHEAD:** The pies can be chilled until firm, then wrapped and frozen for up to 2 weeks. Thaw before baking.)
4. Bake the pies on the bottom shelf of the oven for about 1 hour, or until golden and bubbly and the apples are tender when pierced; cover the pies with foil halfway through if browning too fast. Let cool for about 1 hour before serving.—WALDY MALOUF ➤

Deep-Dish Apple Pie with a Cheddar Crust

INDIAN APPLE PIE

This homespun pie is a cross between Indian pudding and apple pie. Serve it with vanilla or caramel ice cream.

MAKES ONE 9-INCH PIE

TOPPING:

- ¾ cup light brown sugar
- ½ cup all-purpose flour
- ¼ cup coarse cornmeal or polenta
- 1 teaspoon cinnamon
- 4 tablespoons unsalted butter, cut into ½-inch pieces
- 1½ tablespoons heavy cream

FILLING:

- 2 pounds Granny Smith apples, peeled, halved, cored and cut into 12 wedges each
- 1 teaspoon all-purpose flour
- 4 tablespoons unsalted butter, softened
- 2 tablespoons granulated sugar
- ⅓ cup mild unsulphured molasses
- 1½ teaspoons cinnamon
- ¼ teaspoon ground ginger
- Maury's Pie Shell (recipe follows)

1. Make the topping: In a large bowl, rub together the brown sugar, flour, cornmeal and cinnamon between your fingertips. Add the butter and rub into the mixture to form pea-size lumps. Using a blunt knife, stir in the cream.

2. Preheat the oven to 375°. **Make the filling:** In a large bowl, toss the apples with the flour. In another large bowl, combine the butter, sugar, molasses, cinnamon and ginger; whisk until smooth. Add the apples and stir well. Pour the filling into the pie shell, mounding it in the center. Scrape the sticky topping over the apples; it will melt and cover most of them as it cooks.

3. Bake the pie on the middle shelf of the oven for 30 minutes, then cover loosely with foil and place a baking sheet on the lower shelf to catch any drips. Bake for 30 to 40 minutes longer, or until the apples are tender when pierced. Let the pie cool for 30 minutes and serve it while it is still warm.

Maury's Pie Shell

MAKES ONE 9-INCH PIE SHELL

- 1¼ cups all-purpose flour
- 1 tablespoon sugar
- ⅛ teaspoon salt
- 6 tablespoons cold unsalted butter, cut into pieces
- 2 tablespoons cold vegetable shortening
- 2½ to 3 tablespoons ice water

1. In a food processor, pulse together the flour, sugar and salt. Add the butter and shortening and pulse until the pieces are the size of small peas. Drizzle in 2½ tablespoons of the ice water and pulse a few times, adding a little more water if necessary until the dough can be gathered into a ball. Pat the dough into a 6-inch disk. Wrap it in plastic wrap or wax paper and refrigerate for at least 1 hour or overnight. Let the dough soften at room temperature for 5 minutes before rolling it out.

2. On a lightly floured work surface, roll the dough into a 12-inch round. Fit it into a 9-inch pie pan without stretching it. Tuck in the overhang to reinforce a generous rim; crimp the rim decoratively. Refrigerate the pie shell until firm, at least 1 hour or overnight, before serving.—MAURY RUBIN

CHEF'S TIP

Granny Smith apples are the best choice for Indian Apple Pie. They hold their shape during cooking—essential for baking apples—and offer a pleasantly tart contrast to the sweet blend of molasses and granulated sugar in the filling and the brown sugar in the topping. Other baking apples to look for, especially at local farmers' markets, include Mutsu, Golden Delicious, Greening and Idared.

MÉMÉ'S APPLE TART

I remember well the apple tart my mother made every day as a dessert offering in her small Lyons restaurant. Unlike any other dough, hers achieved its tender, crumbly, airy texture from the combination of vegetable shortening, baking powder and warm milk mixed with the flour. This recipe is from Jacques Pépin's Kitchen: Cooking with Claudine *(KQED).*

MAKES ONE 9-INCH TART

PASTRY:

- ¼ cup milk
- 1¼ cups all-purpose flour
- 1 teaspoon sugar
- ½ teaspoon baking powder
- ⅛ teaspoon salt
- 6 tablespoons solid vegetable shortening, such as Crisco

FILLING:

- 2 pounds sweet medium apples, such as Golden Delicious
- 3 tablespoons sugar
- 2 tablespoons unsalted butter, cut into small pieces

Indian Apple Pie

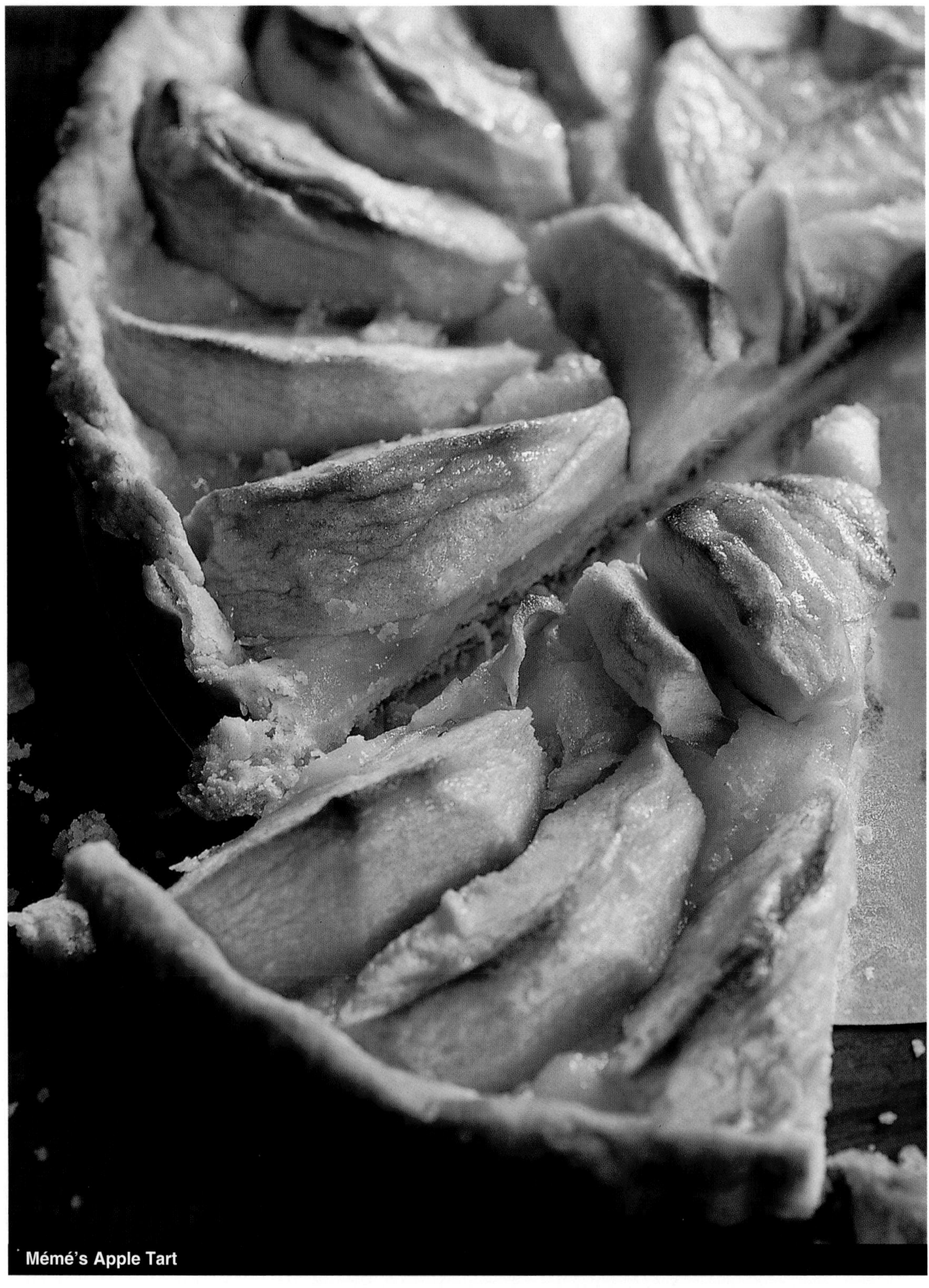

Mémé's Apple Tart

1. Make the pastry: In a small pan, heat the milk to lukewarm. In a bowl, mix the flour, sugar, baking powder and salt. Add the shortening; mix with a spoon or your hands until the dough feels and looks sandy. Add the milk and mix rapidly until the dough forms a ball. (**MAKE AHEAD:** The pastry dough can be refrigerated for up to 1 day.)

2. Roll the dough between two sheets of plastic wrap to an 11- to 12-inch round. Remove the top piece of plastic. Using the bottom piece, invert the dough into a 9-inch tart pan with removable bottom; peel off the remaining plastic.

3. Make the filling: Preheat the oven to 400°. Peel, quarter, core and cut the apples into 1-inch-thick wedges. Arrange the wedges in a concentric circle on the dough. Sprinkle evenly with the sugar and the butter.

4. Set the tart on a baking sheet. Bake for about 1 hour, until the fruit is tender, the pastry golden. Cover the tart loosely with foil after 45 minutes to prevent overbrowning. Cut into wedges and serve warm.—JACQUES PÉPIN

MAKING A TART SHELL

Roll out the pastry dough between two sheets of plastic wrap. Use the tart pan as a guide for the size of the dough round.

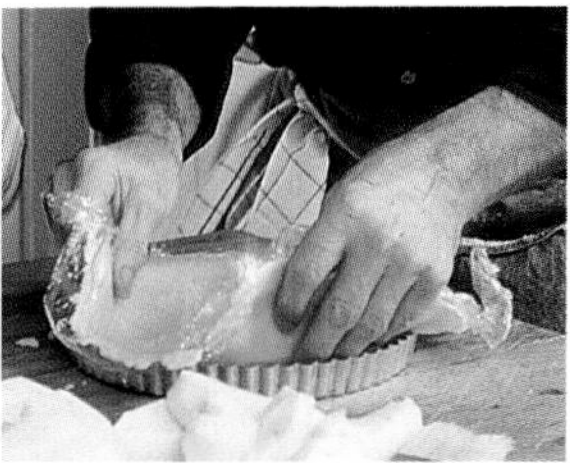

Remove the top sheet of plastic wrap and, using the bottom sheet to lift the dough, carefully invert it into the tart pan.

Once the dough is pressed up the sides, run a rolling pin over the top of the pan to remove the excess dough.

TOFFEE APPLE TART

MAKES ONE 9½-INCH TART

4 tablespoons unsalted butter
¾ cup light brown sugar
4 large Granny Smith apples (about 2 pounds), peeled, quartered and cored

ALMOND PASTRY:
⅓ cup almonds
2 tablespoons sugar
1 cup all-purpose flour
Pinch of salt
1 stick cold unsalted butter (4 ounces), cut into bits
1 large egg, lightly beaten
1 to 3 teaspoons ice water

1. In a 9-inch cast-iron skillet, melt the unsalted butter and the light brown sugar over moderate heat, stirring to combine. Turn off the heat.

2. Fit the apple quarters snugly on their sides in the skillet and cook over moderately high heat until the juices bubble, about 5 minutes. Turn the apples and cook them for 5 minutes longer. Turn the apples rounded-side up, reduce the heat to moderate and cook for 5 minutes; then turn them rounded-side down and cook for 4 to 5 minutes longer. The apples should be soft but not falling apart. Remove the skillet from the heat.

3. Make the almond pastry: Process the almonds and the sugar in a food processor until finely ground. Add the flour and the salt; pulse to combine. Add the butter; pulse until the mixture resembles coarse meal. Add the egg and pulse briefly to incorporate. Add the water 1 teaspoon at a time and pulse until the pastry dough can be gathered into a ball. Transfer the dough to lightly floured wax paper and, with floured fingers, pat it into an even 9½-inch round. Slide the paper with the crust onto a cookie sheet. Refrigerate until firm or for up to 4 hours.

4. Preheat the oven to 400°. Allow the pastry dough to stand at room temperature for about 10 minutes, and then peel off the wax paper and cover the apples with the dough round. Bake the tart for about 25 minutes, or until the pastry is golden. Let the tart sit for 10 minutes. Invert it onto a large flat platter and serve warm.—DIANA STURGIS ➤

Apple Pineapple Pie

APPLE PINEAPPLE PIE

MAKES ONE 8-INCH PIE

PASTRY:

- 2 cups all-purpose flour
- ½ teaspoon salt
- 14 tablespoons vegetable shortening (7 ounces)
- 4 to 5 tablespoons ice water

FILLING:

- 2 pounds tart apples (about 6), peeled and thinly sliced
- ¾ cup finely chopped fresh pineapple
- 2 tablespoons fresh lemon juice
- ½ cup sugar
- 2 tablespoons all-purpose flour
- 1 teaspoon freshly grated nutmeg
- ½ teaspoon cinnamon

- 1 tablespoon milk
- 1 tablespoon sugar

1. Make the pastry: In a large bowl, toss the flour and the salt. With a pastry blender or two knives, cut in the shortening until mealy. Sprinkle in 4 tablespoons ice water. Stir with a fork until the dough comes together. If it is too dry and crumbly, add the remaining water, 1 teaspoon at a time.

2. Halve the dough and pat it into two 7-inch disks. Wrap each disk in wax paper and refrigerate until chilled, about 30 minutes.

3. Put one rack in the bottom third of the oven, one in the middle; preheat to 450°. On a lightly floured surface, roll one dough disk to a 10-inch round. Transfer to an 8-inch pie pan. Roll the second disk to a 12-inch round and move it to a parchment-lined baking sheet. Refrigerate the pastry.

4. Make the filling: In a bowl, mix the sugar, flour, nutmeg and cinnamon. Toss in the apples, pineapple and lemon juice.

5. Put the filling in the pie shell. Moisten the overhanging pastry. Place the top crust over the filling. Trim the edge and crimp to seal. Cut vents in the top. Brush with the milk; sprinkle with sugar.

6. Bake on the bottom rack for 20 minutes, then the middle rack for 40 to 45 minutes longer, until the crust is golden brown and the apples are tender when pierced. Transfer to a rack; cool before serving.—JESSICA B. HARRIS

APPLE CRANBERRY PIE

MAKES ONE 9-INCH PIE

PASTRY:

- 2 cups all-purpose flour
- ¼ teaspoon salt
- ½ cup plus 1 tablespoon cold vegetable shortening
- 4 tablespoons cold unsalted butter, cut into ½-inch pieces
- ¼ cup ice water

FILLING:

- 6 large Golden Delicious apples, peeled, halved, cored and cut into 8 wedges each
- 1 cup fresh or frozen cranberries

Apple Cranberry Pie

Gooseberry Tart

2 teaspoons finely grated orange zest
1 cup sugar
3 tablespoons all-purpose flour
1/8 teaspoon salt
1 large egg, beaten with 1 tablespoon milk

1. Make the pastry: In a large bowl, combine the flour and salt. Using a pastry blender or two knives, cut the shortening and butter into the flour until it resembles coarse meal. Refrigerate the mixture for a few minutes if the butter gets too soft to work with.

2. Drizzle the ice water over the flour mixture and, using a wooden spoon, stir just until the dough can be gathered into a ball. Divide the dough in half and pat each piece into a 6-inch disk. Wrap each disk in plastic wrap and refrigerate until firm, at least 2 hours or overnight, before using.

3. Preheat the oven to 400°. Roll each disk of dough into a 12-inch round. Line a 9-inch pie pan with one of the rounds of the dough and refrigerate both this and the second dough round until ready to fill.

4. Make the filling: In a large bowl, toss the apples, cranberries, orange zest, sugar, flour and salt; transfer to the pie shell. Brush the edges of the shell with the egg wash and cover with the second dough round, lightly pressing the edges together. Trim any overhang to 1 inch, fold under and crimp to seal. Brush the top crust with the egg wash, avoiding the rim as it tends to brown more quickly. Make four small slashes in the top of the pie for venting.

5. Set the pie on the middle shelf of the oven, with a baking sheet below to catch drips. Bake about 1 hour and 10 minutes, or until the crust is light golden and the juices bubble. Cover the pie loosely with foil during the last 15 minutes to prevent excessive browning. Let the pie cool on a rack for 20 minutes and serve warm.—CATHIE GUNTLI

GOOSEBERRY TART

MAKES ONE 9-INCH PIE

PASTRY:

1 cup all-purpose flour
1/4 teaspoon salt
1/4 teaspoon sugar
6 tablespoons cold unsalted butter, cut into 1/2-inch dice
About 3 tablespoons ice water

FILLING:

1/2 cup plus 3 tablespoons sugar
1/4 teaspoon cinnamon
1 tablespoon all-purpose flour
1 pint gooseberries (about 3 cups), stems and tails removed
Vanilla ice cream, for serving

1. Make the pastry: In a large bowl, mix the flour, the salt and the sugar. With a pastry blender, two knives or your fingers, cut in half of the butter until the mixture resembles coarse cornmeal with particles the size of peas. Cut in the remaining butter until it forms chunks the size of peas. Stir in the ice water with a fork. The dough should hold together when pressed; if not, add a little more ice water. Pat into a disk, wrap and refrigerate at least 30 minutes or overnight.

2. On a large sheet of parchment paper lightly dusted with flour, roll the dough into a round about 14 inches in diameter (it doesn't have to be perfect around the edges). Lay it on a large baking sheet or pizza pan and refrigerate.

3. Make the filling: Preheat the oven to 400°. In a small bowl, mix the sugar and cinnamon. Mix 1 tablespoon of this cinnamon-sugar with the flour, sprinkle over a 9-inch area of the pastry and top with the berries. Reserve

1½ tablespoons cinnamon-sugar; sprinkle the rest over the berries. Fold the pastry edges up over the berries to form a 9-inch free-form tart, making pleats and pressing them together lightly. Brush with water; sprinkle with the cinnamon-sugar.

4. Bake in the center of the oven 40 to 50 minutes, or until the fruit is bubbling and lightly browned and the pastry is caramelized in spots and browned on the bottom. Cut the tart into wedges and serve it with vanilla ice cream.—LINDSEY SHERE

WALNUT AND DRIED-CRANBERRY TART

MAKES ONE 11-INCH TART

PASTRY:

- 1¼ cups plus 2 tablespoons all-purpose flour
- 1 tablespoon plus 1 teaspoon sugar
- ⅛ teaspoon salt
- 1 stick cold unsalted butter (4 ounces), cut into pieces
- 1 large egg yolk, beaten with 1 tablespoon milk
- 1 large egg white, lightly beaten

FILLING:

- 1½ cups walnut pieces (about 6 ounces), coarsely chopped
- 4 large eggs
- ½ cup sugar
- 1 cup light corn syrup
- 1 stick unsalted butter (4 ounces), melted and cooled
- 1 tablespoon all-purpose flour
- 2 tablespoons Grand Marnier
- 1 tablespoon frozen orange-juice concentrate
- Grated zest of 2 oranges
- 1 teaspoon pure vanilla extract
- ⅛ teaspoon salt
- 1¾ cups dried cranberries (½ pound)
- 1 cup chilled heavy cream, whipped with 1 tablespoon sugar
- Cranberry Orange Compote (recipe follows)

1. Make the pastry: In a food processor, pulse the flour, sugar and salt. Add the butter; pulse until the mixture resembles coarse meal. Add the egg yolk and pulse just until the dough can be gathered in a ball. On a lightly floured work surface, pat the dough into a 6-inch disk. Wrap in plastic; refrigerate until chilled, at least 1 hour or overnight. Let soften slightly at room temperature before using.

2. Preheat the oven to 350°. On a lightly floured surface, roll the dough to a 13-inch round. Transfer to an 11-inch tart pan with a removable bottom, pressing it evenly into the pan and fitting together any cracks. Trim the dough flush with the rim and freeze until firm, about 10 minutes.

3. Line the shell with foil; fill with pie weights, rice or dried beans. Bake for 20 minutes, or until set. Remove the foil and weights and bake for 10 to 15 minutes longer, or until golden. Immediately brush the hot pastry with the beaten egg white and set aside.

4. Make the filling: Spread the walnuts on a baking sheet and toast in the oven for about 5 minutes; let cool before using.

5. In a large bowl, whisk together the eggs, sugar, corn syrup, butter, flour, Grand Marnier, orange juice, orange zest, vanilla and salt until the sugar is completely dissolved. Stir in the cranberries and walnuts.

6. Pour the filling into the tart shell and bake for about 35 minutes, or until the filling is puffed, set and lightly browned. Let cool completely on a rack. Unmold before serving. Pass the whipped cream and compote separately.

Cranberry Orange Compote

MAKES 1½ PINTS

- 4 navel oranges
- 1½ cups fresh cranberries, picked over
- ½ cup sugar
- 1 tablespoon Grand Marnier

1. Using a sharp paring knife, peel the oranges, removing the skin and all the bitter white pith. Working over a bowl to catch the juice, cut in between the membranes to release the sections. Reserve the orange sections and juice in separate bowls.

2. In a nonreactive medium saucepan, combine the cranberries, sugar and ¼ cup of the orange juice. Cook over low heat, stirring often, until the berries pop and soften, about 4 minutes. Remove from the heat. Stir in the oranges and Grand Marnier. Refrigerate until cool.—KAREN BARKER

MAPLE WALNUT PIE

MAKES ONE 9-INCH PIE

- 3 large eggs
- 1 cup pure maple syrup
- ⅓ cup sugar
- 4 tablespoons unsalted butter, melted
- 1 teaspoon pure vanilla extract
- ¼ teaspoon salt
- 1¼ cups walnut halves
- One unbaked 9-inch pie shell
- Sweetened whipped cream

Chocolate Hazelnut Tartlets

1. Preheat the oven to 400°. In a large bowl, whisk together the eggs, maple syrup, sugar, butter, vanilla and salt. Arrange the nuts evenly over the bottom of the pie shell; pour the filling on top.

2. Set the pie in the oven. Reduce the heat to 350°. Bake about 40 minutes, or until puffed and golden. Let cool on a rack before serving. (**MAKE AHEAD:** The pie can be refrigerated for up to 1 day.) Cut in wedges and pass the whipped cream separately.—JANINE BJERKLIE

CHOCOLATE HAZELNUT TARTLETS

MAKES EIGHT 3½-INCH TARTLETS

CHOCOLATE PASTRY:

- 1½ cups all-purpose flour
- ⅔ cup confectioners' sugar
- ½ cup unsweetened cocoa, preferably Dutch process
- ½ teaspoon salt
- ¼ teaspoon baking soda
- 1½ sticks cold unsalted butter (6 ounces), cut into ½-inch dice
- 2½ tablespoons ice water

FILLING:

- 1 cup whole shelled hazelnuts (about 5 ounces)
- 3 large eggs, at room temperature
- 1 cup light corn syrup
- ½ cup granulated sugar
- 4 tablespoons unsalted butter, melted
- 1 teaspoon pure vanilla extract
- ⅓ cup each of ½-inch squares of bittersweet, milk and white chocolate (about 5 ounces total)

1. Make the chocolate pastry: In a food processor, pulse the flour, sugar, cocoa, salt and baking soda. Add the butter and pulse until the mixture resembles coarse meal. Drizzle in the ice water and pulse until the dough can be gathered into a ball. On a work surface, roll the dough into an 8-inch log. Wrap the log in plastic wrap and refrigerate it for at least 1 hour or overnight.

2. Butter eight ⅔-cup ramekins (3½ by 1½ inches). Cut the log in eight equal pieces; roll them into balls. Pat into 4-inch rounds and line the ramekins with the dough, pressing it evenly over the base and up the sides to the top of the ramekins. Refrigerate until firm.

3. Make the filling: Preheat the oven to 350°. Spread the nuts on a baking sheet. Bake for 12 minutes, or until the skins blister. Wrap in a towel and rub vigorously to remove most of the skins.

4. In a large bowl, whisk the eggs lightly, then whisk in the corn syrup, sugar, butter and vanilla until the sugar dissolves, about 1 minute. Stir in the nuts and the chocolate. Set the ramekins on a large baking sheet. Spoon in the filling.

5. Bake the tartlets for 30 minutes. Cover lightly with foil and bake for 15 minutes longer, or until the nuts are browned and the filling is bubbling in the center. Let cool, and then serve in the ramekins.—JENNIFER WELSHHONS

PUMPKIN CHESS TART

MAKES ONE 10-INCH TART

CHOCOLATE PASTRY:

- ½ cup plus 1 tablespoon all-purpose flour
- 3 tablespoons unsweetened cocoa, preferably Dutch process
- 3 tablespoons sugar
- ⅛ teaspoon salt
- 6 tablespoons cold unsalted butter, cut into ½-inch pieces
- 1 large egg yolk
- Vegetable cooking spray

FILLING:

- 1½ cups heavy cream
- 2 tablespoons milk
- 1 vanilla bean, split lengthwise, seeds scraped, pod reserved for another use
- ½ teaspoon pure vanilla extract
- 1 large egg
- 1 large egg yolk
- ½ cup plus 2 tablespoons sugar
- 3 cups kabocha puree (see box, right) or pumpkin puree
- 1 tablespoon all-purpose flour
- 1 tablespoon semolina
- 4 tablespoons unsalted butter, melted

SAUCE:

- 1 cup ruby port
- ¼ cup dried cherries
- 2 tablespoons sugar

1. Make the chocolate pastry: In a food processor, pulse the flour, cocoa, sugar and salt. Add the butter; process until the mixture resembles coarse meal. Add the egg yolk. Pulse just until the dough can be gathered into a ball. Wrap in plastic wrap. Refrigerate until firm, at least 1 hour or overnight.

2. Preheat the oven to 350°. Spray a 10-inch springform pan with vegetable cooking spray. Roll the dough between two sheets of wax paper to a 10½-inch round. Fit in the prepared pan, gently pressing over the bottom and about ¼ inch up the sides. Bake for 12 minutes, or until puffed and set slightly. Remove from the oven. Reduce temperature to 325°.

Pumpkin Chess Tart

KABOCHA

Japanese kabocha is drier than ordinary pumpkin and lends a creamy texture and sweet yamlike flavor. A three-and-a-half to four-pound kabocha, quartered, seeded and steamed until tender, yields about three cups of puree. For the best results, scrape the cooked flesh from the skin, then pass the flesh through a sieve for a smooth puree.

3. Make the filling: In a medium bowl, combine the cream, milk and vanilla seeds and extract. In a large bowl, beat the egg, egg yolk and sugar until pale and thick, about 2 minutes. Add the vanilla cream, kabocha puree, flour, semolina and butter and blend well; pour the filling into the springform pan.

4. Bake the tart for about 1 hour and 30 minutes, or until small cracks form in the top and the top is pale golden and set. Cover loosely with foil if it appears to be darkening too quickly. Let cool in the pan for 20 minutes; remove the springform. Refrigerate until chilled. (**MAKE AHEAD:** The tart can be refrigerated for up to 1 day.) ➤

5. Make the sauce: In a small nonreactive saucepan, boil the port until reduced to ½ cup. Add the dried cherries and the sugar and cook over high heat until the sauce is slightly thickened, about 3 minutes. Serve the tart in wedges and pass the cherry port sauce separately.—NELLI MALTEZOS

PUMPKIN PECAN TART

MAKES ONE 10-INCH TART

SHORTBREAD PASTRY:

- 2 cups all-purpose flour
- ⅔ cup confectioners' sugar
- 2 sticks cold unsalted butter (½ pound), cut into pieces

PUMPKIN FILLING:

- 3 large eggs
- ⅓ cup light brown sugar
- One 15-ounce can pumpkin puree (1⅔ cups)
- 1 teaspoon cinnamon
- ½ teaspoon salt
- ½ teaspoon ground nutmeg
- ¼ teaspoon ground cloves
- ¼ teaspoon ground ginger

PECAN TOPPING:

- 3 large eggs
- ½ cup light brown sugar
- ¾ cup light corn syrup
- 2 tablespoons unsalted butter, melted
- 2 teaspoons all-purpose flour
- ⅛ teaspoon salt
- 1⅔ cups pecan halves (about 6½ ounces)

Sweet-Potato Chocolate Pie

1. Make the shortbread pastry: In a food processor, pulse the flour and sugar. Add the butter; pulse until the dough can be gathered in a ball. Roll into a 9-inch log on a lightly floured work surface. Divide into a 5-inch log for the sides of the shell and a 4-inch piece for the base. Pat the base into a 6-inch disk; wrap in plastic. Wrap the log separately and refrigerate both until chilled, 1 hour or overnight.

2. On a lightly floured surface, roll the disk evenly into a 10-inch round. Press into the base of a 10-inch springform pan. Divide the log in half crosswise and roll into two 13-inch ropes. Fit them into the pan around the base and join the ends to make one continuous rope. Evenly press the dough 2 inches up the sides of the pan to form a seamless shell; refrigerate.

3. Preheat the oven to 350°. Set a large heavy baking sheet on the lowest shelf of the oven to preheat.

4. Make the pumpkin filling: In a large bowl, whisk the eggs, brown sugar, pumpkin, cinnamon, salt, nutmeg, cloves and ginger.

5. Make the pecan topping: In a large bowl, whisk together the eggs, brown sugar, corn syrup, butter, flour and salt.

6. Stir the filling, pour into the shell and arrange the nuts on top. Stir the topping; pour over the nuts. Bake on the preheated sheet for 1 hour and 10 minutes. Cover loosely with foil; bake about 15 minutes longer, or until the filling in the center looks set when you lift a pecan. Cool on a rack. (**MAKE AHEAD:** The tart can be refrigerated up to 1 day.) —SHERRY FAHEY

SWEET-POTATO CHOCOLATE PIE

MAKES ONE 9-INCH PIE

PASTRY:

- 2 cups all-purpose flour
- 1 teaspoon granulated sugar
- ½ teaspoon salt
- 1½ sticks cold unsalted butter (6 ounces), cut into ½-inch dice
- ⅓ cup cold vegetable shortening
- 3 to 4 tablespoons ice water

FILLING:

- 2¾ pounds sweet potatoes
- 1¼ cups granulated sugar
- ⅓ cup light brown sugar
- ¼ teaspoon cinnamon
- ⅛ teaspoon freshly grated nutmeg
- ⅛ teaspoon salt
- 5 large eggs
- 2 ounces semisweet chocolate at room temperature, cut into 1-inch-long matchsticks

WHIPPED CREAM:

- 1 cup cold heavy cream
- 1 tablespoon granulated sugar
- 1 tablespoon bourbon
- ½ teaspoon cinnamon

1. Make the pastry: In a food processor, pulse the flour, sugar and salt to blend. Add the butter and shortening and pulse until the mixture resembles coarse meal. Drizzle in 3 tablespoons of the ice water and pulse just until the dough can be gathered into a ball; if necessary, gradually add the remaining water. Turn the dough out onto a lightly floured surface and form it into a 9-inch log. Cut off a 4-inch section of the log and pat it into a 6-inch disk for the bottom crust. Wrap the disk in wax paper. Cut the remaining dough in half and wrap each piece separately in wax paper. Refrigerate all of the dough until chilled, at least 1 hour, or overnight.
2. On a lightly floured surface, roll the disk into a 9-inch round. Fit it into the base of a 9-by-2½-inch springform pan. With your hands, roll each of the remaining dough pieces into a 13-inch rope. Fit them around the base of the pan and join the ends to make one continuous rope. Using your fingers, evenly press the dough 2 inches up the sides of the pan to form a seamless shell. Refrigerate.
3. Make the filling: Preheat the oven to 350°. Bake the sweet potatoes on a baking sheet for about 1 hour, or until soft when pierced. Let cool; remove the skins. Puree the potatoes in a food processor. (**MAKE AHEAD:** The shell and potatoes can be refrigerated for 1 day.)
4. In a medium bowl, combine the sugars with the cinnamon, nutmeg and salt. In a large bowl, lightly whisk the eggs. Whisk in 3 cups of the sweet potatoes, then the sugar mixture. Spoon half the custard in the pie shell; top with half the chocolate. Cover with the rest of the custard. Arrange the remaining chocolate decoratively on top.
5. Bake in the center of the oven for about 1 hour, or until almost set in the middle. Turn the oven off; leave the pie inside until cool.
6. Make the whipped cream: Beat the ingredients until stiff. Serve the pie at room temperature; pass the cream separately.—JAMIE SHANNON

Fig Tart

FIG TART

Fans of Fig Newtons will love this fig "linzer torte." Serve cups of espresso with small slices of this intensely flavored tart.

MAKES ONE 9-INCH TART

⅔ cup shelled pecans
¾ cup sugar
2¾ cups all-purpose flour

1 teaspoon baking powder
½ teaspoon cinnamon
2 sticks (½ pound) unsalted butter, softened
3 large eggs, at room temperature
¼ teaspoon pure vanilla extract
2½ cups fig jam (about 27 ounces; see Note)
1 teaspoon milk
Vanilla ice cream, for serving

1. In a food processor, grind the pecans and the sugar until the nuts are very fine. Sift together the flour, baking powder and cinnamon. In a medium bowl, using an electric mixer, beat the butter with the ground nuts until light and fluffy. Add two of the eggs and the vanilla and beat until smooth. Using a wooden spoon, stir in the dry ingredients in three batches, mixing just until the flour is incorporated; the dough will still be sticky.
2. Divide the dough in half. Pat one half into a 6-inch disk for the tart base and wrap it in wax paper. Roll the remaining dough into a log and cut it in half crosswise. Pat one of the pieces into a 5-inch disk for the lattice top and wrap it in wax paper. Cut the remaining dough log in half again and wrap each piece separately for the pan sides. Refrigerate all of the dough until chilled, about 2 hours, or overnight.
3. Preheat the oven to 375°. Line the bottom of a 9-by-2½-inch springform pan with a round of parchment paper. On a lightly floured surface, roll the 6-inch disk into a 9-inch round and fit it into the bottom of the pan. Using your hands, roll each small piece of the dough log into a 13-inch-long rope. Fit the ropes into the pan around the base and join the ends to make one continuous rope. Evenly press the dough 1½ inches up the sides of the pan, forming a seamless shell. On a sheet of wax paper, roll the remaining disk into a 9-inch round, then transfer it to a rimless baking sheet and refrigerate.
4. Spoon the fig jam into the tart shell. The filling should come almost to the top of the pastry. Cut the chilled round of dough into ½-inch-wide strips and lay the strips, lattice-fashion, on top of the jam, anchoring them on the dough rim. Lightly beat the remaining egg with the milk and brush on the lattice. Bake on the bottom shelf of the oven for about 50 minutes, or until the lattice is golden. Let cool on a rack before removing the sides of the pan. Serve with vanilla ice cream.
NOTE: This tart can be made with thick, sweet Kadota fig preserves.—JAMIE SHANNON

BANANA, CHOCOLATE AND COCONUT-CREAM PIE

The sweet, crunchy brittle that tops this pie makes a fun snack on its own or a decoration for sundaes, cakes and pies.

MAKES ONE 9-INCH PIE

PASTRY:
1¼ cups all-purpose flour
½ teaspoon sugar
Pinch of salt
¼ cup plus 1 tablespoon chilled vegetable shortening
About ¼ cup ice water

FILLING:
1 cup heavy cream
6 ounces coarsely chopped semisweet chocolate
Pinch of salt
3 large ripe bananas, sliced crosswise 1½ inches thick
1¼ cups milk
¼ cup sugar
2 tablespoons plus 2 teaspoons cornstarch
2 large egg yolks
½ cup shredded sweetened coconut
¼ teaspoon pure vanilla extract
2 cups Banana Brittle (recipe follows), optional

1. Make the pastry: In a bowl, combine the flour, sugar and salt. Cut in the shortening until the mixture resembles coarse meal. Add the water and stir just until the dough comes together. Shape into a disk, cover with plastic wrap and refrigerate until chilled, at least 30 minutes or overnight.
2. Preheat the oven to 375°. On a floured surface, roll out the dough to an 11-inch round. Transfer to a 9-inch pie plate. Trim the overhang to ½ inch, fold it under itself and crimp decoratively. Freeze the pie shell until firm, about 10 minutes. Bake the pie shell for about 25 minutes, or until golden. Let cool on a rack.
3. Make the filling: In a small saucepan, heat the cream just until boiling. Remove from the heat; stir in the chocolate until melted. Transfer to a bowl and add the salt. Refrigerate, stirring often, until cooled and thickened, about 45 minutes. Arrange the banana pieces vertically in the pie shell in concentric circles. Pour the chocolate over them and refrigerate until firm, about 2 hours.
4. Meanwhile, heat the milk in a heavy saucepan. In a bowl, mix

the sugar and cornstarch. Stir in the egg yolks, then whisk the mixture into the milk. Whisk over low heat until the custard thickens and almost boils, about 4 minutes. Transfer to a bowl, add the coconut and vanilla and let stand until cooled, stirring. Refrigerate until chilled, about 20 minutes.

5. Spread the coconut custard over the pie and refrigerate until firm, about 2 hours. Just before serving, arrange the Banana Brittle over the top of the pie.

Banana Brittle

MAKES ABOUT 4 CUPS

- 2 tablespoons unsalted butter
- 1 tablespoon vegetable oil
- 5 tablespoons sugar
- 3 semiripe medium bananas, very thinly sliced crosswise
- ¾ teaspoon cinnamon
- ¼ cup minced unsalted peanuts

Preheat oven to 350°. On a large baking sheet, melt the butter in the oil. Spread to coat the pan evenly and sprinkle with 3 tablespoons of the sugar. Cover with the banana slices in a slightly overlapping layer and sprinkle with the remaining 2 tablespoons sugar, the cinnamon and the peanuts. Bake for about 20 minutes, or until the slices around the edge are crisp and golden. Let cool slightly so they firm up. Transfer the browned slices to a plate and bake the rest for about 3 minutes, or until browned. (MAKE AHEAD: The Banana Brittle can be wrapped in wax paper and stored in an airtight container for up to 5 days.) —MARCIA KIESEL

Banana, Chocolate and Coconut-Cream Pie

TOASTED-COCONUT CHOCOLATE ICE-CREAM PIE Q

Here's an impressive ice-cream pie that you can whip up using only three ingredients.

MAKES ONE 9-INCH PIE

- One 7-ounce bag shredded sweetened coconut
- 2 tablespoons unsalted butter, melted
- 2 pints chocolate ice cream, slightly softened

1. Preheat the oven to 375°. Spread out the shredded coconut on a baking sheet and toast for 8 to 10 minutes, stirring occasionally, until golden. Transfer the toasted coconut to a bowl and allow it to cool slightly. Add the butter to the bowl and stir until incorporated. Press the coconut mixture evenly over the bottom and up the sides of a 9-inch pie pan. Cover and freeze until the coconut shell is firm, about 15 minutes.

2. Spoon the softened chocolate ice cream into the coconut shell, mounding the ice cream slightly in the center and spreading it out to the edges; be careful not to dislodge any of the coconut shell. Cover the pie and freeze for at least 45 minutes, or until ready to serve. (MAKE AHEAD: The ice-cream pie can be frozen for 2 days.)—JUDITH SUTTON

CHAPTER 19

~

FRUIT DESSERTS

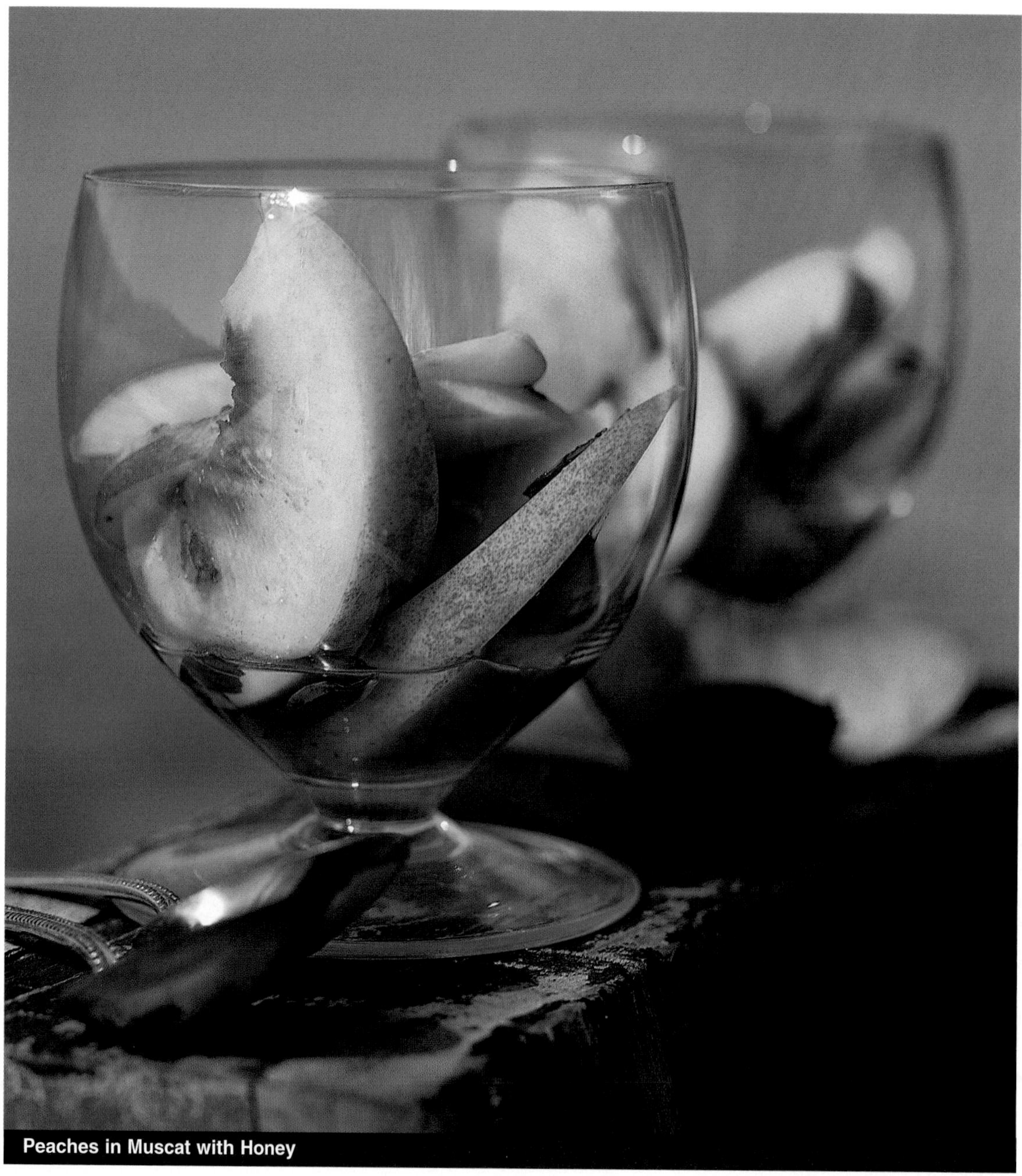
Peaches in Muscat with Honey

PEACHES IN MUSCAT WITH HONEY

Use your hands to crush the fresh basil leaves lightly and release their fragrance into this elegant dessert of peaches and wine.

3–4 SERVINGS

- ½ cup dessert wine, such as Beaumes de Venise or California Muscat
- ½ cup crushed fresh basil leaves
- 2 tablespoons honey
- 3 large ripe peaches, preferably white, sliced ⅓ inch thick

In a large glass bowl, combine the wine, the crushed basil and the honey. Add the peaches and let macerate at room temperature for 1 hour. Refrigerate for at least 1 hour or up to 4 hours before serving.—MARCIA KIESEL

PEACHES IN BLUEBERRY SYRUP

Peaches, plums and blueberries combine for a colorful, summery dessert.

8 SERVINGS

1½ cups blueberries
½ cup sugar
¼ vanilla bean, split lengthwise
2½ tablespoons fresh lemon juice, plus more to taste
5 medium peaches, cut into eighths
5 medium plums, cut into eighths
Scant 1 tablespoon coarsely chopped fresh mint

1. In a nonreactive medium saucepan, combine 1 cup of the blueberries with the sugar, the split vanilla bean and ¾ cup of water. Bring the water to a boil over moderately high heat, and then reduce the heat to moderately low and simmer until the blueberries start to fall apart, about 5 minutes.

2. Remove the vanilla-bean halves from the blueberry mixture and discard them. Transfer the blueberry mixture to a blender or a food processor. Add the 2½ tablespoons lemon juice, or more if desired, and blend until the blueberry syrup is smooth.

3. Strain the syrup into a large bowl, add the peaches and plums and gently toss the fruit with the syrup to combine. Sprinkle with the remaining blueberries. (**MAKE AHEAD:** The dessert can be refrigerated for 4 hours.) Serve the fruit chilled or at room temperature garnished with the chopped mint.—PAMELA MORGAN

ICE CREAM WITH CARAMELIZED PEACHES Q

This quick and easy peach topping is delicious over ice cream and great with angel food or pound cake.

4 SERVINGS

1½ tablespoons unsalted butter
3 firm, ripe peaches, peeled and sliced ½ inch thick

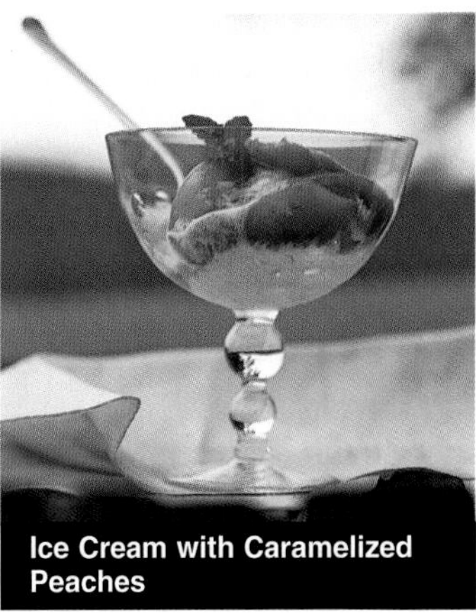

Ice Cream with Caramelized Peaches

Peaches in Blueberry Syrup

3 tablespoons (packed) light brown sugar
1 pint good-quality vanilla ice cream

1. In a heavy medium skillet, melt the butter over moderate heat. Add the peaches, sprinkle with the light brown sugar and stir until the sugar dissolves.
2. Cook the peaches, stirring occasionally, until they are tender and the juices are slightly reduced, 5 to 7 minutes longer. Remove the skillet from the heat and let the peaches cool slightly. Spoon the vanilla ice cream into four dessert bowls and top each serving with the caramelized peaches.—JUDITH SUTTON

Plum and Almond Potstickers

PLUM AND ALMOND POTSTICKERS

Be sure to use ripe plums for these Asian-style fruit dumplings. Serve them with homemade Vietnamese-cinnamon ice cream—a quick version appears below—or substitute vanilla ice cream.

4 SERVINGS

6 ripe medium red plums, 3 finely chopped and 3 quartered
½ cup Japanese plum wine
2 tablespoons almond paste
3 tablespoons unsalted butter
2 tablespoons all-purpose flour
1 tablespoon sugar
Pinch of freshly grated nutmeg
1 large egg, separated
12 egg-roll wrappers
1 tablespoon vegetable oil
¼ cup honey
¼ cup coarsely chopped walnuts
1 quart vanilla ice cream, softened
2 teaspoons cinnamon, preferably Vietnamese
4 fresh cilantro sprigs (optional)

1. In a small nonreactive saucepan, bring the chopped plums and wine to a simmer over moderate heat. Cover and simmer until the plums are soft, about 5 minutes. Transfer to a food processor and puree until smooth; strain.
2. In a bowl, combine the almond paste with 2 tablespoons of the butter, the flour, sugar and nutmeg. Blend in the egg yolk.
3. Using a 4-inch round biscuit cutter or a glass, cut out a round from each egg-roll wrapper. Beat the egg white until foamy and lightly brush each round. Spoon 1½ teaspoons of the almond filling in the center of each round and top with a plum quarter. Fold the rounds over to form half-moons and enclose the plums. Make five pleats along the rounded edge to seal each potsticker.
4. Meanwhile, bring a pot of water to a boil. Add the potstickers. Cook for 45 seconds. Transfer to a bowl of ice water to cool; drain well. (**MAKE AHEAD:** The potstickers and puree can be refrigerated separately for up to 6 hours.)
5. In a large nonstick skillet, melt the remaining 1 tablespoon butter in the oil. Add the potstickers and sauté over moderately high heat until lightly browned and warmed through, about 5 minutes. Stir in the honey and walnuts.
6. Mix the ice cream with the cinnamon. Spoon the plum sauce on four plates. Place a scoop of ice cream in the center of each and arrange three potstickers around it. Garnish with a cilantro sprig and serve.—GEORGE MAHAFFEY

ITALIAN PLUM BETTY Q

6 SERVINGS

1 pound Italian plums, pitted and cut into ¼-inch wedges
3 tablespoons sugar
1 tablespoon rum
2 large anisette toasts
1½ tablespoons unsalted butter, melted
1 pint vanilla ice cream

Preheat the oven to 400.° Generously butter a 9-inch round or 8-inch square nonreactive baking dish. Toss the plums with the sugar and rum; arrange in the prepared dish in an even layer. With a rolling pin, crush the toasts in a bag to make ¼-inch crumbs. (Or pulse in a food processor.) Toss the crumbs with the butter;

scatter over the fruit. Bake for about 15 minutes, until the plums are soft and the top is golden. Serve warm or at room temperature over ice cream.—GRACE PARISI

ICE CREAM WITH STRAWBERRIES AND BALSAMIC GLAZE Q

Balsamic vinegar, tempered with brown sugar and reduced to a glaze, makes a sweet, tangy topping for the ice cream and strawberries.

8 SERVINGS

- 2 pints fresh strawberries, hulled and quartered
- 1 tablespoon granulated sugar
- 1 cup coarsely chopped walnuts (about 3½ ounces)
- 1½ cups balsamic vinegar
- ⅓ cup dark brown sugar
- ¼ teaspoon cinnamon
- Pinch of ground allspice
- Pinch of ground cloves
- 2 pints vanilla ice cream

1. In a medium bowl, sprinkle the berries with the granulated sugar. Let stand at room temperature at least 1 hour and up to 2 hours.
2. Preheat the oven to 350°. Spread the walnuts on a baking sheet; toast for about 10 minutes, or until fragrant. Let cool slightly, then coarsely chop the nuts.
3. In a nonreactive medium saucepan, combine the vinegar, brown sugar, cinnamon, allspice and cloves. Bring to a boil over high heat. Cook until reduced to ½ cup, 7 to 10 minutes. Pour into a bowl; refrigerate until chilled.
4. Scoop the ice cream into eight bowls. Top with the berries and their exuded liquid; drizzle with the glaze. Garnish with the walnuts and serve.—NICO MARTIN

Individual Warm Berry Gratins

INDIVIDUAL WARM BERRY GRATINS

You can use any assortment of berries in these gratins.

6 SERVINGS

- ¾ pint strawberries, rinsed and dried
- ½ pint boysenberries or blackberries, picked over
- ½ pint raspberries, picked over
- 1 teaspoon kirsch or brandy
- 10 tablespoons sugar, or more to taste
- 4 large egg yolks
- ½ cup dry Champagne
- Ice water
- ¼ cup heavy cream

1. Hull the strawberries and slice lengthwise ¼ inch thick. In a large bowl, toss the strawberries, boysenberries, raspberries, kirsch and 2 tablespoons sugar. Add a little more sugar depending on the berries' sweetness (remember the topping will also add sweetness).
2. Place a heatproof bowl over a saucepan of simmering water; do not allow the bottom of the bowl

to touch the water. Add the egg yolks, Champagne and 4 tablespoons sugar and whisk together until the mixture holds its shape when the whisk is raised, about 6 minutes. Do not overcook or the eggs will scramble. Remove the bowl of sabayon from the heat and place it in a bowl of ice water to cool, whisking occasionally.

3. In a medium bowl, whip the heavy cream to soft peaks. Fold it into the sabayon.

4. Preheat the broiler. Divide the berries among six 5-inch gratin dishes and set the dishes on a baking sheet. Spread 2 tablespoons of the sabayon over each serving. Sprinkle the remaining 4 tablespoons sugar over the gratins. Slide the baking sheet under the broiler and cook for 3 to 4 minutes, just until the tops turn golden brown. Watch carefully; turn the baking sheet if necessary. Serve at once.—LINDSEY SHERE

Fruit Soup with Champagne

RASPBERRY FIRECRACKERS

For a simpler stuffing, fill each wonton with three small whole raspberries.

MAKES 36 FIRECRACKERS

- ½ pint fresh raspberries
- 2 ounces semisweet chocolate, finely grated
- 1 tablespoon granulated sugar
- 1 teaspoon finely grated orange zest
- 36 wonton skins
- 3 cups vegetable oil, for frying
- 1 tablespoon confectioners' sugar
- Ginger Caramel Sauce (optional; recipe follows)

1. In a small bowl, toss the raspberries with the chocolate, sugar and orange zest.

2. Place a wonton skin on a work surface; keep the remaining skins covered. Place ½ teaspoon filling in one corner and roll up diagonally to tightly enclose the filling. Twist the ends in opposite directions and pinch together to form a "firecracker." Repeat with the remaining skins and filling.

3. In a medium skillet, heat the oil to 375°. Fry the firecrackers, four at a time, until they are lightly browned, about 1 minute. With a slotted spoon, transfer to paper towels to drain and cool slightly.

4. Dust the firecrackers with confectioners' sugar. Serve warm on their own or with the sauce.

Ginger Caramel Sauce

MAKES ABOUT 1 CUP

- ½ cup plus 2 tablespoons heavy cream
- 2 teaspoons finely grated fresh ginger
- 1 cup sugar
- 1 teaspoon fresh lemon juice

1. In a small saucepan, simmer the ½ cup heavy cream with the ginger for about 10 minutes. Set the mixture aside.

2. In a second small heavy saucepan, cook the sugar with the lemon juice over low heat, stirring frequently, until the sugar caramelizes to a light brown color, 10 to 15 minutes. Being careful to avoid spatters, stir in the remaining 2 tablespoons of heavy cream and remove the caramel from the heat.

3. Strain the ginger cream into a bowl and whisk in the caramel until the sauce is smooth. Serve warm. (**MAKE AHEAD:** The sauce will keep refrigerated for up to 1 month. Rewarm over low heat before serving.) —ROSA ROSS

FRUIT SOUP WITH CHAMPAGNE LF

Any banana berry juice from the supermarket will work for this dessert.

6 SERVINGS

- 1 cup fresh pineapple juice
- 1 cup strawberry orange banana juice
- ½ cup fresh orange juice
- 2 tablespoons fresh lime juice
- 1 medium tart apple, peeled and cut into ½-inch balls or dice
- 1 star-anise pod
- 2 cups assorted berries, such as raspberries, blueberries, blackberries and strawberries
- 1 pint lemon sorbet
- ¾ cup Champagne
- 1 tablespoon shredded fresh basil

1. In a nonreactive medium saucepan, simmer the pineapple juice, strawberry juice, orange

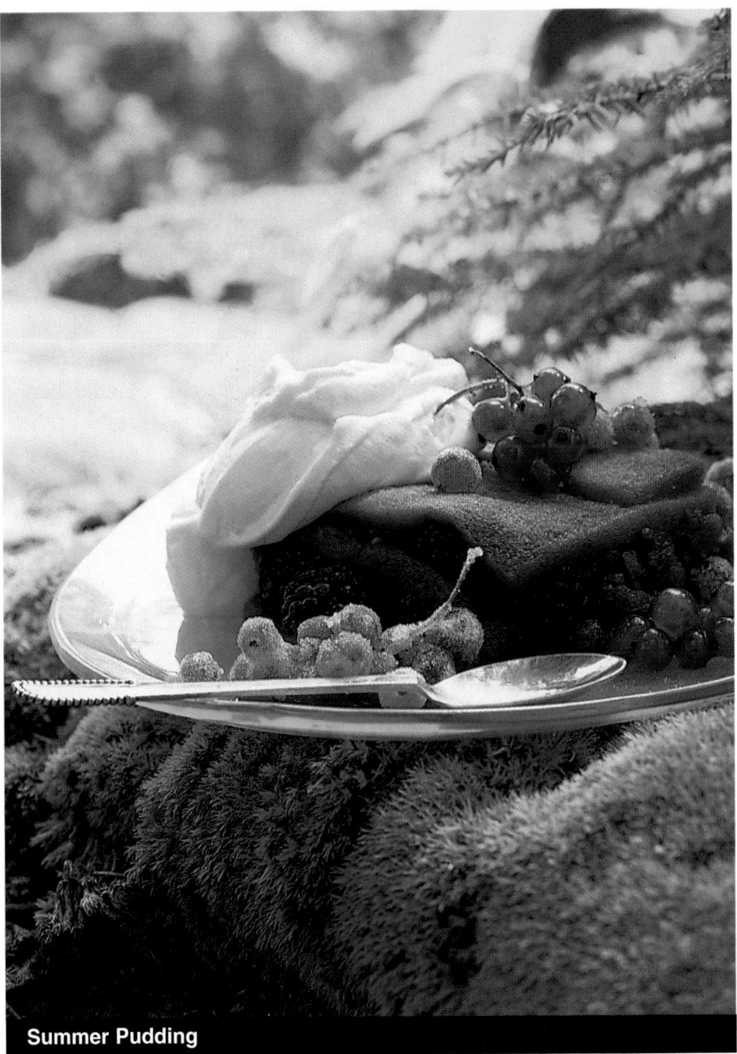
Summer Pudding

juice, lime juice, apple and star-anise pod over low heat until the apple is just tender, about 12 minutes. Transfer the fruit soup to a large bowl and refrigerate until chilled.

2. Discard the star anise and stir the berries into the soup. Divide the fruit soup among six bowls. Add a scoop of lemon sorbet and about 2 tablespoons of Champagne to each of the bowls and garnish with the basil.—HANS RÖCKENWAGNER

SUMMER PUDDING

This classic English dessert consists of layers of cooked berries and bread, which absorbs the sweet berry juice as the pudding sits overnight. To decorate the top of the pudding, crystallize red currants: Dip them in beaten egg white, sprinkle with sugar and then let dry on parchment paper at room temperature.

9 SERVINGS

18 very thin slices of white bread, such as Pepperidge Farm sandwich (about 10 ounces)
1½ pints red or black raspberries (about 4 cups), picked over
½ pint blackberries or boysenberries (about 2 cups), picked over
½ pint red currants (about 1 cup), stems removed
1 cup sugar
1 tablespoon kirsch or brandy
Lightly sweetened whipped cream, for serving

1. Line a 9-inch-square glass baking dish with plastic wrap, leaving enough overhang on all four sides to cover the finished pudding.

2. Trim the crusts from the bread. Place six slices in a tight overlapping layer in the bottom of the prepared dish. Place the raspberries, blackberries and currants in a heavy, medium, nonreactive skillet. Add the sugar and cook over moderate heat, stirring occasionally, until the berries yield some of their juices, about 5 minutes. Sprinkle the kirsch over the berries; remove from the heat.

3. Using a slotted spoon, spread a third of the berries over the bread in the dish. Cover with another layer of bread. Repeat the layering with the remaining berries and bread. Spoon half of the berry juice over the pudding. Refrigerate the remaining juice. Cover the pudding with the overhanging plastic wrap. Place another dish or pan on top of the pudding and weigh it down with some cans. Refrigerate the pudding overnight.

4. To serve, unwrap the top of the pudding and invert onto a platter. Cut into squares. Serve with the whipped cream and the reserved berry juice.—LINDSEY SHERE ➤

RED-CURRANT GELÉE WITH BLACKBERRIES

This is the ne plus ultra of gelatin desserts, a sophisticated combination of fresh berries and a soft jelly flavored with the juice of the berries.

10 SERVINGS

1½ pints red currants (3 cups), stems removed
9 tablespoons sugar
One ¼-ounce envelope gelatin
1½ pints blackberries (about 4½ cups), picked over
½ teaspoon kirsch
Mint sprigs, for garnish

1. In a nonreactive saucepan, bring the currants and 1½ cups of water to a boil over high heat. Reduce the heat and simmer for about 20 minutes. Line a strainer with a double layer of moistened cheesecloth and set over a nonreactive saucepan. Pour the currants into the strainer and let drip for 1 hour. Squeeze the cheesecloth gently to extract excess juice. You should have 2½ cups. If you don't, add a few tablespoons of water to make up the difference.

2. Place the currant juice over moderately low heat to warm slightly. Stir in 6 tablespoons of the sugar until dissolved. In a small saucepan, sprinkle the gelatin over ¼ cup of cold water and let stand 5 minutes to soften. Warm over low heat, stirring, until dissolved. Stir into the currant juice. Pour into a bowl, cover and refrigerate until set.

3. In a large bowl, crush about ¼ cup of the blackberries; stir in the remaining whole berries. Sprinkle the remaining 3 tablespoons sugar on top and toss. Let stand until the berries exude some of their juice, about 5 minutes. Stir in the kirsch.

4. To serve, scramble the chilled gelée with a fork (the mixture will be very loose) and spoon into dessert glasses or wineglasses. Spoon the berries and their juice on top, garnish with a mint sprig and serve.—LINDSEY SHERE

Red-Currant Gelée with Blackberries

KIRSCH

Kirsch, an eau-de-vie made from the fermented mash of small black wild cherries and their stones, heightens the flavor of many berries and other fresh summer fruits, such as cherries, apricots, peaches and nectarines. A touch is all that's needed to enhance the natural goodness of fruit.

BERRY REHAB

If you must use berries that haven't fully ripened, try one or more of the following to improve their flavor.

- **Spread the berries out in one layer on a baking sheet covered with a cloth towel; pick over and discard any bad ones. Leave uncovered at room temperature overnight or as long as their taste and texture continue to improve.**
- **Place berries on a baking sheet and put them in a 350° oven for five minutes. The heat releases their perfume; the effect lasts even after the berries have cooled.**
- **Intensify the flavor of bland berries by adding a bit of sugar and either lemon juice or balsamic vinegar.**
- **Mix several different berries to complement each other's flavors. Strawberries, blueberries and black raspberries add sweetness; currants and blackberries, tartness.**

Blackberry Soup with Peaches and Berries

BLACKBERRY SOUP WITH PEACHES AND BERRIES

Try this luscious fruit soup as a refreshing alternative to a rich dessert. Serve with your favorite crisp cookies.

6 SERVINGS

- 1½ pints blackberries, picked over (about 4½ cups)
- 6 tablespoons sugar, or more to taste
- ½ teaspoon kirsch, brandy or cassis (optional)
- 3 large ripe peaches (about 1½ pounds)
- 1 pint vanilla ice cream

1. Set aside 1½ cups of the blackberries. Place the remaining 3 cups berries and ½ cup of water in a nonreactive 3½-quart saucepan. Cover, bring to a simmer over moderate heat and cook until the berries have softened slightly and exuded their juices, about 5 minutes.

2. Transfer the cooked berries to a strainer and press through to remove the seeds. Stir in 3 tablespoons of the sugar until dissolved; sweeten with more sugar if desired. Refrigerate for 1 hour. Stir in the kirsch, if using.

3. Up to 2 hours before serving the dessert, peel the peaches, halve them and remove the pits. Working over a bowl, slice the peaches ⅛ to ¼ inch thick. Sprinkle the remaining 3 tablespoons sugar over the peach slices and toss them gently.

4. Ladle the chilled blackberry soup into six soup plates, arrange the peach slices in the soup and add a scoop of the vanilla ice cream and about six or seven of the reserved blackberries to each of the servings. Serve the soup at once.—LINDSEY SHERE ➤

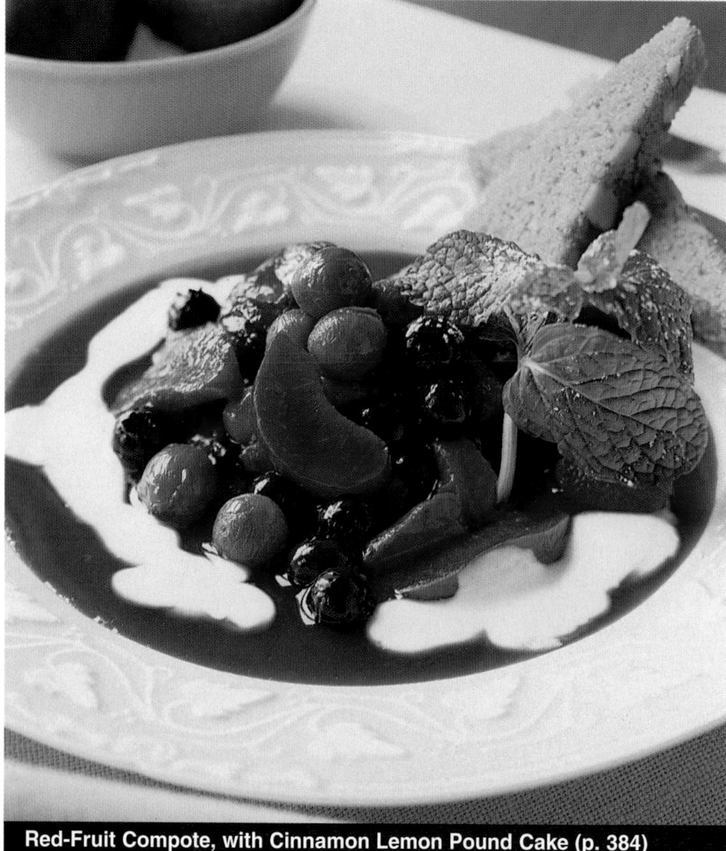
Red-Fruit Compote, with Cinnamon Lemon Pound Cake (p. 384)

BERRY ABC'S

• Use local fresh fruits in season for the most flavor.
• Choose the ripest, most fragrant berries with no soft spots or mold and no smell of fermentation.
• Buy organic berries so that you won't have to wash them (unless they're sandy or dirty). Washing will leach out the juice—and with it the flavor. The only berries that will survive washing with their taste more or less intact are the firmer ones, such as blueberries and strawberries. Raspberries and other delicate berries won't make it.
• If you must wash berries to remove dirt or pesticide residue, don't hull them first; a berry without its stem collects water. Rinse a few berries at a time in a colander, using lukewarm water. Gently pat dry with a soft cloth towel.
• Try to use the berries right away. Although most can be refrigerated for up to three days in a bowl or a basket lined with a paper towel, they'll lose some fragrance and taste.

RED-FRUIT COMPOTE

This delicious stew of plums, cherries, grapes, blueberries and strawberries is simple to assemble, cooks in minutes and, best of all, tastes even better if it's made ahead of time. If I'm short on time, I serve the compote with a wedge of store-bought buttery brioche or pound cake. If not, I make Cinnamon Lemon Pound Cake (p. 384).

8–10 SERVINGS

- 1 cup dry white wine
- 1 cup black-currant syrup or crème de cassis
- ⅓ cup fresh orange juice
- ¼ cup good-quality strawberry jam
- 1 tablespoon finely grated orange zest
- 1 pound red plums, such as Santa Rosa, halved, pitted and cut into wedges
- 1 pound Bing cherries, pitted
- 1 large fresh basil sprig
- 1 pound seedless red grapes, stemmed
- 1 pound blueberries
- 1 pound strawberries, hulled and quartered
- 1 cup sour cream or crème fraîche
- 2 tablespoons granulated sugar

Fresh mint sprigs, for garnish

1. In a nonreactive medium saucepan, combine the wine, black-currant syrup, orange juice, strawberry jam and orange zest. Bring to a boil over moderate heat; boil for 1 minute, stirring to thoroughly dissolve the jam.

2. Add the plums, cherries and basil to the pan and bring to a rolling boil; boil for 1 minute. With a slotted spoon, transfer the plums and cherries to a bowl. Add the grapes to the pan and boil for 30 seconds; transfer the grapes to the bowl of fruit.

Finally, add the blueberries and strawberries to the pan and bring just barely to a boil. Transfer the berries to the bowl with the slotted spoon.

3. Drain the juices from the fruit back into the saucepan and boil over moderate heat until reduced to 2 cups, about 10 minutes. Pour the reduced syrup over the fruit and let cool. Cover and refrigerate for a few hours or overnight.

4. Remove the basil sprig from the fruit. In a small bowl, combine the sour cream with the sugar and 2 tablespoons of water. Spoon 2 to 3 tablespoons of the fruit syrup onto each serving plate and spoon the fruit into the center. Garnish each serving with a mint sprig and 1 to 2 tablespoons of the sweetened sour cream.—JACQUES PÉPIN

BLUEBERRY COBBLER

Here's a simple-as-can-be, not-too-sweet version of this homey dessert and breakfast dish.

6–8 SERVINGS

- 2 pints blueberries (about 5 cups)
- 1 cup plus 2 teaspoons flour
- 5 tablespoons plus 2 teaspoons sugar
- 1 teaspoon kirsch
- ½ teaspoon finely grated lemon zest
- 2 teaspoons baking powder
- ¼ teaspoon salt
- 5 tablespoons unsalted butter
- ½ cup plus 1 tablespoon milk

Vanilla ice cream, for serving

1. Preheat the oven to 375°. Toss the blueberries with the 2 teaspoons flour, 4 tablespoons of the sugar, the kirsch and the lemon zest. Pour the blueberry mixture into a 9-by-12-inch oval baking dish.

2. Mix the remaining 1 cup flour with 1 tablespoon of the sugar, the baking powder and the salt. Cut the butter into the dry ingredients until the mixture resembles coarse meal. Stir in the ½ cup of milk to make a very soft dough.

3. Drop the dough by spoonfuls on top of the blueberry mixture. Dampen your hands with half of the remaining milk and spread out the dough to cover most of the fruit. Brush the top of the dough with the remainder of the milk. Sprinkle the surface of the cobbler with the remaining 2 teaspoons sugar.

4. Bake the cobbler for about 35 minutes, or until it is golden brown and the berries are bubbling. Serve warm with vanilla ice cream.—LINDSEY SHERE

ROSY APPLE CRISP

8 SERVINGS

One 10-ounce package of frozen raspberries in syrup, thawed

- 6 large Golden Delicious apples
- 2 tablespoons fresh lemon juice
- 1 cup packed old-fashioned rolled oats
- ⅓ cup packed light brown sugar
- 2½ tablespoons unsalted butter, cut into bits
- 1 teaspoon cinnamon

Lightly sweetened whipped cream or vanilla frozen yogurt

1. Drain the raspberries in a strainer set over a bowl to catch the syrup. Peel the apples and rub them with 1 tablespoon of the lemon juice. Quarter and core the apples, and then slice them crosswise ¼ inch thick. ➤

BLUEBERRIES FOR BREAKFAST

Tired of berries on your morning cereal? Here are three quick fixes:

BLUEBERRY SAUCE

In a nonreactive saucepan, mash 1 cup of blueberries with ¼ cup sugar. Add 1 cup of water and two 1-inch lemon zest strips. Cover and simmer for 15 minutes. Strain, return the berries to the pan and simmer until slightly thickened. Serve over pancakes or ice cream. (MAKES 1 CUP)

BLUEBERRIES IN CUSTARD SAUCE

Bring 1 cup of milk to a boil. In a bowl, whisk 1 large egg, 3 large egg yolks and 3 tablespoons sugar; gradually whisk in the hot milk. In a small saucepan, stir the mixture over low heat until it is slightly thickened. Strain and stir in 1 teaspoon vanilla extract and 1 cup blueberries. Serve warm or chilled. (2 SERVINGS)

BLUEBERRY BRÛLÉE

In a heatproof bowl, cover ½ cup of plain low-fat or nonfat yogurt with ⅓ cup blueberries. Mix 1 tablespoon each rolled oats and brown sugar with a pinch of cinnamon and sprinkle on top of the berries. Broil until toasted on top. (1 SERVING)

Rosy Apple Crisp

2. In a heavy nonreactive saucepan, toss the apples and the remaining 1 tablespoon lemon juice. Add the raspberry syrup, cover and cook over moderately low heat for 10 minutes. Stir gently, cover and cook for 5 minutes longer. Uncover and simmer, stirring occasionally, until just tender, about 5 minutes. Stir in the berries and remove from the heat.
3. In a large bowl, rub together the oats, sugar, butter and cinnamon. (**MAKE AHEAD:** The apples and oats can be refrigerated separately, covered, for up to 4 days.)
4. Preheat the oven to 350°. Spread the apple mixture in a 10-inch ceramic baking dish. Sprinkle the oats in a wide ring over the apples and bake the crisp for 30 to 35 minutes, or until the oats are toasted and the apples are bubbling around the edges. Serve warm with whipped cream or frozen yogurt.—DIANA STURGIS

APPLE BEIGNETS

These fritters are irresistible for dessert, breakfast or a snack.

4 SERVINGS

- 1½ cups plus 2 tablespoons all-purpose flour
- Salt
- 1¼ cups pale ale
- Vegetable oil, for deep-frying
- 2 Golden Delicious apples, peeled, cored and cut crosswise into ¼-inch rings
- Granulated or confectioners' sugar, for dusting

1. In a bowl, whisk the flour with a pinch of salt; gradually whisk in the ale until completely smooth. Let the batter rest for at least 30 minutes or up to 1 hour.

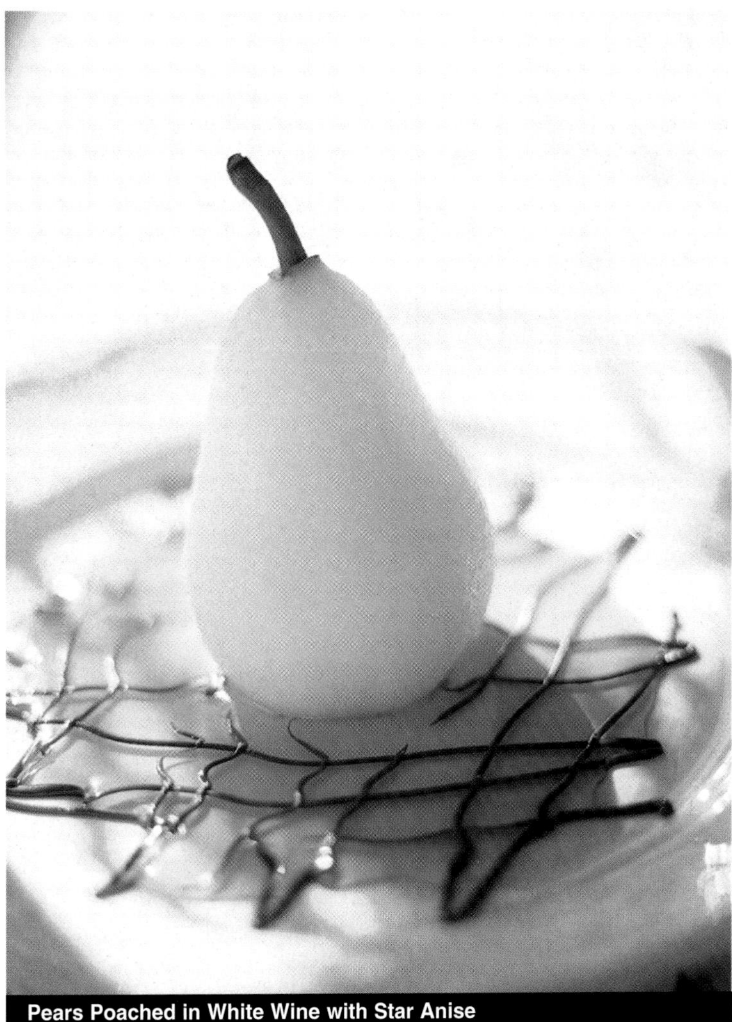

Pears Poached in White Wine with Star Anise

2. In a large deep skillet, heat 3 inches of oil to 370° over moderate heat. Stir the batter. Working in batches, dip the apples in the batter; fry, turning occasionally, until golden and crisp, about 6 minutes.
3. Using a slotted spoon or a wire skimmer, transfer the *beignets* to a baking sheet lined with paper towels to drain. Keep the cooked *beignets* warm in a low oven while frying the rest. Sprinkle the *beignets* with granulated sugar or sift confectioners' sugar over them and serve hot.—DOMINIQUE LALANDE

PEARS POACHED IN WHITE WINE WITH STAR ANISE

6 SERVINGS

- 6 firm ripe pears with stems
- 3 cups Riesling or Gewürztraminer
- ¼ cup sugar
- Zest of 1 lemon
- 2 star-anise pods, broken up
- ¼ cup mascarpone cheese
- 2 ounces semisweet or bittersweet chocolate, melted

1. Cut a thin slice from the base end of the pears so that they will stand upright. Peel the pears.
2. In a nonreactive saucepan just large enough to hold the pears, combine the wine and sugar and cook over low heat until the sugar dissolves. Stand the pears upright in the pan and add the lemon zest, star anise and enough water to just cover the fruit. Simmer over moderate heat, partially covered, until the pears are tender when pierced with a knife, about 30 minutes.
3. Transfer the pears to a plate. Boil the poaching liquid over moderately high heat until it has been reduced to ½ cup, about 30 minutes; strain. (MAKE AHEAD: The pears and syrup can be refrigerated for up to 1 day. Return to room temperature before proceeding.)
4. Using a melon baller, scoop out the core from the underside of each poached pear. Fill the cavities with the mascarpone. Stand the pears on six plates and spoon the syrup over them. Drizzle the melted chocolate on the plates and serve.—BRIGIT LEGERE BINNS

HOW TO BUY AND STORE PRODUCE

PEARS Summer pears turn yellow or crimson as they mature; most varieties you'll find in winter remain brown or green. To tell if a pear is ready to eat, see if it gives slightly near the stem when pressed. If the base is soft, the pear is probably overripe.
GRAPES Refrigerate in pierced plastic bags. Don't wash them first—the dusty residue provides protection.
PEACHES, NECTARINES, PLUMS The flesh should give a bit near the stem when pressed. If the fruit is hard, put it in a loosely closed paper bag at room temperature for several days; the fruit will emit ethylene gas, which speeds ripening.—JULIA CALIFANO

PEARS POACHED IN RED WINE

10 SERVINGS

- 5 cups dry red wine
- ½ cup plus 2 tablespoons sugar
- 10 firm but ripe pears

1. In a large nonreactive saucepan, combine the wine and sugar and bring to a simmer over moderate heat. Stir briefly to dissolve the sugar.
2. Peel the pears; if they don't stand upright, trim the bottoms slightly. Stand the pears in the saucepan and add just enough water to cover them. Place a heatproof plate on top of the pears to help keep them submerged in the liquid. Bring to a simmer over moderately high heat and cook until the pears are tender when pierced with a knife, about 20 minutes.
3. Using a slotted spoon, transfer the pears to a plate and let the poaching liquid cool completely. Return the pears to the liquid, cover with the plate and refrigerate at least 3 hours or overnight.
4. Transfer the chilled pears to a platter or plates. Strain the pear-poaching liquid into a clean nonreactive saucepan and boil over high heat until syrupy, about 35 minutes. Spoon the syrup over the pears.—F&W TEST KITCHEN

MELON BALLERS

Ask any cook to name a useless cooking gadget, and you are likely to hear more than a few unkind words about the humble melon baller. Okay, it's not as versatile as, say, a chef's knife. But in the spirit of fair play, FOOD & WINE would like to sing its praises. Besides coring poached pears for Pears Poached in White Wine with Star Anise, melon ballers are perfect for:

- **Neatly coring halved apples and pears.**
- **Stripping seeds from cucumbers and zucchini.**
- **Making tiny, elegant balls of ice cream.**
- **Scooping the seeds from cherry tomatoes in order to stuff them.**

PURE PEAR SOUFFLÉS

6 SERVINGS

- 4 large ripe Bartlett pears, peeled, cored and cut into thin wedges
- ¼ cup superfine sugar, plus more for dusting
- 2 large egg yolks
- 1 teaspoon kirsch or pear brandy
- ½ teaspoon fresh lemon juice
- 4 large egg whites
- Pinch of cream of tartar

1. In a heavy, nonreactive, medium saucepan, combine the pears with 2 tablespoons of water. Cover and cook the pears over moderate heat until they are tender, about 5 minutes. Put the cooked pears in a food processor and puree.

2. Return the pear puree to the saucepan. Cover the pan partially and cook the puree over moderately low heat, stirring often, until is very thick, about 25 minutes. Uncover the pan and cook, stirring, until the puree has been reduced to ¾ cup, about 10 minutes longer.

3. Scrape the pear puree into a large bowl. Stir in 2 tablespoons of the sugar and the egg yolks and let cool. Stir in the kirsch and the lemon juice.

4. Preheat the oven to 400°. Butter six ½-cup ramekins and dust them with superfine sugar. In a large stainless-steel bowl, combine the egg whites with the cream of tartar. Hold the bowl over low heat for about 30 seconds to warm the egg whites; do not allow the bowl to touch the heat source. Remove the bowl from the heat and beat the egg whites until firm peaks form; add the remaining 2 tablespoons sugar and beat the egg whites until glossy.

5. Using a large rubber spatula, fold one-third of the beaten egg whites into the pear puree to loosen it, then fold in the remaining egg whites just until blended. Spoon the mixture into the prepared ramekins and run your thumb and index finger around the rims to remove any drips and to help the soufflés rise evenly.

6. Bake the soufflés in the upper third of the oven for about 15 minutes, until golden and well risen. Serve at once.—MARCIA KIESEL

POMEGRANATE SORBET IN CHAMPAGNE

Look for large, heavy pomegranates to yield dark red juice. Serve the sorbet in shallow bowls in a pool of Champagne or pass glasses of Champagne alongside.

MAKES ABOUT 4 CUPS

- 7 large pomegranates, 6 halved crosswise, plus 1 peeled and separated into seeds (for garnish)
- ¾ cup plus 1 tablespoon sugar
- 2 teaspoons fresh lemon juice
- Chilled brut Champagne, for serving
- Candied Clementines (recipe follows)

1. Using a large citrus juicer, ream the pomegranate halves until they yield 2 cups of juice. Strain the pomegranate juice if necessary to remove any seeds or white pith. (**MAKE AHEAD:** The pomegranate juice can be frozen for up to 1 month.)

2. In a small saucepan, combine the sugar with ½ cup plus 2 tablespoons water. Simmer over moderate heat until the syrup is thick and reduced to ¾ cup, about 5 minutes. Let cool to room temperature. Stir the syrup and the lemon juice into the pomegranate juice. Transfer the mixture to an ice-cream maker; freeze according to the manufacturer's instructions. While the pomegranate sorbet is churning, chill a stainless-steel bowl in the freezer. As soon as the sorbet is done, transfer it to the chilled bowl. (**MAKE AHEAD:** The pomegranate sorbet can be frozen, covered, for up to 2 days.) ➤

CLEMENTINES

When making the Candied Clementines for the Pomegranate Sorbet in Champagne, work as fast as you can while dipping the clementine sections—the hot caramel syrup cools very quickly. Have ready a large oiled platter to hold the clementine sections. Also, have a few forks out for dipping the sections, in case the one you start with becomes too sticky.

Pomegranate Sorbet in Champagne

3. To serve, scoop the pomegranate sorbet into chilled dessert bowls or Champagne saucers. Pour Champagne around the sorbet, garnish with three or four clementines and sprinkle with the pomegranate seeds.

Candied Clementines

MAKES ABOUT 33 PIECES

- 3 clementines, peeled and separated into sections
- 1 cup sugar

1. Dry the clementine sections on a work surface until the outer membranes are papery, about 10 minutes.

2. In a small saucepan, combine the sugar with ½ cup of water and stir the mixture over moderate heat until the sugar dissolves. Brush down the sides of the saucepan using a wet pastry brush and simmer the syrup until it becomes a pale amber color and the temperature reaches 300° on a candy thermometer, about 10 minutes. Remove the pan from the heat.

3. Submerge a clementine section in the syrup. Using a fork, gently pick up the clementine section; tilt and shake the fork to drain off as much syrup as possible. Transfer the candied clementine to a large, lightly oiled platter. Shake the clementine section to release it from the fork and continue dipping the clementine sections in the syrup, one at a time.

4. Allow the candied clementine sections to harden in a cool dry place for 1 hour. Gently push the clementine sections to loosen them from the platter when they are ready to serve. (**MAKE AHEAD:** The candied clementines can be prepared up to 4 hours in advance. Keep away from heat and moisture.)—MARCIA KIESEL

Orange Gratin with Sabayon

ORANGE GRATIN WITH SABAYON **Q**

A rich yet airy sauce accented with amaretto envelops juicy citrus segments. If you're short on time, you can cut the peeled oranges crosswise into half-inch-thick rounds rather than sectioning them.

8 SERVINGS

- 5 medium navel oranges
- 6 large egg yolks
- ½ cup sugar
- ½ cup dry white wine
- ¼ cup amaretto liqueur

1. Using a sharp knife, peel the oranges, removing any bitter white pith. Cut in between the membranes to release the orange sections. Arrange the orange sections in a 10-inch gratin dish or quiche pan.

2. In the top of a double boiler set over simmering water, combine the egg yolks, sugar, white wine and amaretto. Whisk the sabayon constantly until thickened and light, about 5 minutes. (MAKE AHEAD: The sabayon can be refrigerated for up to 1 hour. Let the oranges stand at room temperature.)

3. Preheat the broiler. Put an oven rack about 6 inches from the heat. Spoon the sabayon over the orange sections and broil about 1 minute, until browned on top.—PEGGY RYAN

MUSCAT ZABAGLIONE WITH WINTER FRUITS

6 SERVINGS

- 1 navel orange
- 3 kiwis, peeled and thinly sliced
- 1 banana, peeled and thinly sliced
- ½ cup seedless red grapes, halved
- 3 large egg yolks
- ½ cup Bonny Doon Muscat Vin de Glacière
- ¼ cup granulated sugar
- 1½ teaspoons confectioners' sugar

1. Using a paring knife, peel the orange, removing all of the bitter white pith. Working over a bowl, cut in between the membranes to release the orange sections. Add the kiwis, banana and grapes.

2. Preheat the broiler. In a medium saucepan, bring 2 inches of water to a boil over moderate heat. Combine the egg yolks, the Muscat and the granulated sugar in a medium stainless-steel bowl. Using a handheld electric mixer, beat the egg-yolk mixture until foamy. Set the bowl over, but not touching, the boiling water and beat the mixture constantly at high speed until it is as thick as whipped cream, about 10 minutes. Set the bowl in ice water and beat the zabaglione until cool, 2 to 3 minutes.

3. Arrange the fruit mixture on six heatproof dessert plates and dollop the zabaglione on top. Set one dessert plate on a baking sheet and broil 3 inches from the heat until the zabaglione is browned, 5 to 10 seconds. Repeat with the remaining plates. Sift the confectioners' sugar lightly over the plates and serve immediately.—JIM DENEVAN

BANANA BRÛLÉE WITH CITRUS-FRUIT SALSA LF

6 SERVINGS

- 2 tablespoons slivered almonds
- 3 large tangerines
- 2 medium navel oranges
- 1 medium mango, peeled and cut into ½-inch dice
- 2 tablespoons honey
- 3 tablespoons brewed orange pekoe tea
- 1 tablespoon fresh lime juice
- ¼ teaspoon pure vanilla extract
- 9 finger bananas or 6 medium bananas, peeled and halved lengthwise
- 3 tablespoons light brown sugar

Fresh mint sprigs, for garnish

1. Preheat the oven to 350°. Toast the slivered almonds for about 7 minutes, or until they are golden and fragrant. Transfer the toasted almonds to a plate and let cool. ➤

BANANAS

Here are the most widely available banana varieties.

CAVENDISH, OR YELLOW, BANANAS

GREEN: Underripe with dark green skin that fades to pale green and mild white flesh that turns pale yellow and sweetens slightly as the bananas ripen. Cook the bananas before eating, but you don't need to remove the peel—it's edible.

SEMIRIPE: Firm and pale yellow with green-tinged ends; semisweet in flavor. Good for cooking in savory dishes and eating.

RIPE: Firm, rich yellow skin speckled with brown. Good for eating and pies.

VERY RIPE: Soft and fragrant, covered with brown spots. Best mashed, for baking in desserts and for making blender smoothies.

RED BANANAS

Plump with dull red black-streaked peel and pale pink-orange flesh. Very sweet, slightly dry. Good for cooking and eating.

LADYFINGER BANANAS

Short and stubby with sunny yellow flesh; very sweet and dry. Good for eating and cooking whole.

PLANTAINS

Bananas' vegetable cousins.

UNDERRIPE: Green skin and starchy texture; cook them before eating.

RIPE: Dark yellow skin that is streaked with black; usually cooked in both sweet and savory dishes.

2. Using a sharp knife, peel the tangerines and the oranges, removing as much of the bitter white pith as possible. Cut between the membranes of the tangerines and oranges to release the sections, then cut the sections into thirds; discard any seeds. Transfer the tangerine and orange pieces to a bowl, add the diced mango and toss to combine. In a small bowl, stir the honey into the brewed tea until dissolved. Fold the tea mixture into the fruit mixture and refrigerate until chilled.

3. Preheat the broiler. In a bowl, combine the lime juice and the vanilla extract. Arrange the halved bananas, cut-side up, in a single layer in a nonreactive baking dish. Brush the bananas with the lime-juice mixture and sprinkle with the brown sugar. Broil the bananas for about 3 minutes, or until caramelized. Let rest for 1 minute.

4. Fold the toasted almonds into the citrus-fruit salsa and spoon the salsa into six shallow soup bowls. Arrange the caramelized bananas on the salsa and spoon any liquid from the baking dish on top. Garnish with the mint sprigs and serve.—ALLEN SUSSER

GLAZED RED AND LADYFINGER BANANAS

4 SERVINGS

- 2 tablespoons unsalted butter
- 8 ripe ladyfinger bananas
- 4 ripe red bananas, halved lengthwise
- 1 vanilla bean, halved lengthwise
- 1 cup diced ripe pineapple (⅓ inch)
- ½ cup sweetened passion-fruit juice*

*Available at specialty-food stores and Latin American markets.

Melt the butter in a nonreactive skillet. Add the bananas in an even layer, with the red bananas cut-side down. Tuck the vanilla-bean halves between the bananas and cook over moderately high heat for 4 minutes. Turn the ladyfinger bananas so that they brown all over; brown the red bananas on the bottom only. Turn the red bananas, add the diced pineapple and cook until golden, about 2 minutes. Add the passion-fruit juice and boil over high heat until reduced to a glaze, about 4 minutes. Serve warm.—MARCIA KIESEL

WINTER-FRUIT COMPOTE WITH OATMEAL WEDGES LF

Apple juice, molasses and dried fruits sweeten this nutty dessert.

12 SERVINGS

- 1 cup quick-cooking oats
- ¼ cup sliced almonds
- 10 dried apricots, minced
- 10 pitted prunes, minced
- 3 large dried Calimyrna figs, stems removed and minced
- 1¼ cups unsweetened apple juice
- ½ cup all-purpose flour
- 3 tablespoons unsalted butter, softened
- 1 teaspoon cinnamon
- ½ teaspoon baking soda
- Pinch of salt
- 3 tablespoons unsulphured molasses
- 1 teaspoon pure vanilla extract
- Vegetable cooking spray

Winter-Fruit Compote

1. Preheat the oven to 400°. Toast the quick-cooking oats and the sliced almonds on separate baking sheets in the oven for about 7 minutes, or until both are golden. Let cool.

2. In an ovenproof saucepan, bring the apricots, prunes and figs and the apple juice to a boil over high heat. Reduce the heat to low and simmer for 5 minutes. Transfer the saucepan to the oven and bake the fruit for about 30 minutes, stirring occasionally, until most of the liquid has evaporated. Let the fruit cool. Lower the oven temperature to 350°.

3. In a bowl, combine the flour with the softened butter, the cinnamon, baking soda and salt. Add the toasted oats and mix until the butter is distributed. Add the unsulphured molasses and the vanilla extract and mix until a dough forms. Shape the oatmeal dough into a disk, cover the disk with plastic and refrigerate until the dough is chilled, or for up to 2 days.

4. Lightly coat a 10-inch springform pan with cooking spray and line it with parchment paper. Press the oatmeal dough in the bottom of the prepared pan to a ¼-inch thickness. Bake the oatmeal crust for about 15 minutes, or until it is lightly browned. Allow it to cool slightly, then remove the sides of the springform pan. Invert the crust onto a plate and peel off the parchment paper.

5. Cut the oatmeal crust into twelve wedges. Spoon the fruit compote into a bowl, sprinkle with the toasted almonds and serve the compote with the oatmeal wedges.—BOB CHAMBERS

CHAPTER 20

~

OTHER DESSERTS

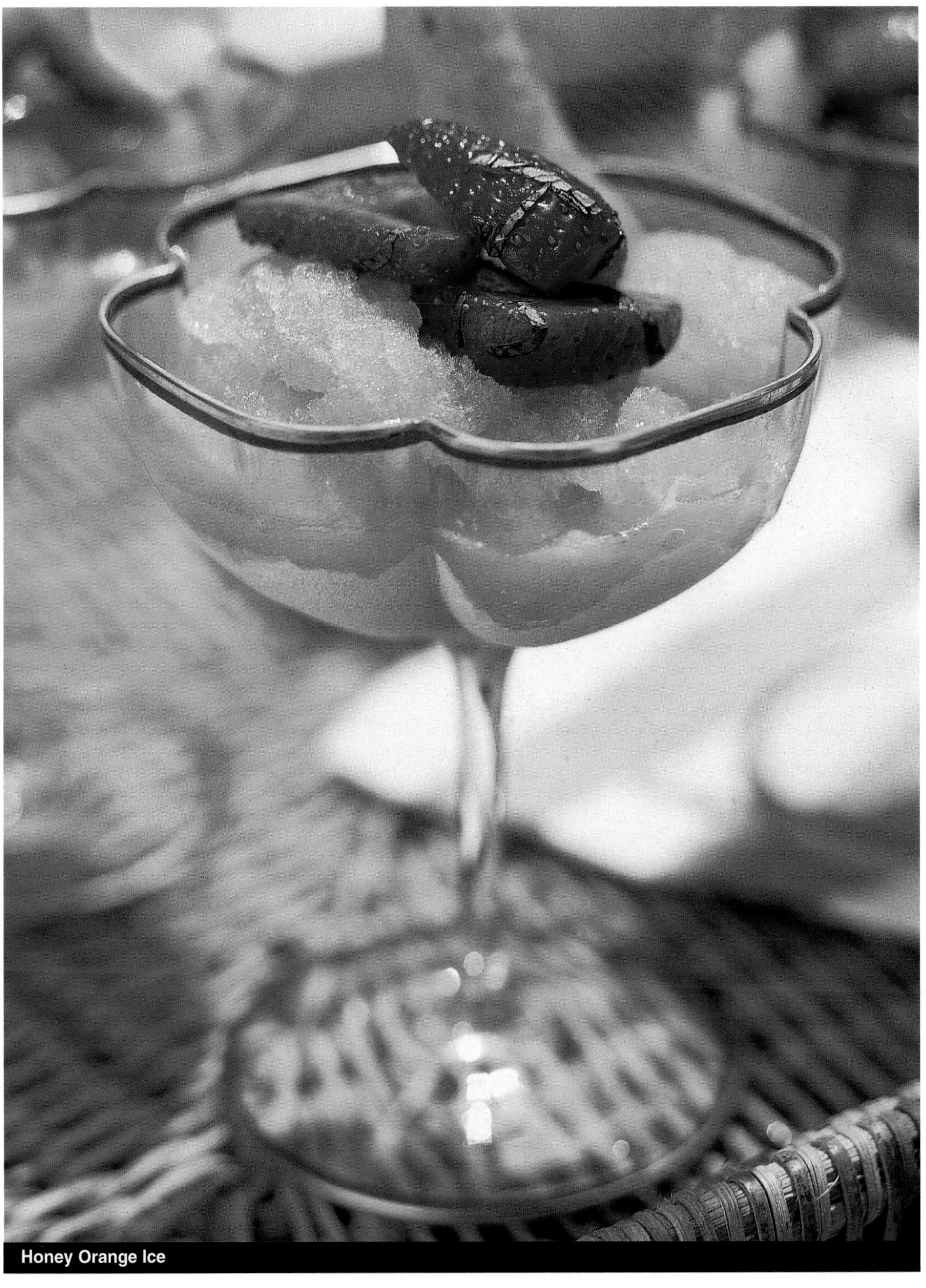

Honey Orange Ice

HONEY ORANGE ICE

MAKES ABOUT 1 QUART

2½ cups fresh orange juice
1 cup honey
1 teaspoon pure vanilla extract

Combine all the ingredients in a bowl. Pour into a 9-by-13-inch nonreactive baking dish and freeze until firm, at least 8 hours or overnight. Just before serving, scrape into fine crystals using one or two forks. Transfer to tall glasses and serve.—WAYNE BRACHMAN

WATERMELON GRANITA LF

To make this simple, refreshing dessert, you'll need about four pounds of watermelon.

6 SERVINGS

⅓ cup sugar
5 cups 1-inch watermelon cubes, seeds removed
2 tablespoons fresh lime juice
6 thin watermelon wedges

1. In a small saucepan, combine the sugar with ⅓ cup of water and bring to a boil over high heat, stirring, until the sugar dissolves. Transfer to a blender or food processor, add half the melon cubes and the lime juice and pulse until smooth. Add the remaining melon cubes and blend until smooth.
2. Pass through a coarse strainer, pressing on the solids. Transfer to a 9-by-13-inch nonreactive baking dish. Freeze, stirring every 30 minutes with a fork, until all the liquid has frozen completely, about 3 hours. (**MAKE AHEAD:** The granita can be frozen up to 2 days. Stir before serving.) Spoon into tall glasses or bowls; garnish with the melon wedges.—JIM ACKARD

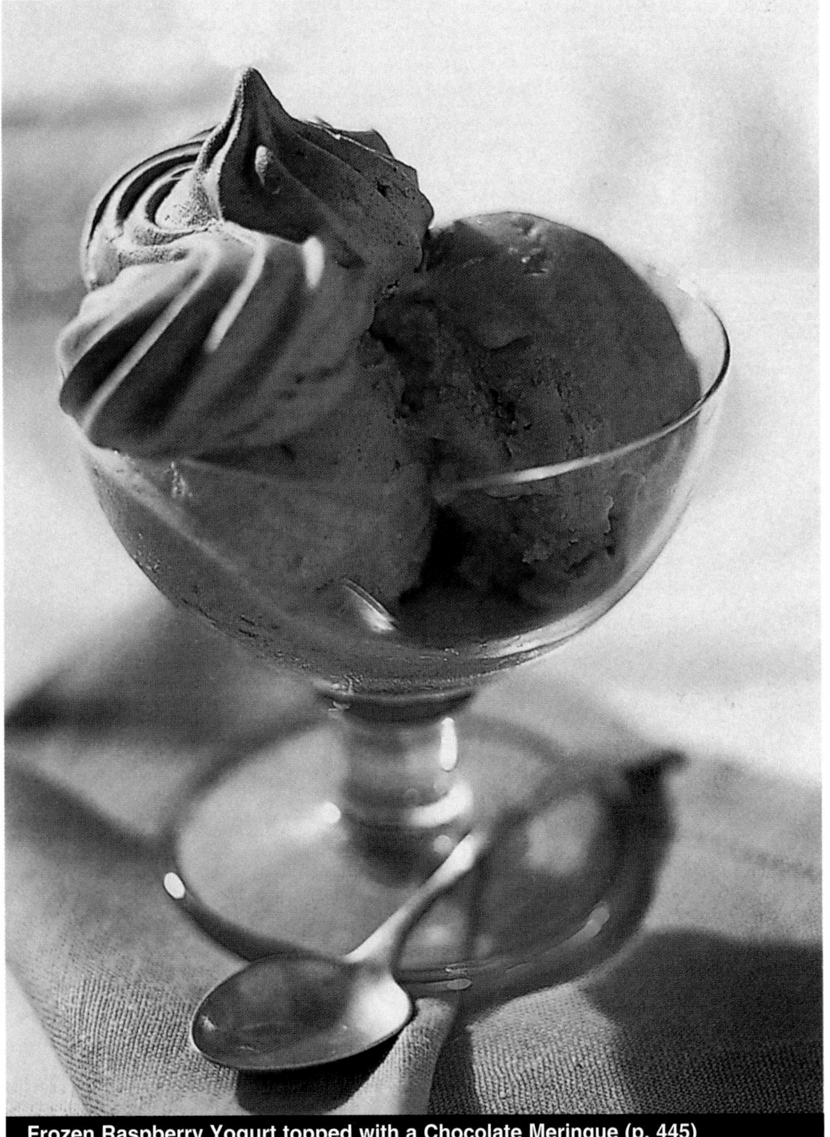

Frozen Raspberry Yogurt topped with a Chocolate Meringue (p. 445)

FROZEN RASPBERRY YOGURT LF

4 SERVINGS

2 pints fresh raspberries
1 cup sugar
2 cups plain low-fat yogurt
Fresh mint sprigs, for garnish

1. In a blender or food processor, puree the raspberries and the sugar. Pass through a fine sieve.
2. In a bowl, whisk the yogurt until smooth and stir in the raspberry puree. Pour into an ice-cream maker and freeze according to the manufacturer's instructions. Transfer the frozen yogurt to a container and freeze until firm. Spoon the yogurt into tall glasses, garnish with mint sprigs and serve.—HUBERT KELLER ➤

RUM SMOOTHIE PARFAITS Q

Before dinner, put four wineglasses and the blender canister in the freezer to chill, and then prepare the ingredients for the parfaits. Make the dessert immediately before serving it.

4 SERVINGS

- ¼ cup dark rum
- 1½ pints (3 cups) hard-frozen good-quality vanilla ice cream
- ½ cup golden raisins or any dried fruit
- 1 tablespoon ground or finely chopped nuts, such as almonds or pecans
- 4 fresh mint sprigs, for garnish
- Crisp sugar cookies, for serving (optional)

1. Add the dark rum to the ice-cold blender canister and scoop in the hard-frozen vanilla ice cream. Blend the ice cream with the rum for 20 to 30 seconds or until the mixture is smooth, stopping now and then to break up the lumps.

2. Pour the softened ice-cream mixture into chilled wineglasses and sprinkle the golden raisins and the chopped nuts over the top. Garnish the ice-cream parfaits with the mint sprigs and serve with crisp sugar cookies, if desired.—PAUL GRIMES

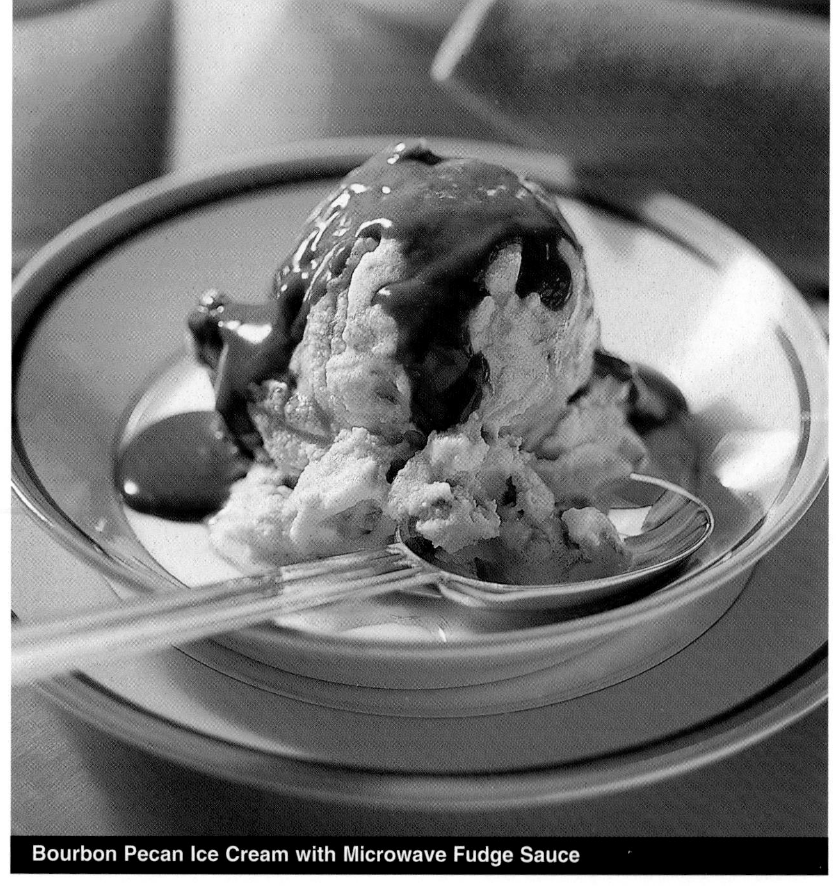

Bourbon Pecan Ice Cream with Microwave Fudge Sauce

BOURBON PECAN ICE CREAM WITH MICROWAVE FUDGE SAUCE

Lightly salted pecans give this whiskey-flavored ice cream an extra dimension that simply adding salt can't equal. If you want the pecans to stay as crisp as possible, add them to the ice cream at the same time you stir in the bourbon. This recipe has been adapted from The Book of Bourbon *(Chapters).*

MAKES ABOUT 1½ QUARTS

- 3 cups half-and-half
- ½ cup (packed) light brown sugar
- ¼ cup granulated sugar
- 1¼ cups broken pecan pieces (4 ounces)
- 3 tablespoons bourbon or Tennessee whiskey
- Microwave Fudge Sauce, for serving (recipe follows)

Q & A

Q: How can I melt chocolate without having it seize up or scorch?

A: Put the chocolate into a Pyrex cup and set the cup in a small pan of simmering water (the water should come halfway up the side of the cup). Stir often; remove when liquefied. Or, if you have a microwave oven, put the chocolate in a Pyrex cup and cook at medium heat for a few seconds. Watch carefully to make sure the chocolate doesn't burn, and stir often to distribute the unmelted pieces.—MARION CUNNINGHAM

1. In a large food processor, combine the half-and-half, brown sugar and granulated sugar and blend for 2 minutes, or until the sugars are thoroughly dissolved. Stir in the pecan pieces and refrigerate until chilled, about 1 hour.
2. Pour the mixture into an ice-cream maker and freeze according to the manufacturer's instructions until moderately set. Stir in the bourbon and continue freezing until the ice cream is firm. Serve immediately with the fudge sauce, or pack the ice cream into an airtight container, cover tightly with plastic wrap and freeze for up to 3 days.

Microwave Fudge Sauce

MAKES ABOUT 3½ CUPS

- ½ pound semisweet chocolate, coarsely chopped
- 2 sticks unsalted butter (½ pound)
- ⅔ cup evaporated skim milk
- ⅓ cup light corn syrup
- ¼ cup packed light brown sugar
- 1 teaspoon pure vanilla extract
- 2 to 5 tablespoons bourbon or Tennessee whiskey

In a heatproof bowl in a microwave oven, heat the chocolate with the butter at medium power until it is almost melted. Remove from the oven and stir until smooth. Add the evaporated milk, corn syrup, light brown sugar and vanilla; stir until the sugar melts and the sauce is completely smooth. Stir in the bourbon just until incorporated. Serve warm. (**MAKE AHEAD:** The sauce can be refrigerated for up to 2 weeks.) —MARDEE HAIDIN REGAN

ICE-CREAM SANDWICHES

Chocolate ice cream and a pair of sauces dress up the humble ice-cream sandwich. The coffee sauce is a delicious alternative to the usual caramel.

8 SERVINGS

ICE-CREAM SANDWICHES:

- 1 stick (4 ounces) unsalted butter
- 3 ounces bittersweet chocolate, coarsely chopped
- ½ cup sugar
- 1 large egg
- 1½ tablespoons strong brewed coffee, at room temperature
- 1¼ teaspoons pure vanilla extract
- ¾ cup all-purpose flour
- 2 tablespoons unsweetened cocoa powder
- ½ teaspoon baking powder
- ⅛ teaspoon cinnamon
- ⅛ teaspoon salt
- 2 pints good-quality coffee ice cream

CHOCOLATE SAUCE:

- 1 tablespoon unsalted butter
- ⅔ cup heavy cream
- 6 tablespoons milk
- ¼ cup tightly packed brown sugar
- ¼ cup plus 1 tablespoon unsweetened cocoa, sifted

COFFEE SAUCE:

- ⅔ cup brewed espresso
- 1⅓ cups plus 2 tablespoons sugar

1. Make the ice-cream sandwiches: Preheat the oven to 325°. Butter a 10-by-15-inch rimmed baking sheet and line it with parchment paper. Butter the parchment paper and refrigerate the baking sheet until the butter is firm, about 15 minutes.
2. In a small saucepan, melt the butter and the chopped bittersweet chocolate over low heat, stirring occasionally. Allow the chocolate to cool.
3. In a medium bowl, beat the sugar and the egg until blended. Beat in the brewed coffee, the vanilla extract and the melted bittersweet chocolate. Sift together the flour, cocoa powder, baking powder, cinnamon and salt. Stir the dry ingredients into the chocolate mixture until combined. Spread the chocolate batter out to the edges of the prepared baking sheet in an even layer and smooth the top. Bake the chocolate wafer for about 15 minutes, or until the center is just set but not dry. Allow the wafer to cool in the baking sheet for 15 minutes.
4. Run a knife around the edge of the chocolate wafer. Cover the baking sheet with a cutting board and invert; peel off the parchment paper. Allow the wafer to cool completely. ➤

CANE VS. BEET SUGAR

Because the chemical composition of sugar from a sugar beet and from sugarcane is identical, it makes no difference if you use cane or beet sugar. They taste, smell and behave exactly the same. Beet sugar is more abundant. Unless a package is marked "pure cane" sugar, it's a good bet that it's beet sugar.—CAROLE BLOOM

Ice-Cream Sandwich

5. Cut the chocolate wafer in half to form two 7½-by-10-inch rectangles. Spread the coffee ice cream evenly on one of the rectangles and cover it with the other rectangle. Poke a few holes in the top of the ice-cream sandwich with a fork or a toothpick for decoration. Wrap the ice-cream sandwich in plastic wrap and freeze it until firm, at least 2 hours. (**MAKE AHEAD:** The ice-cream sandwich can be frozen for up to 2 days.)

6. Make the chocolate sauce: In a small saucepan, melt the butter in the heavy cream and the milk over moderate heat. Stir in the brown sugar and boil, stirring occasionally, until the mixture is slightly thickened, about 3 minutes. Remove the pan from the heat and then whisk in the cocoa until the sauce is smooth. (**MAKE AHEAD:** The chocolate sauce can be refrigerated for up to 2 days. Rewarm before serving.)

7. Make the coffee sauce: In a small saucepan, combine the brewed espresso and the sugar and bring the mixture to a boil. Cook over moderately low heat until the coffee syrup is slightly thickened and coats the back of a spoon, about 18 minutes. Remove the pan from the heat; the sauce will continue to thicken as it cools.

8. To serve, cut the ice-cream sandwich into eight triangles. Drizzle the coffee sauce in a spiral onto each of eight dessert plates. Set one ice-cream-sandwich triangle in the center of each of the plates and spoon some of the warm chocolate sauce over the top of each triangle.—ALI SEEDSMAN

BAKED-ALASKA SNOWBALLS

6 SERVINGS

CARAMEL SAUCE:

- ½ cup granulated sugar
- ¼ teaspoon fresh lemon juice
- ½ cup heavy cream

CHOCOLATE SAUCE:

- 2 ounces bittersweet chocolate, finely chopped
- ¼ cup heavy cream

ICE CREAM AND CHOCOLATE-CRUMB CRUSTS:

- 1 pint coffee ice cream
- 1¼ cups finely ground chocolate wafers (about 5 ounces)
- 1 tablespoon confectioners' sugar
- 5 tablespoons unsalted butter, melted

MERINGUE TOPPING:

- 3 large egg whites, at room temperature
- ½ cup superfine sugar
- ¼ teaspoon cream of tartar

1. Make the caramel sauce: In a small, heavy saucepan, stir together the granulated sugar and lemon juice. Cook over high heat, washing down the side of the pan occasionally with a wet pastry brush, until the sugar is a dark

BASIC MERINGUE TYPES

There are three types of meringues. For all of them, the basic proportion of sugar to egg whites is two to one by weight (one-quarter cup of sugar for each egg white). This can be reduced to as little as one to one for a thinner mixture for topping a pie, for example.

SIMPLE OR COLD MERINGUE **is used in angel food cake, macaroons and delicate baked meringue shells to hold fruit, whipped cream and ice cream, as well as *oeufs à la neige* (snow eggs), a classic dessert consisting of poached meringue in custard. For a simple meringue, beat egg whites until they reach the soft-peak stage, then gradually add the sugar and beat until the whites are stiff and glossy but not dry. Since this meringue isn't cooked, use superfine sugar; it dissolves more easily than granulated.**

COOKED OR WARM MERINGUE **is a stable mixture that is good for pie toppings, baked Alaska, dacquoise layers, icings and dried meringue baskets. Heat the sugar and unbeaten egg whites together until they are warm to the touch and the sugar dissolves, then beat on high speed until the meringue is stiff, glossy and cool. Granulated sugar is fine for cooked meringue, since heating the sugar will dissolve it.**

ITALIAN OR BOILED MERINGUE **is the sturdiest one of all. It is used for unbaked foods, such as marshmallows, icings and buttercreams. To make an Italian meringue, heat a sugar syrup to the firm-ball stage (about 244° to 248°), pour it into the partially beaten egg whites and beat until the whites are stiff and cool. Use granulated sugar when making these meringues.**

brown. Reduce the heat to moderate and pour in the cream in a thin stream, stirring; watch out for spatters. Bring to a boil, washing down the sides of the pan; boil over moderately high heat for 3 minutes. Pour into a bowl.

2. Make the chocolate sauce: Place the chocolate in a small bowl. In a small saucepan, bring the cream to a boil. Pour over the chocolate; stir until melted. (**MAKE AHEAD:** The sauces can be refrigerated for up to 4 days. Rewarm on low heat or microwave briefly. Whisk before serving.)

3. Prepare the ice cream: Scoop six ⅓-cup balls of the ice cream onto a plate lined with plastic wrap. Freeze while you proceed.

4. Make the chocolate-crumb crusts: Preheat the oven to 350°. In a food processor, finely grind the chocolate wafers with the confectioners' sugar; transfer to a bowl. Stir in the butter. Spoon 3 tablespoons of the crumbs into the center of six 3-inch fluted tartlet pans. Press the crumbs firmly and evenly on the bottom and up the sides of the pans. The crusts should be about ¼ inch thick.

5. Place the crusts on a baking sheet and bake for 10 minutes. Transfer to a rack to cool. (**MAKE AHEAD:** The crusts can be made 1 day ahead. Tap the crusts out of the pans, wipe the pans and return the crusts. Stack, wrap in plastic and store at room temperature.)

6. Slip the tartlet shells out of their pans and place on a baking sheet lined with parchment paper. Place an ice-cream ball in the center of each tartlet. Freeze.

7. Prepare the dessert plates: Spoon about 2 tablespoons of the caramel sauce onto each of six warm dessert plates. Dot or swirl the chocolate sauce onto the caramel sauce.

8. Make the meringue topping: Preheat the oven to 500°. Place the egg whites and the superfine sugar in the large bowl of a standing electric mixer and set it over a saucepan of barely simmering water; don't let the bottom of the bowl touch the water. Whisk the whites vigorously until they are warm. Then beat the egg whites with the mixer at high speed until foamy. Without stopping the machine, add the cream of tartar and beat until stiff and glossy, about 5 minutes.

9. Remove the sheet of tartlets from the freezer. Using a metal icing spatula or a pastry bag fitted with a #5 star tip (about ½ inch), completely cover the ice cream with meringue, sealing at the rim of the tartlet shells.

10. Bake the tartlets for about 1 minute, or until the meringues

Baked-Alaska Snowballs

are nicely browned; watch carefully. Immediately place the tartlets on the prepared dessert plates and serve.—PEGGY CULLEN

CHOCOLATE MERINGUES

MAKES 2 DOZEN MERINGUES

- 2 large egg whites
- ¼ cup plus ½ tablespoon granulated sugar
- ¼ cup confectioners' sugar
- 1 tablespoon plus ¾ teaspoon cocoa powder

1. Preheat the oven to 225°. Line a baking sheet with parchment paper. In a bowl, preferably copper, beat the egg whites on medium speed until frothy, 2 to 3 minutes. Gradually add 1½ tablespoons of the granulated sugar and beat for 1 minute. On high speed, beat in the remaining 3 tablespoons granulated sugar; beat until the egg whites are stiff and glossy, about 2 minutes.

2. In a bowl, sift the confectioners' sugar with the cocoa and gently fold into the meringue until incorporated. Transfer to a pastry bag fitted with a large plain or star tip and pipe out two dozen 2½-inch-long swirls, spacing them 1 inch apart.

3. Bake the chocolate meringues in the middle of the oven for about 1¼ hours, until the swirls are dry and puffed. Turn off the heat and leave the meringues in the oven for 10 more minutes. Allow the meringues to cool on the baking sheet, then remove them from the parchment paper. (**MAKE AHEAD:** The chocolate meringues can be stored for up to 1 week in an airtight container.) —HUBERT KELLER ➤

TEN STEPS TO MASTERING MERINGUES

1. START WITH EGGS AT ROOM TEMPERATURE. Warm whites expand more than cold ones; some recipes even call for heating them.

2. SEPARATE THE EGGS CAREFULLY. The yolk contains fat, which prevents the white from reaching full volume when beaten. Separate the eggs one by one, dropping the white into a small clean bowl, then transferring it to your mixing bowl. If a yolk breaks, you won't contaminate an entire batch of whites. If only a tiny speck of yolk gets in, scoop it out with an egg shell.

3. KEEP YOUR UTENSILS CLEAN. Because you want to prevent the egg whites from coming in contact with fat, make sure all your utensils are grease-free. Wash them in warm soapy water, rinse thoroughly and dry. Rub the beater and bowl with a paper towel moistened with white vinegar. Don't use a plastic bowl; it is likely to be coated with residual fat that is hard to remove.

4. STORE THE EGG WHITES PROPERLY. If setting aside for later use, place them in a small bowl and cover with plastic wrap. You can refrigerate whites for up to four days—bring them to room temperature before using—or freeze them in an airtight container up to three months. (To measure for use, remember that there are about seven large egg whites in one cup, and that one large white weighs about one ounce.)

5. USE A STANDING ELECTRIC MIXER. While a thin wire whisk or a hand-held electric mixer works well, a standing electric mixer produces the best volume since it beats strongly and evenly. It is also the most convenient tool for the purpose, because while the eggs beat, which often takes a long time, you can do something else.

6. ADD CREAM OF TARTAR. This crystalline powdery acid, which forms on the inside of wine barrels, makes beaten egg whites more stable. Add it when they become foamy. Use about one-half teaspoon for every eight whites.

7. BEAT SLOWLY AT FIRST. Start on slow or medium speed; as the whites become foamy, move up to high. The gradual increase helps build stability. Without stopping the mixer, add the sugar slowly when the whites reach soft peaks. Continue beating until the whites have reached the full volume specified in the recipe.

8. FOLD THE MERINGUE GENTLY. When folding ingredients into a meringue, such as flour for angel food cake or nuts for dacquoise, the object is to deflate the egg whites as little as possible. Add the ingredients to the bowl and, using a wire whisk, large rubber spatula or clean hand, cut through the mixture and scoop around and under, folding in a rolling motion and rotating the bowl as you work.

9. GET THE MERINGUE INTO THE OVEN FAST. The longer it sits, the more time it has to break down.

10. DON'T MAKE MERINGUE ON A RAINY DAY. Meringues are hygroscopic: They absorb moisture like a sponge. On a wet or humid day, they weep, which means they collapse. For the same reason, fill meringue shells as close to serving time as possible.

Crème au Chocolat

CRÈME AU CHOCOLAT

This recipe comes from the book Jacques Pépin's Kitchen: Cooking with Claudine *(KQED).*

4 SERVINGS

1 tablespoon instant coffee granules
1½ cups milk
1 large egg
1 large egg yolk
¼ cup sugar
1½ tablespoons all-purpose flour
5 ounces bittersweet chocolate, coarsely chopped
1 tablespoon sliced almonds, toasted
Butter cookies, for serving

1. In a medium saucepan, dissolve the coffee in the milk; bring to a boil. Meanwhile, in a bowl, whisk the whole egg, the egg yolk and the sugar. Whisk in the flour.
2. Gradually whisk 1 cup of the hot milk into the egg mixture, then whisk the loosened mixture back into the remaining milk in the saucepan. Bring to a boil and cook over moderate heat, whisking constantly, until the custard is thickened.
3. Strain the hot custard into a bowl. Add the chopped bittersweet chocolate and stir occasionally until the mixture is smooth. Let cool, then refrigerate until cold. (**MAKE AHEAD:** The *crème au chocolat* can be refrigerated for up to 4 days.)
4. Spoon the *crème au chocolat* into four dessert bowls or cups. Sprinkle with the toasted almonds and serve with butter cookies.—JACQUES PÉPIN

CHOCOLATE PÂTÉ WITH CHAMPAGNE SABAYON

The leftover sabayon can be passed separately or served the next day with berries.

4 SERVINGS

5 ounces bittersweet chocolate, coarsely chopped
½ cup cold heavy cream
½ cup milk
2 large egg yolks
2 tablespoons sugar
1 tablespoon orange-flavored liqueur
¼ teaspoon cinnamon
About 1 cup Champagne Sabayon (recipe follows)
½ cup fresh raspberries

1. Butter four ½-cup ramekins and line them with plastic wrap, allowing a 2-inch overhang. In a bowl set over a pan of simmering water, stir the chopped bittersweet chocolate until it is melted. Allow the chocolate to cool. In a bowl, whip the cold heavy cream until it holds firm peaks. Allow the whipped cream to come to room temperature.
2. In a saucepan, bring the milk to a simmer. In a bowl, beat the egg yolks and sugar, then whisk in the hot milk. Return the mixture to the saucepan and whisk over moderate heat until thickened, about 3 minutes; do not let it boil. Whisk in the orange liqueur and the cinnamon.
3. Stir the milk mixture into the melted chocolate and let cool. Gently fold in the whipped cream. Spoon the pâté mixture into the prepared ramekins and refrigerate until very firm, at least 4 hours or overnight.
4. Remove the chocolate pâtés from the ramekins, invert them onto plates and peel off the plastic wrap. Spoon ¼ cup of the Champagne Sabayon around each of the pâtés and garnish with fresh raspberries.

Champagne Sabayon

MAKES ABOUT 2½ CUPS

4 large egg yolks
⅓ cup Champagne
¼ cup sugar
Pinch of salt
½ cup heavy cream

In a bowl, combine the egg yolks, the Champagne, the sugar and the salt. Set the bowl over a saucepan of gently simmering water and whisk constantly until the mixture is thickened, about 5 minutes. Remove the bowl from the heat and whisk occasionally until the sabayon is cool. In another bowl, beat the heavy cream until it holds firm peaks, then fold the whipped cream into the Champagne Sabayon. Refrigerate the sabayon until chilled, for at least 1 hour. (**MAKE AHEAD:** The Champagne Sabayon can be refrigerated for up to 1 day.)—CARINA JOST

CHOCOLATE MOLE BREAD PUDDING Q

10–12 SERVINGS

- 3 cups heavy cream
- 1½ cups half-and-half
- 12 ounces semisweet chocolate chips
- 2 teaspoons pure chile powder, preferably ancho
- 1 teaspoon cinnamon
- ½ teaspoon ground cloves
- ½ teaspoon salt
- 3 large eggs
- 3 large egg yolks
- ½ cup sugar
- 1 medium loaf of French bread (about ½ pound), cut into 1-inch cubes

1. In a medium saucepan, bring the heavy cream and the half-and-half just to a boil over high heat. Put the semisweet chocolate chips in a large bowl, add the hot cream mixture and stir until smooth. Stir in the pure chile powder, cinnamon, ground cloves and salt.

2. Preheat the oven to 325°. In a large bowl, lightly beat the eggs and the egg yolks with the sugar. Stir 1 cup of the chocolate cream into the egg mixture, then add the egg mixture to the remaining chocolate cream, stirring until smooth. Add the cubes of French bread and toss to coat. Allow the bread to soak in the chocolate cream for 15 minutes, stirring occasionally.

3. Pour the bread-and-chocolate mixture into a 9-by-13-inch nonreactive baking dish. Cover with foil and bake for about 45 minutes, or until set. Let stand, covered with foil, until ready to serve.—TANYA HOLLAND

INDIAN PUDDING WITH PEARS AND GINGER

12 SERVINGS

CORN BREAD:

- ¾ cup buttermilk
- ¾ cup cornmeal
- 1 cup all-purpose flour
- ½ cup sugar
- 1½ teaspoons baking powder
- 1 teaspoon ground cinnamon
- ½ teaspoon ground ginger
- ½ teaspoon salt
- 1 stick (4 ounces) unsalted butter, melted and cooled

Indian Pudding with Pears and Ginger

- ½ cup sour cream
- 1 extra-large egg, lightly beaten

PUDDING:

- 6 cups milk
- ¼ cup plus 2 tablespoons thinly sliced fresh ginger
- 8 extra-large eggs
- 12 extra-large egg yolks
- 1 cup unsulphured molasses
- 2 ripe large pears, such as Anjou or Comice, peeled, cored and cut into ½-inch dice

Butterscotch Sauce (recipe follows)

1. Make the corn bread: Preheat the oven to 375°. Butter an 8-inch square cake pan. In a large bowl, combine the buttermilk and the cornmeal and allow the mixture to stand for 5 minutes. In another bowl, sift together the all-purpose flour, sugar, baking powder, ground cinnamon, ground ginger and salt.

2. In a small bowl, whisk the melted butter with the sour cream and the beaten egg and stir into the cornmeal mixture. Stir in the sifted dry ingredients. Pour the corn-bread batter into the prepared pan and bake for about 30 minutes, or until a toothpick inserted in the center of the corn bread comes out clean. Let cool slightly, then unmold the corn bread to cool completely. Cut three-quarters of the corn bread into 1-inch dice and let dry. (You can snack on the rest.) Put the diced corn bread in a food processor; pulse until fine. (**MAKE AHEAD:** The corn-bread crumbs can be made up to 3 days ahead.)

3. Make the pudding: Preheat the oven to 325°. Generously butter twelve 1-cup ramekins and set them in a large roasting pan.

4. In a medium saucepan, combine the milk and the sliced fresh ginger and bring the milk to a boil. Remove the pan from the heat and let the milk steep, covered, for 10 minutes.

5. Put the corn-bread crumbs in a large bowl. In a medium bowl, whisk the whole eggs with the egg yolks and the unsulphured molasses. Bring the milk back to a boil and slowly whisk it into the eggs. Strain the custard over the corn-bread crumbs and stir well. Add the diced pears to the ramekins and spoon the custard mixture on top. Pour enough hot water into the pan to reach one-third of the way up the sides of the ramekins.

Crème Brûlée

6. Cover the roasting pan tightly with foil and bake in the middle of the oven for about 1 hour, or until the puddings are set. (MAKE AHEAD: The puddings can be refrigerated for 1 day. Bring the puddings to room temperature and rewarm in a water bath in a 300° oven, covered with foil, for 20 minutes.)

7. Run a thin knife around the puddings and invert each one onto a plate. Spoon the Butterscotch Sauce on top of the puddings and serve.

Butterscotch Sauce

MAKES ABOUT 3 CUPS

- 1½ cups light brown sugar
- ⅔ cup light corn syrup
- 1 stick (4 ounces) unsalted butter, cut into tablespoons
- 1 cup heavy cream
- ¼ cup brandy

In a heavy medium saucepan, bring the brown sugar, light corn syrup and butter to a boil over high heat. Add the heavy cream and return to a boil. Reduce the heat to moderate and simmer the sauce, stirring, for about 10 minutes or until the temperature reaches 240° and the sauce is thick when a spoonful is cooled on a plate. Stir in the brandy. Serve warm. (MAKE AHEAD: The sauce can be refrigerated for 1 week.) —WALDY MALOUF

CRÈME BRÛLÉE

4 SERVINGS

- 4 large egg yolks
- ⅓ cup plus 1 tablespoon granulated sugar
- 2 cups heavy cream
- 1 vanilla bean, split lengthwise and scraped
- ¼ cup air-dried light brown sugar (see Note)

1. Preheat the oven to 275°. In a medium bowl, whisk the egg yolks with half of the granulated sugar. In a small saucepan, warm the heavy cream with the vanilla-bean scrapings and the remaining granulated sugar until the cream is steaming. Gradually whisk the hot cream into the egg-yolk mixture until blended. Strain the custard and pour it into four 5-ounce ramekins or shallow gratin dishes.

2. Set the ramekins in a small baking dish and add enough hot tap water to the dish to reach halfway up the sides of the ramekins. Bake for about 1 hour and 15 minutes, or until the custards are just set. Let the custards cool in the water bath for 10 minutes, then remove from the baking dish and allow them to cool completely. Cover and refrigerate for at least 4 hours or overnight.

3. Preheat the broiler. Sift a thin even layer of the air-dried brown sugar over each of the custards. Broil one ramekin at a time as close as possible to the heat source until the brown sugar melts, forming a caramelized crust on top of the custard. Serve immediately.

NOTE: To air-dry brown sugar, sift it onto a plate and leave it out, uncovered, for 1 day. Alternatively, if the weather is humid, the sifted brown sugar can also be dried in the oven. Set the temperature at 250° and put the sugar in the oven for 20 minutes. —PAUL BOCUSE

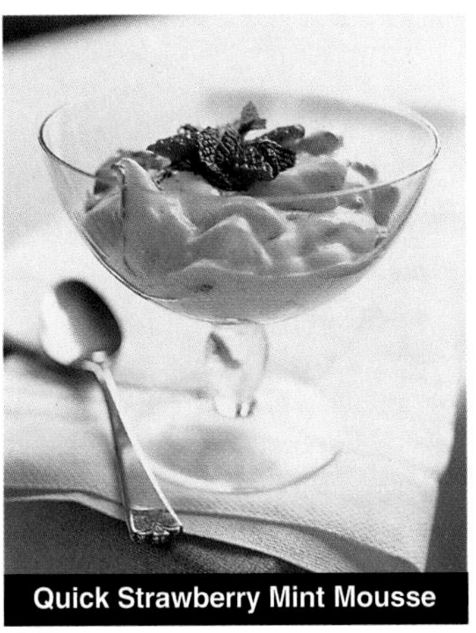

Quick Strawberry Mint Mousse

QUICK STRAWBERRY MINT MOUSSE Q

4 SERVINGS

- 1 pint strawberries, hulled and quartered
- 3 tablespoons sugar
- ½ cup sour cream
- ½ cup heavy cream
- 1 heaping tablespoon slivered fresh mint

1. In a medium bowl, sprinkle the hulled and quartered strawberries with the sugar and mash them lightly with a fork until the strawberries have exuded some juice and the sugar has started to dissolve. Let macerate for 15 minutes.

2. Strain the juice from the strawberries into a bowl. Whisk the sour cream into the strawberry juice. In a medium bowl, whip the heavy cream until it holds soft peaks. Fold in the sour-cream mixture and then gently fold in the sweetened strawberries. Refrigerate the strawberry mousse until it is chilled, at least 20 minutes. Spoon into bowls and garnish the mousse with the slivered fresh mint. —STEPHANIE LYNESS ➤

BRUSCHETTA WITH CANNOLI CREAM

This cream is lighter and considerably less sweet than the version that's typically used as a filling for crisp fried cannoli shells.

4 SERVINGS

½ pound fresh ricotta cheese
3 tablespoons almonds, toasted and coarsely chopped
½ ounce bittersweet chocolate, chopped into small pieces (2 tablespoons)
Zest of ½ orange, minced
1 tablespoon sugar
4 thick slices of country bread (not sourdough)
Unsalted butter (optional)

1. To make the cream, stir together the ricotta, almonds, chocolate, orange zest and sugar. (If you prefer a smooth texture, press the ricotta through a strainer first.)
2. Toast the bread until golden but still soft inside. Butter if desired. Spread with the cream and serve warm.—VIANA LA PLACE

JAM-FILLED CRÊPES WITH ORANGE BOURBON SAUCE

8 SERVINGS

CRÊPES:
¾ cup all-purpose flour
¼ teaspoon salt
1 cup milk
3 large eggs, lightly beaten
3 tablespoons unsalted butter, melted
½ cup raspberry or apricot jam or orange marmalade
½ cup pecan pieces

ORANGE-BOURBON SAUCE:
4 tablespoons unsalted butter
¼ cup sugar
1 cup fresh orange juice
1 to 2 tablespoons bourbon
Vanilla ice cream, for serving

1. Make the crêpes: In a medium bowl, combine the flour and salt. Gradually whisk in the milk until smooth. Stir in the eggs just until blended, then add 2 tablespoons of the butter. Strain the batter.
2. Set a 6-inch crêpe pan or nonstick skillet over moderately high heat. Dip a paper towel into the remaining butter; lightly grease the pan. When it is hot, pour in 2 to 3 tablespoons of the batter and tilt the pan to evenly cover the bottom; pour any excess batter back into the bowl. Cook the crêpe until lightly browned on the bottom, about 1 minute. Flip the crêpe and cook briefly on the other side, about 30 seconds. Turn out onto a plate and continue making crêpes, lightly greasing the pan as necessary. You should have about 24 crêpes.
3. Spread 1 teaspoon jam over each crêpe; fold the crêpes in half and half again to make triangles. Arrange the folded crêpes in a buttered baking dish. (**MAKE AHEAD:** Cover the dish with a double layer of plastic wrap and set aside or refrigerate. Or cover the plastic wrap with foil and freeze for up to 1 month. Let the crêpes thaw at room temperature for 10 minutes before proceeding.)
4. To serve, preheat the oven to 400°. Spread the pecan pieces in a pan and toast them in the oven for about 5 minutes, or until fragrant. Remove and set aside.
5. Cover the dish of crêpes with foil. Warm the crêpes in the oven for about 5 minutes, or until just heated through; do not overbake, or they will dry out.

Silken Tofu in Ginger Syrup

6. Meanwhile, **make the sauce:** In a medium nonreactive skillet, melt the butter over moderately high heat. Add the sugar and cook, stirring, until dissolved. Add the orange juice and boil over high heat until concentrated in flavor and reduced to ⅔ cup. Add the bourbon. Pour the hot sauce over the crêpes and garnish with the pecans. Serve three crêpes per person with a scoop of vanilla ice cream.—MARCIA KIESEL

SILKEN TOFU IN GINGER SYRUP

This tofu dessert is as luscious and creamy as custard.

6 SERVINGS

- 3 juice oranges
- ¾ cup sugar
- ⅓ cup finely slivered fresh ginger (from a 4-inch-long piece of ginger)
- One 1-pound block of silken tofu

1. Using a small sharp knife, peel the oranges, removing the bitter white pith. Holding the oranges over a bowl, cut in between the membranes to release the sections.

2. In a large nonreactive saucepan, combine the sugar with the slivered ginger and 1 cup of water. Bring to a boil over high heat, then lower the heat to moderate, cover and simmer for 5 minutes.

3. Gently place the tofu block in the ginger syrup. Cover the pan and simmer over low heat for 10 minutes to infuse the tofu with ginger flavor. (MAKE AHEAD: The tofu and orange sections can be refrigerated separately overnight. Transfer the tofu to a shallow dish, pour the syrup on top and refrigerate.)

4. Cut the tofu block into six even slices and, using a spatula, transfer them carefully to rimmed serving plates or shallow bowls. Spoon the ginger syrup, along with some fresh ginger slivers, over each serving of tofu. Garnish with the orange sections and serve.—MARCIA KIESEL

GELATINA DI FRUTTA

You might think gelatin went out with TV dinners and maraschino cherries, but this pretty, refreshing dessert is right in step with current tastes. It has the added benefit of being fat-free.

4 SERVINGS

- 2 envelopes unflavored gelatin
- ½ cup sugar
- 3 cups fresh orange juice
- 2 tablespoons orange-flavored liqueur or rum
- Orange slices and fresh mint sprigs, for garnish

1. In a nonreactive medium saucepan, sprinkle the gelatin over ½ cup of cold water. Let stand for 5 minutes to soften. Add the sugar and cook over moderately low heat, stirring constantly, until the gelatin is completely dissolved; don't let it boil. Stir in the orange juice and liqueur. Pour the mixture into four small bowls, ramekins or wineglasses. Cover with plastic wrap and chill until set, at least 4 hours or overnight.

2. If using bowls or ramekins, dip the bottoms in warm water for 30 seconds. Run a small knife around the sides of each mold and invert the gelatin onto small plates. Garnish the gelatin with orange slices and mint sprigs and serve.—MICHELE SCICOLONE

Gelatina di Frutta

Apple Cinnamon Tortilla Strips

APPLE CINNAMON TORTILLA STRIPS LF

Homey cinnamon sugar combines with apple jelly to glaze tortilla strips with a flavor reminiscent of apple pie.

MAKES ABOUT 4 CUPS

- Vegetable cooking spray
- 1 tablespoon sugar
- ¼ teaspoon cinnamon
- Four 6-inch low-fat flour tortillas, cut into ¼-inch-thick strips
- 2 tablespoons apple jelly, melted

Preheat the oven to 350°. Coat a nonstick baking sheet with cooking spray. In a bowl, combine the sugar and cinnamon. In a large bowl, toss the tortilla strips with the apple jelly and the cinnamon sugar. Spread the strips on the baking sheet in a single layer. Bake for about 20 minutes, tossing occasionally, until golden. Let cool on the baking sheet. (**MAKE AHEAD:** The tortilla strips can be stored in an airtight container for 1 week.) —GRACE PARISI

PRALINES

These pralines need your undivided attention for almost an hour, but they're worth it.

MAKES ABOUT 4 DOZEN PRALINES

- 4 cups heavy cream
- 2 cups sugar
- Finely grated zest of 1 orange (2 teaspoons)
- 4 cups shelled pecans (1 pound)

1. Lightly oil four baking sheets. In a large heavy saucepan, combine the cream, sugar and orange zest. Bring to a boil over moderately high heat, stirring constantly with a wooden spoon. Cook, stirring constantly, until the mixture registers 240° on a candy thermometer; this can take up to 50 minutes. The mixture will be thick, bubbly and golden brown. Add the pecans and cook, stirring, for 3 minutes.

2. Meanwhile, place a large bowl of cold water in the sink. Remove the saucepan from the heat and place the bottom in the cold water for 5 seconds to stop the cooking. With two spoons, drop tablespoon-size pralines 1 inch apart on the oiled baking sheets. (**MAKE AHEAD:** The pralines can be stored between sheets of wax paper in an airtight tin for up to 1 week.) —JAMIE SHANNON

ORANGE ALMOND MARSHMALLOWS

Homemade marshmallows are surprisingly easy to make and so much better than their store-bought counterparts. This version is flavored with orange juice and orange zest. For other flavorings, see "Marshmallow Variations," below.

MAKES 4 DOZEN MARSHMALLOWS

- 2 cups sliced natural almonds
- 1½ teaspoons cornstarch
- 1½ teaspoons confectioners' sugar
- Melted or softened butter, for brushing the pan
- 2 packages (about 1½ tablespoons) unflavored gelatin
- ⅓ cup fresh orange juice, strained
- 3 large egg whites, at room temperature
- 1¼ cups granulated sugar
- 2 tablespoons light corn syrup
- ⅛ teaspoon salt
- 1 teaspoon pure vanilla extract or 1 vanilla bean, split and scraped

MARSHMALLOW VARIATIONS

By following a basic marshmallow method but altering the flavorings, you can invent endless variations. Here are three to try. For each, follow the recipe for Orange Almond Marshmallows, but make these changes:

LEMON-MERINGUE MARSHMALLOWS

- **Omit the nuts.**
- **Increase the amount of cornstarch and confectioners' sugar to ¼ cup each.**
- **Substitute lemon juice and zest for the orange juice and zest.**
- **Use 1 tablespoon of the cornstarch mixture to dust the pan and the remainder for rolling the marshmallows.**

TOASTED-COCONUT MARSHMALLOWS

- **Substitute 2 cups unsweetened shredded coconut for the almonds in Step 1. Toast for 5 minutes, or until golden; let cool completely.**
- **In Step 2, substitute ⅔ cup of the coconut for the almonds.**
- **In Step 3, substitute cold water for the orange juice.**
- **In Step 6, add 1 teaspoon of pure almond extract along with the vanilla; omit the orange zest.**
- **In Step 8, substitute the remaining coconut for the almonds.**

CHOCOLATE MARSHMALLOWS

- **Substitute 4 ounces semisweet chocolate for the almonds; grate the chocolate on the coarse side of a grater.**
- **In Step 2, dust the buttered pan with 1 teaspoon of cornstarch mixed with 1 teaspoon of confectioners' sugar and 1 teaspoon of unsweetened cocoa powder. Evenly cover the bottom of the pan with ⅔ cup of the grated chocolate.**
- **In Step 3, substitute cold water for the orange juice.**
- **In Step 4, substitute dark corn syrup for light.**
- **In Step 6, substitute 2 tablespoons unsweetened cocoa powder for the orange zest.**
- **In Step 8, substitute the remaining grated chocolate for the almonds.**

1 tablespoon finely grated orange zest

1. Preheat the oven to 350°. Spread the sliced almonds on a baking sheet and toast for about 10 minutes, or until golden. Let cool; rub the toasted almonds between your hands until finely crushed.

SUGAR SYRUP

Boiling a sugar syrup—a mix of sugar and water—is the first step in making most confections. As the sugar cooks, it reaches different stages that correspond to various uses. To decide if the syrup has reached the right stage, use a candy thermometer, or drop a teaspoon of the syrup into ice water and knead it with your fingers (until the hard-crack stage, when the syrup becomes too hot to test by hand.)

THREAD **(230° to 234° F)**
Makes a limp, thin thread.
SOFT BALL **(235° to 242° F)**
Makes a soft, sticky ball.
FIRM BALL **(244° to 248° F)**
Makes a firm, flexible ball.
HARD BALL **(250° to 266° F)**
Makes a stiff, sticky ball.
SOFT CRACK **(270° to 290° F)**
Separates into firm strands.
HARD CRACK **(300° to 310° F)**
Separates into hard, brittle pieces.
CARAMEL **(320° to 375° F)**
Changes color from light amber to dark brown.

—CAROLE BLOOM

2. In a small bowl, whisk together the cornstarch and the confectioners' sugar. Using a pastry brush, lightly butter the bottom and sides of a 13-by-9-by-2-inch baking pan. Dust the pan with the cornstarch mixture. Evenly coat the bottom of the baking pan with ⅔ cup of the crushed almonds.

3. In a small bowl, sprinkle the gelatin over the juice; make sure the gelatin granules are evenly moistened. Put the egg whites in the large bowl of a standing electric mixer.

4. In a small heavy saucepan, stir together the granulated sugar, the corn syrup and ½ cup of water. Bring the syrup to a boil over high heat, washing down the sides of the pan occasionally with a wet pastry brush. Insert a candy thermometer (be sure the bulb is completely submerged in the syrup).

5. When the sugar syrup reaches 230°, begin beating the egg whites at medium-high speed. When the whites are foamy, add the salt and continue beating until the sugar syrup reaches 245°. Remove the sugar syrup from the heat and quickly whisk in the softened gelatin until completely dissolved.

6. Beat the sugar syrup into the egg whites in a slow stream at high speed. Add the vanilla and beat the whites until just cool, about 5 minutes. Using a large rubber spatula, fold in the orange zest.

7. Spread the meringue in the prepared pan and smooth the surface. Let the meringue stand uncovered in a cool dry place until set, at least 2 hours.

Orange Almond Marshmallows (*top*) and a chocolate variation

8. Sprinkle a work surface with the remaining crushed almonds. Run a knife around the edge of the baking pan to loosen the marshmallow. Turn the marshmallow out onto the almonds. Quarter the marshmallow rectangle. Cut each quarter into twelve even pieces. Roll each piece in the nuts until completely coated. Set the marshmallows on a rack to dry for 2 to 3 hours before serving. (MAKE AHEAD: The marshmallows will keep in an airtight container for up to 1 week.) —PEGGY CULLEN ➤

COCONUT MARSHMALLOW CHICKS AND BUNNIES

Using cookie cutters, you can make wonderful, whimsical marshmallow cut-outs. Here the mixture is thinly spread in a sheet tray, then bunnies and chicks are cut out and rolled in colored sugar and fluffy coconut.

MAKES ABOUT 3 DOZEN MARSHMALLOWS

1. Follow the recipe for Orange Almond Marshmallows (p. 452), substituting water for the orange juice, adding 1 teaspoon of pure almond extract along with the vanilla and omitting the orange zest. Spread the marshmallow mixture in a buttered 17-by-11-inch jelly-roll pan and allow it to stand for 2 hours.

2. In a small bowl, stir together about 1 tablespoon superfine sugar and the food-color powders of your choice (available at cake-decorating-supply stores). Use pink powder for bunny ears and tails and orange powder for chick feet and beaks. In a medium bowl, tint 1⅓ cups unsweetened shredded coconut (available at health-food stores) with yellow powder for chicks; leave the coconut white for bunnies. Adjust the intensity of the colors to your liking.

3. When the marshmallow has set, sprinkle a work surface with 1 cup of the coconut; set aside the remainder in a bowl. Using a bunny or chick cookie cutter, cut out the marshmallow shapes as close together as possible. If the cutter gets too sticky, rinse it under hot water and shake off any excess water; it doesn't have to be completely dry.

4. With dry hands, press the ears, tails, feet or beaks of the figures into the colored sugar; shake any excess sugar back into the bowl. Press the figures into the remaining coconut to coat completely. Set on a rack to dry for 2 to 3 hours. (**MAKE AHEAD:** The marshmallows will keep in an airtight container for up to 1 week.) —PEGGY CULLEN

BEYOND MARSHMALLOWS

Inspired by Peggy Cullen's marshmallow recipes and childhood memories of S'Mores—melted marshmallow and chocolate sandwiched between two graham crackers—Grace Parisi of FOOD & WINE's test kitchen devised these easy marshmallow treats.

• Drizzle melted semisweet chocolate on marshmallow squares. Place on a plate lined with wax paper. Refrigerate for 20 minutes or freeze for 5 minutes to set.

• Drizzle marshmallow squares with caramel and then with melted semisweet chocolate. Place on a plate lined with wax paper and freeze until firm, about 1 hour.

• Cut out 2-inch rounds of marshmallow with a biscuit cutter. Brush one side of two chocolate wafers with melted chocolate; sandwich a marshmallow in between. Repeat with the remaining rounds. Refrigerate for 10 minutes to set.

• Spread a small amount of marshmallow meringue in the bottom of a baked homemade or store-bought graham-cracker or chocolate-wafer pie shell. Refrigerate for 5 minutes to set. Fill with any chiffon pie filling.

• Make your favorite chocolate layer cake and split it horizontally. Spread the bottom cake layer with 1½ cups of the marshmallow meringue. Top with the second cake layer. Working quickly, frost the top and sides of the cake with another 1½ cups of the marshmallow meringue. Allow 15 minutes for the frosting to set before serving.

OVERNIGHT CHEESECAKE

Because it bakes slowly at a low temperature, this cheesecake never cracks, it never dries out and it requires no water bath.

16 SERVINGS

Vegetable cooking spray
½ cup graham cracker crumbs
2 pounds cream cheese, at room temperature
1 cup sugar
5 large eggs
¼ cup brandy
2 tablespoons pure vanilla extract

1. Preheat the oven to 200°. Coat a 2-quart soufflé dish or 9-inch springform pan with vegetable cooking spray and dust with the crumbs (if necessary, spray and dust again to coat well).

2. In a large bowl, using a wooden spoon, mix the cream cheese with the sugar until smooth, scraping as necessary. Mix in the eggs, the brandy and the vanilla until blended.

3. Pour the batter into the prepared pan and bake for 6 to 8

hours, or until the cake barely wiggles in the center. (The cake will firm up as it cools.) Transfer the cake to a rack and cool in the pan for 1 hour.

4. Cover the cake with wax paper, invert onto a plate, remove the pan and refrigerate upside down for at least 1 and up to 24 hours. Invert onto a platter. (**MAKE AHEAD:** The cheesecake can be wrapped well and refrigerated for up to 4 days.) Cut the cake with a long sharp knife; dip it in warm water to prevent sticking. —ANDREW SCHLOSS

INDIVIDUAL POACHED-PEAR CHEESECAKES

9 SERVINGS

- 1½ cups sugar, plus more for the ramekins
- 2 tablespoons pear brandy
- Three ½-inch-wide strips of lemon zest
- 3-inch cinnamon stick
- 1 vanilla bean, split
- 2 star-anise pods
- 2 whole cloves
- 2 ripe Bartlett pears, peeled, halved lengthwise and cored
- 1½ pounds cream cheese, softened
- ½ cup mascarpone cheese, softened
- 1½ teaspoons pure vanilla extract
- 3 large eggs, lightly beaten

1. In a nonreactive saucepan, combine ¾ cup of the sugar with the brandy, lemon zest, cinnamon stick, vanilla bean, star anise, cloves and 1½ cups of water. Bring to a boil over high heat, then add the pears. Lower the heat, set a plate on the pears to submerge them and simmer until tender, about 3 minutes. Transfer the pears to a plate to cool. Boil the liquid until reduced to a syrup, about 4 minutes. Strain and let cool.

2. Butter nine ½-cup ramekins and coat with sugar. Trim the pears so that they're 2 inches long, then slice them ¼ inch thick. Fan the slices, overlapping slightly, in the prepared ramekins and add 1 teaspoon of the poaching syrup to each.

3. Preheat the oven to 325°. Using a standing mixer fitted with a paddle or an electric mixer, beat the cream cheese until light and fluffy. Beat in the remaining ¾ cup sugar until smooth, then beat in the mascarpone. Add the vanilla extract and then the eggs, one at a time. Spoon the batter into the ramekins and set them in a roasting pan. Add enough hot water to the pan to reach two-thirds of the way up the sides of the ramekins. Bake for about 35 minutes, or until just set. Transfer to a rack to cool, then refrigerate overnight.

4. Run a knife around each of the cheesecakes and invert onto a plate. Spoon a little of the reserved poaching liquid around each cheesecake and serve.—NICK MORFOGEN

CHAPTER 21

~

BEVERAGES

Clockwise from top left: **Mint Julep (p. 461), Bourbon Milk Punch (p. 462), Pineapple Rum Coolers (p. 460), Bittersweet Black-and-White Shake**

BERRY SMOOTHIE

Here's a quick fix for fresh blueberries.

MAKES 2 SMOOTHIES

1 cup blueberries
1 ripe banana
1 cup milk

Put the blueberries, ripe banana and milk in a blender and puree them until the mixture is smooth. Fill two tall glasses with ice. Pour the blueberry smoothie over the ice in the glasses and serve.—DIANA STURGIS

SOY-MILK SMOOTHIE

Sprinkle additional cinnamon over the top of this refreshing drink if desired.

MAKES 4 SMOOTHIES

1 cup ice
1 pint soy milk

1 cup fresh orange juice
¾ cup pure maple syrup
1 very ripe banana
½ teaspoon cinnamon

Combine the ice, soy milk, fresh orange juice, pure maple syrup, ripe banana and cinnamon in a blender and blend until smooth. Pour the smoothie over ice in two tall glasses and serve at once.—MARCIA KIESEL

BITTERSWEET BLACK-AND-WHITE SHAKE

MAKES 2 LARGE SHAKES

1 pint vanilla ice cream, softened
¼ cup milk
¼ teaspoon pure vanilla extract
¼ cup Chocolate Syrup (recipe follows)

Combine the softened ice cream, the milk, the vanilla extract and the Chocolate Syrup in a blender and blend until smooth. Stir, pour the shake into a pair of tall glasses and serve.

SHAKE IT UP

For a delicious Vanilla Shake, leave out the Chocolate Syrup when making the Bittersweet Black-and-White Shake Or make a Strawberry Shake: Puree 10 ounces of thawed frozen strawberries in light syrup with 2 tablespoons of superfine sugar, then strain; substitute ½ cup of this strawberry puree for the Chocolate Syrup.

Chocolate Syrup

MAKES ABOUT 1 CUP

3 ounces bittersweet chocolate, coarsely chopped
Pinch of salt
3 tablespoons sugar
½ teaspoon pure vanilla extract

In a small saucepan, combine the chopped chocolate, salt and 2 tablespoons of water and stir over moderate heat until smooth. Add the sugar, the vanilla and ¼ cup plus 1 tablespoon of water; bring to a boil. Cook, stirring, for 3 minutes. Strain the syrup and allow it to cool. (**MAKE AHEAD:** The Chocolate Syrup can be refrigerated for up to 2 weeks.) —GRACE PARISI

DOUBLE-K CRUSH

If you've never used a kiwano, or horned melon, the time has come. Can't find one? Substitute three ripe strawberries.

MAKES 2 DRINKS

1 kiwano
2 kiwis, peeled and coarsely chopped
4 ounces vodka
2 ounces Cointreau
2 cups crushed ice

Cut two thin slices from the center of the kiwano; reserve the slices for garnish. Scoop out the seeds from the kiwano halves and place them in a blender. Add the kiwis, vodka, Cointreau and ice; whir on high speed until smooth. Pour the drink into two highball glasses. Garnish with the kiwano slices.—GARY AND MARDEE HAIDIN REGAN

GINGER TEA

Wherever ginger is used in cooking, you'll find ginger-based folk remedies. From China to America, people have found that ginger can soothe an upset stomach. If you suffer from acid indigestion or a sore throat, try brewing a cup of ginger tea for relief. Simmer one to one-and-a-half teaspoons freshly grated ginger in one cup of water for ten minutes. Strain; season with honey if desired.—LAUREN MUKAMAL CAMP

TEQAYA

MAKES 1 DRINK

1 ounce grenadine
Granulated sugar, for the glass
1 cup cubed ripe papaya
1 ounce fresh lime juice
2 ounces white tequila
1 tablespoon lime-juice cordial, such as Rose's Lime Juice

Pour the grenadine into a saucer. Invert a stemmed wineglass into the grenadine to coat the rim. Hold the glass sideways by its stem over the sink. Sprinkle the outside edge with sugar, twirling the glass to coat just the moistened outside rim with sugar. Set aside to dry a bit. Combine the remaining grenadine with the papaya, lime juice, tequila and lime-juice cordial in a blender and add ice, following the instructions in "Frozen-Drink Basics" (p. 461). Pour the drink into the prepared glass and serve it with two long straws.—GARY AND MARDEE HAIDIN REGAN ➤

TART GIN COOLER

This is a simple, refreshing drink, with flavors so complex you won't believe your taste buds. If you can't find Peychaud's bitters in your area, order it from Sazerac at 1-800-899-9450.

MAKES 1 DRINK

Ice cubes
2 ounces London dry gin
2 ounces fresh pink grapefruit juice
3 ounces tonic water
2 dashes Peychaud's bitters

Fill a collins glass two-thirds full of ice cubes. Pour in the gin, grapefruit juice, tonic water and bitters; stir to blend.—GARY AND MARDEE HAIDIN REGAN

FRUIT COCKTAILS

Follow these simple rules to turn liquor and fresh fruit into great summer drinks.

RULE ONE **Don't choose the least expensive brand of liquor, even though the nuances of the finest spirits may be somewhat masked by the fruits and other ingredients. Name brands are more expensive, but they're also more full-flavored than spirits with names you don't recognize.**

RULE TWO **Keep plenty of fresh citrus fruits on hand. A squeeze of lemon or lime makes flavors sparkle.**

RULE THREE **Don't let dominant fruit flavors make you forget that these drinks generally contain plenty of alcohol. You may want to ease up on refills.**

PINEAPPLE RUM COOLERS

MAKES 8 DRINKS

Crushed ice
About 1 cup white rum
About 2 cups pineapple juice, preferably fresh
About 3 tablespoons superfine sugar
About 3 tablespoons finely shredded fresh mint
8 fresh pineapple wedges, for garnish

For each of the drinks, fill a tall glass with crushed ice. Pour in about 1 ounce of rum and fill the glass with about 2 ounces of the pineapple juice. Stir in about 1 teaspoon of sugar and 1 teaspoon of shredded mint. Garnish each drink with a pineapple wedge.—LAURENCE KRETCHMER

COCONANA

We love both piña coladas and banana daiquiris, so we combined the two. Dark rum works best, but light will suffice.

MAKES 1 DRINK

2 ripe bananas, coarsely chopped
3 ounces dark rum
¼ cup canned coconut cream
2 dashes Angostura bitters

Combine the chopped bananas, dark rum, coconut cream and Angostura bitters in a blender and add ice, following the instructions in "Frozen-Drink Basics" (opposite page). Spoon the frozen drink into a wineglass or a hurricane glass. (Now's the time to bring out that plastic monkey if you have one.)—GARY AND MARDEE HAIDIN REGAN

THE DAIQUIRI

In 1898, according to Charles Baker's *The Gentleman's Companion*, two Americans working in Daiquirí, Cuba, concocted a homemade antidote to malaria: a mix of local rum, fresh lime juice and a little sugar. That first daiquiri may not have done much to bring down fever, but it has inspired legions of drinks, like Coconana.

THE BLOODY MACALLAN

Purists will insist that the subtleties of a fine single-malt Scotch are lost in a mixed drink, but we're convinced that this cocktail is superior in every way. You may want to experiment with other single malts when you make this drink—Highland Park, Laphroaig and the Glenlivet eighteen-year-old all work well—but we are enamored of The Macallan in this particular cocktail; it's rich, smooth and strangely exotic.

MAKES 1 DRINK

2 ounces 12- or 18-year-old The Macallan single malt Scotch
5 ounces tomato juice or vegetable-juice cocktail
1 thin slice of cucumber
1 ruffle of pink pickled ginger

Pour the Scotch and the tomato juice into an ice-filled highball glass and float the cucumber slice on top. Thread the ruffle of pickled ginger on a cocktail pick and suspend it across the top of the glass.—GARY AND MARDEE HAIDIN REGAN

MINT JULEP

To serve this Southern classic to a group of people, simply multiply this recipe by the number of drinks you want to serve.

MAKES 1 DRINK

- ¼ cup lightly packed mint leaves (about 20), plus 1 mint sprig for garnish
- 2 teaspoons Simple Syrup (recipe follows)
- 1½ cups crushed ice
- ¼ cup 90- to 100-proof bourbon
- Splash of brandy

1. Put the mint leaves in a 14-ounce highball glass or goblet. Add the Simple Syrup and 1 tablespoon of water. Crush the mint leaves with a muddler or the handle of a wooden spoon to bring out the flavor.
2. Add the crushed ice and the bourbon to the mixture in the glass and stir briskly until the outside of the glass becomes frosty. Add a splash of brandy and garnish the drink with the mint sprig.

Simple Syrup

MAKES 1 CUP
(ENOUGH FOR 24 DRINKS)

In a small saucepan, stir 1 cup of sugar into ½ cup of water. Bring the water to a simmer over moderately low heat. Reduce the heat and allow the syrup to simmer gently for 5 minutes. Let the syrup cool and then transfer it to a jar. (**MAKE AHEAD:** The Simple Syrup can be kept at room temperature or stored in the refrigerator for up to 1 week.)—COMMANDER'S PALACE, NEW ORLEANS ➤

FROZEN-DRINK BASICS

Here's how to achieve the consistency delivered by a commercial frozen-drink machine. Just follow these five steps:
1. Combine the liquor and the fruit in a blender and whir on high speed until the mixture is thoroughly pureed. Turn off the blender.
2. Add a handful of ice. Remove the "feed hole" from the center of the blender's lid and set the lid in place. Blend until smooth.
3. While the blender is running, slowly add more ice cubes, no more than three at a time. Listen carefully to the sound of the machine. When the machine resumes its normal pitch rather than sounding gravelly, look at the drink. You will notice a vortex in the center of the mixture. Keep adding ice to the blender until the vortex disappears and the mixture looks smooth.
4. Turn off the blender and stir the mixture with a long spoon or a chopstick. Replace the lid and turn on the blender. The vortex will reappear. Keep adding ice cubes, two or three at a time, until it disappears.
5. Once again, turn off the blender, stir, replace the lid and blend for about ten seconds, or until the sound of the motor tells you that all the ice has been thoroughly chopped. *Voila!* Your frozen drink will be as smooth as those made by the pros.

COOL COCKTAILS FROM HOT BARS

CAPARAGÑA

Combine the juice of 6 limes with 1 tablespoon sugar. Add ½ ounce of Triple Sec and 1½ ounces of Brazilian rum. Serve over crushed ice in an old-fashioned glass; garnish with a lime slice.—FROM THE ROSE BAR, THE DELANO HOTEL, MIAMI

CAPTAIN LAMBCHOP

Combine 2 ounces vodka, ½ ounce Chambord, a dash each of Cointreau, Grand Marnier and Rose's lime juice, and 1 ounce sweet-and-sour mix. Add 3 lime slices. Shake vigorously, then strain the drink into a glass; garnish with a lime slice.—FROM THE LORING CAFE, MINNEAPOLIS

COSMOPOLITAN

Soak cranberries in vodka for 4 days. Combine 3½ ounces of the infused vodka, ½ ounce of Triple Sec, a splash of Rose's lime juice and a squeeze of fresh lime. Shake, then serve in a martini glass; garnish with a Maraschino cherry.—FROM THE BAR MARMONT, LOS ANGELES

CALVADOS SIDECAR

Rub the rim of a martini glass with an orange slice, then coat with sugar. Combine 2 ounces Calvados with ½ ounce orange juice, ½ tablespoon sugar and 2 ounces fresh lime juice. Strain into the glass; garnish with an orange slice.—FROM THE TEMPLE BAR, NEW YORK CITY

Q & A: WINE

Q: When you're tasting wine, what is the first thing you look for?

A: First, I check the appearance of the wine, its color and clarity. In general, a white wine should be a light straw yellow, a red should be a medium or brick red. Then I consider aroma. This is crucial, since our sense of smell is so much more acute than our sense of taste. There are more than four hundred aroma and bouquet components in wine. Here I'm interested in fruitiness, varietal character and bouquet development. When I taste the wine, I'm concerned with its primary tastes and basic fruit flavors and whether the tannins, acidity and fruit are in balance. Finally, as I swallow the wine and make my final evaluation, I concentrate on my overall enjoyment. A smooth finish is what I'm looking for. The longer it lingers, the better I like it.—RORY CALLAHAN

Q: In terms of value, what kinds of wines should Americans be drinking now?

A: In spite of escalating prices, there are still lots of bargains. FROM FRANCE: Beaujolais is, year in and year out, a good buy. I like those of Georges Duboeuf and Louis Jadot. Also the new varietals from the south of France are exciting. Look for Merlots from Les Jamelles and Fortant de France. FROM CALIFORNIA: Try wines from good, mid-size wineries like Rodney Strong and Fetzer. For a real surprise, try Gallo's new Sonoma varietals and for a great sparkling wine, Roederer Estate's Brut, a steal at about $14. FROM SPAIN: Torres makes fine wines at great prices in the Penedés near Barcelona. Try their Gran Sangre de Toro. FROM ITALY: Seek out good buys from Antinori, like the Santa Cristina red and Galestro white. FROM CHILE: Choose almost any Sauvignon Blanc.—FRANK PRIAL

Q: What varietals would you recommend for someone who is just starting to explore wine, and why?

A: Stay away from Chardonnay and Cabernet. They have their place, but are really for folks who can appreciate—and grapple with—their enormous complexity. Instead of chardonnay, try a Riesling from Oregon, Washington, Mendocino County or Germany's Kabinett. No Chardonnay has Riesling's electricity, deliciousness or affinity for a wide range of food. Riesling is also a good teacher; you'll find yourself graduating to the better Rieslings, the steely stuff from Alsace and the great German estates. For a red start, try Gamays: Beaujolais from Burgundy or some of the Beaujolais-style Gamays from Sonoma County. They are delicious with almost any food and prepare your palate for richer reds. You'll realize, in time, that they're too frilly or too fruity for serious sipping. Then you'll be ready for Pinot Noir.—BILL ST. JOHN

SOUTHERN SERENITY

There's no need to peel the peaches for this frozen fantasy; the blender chops the skin into fine orange speckles.

MAKES 2 DRINKS

- 2 ripe peaches, pitted and chopped
- 4 ounces straight bourbon
- Peach wedges or diced peaches, for garnish

Blend together the peaches and bourbon. Add ice, following the instructions in "Frozen-Drink Basics" (p. 461). Spoon the drink into stemmed wineglasses and garnish with peach wedges.—GARY AND MARDEE HAIDIN REGAN

THE MARQUIS

MAKES 1 DRINK

- 1½ ounces bourbon
- 1 ounce Lillet rouge
- ½ ounce Grand Marnier
- 1 thin orange slice, for garnish

Fill a cocktail shaker two-thirds full of ice cubes. Add the bourbon, Lillet rouge and Grand Marnier and stir until well-mixed and chilled. Fill a double old-fashioned glass with ice cubes. Strain the drink over the ice. Hang the orange slice over the edge of the glass; serve at once.—GARY AND MARDEE HAIDIN REGAN

BOURBON MILK PUNCH

Try this eggless eggnog-like drink at a holiday get-together.

MAKES 2 QUARTS

- ½ cup pure vanilla extract (4 ounces)
- 1 cup sugar
- 2 cups heavy cream

4 cups milk
1 cup plus 2 tablespoons bourbon
Freshly grated nutmeg

In a large bowl, whisk together the vanilla and sugar. Whisk in the heavy cream, milk and bourbon. Pour into glass jars and refrigerate until chilled, about 2 hours. (**MAKE AHEAD:** The punch can be refrigerated for up to 3 days.) Serve cold in short 9-ounce glasses, garnished with nutmeg.—JAMIE SHANNON

COGNAC COULIS

This is an excellent fresh and flavorful alternative to dessert.

MAKES 2 DRINKS

2 ripe kiwis, peeled and sliced crosswise
6 large ripe strawberries, hulled
5 large ice cubes
3 ounces Cognac
1 ounce Grand Marnier

Reserve two slices of kiwi for garnish. Combine the remaining kiwis, the strawberries, ice cubes and Cognac in a blender. Whir at high speed until the mixture is smooth. Pour the drink into two martini glasses. Drizzle half of the Grand Marnier over each of the drinks and garnish each with a slice of kiwi.—GARY AND MARDEE HAIDIN REGAN

TROPICAL ITCH

Pineapple and passion fruit flavor this potent drink.

MAKES 4 DRINKS

¼ cup rum
¼ cup gin
¼ cup bourbon
2 tablespoons passion-fruit sorbet
1½ cups pineapple juice
¾ cup orange juice
2 tablespoons sweet-and-sour mix
½ tablespoon grenadine
4 pineapple slices, for garnish

Blend the rum, gin, bourbon, passion-fruit sorbet, pineapple juice, orange juice, sweet-and-sour mix and grenadine. Serve the drink on the rocks in tall glasses, garnished with pineapple slices and miniature backscratchers.—JEAN-MARIE JOSSELIN

INDEX

Page numbers in **boldface** indicate photographs

C

D

E

F

I

J

K

L

M

N

O

P

Q

R

S

T

V

W

Y

Z

CONTRIBUTORS

Jim Ackard is chef at the Grill at Reebok Sports Club in New York City.

Catherine Alexandrou is chef/owner of Chez Catherine in Westfield, New Jersey.

Jean Anderson is a food writer and cookbook author based in New York City. Her latest book, co-authored by Barbara Deskins, is *The Nutrition Bible* (William Morrow).

Richard Avedon is a celebrated photographer who has worked at the magazines *Harper's Bazaar*, *Vogue* and *The New Yorker*. His latest book is *Evidence 1944-1994: Richard Avedon* (Random House).

Karen Barker is co-owner and pastry chef at the Magnolia Grill in Durham, North Carolina.

Teresa Barrenechea is chef at New York City's Marichu Restaurant & Tapas Bar.

Rick Bayless is co-owner and chef at Frontera Grill and Topolobampo in Chicago. He is also the author of *Rick Bayless's Mexican Kitchen* (Scribner).

Paul Bertolli is co-owner and chef at Oliveto Cafe and Restaurant in Oakland, California. He was the executive chef of Chez Panisse for ten years and is the co-author, with Alice Waters, of *Chez Panisse Cooking* (Random House).

Brigit Legere Binns has collaborated on cookbooks with some of Los Angeles's top chefs. She recently published her first solo book, *Polenta* (Chronicle Books).

Janine Bjerklie is the owner of Betty's Pies in Two Harbors, Minnesota.

Carole Bloom is the author of *The International Dictionary of Desserts, Pastries and Confections* (Hearst Books), *Truffles, Candies and Confections* (Crossing Press), *The Candy Cookbook* (Chronicle Books) and *Sugar and Spice* (HP Books).

Jackie Bobrow is a cook at the SeaGrill Restaurant in Rockefeller Center in New York City. She is also a freelance recipe developer and editor.

Paul Bocuse is chef/owner of the three-star restaurant Paul Bocuse in Lyons, France.

Susan and Philippe Boulot are pastry chef and executive chef, respectively, at The Heathman Hotel in Portland, Oregon.

Daniel Boulud is chef/owner of Daniel in New York City and co-owner of its catering division, Feasts and Fêtes.

Michel Bourdeaux is executive chef at Tatou in New York City.

Wayne Brachman is executive pastry chef at both Mesa Grill and Bolo in New York City and the author of *Cakes and Cowpokes: New Desserts from the Old Southwest* (William Morrow).

Michelle and Bill Bracken are pastry chef and chef, respectively, at The Peninsula Beverly Hills Hotel.

Scott Bryan is co-owner and executive chef at both Indigo and Luma in New York City.

Julia Califano is a freelance writer based in Hoboken, New Jersey.

Rory Callahan is president of Wine and Food Associates in New York City.

Lauren Mukamal Camp is a freelance writer currently studying the cuisines of the Middle East and Asia.

Penelope Casas is a New York City-based food writer. Her most recent book is *¡Delicioso!: The Regional Cooking of Spain* (Knopf).

Bob Chambers is executive chef at Lâncome-L'Oréal in New York City.

Julia Child is the country's foremost television cooking teacher and the doyenne of French cooking in America. Her books include *Mastering the Art of French Cooking*, *The Way to Cook*, *In Julia's Kitchen with Master Chefs* (all from Knopf) and, most recently, *Baking with Julia* (William Morrow).

Jim Cohen is executive chef at The Phoenecian Resort in Scottsdale, Arizona.

Scott Cohen is executive chef at The Stanhope Hotel in New York City.

Tom Colicchio is chef at Gramercy Tavern in New York City.

Shirley Corriher is a teacher, writer and food consultant who delves into the whys of food. Her latest book, *Cookwise*, is due this spring from William Morrow.

Jessie Cromwell, nicknamed Grandma Dynamite, starts baking her sour-cherry pies at seven a.m. at the Summertime Restaurant in Fish Creek, Wisconsin.

Peggy Cullen is a baker, writer and candymaker living in New York City.

Marion Cunningham is a columnist, cooking teacher and cookbook author. Her books include *The Fanny Farmer Cookbook* and, most recently, *Cooking with Children* (both from Knopf).

Charles Dale is chef/owner of Renaissance in Aspen, Colorado.

Julia della Croce is a cooking teacher whose most recent books are *Pomodoro: Everything You Need to Know About Making Italy's Great Tomato Sauces* (Chronicle Books) and *Classic Italian Cooking* (DK Publishing).

Jim Denevan is chef at the Gabriella Cafe in Santa Cruz, California.

Traci Des Jardins is executive chef at Rubicon in San Francisco.

Cassandra Dooley is a New York City-based writer specializing in food trends.

Tom Douglas is owner of Etta's Seafood in Seattle.

Lissa Doumani and Hiro Sone are the owners of Terra restaurant in St. Helena, California, where he is chef and she is pastry chef.

Naomi Duguid and Jeffrey Alford are location food photographers and the authors of *Flatbreads & Flavors* (William Morrow) and a forthcoming book about rice.

Gilles Epie is chef at L'Orangerie in Los Angeles.

Florence Fabricant is the "Food Notes" columnist for *The New York Times*. Her most recent cookbook is *Venetian Taste* (Abbeville Press), written with Adam Tihany and Francesco Antonucci.

Sherry Fahey is head pastry chef at Cafe Latte in St. Paul, Minnesota.

Dean Fearing is chef at Mansion on Turtle Creek in Dallas.

Bobby Flay is co-owner and chef at Mesa Grill, Mesa City and Bolo, all in New York City.

Jim Fobel is the author of many cookbooks, including the forthcoming *Jim Fobel's Casseroles* (Clarkson Potter).

Susanna Foo is chef/owner of Susanna Foo Chinese Cuisine in Philadelphia.

Anne and David Gingrass are owners of Hawthorne Lane in San Francisco, where she is chef and he is butcher, baker and sausage maker.

Rozanne Gold is the author of *Recipes 1-2-3* (Viking).

Paul Grimes is a freelance chef, teacher and writer based in New York City.

Christopher Gross is chef/owner of Christopher's in Phoenix, Arizona.

Lauren Groveman is a cooking teacher and the author of *Lauren Groveman's Kitchen: Nurturing Food for Family and Friends* (Chronicle Books).

Vincent Guerithault is the chef/owner of Vincent Guerithault on Camelback in Phoenix, Arizona.
Cathie Guntli is owner and pastry chef at the Liberty Cafe in San Francisco.
Gordon Hamersley is chef/owner at Hamersley's Bistro in Boston.
Jessica B. Harris is a cookbook author based in New York City. Her books include *Sky Juice and Flying Fish* (Fireside).
Marcella Hazan is the owner of the cooking school Master Class in Classic Italian Cooking in Venice, Italy, and a renowned author, most recently of *Essentials of Classic Italian Cooking* (Knopf).
Victor Hazan is a frequent contributor to FOOD & WINE. He lives in Venice with his wife, Marcella, and writes about travel, wine and food.
Kerry Heffernan is executive chef at the Polo in New York City's Westbury Hotel.
Maria Helm is executive chef at the PlumpJack Cafe in San Francisco.
Tanya Holland is chef at Mesa Grill in New York City.
Susan Shapiro Jaslove is a food writer and recipe developer.
Nancy Harmon Jenkins is the author of *The Mediterranean Diet Cookbook* (Bantam) and divides her time between the coast of Maine and the hills of southern Tuscany. Her book on the traditional foods of Apulia will be published by Broadway Books in 1997.
Michele Anna Jordan is the California-based author of eight books, including *The Good Cook's Book of Oil and Vinegar* (Addison Wesley).
Jean-Marie Josselin is chef/owner of A Pacific Cafe Maui in Hawaii.
Carina Jost is pastry chef at Renaissance in Aspen, Colorado.
Hubert Keller is chef/owner of Fleur de Lys in San Francisco. His most recent book is *The Cuisine of Hubert Keller* (Ten Speed Press).
Michel Keller is chef/owner of Restaurant du Village in Chester, Connecticut.
Diana Kennedy has written many books on Mexican cooking, including the forthcoming *My Mexico* (Bantam). A longtime resident of Mexico, she has been decorated by the Mexican government for her work on cuisine and culture.
Matthew Kenney is chef/owner of Matthew's and owner of Mezze, both in New York City.
Marcia Kiesel is associate director of FOOD & WINE's test kitchen and the coauthor of *Simple Art of Vietnamese Cooking* (Prentice Hall).
Johanne Killeen and George Germon are chef/owners of Al Forno Restaurant in Providence, Rhode Island, and authors of *Cucina Simpatica* (HarperCollins). They are currently at work on a new cookbook to be published by Scribner.
Bharti Kirchner is a cookbook author whose most recent book is *Vegetarian Burgers* (HarperCollins).
Deborah Krasner, the author of *Kitchens for Cooks*, is at work on the forthcoming *Commonsense Kitchen Adviser* (HarperCollins).
Laurence Kretchmer is part-owner of the restaurants Mesa Grill, Mesa City and Bolo, all in New York City.
Emeril Lagasse is chef/owner of Emeril's and Nola, both in New Orleans, and Emeril's Fish House in Las Vegas, Nevada. He is also an author and host of his own show on the TV Food Network.
Matthew Lake is executive chef at New Heights in Washington, D.C.
Dominique Lalande is a cook and a designer of plates and gardens who lives in Avignon, France.
Susan Lantzius is an assistant editor of FOOD & WINE Cookbooks.
Viana La Place is the author of several cookbooks, most recently *Unplugged Kitchen* (Morrow).
Mary Beth and Roland Liccioni are pastry chef and chef, respectively, at Le Français, their restaurant in Wheeling, Illinois.
Susan Hermann Loomis is a journalist and the author of *The Great American Seafood Cookbook*, *The Farmhouse Cookbook*, *Seafood Celebrations* and *The French Farmhouse Cookbook* (all from Workman). She is working on *The Italian Farmhouse Cookbook* (Workman).
Barbara Lynch is executive chef at Galleria Italiana in Boston.
Stephanie Lyness is a food writer and recipe developer based in Guilford, Connecticut. Her most recent book is *Cooking with Steam* (William Morrow).
George Mahaffey is chef at The Restaurant at The Little Nell in Aspen, Colorado.
Waldy Malouf is chef/director of the Rainbow Room in New York City.
Nelli Maltezos is pastry chef at Zucca in New York City.
Luca Marcato is chef at Ostaria al Doge in New York City.
Priscilla Martel, a former chef and restaurateur, is currently the president of American Almond Products.
Nico Martin is sous chef at 42° in San Francisco.
Zarela Martinez is chef/owner of Zarela Restaurant in New York City and author of *Food from My Heart* (Macmillan).
Robert McGrath is chef at Windows on the Green in Scottsdale, Arizona.
Mark Miller is chef/owner of the original Coyote Cafe in Santa Fe, New Mexico, others in Las Vegas, Nevada, and Austin, Texas, and Red Sage in Washington, D.C.
Jim Moffat is chef/owner of 42° in San Francisco, named for the latitude line which runs through regions of Spain, Portugal, Italy and France.
Susan and Bruce Molzan are pastry chef and chef, respectively, at Ruggles Grill, their restaurant in Houston, Texas.
Nick Morfogen is executive chef at Ajax Tavern in Aspen, Colorado.
Pamela Morgan is owner of Flavors Catering & Carryout in New York City and the author of the upcoming *Flavors Cookbook*, due from Viking Penguin in the fall of 1997.
Charlie Palmer is chef/owner of Aureole in New York City and the author of *Great American Food* (Random House).
Grace Parisi is a recipe tester/developer for FOOD & WINE.
Jacques Pépin is a famed cooking teacher and the author of numerous cookbooks, most recently *Jacques Pépin's Kitchen: Cooking with Claudine* (KQED).
Harlan Peterson is chef/owner of Tapawingo in Ellsworth, Michigan.
Monica Pope is chef/owner of Boulevard Bistrot in Houston.
Alfred Portale is chef/owner of Gotham Bar and Grill in New York City.
Frank Prial is an authority on wine who has written for *The New York Times* since 1970.
Steven Raichlen is the author of *High-Flavor, Low-Fat Vegetarian Cooking* (Viking) and forthcoming cookbooks on appetizers and desserts.
Kevin Rathbun is executive chef and partner at Nava in Atlanta.
Gary and Mardee Haidin Regan are coauthors of *The Book of Bourbon and Other Fine American Whiskies.*
Hans Röckenwagner is chef/owner of Röckenwagner in Santa Monica, California.
Judy Rodgers is owner of the Zuni Cafe in San Francisco.
Rosa Ross is a New York City teacher, caterer and writer whose latest book is *Beyond Bok Choy: A Cook's Guide to Asian Vegetables* (Artisan).
Maury Rubin is chef/owner of The City Bakery in New York City and author of *Book of Tarts* (William Morrow).

Jacky Ruette is the former chef/owner of La Petite Marmite and Prunelle restaurants in New York City.
Peggy Ryan is chef/owner of Va Pensiero in Evanston, Illinois.
Bill St. John, a staff writer for *Rocky Mountain News* in Colorado, has a regular column in *Wine & Spirits* magazine.
Marcus Samuelsson is executive chef of Aquavit in New York City.
Lorna J. Sass is the author of *Cooking Under Pressure* and *Great Vegetarian Cooking Under Pressure* (both from William Morrow).
Amy Scherber is baker/owner of Amy's Bread in New York City.
Chris Schlesinger is chef/owner of the East Coast Grill in Boston.
Andrew Schloss is a food writer, recipe developer, former restaurant chef and the author, with Ken Bookman, of *One-Pot Cakes* (Morrow).
Michael Schlow is chef/co-owner of Café Louis in Boston.
Michele Scicolone is a food and travel writer and the author of the upcoming *A Fresh Taste of Italy* (Broadway Books).
Tracey Seaman, the test-kitchen director of *Great American Home Cooking*, is a cookbook author and food writer living in New Jersey.
Ali Seedsman is chef at Penfolds in Adelaide Hills, Australia.
Jamie Shannon is the executive chef at Commander's Palace in New Orleans.
Lindsey Shere has been the pastry chef at Chez Panisse in Berkeley, California, since 1971. She is the author of *Chez Panisse Desserts* (Random House) and is part-owner of the Downtown Bakery in Healdsburg, California.
André Soltner was chef/owner of Manhattan's famed Lutèce restaurant for thirty-three years.
Diana Sturgis is the test-kitchen director of FOOD & WINE.
Allen Susser is chef/owner of Chef Allen's in Miami.
Judith Sutton, a food writer who has worked at several New York City restaurants, is a frequent contributor to FOOD & WINE.
Elizabeth Terry is chef/owner of Elizabeth on 37th in Savannah, Georgia.
Norman Van Aken is chef/owner of Norman's in Coral Gables, Florida.
Lance Dean Velasquez is executive chef at 1848 House in Marietta, Georgia.
Jean-Georges Vongerichten is chef/owner of the restaurants Vong and JoJo in New York City and Vong in London.
John Frederick Walker is a contributing editor of FOOD & WINE.
Patricia Wells is the restaurant critic of the *International Herald Tribune* whose books include the forthcoming *Patricia Wells at Home in Provence* (Scribner).
Jennifer Welshhons is pastry chef at Wildwood Restaurant and Bar in Portland, Oregon.
John Willoughby is a senior editor at *Cooks Illustrated* and a frequent contributor to *The New York Times*.
Eileen Yin-Fei Lo teaches cooking at the China Institute in America in New York City. Her most recent book is *The Dim Sum Dumpling Book* (Macmillan).
Nina Zagat is co-publisher of Zagat Surveys.
Josu Zubikarai is executive chef at Taberna del Alabardero in Washington, D.C.

PHOTO CREDITS

Melanie Acevedo: 12 (*top right and bottom left*), 80 (*bottom*), 92 (*left*), 98, 106, 108, 109, 111 (*bottom*), 114, 115, 118, 127, 130, 149, 153, 156 (*top*), 172, 189, 203, 210, 229, 231 (*left*), 233, 281, 282, 329, 340, 343, 355, 356, 359, 406; **Willie Alleyne:** 187; **Bill Bettencourt:** 51, 54, 55, 59 (*top*), 89, 116, 143, 152, 160, 164, 167, 169, 184, 197, 199, 224 (*bottom*), 228, 240, 241, 247, 254, 261, 276, 278, 299, 300 (*bottom*), 301, 304, 316, 342, 404, 405, 446, 458 (*bottom left*); **Antoine Bootz:** 307, 310, 339; **Michael Calderwood:** 16, 111 (*top*), 231 (*right*), 357; **Mitch Epstein:** 39; **Stewart Ferebee:** 46, 59 (*bottom*), 93, 323, 368; **Mark Ferri:** 25, 120, 131, 142, 217, 230, 451 (*top*); **Owen Franken:** 87, 134 (*top*), 170, 186, 246, 263; **Dana Gallagher:** 178; **Gentl & Hyers:** 6, 12 (*bottom right*), 15, 21 (*right*), 60, 72, 91, 121, 161, 176, 177, 198, 268, 269, 272, 275, 277, 297, 305, 331, 392, 401 (*top*), 426, 449, 450, 451 (*bottom*); **Ruedi Hofmann:** 45, 80 (*top*), 140, 175 (*top*), 192, 224 (*top*), 255, 296, 408, 419 (*bottom*), 421, 423, 424, 425, 432, 448; **Matthew Hranek:** 19, 24, 29, 165; **Jeff Jacobson:** 70, 156 (*bottom*), 252, 420; **Kit Latham:** 57, 158, 162, 163, 225, 262, 376, 384; **Geoff Lung:** 8, 63, 250, 386, 442, back cover; **Joshua McHugh:** 119, 243, 308, 385, 434; **Victoria Pearson:** 52, 123, 244, 259, 311, 346, 349, 350, 351, 352, 359 (*right*), 398, 429; **Steven Rothfeld:** 50, 84, 309, 399; **Laurie Smith:** 154, 288, 289, 400 (*top and bottom*), 403, 407, 410, 411; **Bill Steele:** 34, 41, 58, 129, 132, 146, 150, 171, 174 (*top and bottom*), 190, 193, 200, 204, 216, 219, 226, 239, 256, 260, 270, 279, 334, 363, 369, 371, 372 (*top and bottom*), 373, 374, 375; **Ann Stratton:** front cover, 2, 12 (*top left*), 21 (*left*), 22, 32, 35, 36, 38, 40, 53, 56, 62, 65, 68, 71, 76, 77, 78, 79, 82, 85, 88, 92 (*right*), 94, 97, 104, 107, 112, 125, 133, 134 (*bottom*), 135, 136, 147, 166, 175 (*bottom*), 182, 194, 201, 208, 214, 222, 232, 248, 258, 283, 284, 300 (*top*), 306, 314, 319, 320, 322, 328, 332, 335, 338, 366, 377, 379, 382, 389, 396, 401 (*bottom*), 412, 413, 415, 418, 419 (*top*), 428, 438, 439, 440, 444, 447, 453, 458 (*top left and right, bottom right*); **Jonelle Weaver:** 81, 151, 238, 330, 391, 422, 431.